MACMILLAN'S HISTORY OF THE
GREEK AND ROMAN WORLD

General Editor: M. CARY, M.A., D.LITT.

II
A HISTORY OF THE GREEK WORLD
FROM 479 TO 323 B.C.

# MACMILLAN'S HISTORY OF THE GREEK AND ROMAN WORLD

GENERAL EDITOR : M. CARY, M.A., D.LITT.

DEMY 8VO

I. *A HISTORY OF THE GREEK WORLD FROM 776 TO 479 B.C.* *In preparation.*

II. *A HISTORY OF THE GREEK WORLD FROM 479 TO 323 B.C.* By M. L. W. LAISTNER, John Stambaugh Professor of History in Cornell University ; Hon. Fellow of Jesus College, Cambridge. With four maps.

III. *A HISTORY OF THE GREEK WORLD FROM 323 TO 146 B.C.* By M. CARY. With three maps.

IV. *A HISTORY OF THE ROMAN WORLD FROM 753 TO 146 B.C.* By HOWARD H. SCULLARD. With four maps.

V. *A HISTORY OF THE ROMAN WORLD FROM 146 TO 30 B.C.* By FRANK BURR MARSH. Revised by H. H. SCULLARD. With five maps.

VI. *A HISTORY OF THE ROMAN WORLD FROM 30 B.C. TO A.D. 138.* By EDWARD T. SALMON, Professor of Ancient History in McMaster University, Hamilton, Ontario. With five maps.

VII. *A HISTORY OF THE ROMAN WORLD FROM A.D. 138 TO 337.* By H. M. D. PARKER. With four maps.

# A HISTORY OF THE GREEK WORLD

## FROM 479 TO 323 B.C.

BY

M. L. W. LAISTNER

M.A.

JOHN STAMBAUGH PROFESSOR OF HISTORY IN CORNELL
UNIVERSITY; HON. FELLOW OF JESUS COLLEGE, CAMBRIDGE

WITH FOUR MAPS

NEW YORK
THE MACMILLAN COMPANY
1957

*First published February 13th 1936*
*Second edition 1947*
*Third edition 1957*

PRINTED IN GREAT BRITAIN

# CONTENTS

| | PAGE |
|---|---|
| LIST OF ABBREVIATIONS . . . . . . . . | xii |
| INTRODUCTION . . . . . . . . . | xiii |

## PART I

### CHAPTER I

GREECE AND PERSIA, 479 TO 448 B.C. . . . . . . 1–20

- § 1. The aftermath of the Persian invasions . . . . 1
- § 2. The confederacy of Delos . . . . . . . 5
- § 3. Cimon's operations against Persia . . . . . 7
- § 4. Athens and her allies . . . . . . . 9
- § 5. The Egyptian expedition . . . . . . 15
- § 6. Cimon's last campaign and the peace of Callias . . . 19

### CHAPTER II

THE GREEK HOMELAND, 479 TO 432 B.C. . . . . . 21–53

- § 1. Sparta and the Peloponnesian League . . . . 21
- § 2. The Helot revolt . . . . . . . . 25
- § 3. Athens: party struggles and the exile of Themistocles . 27
- § 4. Athens: Ephialtes' and Pericles' programme of reform . 31
- § 5. The First Peloponnesian War, 459–445 B.C. . . . 34
- § 6. The later régime of Pericles . . . . . . 44

### CHAPTER III

THE GREEKS OF THE WEST . . . . . . . . 54–70

- § 1. The tyrants of Syracuse and Acragas . . . . 54
- § 2. Unrest in the Sicilian cities and the rise of Ducetius . . 61
- § 3. The Greeks of Magna Graecia and their neighbours . . 66

### CHAPTER IV

THE GREAT PELOPONNESIAN WAR: FIRST STAGE, 431 TO 421 B.C. 71–115

- § 1. The antecedents of the war . . . . . . 71
- § 2. The outbreak of the war and the resources of the combatants 78
- § 3. The war in Central Greece and the Peloponnese, 431–427 B.C. 82
- § 4. The secession of Lesbos . . . . . . . 86
- § 5. Operations in north-western Greece, 430–426 B.C. . . 91
- § 6. Pylos and Sphacteria . . . . . . . 99
- § 7. The Delium campaign . . . . . . . 103
- § 8. Financial stringency at Athens . . . . . . 106
- § 9. Brasidas in Thrace . . . . . . . . 107
- § 10. Peace of Nicias . . . . . . . . 113

## viii THE GREEK WORLD FROM 479 TO 323 B.C.

### CHAPTER V

THE PELOPONNESIAN WAR: SECOND AND THIRD STAGES, 420 TO 404 B.C. . . . . . . . . 116–165

- § 1. Discontent of Sparta's allies and renewed warfare . . 116
- § 2. Athenian affairs at home and in the empire . . . 123
- § 3. The Athenian expeditions to Sicily . . . . . 126
- § 4. Athens in straits . . . . . . . . 139
- § 5. The intervention of Persia . . . . . . 141
- § 6. The oligarchic revolution of 411 B.C. . . . . 146
- § 7. The restored democracy at Athens . . . . . 151
- § 8. The closing years of the war: Lysander and Cyrus . . 154
- § 9. The Thirty at Athens and the restoration of the democracy . 162

### CHAPTER VI

SPARTA AS AN IMPERIAL STATE . . . . . . 166–203

- § 1. Sparta and her empire . . . . . . . 166
- § 2. The expedition of Cyrus the Younger . . . . 169
- § 3. Sparta and Persia at war . . . . . . . 173
- § 4. Anti-Spartan coalitions in Greece . . . . . 179
- § 5. The King's peace . . . . . . . . 183
- § 6. Spartan policy in Greece . . . . . . . 187
- § 7. The rise of Thebes and the Second Athenian Confederacy . 191
- § 8. Jason of Pherae . . . . . . . . 198
- § 9. Abortive peace of 371 and the campaign of Leuctra . . 200

### CHAPTER VII

THE HEGEMONY OF THEBES . . . . . . . 204–219

- § 1. Epaminondas in the Peloponnese . . . . . 204
- § 2. The Arcadian League and the war in the Peloponnese to 364 B.C. 207
- § 3. The relations between Thebes and northern Greece . . 211
- § 4. Athenian naval operations . . . . . . 213
- § 5. The campaign of Mantinea . . . . . . 216

### CHAPTER VIII

THE RISE OF PHILIP OF MACEDON . . . . . . 220–248

- § 1. Macedonia before the time of Philip . . . . . 220
- § 2. Succession and early campaigns of Philip II . . . 222
- § 3. Philip's reforms and earlier relations with Athens . . 224
- § 4. Athens and her allies . . . . . . . 228
- § 5. The rise of Phocis and the Sacred War . . . . 233
- § 6. Philip in Chalcidice and his war with Athens . . . 239
- § 7. The peace of Philocrates . . . . . . . 243

### CHAPTER IX

THE TRIUMPH OF PHILIP . . . . . . . 249–264

- § 1. The rival diplomacies of Demosthenes and Philip . . 249
- § 2. Philip in Thessaly and Thrace . . . . . . 252
- § 3. Renewed war between Athens and Philip . . . 254
- § 4. A new Sacred War and the campaign of Chaeronea . . 256
- § 5. Congress of Corinth and death of Philip . . . . 260

# CONTENTS

## CHAPTER X

**THE GREEKS IN THE WEST DURING THE FOURTH CENTURY** . 265–290

§ 1. Sicily after the Athenian expedition . . . . . 265
§ 2. The rise of Dionysius . . . . . . . 268
§ 3. The first Punic War . . . . . . . 273
§ 4. Dionysius in Italy . . . . . . . . 276
§ 5. The later years of Dionysius . . . . . . 279
§ 6. The western Greeks after the death of Dionysius I . . 281
§ 7. Expedition of Timoleon . . . . . . . 285
§ 8. The Italian Greeks after the death of Dionysius II . . 289

## CHAPTER XI

**THE CONQUESTS OF ALEXANDER** . . . . . . 291–317

§ 1. The Persian Empire in the fourth century . . . . 291
§ 2. Early training and career of Alexander . . . . 292
§ 3. The campaigns against Darius III . . . . . 294
§ 4. Conquest of Media and Persis . . . . . . 303
§ 5. The campaigns in central Asia . . . . . . 305
§ 6. Alexander in India . . . . . . . . 309
§ 7. The last phase: return and death of Alexander . . . 314

## CHAPTER XII

**THE EMPIRE OF ALEXANDER** . . . . . . 318–327

§ 1. Alexander's achievement and its effects . . . . 318
§ 2. The imperial administration . . . . . . 320
§ 3. Alexander and the Greeks . . . . . . 322

## PART II

## CHAPTER XIII

**GREEK WARFARE** . . . . . . . . . 328–345

§ 1. Recruitment of armies and conditions of service . . . 328
§ 2. Strategy and tactics: siege operations . . . . 333
§ 3. The innovations of Philip and Alexander of Macedon . . 337
§ 4. Naval warfare and tactics . . . . . . 340
§ 5. The rules of war . . . . . . . . 344

## CHAPTER XIV

**THE GOVERNMENT OF THE CITY-STATES** . . . . 346–370

§ 1. Tyranny and oligarchy . . . . . . . 346
§ 2. Athenian democracy in the fifth century . . . . 350
§ 3. Changes in the Athenian government during the fourth century 356
§ 4. Financial administration in Athens . . . . . 360
§ 5. Leagues and federations . . . . . . . 365

x THE GREEK WORLD FROM 479 TO 323 B.C.

CHAPTER XV

|  | PAGE |
|---|---|
| GREEK ECONOMIC LIFE | 371–386 |
| § 1. Geographical features and natural resources | 371 |
| § 2. Resident aliens and slaves | 373 |
| § 3. Agriculture | 376 |
| § 4. Industry and commerce | 379 |
| § 5 Money-dealing | 384 |

CHAPTER XVI

|  | |
|---|---|
| GREEK ART | 387–406 |
| § 1. Architecture | 387 |
| § 2. Sculpture | 393 |
| § 3. Painting and the minor arts | 401 |
| § 4. Greek music | 405 |

CHAPTER XVII

|  | |
|---|---|
| GREEK LANGUAGE AND LITERATURE | 407–434 |
| § 1. Spoken and written dialects | 407 |
| § 2. Elementary education | 408 |
| § 3. Lyric poetry | 412 |
| § 4. The drama | 413 |
| § 5. History and geography | 420 |
| § 6. Oratory | 430 |

CHAPTER XVIII

|  | |
|---|---|
| GREEK SCIENCE AND PHILOSOPHY | 435–460 |
| § 1. The Eleatics and the Atomists | 435 |
| § 2. Mathematics and astronomy | 438 |
| § 3. Hippocrates and scientific medicine | 440 |
| § 4. The Sophists | 442 |
| § 5. Isocrates | 445 |
| § 6. Socrates and the minor Socratic schools | 447 |
| § 7. Plato | 451 |
| § 8. Aristotle | 454 |

CHAPTER XIX

|  | |
|---|---|
| GREEK RELIGION | 461–469 |
| § 1. The state religion | 461 |
| § 2. Religious festivals | 465 |
| § 3. Mysteries and foreign cults | 467 |
| SOURCES AND AUTHORITIES FOR THE PERIOD, 479 TO 323 B.C. | 470 |
| SELECT BIBLIOGRAPHY | 474 |
| INDEX | 481 |

## MAPS

| | | PAGE |
|---|---|---|
| I. | GREECE AND THE AEGEAN AREA | facing 1 |
| II. | SICILY AND MAGNA GRAECIA | 55 |
| III. | ANCIENT SYRACUSE | 133 |
| IV. | THE EMPIRE OF ALEXANDER | facing 294 |

*From Drawings by Richard Cribb*

## LIST OF ABBREVIATIONS

| | |
|---|---|
| *A.T.L.* | = B. D. Meritt, H. T. Wade-Gery, and M. F. McGregor, *The Athenian Tribute Lists*. |
| *C.A.H.* | = *Cambridge Ancient History*. |
| Grose | = *Catalogue of the McClean Collection of Coins*, Vol. I. |
| Hill, *H.G.C.* | = G. F. Hill, *Historical Greek Coins*. |
| *I.G.* | = *Inscriptions Graecae, editio minor*. |
| *J.H.S.* | = *Journal of Hellenic Studies*. |
| P.-W. | = Pauly - Wissowa - Kroll - Mittelhaus, *Real - encyclopädie der klassischen Altertumswissenschaft*. |
| *Syll.* | = W. Dittenberger, *Sylloge Inscriptionum Graecarum*, 3rd edition. |
| Tod | = M. N. Tod, *A Selection of Greek Historical Inscriptions*. Inscriptions 1 to 96 are in Vol. I (2nd edition, 1946), 97 to 205 in Vol. II. |

# INTRODUCTION

THE period of Greek history from the end of the Persian Wars to the death of Alexander the Great can claim to be in some of its aspects unique in the history of the world. Where else could one find crowded into the brief space of five generations such a galaxy of great poets, artists, and thinkers; in short, of men whose creative achievement directly or indirectly has exerted an unparalleled influence on Western civilisation for two thousand years, and in some of its manifestations at least is still unsurpassed?

Yet the very magnitude of what was then accomplished in literature, philosophy, and art has all too often so overpowered those who have set themselves to portray the age as a whole, that it has paralysed their critical faculty. The less admirable features of Greek civilisation have been ignored or glossed over, the Athenians of the Periclean Age represented as a society of paragons and supermen. The truth, of course, is very different. Dispassionately considered, the political history of the Greeks during the fifth and fourth centuries makes sad reading. Pericles and Isocrates might indeed envisage some kind of larger political organism than the city-state, which should knit the Greek nation together, cause the Greeks to live in harmony, and enable them to present a united front at all times to extraneous enemies. In practice, though the fourth century especially saw many experiments in bringing together groups of city-states to effect greater security and stability over a larger area, all of them were shattered on the rock of particularism, a blind adherence to the cherished αὐτονομία which, in view of the selfish policy pursued by a few states stronger than their neighbours, had degenerated into a mere catchword. Disunion prevailed and the Macedonian conqueror came, saw, and conquered before any true federation had been evolved by the Greeks.

Again, one must not blind oneself to the essentially primitive character of economic life in this period. The methods of agriculture followed in the fourth century were little more scientific than in the sixth; industry and commerce, though more intensive than in the archaic period, were undeveloped and on a small scale when compared with the more advanced economy of the Hellenistic and Graeco-Roman epochs, not to speak of more recent times. And, moreover, one of the cancers in Athenian, and probably in many other Greek societies, was the growing parasitism of the citizens, supported wholly or in part by the state to fulfil their civic duties of government and dispensing justice, which left so much of production and trade to the foreigner and the slave.

That the standard of living was generally low in Greece during this era is doubtless true;[1] but this is only of secondary importance, save perhaps to those ultra-moderns to whom material comfort is the sole criterion of culture. More essential for a proper estimate of Greek civilisation is the knowledge that the same age that produced the finest flower of the Attic drama, the profound speculations of Plato, or the masterpieces of Phidias, Ictinus, and Praxiteles, was characterised by not a little cruelty and barbarism. The treatment of large sections of the slave population, the butchery and enslavement often attendant upon the capture of cities in time of war, and the practice of infanticide, which contrary to a commonly held belief was by no means confined to Sparta, bear eloquent testimony to a repulsive side of Hellenic history.

To interpret fairly an epoch presenting so many and such apparently contradictory aspects is at best a difficult, if a fascinating, task. But there is a further handicap under which any modern historian of ancient Greece must needs labour. The surviving material, particularly the literary sources, is vastly fuller for Athenian history than for that of any other Greek state. Nor is it only about the little city-states of the third rank that precise information is often entirely lacking; it is still impossible to compose even in outline a continuous history of so leading a state as Corinth. Thus it is inevitable

[1] This unpleasing aspect of Greek society has recently been stressed by Ch. Picard in his essay, *La vie privée dans la Grèce classique* (Paris, 1930).

that modern histories of Greece might with almost greater accuracy be described as histories of Athens. The fact that Athens was for virtually the whole period the intellectual leader of Greece and for a great part of it exercised a preponderating influence also in economic and artistic life, to a considerable extent redresses the balance; it makes the narrative which assigns one-half or even two-thirds of the space to Athens less out of perspective than a superficial observer might suppose.

# PART I

## CHAPTER I

## GREECE AND PERSIA, 479 TO 448 B.C.

### 1. THE AFTERMATH OF THE PERSIAN INVASIONS

THE end of the normal campaigning season in 479 had seen the withdrawal of the Persian army from European Greece after their defeat at Plataea, and, s to the timely secession to the Greek side of the ins, Milesians, and other Greek subjects of Xerxes, in arms had suffered a reverse of equal magnitude in Minor. Moreover, apart from the casualties at Mycale, irning of the fleet for the time being completely crippled reat King's naval strength. After this success the in King, Leotychidas, who had been in command of the c expedition, had returned home with the Peloponi contingent. The newly liberated islanders and Greeks a Minor, however, rightly regarded the expulsion of the in garrison in Sestos, controlling, as it did, the entry he Hellespont (Dardanelles), as essential to their immesecurity. Their view was shared by the Athenians, led inthippus. Thus, contrary to the usual practice, active ry operations were continued into December, until the re of Sestos was followed by the withdrawal of the il allies to their respective homes.
Greek state, least of all Sparta, whose leading position een generally acknowledged for the past three or four es, could doubt that the declaration of independence by the cities of Aeolis and Ionia could only be upheld, ive support from the Greek homeland continued to be ed to them. What the Spartan government's deliberaon foreign affairs during the winter may have been, we

do not know ; but, to judge by its conduct at other times, we may well doubt whether it looked beyond the immediate future. It was one thing for Sparta, in view of her military primacy in the Peloponnese, to take over during the emergency of the late war the direction of a larger military and naval alliance ; quite another to promote and direct a Panhellenic federation which would include not only European Greece but the islands of the Archipelago and the Greeks of Asia Minor. We can be sure that no Spartan in 478 contemplated such a development ; for before it could even have been begun, Sparta would have needed to become a naval power, a responsibility for which she had neither the resources nor the geographical position. The story that the Ionian Greeks were urged by Sparta to leave their Asiatic homes and emigrate to European Greece, a proposal that they rejected on the advice of the Athenians, is very possibly unhistoric ; but it is not wholly without value, because it reflects what a later generation of Greeks conceived to be a characteristic Spartan attitude.[1]

The winter, 479–478, was, it may be imagined, spent in setting their home affairs in some kind of order by all those cities which had actually been situated in the war area, whether in Europe or Asia. At Athens at least we know that immediate steps were taken to bring back the non-combatants from their temporary refuge in the Argolid, Salamis, and Aegina. Then, as soon as circumstances allowed, the Athenians at the instance of Themistocles proceeded to rebuild and enlarge their city-walls.[2]

That an expedition of moderate size was sent to eastern waters in the spring of 478 may have been partly due to the influence of Pausanias, who saw in it a means to further his own ends, partly to a feeling among the ephors that immediate abandonment of the Asiatic Greeks would be neither politic nor honourable. The expedition was put under the command of Pausanias and was composed of twenty Peloponnesian and thirty Athenian vessels, reinforced by an unknown number of ships supplied by the Ionian Greeks. The instructions received by the king were presumably definite—to increase the difficulties of Persia by instigating fresh revolts amongst his subjects. The armada sailed to Cyprus which,

[1] Herodotus, IX, 106 ; Diodorus, XI, 37.    [2] See below p. 22 ff.

owing to its proximity to Syria and Egypt, was a specially vulnerable spot, and conquered the greater part of the island.[1] Later in the season Pausanias proceeded to follow up the advantage won by Athens and the Ionian confederates during the winter by besieging Byzantium. This, the most important of the few strongholds still held by Persia in Europe, does not appear to have offered a prolonged resistance before it was captured.

After these successes, all the ancient authorities are agreed, the trouble began. Pausanias, instead of working hand in hand with his allies from both sides of the Aegean to consolidate the Greek position against Persia, laid plans to make himself despot of Byzantium. He began actively to intrigue with Persia. Amongst the prisoners taken in the city were certain relatives of Xerxes. These he caused to be smuggled out of the city and despatched with a letter to the Persian king. Pausanias' manœuvre met with more success than it deserved. The newly appointed satrap of Dascylium, Artabazus—Thucydides even suggests that he was specially sent out to supersede Megabates—was instructed to enter into conversations with Pausanias and to promise him ample support if he would betray the Greek cause to the enemy. The traitor might well have succeeded had he not in singularly stupid fashion antagonised his Greek allies, especially the Ionians, by harsh and insulting treatment, before his own plans were ripe. Moreover his adoption of Oriental dress and manners, and the bodyguard of Persian and Egyptian soldiers that attended him, aroused the utmost resentment. Complaints reached the Spartan ephors, who recalled their king to stand his trial on various charges. At the same time the Asiatic Greeks turned to the commanders of the Athenian squadron, whose attitude had been consistently sympathetic, and invited Athens to take over the leadership of the maritime alliance. On his return to Sparta Pausanias was arraigned and fined for some minor offences. But he was acquitted of the major indictments, of which the worst was treason. In the meanwhile the Spartan government rather injudiciously,

---

[1] The defection of the Cypriotes from the Great King cannot have endured very long. At all events, at the time of Cimon's expedition to Pamphylia (see below, p. 8), Cyprus was again a Persian base (cf. Diodorus XI, 60; Plutarch, *Cimon* 12).

unless it be that they failed to realize the full bitterness of the Greeks who had lately served under Pausanias, sent Dorcis with a small force to take over the command at Byzantium. But as the allies refused to serve under him, the humiliated officer could only return home. The last years of Pausanias, however, could serve moralists as an historical instance of that ὕβρις—unbridled arrogance towards human and divine institutions—which in the end brought down the wrath of Heaven on the offender. Managing to withdraw from Laconia once more, Pausanias in a single galley made his way to Byzantium, there to continue his negotiations with Persia. He appears to have remained in control of Byzantium for several years, but ultimately he was expelled from the city of Athenian action.[1] He escaped to Colonae in the Troad, where he must have passed at least some months. In the meanwhile the ephors received information that he was again engaged in treasonable designs. They sent an emissary to recall him to Sparta, threatening military action if he did not obey their summons. Pausanias acquiesced, apparently because he thought that by bribery he could obtain a favourable verdict or even escape legal action entirely; it may be inferred that he owed his former acquittal to the same corrupt tactics. At all events these and his prestige, coupled with the difficulty of mustering sufficient reliable evidence against him, saved him from prosecution after a short period of imprisonment. Some years were still to elapse before additional information and real or suspected complicity with a domestic revolution enabled the ephors to take extreme measures.[2]

[1] E. M. Walker (*C.A.H.*, V, p. 467) rightly rejects the statement of some modern writers that Pausanias seized Sestos and was expelled therefrom by Cimon after a siege. For this story is a false inference from a single passage in Plutarch (*Cimon* 9), where the biographer has confused Aristides with Cimon (in an earlier passage he had named them together), and finds no confirmation in Thucydides or elsewhere. Glotz, however, repeats the tale (*Histoire grecque*, II, p. 120).

[2] The chronology is most unsatisfactory. If, as is possible, Pausanias returned to Sparta for the second time before the end of 472, he would have been in Byzantium for about five years. His complicity in the Helot Revolt and his death then occurred in 468 or 467. See below, p. 25.

## § 2. THE CONFEDERACY OF DELOS

During the time that Pausanias was in charge of the allied forces in the Aegean Aristides and his understudy, Cimon, laid themselves out to treat their Asiatic allies as friends and equals. Such courtesy was particularly noticeable because of its contrast to the brutalities of the Spartan king; it overcame any lingering hesitation that the Ionians may still have felt regarding their future conduct. Not only was Athens, thanks to the efforts of Themistocles in the years immediately preceding Xerxes' invasion, the leading naval state in Greece, but, by helping to reduce Sestos in 479, she had quite recently earned the special gratitude of the allies. They now (478–477) formally invited the Athenians to take over the general direction of the maritime League.[1] Unfortunately the ancient sources leave a great deal unsaid, so that information, particularly about the earliest years of the Confederacy, is very scanty. It was both defensive and offensive in character, since its purpose was both to protect the autonomy of the islanders and Asiatic Greeks and to revenge the Persian invasions of Greece by harrying the Great King's possessions. In the beginning the League was an alliance entered into for war purposes and without elaborate organization. In fact, all that is known of it in this early stage suggests that it was an improvization to meet a temporary situation rather than a well-balanced scheme intended to pave the way to a true confederation of states. It was, however, necessary to have funds in order to carry out the purposes of the League. The temple of Apollo on Delos, the little islet surrounded by the larger Cyclades, was selected to be the Treasury, a choice dictated partly by the fact that it had long been the meeting-place of a religious festival supported by the Ionians, partly no doubt by its position midway between Athens and the coast of Asia Minor. The assessment of the tribute ($\phi \acute{o} \rho o s$) to be paid by the members was entrusted by general consent to Aristides, whose reputation for incorruptible fair-dealing was universally recognized. Delos was

---

[1] Aristides' assessment was made " in the third year after the battle of Salamis during the archonship of Timosthenes " (Aristotle, *Const. of Athens*, 23). This is one of the few precise and reliable dates for the period from 479 to 432 that has come down to us.

also the place where the delegates periodically met to discuss the general policy of the League ; but how often such congresses were held and what system of representation was adopted is unknown.[1] It may be suspected that, since the entire executive was from the first left to the Athenians, it was they who initiated offensive and defensive measures, even as was the case with Sparta as head of the Peloponnesian League. The commandership-in-chief was thus invariably held by an Athenian ; Athenian, too, were the financial officers (ἑλληνοταμίαι), ten in number, who supervised the funds of the League. The ancient writers are very vague, too, about the original or early members of the Confederacy ; for it is only from 454–453 onwards that more precise *data* are available. The cities of Ionia, Aeolis, and the Hellespontine region seem to have joined at the outset ; similarly a majority of the islands in the archipelago, headed by Chios, Samos, and Lesbos, were either original members or else came in very soon. As the number of tributaries recorded for 454–453 was probably about 140, it is unlikely that the total number of members during the first decade of the League's existence much exceeded one hundred.[2] From the first certain of the larger island-states, Chios, Lesbos, Samos, Naxos, Thasos, occupied a somewhat different position from the other allies. Like Athens herself, they placed a certain proportion of their naval forces at the disposal of the League. The rest met their liabilities by payment of the tribute. The grand total which Aristides' assessment was supposed to bring into the treasury annually was the very respectable sum of four hundred and sixty talents, but there is good reason for doubting whether this amount was ever collected in any given year during the earlier days of the Confederacy. In addition, the tribute-paying allies must have been under the obligation of providing a certain percentage of fighting men, although it is likely that some system of rotation was devised whereby the burden of service was more equitably distributed.[3] When

[1] As there is no doubt that all the cities in the League were at the outset autonomous, it is a reasonable inference that each had the same voting power at the congresses.

[2] For the tribute-lists and the light that they throw on the later history of the Confederacy see below, p. 14.

[3] Thucydides (I, 99), in discussing the secession of Naxos, mentions amongst the causes which led Athens to use compulsion against some of her allies their refusal to serve (λειποστράτιον).

all the terms of the alliance had been satisfactorily settled the solemn oaths were ratified to the accompaniment of an ancient and picturesque ceremonial. Lumps of iron were cast into the sea to signify that adherence to the covenant would endure until the iron should rise or float, that is to say, for ever.[1]

### § 3. CIMON'S OPERATIONS AGAINST PERSIA

The first campaign against Persia recorded in the sources was directed against Eion, a town lying at the mouth of the River Strymon (Struma) and occupied by a determined Persian garrison (summer of 476). Cimon, son of Miltiades, who commanded the expedition, and indeed continued to direct the military and naval operations of the allies down to 461, was at this time in his early thirties. He had been a mere stripling when he first came into public notice by paying the heavy fine imposed on his father after the failure of the Parian expedition (489), More recently he had won distinction by his conduct at Salamis. Apart from the need of reducing what Persian strongholds still remained in Europe, the Athenians were impressed with the value of Eion, for control of it would give them access to the Thracian hinterland with its wealth of timber and rich mineral deposits. The siege of the city seems to have been protracted owing to the stubborn resistance offered by the Persian commandant, Boges. When at last the place could hold out no longer he preferred immolation on a funeral pyre to surrender. In grateful memory for their father's gallantry Xerxes, we are told, showed exceptional favour to Boges' children.[2]

The expulsion of other Persian detachments in Thrace followed in this year or the next so that the allies secured complete control over the Thracian Chersonese. On the other hand they failed to take Doriscus from the Persians, and an Athenian detachment operating inland from Eion seems to have been destroyed by native tribes.

The attack on Scyros (475-474?) was unconnected with the anti-Persian objective of the League. But, even though

[1] An earlier instance of this ceremonial is recorded by Herodotus (I, 165) in the case of the Phocaeans.
[2] Herodotus VII, 107. There seems no reason for doubting the truth of the tale, which Herodotus can easily have learnt from a reliable Persian source.

Athens primarily benefited by the result, it could reasonably be interpreted as an undertaking that was in the common interest. The Dolopian inhabitants of the island lived from piracy and accordingly were a menace to peaceful and legitimate trade in the Aegean. Cimon captured the island and sold the inhabitants into slavery. The place was then settled by a body of Athenian cleruchs.[1] This exploit, moreover, added greatly to Cimon's reputation owing to an opportune archæological discovery. According to an ancient oracle, Scyros was the last resting-place of the Attic hero, Theseus. Exploration of an old tumulus brought to light a skeleton of great size of some long-forgotten warrior who had been laid to rest in full panoply of war. After this there could be no doubt that the oracle had spoken truly. The venerable remains were brought with solemn rites to Athens and there interred.

Serious hostilities against Persia appear to have been suspended for several years. At last, in 468 according to the most likely computation, an armament of about two hundred vessels under Cimon's direction took to the high seas. The reason for assembling this formidable array—and it was the first occasion on which approximately the full resources of the Confederacy were brought into play—was that the Great King himself, after a long period of preparation, was about to launch a naval attack on the Greeks with the object of recovering his lost dependencies in Asia. Cimon's immediate objective was Phaselis on the Gulf of Pamphylia, an important city subject to Persia, which he must needs occupy before trying conclusions with the Persian fleet stationed in those waters. Once in his grasp, Phaselis would serve as a much-needed base of operations. After some preliminary skirmishing the place surrendered because the inhabitants, after some hesitation engendered by fear of the Great King, were persuaded by the Chian contingent serving under Cimon to throw in their lot with the Greeks; for Chios and Phaselis had long been on friendly terms. After this initial success the Greek commander hastened to engage the main Persian fleet. Whether it was about equal, or, as seems more probable, slightly inferior numerically to his own forces, Cimon was

[1] For the character and organization of cleruchies in general see below, pp. 14 and 45.

anxious to force an engagement before a reinforcement of eighty Phoenician galleys could arrive from Cyprus. He found the enemy entrenched in a naval camp near the mouth of the River Eurymedon, the Persian commanders with questionable wisdom having followed the Persian tactics at Mycale. The Greeks succeeded in storming the camp and cut the Persians to pieces. Their ships were either captured or destroyed. Amongst those who did yeoman service for Cimon was the Samian Maeandrius and his companions. They were responsible for scuttling eight Persian galleys.[1] Cimon followed up this striking victory by putting to sea and intercepting the squadron of eighty vessels near Hydros. It suffered a similar fate to the main fleet. Thucydides (I, 100) puts the total of Persian galleys captured or destroyed by the Greeks at two hundred. Besides this, much booty fell to the lot of the conquerors. To commemorate the achievement of Cimon and his men the Athenians soon after made a dedication at Delphi from the proceeds of part of the spoil—a bronze palm surmounted by a gilded image of Athena. Two important consequences flowed from Cimon's victorious campaign: the fleet of Athens and her allies now held undisputed mastery over the Aegean, and the League received many new members by the inclusion of Phaselis and a number of cities in Caria and Lycia. Many of these under the influence of the Greek victory joined voluntarily, some others were taken by force.[2]

### § 4. ATHENS AND HER ALLIES

For some years before the successful Greek expedition to Asia Minor there had been ominous signs that Athenian statesmen were prepared, in order to further Athenian interests, to ignore or go beyond the terms on which the League of Delos had been founded. Of the several city-states on Euboea

---

[1] G. Klaffenbach in *Ath. Mitt.* 51 (1926), 26–28; Wade-Gery in *J.H.S.*, 53 (1933), 97–99.

[2] The account in Plutarch (*Cimon* 12) implies that the defection of Caria and Lycia followed the Eurymedon campaign, as Beloch (*Griech. Geschichte*, II, 2, p. 159) rightly pointed out. Diodorus (XI, 60–61), however, reverses the order of events. But it is inherently improbable that the cities of southern and south-western Asia Minor would throw off their allegiance to Persia while the Persian armament was not only intact but in the vicinity. Even a strong city like Phaselis hesitated at first to join the Greeks.

only Carystus had remained outside the Confederacy, whether through jealousy of Chalcis and Eretria or for some other cause, such as racial differences, is unknown.[1] From the allied, and especially from the Athenian, point of view, owing to the proximity of Carystus to the Attic coast, the aloof attitude of this city was a serious handicap. Hence it is understandable that when, some time between 474 and 470, persuasion failed, Athens declared war on the Carystians and coerced them into joining the League. But, since at its inception membership had been voluntary, the Athenian government showed by its action that it was beginning to regard the Confederacy in a new light. Its next action made it clear that the Athenians were preparing to change the position of Athens in the League. Some of the members showed signs of tiring of their obligations. Their growing unwillingness to furnish their quota in ships or tribute was perhaps due in part to a false sense of security promoted by the apparent inaction of Persia.[2] In 470 or 469 one of the leading allies, Naxos, withdrew from the Confederacy. Athens promptly treated this action as a *casus belli*. After a brief blockade the islanders were forced to capitulate. The terms imposed by Athens on the Naxians are not recorded; but Thucydides' statement (I, 99), that "Naxos was the first allied city to be enslaved contrary to the terms of the alliance," would seem to suggest some loss of autonomy and, to judge from later instances, destruction of Naxos' fortifications and confiscation of her navy.

No more is heard of trouble between Athens and other cities in the League until 465, when Thasos seceded. But, whereas the Naxians, as far as is known, attempted to withdraw merely because they were weary of their responsibilities as members of the Confederacy, the people of Thasos took the rash step on account of a quarrel with Athens over their mining rights in that part of the Thracian mainland which lay nearest to their island. Like the Naxians, they belonged to the small group of islanders who put their navy at the disposal of the League. Indeed, in material resources and

---

[1] Thucydides (VII, 57, 4) calls the people of Carystus Dryopians in distinction from the rest of Euboea which was Ionian.

[2] Thucydides (I, 99), in commenting on the revolt of Naxos, implies that secessions from the League had been attempted before.

naval strength they were probably little inferior to Chios, Lesbos, and Samos. Their prosperity was derived partly from their trade in wine, partly from the working of gold mines in Thasos and in Thrace. The Athenians on their part were making fresh plans, after their initial failure in 476, to exploit the territory inland from Eion. The Thasians, seeing their interests threatened, expostulated and, when this availed nothing, seceded from the League. They must have been fully conscious, in view of the fate of Naxos, that this step would mean war. It seems reasonable to assume, however, that from the first they hoped to embroil Athens in a quarrel with the Peloponnesian states. The Athenians acted promptly and despatched Cimon with a fleet to the island. He defeated the Thasian galleys that ventured to oppose him and captured thirty-three of them. Then he landed his men and, after several skirmishes, invested the city. The citizens nevertheless managed to smuggle through a message to Sparta imploring her aid, to take the form of a Peloponnesian invasion of Attica, in the hope that Cimon would be recalled and the blockade of Thasos raised. Whether even in normal times the Spartans would have acceded to this request is problematic. But a severe earthquake followed by a rising of the serfs and dependent population of Laconia and Messenia made any foreign commitment out of the question. Left to their own resources, the Thasians held out gallantly for two years. At last, in 463, they capitulated and paid a heavy penalty for their boldness in opposing Athens. They were required to raze their fortifications and hand over their galleys, to pay an indemnity at once and tribute hereafter,[1] and to give up their mainland possessions. The exploitation of Thrace by Athens had, however, to wait for another quarter of a century. An Athenian colony of ten thousand —an unusually large number—had been sent out in 465 to Nine Ways ('Εννέα ὁδοί), a few miles up the river from Eion. But the Edones, whom they dispossessed, stirred up other Thracian tribes, and when the colonists attempted to bring a wider area under control they were surrounded and cut to pieces.

After the treatment of Naxos and Thasos the Athenian

[1] Thasos' name duly appears on the first of the quota-lists in 454–3. Cf. Tod 30, col. v, 14.

government's attitude towards the Confederacy could no longer be in doubt. Many of the states who had joined in 478 may then have regarded it as a temporary alliance, to be dissolved as soon as danger from Persia appeared to be over. But those who guided Athenian policy, if not from the first, at least very soon, saw in the League a means of ensuring for their city a leading political position in the Hellenic world and of promoting her economic growth, if for no other reason than that only in some such way as this could the safety and freedom of the seas be secured. To have allowed the withdrawal of even a few of the most prominent members would have led quickly and inevitably to the complete dismemberment of the alliance. In 454–453, perhaps as a measure of safety when Athens' naval power was temporarily weakened by the disaster in Egypt (p. 18), the Treasury of the League was moved from Apollo's temple on Delos to that of Athena on the Athenian Acropolis. The oft-repeated statement that this transference marked the transmutation of the Delian Confederacy into an Athenian maritime empire is, however, erroneous. For, in the first place, the change was gradual and not sudden, and, again, it was approximately complete by 461. In addition to the two classes of autonomous allies, one providing ships the other paying tribute, there was now a third group—the tribute-paying subjects (ὑπήκοοι) of Athens. This last class grew steadily and, by 431, most of the cities belonged to it *de facto*, if not *de iure*. It was the policy of Athens to make separate agreements with the city-states, and there appears to have been considerable variation in their status; yet the few cases where the process can be seen actually at work do not suffice to give anything but a very incomplete picture of the whole organization. Thus an extant decree, passed in 450 or a little earlier, regulates the commercial relations between Athens and Phaselis;[1] another, of approximately the same date but very badly damaged, seems to deal with the procedure to be followed in judicial disputes between citizens of Athens and of Miletus.[2] The fact that the last-named city about the same time passed ordinances outlawing members of two families and their descendants perhaps because they were suspected of aiming at tyranny, seems to show that the Milesians were in some

[1] Tod 32.   [2] *I.G.*, I², 22.

anxiety for the safety of their democratic constitution.[1] A very fragmentary decree which can now be assigned to the year 447–446 refers to the affairs of Colophon. The only parts that can be restored with any certainty reproduce an oath to be taken by members of the Colophonian council. They swear to carry out their duties according to the laws of the city, to deliberate in the best interests of Athens and her allies, and to be faithful to the Athenian alliance and resist any effort to subvert the democratic constitution.[2] Judicial regulations and extreme penalties against any promoters of tyranny are also found in the last part of an Athenian decree relating to the affair of Erythrae (passed in 453–452). The earlier portion of the same inscription lays down the rules that are to govern the election of the Erythraean council together with the oath to be taken by each newly elected member. Its terms are similar to that found on the Colophonian inscription and elsewhere.[3]

On the strength of this epigraphic evidence, coupled with the generalizations of several Greek writers, of whom Aristotle is the most authoritative (*Politics*, 1307, b 20), it has commonly been stated that Athens, once her ascendancy in the League was completely assured, compelled her allies and subjects to adopt constitutions similar to her own. But, while it is no doubt true that democratic governments were to be found in most of these city-states, it by no means follows that the Athenians invariably or even frequently used force. The decrees concerning Erythrae and Miletus have been interpreted as showing secession from the League by the two cities. When they rejoined, the Athenians intervened and introduced a democratic constitution somewhat similar to their own. This conjecture is attractive but cannot be regarded as proved in the light of the extant evidence. But the earliest example recorded of a state, which had not tried to secede from the League, having a democratic constitution forced upon it is that of Samos.[4] This, moreover, was a

[1] Tod 35.
[2] *A.T.L.* II, D 15.
[3] Tod 29. The oath which Athens required every adult male citizen of Chalcis to take after the suppression of the Euboean revolt in 446–445 will be found in Tod 42.
[4] Cf. R. Meiggs in *J.H.S.* 63 (1943), pp. 21–34; *A.T.L.* II, pp. 54–60, and further references there given.

special case, because the Athenians forcibly intervened in a war between two of their allies at the request of one of them. As time progressed, Athenian sentiment undoubtedly hardened, and their treatment of allied and subject states became more arbitrary. This change is to some extent illustrated by the more frequent despatch of cleruchies.[1] These groups of Athenian settlers acted, as it were, as a garrison in the area where they were established. Sometimes at least the former inhabitants were depressed to the status of dependents ;[2] in extreme cases they were dispossessed entirely.[3] It is further significant that small bodies of Athenian troops under a commandant ($\phi\rho o \acute{v} \rho a \rho \chi o s$) and permanently quartered in a subject city-state are heard of more frequently after 440.[4]

Much light is shed on the financial organization of this maritime empire by a long series of lists that were originally inscribed on stone and set up on the Athenian Acropolis. Beginning in the year 454–453 and extending to 415–414, they record the offering of one-sixtieth that was set aside for the goddess Athena from the tribute of the allies and subjects. The names of the contributing cities are inscribed in long columns and opposite to each is the quota. A simple sum in multiplication will thus give the actual amount of tribute paid by each community. Owing, however, to the very damaged condition of many of the lists, not a single one being in fact complete, many uncertainties still exist. Normally, and until the time of the Second Peloponnesian War, a reassessment was made every four years during the year of the Greater Panathenaea at Athens. Estimates both of the number of contributors and of the total sum collected in a given year are necessarily more approximate than exact.[5]

[1] For these settlements see below, p. 45.
[2] As, for example, in Lesbos after the revolt of 428–427. See Thucydides, III, 50, and an inscription of 427–426 (Tod 63).
[3] This was the fate of the people of Hestiaea in Euboea (Thucydides, I, 114).
[4] Even so, as H. G. Robertson has shown (*Classical Philology*, 28, 50–53), the cities continued sometimes to be free to choose their own form of government.
[5] Though long known, these quota lists have only been correctly reconstructed during the last thirty years. For the complete series, see *A.T.L.* I and particularly II, where the lists have been reprinted from *A.T.L.* I with some recent additions and emendations and with full references to recent articles. Cf. also Tod I, pp. 52–56 and 260.

Two general conclusions that emerge from comparison of these documents are noteworthy. While the complete index of communities found in all the lists taken together totals about 400 names, it is clear that the total number of contributing states in any single year fell far short of two hundred.[1] In the second place, although we are told on the authority of Thucydides (I, 96) that Aristides' assessment was calculated to bring in four hundred and sixty talents annually, the quota lists show that this sum was never realized in any year before the drastic reassessment imposed by Athens in 425-424. Indeed, save in the year 444-443, when the total may have reached between four hundred and twenty-six and four hundred and twenty-seven talents, the income that can be tentatively estimated for each year is less than four hundred. For convenience in collection the Athenians, after some experimental years, sought to group the tributaries into separate geographical areas. From 443-442 to 439-438 there were five—Ionia, Caria, Thrace, Hellespont, and the islands.[2] In 438-437 Caria and Ionia were joined into one group; hereafter the four geographical divisions remain unchanged, although the order in which they are entered in the lists is not constant.

## § 5. THE EGYPTIAN EXPEDITION

The success of Cimon in south-western Asia Minor had assured to Athens the naval control in the Aegean, so that in effect the reduced Persian fleet was confined to the restricted area between the Syrian coast and Cyprus. Not many years after the Eurymedon campaign there occurred one of those palace revolutions which were so familiar a feature in the despotic kingdoms of the Orient. The commandant of the king's guard, Artabanus, together with one of the royal eunuchs, formed a plot to assassinate Xerxes (464). Having killed the king they secured the succession for his second son, Artaxerxes. They further persuaded him to believe that the murder had been done by his elder brother, Darius, whose

---

[1] The complete index of names will be found in the Register in *A.T.L.* I, pp. 215 ff., together with the amount assessed against each city, insofar as it is recorded or can be restored with reasonable certainty.

[2] Cf. H. Nesselhauf, *Untersuchungen zur Geschichte des Delisch-Attischen Symmachie* (*Klio*, Beiheft 30), pp. 36-37.

execution was thereupon ordered by the new ruler.[1] Artabanus, however, was evidently aiming at supreme power for himself, for he soon entered into a conspiracy with Megabyzus to assassinate Artaxerxes. But Megabyzus betrayed the secret and Artabanus was executed. His fellow-conspirators were overpowered after a fight and killed, amongst them Artabanus' three sons. The loyal Megabyzus was desperately wounded, but, thanks to the skill of a Greek physician from Cos, ultimately recovered.

A rising organized by the satrap of Bactria inaugurated Artaxerxes' reign. Such disturbances were by no means uncommon when there was a change of ruler in an Oriental empire, and were most likely to be attempted in an outlying province. The first engagement between the insurgents and Artaxerxes' forces was indecisive ; but in a second battle the king's army triumphed and the revolution collapsed. Far more serious was the rebellion which broke out in Egypt, probably not later than 461. Its leading spirit was the Libyan prince, Inaros, who entered Egypt and won over a goodly proportion of the inhabitants to his cause. They proclaimed him king of Egypt and abruptly expelled the Persian officials who arrived soon after to collect the annual tribute due from the province. Although momentarily successful against the weak Persian force quartered in Egypt, Inaros was quick to recognize that the Persian government would mobilize a large force to recover so valuable a dependency. He therefore augmented his native army by enlisting foreign mercenaries.[2] At the same time he sent an embassy to the Athenians inviting their active co-operation. Unfortunately it is not known what material inducements he may have offered. Yet it is not difficult to understand that the Athenians, in view of their past successes against the ancestral enemy, saw in the Egyptian enterprise a fair chance of detaching the Nile province permanently from the Persian empire, and then drawing the ruler of Egypt into an alliance with

---

[1] This is the version given by Ctesias, *Persica* (ed. J. Gilmore), § 60. Ctesias, in view of his long residence at the Persian court, is likely to be accurately informed. Somewhat different accounts will be found in Diodorus (XI, 69) and Justin (III, 1).

[2] Diod., XI, 71—μισθοφόρους ἐκ τῶν ἀλλοεθνῶν ἀθροίζων. These mercenaries were presumably Greeks, but they find no mention in H. W. Parke, *Greek Mercenary Soldiers* (Oxford, 1933).

themselves that would be both politically and commercially advantageous. Nor must it be forgotten that Pericles at this time had had but little experience of foreign affairs. And it is open to doubt whether, if Cimon, who had been ostracized in 461, had still been influential at Athens, the Egyptian proposal would have been accepted. And had it been, and had the resulting expedition been under the experienced guidance of Cimon, the result would probably have been very different.

A large expedition of two hundred vessels which had recently been ordered to Cyprus was instructed to sail for Egypt ; but only a portion of this force—some fifty vessels— remained to co-operate with Inaros. The greater part returned to Cyprus to hold the Persians in check by sea.[1] The allies in Egypt began brilliantly. A Persian army, which probably outnumbered them, was defeated in a pitched battle, and its commander, Achaemenes, the Great King's uncle, fell fighting with many of his men. The rest of the Persians managed to cover their retreat and shut themselves up in the strongly fortified quarter of Memphis, known as the White Castle (Λευκὸν τεῖχος). It is indicative of the undeveloped character of siege warfare at this period that their enemy, though they occupied the rest of Memphis, completely failed to force their surrender. If we accept Thucydides' statement (I, 110) that the Athenian operations in Egypt lasted six years, some years must have passed before a fresh Persian army appeared to recover the lost province. Artaxerxes' efforts to bring about the withdrawal of the Athenian force by stirring up Sparta to invade Attica, though unsuccessful, must have caused considerable delay. Furthermore, means of communication in the ancient world were necessarily slow, so that the mobilization of troops in so vast an Empire as the Persian always consumed much time. In the interval, though they failed to dislodge the garrison in the White Castle, Inaros and his allies, to whom

[1] That there was some fighting in or near Cyprus is proved by the casualty list of the Erechtheid tribe at Athens, which contains the names of some who fell in the island in 459 or 458. See Tod 26. That only a part of the Cypriote expedition operated in Egypt, and that the disaster to Athens in 454 was not as great as suggested by Thucydides, has been demonstrated by M. Caspari in *Classical Quarterly*, VII (1913), pp. 198 ff., and by F. E. Adcock in the *Proceedings of the Cambridge Philological Society* for 1926.

was added Amyrtaeus, a chief ruling in the fen district of the Egyptian Delta, probably secured complete control of Upper Egypt. At length, in 456, a Persian army commanded by Megabyzus advanced through Syria into the Delta. The enemy was probably waiting to bar his progress not far from the frontier. A pitched battle was the sequel, in which the complete victory of Megabyzus avenged the disaster that had befallen Achaemenes some years before. The relief of Memphis followed swiftly. Inaros with his allies was steadily and relentlessly driven back into Prosopitis, territory formed into an island by two branches of the Nile and a communicating canal. Here the insurgents were blockaded for eighteen months until Megabyzus in April or May, 454, when the Nile stream was at its lowest, succeeded in diverting the waters of the canal. The Athenian ships which were moored in it were left high and dry, and Megabyzus was able to turn the blockade into an assault. His manœuvre was perfectly successful and the enemy were crushed. The Athenians, who by setting fire to their galleys had deprived the Persian of part of the fruits of victory, seem to have perished fighting. Only a few stragglers managed to escape and eventually found their way to Cyrene.[1] Inaros was taken alive and led off to Persia ; he was subsequently put to death by impaling. Amyrtaeus held out for some time longer in his marshes.

Serious though this loss in men and material was to Athens, it was almost doubled by the disaster which overtook a relief expedition of fifty Athenian and allied vessels. This squadron reached the African coast in ignorance of the calamity at Prosopitis ; its admiral was consequently off his guard. As the Athenians entered the mouth of the Mendesian branch of the Nile, they were attacked by Phoenician galleys which drove them on to the shore. Here a Persian army was in waiting and cut them in pieces. The majority of the Greek vessels was destroyed, only a very few making good their escape.

[1] This is the explicit statement of Thucydides (I, 110). The assertion of Ctesias (*Persica*, § 65), that Megabyzus captured six thousand Athenians, is impossible. Diodorus, apparently trying to combine the two versions, relates (XI, 77) that the Athenian prisoners by agreement with the Persian commander were allowed to escape to Cyrene.

## § 6. CIMON'S LAST CAMPAIGN AND THE PEACE OF CALLIAS

Very decidedly Persia had won the second round of the contest. The resources and naval power of Athens were temporarily weakened; consequently her conduct of the war in which she was engaged with the Peloponnesian League was strictly defensive. In 452-451 Cimon returned from exile to Athens at a critical time. The policy of Pericles and his associates had been far from uniformly successful, while the bitterest blow to Athenian pride had doubtless been their recent humiliation by the Great King. It was, then, not surprising that Cimon immediately regained his old ascendancy in the assembly. Retaliation on Persia would be the wish of every patriotic Athenian, but recent events had shown that this would only be possible if Athens were at peace with her Greek neighbours. With the philo-Laconian Cimon once more exerting a predominant influence, an accommodation was reached with Sparta, and a five years' truce was concluded in 451 between the two states and their respective allies.

In the following year a fleet of two hundred Athenian and allied vessels set sail for Cyprus, with the double object of exhibiting Athenian supremacy in the Aegean and inflicting suitable losses on the Great King within his own waters. Sixty of the galleys were detailed to sail for Egypt, there to co-operate with Amyrtaeus, who was still maintaining his independence. The rest laid siege to Citium on the south coast of Cyprus. In what was to prove his last undertaking Cimon's good fortune deserted him. Citium put up a spirited defence, so that the siege was protracted until Athenian supplies ran seriously short. Cimon himself fell dangerously ill and died. Though the ancient accounts are vague and do not specify the disease, the cause of death may well have been enteric fever. The Athenians, apparently acting on the last instructions of their admiral, abandoned the blockade. They circumnavigated Cyprus, however, on their way home, and off Salamis encountered and engaged a fleet of Phoenician and Cilician warships. Spurred on by the memory of their late commander, they carried all before them. They drove the enemy vessels ashore and then, following up their advantage, inflicted a crushing defeat on the Great King's men on land.[1] After this the expedition sailed home, the squadron in Egypt being recalled at the same time.

It is reasonably clear that an understanding was now reached by Athens and Persia; but which side took the initiative must remain undecided. At all events an Athenian embassy headed by Callias—possibly Cimon's brother-in-law of that name—reached Susa in the winter of 449-448. There an agreement is supposed to have been concluded on terms suspiciously favourable to Athens. For while the Athenians merely consented to abstain from attacking or interfering in territory subject to Persia, Artaxerxes agreed to recognize the independence of the Greek cities in the Asia Minor littoral and to keep his men-of-war out of the Aegean. It is in the highest degree improbable that the ruler of the Persian empire gave any such definite undertaking to the leader of a group of Greek city-states. But even if no formal treaty was drawn up and little more than a cessation of present hostilities was arranged, the result remained the same. The two states were at peace with one another for thirty-six years, a peace that was not seriously endangered by an occasional "frontier incident."[2]

Thus after three decades the purpose for which the Delian Confederacy had been formed was at last achieved. A dispassionate observer might have commented that, if Athens had gained much, the Asiatic Greeks had also increased their material prosperity under the new *régime*. They themselves, however, were more conscious that politically they had but exchanged one master for the other. That consciousness was the germ which was ultimately to disintegrate the empire of Athens.

[1] Diodorus (XII, 3-4) and Plutarch (*Cimon* 18) reverse the order of events, attributing the naval victory to Cimon. Plutarch wastes a page on omens and apparitions portending Cimon's death, and introduces a highly improbable story how Cimon sent to consult the oracle of Zeus Ammon at Siwah.

[2] Thus Pissuthnes helped the Samians in 440 (Thuc., I, 115) and a medizing party in Colophon in 428 (*ib.*, III, 34). Some years later the Athenian Lamachus, when in Pontus, marched through Persian territory to Chalcedon with a body of troops (*ib.*, IV, 75).

## CHAPTER II

## THE GREEK HOMELAND, 479 TO 432 B.C.

### § 1. SPARTA AND THE PELOPONNESIAN LEAGUE

IT would not be easy to point to a greater contrast than that afforded by the political histories of Sparta and of Athens for two decades after the Persian wars. While Athens, as has been seen, advanced from strength to strength, the Spartan government was faced with a succession of problems, any one of which occurring singly would have been far from negligible. Their cumulative effect threatened to shatter the solidarity of the Peloponnesian League and to deprive Sparta herself of her military hegemony. Whatever judgment one may form of her political ideal, one cannot withhold admiration of the iron discipline and efficient organization by virtue of which in the end her authority was established as firmly as before.

The scanty and unreliable sources record a military intervention by Sparta in Thessaly, which was entrusted to the Spartan king, Leotychidas, the same who had commanded the allies at Mycale. This expedition is most likely to have occurred in 479–478, its purpose being to put an end to the despotism of the Aleuad clan, its excuse, besides the Spartan dislike of tyrants, the pro-Persian policy recently pursued by these Thessalian princes. But it failed to achieve its object, ostensibly because Leotychidas allowed himself to be bought off. This at least was the charge brought against him some eight or nine years later; rather than face an impeachment he fled to Tegea, where he ended his days.[1]

Of greater interest and moment are the relations at this period between Sparta and Athens, which was still technically a member of the Panhellenic alliance formed in 481–480, if

[1] A discussion of the chronological difficulties in the extant accounts of this episode will be found in *C.A.H.*, V., Appendix I.

not actually of the Peloponnesian League. For several years
after Salamis Themistocles continued to exercise considerable
influence in Athenian affairs; it was only after 474 that his
authority began rapidly to wane. About few men in antiquity
were more stories told at a later time than about him. Most
of these are probably apocryphal; but, even so, they are not
without value in that they illustrate the judgment formed by
posterity of his character and methods. One of these tales
attributes to him a plan to burn the Peloponnesian fleet
while it lay at anchor in the Gulf of Volo at the time of
Leotychidas' Thessalian venture. On the advice of Aristides
the virtuous Athenian *demos* rejected a proposal that, translated into successful action, would have left the Athenian
navy at least temporarily without rival in European Greece.
Again, we are told that when the Spartans tried to force the
exclusion from the Delphic Amphictiony of all those states
that had gone over to Persia during the late war, Themistocles succeeded in bringing about the rejection of this motion
which, if carried, would have given Sparta control of the
majority of votes on the Amphictionic Council. Whatever,
then, the precise historical truth underlying these later
traditions about the Athenian statesman may be, at least
they mirror his political activity and the fact that in external
affairs it was directed against Sparta. This is even more
apparent in an episode vouched for by so rigorous a critic of
historical fiction as Thucydides. There is no doubt that one
of the first acts of the Athenians after the war with Persia
was over was to repair the material damage done to Athens
during two hostile invasions of Attica. By the use of every
available person of either sex the fortifications were rebuilt
in a remarkably short time, the city area being somewhat
enlarged on the same occasion. This action of the Athenians
called forth a protest from the Spartan government, which
argued that, in case of another foreign attack, the invader
would find a strongly fortified Athens an admirable base, and
that it would be in the interests of Greece as a whole in the
event of such an attack, if the inhabitants of central Greece
took refuge behind the Isthmus of Corinth. Rather than face
the issue directly with the Spartans, the ancient narrative
continues, the Athenians followed the advice of Themistocles
and sent him to Sparta. There he temporized and delayed

the negotiations for several months until the most necessary fortifications had been built. Then the Athenians came out into the open and confronted the Spartans with a *fait accompli*. If one hesitates to accept the story in all its elaborate detail, even on the high authority of Thucydides, there can at least be no reasonable doubt that the Spartans were piqued at the independence shown by the Athenians, whom they chose to put in the same category as their Peloponnesian allies, and for that reason they had felt entitled to register a protest. That Athens was following the guidance of Themistocles, moreover, is proved by the circumstance that the rebuilding of the city walls was only the first part of a more elaborate plan of defence-works.

He had long urged that the whole peninsula of Acte, with the fine harbour of Piraeus on the north-west and the two adjacent smaller ports of Zea and Munychia on the south-east, be fortified. The building operations had been begun in 493–492, but had been interrupted by Darius' invasion and apparently not resumed afterwards. At last, between 477 and 476, this very considerable undertaking was completed. The total length of the walls was about seven and a half miles ; in addition, each of the harbours was protected on the sea side by strong moles. It was the last notable achievement of Themistocles that he heartened his countrymen thus to construct a port and naval base worthy of a great maritime *polis* and second to none in the eastern Mediterranean. It was a fitting climax to the policy that he had consistently pursued for sixteen years or more, that of making Athens the leading naval state in the Hellenic world.

The wave of optimism and increased political consciousness which was the legitimate sequel to the defeat of the Persian invader was by no means confined to Athens ; nor was it there alone that the older form of government, in which responsibility and prerogative were restricted to a minority, broke down before the demands of the citizen body as a whole for a share in the control of affairs. Such developments could not but be objectionable to the Spartans, who with rare exceptions were the most conservative of the Greeks and the least receptive of new ideas.

Elis hitherto had been an agrarian state composed of a number of scattered communities and governed by its landed aristocracy. During the decade after Xerxes' invasion the Eleans under the impetus of a strong democratic movement abandoned their loose political organization and created a single city-state of Elis. This unification (συνοικισμὸς), accompanied, as it was, by the adoption of a democratic government, put Elis in a stronger position in relation to her neighbours than she had ever been. Unwelcome though this development was to the Spartans, they did not intervene; for internal problems—the deposition of her kings and unrest amongst her serf population—and ominous changes in neighbouring Arcadia demanded all their attention. Initiated by the people of Tegea, a movement was afoot for creating an Arcadian alliance of city-states and breaking away completely from Sparta and the Peloponnesian League. This threat to Sparta was the more formidable because Tegea had been able to enlist the support of Argos.

This state had recovered but slowly from the shattering defeat inflicted by Cleomenes I and his Spartans about the year 494. Her citizen body had been so depleted by that war that she was powerless to interfere when communities in the Argolid hitherto dependent on her reasserted their autonomy. Indeed, the remnant of Argive citizens had been forced to enfranchise a portion of the serf population.[1] At last, after about a quarter of a century, they felt themselves strong enough to try and recover some of their old influence in the Peloponnese. Filled with hatred of their ancient enemy, Sparta, they supported the Arcadians in their bid for independence. But the Spartans, putting forth their maximum effort, in two campaigns (c. 471 and 469?) proved once more the superiority of their training and organization. Close by Tegea they defeated a combined force of Tegeans and Argives, and the latter gave up active military intervention in Arcadia. Even more decisive was a Spartan victory at Dipaea two years later over an army of all the Arcadian cities except Mantinea, for it delayed for a century the formation of an Arcadian League, and Tegea and the rest returned to their allegiance to the Peloponnesian League. The refusal of Mantinea,

[1] Herodotus, VI, 83; Aristotle, *Politics*, 1303, a 6. As W. L. Newman in his commentary on the *Politics* points out, Aristotle by περίοικοι means serfs, not a free though dependent population like the Laconian and Messenian Perioeci. Hence Plutarch (*Moralia*, 245 F) is not justified in his criticism of Herodotus' statement with which Aristotle's is in agreement.

probably the strongest of all the Arcadian communities, to take up arms against Sparta, had probably been the deciding factor in the struggle. Her reward was that she about this time carried through a unification of neighbouring villages, similar to that at Elis, without Spartan protest. At the same time a democratic government was established at Mantinea.

Meantime the Argives, besides giving some assistance to the Mantineans in carrying out their reforms, recovered control of the Argolid. First a number of smaller communities were overawed or compelled without much trouble to acknowledge Argive authority. Then Mycenae and Tiryns were attacked. With some help from Cleonae the Argives reduced both cities. Mycenae was levelled to the ground and its people enslaved. Tiryns also ceased to exist as a separate town; its surviving citizens appear to have gone free and found a new home in Halieis.

### § 2. THE HELOT REVOLT

A far more formidable danger to Sparta than any challenge levelled against her by neighbouring states was the growing restiveness after the Persian wars of the serfs in Laconia and Messenia. After their final conquest in the seventh century the Helots seem to have been kept sufficiently in subjection to prevent for many years any serious trouble to the citizen body. Perhaps they would have continued in their mood of hopeless resignation even now, if their hopes of an all but forgotten freedom had not been roused to the highest pitch by no less a person than a Spartan king. Pausanias, foiled in his plans for becoming an Oriental despot outside the boundaries of Laconia, began, after the second failure of the ephors to bring his treason home to him, to frame a plot for overthrowing the existing Spartan constitution, and with the help of the Helots, to whom he promised admission to the civic body, establishing himself in a position of absolute authority. At the same time he was continuing his treasonable correspondence with Persia. This was his undoing. The ephors, although they had obtained incriminating information from some Helots, withheld action until a young Thracian slave, who was the king's trusted messenger, began to fear for his own skin and divulged all he knew. By arrangement with this informer a trap was laid for the king, who, when he realized that the game was up, took sanctuary in the temple of Athena of the Brazen House. The ephors caused the place to be barred up, allowing Pausanias to perish of starvation. When he was on the point of death they had him carried out into the open so that the shrine of the goddess might not be polluted (c. 468).

Bitterly disappointed at their frustrated hopes but without a leader of weight, the Helots for the moment remained quiescent. But in 464 a severe earthquake shook Laconia. It was especially severe in the city of Sparta, where all but five of the dwelling-houses were said to have been levelled to the ground and more than twenty thousand persons killed.[1] The young king, Archidamus, kept his head admirably in the emergency, and summoned all able-bodied Spartans under arms. His action, equivalent to putting the country under martial law, prevented a panic. But the Helots, who were soon joined by some of the Perioeci, saw in this catastrophe a heaven-sent opportunity to rise against their masters. So meagre, however, are the sources that it is impossible even to sketch the progress of the war. Most, if not all, of Laconia and Messenia was probably involved. The insurgents, finding that owing to Archidamus' presence of mind they would meet with a desperate resistance there, abandoned their plan of trying to seize the city of Sparta. On the other hand they cut to pieces a company of three hundred Spartans near Stenyclarus, and they must have had other successes. After the first few months the Spartans who had received timely help from a detachment of Mantinean troops, probably regained full control in Laconia. The struggle in Messenia was more bitter and long drawn out. In 462 the Spartans appealed for military assistance to their allies in the Peloponnese and to Athens. By the time that the request was sent to the Athenians the tide of war had already turned; but there remained the reduction of those insurgents who obstinately refused to yield and had fallen back on Mount Ithome, the scene of their ancestors' struggle against Sparta two centuries earlier. The Athenians responded

---

[1] This figure for the casualties caused by the earthquake is given in Diodorus (XI, 63), and must therefore be regarded with some suspicion.

by sending Cimon at the head of a considerable body of troops. But even with the help of the Athenians, who were reputed to be especially versed in siege warfare, the Spartans were unable to capture Ithome. To make matters worse, disagreements arose between the two allies which culminated in an abrupt intimation by the Spartan government to Cimon that the services of the Athenians were no longer needed. The snub caused bitter feelings in Athens which recoiled on Cimon, who had been the chief advocate of the Athenian expedition to Messenia as well as being its military head. The Helots were eventually compelled by starvation to surrender. That they were able to hold out all together for nine years is difficult to believe. If we can accept a probable emendation in the text of Thucydides (I, 103, 1), the war ended in the fourth year, that is to say, in 460–459.[1] When finally they surrendered, they were allowed to go free on condition that they left the country and made no attempt, singly or collectively, to return; for in that event the penalty would be immediate enslavement. The Athenians, partly out of pique against Sparta, but mainly because they saw in the Messenians serviceable and thrifty settlers, established them at Naupactus on the north shore of the Corinthian Gulf, a place from which they had just ousted a body of Ozolian Locrians.

### § 3. ATHENS: PARTY STRUGGLES AND THE EXILE OF THEMISTOCLES

Nothing is more tantalizing than the almost complete silence of our sources concerning the internal history of Athens during the decade after Salamis, for it was during those years that the way was prepared for reforms which, when completed, left the Athenian government a very different thing from that associated with the venerated name of Clisthenes. Of Athens' "elder statesmen" nothing further is heard of Xanthippus after his archonship in 479–478.[2] Aristides, on

[1] Cf. H. Bengtson, *Griechische Geschichte*, p. 183, note 4.
[2] There is no ancient evidence to suggest that Xanthippus took part in the agitation that led to the ostracism of Themistocles. When Diodorus (XI, 41) couples the name of Xanthippus with that of Aristides in relating the rejection of Themistocles' proposal to burn the Peloponnesian fleet (cf. above, p. 22), he is writing of an event which, if it took place at all, occurred in 478.

the other hand, was for some years too fully occupied with the organization of the newly created Confederacy to permit his taking a prominent part in internal affairs. Thus it would seem that for a while Themistocles continued to wield more influence than any other over his countrymen. It has been seen how he left an enduring memorial of the policy that he had unswervingly advocated for many years in the fortification of Athens and Peiraeus. Once the Confederacy of Delos was firmly established, however, Aristides was free to give his attention to home affairs, leaving the military direction of the League to a younger man. It is thus possible that, as one ancient writer suggests,[1] Aristides, bearing in mind the possibilities and needs of Athens' recently acquired maritime ascendancy, helped on the process by which the number of urban citizens in Athens and Peiraeus increased steadily while the free agricultural population of Attica declined.

It is well attested that he continued to be Themistocles' political opponent in the assembly; we do not know the questions of policy on which they chiefly disagreed. The differences must in time have become acute and the influence of Aristides and of younger men have prevailed over the counsels of Themistocles. It was probably in 471–470 that matters reached a crisis on the annual occasion when the people had to decide whether it wished to vote on the ostracism of any of the citizens. A majority was in favour of testing popular sentiment; the sequel was the ostracism of Themistocles. He retired to Argos, and in two or three years that he passed there did what he could to foster anti-Spartan sentiment in the Peloponnese. He received communications, too, from Pausanias; but while he was no doubt cognisant of the king's plans, there is no ground for believing that he favoured any anti-Hellenic projects which Pausanias may have formed. The downfall and death of the king compromised the Athenian owing to the discovery of certain correspondence. The Spartan government lodged a formal protest at Athens; the Athenians, instead of declining to interfere, took steps to have Themistocles extradited. Realizing that it would go hard with him, if he were arraigned in the existing state of public opinion at Athens, he withdrew

[1] Aristotle, *Const. of Athens*, 24.

to Corcyra. But there and elsewhere he found men unwilling to harbour him indefinitely. By devious routes he finally made his way to Asia Minor. There he remained for a time in obscurity; then he made his way to Susa and appeared at the Persian court after the accession of Artaxerxes I (464). His reception by the Great King was gracious and he was entrusted with the government of Magnesia-on-the-Maeander. In addition he was assigned considerable revenues from the cities of Myus and Lampsacus. At Magnesia he seems to have lived another dozen years, held in high honour by the inhabitants as well as by the Oriental despot whose retainer he had become. Extant coins of the city from this period bear his name.[1]

It is idle to moralize on the later years of this great man. To him more than to any other man Athens owed her imperial position in the fifth century. The earliest surviving judgment of him as a statesman stresses his native intelligence, his unerring power of foreseeing political developments in the Greek world and beyond, and his resourcefulness in the face of them and in any emergency.[2] Such praise from the most reserved of philosophic historians silences criticism and reduces the last stage of his career to its true proportion. It was a trivial episode without great historic importance except to those sentimental souls who to every story demand a happy ending. They would do better to ponder the ingratitude of the Athenian democracy rather than the Persian exile of its greatest citizen.

Of the younger politicians at Athens the more radical were to some extent the heirs of Themistocles' ideas. They sought to make their city the rival not the equal ally of Sparta, and, at home, they strove to widen the basis of democratic government by weakening the hold which the members of the old aristocratic families in Attica still had upon the higher offices in the state. Cimon, on the other hand, was among the younger men the outstanding representative of the ruling class. His personal popularity he owed in part to a frank and generous nature. His fellow-demesmen saw in him a *grand seigneur*, but one who could dispense hospitality with a lavish hand without assuming an air of patronage. But

---

[1] Cf. *C.A.H.*, Plates II, 3 h.
[2] Thucydides, I, 138.

it was to those more solid qualities, shown by him as *generalissimo* of the Delian League, that he owed his position as the acknowledged leader of the more conservative group in the *ecclesia*. Characteristic of his class and traditions was the foreign policy that he advocated. Its basic principle was the continued maintenance of cordial relations with Sparta, and its ultimate aim, therefore, that dual hegemony in Greece—Sparta's military, allied to Athens' naval leadership—to which political thinkers of the fourth century like Isocrates looked back regretfully as the ideal of Athens' and Greece's golden age. But this was not a popular doctrine at Athens; that Cimon was able to command sufficient support to translate his views into action for a while must be attributed in the main to the prestige which he deservedly derived from his steady enlargement of the League and his successes against Persia. The first sign of waning authority occurred in 463. On his return from Thasos a group of his political opponents, amongst them Xanthippus' son, Pericles, instigated a prosecution against him on the ground that, when he had the opportunity to add to the Athenian dependencies at the expense of Macedonia, he was bribed by Alexander of Macedon to desist. He was able to make a successful defence against what was no doubt a trumped-up charge and was acquitted. It may be surmised that his accusers had hoped to make capital out of Cimon's well-known friendliness to Sparta; for, though the attempt of the Thasians to provoke a war between Sparta and Athens failed, popular irritation in Athens, once the facts became known, is not likely to have been confined to Thasos.

Within a year of his trial and acquittal Cimon faced the greatest test in his political career triumphantly. In the face of the strongest opposition he urged compliance with the Spartan request for military aid against the Helots. Of the speech by which he carried a majority in the assembly with him a younger contemporary recorded the most famous sentence. It may be said to crystallize his political faith: " They (the Athenians) ought not to suffer Greece to be lamed, nor their own city to be deprived of her yoke-fellow."[1] The abrupt dismissal of the Athenians at Ithome a few months later concentrated the full indignation of the Athenians on

[1] Ion quoted by Plutarch, *Cimon* 16.

the man who had advised the unfortunate expedition, and Cimon was ostracized in the spring of 461.

§ 4. ATHENS: EPHIALTES' AND PERICLES' PROGRAMME OF REFORM

About the same time the constitutional issues between the progressives and the conservatives in the Athenian assembly came to a head ; indeed, the enforced withdrawal from politics of Cimon was a necessary condition for the passing of the progressive programme, because the conservatives were deprived of an effective leader.

The council of the Areopagus, whose beginnings reached back far into the seventh century, was much the most important survival at Athens of an older *régime*. Recruited exclusively from the two wealthiest of the four Solonian classes, the council was the exclusive preserve of a minority ; its members with few exceptions belonged to the landed proprietors.[1] It is true that in the interval between the first and second Persian invasions election to the archonship by the Athenian *ecclesia* had been abandoned. In a preliminary election five hundred eligible persons under the new system were chosen by the demes. From this group three archons and six thesmothetae were appointed by lot from each tribe. The tenth tribe provided the secretary to the thesmothetae. This reform introduced a certain element of chance into the appointment of the archons ; under normal conditions it would have tended somewhat to lower the importance of the office. But this deterioration was arrested or retarded by the crisis of the Second Persian War ; for it was the council of the Areopagus which kept its head in the emergency before Salamis. When the military and naval leaders were fully engaged on the problems of defence and the population was dangerously near hysteria, the council rallied them and supervised the transportation of the non-combatants to a safety zone.

It would be difficult to name any notable institution in ancient Greece about which there is so little precise information as about the powers and functions of this council. That

[1] The ἱππεῖς had become eligible for the archonship, and consequently for membership of the council at the expiration of their year of office, about 500 B.C.

it exercised a general supervision or censorship over the community is clear, and in connection therewith its judicial powers were extensive. The prestige that it gained in the anxious weeks of 480 survived after the crisis had passed ; and for some time its influence appears to have been greater after 480 than in the two decades before that date. Thus, even if the sovereignty of the *ecclesia* had been regarded as an axiom of the constitution since the days of Clisthenes, the exercise of a real, if less clearly defined authority by an oligarchy of ex-magistrates was felt by the progressives to be an intolerable infringement of the people's will. We know nothing of the manner by which they paved the way for their drastic reforms ; but the departure of Cimon for Messenia in the summer of 462 coincided with the beginning of the attack on the council of the Areopagus by his political opponents. Their leader was Ephialtes, about whom little is known beyond his political honesty and his democratic principles. Legal proceedings were instituted against many individual members of the council, who were accused and convicted of irregular practices. Then, in the following year, after Cimon had gone into exile, the people, on the advice of Ephialtes and his younger contemporary and chief supporter, Pericles, deprived the council of all its prerogatives save one. Hereafter it continued to function solely as the chief court for the trial of homicide. Its jurisdiction in such cases was probably as old as the council itself. That it was left untouched by Ephialtes is not surprising, for by continuing to act as judges in such trials the council of the Areopagus could perform a valuable service, yet one quite remote from politics. Besides, in Greek law the slaying of a man and the atonement for the crime involved certain religious taboos ; to have transferred the trial of a homicide from the venerable body that had dealt with such for centuries to the popular law-courts would have shocked and alienated many citizens who were willing enough to see the council shorn of all political influence.[1] Two years later, in the spring of 458, Aeschylus in the

---

[1] The account in Aristotle's *Constitution of Athens* (25), in which Themistocles is associated with Ephialtes in the proceedings against the Areopagus, has been rightly rejected by the majority of modern scholars. It is quite irreconcileable with the other sources for the life of Themistocles and raises insurmountable chronological and other difficulties.

concluding scenes of his *Eumenides* pronounced a noble panegyric on this ancient and impartial court of justice.

Ephialtes did not long survive these initial victories of the progressive campaign. Like Scipio Aemilianus and Livius Drusus, the Younger, he fell by the hand of an assassin. And, though the agent of murder was known—Aristodicus, a citizen of Tanagra—the real instigators of the crime were never unmasked.[1] The leadership of the progressives passed to Pericles, who at this date was about thirty-three years of age. Although he chose the more popular side in politics, he was himself through his mother, Agariste, the great-niece of Clisthenes, closely connected with one of the oldest clans in Attica, the Alcmaeonids. His education had been of the best and engendered a love of abstract thought that in his middle years brought him the friendship of Anaxagoras. A natural readiness of speech was transformed by assiduous practice into an unrivalled eloquence. Shy and diffident in his youth, he later seemed to some of his contemporaries excessively reserved, whilst his enemies pronounced him haughty and proud. But this reserve, which was from the first a natural characteristic of the man, was in time used as an instrument of policy by the most dominating personality of his age. During the nine years following the death of Ephialtes Pericles carried through a number of drastic reforms which radically altered the character of the Athenian democracy. Eligibility to the archonship was accorded the third Solonian class ($\zeta\epsilon\upsilon\gamma\hat{\iota}\tau\alpha\iota$) in 457–456. Then a measure was passed which substituted sortition for election in the preliminary choice by the demes of candidates for the archonship. Thus the nine archons, being selected entirely by lot, soon became purely administrative officials; politically they exercised little power, though tenure of the office continued to be regarded as conferring distinction on the holder. While the board of ten *strategi* were the chief executive magistrates, the council of five hundred ($\beta o \upsilon \lambda \acute{\eta}$) greatly increased in importance, the more so as it inherited much of the power formerly wielded by the council of the Areopagus.

---

[1] Antiphon, *On the murder of Herodes*, 68. But Plutarch (*Pericles* 10) is probably right in attributing it to the oligarchs, that is to say, to one of those oligarchical clubs of which more is heard in the latter part of the century.

But the most thoroughgoing innovation was the introduction of payment to jurors in the popular courts, to all magistrates except the *strategi*, and to the members of the council of five hundred. In this manner Pericles and the progressives ensured that poverty would be no bar to the full exercise of civic responsibilities. Nor were those citizens forgotten who were at any time withdrawn from civil life on military and naval duties; to them also a small payment *per diem* whilst on active service was voted. It was the logical outcome of this conception of citizenship in the Athenian democracy that Pericles in 451–450 procured the passing of an act limiting the citizen body to those of Athenian descent on both sides. In doing this he went directly counter to the policy of Clisthenes, who had enlarged the civic body by admission of many who were only partially of Athenian birth and perhaps of some who were entirely foreign.[1]

§ 5. THE FIRST PELOPONNESIAN WAR, 459–445 B.C.

During the years in which the internal reforms sketched in the preceding section were being introduced, the Athenians were engaged in wars which for a short time involved directly a majority of states in the Peloponnese and central Greece. Athens' immediate reply to Sparta's curt dismissal of Cimon's expeditionary force at Ithome was to repudiate her membership of the Hellenic alliance formed in 481 under the presidency of Sparta, and then to conclude an alliance with Sparta's bitterest enemy in the Peloponnese, Argos. Both states next allied themselves to the Thessalians, a step which in the military sphere at least was soon to prove of questionable value. The actual outbreak of hostilities resulted from the decision of the Megarians to ally themselves to Athens as a protection against their neighbours of Corinth with whom they had fallen into a quarrel. The progressives in Athens welcomed this opportunity of extending their influence to the Isthmus. They sent garrisons to Megara and Pagae, its port on the Corinthian Gulf; they further made Nisaea, the harbour on the Saronic Gulf, secure by building two walls a little distance apart from it to Megara. The sequel to this energetic response of Athens to the Megarian appeal for help

[1] The actual working of the Periclean democracy is considered more fully below, Chapter XIV, § 2.

was war between her and Corinth, supported by Corinth's ally, Epidaurus. The Athenians made a raid on Halieis but were repulsed; later in the season, however, the Athenian naval forces defeated their Peloponnesian opponents off Cecryphaleia (spring and summer, 458). In the meanwhile Aegina had been added to the active enemies of Athens. The relations between the two states had for many years been as bad as those existing between Sparta and Argos. The prosperity of the Aeginetans, derived primarily from their carrying trade, was more than ever an offence to the Athenians now that they themselves were well launched on a programme of maritime expansion. The Aeginetans, for their part, had become increasingly apprehensive of their neighbour's growing power. In these circumstances it needed only a slight episode to precipitate war, but it is not clear from the sources which side was the aggressor in 458. A decisive naval engagement between the Athenians and the Aeginetans was fought in the Saronic Gulf before the end of this summer. The latter, though reinforced by Corinthian and Epidaurian vessels, not merely suffered defeat but lost seventy of their galleys by capture. Leocrates, the Athenian commander, followed up his victory by landing his fighting men and investing the city of Aegina.

The Peloponnesian allies of Aegina tried to raise the blockade by landing three hundred mercenaries to co-operate with the islanders and by invading the Megarid, in the expectation that they would in this way compel the Athenians to withdraw part or all of their troops from Aegina. In this they were disappointed. The Athenian *strategus*, Myronides, collected a force composed of those who under normal conditions would only be used for home defence—men past their prime and *ephebi* between eighteen and twenty years of age— and entered the territory of Megara. After the ensuing fight both sides claimed the victory; yet, if the encounter was indecisive, it was at least followed by the retirement of the Corinthians. In the second skirmish a few days later Myronides and his men indisputably came off best. Meanwhile the blockade of Aegina continued, and it was not until the early summer of the next year (457) that the islanders were obliged to capitulate. Under the terms imposed by the victor the Aeginetans lost their navy and were required to raze their fortifications. Worst of all, they were enrolled as tribute-paying subjects of Athens.[1]

It was probably during the winter of 458–457 that Pericles prevailed upon his countrymen to make Athens and Peiraeus a single defensible unit by constructing two walls connecting Athens with Peiraeus. The experience which the Athenian engineers had recently acquired in joining up Nisaea with Megara was no doubt of great value in this even greater piece of construction. It was no easy task because much of the ground traversed was soft and marshy, necessitating the sinking of boulders and rubble below the lowest courses of the wall. These two walls—the northern and the Phaleric—were probably completed not later than 456. The North Wall ran in a straight line from the city wall to the Piraeus defences and was approximately three and three-quarter miles long. The course of the Phaleric Wall is less certain; but, since it made a slight curve and joined the Piraeus Wall on the hill of Sicelia, north-west of Munychia, its length must have been appreciably greater. Eleven or twelve years later (c. 445) it was found more expedient to construct a wall—the Middle Wall—running parallel to the North Wall and of almost identical length, the Phaleric Wall being hereafter allowed to fall into disrepair. While the amount of territory within the fortified area was thus reduced—the distance in a straight line from the North to the Middle Wall was about one furlong—the loss of space for refugees from the countryside in time of war was offset by the greater ease with which the parallel lines of fortification could be defended.[2] A casualty list of members of the Erechtheid tribe records 177 names of those who fell fighting in 458 in Cyprus, Egypt, Phoenicia, at Halieis, in Aegina, and in the Megarid.[3] While it cannot be assumed that the losses incurred by the other nine tribes were as heavy, the inscription at least bears eloquent testimony to the many fronts on which Athenian

---

[1] They appear in the quota list of 454–453, the tribute paid by them being 60 × 3000 drachmae, that is to say, 30 talents. Cf. Tod, p. 51, col. vi, 18.

[2] A detailed description of the three walls, together with full references to the ample modern literature on the subject, will be found in W. Judeich, *Topographie von Athen* (new edition, Munich, 1931), pp. 155 ff.

[3] Tod 26. The absence of Cecryphaleia from the list of places may mean either that no men of the Erechtheid tribe fell there or that this action was tacitly joined with the preceding fight off Halieis.

## THE GREEK HOMELAND, 479 TO 432 B.C.      37

citizens were laying down their lives at this date and to the heavy drain on the man-power of Athens.

With the year 457 the number of her enemies was swelled by the entry of Sparta and the Peloponnesian League as a whole into the war. The Spartans intervened in a dispute in central Greece between Doris and Phocis, compelling the Phocians to surrender the territory that they had recently wrested from their opponents. But the unusual size of the Peloponnesian army—eleven thousand five hundred hoplites[1] —shows that it had a more important purpose than forcible arbitrament in a quarrel between two states of the second rank. The Spartans, in short, planned to support the aristocratic and anti-Athenian factions in Boeotia in their aim of reconstituting the Boeotian League under the hegemony of Thebes. A number of discontented Athenian oligarchs were also involved in the plot. As happened so frequently, the Spartan government on this occasion also miscalculated the reaction which its policy would arouse amongst its enemies; and, further, it shrank from carrying through an enterprise to its logical conclusion. The Athenians, instead of being overawed by and accepting the formation of a hostile *bloc* beyond their northern frontier, decided to take the offensive. The Peloponnesian forces had crossed the Corinthian Gulf in boats, but proposed to march back to the Isthmus by the Megarid. While an Athenian naval squadron operating from Pagae was prepared to stop the return of Peloponnesian transports across the Gulf, an army of fourteen thousand Athenian and allied infantry, including one thousand hoplites from Argos and some from Cleonae, supported by a detachment of Thessalian cavalry invaded Boeotia. The two armies met close by the city of Tanagra. The tactics appear to have followed the usual plan in Greek warfare at this period, namely, a direct frontal attack. The fighting lasted till nightfall. The numerical inferiority of the Peloponnesian army was counterbalanced partly by its superior discipline, partly by the defection from the Athenian side of their Thessalian allies. Sparta and her confederates in arms won a decisive victory, but the casualties on both sides were heavy.[2] At this point the action of the Spartans becomes

[1] The figure is vouched for by Thucydides (I, 107).
[2] Some very mutilated fragments of an inscription record the names of some of the Argives and Cleonaeans who fell in the battle. See Tod 28.

hardly intelligible. Instead of following up their success in the field by seeing the Boeotian League firmly established and, if necessary, lending it some military support, they withdrew across the Gerania hills into the Megarid. There they did as much damage as they could on their return march to the Isthmus. The Boeotians, left to their own resources, now appear to have made some progress with their scheme of reconstituting their League. Then, two months after Tanagra, the Athenians invaded their neighbours' territory a second time with the express purpose of putting a stop to those anti-Athenian developments. No ancient writer has left even a brief description of the engagement victoriously fought by the Athenians under Myronides on the field of Oenophyta. Its political results, however, were striking. The city of Tanagra was stormed and its walls razed. Then all Boeotia save Thebes and also the neighbouring country of Phocis joined the Athenian alliance. The Opuntian Locrians also submitted to Athens' demands, and, as a punishment for their previous hostility, were required to hand over one hundred hostages from amongst their leading men.

The next two years were marked by Athenian naval activity in Peloponnesian waters and by operations in north-western Greece which, if successful, might well have made all central Greece to the Gulf of Arta dependent on Athens. The Peloponnesian states for their part embarked on no further offensive, not even, which is remarkable, after 454 when the Athenians suffered their disastrous reverse in Egypt. In 456 the strategus, Tolmides, with fifty galleys and a body of one thousand hoplites made a series of raids on the Peloponnese.[1] The attack on Methone with which he began his campaign was perhaps calculated solely to bring the Spartans down into southern Messenia. Having succeeded in bringing this about, he put rapidly to sea and sailed for Gythium. This place he raided and in particular set fire to the Spartan arsenal and ship-sheds. Next he sailed into the Corinthian Gulf; there he made a descent on a dependency of Corinth and into the territory of Sicyon, where he had the

[1] Aeschines, *On the false embassy*, 78. Diodorus (XI, 84) enlarges the figure to 4000. But there is no reason to suppose that Tolmides' resources were greater than those of Pericles in the following year. Pericles' hoplites in the Acarnanian expedition numbered 1000 (Thucyd., I, 111).

best of a skirmish with the citizens.[1] These exploits, though an ocular demonstration of the value of sea-power for embarrassing an enemy, were ephemeral in their results. Of greater importance were the operations conducted probably in 455 by an Athenian expedition under the command of Pericles. Its objective was Oeniadae, a strong Acarnanian city situated close to the mouth of the Achelous. The naval squadron, which was probably fifty triremes strong as in the previous year, started out from Pagae with one thousand hoplites on board. After raiding Sicyon, as in 456, and defeating the inhabitants in the open, the Athenians sailed for Acarnania.[2] But the efforts of Pericles to capture Oeniadae were fruitless; for the surrounding country was low-lying and marshy because at certain seasons it was flooded by the river. Hence the place was exceedingly difficult to take by assault, while a prolonged blockade lasting into the winter months was impossible owing to the physical conditions.[3] Had Pericles been successful, the results would have been as far-reaching as the sequel to Oenophyta. Acarnania and southern Aetolia, where Athens had already a base at Naupactus, could scarcely have failed to pass under her control.

An expedition to Thessaly against Pharsalus about this time was equally unproductive of results. Although Thucydides mentions it in connection with the appeal of the exiled Thessalian prince Orestes, who hoped to return to his country with Athenian help, it may be surmised that the undertaking was in the nature of a retaliation for the treachery of the Thessalian detachment which fought at Tanagra.

The war now languished for several years and Athenian attention was centred chiefly on the maritime league. The Egyptian disaster not merely made renewed naval activity in the Aegean on the part of Persia a possibility, but the shock to Athenian prestige might well produce disaffection amongst

[1] Diodorus (XI, 84) also records an attack on Cephallenia and adds that the islanders were constrained to join the Athenian alliance. This must be a confusion with later events; for Cephallenia was one of the states that the Athenians approached with a view to alliance in 432–431 (Thucyd., II, 7).

[2] Thucyd., I, 111. Diodorus (XI, 88) embroiders the narrative by stating that Pericles assaulted the walls of Sicyon. Plutarch (*Pericles*, 19) is more cautious. He narrates that the raid was carried further inland than that made by Tolmides, and mentions a skirmish near Nemea.

[3] Cf. the instructive remarks of Thucydides (II, 102) on the physical geography of this region.

the allies. It is at least noteworthy that the earliest surviving quota-lists, insofar as they permit an approximate estimate of the φόρος, imply a total far lower than might have been expected. It is thus not unreasonable to suppose that Athens, to forestall possible difficulties with her allies and subjects, remitted some portion of what had previously been the normal assessment. In the sphere of party politics, too, we can postulate a distinct change and a greater amount of opposition in the *ecclesia* on the part of the conservative group. All that was needed was a leader comparable to the leader of the progressives. In 451 Cimon returned from exile and immediately made his presence felt. Pericles' influence temporarily suffered eclipse, and the Athenians, acting on Cimon's advice, entered into negotiations with Sparta. In the winter of 451–450 a five years' truce was concluded between Athens and the Peloponnesian states. While the cessation of hostilities could only be welcome to both sides, the ensuing conversations between Sparta and Argos, which culminated in the establishment of a treaty of peace for thirty years between these two ancient enemies, must have aroused many bitter feelings in Athens. The increased influence of Argos at this time, compared with the relative insignificance earlier in the century, is mirrored in an inscription that shows her acting as arbiter in a dispute between two Cretan communities.[1]

The death of Cimon on active service once more deprived his party of its strong man. His successor, Thucydides, son of Melesias, a man of respectable talent, was indeed able to command sufficient support in the assembly to embarrass his opponents for several years; but he could not stop the renewed ascendancy of Pericles in that body.[2] The withdrawal of the Athenian expedition from Cyprus and the subsequent negotiations with Persia were the first result of Pericles' renewed authority. Then, perhaps even before the conversations with Persia were complete, he issued invitations to the Greek city-states at large to join with Athens in a

[1] Tod 33. The inscription was found at Argos and is in the Argive dialect.
[2] The article of H. T. Wade-Gery (*J.H.S.*, 52 [1932], pp. 205–227) is valuable inasmuch as it presents all the known facts of Thucydides' career. But the present writer is unable to accept many of its conclusions which depend largely on guess-work, or seem to him to misinterpret the ancient evidence.

Panhellenic congress (449–448). The subjects to be submitted to the delegates for discussion were the restoration of sacred buildings destroyed during the Persian wars, the fulfilment of religious vows made by the Greeks at that time, and the freedom of the seas. Two distinct aspects of this impressive manifesto deserve consideration. Towards the European Greeks it was a gesture signifying the willingness of Athens not merely to live in amity with her neighbours, but to resuscitate under another form and in time of peace the Panhellenic union which had been partially achieved thirty-three years before in face of a common enemy. Regarded in this light Pericles' proposal failed, because Sparta and her Peloponnesian confederates were unwilling to lend their support to any scheme which, however laudable in itself, would inevitably transfer the presidency amongst the Greek states to Athens. Nor can we blame them if they were sceptical of Athens' good faith; indeed, though Pericles' desire for a Panhellenic understanding was no doubt perfectly genuine—it would have been of benefit to all—he was also working for the greater glory of Athens. He was probably sufficient of a realist in politics to have foreseen from the outset that his invitation would be ignored or refused by the Peloponnesian states. On the other hand, if the proposal failed in its main purpose, it may nevertheless have been of some value to Athens in her relations with her allies and subjects. Cessation of hostilities with Persia had made the primary purpose for which the maritime league had come into being an anachronism, and it is probable that even before the end of the war there had been serious unrest among the allies. It is significant that for several years after 450–449 the tribute assessments were lower, and, as no list survives for 449–448, there may have been no collection at all in that year. Pericles intended to show that the League was still advantageous to all the members, and, to prove that their interests were being kept in view, the " freedom of the seas " was made one of the chief items on the proposed agenda for the congress.

But on the mainland peace was not likely to be of long duration so long as the authority of Athens was paramount in central Greece. Sparta, although her military reputation had been upheld and even augmented on the field of Tanagra, had not forgotten her loss of political influence in that area. Her real reply to Pericles' project for a Panhellenic congress was an expedition to Phocis to deprive the Phocians of the custody and direction of Greece's most revered sanctuary, Delphi, and transfer it to the Delphians. Pericles' reply was prompt—a counter-expedition to reinstate the Phocians;[1] at the same time the alliance between them and Athens concluded in 454–453 was reaffirmed.[2] Less than a year later (summer, 447 ?) the latent discontent in Boeotia became overt. The exiled oligarchs gained control of Orchomenus, Chaeronea, and some other places. The Athenians, fearing that a Boeotian confederacy hostile to Athens would be established, sent Tolmides at the head of a thousand hoplites and an uncertain number of allied troops to intervene by force. Tolmides captured Chaeronea, but he can hardly have realized how general the movement of the Boeotians to recover their independence had become. Near Coronea the Athenians and their allies were caught in a trap and surrounded. In the desperate action that ensued Tolmides and many of his men were killed, the remainder were taken prisoner. In order to ransom them the Athenian government was obliged to agree to the withdrawal of the Boeotians from their alliance. The reconstituted Boeotian Confederacy under Theban leadership was for the next century a formidable neighbour to Athens, and, save for one or two brief intervals, its policy was opposed, when not actively hostile, to the Athenian. To Pericles and his countrymen the loss of Boeotia, which was followed by the defection of Phocis and Locris, spelt the loss of the land " empire " that they had controlled for just a decade. But, though a severe disappointment at the time, it was probably in the long run a benefit. For the remainder of his career Pericles concentrated on knitting together more securely the maritime empire of Athens and avoiding responsibilities and commitments on the Greek mainland, to shoulder which indefinitely was undoubtedly beyond the powers and resources of a Greek πόλις, even one as considerable as Athens.

[1] The language of Thucydides (I, 112) suggests that no great interval elapsed between the Spartan and Athenian expeditions. Hence the statement of Philochorus (cited by the Scholiast on Aristophanes, *Birds*, 556) that two full years elapsed between them can hardly be correct.
[2] Tod 39.

# THE GREEK HOMELAND, 479 TO 432 B.C. 43

The Boeotian fiasco had an immediate sequel which hit Athens in a most vulnerable point. Euboea revolted in 446;[1] then, while Pericles was absent with an army to bring the islanders to submission, the Megarians threw over their alliance with Athens, killed the Athenian garrison in Megara, and joined the Peloponnesian states. An Athenian detachment was sent at once to the Megarid. Meanwhile a Peloponnesian army led by the Spartan king, Pleistoanax, crossing the Megarid, invaded and ravaged the Thriasian plain. The Athenian force, in danger of being cut off by a greatly superior army, managed to escape into southern Boeotia. From there by a devious route it returned into Attica and effected a junction with the main Athenian army which had been recalled in all haste from Euboea.[2] Then Pericles, instead of venturing on a trial of arms, used all his diplomatic skill and came to an understanding with the Spartan commander. The Peloponnesians withdrew from Attica, but Megara, like Boeotia, ceased to be within the Athenian ἀρχή and hereafter ranked amongst the active enemies of Athens. The recovery of Euboea followed rapidly. A part of the population of Chalcis—the Hippobotai—was expelled and their land became the property of the Athenian state. Eretria and perhaps other communities are likely to have received similar terms. Only Hestiaea in the north of the island was treated more severely. The entire population was evicted and ultimately found a home in Macedonia. Soon after Hestiaea was settled by a thousand Athenian cleruchs, and these were perhaps joined by a further thousand after a short interval.[3] An extant document in an unusually good state of preservation records the conditions by which the Chalcidians were hereafter bound as members of the Athenian empire.[4] The terms of the oath which each adult male

---

[1] The guess of H. T. Wade-Gery (*J.H.S.*, 52, p. 207, note 9) that the revolt of Euboea was planned by Sparta in 448 is unconvincing. The presence of Athenians in Boeotia in 447 resulted from the activities of the Boeotian oligarchs.     [2] Cf. the epitaph of the guide Pythion, Tod 41.

[3] This is the probable suggestion of M. Cary, *J.H.S.*, 45 (1925), p. 248.

[4] There is no satisfactory evidence that cleruchies were sent to Chalcis and Eretria; indeed Thucydides' account (I, 114) of the revolt is decisive against such an assumption. Nor does the important inscription, Tod 42, make any reference to cleruchs. Cf. the general discussion in H. Nesselhauf, *Untersuchungen zur Geschichte der Delisch-Attischen Symmachie* (*Klio*, Beiheft 30), pp. 133–139.

citizen of Chalcis was required to take, swearing loyalty to Athens, are similar to those met with elsewhere.[1] The land confiscated by the Athenian government in Euboea was subsequently leased out and the proceeds formed an important addition to the Athenian exchequer.

The latter part of the year was taken up with negotiations between Sparta and Athens. A thirty years' peace was concluded between the Peloponnesian states headed by Sparta and Athens and her " allies." The Athenians gave up Nisaea and Pagae ; Troizen and Achaea also ceased to be members of the Athenian ἀρχή. But they retained Naupactus and, though they appear to have agreed to recognize the autonomy of Aegina, in fact they continued to treat the islanders as subjects.[2] If the Athenians were thus forced to give up their plans for extending their ascendancy over portions of the Peloponnese, even as they had had to abandon their hold on central Greece after Coronea, they still had some grounds for satisfaction in the open and official recognition accorded to their maritime empire at long last by Sparta and her confederates.

§ 6. THE LATER RÉGIME OF PERICLES

The checks and reverses suffered by Athens outside Attica between 448 and 445 synchronized with the last and acutest stage of the party struggle between Pericles and Thucydides. The differences between the two statesmen and their supporters centred on the future policy of Athens towards her maritime allies and dependents. Thucydides himself appears also to have been hostile to the building programme in Athens inaugurated by Pericles in 447 and continued steadily for a dozen years and more. Pericles, determined at all cost to keep the ἀρχή intact and, if possible, to extend it, had been responsible for strengthening Athens' position by sending out Athenian settlers to various points. Andros, which in 451–450 was assessed at twelve talents, in the next year was

[1] Tod 42. Cf. above, p. 13.

[2] In referring to the peace treaty Thucydides (I, 115) ignores Aegina. Yet in 432 the Aeginetans were amongst those who urged Sparta to make war on Athens and complained that they " were not independent according to the treaty " (Thucyd., I, 67). However, Aegina appears in the quota-lists for 445–444, 443–442, 442–441, 441–440, 433–432. In the remaining lists before 431 the Nesiotic φόρος is lost.

required to pay only half that amount. But since a body of Athenian cleruchs proceeded to the island not later than 448, one is tempted to surmise that Athens feared serious unrest in that quarter. About the same time the near-by island of Naxos also received settlers, although its assessment was left unchanged.[1] The quota-list for 448–447 shows that some cities paid no tribute at all in that year or only a part of the assessment. In short, all the evidence suggests that the ἀρχή was passing through a crisis which had its origin in the change of the political situation after the peace with Persia, and which received encouragement from the gradual realization that the Conservative Party in Athens itself was unfriendly to the imperial policy of Pericles. It was not in the archipelago alone that Pericles' " colonial " programme was applied. In 447–446 one thousand cleruchs migrated to the Thracian Chersonese, and we may probably date in 446 the Athenian colony founded at Brea in Thrace.[2] This enterprise would be unknown but for an Athenian decree which lays down certain regulations for the colonists.[3] The site of Brea is uncertain, but it may have been in the territory of the Bisaltae, that is to say, in western Thrace.[4] Nor is it known whether the new city flourished for any length of time or was soon wiped out by hostile natives. According to the official decree it was the duty of ten surveyors, after they had set aside certain territory as sacred lands, to parcel up the rest for the new citizens. The colonists undertook to send offerings to the Greater Panathenaea and the Dionysia at Athens. In case of hostile attacks they were to receive succour from the members of the Athenian empire in the vicinity. From a rider to the main decree we also learn the interesting fact that the colonists were picked from Athenians of zeugite and thetic census. It is to be noted that, whereas the cleruchs, wherever situated, retained their Athenian

---

[1] The sending of cleruchs to Euboea a year or so before the revolt rests on very poor evidence. For the passage of Diodorus (XI, 88) is corrupt, a fact which Wade-Gery (*op. cit.*, p. 207, note 9) does not point out. Nor does he cite Pausanias, I, 27, 5, who mentions such a cleruchy in a general way. The allusion in Andocides, *De pace*, 9, merely says that Athens controlled two-thirds of Euboea, but says nothing of Athenian settlers.

[2] For these dates cf. Nesselhauf, *op. cit.*, pp. 121–128 and 130–132.

[3] Tod 44.

[4] That is, if the vague statement in Plutarch, *Pericles*, 11, alludes to Brea.

citizenship and did not therefore form independent political communities, the Athenians who went to Brea were colonists. Nevertheless, as the obligation to despatch gifts periodically to Athenian festivals shows, the intention of the *ecclesia* was to ensure somewhat closer relations between the mother— and the daughter—city than was normally the case.

Again, the progressives in Athens would seem not to have been averse from cementing good relations, when opportunity offered, with the Greeks of the West. A mutilated inscription of 458–457 records an alliance between Athens and Segesta.[1] Perhaps nine or ten years later treaties were concluded with Leontini and with Rhegium, and these were renewed in 433–432.[2] In 446–445 the inhabitants of Sybaris, which had only been established a few years before, were again dispossessed by Croton and appealed for help to their kinsmen in Greece.[3] Their envoys met with little immediate success in the Peloponnese, but they were well received in Athens. Within a few months some Athenian settlers, now reinforced with some from other parts of Greece, started for Italy to strengthen the recently founded city. But the older and the new settlers failed to live in harmony; civil war ensued and the Sybarites were expelled or killed. The answer to a new appeal for colonists from Greece was a large contingent composed partly of Athenians, partly of persons from Arcadia, Achaea, and Elis, and a few from central Greece and the islands. The active participation of Athens in both these projects is best interpreted as a further step in the policy of establishing contacts with the western Greeks. In short, it is reasonable to view all these western relations of Athens between 454 and 440 as part of a whole, and to see in Pericles their inspirer. Indeed Plutarch attributes to him the foundation of Thuria, as the western city was called after it had received its second body of settlers, but he does not there distinguish between the first and second colonies.[4]

---

[1] Tod 31.   [2] Tod 57 and 58.   [3] See also below, p. 70.
[4] Plutarch, *Pericles*, 11. The hypothesis of Wade-Gery (*op. cit.*, pp. 218–219) that Thucydides took a leading part in the " execution of the Thuria project," was responsible for inviting Peloponnesian co-operation, visited the new settlement in person, and was soon after ostracized for his trouble, is ingenious but unconvincing. It rests in part on the unproved assumption that Pericles was out of office in 444–443, in part on the confused statements made by the anonymous author of the life of Thucydides, the historian. It

Although the danger of a general collapse of Athens' maritime empire passed quickly—already in 446 the number of tribute payers was about one hundred and seventy—the hostility to Pericles from a section of the assembly continued. It is possible that his opponents essayed in 445 to make capital out of the peace terms that he had been obliged to accept. It has even been suggested, though with little probability, that Pericles failed to be elected on the board of *strategi* for 444–443.[1] At all events in the spring of 443 this bitter rivalry came to an end; for Thucydides was ostracized. If one can judge from a collection of forty-six *ostraka* that may have been used on this occasion, his " runner-up " was Cleippides, a supporter of Pericles.[2] With the departure of Thucydides Pericles' position became unassailable. He was re-elected annually to his death on the board of *strategi*, and, as the one *strategus* chosen to represent the whole citizen body, not merely his tribe, he was accorded precedence and some additional authority. This was expressed by his official designation of στρατηγὸς αὐτοκράτωρ.

It is possible that already at the beginning of his final period he was planning to strengthen Athenian connections in the Propontis and the Black Sea region. But if so, his projects were postponed owing to unexpected and serious trouble within the empire, in which one of Athens' few remaining independent allies was deeply involved. In the summer of 441 Samos and Miletus quarrelled over the affairs of Priene and went to war.[3] When the Milesians were beginning to have the worst of the fighting, they complained to Athens; associated with them were some disaffected Samians. An Athenian naval force of forty galleys proceeded to the island,

also ignores the statement (Diodorus, XII, 10) that the Sybarites had originally invited help from Sparta as well as from Athens. Sparta had declined to act, but the co-operation of others with Athens was surely the logical result of the original Sybarite appeal to the two leading states in Greece and accepted as such by Pericles.

[1] Wade-Gery, *op. cit.*, p. 206. Yet he doubts (p. 222) whether Thucydides was himself *strategus* in 444–443. Are we then to believe that he was προστάτης τοῦ δήμου without holding an executive office ? Such a situation would be highly unusual at this time and should not be assumed without the strongest proofs.

[2] For these sherds cf. Tod 45.

[3] Why either state should have the right to control Priene, if that was the cause of the disagreement, is obscure. Priene appears as a separate tribute-paying city in the quota lists from 450–449.

replaced the existing oligarchy by a democratic government, and carried off one hundred hostages, whom they transported to Lemnos and left in charge of a guard. A small garrison was also placed in Samos. But during the winter 441–440 civil war broke out in Samos. The anti-Athenian faction sought for help from Pissuthnes, satrap of Sardes, who gave them a substantial subsidy. This they used to hire a body of seven hundred mercenaries, with whose aid they made themselves master of the island and overthrew the pro-Athenian government. A raid on Lemnos followed. The hostages were rescued and the Athenian garrisons in Lemnos and Samos were given into the safe-keeping of Pissuthnes. In the spring the insurgents planned to resume hostilities against Miletus. Moreover, the disaffection to Athens spread; for Byzantium revolted and there was unrest amongst the coastal cities of Thrace. But when the campaigning season began, Pericles took personal charge of a naval expedition against the Samians. Having detailed sixteen vessels to collect additional triremes from Chios and Lesbos, and also to keep a look-out for a Phoenician squadron rumoured to be in the offing, he intercepted the Samian fleet of fifty triremes and twenty transports as it made its way from Miletus to Samos, and defeated it. Reinforced by a further forty ships from Athens and by twenty-five from Chios and Lesbos, he next invested Samos. But soon, in view of persistent rumours that a Phoenician fleet was coming from Cyprus to help the insurgents, Pericles, unwisely, as it happened, divided his forces. He sailed for Caria with sixty vessels, leaving the rest to carry on the blockade. The Samians were not slow to see their advantage; they broke the blockade and inflicted a defeat on the Athenians. Then for a fortnight they continued to control the sea-approach to their island and were thereby enabled to replenish their commissariat. With the return of Pericles, however, and the arrival of further reinforcements from Athens under three *strategi*—one of them may have been the historian Thucydides—an effective investment of Samos was re-established. The attempts to take the city by assault, however, failed, so that Pericles was reduced to the time-honoured expedient of starving out the population. After nine months the Samians capitulated (winter, 440–439). They lost their navy and their fortifications and were required to give hostages and pay a heavy war indemnity. In Byzantium and Thrace Athenian authority was also restored before the end of 439.[1] The cost of the Samian operations had been heavy. A partially preserved inscription records a total expenditure during two years of 1404 talents. If the latest editor is correct in his interpretation, 1276 talents were spent on the Samian War and 128 on the fighting at Byzantium.[2] About the same time Athens suffered a diminution of her tributaries by the defection of many communities in southern Caria. From 438–437 we find the five geographical groups within the empire reduced to four, the remnant of the Carian district being united to the Ionian. The payments which had been made by those Carian members who seceded had been relatively small, and the Athenian government evidently did not feel that coercion would be expedient. The cost might have been considerable, and naval or military action in that region might have provoked a fresh conflict with Persia.

Two undertakings of great importance marked the year 437, the despatch of a new Athenian colony to Thrace and a cruise of the Athenian navy under Pericles' personal direction to the Propontis and Black Sea. The Greek communities on the coast of Thrace and along the European shore of the Propontis had always lived in a certain state of insecurity owing to the periodic hostility of the natives in the interior. The disaster of Ennea Hodoi in 465, moreover, had shown the dangers confronting settlers who ventured to advance into the Thracian hinterland. If the problem was serious enough while each of the Thracian tribes was an independent political unit, it became doubly so about the middle of the fifth century when Teres, king of the Odrysae, created a larger Thracian kingdom by bringing many of the other tribes under his single control. Under his son Sitalces the kingdom was

[1] Thucydides (I, 115 and 118) briefly mentions the defection of the Byzantines and their re-enrolment in the empire. For the fighting there and the disturbances in Thrace there is also the evidence of a casualty list containing the names of fifty-eight Athenians who fell fighting in 440–439 in the Chersonese, at Byzantium, and in " other wars." See Tod 48.

[2] B. D. Meritt, *Athenian Financial Documents* (*Univ. of Michigan Studies: Humanistic series*, XXVII [1932]), pp. 42–46. Meritt refers the 128 talents to Byzantium alone, but, as the sum is large, may it not represent the cost of all the fighting in Thrace and the Hellespont? For the treaty with Samos after the war, see *A.T.L.* II, D 18.

still further enlarged so that it extended from the confines of Abdera to the Danube, and from the neighbourhood of Byzantium in the east to the Strymon in the west. Thus in modern terms it was approximately equivalent to European Turkey, Bulgaria, and a small portion of Greece. West of the Strymon lay Macedonia. This kingdom also had been enlarged and unified after the Persian wars by its able ruler, Alexander I. On his death (c. 450 ?) a partition of the realm between several sons was a source of political weakness. Perdiccas II, although he ended by becoming sole ruler, was for many years hampered by this division of power. Moreover, in addition to Athenian expansion in Chalcidice, which had already been regarded by his father as a menace to Macedonian interests, the growth of the Odrysian kingdom was a formidable obstacle to the development of a greater Macedonia. Certainly when a large body of Athenian colonists in 437 founded a city on the site of Ennea Hodoi, Perdiccas was not able to prevent them. It is reasonable to assume that this settlement was carried out with the goodwill of the Odrysian king. Amphipolis, as the new colony was named because it stood in a semicircular bend of the Strymon so that it was all but surrounded by water, was an ideal site. It controlled one of the main highways into the interior with its vast reserves of timber, and it was close to the Pangaeus range, with its extensive mineral deposits.

The Pontic expedition of Pericles in the same year had several important objects in view. The recent defection of Byzantium must have brought home to the Athenians a grave danger to which they were always exposed unless they could control the Bosphorus and insure the unobstructed passage of grain ships from the Black Sea. Attica had long since ceased to be self-supporting; more than half of the wheat and barley needed to feed its population had to be imported, and for cereals as well as for dried fish the districts bordering on the north shore of the Euxine were Athens' primary source of supply. Moreover, the presence of an Athenian fleet, although without hostile intent, was calculated to impress not only the Byzantines and other Greek cities in that area with the might of Athens, but also the ruler of the Thracian kingdom.

Proceeding along the southern shore of the Black Sea the

fleet visited Sinope. There Pericles assisted the inhabitants to expel their tyrant. Subsequently six hundred Athenian volunteers were sent out to join in the resettlement of the city. Small bodies of Athenian settlers were also drafted to Amisus, south-east of Sinope, and to Astacus on the Propontis. The former changed its name to Peiraeus, and coins of the period not only bear this name but show Athenian influence in the owl symbol on the reverse.[1] Astacus, on the other hand, had been a tribute-paying member of the empire ever since 454–453. Finally Pericles visited the Cimmerian Bosporus which had just passed into the control of a Thracian mercenary captain, Spartocus, who became the founder of a long and prosperous dynasty. The extent of his kingdom is uncertain, but it was certainly enlarged by the inclusion of several prosperous Greek or semi-Greek cities during the long reign of his successor, Satyrus I (432–392). It is probable that a friendly agreement was reached between Pericles and Spartocus, and this success alone was enough to justify the voyage to Pericles. At all events we find that Athens subsequently received from the ruler of Bosporus certain commercial privileges relating to the export of grain. With this guarantee and the safe control of the straits into the Black Sea the supply of Athens' essential food-stuff was assured.

Thus in the last decade of Pericles' life the Athenian empire reached its final form though not its greatest extent. While we can see the magnitude of his achievement, it is not so easy to form a just estimate of it. Certainly, as time went on, many features of it were criticized not merely by the opponents of Athens but by its members. Much of the jurisdiction had passed into Athenian hands; for many civil cases, especially commercial litigation, were tried in the Athenian courts, as well as all serious criminal offences in which persons belonging to an allied or subject state were involved. Doubtless it was not only inevitable, but in the common interest desirable, that this should be so; and it is probably fair to say that, in spite of cavillers, the majority of litigants and defendants were treated with equity by the Athenian juries. Yet it is easy to understand the discontent voiced from time to time by the allies or subjects, because their subordination

[1] *British Museum Catalogue of Greek Coins: Pontus*, Plate II, 9.

to the Athenian courts spelled for them a partial loss of independence.

Again, the use by Pericles of considerable sums from the tribute monies on the beautification of Athens, and especially the Athenian Acropolis, was another of their grievances. From 447–446 to the outbreak of the Peloponnesian War in 431 Pericles set himself steadily to make Athens a worthy capital city for all the Hellenic world to see and to admire. The building of the Parthenon was begun in 447–446 and finished fourteen years later. A new gold and ivory cult-statue of Athena of colossal size was completed by 437 and placed in the new temple. Then an elaborate entrance gateway, the Propylaea, was begun; the main structure was completed by 431. But with the outbreak of war further work on it was suspended and the complete design of the architect was never carried out.[1] The cost of these structures and others in the city, like the Odeum, was at first defrayed from the accumulated treasure of Athena and of the other gods. But when these resources ran dry, Pericles did not hesitate to use part of the tribute monies. While one can understand that this action provoked the resentment of the allies, the Athenians could point to the security and increased prosperity enjoyed by all the members of the empire owing to the initiative and energy of Athens. Hence, provided that she fulfilled her duty to all, they could not fairly complain if they contributed to her material prosperity.

The complaint that the assessment of the tribute was, with very few exceptions, controlled by Athenian officials was less justifiable. For the executive had from the very beginning been in Athenian hands. Besides, the evidence of the extant quota-lists is decisive. Every four years from 454–453 a general revision of the assessments was made, and Athenian practice appears to have been reasonably equitable. Certainly there was no great increase in the total amount of *phoros* before 425. As regards the individual contributory states, there was, it is true, a fair amount of variation. Yet this very fact, whether inspired by equity or mere political caution, is proof that the Athenian assessors did not proceed arbitrarily. Moreover, it is remarkable how many cities continued to pay the same sum year after year, even when

---

[1] For these buildings see further below, Chapter XVI, § 1.

other evidence suggests that their prosperity and consequently their ability to pay had increased in the interval.

But the most unpopular feature of Athens' imperial policy was the sending out of cleruchies, a policy with which, as we have seen, Pericles was particularly identified. Whether viewed from the military standpoint as Athenian garrisons, or from the social and economic point of view as a privileged aristocracy in the communities where they lived, the cleruchs were with some justice regarded by the allies and subjects of Athens as offensive. But, apart from these objections, of which the contemporaries of Periclean Athens were fully sensible and which were of greater or less cogency, the modern student of Hellenic history will not without reason pass an adverse judgment on the Athenian empire because it lacked organic unity and because it was essentially a selfish creation which never developed into something better. True, Athens in the fifth century was both more equitable and more successful in her imperial policy than Sparta or Thebes in the fourth. But the advantage and interests of Athens were always paramount, and it is difficult to believe that, had its empire endured three times as long as it did, it would have brought the Greek world or the greater part of it nearer to a national and permanent unity.

# CHAPTER III

# THE GREEKS OF THE WEST

### § 1. THE TYRANTS OF SYRACUSE AND ACRAGAS

THE repulse of the Carthaginian attack on Sicily in 480 may be attributed in the first place to the effective alliance in the hour of danger of the two leading states in the island, Syracuse and Acragas, and, secondly, to the military genius of the Syracusan tyrant, Gelon. He and the ruler of Acragas, Theron, were related by marriage, and the friendly relations between their states were strengthened by their joint success before the battlements of Himera. Of the two cities Syracuse was somewhat smaller;[1] but it was superior in natural advantages owing to its two excellent harbours and its position on the east coast in greater proximity to the straits of Messana and to Italy. The peninsula or " island " of Ortygia and the quarter, Achradina, opposite on the north side of the little harbour were probably fortified by Gelon.[2] In any case he must have enlarged the inhabited area of the city to make room for the numerous persons whom he transplanted there from Gela and other places. That Syracuse was politically the foremost city in the island was also Gelon's work. In the years immediately preceding the Carthaginian invasion he had, partly by conquest, partly by alliance, established his authority over more than half of Sicily. His various allies, after their common campaign against Hamilcar, renewed their alliances with him.

The spoils taken from the Carthaginians were vast and, while much was retained by Gelon, much was also divided amongst the Acragantines and other allies in the late war.

---

[1] That the size of ancient Syracuse has been greatly exaggerated by modern writers has recently been demonstrated by K. Fabricius in his brief but important monograph, *Das antike Syrakus* (*Klio*, Beiheft 28 [1932]).

[2] The so-called wall of Gelon on the plateau of Epipolae is not a fortification but part of an ancient quarry. See Fabricius, *op. cit.*, p. 14.

MAP II

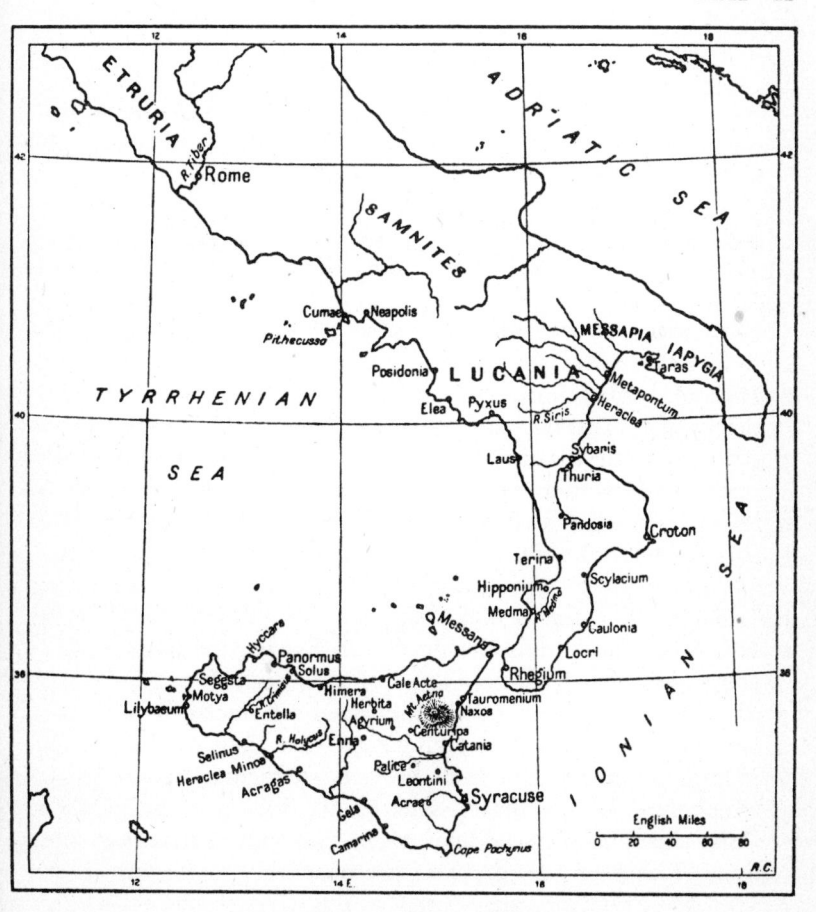

SICILY AND MAGNA GRECIA

To commemorate his great victory Gelon built a temple to Demeter and Kore in Syracuse and dedicated a gold tripod at Delphi.[1] A further memorial of victory were the fine silver decadrachms issued by him at this time and named Damareteia in honour of his wife.[2] But he survived his triumph by two years only. Although his earlier career had been marked by many ruthless actions and his seizure of power in Syracuse had not passed off without opposition, his prestige was immensely increased by the victory at Himera, and in the last years of his reign he commanded the universal admiration and good will of the Syracusans.

Hieron, his brother, succeeded him. A man of considerable ability, he was nevertheless much inferior to Gelon both as a ruler and as a man. Indeed, in the pages of Diodorus he is depicted as a typical Greek τύραννος, a picture that is not necessarily at variance with the idealized portrait of the Syracusan ruler in Pindar's odes. It is the magnificence of Hieron's court, and the wealth which made possible the patronage of artists and participation on a lavish scale in the athletic festivals of Greece, that have inspired some of the finest compositions of the aristocratic poet. For the rest, he is content to moralize along conventional lines, though in superb language, on the vicissitudes and fleeting happiness of human life.[3] According to Gelon's last dispositions, his younger brother, Polyzalus, was to marry his widow, Damareta, and take charge of the Syracusan army.[4] It is conceivable that this division of authority between Hieron and Polyzalus would have functioned satisfactorily, had both brothers enjoyed equal popularity with their subjects. But Hieron's appears to have been a suspicious temperament which reacted on the citizens to his disadvantage, whereas Polyzalus was a general favourite. The reasons for the ensuing quarrel between the brothers are obscure. According to one account Polyzalus suspended a punitive campaign against some Sicels without Hieron's knowledge. Another version relates that the tyrant sent Polyzalus on a military mission

---

[1] Tod 17.   [2] Hill, *H.G.C.*, 20. *C.A.H.*, Plate II.
[3] Cf. Pindar, *Pyth.* 3, 104–6 :   ἄλλοτε ἀλλοῖαι πνοαὶ
ὑψιπετᾶν ἀνέμων. ὄλβος οὐκ ἐς μακρὸν ἀνδρῶν ἔρχεται
σάος, πολὺς εὖτ' ἂν ἐπιβρίσαις ἕπηται.
[4] It has been suggested that Polyzalus was given charge of the city of Gela seeing that there is an allusion to him and that city on the base of the Delphic Charioteer. Even so he would be subordinate to the ruling prince.

to southern Italy, so as to remove him for a time from
Syracuse. But Polyzalus, being suspicious of his brother's
motives, took refuge with his father-in-law, Theron of Acragas.
The differences between the two Syracusan princes nearly
precipitated war between the two states that had but lately
fought side by side as allies. Wiser counsels prevailed in the
eleventh hour, the result of an unexpected complication.
Himera, which was a dependency of Acragas, was mis-
governed by Theron's son Thrasydaeus. A delegation from
Himera appealed to Hieron and offered to surrender the city
to him. The Syracusan ruler, to whom the people of Himera
were only a pawn in the game, communicated what he knew
to Theron and thereby paved the way for an adjustment of
their family quarrel. According to one tradition the poet
Simonides acted as intermediary in the negotiations between
Theron and Hieron. Polyzalus, however, continued to reside
in Acragas. The unhappy citizens of Himera, after the ringleaders of the attempted rebellion had been executed, were
compelled to endure the misrule of Thrasydaeus for some
years longer.

During the early years of his reign Hieron intervened more
than once in the affairs of Rhegium. This city was still held
by Anaxilaus—its actual governor was the tyrant's eldest
son, Leophron—and he also occupied Messana across the
straits. Since, moreover, Anaxilaus had been related by
marriage to Terillus of Himera, who had been responsible for
bringing the Carthaginians to Sicily and had subsequently
been driven out, the relations between him and the tyrant
of Syracuse are not likely to have been very cordial. It was
therefore in the interests of Hieron to lend his support to
the nearest neighbour of Rhegium, Locri. When Anaxilaus
began a war with the Locrians (c. 477), Hieron promptly
interfered and threatened him with active hostilities. His
kinsman, Chromius, carried out his duties as legate well, and
Anaxilaus abandoned his plan to add Locri to his kingdom.
Only a year later the despot died, and since his sons were
minors, the government of Rhegium passed into the hands
of a regent, Micythus, a member of the deceased tyrant's
household.[1]

[1] It is to be assumed that the eldest son, Leophron, predeceased his father.
The hypothesis of Beloch (*Griech. Gesch.*, II, 2, 176) that Leophron ultimately
succeeded Micythus as ruler of Rhegium is impossible. It is inconceivable

In 474 Hieron was again drawn into Italian affairs, indeed his achievement in this year is the one outstanding event of his reign. The ancient Greek city of Cumae, partly perhaps as the result of internal dissensions, had fallen on evil days. But its geographical position lent it exceptional importance in the eyes of the Etruscans at this time. The recent formation of a federation of Latin cities under the leadership of Rome had closed the land communications between Etruria and the Etruscan dependencies in Campania. Possession of Cumae and control of the sea-route to Campania were consequently of vital moment to the Etruscans. They blockaded the city, whereupon the Cumaeans, in face of this threat from a formidable and alien people, appealed to Syracuse for help. Hiero acted swiftly. A Syracusan fleet was despatched to Italy and in conjunction with the galleys of Cumae inflicted a crushing defeat on the Etruscans off Cumae. The ultimate effect of this victory on the history of Italy was far-reaching, for it not only rid the Greek cities on the west coast of Italy for ever from the peril of Etruscan domination, but so weakened the Etruscan hold on Campania that the loss of this fertile region was only a matter of time. Hieron followed up his success by occupying the island of Pithecusa (Ischia), where he left a garrison. It is tempting to surmise that he was planning an extension of his power by bringing Cumae and other Greek cities along the coast into alliance with, or dependence on, Syracuse. Within a short time, however, the troops there were forced to flee before an earthquake. Hieron, who by then was fully occupied with unwelcome developments nearer home consequent upon the death of Theron of Acragas, made no further attempt to hold this outpost or to advance his power in Italy. Ischia was soon after occupied by Neapolis; for this city was rapidly outstripping its neighbour and mother-city Cumae, which, in spite of the victory over the Etruscans, failed to recover its former prosperity. A portion of the spoil taken by Hieron at Cumae was dedicated by him at Olympia and Delphi. One item discovered at Olympia survives to this day, a bronze

that Leophron, whatever his father's dispositions, tamely allowed Micythus to act as regent for his younger brothers and so disinherited himself. Ciaceri (*Storia della Magna Grecia*, II, 294) also assumes that Leophron died before Anaxilaus, helmet inscribed, " Hieron and the Syracusans dedicated these spoils from Cumae to Zeus."[1] Delphi also received a tripod and golden statue of Victory.

In Sicily Hieron, like his predecessor, more than once forcibly transplanted the inhabitants of the smaller Sicilian cities within his realm. Thus the people of Naxos and Catana were expelled from their towns and moved to Leontini. In Catana he established a new body of settlers, ten thousand strong, part of whom came from Syracuse, while the rest were imported from Greece. He enlarged the territory of the city, which he renamed Aetna, by confiscating some land belonging to native Sicels. The government he entrusted nominally to his young son, Deinomenes, actually to the boy's guardian, Chromius, the same who had served Hieron well as ambassador to Rhegium and whose victories in chariot races at Nemea and Sicyon were hymned by Pindar.[2] A separate coinage for this city was also struck; a solitary specimen has survived.[3] The purpose of this foundation was to provide Hieron with a second stronghold in case his position at Syracuse should at any time prove untenable. At the same time he may have striven to strengthen the Dorian elements in Sicily at the expense of the Chalcidic-Ionian settlements of which Catana was one.

What is known about Acragas at this time is even more scanty than the tenuous stream of information that we possess for the history of Syracuse. Its tyrant, Theron, used the numerous captives and other spoil that fell to his share after Himera to enlarge and adorn his city. Improved fortifications and a row of temples close to the southern wall, added to the security and beauty of Acragas.[4] A newly constructed drainage system contributed to the health and material comfort of the townsfolk. A large artificial lake for breeding fish was also constructed at this time. The attempted secession of Himera, which, as we saw, was averted by the intervention of Hieron, was the only political crisis to disturb the last eight years of Theron's reign. The prosperity of Acragas, derived largely from the produce of vineyards and orchards, increased steadily. On Theron's death (472–471) his son,

[1] Cf. Tod 22 and *Syll.*, 35 Bb and C.     [2] Pindar, *Nem.* 1 and 9.
[3] Hill, *H.G.C.*, 22; *C.A.H.*, Plates II, 2 l.
[4] Actually many of these buildings were not finished till after the passing of the tyranny at Acragas.

Thrasydaeus, came to the throne. Having already misruled Himera, he now applied the same principles of despotic government to Acragas. Even so he might with the help of mercenaries have maintained his authority for some time. But within a year he used these and levies from Acragas and Himera to attack Syracuse. He was defeated in a pitched battle—the site of the encounter is not known—and his losses were twice as heavy as Hieron's. Rightly distrusting the temper of his subjects, he fled to Megara in Greece, whose government promptly executed him. The Acragantines for their part made peace with Hieron and then established an oligarchic government in their city. Himera, too, recovered its independence at this time; its coins ceased to bear the symbol of Acragas on the reverse as they had done during the years of Theron's domination.[1]

The last recorded political act of Hieron was a renewed intervention in the government of Rhegium. For reasons that are obscure, though we may guess that the growing prosperity of the place under the regency of Micythus caused him uneasiness, he invited the sons of Anaxilaus to his court and then advised them to take over the government of their city themselves. On their return to Rhegium the account that Micythus rendered of his stewardship and his influence and popularity with the people weighed so heavily with Anaxilaus' sons that they wished to disregard the counsel of Hieron. But Micythus insisted on resigning and withdrew to Greece, to end his days in Tegea. The last records that survive of him are very human documents. Two inscriptions at Olympia refer to dedications that he made there to all the gods and goddesses in gratitude to them for the recovery of his son, who had suffered from tuberculosis and had not improved although his father had spent much of his wealth on physicians.[2]

A few months after his entertainment of Anaxilaus' sons Hieron passed away (466). He had maintained intact the realm bequeathed to him by his elder brother and he had humbled the Etruscans. But his government of Syracuse had been despotic, not the least irritating feature to his

---

[1] Cf. Hill, *op. cit.*, 19; Grose, pp. 270-1.

[2] The restored portions of the inscriptions may be regarded as reasonably certain. For the text of one see E. Schwyzer, *Dialectorum Graecarum Exempla* (Leipzig, 1923), no. 794.

subjects being an elaborate system of espionage on private
citizens. At the same time it must be admitted that for a
few years he made the Syracusan court an unrivalled centre
of literary talent. Besides Pindar, Hieron numbered amongst
his guests Aeschylus, whose *Persae* was represented in the
city, Simonides, and Bacchylides. Native talent, too, was
encouraged in the persons of Epicharmus and Phormis.[1]
Although his death probably caused little sorrow to his
subjects they made no immediate attempt to oust his brother
Thrasybulus. But the new ruler began at once to oppress
the Syracusans by putting to death or driving into exile
wealthy citizens in order to confiscate their property. With
some of the proceeds he increased the number of his mercenaries. But already in 465 a general uprising of the citizens
was the answer to his misrule. At first he tried to parley
with them. When this availed nothing, he had recourse to
the population settled by Hieron in Aetna. With them and
his mercenaries he managed to hold Ortygia and Achradina.
But the citizens sent round a successful appeal for help to
Acragas, Gela, Himera, Selinus, and even to the Sicel communities in the interior of the island. In spite of the large
accession which they thus received to their strength,
Thrasybulus was able to hold out for some time longer. At
last after being defeated in a pitched battle with his late
subjects in the suburbs of Syracuse, he came to terms and
was allowed to withdraw from the city. He retired to Locri,
there to end his days as a private citizen.

### § 2. UNREST IN THE SICILIAN CITIES AND THE RISE OF DUCETIUS

The end of the tyrannies in Sicily was followed by a general
return of political exiles' to their respective cities. There
was also a strong movement to undo the arbitrary acts of
Gelon and Hieron in transporting large numbers of persons
from their native place to other sites. Not unnaturally,
these changes were not effected without dissension and hardship to many; in particular they were accompanied by
enmity to the strangers imported in previous years by the

---

[1] The Sicilian origin of Epicharmus is not certain. According to Diogenes
Laertius (VIII, 78) he came originally from Cos; but Suidas (s.v.) says he
was a native of either Crastus or Syracuse.

tyrants. Nor was it to be expected that in this warring of diverse interests the establishment of constitutional government in the different cities should pass off without *stasis*.

In Syracuse the struggle was especially bitter. After their first rapture at liberation from the despot had been celebrated by the institution of a yearly festival in honour of Zeus, to be called the Eleutheria, the citizens settled down to devising a system of more equitable government. The mercenaries and other foreigners who had been incorporated in the civic body by Gelon were suspect because they were believed to be sympathetic to a continuation of absolutism. Hence they were excluded from office which was reserved for the true Syracusans. A civil war thereupon broke out, and the foreigners, like the last tyrant before them, occupied the Island and Achradina. The intermittent fighting between them and the citizens must have continued for some time, and the former fully held their own in the many skirmishes and hand-to-hand encounters that ensued. In the end the citizens were able to keep them shut up in the quarters that they had first seized; then starvation did the rest. A last desperate sortie developed into a general engagement in which many fell on both sides, but the citizen army at last carried off the victory.

In Acragas similar scenes appear to have been enacted, but the ancient references are confused and contradictory. It would seem, however, that even after the expulsion of foreign elements the dissensions between the citizens were prolonged for some years. The government was exercised for a while by an oligarchy; then a democratic revolution was successfully effected, the leading spirit in it being the philosopher and scientist Empedocles. That he gained a striking ascendancy over his fellow-citizens for some years is evident from the numerous legends subsequently current about him. In the end, however, he left or was driven out of Acragas. He withdrew to Greece, where he ended his days (*c.* 445). The kernel of one story, which illustrates his scientific reputation, may well be historic fact. The city of Selinus was visited by a severe epidemic. It caused a high mortality among the population and miscarriages amongst the women, the result, it was believed, of the evil effluvia arising from the near-by river. Empedocles was consulted, and at his own expense diverted two neighbouring streamlets into the main stream, thereby putting an end to the noisome exhalations.[1] Clearly the philosopher carried out some draining operations which reduced the number of stagnant pools and produced a more rapid flow in the river. While this would reduce the odours, it would also, of course without his knowledge, get rid of admirable breeding-places for anopheline mosquitoes; for it can scarcely be doubted that the epidemic was a severe type of malaria.[2]

Elsewhere in Sicily, too, the cities were setting their house in order. Camarina, which had been destroyed by Gelon, was rebuilt by the people of Gela, and the old inhabitants were as far as possible restored (c. 460). Amongst them was Psaumis who in later years won victories in the chariot and mule-car races at Olympia.[3] Megara Hyblaea, another of the communities destroyed by Gelon, was retained by Syracuse, but Naxos regained its independence and resumed the issue of its own currency.[4] Nor was Hieron's foundation, or, as one modern writer has aptly called it, military colony, Aetna, left undisturbed. The expulsion of the mercenaries there was the first known achievement of a unique personality in Sicilian history, Ducetius. A native Sicel, he succeeded in the course of a decade in building up a considerable kingdom. About 460–459 he came to an understanding with the Syracusans and with some support from them expelled the inhabitants of Aetna. Having recovered the Sicel territory which had been filched by Hieron he allowed the former inhabitants to return to the site and the city resumed its old name of Catana. The military colonists of Hieron were permitted to take up their abode at Inessa, which was renamed Aetna and was situated near the foot of the mountain of the same name. A year or two later Ducetius founded

---

[1] Diogenes Laertius, VIII, 70. Contemporary coins commemorate this purification of the city. Cf. Grose, I, 304.

[2] The allusion to the mortality amongst pregnant women is specially valuable as a possible indication of the disease. " Severe malaria, especially aestivo-autumnal fever, if untreated, is a serious complication of pregnancy. It is a frequent cause of abortion, premature labour, and still-birth, the interruption of pregnancy occurring most commonly in the latter months." (Byam and Archibald, *The Practice of Medicine in the Tropics*, 3, 2483.) Cf. also Blacklock and Gordon, " Malaria infection as it occurs in late pregnancy " in *Annals of Tropical Medicine and Parasitology*, X (1925), 327–363. I am indebted to my friend and colleague, Professor Robert Matheson, for these references.   [3] Pindar, *Ol.* 4 and 5.   [4] Cf. Grose, I, 291–293.

a city on the hill of Menaenum and then enhanced his military reputation by capturing the Sicel town of Morgantina lying in the fertile valley watered by the Symaethus and its tributaries. By 453 he had brought all the native communities except Hybla into a Sicel federation controlled by himself. To mark the completion of the first part of his ambitious programme he now built a new capital at the foot of the hill of Menaenum, calling it Palice after the sanctuary of the native divinities, the Palici, close by.[1] So far Ducetius seems to have lived on terms of amity with the Greek cities; but now he planned to enlarge his federation by coercing some of these. He began by swooping down on Aetna and capturing it. Next he seized Motyum, a hill fortress in Acragantine territory. This brought upon him concerted action by Acragas and Syracuse. Nevertheless he inflicted a severe defeat on these allies. The Syracusan commander was subsequently found guilty of collusion with the enemy and executed. In the following spring (450 ?) the fortunes of war were reversed. The Syracusan army, after a long and bloody affray, routed the forces of Ducetius, while the Acragantines recovered their fortress. Most of Ducetius' followers now fled to their hill-towns, and the unhappy man seems to have grown suspicious even of the few friends who stayed with him. One night he slipped away unobserved and rode for Syracuse, trusting in the generosity of its citizens. Nor was he mistaken, for after a lengthy debate in the assembly they voted that the suppliant be spared. He was sent to Corinth, where he seems to have spent several years as a private individual.

During the years of Ducetius' short-lived hegemony in Sicily the internal development and growing prosperity of Syracuse had once more been retarded by *stasis*. Nor, if we can trust the vague generalizations of Diodorus (XI, 86), was the evil confined to this city-state alone. The attempt of one, Tyndarion, to seize the tyranny with the help of the neediest class of citizen seems to have occurred at Syracuse in 454. The attempt was promptly suppressed and the would-be despot with a number of his followers was put to death. After this the Syracusans tried the experiment of

[1] On the cult of the Palici see Roscher, *Lexikon der Griech. und Röm. Mythologie*, 3, 1281–1295.

introducing a procedure (πεταλισμὸs) similar to the ostracism practised at Athens. But the hope that this might prove a remedy for civil disturbances by removing the potential instigators of them was disappointed. In part this was due to the absence of such safeguards as were in force at Athens and the fact that a bare majority of votes sufficed to send a man into exile. Thus the main effect produced appears to have been the partial or complete withdrawal from political life of the better class of citizen. Petalism was soon abolished and periodical outbreaks of violence continued to occur for some time. It is therefore somewhat surprising that, only a year after Tyndarion's attempt, two naval raids against Etruria were carried out by the Syracusans. They were a retaliation for Etruscan privateering off the Sicilian coast. The first expedition produced little result, the Syracusan commander being found guilty of accepting bribes from the enemy. The second, however, under Apelles, was more successful. Descents were made on the coast of Corsica and Aethalia (Elba) was temporarily occupied. The Syracusans returned home with many captives and a considerable quantity of booty.

About 446 the good relations which had existed for so long between Syracuse and Acragas suffered a brief interruption. The proximate reason was Ducetius, but there may have been other causes of disagreement. The Sicel leader had broken his parole and returned to Sicily ; but the Syracusan government does not seem to have put any obstacles in his way when he proceeded to found a new city on the north coast of Sicily, about half-way between Himera and Messana, which he named Cale Acte. Some of the settlers had accompanied Ducetius from Greece, others were native Sicels. This venture was strongly disapproved by the people of Acragas, who were already irritated that the Syracusans five years before had treated Ducetius with such clemency. They now treated Syracuse's action as a *casus belli* and declared war. The armies of the two states, each reinforced by some allies, met on the banks of the river Himera. The Syracusans had the best of the fight and their opponents, who lost a thousand men, then sued for peace. Ducetius survived for a few more years, dreaming perhaps of a new Sicel federation. But about 440 death put an end to his plans.

In the next few years the Syracusans established their authority over the numerous Sicel communities, only one of which offered a stubborn resistance. They also increased their naval forces and began to envisage a future when all Sicily would obey their behests. It is perhaps legitimate to see in these plans, though they were never more than partially fulfilled, a desire to counteract the growing influence of Athens in western affairs, the more so as all the states with which Athens had allied herself in the west—Segesta, Leontini, Rhegium—were non-Dorian.

### § 3. THE GREEKS OF MAGNA GRAECIA AND THEIR NEIGHBOURS

The superficiality and lack of continuity in the sources for Sicilian history during the greater part of the fifth century are surpassed by the poverty of existing information concerning the Greek settlements in Italy during the same period. The number of these was considerable, and many were of great antiquity. At no time, however, was even a partial unity amongst them achieved as happened for one or more generations in Greece and for shorter spans, as we have seen, even in Sicily. The absence of any central power, like Sparta, or Athens, or even Syracuse, produced a constant bickering amongst the Hellenic cities of Magna Graecia, besides being a source of weakness in face of non-Hellenic peoples, whether Etruscans or hill tribes of Italic stock. The most powerful states were situated in the south of the peninsula—Croton, Taras (Tarentum), and Rhegium. Those on the west coast were cramped in their economic development, depending, as it did, largely on maritime carrying-trade, by the still substantial power of Etruria. Thus, it is significant that after the battle of Cumae even Posidonia, where Etruscan influences had been strong and material welfare had been greatly dependent on trade with the Etruscans, was, to judge by her admirable currency in the second half of the century, more prosperous than before.[1]

The rise of Croton to first place amongst these cities dated from the destruction of her old rival, Sybaris (c. 510). At that time and for many years to come, the government of Croton was dominated by members of the Pythagorean brotherhood

[1] Cf. Grose, pp. 137 ff.

and their supporters amongst the aristocratic families. The fame of her athletes and the reputation of her physicians, who were in the west what the healers of Cos and Cnidus were in the eastern Mediterranean, she owed very largely to the brotherhood. Early in the fifth century their *régime* produced a short-lived reaction. The Crotoniate oligarchs were expelled and the government passed into the hands of the popular leader, Cylon, who ruled autocratically. But he was unable to maintain himself for long against the aristocratic faction, mainly perhaps because the Pythagoreans had so many sympathizers and adherents in neighbouring communities. Under the restored oligarchy Croton reached the zenith of her influence. She had added the territory of Sybaris to her own and, in addition, controlled a number of smaller cities which were nominally independent. For the extant coinage of the period suggests the existence of commercial alliances between Croton and weaker states, such as Caulonia, Temesa, Pandosia, and perhaps even Locri.[1] An attempt of the exiled Sybarites to recover some of their old lands (*c.* 477) failed, even though they may have had some support from Hieron of Syracuse. Croton was thus a formidable neighbour to Taras on the north and to Rhegium on the south-west.

The people of Taras were less fortunately situated owing to their proximity to troublesome Calabrian tribes. It is, however, not without significance that, when their own power to cope with the danger was insufficient, they turned for help against the Iapygians and Messapians in southern Apulia and Calabria, not to Croton but to Rhegium. The attempts of the Tarantines at northward expansion had already involved them in a Messapian war at the beginning of the fifth century, but this war does not seem to have produced any appreciable territorial or political changes. About 473 the regent of Rhegium, Micythus, was instrumental in establishing a colony or trading-station in Pyxus at the head of the Gulf of Policastro.[2] It is a reasonable conjecture that

[1] Cf. Grose, p. 199, who gives additional references to recent numismatic literature.

[2] That there had been a city of Pyxus in the sixth century is proved by extant alliance coins of Siris and Pyxus. As Siris was destroyed *c.* 512 by Croton and Sybaris, this earlier settlement at Pyxus may have shared the same fate.

this venture was undertaken with the knowledge and goodwill, if not the active co-operation, of Taras, since both she and Rhegium would thereby more effectively control the most direct route between the Tyrrhenian and Adriatic. The Tarantines next asked Rhegium for military assistance in the fresh war in which they had lately become involved with their neighbours in the interior. From a strategic point of view also Pyxus might prove a valuable asset.

The hostilities between the two Greek communities and the Messapian-Iapygian coalition probably lasted fully two years. The earlier operations consisted of raids and counter-raids; in the meanwhile the strength of the Messapians and Iapygians steadily grew, so that in the end they could put twenty thousand men into the field. This force utterly defeated the joint armies of Taras and Rhegium, whose losses were much increased in the rout that followed the battle. The site of the engagement is uncertain, as the ancient notices are vague and cannot be brought into harmony; but it is likely to have been in the vicinity of Taras, and in a northerly or westerly direction from that city.[1] The immediate sequel to this defeat, which Herodotus describes in the language of hyperbole as " the greatest Greek carnage known to him,"[2] was the overthrow of the oligarchic government in Taras. The democratic party signalized its accession to power by minting coins with a new type on the reverse, a seated figure of Demos, to symbolize their victory.[3] In Rhegium, however, Micythus was strong enough to retain his hold on the reins of government in face of this serious disaster. About a decade later (c. 461 ?), that is, several years after Micythus' retirement to Greece, the people of both Messana and Rhegium drove out the sons of Anaxilaus, and Messana seems for a short time to have resumed its older name of Zancle.[4] The people of Rhegium, for their part, had remained on friendly terms with Taras, whence they received

---

[1] Cf. Ciaceri (II, 281–283), who conjectures that the Rhegians were driven back on Pyxus not on Rhegium, as stated by Diodorus. Even so the distance to be covered by pursued and pursuers, partly over mountainous country, seems impossibly great. As the crow flies the distance from Taras to Pyxus is about eighty-five miles.
[2] Herod., VII, 170.     [3] Cf. Grose, p. 74, no. 549.
[4] Cf. the unique coin with the inscription ΔΑΝΚΛΑΙΟΝ, figured in G. Macdonald, *Coin Types*, Plate V, 12.

some aid when expelling the tyrants.[1] But in a fresh war with the Iapygians and Peucetians the people of Taras fought without their ally. Nevertheless it is evident that they to some extent revenged the defeat of 471, for they dedicated a group of statuary at Delphi from the spoils of victory.[2]

Approximately contemporary with the revolutions in Sicily and Rhegium was the concluding stage in the prolonged struggle between the two factions in Croton. The circumstance that this acute political rivalry had been in progress for a quarter of a century and more makes it improbable that it was directly connected with the internal revolutions in other city-states. At the same time the steadily growing sentiment throughout the Hellenic world in favour of popular government did not pass Croton by and may have helped to precipitate the gruesome finale of the political drama. A meeting-house in which forty members of the Pythagorean brotherhood were assembled was surrounded by their political opponents and set alight. All but two of the brethren perished in the flames (c. 453 ?). A general persecution of Pythagoreans and oligarchs followed, which, as far as the former were concerned, was by no means confined to Croton. But the Crotoniates paid a heavy price for their ruthless extermination of Pythagoras' followers, to whom much of Croton's prosperity and political influence had been due. From this time the decline of the city was rapid and Croton sank back into the second rank of states. The issue of a separate coinage by Pandosia may belong to this period and perhaps also the appearance of a new type on Caulonian coins, symptoms suggesting a diminution of Croton's authority among her neighbours.[3] Nor can the view that Croton at this time was drawn into closer relations with Messana be upheld on the existing evidence.[4] But the clearest proof of Croton's political decline is to be found in the renewed efforts of the exiled Sybarites and their descendants to recover their

[1] This is suggested by the similarity, even to the encircling olive wreath, of the reverse types of Tarantine and Rhegian coins. Cf. Grose, nos. 550 and 1860.    [2] *Syll.*, 40.

[3] Cf. Ciaceri, *op. cit.*, p. 336.

[4] Ciaceri (*op. cit.*, p. 302, note 2) still adheres to the theory that certain Crotoniate coins are evidence of an alliance between Croton and Messana, c. 460–450. But Grose (p. 198, note 2) has pointed out that the inscription on the reverse is imperfectly preserved on several specimens and that the supposed reading ΔA (for ΔANKΛAION) is really PA.

own. While some of these had remained in the old territory of Sybaris as tillers of the soil and subjects of Croton, others had found homes in Scidrus and Laus. About 453 they felt themselves strong enough, with some assistance from Posidonia, to reoccupy the old site and proclaim their independence. Yet it soon appeared that, without more substantial support from outside, the Sybarites were still too weak to hold their own against the old enemy, for in 448 they were once more dispossessed by the Crotoniates. This reverse was followed, as we have seen, by an appeal to their kinsmen and others in Greece.[1] The foundation of New Sybaris a few miles away from the old city was, it is true, not a success, but Thuria endured. The new colony was probably laid out according to the plans of Hippodamus of Miletus, the friend of Pericles, who had already carried some of his novel ideas on town-planning into effect in rebuilding parts of Peiraeus. The form of Thuria's constitution is more doubtful. The ancient traditions are confused, for the laws of Charondas and Zaleucus, as well as the sophist, Protagoras of Abdera, are named in this connection. Probably the government began by being modelled on the Athenian pattern; but after about a decade the Athenian influence in the city declined and the constitution also underwent a gradual change, so that it took on a more " Dorian " character, a blending of oligarchic with democratic institutions. Internal dissension during the early years of its existence was not the only danger to which the young city-state was exposed. Its most hostile neighbour was not Croton but Taras. The two states carried on a dispute and fought intermittently for a decade over the possession of Siris and its territory on the coast half-way between Taras and Thuria.[2] The dispute was at last settled in favour of Taras. In 432 a little to the north of the old Siris a new colony was established by Taras, with some participation by the surviving Sirites and possibly by Thuria, and was named Heraclea. Like Thuria, Heraclea maintained her independence for more than a hundred and fifty years until all southern Italy passed under the control of Rome.

[1] See above, p. 46.
[2] Cf. Tod 49 for spoils taken from the Thurians and dedicated by the people of Taras at Olympia.

## CHAPTER IV

## THE GREAT PELOPONNESIAN WAR: THE FIRST STAGE, 431 TO 421 B.C.

### § 1. THE ANTECEDENTS OF THE WAR

THE peace of 445 had been in effect an admission that the majority of Greek cities had been brought into one or other of two spheres of political influence, the Spartan or the Athenian. The treaty, moreover, recognized the right of any state that was neutral in the sense of not belonging to either federation to join one or the other when it wished. The settlement of disputes by arbitration was also provided for, although we do not know the exact methods to be followed in such cases.[1] Certainly, however, such interstate arbitration was not applicable to cities in relation to their subjects or allies. The Corinthians, indeed, a few years after the revolt of Samos reminded the Athenians that Corinth had successfully opposed an armed Peloponnesian intervention on that occasion on the ground that the differences between Athens and the islanders were a domestic quarrel within the empire.[2] They themselves elected to regard their differences with Corcyra in 435 in the same light. It is customary to blame the Greeks for their inability to adhere to a peaceful solution of political disagreements which they had thus theoretically acknowledged to be desirable. Yet it is difficult to see why they are to be censured for failing to attain what has ever since proved unattainable. It is also easy to criticize the jealous individualism or particularism of the city-states, which wrecked every attempt at federal

---

[1] Corcyra in 435 was ready to submit her case against Epidamnus to arbitration (Thucydides, I, 28). In 432 Pericles complained (*id.*, I, 140) that, while Athens was willing to follow a similar course, Sparta had refused to do so.

[2] Thucydides, I, 41.

government before the Hellenistic period; but to do so is to expect a majority, not merely a few men with ideas ahead of their time, to have discarded the basic principle of the political life familiar for centuries to oligarch and democrat alike. Complete autonomy of the city-state was incompatible with federalism; and let it not be forgotten that to both Plato and Aristotle the city-state was the ideal state. Too much stress, then, must not be laid on the agreement reached in 445. On the Peloponnesian side the leading states viewed Athens and her empire with a jealous uneasiness, and so Thucydides is careful to separate this fundamental cause of the war from the several events which served to precipitate the conflict.[1]

Pericles himself can have been under no illusions about the possibility of maintaining the thirty years' peace for the full period. Indeed, while the Athenians showed their confidence in him by accepting him as a virtual autocrat, he repaid their trust by keeping Athens at peace with her neighbours for a dozen years. His authority was unassailable, and the attempts of a discontented and unscrupulous few in Athens to embarrass him by striking at his friends, though vexatious, did not undermine his position. In 438 Phidias, the sculptor of the chryselephantine statue of Athena, was impeached for embezzling part of the sacred funds of the goddess and for sacrilege in representing Pericles and himself amongst the figures on Athena's shield. He was exiled or else withdrew voluntarily from the city. Soon after Pericles' mistress, Aspasia, was accused of impiety, but through his influence was acquitted. Probably about the same time (*c.* 433?) the philosopher Anaxagoras, a close friend of the statesman, was brought to trial on the same charge and was forced to leave the city.[2] If Thucydides, son of Melesias, who returned to Athens in 433, was really implicated in this prosecution,[3] he stooped to dirty methods which his great predecessor, Cimon, would have abhorred.

No one could have foreseen the first of the events that were

[1] Thucydides, I, 23; cf. I, 118.
[2] On the trial of Phidias cf. Adcock in *C.A.H.*, V., 175; on that of Anaxagoras see the full account in E. Derenne, *Les procès d'impiété intentés aux philosophes à Athènes* (Liège and Paris, 1930), pp. 13–43, and the remarks of Wade-Gery in *J.H.S.*, 52 (1932), 220–221.
[3] As suggested by Wade-Gery, *loc. cit.*

the prelude to a general renewal of hostilities in Greece. The city of Epidamnus on the Illyrian coast—on the site of the later Dyrrachium—was a Corcyraean colony, but its actual founder and a few of the original settlers had come from Corinth. Epidamnus had developed into a flourishing Greek *polis* surrounded by non-Hellenic or semi-Hellenic neighbours who were at times troublesome. Furthermore like many another city-state, Epidamnus was frequently disturbed by violent dissensions between oligarchs and democrats. These two adverse factors had arrested or even reduced its prosperity during the fifth century. About 436–435 a civil war was followed by the expulsion of the oligarchic faction which thereupon made common cause with some Illyrian tribes in a concerted attack on Epidamnus. The democrats there finding themselves too weak to contend against the coalition, appealed to Corcyra for help. But the mother-city—whether from jealousy or for some other cause—refused to take any action. After consulting the Delphic oracle and receiving an encouraging response, the Epidamnians turned for assistance to Corinth. Here they met with more sympathetic treatment because the Corinthians regarded themselves as part-founders of this north-western outpost of Hellenism. At the same time the Corinthians saw a chance of humiliating the Corcyraeans with whom they had long been on bad terms. A Corinthian expedition, reinforced by detachments from Corinthian colonies or allies in the north-west, made its way to Apollonia. The Corcyraeans, seeking a quick decision, protested vigorously to the Epidamnians; when this had no result they blockaded the city. But very soon, when they learnt that Corinth was equipping a supplementary expedition and was even receiving assistance in the form of money or ships from other Greek states, they in turn became alarmed and sent representatives to Corinth. They offered to submit their disputes to arbitration if only Corinth would first withdraw the armed force that she had placed into Epidamnus. The Corinthians refused the proposals, and their seventy-five galleys with two thousand hoplites on board sailed for Corcyra. Eighty Corcyraean vessels barred their progress off the Actian promontory and inflicted a decisive defeat on them. Meantime forty Corcyraean ships had been blockading Epidamnus with good effect, for the city capitulated—if Thucydides may be believed—on the very day on which the naval action was fought to the south.

It was not to be expected that the Corinthians would lie down under this ignominious reverse. For the next two years they were engaged in building ships and in hiring mercenary rowers from different parts of Greece. In face of these preparations the people of Corcyra became sensible of their own precarious position of political isolation in Greece. Since any approach to the Peloponnesian League was obviously impossible, they sent envoys to Athens. This move did not remain unknown to Corinth, which promptly sent a delegation to Athens in order to dissuade the Athenians from supporting her objectionable daughter-city. The Corcyraeans, in presenting their case at Athens, assumed that a general conflict in Greece was shortly to be expected. For, besides stressing the advantage of an alliance with a state situated on the direct route to Italy and Sicily, they pointed out how Athens, confronted by a hostile Corcyraean navy, in addition to the Peloponnesian naval forces headed by Corinth, would be at a grave disadvantage from the outset. The arguments of Corinth, as presented by Thucydides, were less forceful. Besides recalling Corinthian aid to Athens at the beginning of the century and Corinth's refusal to embarrass the Athenians at the time of the Samian revolt, the envoys, apart from uttering generalities, could do little beyond emphasizing the danger to the peace of 445, if Athens gave active support to Corcyra. That the issues were of the gravest was clear to Pericles and his countrymen. The assembly met twice and then voted for what was really an impossible compromise. A defensive alliance was made with Corcyra. A few days later a squadron of ten galleys was ordered to Corcyra to watch events but abstain from active intervention, unless Corcyraean territory was directly attacked by the Corinthians. Thus the letter of the agreement of 445 was momentarily preserved; but an active violation of the treaty was unavoidable unless Corinth abandoned her case and desisted from attacking her daughter-city.

However, after the failure of the negotiations, an armament of ninety Corinthian and sixty allied galleys sailed for the Adriatic. They made their headquarters on the mainland off the southern end of Corcyra, in the plain between

# THE GREAT PELOPONNESIAN WAR

Chimerium and Ephyra, while the former place afforded an adequate harbour for the ships. On receiving news of their approach one hundred and ten Corcyraean triremes proceeded to one of the islets, called Sybota, to the south of Corcyra. The Corinthians setting sail by night from Chimerium planned a surprise attack, but it miscarried. Instead of taking the enemy unawares, they found the Corcyraean fleet at dawn on the high seas ready to fight. The ensuing engagement made up in vigour what it lacked in scientific naval tactics.[1] Before the end of the day the ten Athenian vessels participated in the fighting in order to save their allies from defeat. Even so the Corinthians had had the best of the contest. But the appearance of a second Athenian squadron, twenty triremes strong, caused them to abandon their plan for a renewed attack next day, and to sail home with a number of Corcyraean prisoners. Thus, apart from the poor return which Corinth reaped for two years of intensive preparations, the treaty of 445 had been openly violated when the Corinthian and Athenian galleys came into conflict.

The dangerous political situation thereby created was immediately aggravated by Athens' treatment of one of the Chalcidic members of the empire. Potidaea, a colony of Corinth situated at the northern end of the peninsula of Pallene, had certainly been paying tribute since 446–445, being assessed for six talents.[2] Nevertheless the city had maintained closer relations than usual with the mother-state, seeing that each year a Corinthian magistrate took office there. In the spring of 432 the Athenian government presented an ultimatum to the people of Potidaea. They were required to raze their southern fortifications, which would give the Athenians free access to the city at any time, to exclude for the future annual Corinthian magistrates, and to render hostages to Athens. Moreover, their tribute was raised to fifteen talents.[3] These demands, besides being in the nature of a challenge to Corinth, were presumably made with a full realization on the part of Pericles of the probable consequences in the Hellenic world generally and in north-

---

[1] For the " old fashioned " strategy of this battle see below, p. 342.

[2] The name appears first on the quota-list for 445–444, but can be restored with certainty on that for the previous year. Cf. *A.T.L.* II, 9 and 10.

[3] This is the sum in the list for 433–432. The amount in the previous year's list is not preserved.

eastern Greece in particular. The good relations between Perdiccas II of Macedon and Athens had probably come to an end some years before, though no actual hostilities between the two powers had ensued.[1] But now Perdiccas entered into relations with Sparta and Corinth; at the same time he sought to undermine Athenian control of Chalcidice by inciting a number of small communities to secede from Athens and to form a joint settlement some miles inland at Olynthus. The Athenians at once sent a small squadron to Potidaea to enforce their demands, but meanwhile the Potidaeans sent legates in order to dissuade the Athenian assembly from its purpose. Failing in this, they went on to Sparta in the hope of enlisting the active help of the Peloponnesian states in their struggle against Athens. The Athenian squadron of thirty vessels being too weak to deal adequately with the Chalcidic situation and Perdiccas as well, attacked Macedonia. It received some support from Perdiccas' brother, Philip, who had taken refuge with the Athenians, and from Derdas, ruler of Elimaca, who did not recognize the Macedonian overlordship of Perdiccas. After capturing Therma they proceeded to lay siege to Pydna. By this time a Corinthian expeditionary force, commanded by Aristeus, had reached Potidaea, while Athens at the same time despatched forty triremes and two thousand hoplites to Chalcidice. The commander of the first Athenian detachment abandoned the attack on Pydna and patched up a truce with Perdiccas. Then he joined forces with the second squadron. The combined Athenian expedition then advanced into the vicinity of Olynthus and was joined by some Macedonian cavalry from amongst the supporters of Philip and Pausanias. Presumably for this reason Perdiccas almost at once repudiated his recent agreement with the Athenian commander and was again numbered among the opponents of Athens. The Athenian commander-in-chief, Callias, next detached his Macedonian horsemen and a body of allies to hold Olynthus in check, while he led his main army against Potidaea. A battle was fought hard by Potidaea. While the Corinthians more than held their own against the troops opposed to them, the Potidaean army was overwhelmed. The Athenians whose casualties were light, although Callias himself was amongst them, now invested

[1] Cf. F. Geyer, *Makedonien bis zur Thronbesteigung Philipps II*, p. 55.

the town.[1] Since the troops on the spot were too few to do this with complete effectiveness, the home government despatched a reinforcement of seventeen hundred men under Phormio to Potidaea.[2]

The vigorous conduct of the Athenian operations against that city demonstrates very clearly how the re-establishment and maintenance of full authority in Chalcidice was a leading principle of Periclean policy. In reply the Corinthians strove to their utmost to precipitate a general war against Athens. They were joined in their urgent representations at Sparta, to present the Athenians with an ultimatum, by the Aeginetans and Megarians. The former complained that contrary to the peace of 445 they were still treated by Athens as tributaries.[3] The plight of the Megarians was more acute, for the Athenian assembly had recently replied to the Peloponnesian challenge in Chalcidice by passing a decree to shut out Megarians from all the harbours and markets of the Athenian empire. Granted that Athens had a legitimate grievance against the Megarians, because in 446 they had massacred the Athenian garrison then quartered in Megara and had assisted Corinth in the recent operations against Corcyra, the action of Pericles in using economic pressure of the sharpest kind against them was a declaration of war against the whole Peloponnesian Confederacy and was clearly made on the assumption that war was inevitable.

The autumn and winter of 432–431 were, however, taken up with deliberations and diplomatic conversations. At Sparta opinions were divided, an influential minority whose chief spokesman was the king Archidamus being reluctant at this time to try conclusions once more with the Athenian empire. But a majority of the ephors thought otherwise, partly because they feared that, if Sparta held back at this juncture, her leadership in the Peloponnese might soon be in jeopardy,[4] partly from jealousy and alarm at Athenian power. When

[1] A tombstone with metrical inscription mourning the Athenians who fell at Potidaea survives to this day (Tod 59).
[2] Epigraphic records of the expenses (26 talents) for the Corcyraean expedition: Tod 55=Meritt, *Athenian Financial Documents*, p. 69. For the cost of Athenian operations in Macedonia and Chalcidice cf. Meritt, *op. cit.*, pp. 71–81.
[3] See above, p. 36.
[4] Cf. the exceedingly bitter criticisms of Sparta placed by Thucydides (I, 70–71) in the mouth of the Corinthian envoys.

the vote was put to the citizen assembly at Sparta a majority voted that Athens had violated the peace of 446. Then after a formal consultation of the Delphic oracle whose reply was considered satisfactory, a congress of the Peloponnesian League was summoned and the issue laid by Sparta before the delegates. A large majority voted for a declaration of war against Athens. There followed an interchange of recriminations between Sparta and Athens, the only purpose of which, from the Spartan point of view, was to gain time. But a second delegation put the issue squarely. It demanded that Athens rescind the Megarian decree, that Aegina be restored to full autonomy, and that the siege of Potidaea be abandoned. Pericles, however, was not prepared to make any concessions. When a third delegation from Sparta arrived in Athens, bluntly threatening war unless the Athenians allowed the Greeks to remain autonomous, he had no difficulty in carrying the great majority of his countrymen with him. Indeed, logically interpreted, acceptance of Sparta's final demands would have meant neither more nor less than the disbandonment of the Athenian empire. Pericles' answer to Sparta was to the effect that Athens would annul the decree against Megara, if Sparta would raise her embargo on strangers within her territory, that she would permit cities that were autonomous before 445 to resume their full independence, if the Spartans would follow a similar course in the Peloponnese, and that she was ready to submit disputed matters to arbitration in so far as this was provided for in the treaty of 445. To such a declaration from the Athenian statesman Sparta could make but one reply—mobilization.

### § 2. THE OUTBREAK OF THE WAR AND THE RESOURCES OF THE COMBATANTS

The first blow at the enemy had been dealt by the Athenians when they passed the decree against Megara. But the formal opening of hostilities was delayed until the season was already well advanced; for it was not until the beginning of June that a Peloponnesian army passed the Isthmus and invaded Attica. Already before the end of March, however, the peace had been broken by a Theban attack on Plataea. This was a gross and indefensible violation of the treaty of 445. Ever

# THE GREAT PELOPONNESIAN WAR

since the sixth century this city had steadfastly refused to join the Boeotian League, a course of action only made possible by its friendly relations with Athens. The Plataeans had fought side by side with the Athenians at Marathon, and in the years that followed the friendship between the two states was closer than ever. But in 431 a small faction in this otherwise pro-Athenian town intrigued with Thebes and on a dark night admitted an advance body of three hundred men within the walls. The Plataeans, being taken by surprise and under the impression that a much greater number of the enemy were within the gates, began to parley. When, however, they discovered that their opponents were not so formidable as they had first imagined, they took courage and barricaded the streets. Then they rounded up one hundred and eighty of the Thebans, while the remainder were either killed in the fighting or escaped. When the main army of Thebes arrived outside the walls the Plataeans announced that they held their prisoners as hostages for the withdrawal of the enemy. Unfortunately, when they had brought all their effects inside the town and were ready to stand a siege, their intense hatred of Thebes led them to commit a breach of good faith. The prisoners were put to death and the urgent instructions from Athens, whither the Plataeans had sent a messenger asking for immediate help, not to harm their captives, came too late. The Athenian government, however, despatched provisions and eighty hoplites to their ally and at the same time brought away the non-combatants to Athens.

In respect of man-power the two groups of states between whom formal hostilities were about to begin were perhaps fairly evenly matched. Unhappily, however, reliable figures are few and incomplete. Athens' army comprised 13,000 hoplites for foreign service and 16,000 for home and garrison duties. The latter were composed partly of *ephebi* between eighteen and twenty, partly of middle-aged men, partly of resident aliens. Besides this there were 1200 cavalrymen and mounted archers and 1600 archers on foot. The total of seaworthy galleys in 431 was three hundred. To man all that number at once would have needed 60,000 men. Actually the number of ships in commission at any one time during the war was always less, in fact, the maximum mentioned by Thucydides of 250 vessels at sea at one time was quite exceptional.[1] On the Athenian side were all the cities, large and small, that made up the empire, Corcyra, Zacynthus, most of Acarnania, the Messenians in Naupactus, Plataea, and the Thessalians, who sent a cavalry detachment to Attica at the beginning of the war. But the ancient writers are silent about the resources actual or potential of these allies. Equally in doubt is the strength of Athens' enemies. They comprised the Peloponnesian League, that is all the states in the Morea except Argos and Achaea, Boeotia, Locris, Phocis, and Megara in central Greece, Ambracia, Anactorium, and Leucas in the west. But the recorded figures of Peloponnesian armies are unreliable.[2]

Financially the position of Athens was incomparably stronger than that of Sparta, for besides the regular income provided by the tribute monies, a reserve of six thousand talents lay on the Athenian acropolis. Of these one thousand, in addition to a hundred triremes, were set aside by Pericles in the first year of the war, to be used only in case of grave emergency. Even so it was not many years before the continuous upkeep of a large naval force on a war footing, and the expense of contemporaneous operations in several theatres of war caused serious embarrassment to the government, necessitating unusual measures. How the enemies of Athens financed their military and naval undertakings is very uncertain. The Corinthians seem at the very outset to have suggested that the treasures of Delphi and Olympia be used or at least borrowed for war purposes, but the plan was not adopted. Religious sentiments on the part of a majority amongst the allies may help to account for this abstention; we shall see that the Phocians eighty years later were not so scrupulous. The Spartan government, however, organized a war fund to which contributions could be made either in money or food-stuffs. The contributors sometimes included

---

[1] Thucydides, III, 17. In the two expeditions to Sicily in 415–413 the total number of triremes was 207. At the battle of Arginusae 150 galleys were engaged on the Athenian side, but some of them were furnished by allies.

[2] Plutarch, *Pericles*, 33, says 60,000 men invaded Attica in 431, an impossible figure. The total force of Sparta and her allies at the battle of Mantinea in 418 was nearly 12,000. At Delium in 424 the allied Boeotian army numbered about 7000 hoplites, over 10,000 light-armed troops, 500 peltasts, and 1000 cavalry (Thucydides, IV, 93).

even neutrals like the Melians or disaffected citizens of Athenian allied states like Chios.[1] Yet a voluntary fund of this kind was at best uncertain, so that one is tempted to conjecture that the occasional failure of the Peloponnesians properly to follow up a military advantage was attributable to a shortage of the " sinews of war." Nor was their more vigorous conduct of the war after 412, when most of their fighting was also done far from home, unconnected with the ample, though not always regular funds provided by the Great King and his representatives in western Asia.

Although the Peloponnesian War lasted twenty-seven years and was rightly regarded by its historian, Thucydides—he himself did not live to carry his narrative further than 411 —as a single whole, since hostilities were never at any time completely suspended, it nevertheless falls into three clearly marked stages. This division is most apparent in the shift of the main theatre of operations. In the first decade—the so-called Archidamian War, though the Spartan king was scarcely eminent enough to deserve this form of immortality —from 431 to the abortive Peace of Nicias the struggle chiefly centred in various regions of the Greek homeland. In the next stage (421–413) the main fighting at first was still in Greece. But very soon the scene shifted; for the crucial and dramatic episode of that period, whose disastrous end foreshadowed the ultimate outcome of the war, was laid in the West—Athens' attack on Syracuse. Then between 412 and 405 the centre of operations was in Asia Minor and the adjacent waters of the Aegean, and it was there that the final decision was reached.

To understand the course of the Archidamian War one must bear in mind that the contest was between two groups of states of which one was predominantly maritime, the other in the main military. The strategy which Pericles imposed on his countrymen was thus fundamentally sound, to maintain a strictly defensive position in Attica and on land, while using the naval strength of Athens to the full, with the double purpose of enforcing as far as possible the economic isolation of the Peloponnese and of carrying out offensive operations at suitable points to give Athens fresh bases and additional

---

[1] Tod 62. For the probable date (427) of this inscription cf. F. E. Adcock in *Mélanges Glotz*, I, 1–6.

allies. To make the first part of his plan truly effective, Pericles prevailed on the rural population of Attica to forsake their farmsteads and seek refuge within the fortified area of Athens and Peiraeus. There can be no clearer proof of the unlimited confidence reposed by the Athenians in their leader at the beginning of the war than this. Their food-supply was assured so long as their navy remained supreme in the Aegean. In addition, a strict control was in force at the Hellespont on all grain shipped from Black Sea ports, while in Peiraeus a special board of superintendents (ἐπιμεληταί) enforced the regulation that two-thirds of the imported corn must be reserved for Athens. The rest could be re-exported to states within the empire.[1]

### § 3. THE WAR IN CENTRAL GREECE AND THE PELOPONNESE, 431–427 B.C.

Formal hostilities opened at the beginning of June with a Peloponnesian invasion of Attica. The invaders, after failing to reduce the fort of Oenoe, did as much material damage as they could in the plains. Then, since the Athenians remained obstinately behind their walls, they withdrew into Boeotian territory. Inroads into Attica were repeated in the following year, when the visitation was actually prolonged for six weeks, and again in 428, 427, and 425. The Athenians retaliated by annual incursions into the Megarid. The Peloponnesian manœuvre seems particularly pointless since the yearly destruction of crops and damage to orchards in Attica, though exasperating to the inhabitants, could make no appreciable difference. The attacks of Athens on Megarian territory were more serious in so far as that city was already in economic difficulties owing to the operation of the Athenian decree. To make their position in the Saronic Gulf even more secure than it was already, the Athenians in 431 expelled the population of Aegina and sent a body of their own settlers to the island. The old inhabitants either settled with the goodwill of Sparta in the mountainous region of Thyrea or else found homes in other parts of Greece.

---

[1] Cf. Tod 61, lines 35 ff. This particular decree was passed in the summer of 426. It granted to Methone certain exemptions from the strict regulations then in force. For the ἐπιμεληταί cf. Aristotle, *Const. of Athens*, 51.

# THE GREAT PELOPONNESIAN WAR

Substantial results were gained in 431 by the Athenian navy. A fleet of one hundred galleys circumnavigated the Peloponnese. A raid on Methone was repulsed by a Spartan force under Brasidas, but elsewhere the Athenians were more successful. They seized Sollium, a Corinthian dependency, and handed it over to their allies in Acarnania. They also expelled the tyrant of Astacus and compelled the city to join their side. The island of Cephallenia about the same time, as a result of a visit by the Athenian squadron, voluntarily abandoned its neutrality in favour of Athens. In 430 a naval force of the same strength, but reinforced by four thousand heavy infantry and three hundred cavalry as well as by fifty triremes from Chios and Lesbos, made a determined attack on the cities of the Argolic peninsula. Pericles in person took charge of the operations, but failed completely in his main objective, the capture of Epidaurus. Some flying raids on other Argolic communities were hardly a sufficient return for so costly an undertaking, and Thucydides is discreetly silent about the causes of Pericles' lack of success. A beginning was also made this year with more ambitious undertakings in north-western Greece,[1] while in Chalcidice the siege of Potidaea at last came to an end (late autumn, 430). The inhabitants were allowed to leave, taking with them only the barest necessaries. Athenian colonists subsequently arrived to occupy the town.[2]

These military events, however, fade into insignificance before the blow that befell the Athenians in their own territory. The emergency measures of Pericles which brought the population of Attica within the fortified city area were fully justified on military grounds. But the consequent overcrowding, accompanied by exceptionally unsanitary conditions even for a Mediterranean town, provided an ideal field for the propagation of disease. In 430 an epidemic, which was believed to have been introduced from north Africa, attacked the dwellers in Peiraeus and then spread rapidly to Athens. The disease was virulent and highly contagious. Many victims died after six or eight days, if not sooner, racked by a burning fever; others, who survived this hyperpyrexia, later succumbed from intestinal complications because in their weakened condition they had little

[1] See below, pp. 91 ff.  [2] Cf. Tod 60.

power of resistance left.  Some again put an end to their
sufferings by suicide, while of those that recovered not a few
remained partially maimed.  Many of the dead were left
unburied, and the contamination of the air and the water
supply helped greatly to spread and prolong the sickness.
Thucydides, who himself fell ill but made a complete recovery,
has in his *History* left a careful clinical account of this disease
in its various stages.  Nevertheless it cannot be certainly
identified with any contagion now known.[1]  Birds and beasts
who fed on the unburied corpses were not immune but
frequently died.  In 429 and 428 there were fresh outbreaks.
The total mortality must have been exceedingly high, the
more so as in 430 the Athenian troops at Potidaea were
infected by reinforcements coming from Athens.  If Thucydides' statement that 4400 hoplites and 300 cavalrymen
perished from the pestilence in one year, and that Hagnon
at Potidaea lost 1050 out of 4000 men, is approximately
accurate, the total death-roll can hardly have been less than
30,000 and probably was considerably higher.[2]  It is remarkable
that, apart from Potidaea, the disease scarcely passed beyond
the confines of Attica.  Thucydides emphasizes that worse
than the actual sufferings and destruction of human life was
the disastrous effect of the pestilence on the *morale* of the
people.  While it roused some to heroic self-sacrifice in helping the victims, it engendered hopeless depression in others;
and again there were many who " disregarded all the ordinances of gods and men " to indulge in all manner of excess
because on the morrow they too might be dead.

The desperation of the Athenians, moreover, caused them
to sue for peace at Sparta, but without success.  Their disappointment, added to the misery that they had endured and
were enduring, then turned to fury against their leader, whom
with pardonable lack of logic they regarded as the cause of all
their troubles.  Pericles was arraigned for misappropriation
of public funds.  Though there is no reason to suppose that
there was the slightest truth in the charge, he was found guilty,
fined, and deposed from office.  Before this, however, he had

---

[1] It is unfortunate that this epidemic is still frequently referred to as the plague, for whatever else it may have been, it was not bubonic plague.  Nor yet was it cholera.  To judge from some at least of the recorded symptoms, it was allied rather to typhus or to the typhoid fevers.

[2] Thucydides, III, 87 ; II, 58.

still been able to exercise sufficient authority in the assembly
to persuade his hearers to prosecute the war with the same
energy and on the same lines as hitherto.[1] A few months
after the trial popular exasperation had died down. There
was a revulsion of feeling, and Pericles was re-elected in the
spring of 429 to the στρατηγία. Near the close of the year
he died. His loss was a great disaster for Athens; for, although
his general policy was followed to a great extent down to
421, there was no one to take his place, no one who could
exercise the same unquestioned authority resulting partly
from thirty years' experience of public affairs, partly from
personal attributes—force of character, unswerving integrity,
and profound knowledge of mass psychology. The inevitable
sequel was a return to the uncertainties and sometimes bitter
wrangles of party government. This had worked well enough
in former days; but in 429 and after, when the Athenians,
besides having far greater imperial responsibilities than in the
first part of the century, were in the midst of a veritable life
and death struggle, it might spell delay, loss of efficiency,
perhaps even disastrous defeat. Indeed, the ancient historian
frankly attributes the later misfortunes of Athens to this
lack of an outstanding leader, whose force of character and
prestige were sufficient to enable him to dispense with those
arts of flattery and time-serving measures, on which Pericles'
successors depended in order to keep their influence with the
people.

In 429 the annual Peloponnesian attack was directed not
against Athens but against her ally, Plataea, which had been
left unmolested for two years. The Plataean territory had
been declared sacred soil in 479 to commemorate the deliverance of Greece from Persian aggression brought about by
the victory fought there. But the action of the Plataeans
in 431 in putting their Theban prisoners to death had put
them in the wrong and afforded a pretext to the Spartan
king, Archidamus, and his army for marching into their land.
That his real purpose was to become master of a geographically
important place controlling the direct road from the Isthmus
and the Megarid across Mount Cithaeron into Boeotia, is
shown by his offer to let the Plataeans go free if they would
evacuate their land for the duration of the war. The

[1] Cf. the speech put in Pericles' mouth by Thucydides (II, 60–64).

Plataeans, after applying to Athens and being promised support from that quarter, refused. The rest of the campaigning season was spent in active siege operations, each of which was successfully repulsed by the defenders.[1] In the autumn the Peloponnesians constructed a wall of circumvallation and, leaving a sufficient force to guard it, thus changed the siege into a blockade. The Plataean garrison held out for a year, but their hope of receiving help from Athens was never fulfilled. In the winter of 428–427, as their plight became desperate, their counsels were divided. Somewhat less than half the garrison determined to attempt escape, and their plan though full of hazard was justified by results. Two hundred and twelve men succeeded in reaching Athens in safety. The rest of the Plataeans continued to hold out until the summer of 427, when starvation at last compelled surrender. All of them, to the number of 225—twenty-five of these were Athenians—were put to death. They could have expected no other fate seeing that their bitterest enemies, the Thebans, had won over Sparta to take extreme measures. Their city was razed to the ground. Thucydides fails to explain the conduct of the Athenian government in omitting to succour their ally. Apart from the sentimental ties between the two cities and the gratitude that the Athenians owed to their neighbour across the border, the strategic value of Plataea was, one would have supposed, sufficient to make Athenian intervention imperative. That it was nevertheless not forthcoming at the beginning can only have been due to the pestilence still raging in Athens, and, later on, to the financial difficulties, which at the end of the fourth year of the war were becoming acute, coupled with the secession of Lesbos. This event which threatened the basic structure of the empire demanded the maximum effort that Athenian power could exert.

### § 4. THE SECESSION OF LESBOS

The only two completely autonomous allies of Athens that remained after the suppression of Samos in 440–439 were Chios and Lesbos. The most powerful of the five communities in Lesbos was Mytilene. Antissa, Eresus, and Pyrrha, being

---

[1] For the siege-craft displayed by both sides see below, p. 336.

smaller, maintained close relations with her; but the fifth city, Methymna, pursued a policy of her own and during the events of 428-427 held staunchly to Athens. The government of Mytilene which was oligarchical appears to have meditated secession from Athens some years before, but, receiving no encouragement from Sparta, postponed action. In the midsummer of 428, no doubt calculating that the Athenians were too distracted by the epidemic and beset with enemies in Greece to follow up active protests by a considerable display of force, the Mytilenaeans openly seceded, although the defensive measures that had been in progress for some time—improvements in the fortifications and harbour works—were not quite completed. The three smaller communities on the island, moreover, consented to become members of the Mytilenaean state. Rumours of this συνοικισμὸς and of the other preparations reached Athens through various channels. The Athenian government, though unwilling to credit such serious tidings, took no risks but sent representatives to Lesbos. When their efforts failed to avert a rupture, an Athenian squadron of forty triremes which was to have operated in Peloponnesian waters was at once dispatched to the island instead. Cleippides and his two fellow-admirals were instructed to take the Mytilenaeans by surprise on the day when they were celebrating a religious festival outside the city. Some news of this amiable plot, however, leaked out at Athens, for a Mytilenaean then in Athens succeeded in hastening home by way of Euboea and warning his countrymen, before Cleippides arrived. The Athenian commander, finding the city closed against him, declared war and drove the Mytilenaean ships which sallied out against him back into their harbour. Then, rather unwisely as it proved, he agreed to an armistice to enable the Mytilenaeans to send a delegation to Athens. To make matters worse, the vigilance of the Athenian fleet anchored to the north of the city under the lee of Cape Malea was relaxed, so that a Mytilenaean galley was able to slip away unnoticed and sail for the Peloponnese.

The Athenian reply to the Mytilenaean envoys was categorical—complete submission or war; hence on their return home hostilities recommenced. Although Cleippides was now able effectively to blockade Mytilene from the sea, he had not the men at his disposal to shut the enemy in on the land side. They on their part helped to strengthen the defences of Antissa, Pyrrha, and Eresus. The Methymnaeans too were drawn into the war but suffered a severe reverse at the hands of the people of Antissa. With the arrival of Paches, who appears to have superseded Cleippides and his colleagues, and one thousand hoplites from Athens the situation underwent a marked change. He built defence works on the land side and thereby cut off the Mytilenaeans completely from the outer world. The blockade lasted through the winter.

Meantime the deputation to Sparta had effected nothing beyond the formal admission of Mytilene to membership in the Peloponnesian League and the promise of assistance in the spring. In February, 427, a Spartan, Salaethus, reached Lesbos and smuggled himself into the city. He brought the news that a Peloponnesian fleet of forty vessels under the command of Alcidas would shortly arrive on the scene. But by this time the citizens were in imminent danger of starvation. Salaethus therefore advised the Mytilenaean government to stake all on a desperate bid for victory and organize a general sortie of the able-bodied Mytilenaeans. With this end in view the oligarchs issued out arms to the population. But they were discredited in the eyes of the citizen body, the more so as they were suspected of having secreted stores for their own use while others went hungry. Once they were armed the Mytilenaeans turned against their rulers and refused to face the enemy. At the same time they demanded that the hoarded supplies be distributed, otherwise they threatened to treat with Paches. In this dilemma the oligarchs preferred themselves to open negotiations with the Athenian commander. Paches took possession of Mytilene, but agreed to suspend further action until the Athenian assembly had been consulted. The fleet of Alcidas was still some distance from Lesbos when news of the fall of Mytilene arrived. Although some of his companions advocated either a surprise attack on the Athenians or alternatively the occupation of some city in Ionia or Aeolis with a view to stirring up a general revolt against Athens, Alcidas was too cautious for any such venture. He touched at one or two points on the Asiatic coast; but when he was sighted by Paches' look-out ships and pursued he hastily withdrew across the Aegean to home waters.

Paches, when he sent for instructions, also despatched Salaethus and certain Mytilenaean ringleaders as prisoners to Athens. The Spartan was immediately put to death. Then the assembly, roused to the utmost fury against their late ally, voted that the entire male population be put to the sword and to sell the women and children into slavery. A galley was then sent off to Paches with instructions to carry out this fearful decision. The next day public sentiment in Athens underwent some change and the board of *strategi* took the unusual step of summoning a special meeting of the assembly. To do this required some courage as the magistrates in question thereby laid themselves open to prosecution for unconstitutional procedure.

It is in the tragically dramatic setting of the second Mytilenaean debate that Cleon, who had been foremost in urging the extreme penalty on the previous day, first makes his appearance in the pages of Thucydides. Little is known of his earlier career. He may have been one of Pericles' accusers in 430. In the year of the Lesbian revolt his official position was that of a member of the council. In 427–426 he was one of the ten Hellenotamiae and it is probable that thereafter to the year of his death (422–421) he was annually elected to the $\sigma\tau\rho\alpha\tau\eta\gamma\iota\alpha$. Certainly from 427 he was the unofficial but acknowledged leader of the *ecclesia*. His reputation has suffered because of the adverse judgment passed on him by Thucydides and the brilliant scurrilities of Aristophanes at his expense. It is thus not easy to form a fair estimate of this most violent yet most influential citizen, the exponent of a new style of popular oratory, who slapped his thigh, disarranged his dress and ran up and down the while he declaimed torrentially, until his voice rose to the squeal of a singed sow.[1] Yet a dispassionate weighing of all the evidence suggests that he was an administrator of marked ability, especially in the sphere of finance, and that even as a military leader he was at least not below the average. In his imperial policy he upheld with brutal frankness the doctrine that might is right. In the pages of Thucydides he is made to remind the Athenians that their empire

---

[1] Cf. Thucydides, III, 36; Plutarch, *Nicias*, 8; Aristophanes, *Wasps*, 34.

is no more nor less than a tyranny. He argues that the people of Mytilene as a whole, not merely a minority, were responsible for the secession from Athens. Moreover, since this ally had always enjoyed all the privileges due to a free and autonomous state, repudiation of the long-standing and friendly relations between the two cities was peculiarly culpable. The Athenians before this had punished severely allies who had been forced into revolt. The punishment of the Mytilenaeans, whose defection was quite unprovoked, should be all the more severe. In short, Cleon argued that if the Athenians were to incline to leniency in this crisis and refuse to make an example of Mytilene, they might as well give up their empire at once.

The reply to Cleon's indictment of Mytilene and his insistent demand that the previous day's decree of the assembly be left unchanged is assigned by the historian to Diodotus—a speaker otherwise unknown. Diodotus enters no humanitarian plea for the islanders; like Cleon, he is concerned only with what it is expedient for Athens to do. Not what the Mytilenaeans deserve—he does, indeed, argue that it was the oligarchy not the *demos* which was responsible—but what prudence demands that the Athenians should do is the subject of his argument. He warns against the danger in a democratic state like Athens of precipitate action under the spur of momentary passion. Then he contends with great force that terroristic methods defeat their own end. No punishment, not even death, has ever sufficed to end wrong-doing. In the case under consideration the ultimate result of inflicting the extreme penalty on Lesbos, so far from ensuring the future solidarity of the empire, would be to hasten its disintegration by alarming and antagonizing in the various city-states the democratic majorities whose feelings to Athens were friendly. The orator's arguments, doubtless because they avoided all sentiment and enlarged only upon what he believed to be in the long run in the Athenian interest, were powerful enough to win sufficient votes to give him a small majority. The decision of the previous day was rescinded and a second vessel was despatched at once to countermand the orders already transmitted to Paches. The Mytilenaean representatives in Athens provided rations and promised rewards if the rowers reached their destination in time. By dividing the crew into shifts rowing day and night—the rowers even took their food as they worked at the oars—the commander of the second ship brought her to Lesbos almost in the wake of the first, whose captain sent on a painful errand had not made particular haste to reach his destination. Only the ringleaders of the revolt were put to death—their number is uncertain—the rest forfeited their political independence. The land of the Lesbian cities, other than loyal Methymna, was parcelled out into lots. After certain of these had been set aside as sacred lands, the remainder were assigned to cleruchs who came from Athens to settle in the island. The defeated inhabitants farmed the lots and paid an annual rental to their conquerors.[1] Thus the Athenians had extricated themselves from a dangerous situation; but the cost had been great. The unexpected addition to the heavy expenses incurred in other theatres of the war compelled the government to institute an extraordinary tax on property (εἰσφορά). So far as is known, that was the first occasion on which the Athenian state had recourse to such direct taxation.

### § 5. OPERATIONS IN NORTH-WESTERN GREECE, 430–426 B.C.

It will be recalled how in 431 and 430 the Athenians had with varying success carried out naval raids on various points of the Peloponnese. Amongst the more substantial results had been the voluntary accession of Cephallenia and the conquest of some towns on the Acarnanian coast. North-western Greece then seemed a promising area for further Athenian expansion, perhaps with the ultimate hope of completely hemming in Boeotia and Phocis; for on the south was the Corinthian Gulf while the Thessalians in the north were already numbered amongst the enemies of Thebes and her confederates. Of these more backward Greeks in the north-west the Aetolians maintained their neutrality at this time. Much of Acarnania was on the Athenian side; but Oeniadae in the extreme south, as well as the north-western corner of Acarnania with the adjacent island of Leucas, was allied to Sparta. So, too, were the Ambraciots on the north side of the Gulf of Arta. The Athenians had an initial advantage in their control of a first-class base for naval operations,

[1] Thucydides, III, 50, supported by an inscription of 427–426 (Tod 63).

Naupactus. Before the end of the campaigning season of 430 a beginning was made with plans that presumably originated with Pericles.[1]

Actually the initiative came from the Amphilochians of Argos on the eastern side of the Gulf of Arta. As a result of a feud with their neighbours of Ambracia, they had been driven out of their city and had temporarily found a home with the Acarnanians further south. A joint petition to Athens was answered by immediate instructions to Phormio to restore the exiles. With a squadron of thirty triremes the Athenian admiral carried out his orders efficiently. Argos was taken and then resettled by Amphilochians and Acarnanians. The reduced Ambraciots were sold into slavery. After this Phormio withdrew to Naupactus, where he remained on guard for the winter months.

That the Athenians entertained high hopes of advancing their interests in the north-west is suggested by the fact that, in spite of the epidemic and more urgent calls elsewhere on their resources, they continued their operations to the north of the Corinthian Gulf for the next four years. An additional reason for their action, however, was the intervention of Sparta in this theatre of war. After their reverse at Argos the Ambraciots appealed to the enemies of Athens. The Spartans despatched an advance force under Cnemus, while a larger Peloponnesian fleet was made ready. He succeeded in crossing to Leucas unbeknown to Phormio who was on guard at Naupactus and in the vicinity. Cnemus now received reinforcements from various enemies of Athens in the north-west and some also from the tribes of southern Epirus. Perdiccas even sent a thousand of his Macedonians to co-operate, but they did not arrive in time for the business in hand. This was an attempt to capture the important Acarnanian town of Stratus. It failed mainly, it would seem, because of the indiscipline and lack of co-operation shown by Cnemus' miscellaneous allies. He withdrew his men into the territory of Oeniadae, where the allies disbanded. Meanwhile the Peloponnesian fleet of forty-seven galleys was on its way to support him. But it was followed by Phormio and

---

[1] It will be remembered that Pericles had tried without success more than twenty years before to strengthen the Athenian position on the northern shore of the Corinthian Gulf. Cf. above, p. 39.

his twenty triremes as far as the open sea just outside the entrance to the gulf. Here, aided by a favourable wind, he was able to use the Athenian naval tactics to full advantage and completely defeated his adversaries although they were more than twice as strong numerically. Later in the summer of 429 Cnemus, whose failure had formed the subject of an official inquiry at Sparta, tried to retrieve his reputation by an attack on Naupactus. But once more the Athenian admiral, though some of his ships were driven ashore, saved his base and turned an imminent defeat into a victory not less brilliant than the first.[1] During the winter he conducted a raid against Astacus and deported some disloyal elements in Stratus and other Acarnanian communities. Then he withdrew to Athens, where he probably died soon afterwards.

In the summer of 427 his son, Asopius, was put in charge of a squadron which, following the precedent set in previous years, raided the Laconian coast. While the rest of the fleet then returned to home waters, the admiral proceeded with twelve galleys to Naupactus. It is a tribute to Phormio that, after his withdrawal, the Acarnanians petitioned Athens to send some relative of his to take charge. Asopius now led his Acarnanian allies against Oeniadae, which being unassailable during the winter months had not been attacked by his father during his last campaign. But the career of Phormio's son was almost immediately cut short. Devastation of Oeniadae's territory did not intimidate its citizens into joining Athens. When Asopius went on to attack Leucas, he himself was killed and his men were repulsed with heavy loss.

But the chief event amongst the north-western Greeks in this year was a civil war in Corcyra. Few episodes in ancient history can compare with it for stark Aeschylean horror, so that Thucydides was moved to append to a characteristically restrained, though vivid, narrative of its progress and end a searching analysis of revolution ($\sigma\tau\acute{\alpha}\sigma\iota\varsigma$), and of the spirit of faction in party government which in given circumstances might degenerate into anarchy and a complete destruction of ordered political life. The trouble on the island began soon after the arrival there of the Corcyraean prisoners taken by Corinth in 433–432. They had been

[1] On the Athenian naval tactics cf. below, p. 343.

released on the understanding that they would work for the defection of Corcyra from the Athenian alliance. After failing to bring about the legal condemnation of Pithias, the leader of the democratic government, the oligarchic conspirators, some of whom were prosecuted in their turn for sacrilege, carried out a raid on the council-house. There they slew Pithias and about sixty of his supporters. Next they succeeded in obtaining temporary control of the city, save for the acropolis and one of the two harbours. There their opponents maintained themselves until they received reinforcements from the agricultural serfs in the island, to whom in return for loyal help they promised their freedom. The oligarchs, however, through possessing one of the two harbours, were able to introduce some eight hundred mercenaries from the mainland, presumably Epirot mountaineers. Renewed fighting attended by much material damage in the city was suspended for a short time owing to the arrival and intervention of some Athenian galleys from Naupactus. Many of the oligarchs nevertheless were distrustful of their opponents and of the Athenian commander. They took sanctuary in temples and later withdrew to a small island off the coast. The arrival of fifty-three Peloponnesian ships under the Spartan admiral Alcidas, who after his fruitless cruise to Asia Minor had been sent off to support the Corcyraean oligarchs, must have raised their hopes. But, although Alcidas engaged the Corcyraean fleet and came off best, he withdrew after a few days on receiving intelligence of the approach of a superior Athenian armament. He showed the same excess of caution and inability to exploit an initial advantage as when he was ordered to the relief of Mitylene. Had he followed the plan of Brasidas, who accompanied him to Corcyra in an advisory but subordinate capacity, he might well have occupied the city and have been in a strong position to repulse the Athenians when they came, in spite of their slight numerical superiority.

On the departure of Alcidas the Corcyraean *demos* proceeded with pitiless ferocity against the oligarchs and against all suspected of being in sympathy with them. Many, too, anticipated certain execution by committing suicide or killing each other. Only some six hundred effected a withdrawal to Mount Istone. The Athenian squadron under Eurymedon stood by for some days, but he took no steps to stop the carnage. In their stronghold in the north-eastern corner of the island the oligarchs held out for two years, making periodical raids into the lowlands and even against the city itself. The end came in the summer of 425. Then the democrats, aided by another Athenian fleet which, commanded by Eurymedon and Sophocles, was on its way to Sicily, stormed the fastness on Istone. The oligarchs surrendered on the understanding that their fate should be decided by the Athenian people. The Athenian commanders segregated them on a small island near by, it being stipulated that any attempt to escape would negative the agreement. The Corcyraeans, not to be baulked of their vengeance, trapped certain oligarchs by false statements into attempting to escape from custody. It is impossible to condone the action of Eurymedon and his colleague in handing over the prisoners to their fellow-citizens and making no move to intervene when the wretched oligarchs were butchered to a man.

The next year brought to the front an Athenian soldier who for more than a decade was to serve his country loyally and with substantial success. Demosthenes, so far as is known, first held the office of *strategus* in 426. He was an officer gifted with imagination and ready to adapt his military tactics to the special needs of the occasion rather than rigidly to adhere in all circumstances to the traditional usages of Greek warfare at this date. Such a man, however, was not " safe " ; and if he had some brilliant successes, he also suffered reverses which a more cautious and orthodox commander would have avoided. Again, he was not a politician ; and so, from one cause or the other, he never enjoyed the degree of confidence and support from the Athenian *demos* to which his real abilities entitled him. In the last and most critical campaign of his life we shall see that an unparalleled disaster for Athens would probably have been avoided, if he had had a free hand to carry out his plans instead of being overruled by an older and politically more influential colleague.

In the summer of 426 he and another commander were put in charge of a modest naval squadron of thirty vessels with orders to operate in western Greece. In conjunction with the Acarnanian allies and others from Zacynthus, Cephallenia, and even Corcyra he directed an attack on Leucas. The inhabitants were hard pressed and driven to take refuge within their chief town. A blockade would probably have reduced them within a short time, but, in spite of the protests of the Acarnanians, Demosthenes changed his plans, lured by the prospect of carrying out a far more ambitious undertaking. This was no less than the conquest of Aetolia. This once achieved, the isolation of Boeotia and neighbouring Doris would have been all but complete; for the Phocians were only through force of circumstance on the Peloponnesian side and would have joined Athens once they could safely do so. At the same time direct communication between the Gulf of Corinth and the Maliac Gulf would be opened to the Athenians and their allies. The Spartans had, however, not lost sight of the situation in central Greece. The tribes of Trachis and Doris had appealed to them for assistance against their neighbours in the hills. A colony, Heraclea, was established in Trachis, a few miles west of Thermopylae, which commanded the road from Delphi and Amphissa to Thessaly. The settlers were drawn partly from Laconia, partly from the Peloponnesian allies. The town's vicinity to the sea and to the northern end of Euboea flattered the hopes of the Spartans that they might use it to strike at Athens in a most vulnerable spot; but they reckoned without the hostility of the Thessalians on the north, who prevented Heraclea from ever developing into a place of importance. Moreover, the harsh government of the Spartan leaders there called forth the discontent of the remainder of the population, and internal disharmony made for weakness against outside foes.

In 426, however, when Heraclea was first founded, the threat to Athenian interests seemed serious. A successful occupation of Aetolia would go a long way towards neutralizing the value of the new colony. Nevertheless Demosthenes was guilty of underestimating the difficulties of his undertaking. Aetolia was mountainous and had few roads and passes suitable for movements of bodies of troops. Its inhabitants were skilled at the type of fighting and skirmishing requisite in such country and with the right tactics could hold their own against greatly superior numbers. They knew every inch of the ground, a knowledge which no invader, even with native guides, could hope to equal. The Acarnanians refused to co-operate with Demosthenes, because he had refused to complete the conquest of Leucas. He depended, therefore, on his own men and such other allies as he could muster. Chief of these were the Ozolian Locrians whose country physically resembled Aetolia and who, like the Aetolians, were versed in mountain warfare. But the Athenian general showed too much haste. Instead of waiting for the Locrians, he thought he saw an opportunity of striking an effective blow at some of the tribes in southern Aetolia before the whole of that country could mobilize against him. Instead he suffered a severe reverse near Aegitium, losing many of his allies and one hundred and twenty picked Athenian hoplites. Speedy withdrawal to Naupactus was then the only feasible course.

The Aetolians, not content with their momentary success, turned to Sparta. The answer to their appeal was an expeditionary force under Eurylochus and two other commanders. It consisted of 2500 hoplites from the cities of the Peloponnesian League and five hundred from Heraclea. Their immediate objective was Naupactus. Joining forces at Delphi, the two detachments passed through the territory of the Ozolian Locrians, from whom hostages were taken to ensure their neutrality, and advanced to the assault of the Athenian naval base. Had its defence depended on its inhabitants and Demosthenes alone, it could scarcely have escaped capture. But Demosthenes' influence with the Acarnanians was still sufficient to persuade them to forget past disagreements and come to the rescue. Thus reinforced by a thousand additional hoplites he was able to beat off the enemy. Eurylochus made no attempt to repeat his assault but withdrew into Aetolia. His object now was to embarrass the Acarnanian allies of Demosthenes by bringing in the Ambraciots on the Spartan side. In this he succeeded, and the ensuing operations were prolonged through the autumn into the winter of 426–425.

Meanwhile, however, a welcome Athenian reinforcement of twenty vessels, which had been in Peloponnesian waters and there received an urgent message from Demosthenes, sailed up the Acarnanian coast and effected a junction with him in the Gulf of Arta. The opposing armies were stationed in the neighbourhood of Olpae, which the Ambraciots had seized, for nearly a week before a battle took place. Demosthenes, fearing to be surrounded by superior numbers, departed so far from normal Greek tactics as to post in an ambush a mixed force of four hundred heavy and light-armed Acarnanian infantry. These, when the right wing of the Athenians was in danger of being surrounded, suddenly swooped on the Spartans from the rear and routed them. At the same time their centre gave way. The Ambraciots, however, carried all before them on the other wing; but when they returned from pursuing their opponents they found themselves exposed to a fresh attack by the victorious troops of Demosthenes. They only covered their retreat into Olpae with the greatest difficulty. The Athenian commander had won a striking victory which fully atoned for his costly errors earlier in the year. The casualties of his opponents had been very heavy, amongst them being Eurylochus himself. The Spartans, moreover, now desired to extricate themselves from a perilous commitment. They reached a secret understanding with Demosthenes and then slunk away from Olpae one by one under pretext of gathering kindling wood and herbs. When their late allies realized their treachery they hurried out in pursuit, but they were set upon by the Acarnanians and repulsed with heavy losses. Finally Demosthenes waylaid and all but annihilated Ambraciot reinforcements hastening to Olpae. Thoroughly defeated and deserted by their Peloponnesian allies, the Ambraciots were glad to come to terms with their neighbours. Although they did not become Athenian allies, they hereafter remained neutral in the war. About nine months later (autumn, 425) Anactorium was betrayed into the hands of a mixed Athenian and Acarnanian force, and in the next year Oeniadae was at last constrained into standing in with the rest of Acarnania. Both these events, however, took place after Demosthenes had been transferred to another theatre of war. The hope of coercing Aetolia was never fulfilled. Even had the Athenians been willing or able to send a far greater army to its conquest, the enterprise would have been lengthy and its ultimate success far from certain. But in the next few years their vital interests demanded attention elsewhere, while in the second stage of the war under the influence of younger politicians the Athenian *demos* embarked on more spectacular undertakings. The inhabitants of Naupactus meanwhile had commemorated their successes in 426 and 425 by setting up dedications at Delphi and Olympia.[1]

### § 6. PYLOS AND SPHACTERIA

The surrender of Mytilene in 427 had aroused a keen division of opinion in the Athenian assembly. Two years later our sources afford us another glimpse of the party struggles which, familiar enough in earlier days, had been in abeyance during the later part of Pericles' *régime*. Cleon's ascendancy in the *ecclesia* was far from complete, as the outcome of the Mytilenaean debates had clearly shown. The more conservative or moderate group (οἱ μέσοι) in the assembly had as its chief spokesman Nicias, son of Niceratus. A man of considerable wealth, he was at this time probably close to fifty years of age. He appears to have served as *strategus* in Pericles' lifetime and certainly several times since. In the late summer of 427 he had been in charge of a military contingent which captured Minoa, an islet lying off the coast of Megara. In the next year he commanded sixty ships which first raided Melos, whose population abided obstinately by their neutrality, and then the coast of Locris. This second venture was timed to coincide with an Athenian sortie into Boeotia that culminated in a successful skirmish against Boeotian troops near Tanagra. The ancient writers stress the political integrity, the liberality, the high sense of duty, and the piety, sometimes verging on superstition, of Nicias. He enjoyed the respect even of his political opponents, while his popularity with the general public was great. But while these excellent qualities were of outstanding value to his countrymen in time of peace, he lacked the initiative, energy, and far-sightedness indispensable in a statesman who would guide Athens to victory over her enemies. It was his tragedy, and Athens', that the implicit trust of his fellow-Athenians assigned to him tasks and responsibility to which his capacity was unequal.

An Athenian fleet was sent off to the west in the spring of 425, its final destination being Sicily. The two admirals, Eurymedon and Sophocles were, however, under orders to put in at Corcyra on the way. It has already been related how

---

[1] For the inscriptions recording these dedications see Tod 65.

they stood by during the final reckoning of the Corcyraean *demos* with its oligarchic opponents. The arrival of the Athenians in the island had been delayed by bad weather. Moreover, Demosthenes had sailed with them when they left Athens. Though not holding office in this year, he seems to have had the support of Cleon to call upon the two commanders for assistance, if he saw a suitable occasion of inflicting a telling blow on the enemies of Athens. It is possible that on his previous cruises he had formed some plan for establishing a strong post in Spartan territory. At all events, when the fleet was caught in a storm and driven to shelter for several days in the harbour of Pylos on the west coast of Messenia, Demosthenes proposed to turn the rocky peninsula of Pylos into a fort by strengthening artificially three places which were not by nature unassailable. The admirals were opposed to what they deemed a hare-brained scheme; nevertheless, as they could not leave at once, they acquiesced in the employment of their men on this task. At the end of six days the bad weather had abated, but the building of the three pieces of wall was also finished. Demosthenes was left with five triremes to hold the fort as best he could, while the main fleet proceeded on its way to Corcyra.

The Spartan government looked seriously on what they might have been excused for regarding as an impudent, but negligible escapade. The Peloponnesian army that was ravaging Attica was recalled and orders were sent to a fleet which had been despatched to Corcyra to hasten to Pylos. An advance body of troops was detailed at once to blockade Demosthenes. It was joined soon after by a larger Peloponnesian army and by the fleet which had eluded Eurymedon and Sophocles in the neighbourhood of Zacynthus. But, though Demosthenes had realized his danger in time and despatched two of his galleys to bring back the Athenian fleet, he was blockaded by the enemy on both elements before its arrival. The Spartans, to prevent any attempt at occupation by the Athenians, stationed some of their men on the island of Sphacteria which all but shut off the bay from the open sea. Immediately to the north of it and separated from it only by a narrow channel was the promontory of Pylos. The strait to the south of the island was three-quarters of a mile wide. To block this entry into the bay effectively against the Athenians, while continuing the siege of Pylos, would have required more vessels than the Spartans had at their disposal. The Spartan admiral strove hard to reduce Demosthenes before the Athenian fleet could return. On three separate days he assaulted the Athenian position. But the strength of the little peninsula and the reefs inshore which made navigation for the Peloponnesian ships dangerous compensated the gallant defenders for their numerical inferiority. Thus when the Athenian fleet arrived on the scene Pylos was still unconquered. After one day's delay the Athenians sailed into the bay early in the morning, taking the enemy, who were just preparing to launch their triremes, at a serious disadvantage. They captured or disabled enough of the Peloponnesian boats to give them a marked superiority and enable them not merely to relieve Demosthenes but to blockade the 420 Spartans and a body of Helots on Sphacteria.

The Spartan government, seeing no means of rescuing their men on the island, proposed a truce while they sent legates to Athens to negotiate. In the interval the Athenian admirals agreed to allow regular food rations to be introduced into the island under supervision. But the reply to the Spartan peace proposals given by the Athenian assembly was far from conciliatory. Cleon commanded sufficient support to demand the cession of Achaea, Troizen, Pagae, and Nisaea as the price for the surrender of the Spartans on Sphacteria; in other words, he would have recovered at one stroke all that Athens had forfeited or lost by the peace of 445. Thus the negotiations came to nothing and the truce ended. The Athenians, moreover, alleging that their opponents had been guilty of a small infraction of the truce, retained the Peloponnesian ships of which they had taken charge when hostilities were temporarily suspended. But to carry out a complete blockade of Sphacteria proved more difficult than had been anticipated, partly because the prevailing winds made patrolling difficult, partly because food was running short and fresh supplies being sea-borne arrived irregularly, partly because the Spartans on the mainland offered rewards to swimmers who would carry skins filled with food across the bay by night. This delay in due course produced a change of public sentiment in the Athenian *ecclesia*. Criticism of

Cleon was voiced, to which he replied by denying the reports that had come through from Pylos and then taunting Nicias and his military colleagues with lack of energy, adding that with a detachment of troops he could do better himself. Nicias and the assembly thereupon took Cleon at his word and the direction of the expedition was entrusted to him against his will, Demosthenes to be associated with him in the command. He put the best face he could on an unwelcome responsibility and even guaranteed to capture or kill off the Spartans on Sphacteria within three weeks.

Demosthenes, even before Cleon reached Pylos, had been planning to land on the island. It was a difficult undertaking, because the points at which troops could be disembarked at all were few and dangerous; besides, much of Sphacteria was covered with thick brushwood which afforded protection to the defenders. Most of them were encamped in the middle of the island near the only well, but there were two outposts, one to the south, one on a steep hill near the northern end. An accidental bush-fire, however, destroyed much of the thick undergrowth, so that the main Spartan position became more distinct for any landing party. Soon afterwards Cleon arrived and the capture of the island was attempted without delay. The troops, heavy- and light-armed, were disembarked early in the morning at two points near the south-eastern and south-western extremities of Sphacteria. Although the total number cannot be determined with certainty, it is probable that they outnumbered their opponents by at least ten to one. Against this mass attack of hoplites, flanked by archers and other light infantry, the Spartans and their helots fought with magnificent doggedness. When at last their position in the central encampment became untenable they slowly retired to the hill in the north. From this inaccessible spot they continued to beat off their assailants until a detachment of light-armed Messenians was despatched by the Athenian commanders up a narrow gorge which led them to the rear of the Spartan position. Only then the surviving Spartans to the number of 292 capitulated.

The unusual character of these operations, combined perhaps with the epic quality of the Spartan stand, influenced the Athenian historian to relate them at a length disproportionate to their military importance. The occupation of

Pylos, however galling to Spartan pride, did not prove of great strategic value. On the other hand, the detention at Athens of nearly three hundred Spartan prisoners of war was an event without parallel in Greek history and proved of great value to the Athenians in later negotiations. Besides this, the exploit completely rehabilitated Cleon, and his authority for the remainder of his life was greater than it had ever been.

### § 7. THE DELIUM CAMPAIGN

The occupation of Pylos was followed by the capture of two other Peloponnesian bases. In midsummer 425 an expedition led by Nicias and two other commanders began by a raid into Corinthian territory. Though indecisive in character, it cost them less than fifty lives, whereas their opponents' casualties numbered two hundred and twelve. They next occupied the peninsula of Methone on the southeastern side of the Argolic peninsula, and fortified the narrow strip of territory connecting it with the mainland. In the following spring Nicias, again in association with two colleagues, inflicted a grave loss on Sparta by seizing Cythera. The island was chiefly inhabited by *Perioeci*. It was important for its local fisheries and as a port of call for merchantmen on their way to and from the African coast. Hence a Spartan magistrate was in charge and a garrison was maintained there. The Athenians at once used the island as a centre from which to make descents on the coast settlements of Messenia and Laconia.

Another capture nearer home the Athenians owed to a civil disturbance in Megara. It had led to the expulsion of one faction, which seized Pagae and held it against its rivals. Some of the Megarians then opened secret negotiations with Athens, asserting their willingness to hand over the city and the port of Nisaea. Demosthenes and another general, Hippocrates, who were again but less happily to be associated later in the year, were entrusted with this operation. Their attempt to surprise and occupy Megara failed, thanks to the timely arrival of a Peloponnesian relief force under the Spartan, Brasidas. But they reduced Nisaea and gained control of the Long Walls, which the Athenians themselves had constructed thirty years before. Renewed civil war in

Megara brought the secessionists at Pagae into power. After a ruthless persecution of their political opponents they established an oligarchic government of a narrow type.

But now the series of Athenian successes, all but unbroken through two seasons of fighting, received an abrupt check. The summer of 424 saw the beginning of operations under a Spartan commander in Chalcidice which threatened to deprive the Athenians of an important section of their maritime empire. At the very end of that year's campaigning an Athenian army in the field suffered a severe defeat in central Greece, for in October Hippocrates and Demosthenes prepared to make a concerted attack on Boeotia. Although both were on the board of *strategi* for 424–423, they could not have undertaken this campaign without the backing of the political leaders; in other words, while the plans no doubt originated with one or both of them, the decision to carry them into effect was Cleon's. This circumstance deserves to be emphasized because the invasion of Boeotia was the first substantial departure from Periclean strategy during the war. Having failed to isolate Boeotia by the acquisition of Aetolia, Demosthenes and Hippocrates, who had been in communication with disaffected persons in Boeotia, hoped that the appearance of an Athenian army there would encourage them to attempt a pro-Athenian revolution. The plan that was evolved was strategically sound enough, provided absolute secrecy could be maintained till it was time to strike. But a leakage of information ruined it and the Boeotarchs were able to take precautionary measures. Demosthenes with a fleet of forty ships sailed for Naupactus. There he raised levies among his Acarnanian friends and with their help he proposed to seize Siphae on the Gulf of Corinth. Hippocrates, who in the meantime had collected all the available men in Attica—even foreigners permanently or temporarily resident in Athens were summoned under arms—was on the same day to cross the border and seize Delium, some five miles east of Tanagra. Contemporaneously a democratic revolution was to be staged in Chaeronea. Only one part of this plan succeeded. Hippocrates led his army of seven thousand heavy- and about twenty thousand light-armed infantry across the frontier. They occupied and then proceeded to fortify the sanctuary of Apollo at Delium. But the Boeotarchs, acting on a warning that they had received, had placed troops in Chaeronea and Siphae. Thus the democratic rising in the one and the seizure of the other by Demosthenes were alike frustrated. The Athenian commander was not strong enough to attempt to take the Boeotian port by assault and hold it afterwards. He had perforce to retire, but he still hoped that the disaffected Boeotians in Siphae might play into his hands. When he was convinced that there was no chance of this he crossed the Corinthian Gulf and descended on Sicyon. But the raid was beaten off with some loss to the Athenians in dead and prisoners.

Shortly before this the expedition of Hippocrates had ended disastrously. While he was putting Delium into a state of defence the majority of the Boeotarchs were undecided whether to take the field against him, but in the end one of their number, Pagondas, persuaded his colleagues that the boldest course was the best. When the fortification of Delium was completed the Athenian general left a garrison there and then prepared to lead his army back into Attica. The Boeotian forces which had been collected at Tanagra marched out to attack the Athenians as they withdrew into Attica. The two armies engaged about a mile to the east of Delium. The Boeotian heavy infantry was numerically about the same as the Athenian, but their light-armed troops were fewer. This disparity was more than equalized by a thousand cavalry. The Athenian right wing more than held its own against the Boeotian left, but the Athenians who formed the left wing were confronted by the Theban hoplites drawn up twenty-five deep, a mass formation on one wing that foreshadowed the infantry tactics perfected by Epaminondas in the fourth century. Before this pressure of men the Athenian left wing was driven steadily back. Then at the critical moment Pagondas sent a part of the cavalry stationed on his right flank round a low hill, which concealed the movement. The horsemen suddenly appearing in the rear of the victorious right wing of the Athenians won the day for Pagondas, for this new development misled the Athenians into believing that the cavalry were the vanguard of a second Boeotian army. A panic seized them and they broke into a run. The enemy followed up the fugitives till nightfall and inflicted heavy casualties on them. A little more than a fortnight later the

Boeotians, who had failed to recover Delium by negotiation, expelled the Athenian garrison. The Boeotian misadventure had cost Athens dear. Nearly a thousand hoplites were killed and the casualties amongst the light-armed troops were proportionately even heavier. Two hundred, moreover, of the garrison left in Delium were taken prisoner. The Boeotian losses were less than five hundred. Pagondas, to whose unusually skilful handling of the Boeotian army the Athenian debacle was entirely due, is not heard of again.

### § 8. FINANCIAL STRINGENCY AT ATHENS

The loss in man power incurred by Athens in this ill-starred campaign was so serious as to offset in a great measure the recent gains in other theatres of war. Furthermore, the heavy cost of the war added to the difficulties of the government, which had already faced a financial crisis in 427. The sums borrowed from the treasuries of Athena Parthenos and of the other gods between 433–432 and 423–422 totalled nearly 5600 talents, and it is probable that this sum was spent on the prosecution of the war in addition to the regular income from the tribute and other sources.[1] In the Attic year 425–424 a drastic revision of the tribute was instituted, an occurrence passed over in silence by Thucydides, but recorded on an extant inscription. In view of its importance one must regret that much of this document, especially the assessment list itself, is very imperfectly preserved.[2] It contains two decrees which lay down the procedure to be followed in making the reassessment, provide for a special body of jurors to try suits arising out of it, and set out the duties of the several officials concerned, as well as the religious obligations imposed on various states in the empire. The fragmentary character of the lists that follow leaves much in doubt. Nevertheless it is clear that the total number of cities enrolled was far greater than in previous years. This increase was primarily due to a change in procedure. In the past there had been many cases where a group of small communities had been assessed to pay a single sum. These groups were now

---

[1] Tod 64. Meritt, *Athen. Financial Documents*, Chapter VIII.

[2] Tod 66. B. D. Meritt and A. B. West, *The Athenian Assessment of 425* (Ann Arbor, 1934).

dispensed with and each member of a group was required to make a separately assessed payment.[1] Two new districts also make their appearance in this list and the lists for two later assessments, the Pontic and the so-called Actaean, embracing certain cities in the Troad. The total assessment for 425–424 in all probability amounted to slightly under fifteen hundred talents. The action of Athens in doubling and trebling the φόρος has been severely criticized as an act of despotic harshness. But, apart from the urgent requirements of the war, whose successful issue for Athens would also ensure the continued prosperity of her subjects and allies, it is fair to say that a majority of these had materially benefited during the years that they had been enrolled in the empire. Many of them had, however, been paying the same amount for years, although their revenues had increased, so that the change in the ratio between their income and what they were required to pay in 425–424, compared with the ratio between income and tribute payment at the time when they were first assessed, was in all likelihood not nearly so great as the total increase in tribute from the whole empire would suggest. The steps taken by the Athenians as early as 449 to establish the uniform use of Athenian currency, weights, and measures throughout the empire were in principle a far more arbitrary use of power.[2]

## § 9. BRASIDAS IN THRACE

Perhaps no feature in Athens' conduct of the war is more puzzling than her relative neglect of the dependencies in Chalcidice and Thrace. In part this may be explained by a false belief that the reduction of Potidaea had sufficed to restore her authority and prestige permanently in that area. At that time there was no sign that the synoecism of Olynthus would give rise to any serious problems. Nevertheless the variable policy of the Macedonian king should alone have been a warning of possible danger. It has already been seen how, at a time when he was ostensibly at peace with Athens, he sent a detachment of Macedonians to co-operate

---

[1] This breaking up of a group and assessing each member separately was technically known as ἀπόταξις.

[2] By the decree of Clearchus, fragments of which have been found in Syme, Cos, Aphytis, and Siphnos. See Tod 67 and particularly *A.T.L.* II, pp. 61–68.

with the Peloponnesians in Acarnania.[1] Perdiccas, it is true, had trouble enough to maintain his position in his own realm. A temporary accommodation with his most dangerous neighbour, the Odrysian king Sitalces, who had recently concluded an alliance with Athens, was brought to an end by a thirty days' raid, in which the Thracians devastated extensive tracts of country on both sides of the River Axius (autumn, 429). Perdiccas wisely abstained from taking the field against the invaders, but concentrated on holding his fortresses. After this hostile interlude the two monarchs settled down to a more lasting peace. For several years, however, there was friction between Perdiccas and Athens, of which the sole cause was apparently Methone on the coast of Pieria. This city had been a member of the Athenian empire for some time, but the Macedonian king was eager to have this valuable seaport in his hands. His efforts to bring the city over to his side by economic and military pressure failed; the Athenians sought to ease the position of the Methonaeans by making strong protests to Perdiccas, by remitting a part of the city's tribute, and by granting its citizens preferential treatment in the matter of importing grain direct from the Black Sea.[2] This last-named concession was not unique, for the people of Aphytis at this time or a little earlier were accorded a similar privilege.[3] Possibly they had been of service at the time of the Athenian operations against Potidaea. Outwardly, at least, the relations between Athens and Macedonia remained friendly until 424. Then at last the striking successes recently won by the former in the Peloponnese, one at least of which had influenced Sparta to make overtures for peace, so alarmed Perdiccas that he once more approached the head of the Peloponnesian League. The increased tribute levied from the Athenian dependencies in 425–424 was causing discontent,[4] and to Perdiccas it seemed a good occasion for encouraging disaffection from Athens. He felt renewed anxiety, too, in his own kingdom, for the district of Lyncestis, a Macedonian frontier province abutting

[1] See above, p. 92.
[2] Cf. the two decrees of 429 and 426 in Tod 61.
[3] Cf. *I.G.*, I², 58.
[4] Cf. *Syll.*, 77. This is a list of Athenian casualties in 425–424, which includes names of men who fell at Amphipolis, Potidaea, Sermylia, and Singus, in addition to those who were killed in other theatres of the war.

on Illyria, had become virtually an independent state under its prince, Arrhabaeus.

When Perdiccas appealed to Sparta to intervene in Thrace, his arguments were seconded by envoys from the Chalcidic League centred in Olynthus. The ephors instructed their best commander, Brasidas, who had already distinguished himself several times during the war, to proceed to Macedonia; but his military force was modest enough. Seven hundred Laconian Helots trained for hoplite service and one thousand mercenaries from the Peloponnese were conducted by him to Heraclea in Trachis. From here he made his way through Thessaly without hostile incident, although this region was as a whole friendly to Athens; but the charm of his address and his persuasive tongue overcame all obstacles. His relations with Perdiccas quickly became strained, since the Macedonian king wished to use the Spartan wholly for his own purposes against Arrhabaeus. Brasidas, however, listening to the Chalcidic League and bearing the interests of Sparta in mind, was more disposed to promote with the least delay a general secession of the Thracian cities from Athens. His main objective was Amphipolis, but prudence demanded that he should first ensure the neutrality or friendship of those cities which might otherwise cut off his line of retreat. Hence he first appeared at Acanthus (early autumn, 424) and persuaded its citizens to allow him to address their assembly. The impression made by him was so favourable that a majority of the Acanthians, though not hostile to Athens, voted for secession. The example of Acanthus was soon followed by Stagirus and Argilus. The last-named city, however, had a special reason for joining Sparta. Its prosperity had been seriously impaired by the foundation and rapid growth of Amphipolis, so that Brasidas' plans for capturing this important Athenian base sounded pleasant in the ears of the Argilians.

The unpreparedness of Amphipolis is inexplicable, when it is remembered that Brasidas had been in Thrace for several months and the news of what had happened at Acanthus cannot have remained unknown to the Athenian commander in Amphipolis. One dawn the Spartan general reached the bridge over the Strymon and found it defended only by a small posse of men. Having overpowered the guard and seized the bridge-head, he began to parley with the townspeople. Eucles, the Athenian officer in charge, sent a hasty message to the nearest Athenian naval squadron. It was at Thasos and in charge of the historian Thucydides. But, although he sailed at once with seven triremes to the Strymon, he found that the Amphipolitans had already succumbed to the blandishments of Brasidas and had opened their gates to him. Eion remained in Athenian hands, but Thucydides on his return home was prosecuted for negligence, found guilty and banished.[1] He remained in exile till the end of the war. To this enforced abstention from the duties of civic life we owe the composition of his historical masterpiece.

Brasidas' spectacular success caused political unrest in many of the Thracian communities. When he next turned his attention to the rocky peninsula of Acte, most of the smaller settlements, whose population was part Greek, part Thracian, made their submission to him. Only Sane, close to the canal dug in 481 by Xerxes' engineers, and Dium shut their gates against him. To reduce them by siege operations would have taken time and more resources than he had available. He therefore passed to the central peninsula of Chalcidice and with the help of an anti-Athenian faction in the town made himself master of Torone and its citadel in a few days. The small Athenian garrison was either captured or killed. Anti-Athenian sentiment grew apace and in the spring of 423 first Scione, and a little later Mende, openly seceded from Athens and allied themselves to Brasidas.

But these rebellions were almost as unwelcome to Sparta as to Athens. During the winter a strong desire for peace had made itself felt in both states, in Sparta primarily for the sake of the Sphacterian prisoners still held captive by the enemy, in Athens because the reverses in Boeotia and Chalcidice had temporarily numbed the people's will to energetic action. The authority of Cleon was for the moment in eclipse and his political opponents led by Nicias could command a majority of the votes in the assembly. A truce for one year on the basis of the *status quo* was drawn up and

[1] It is assumed in the text that Thucydides was banished after a formal trial. But his own reference to the event (V, 26) is vaguely worded. It is therefore possible that, like Conon after Aegospotami, he feared the death penalty, if he returned home, and went into voluntary exile immediately after his failure to save Amphipolis. Eucles' fate is unknown.

signed, it being understood that this was only a preliminary to a more permanent settlement. When official news of the truce reached Chalcidice, Scione had just gone over to Brasidas; the revolt of Mende actually occurred subsequently. Neither of the cities was therefore technically included in the recent agreement; at the same time Brasidas refused to be bound by it. Thus, although hostilities in Greece were suspended, the war in Thrace went on. The defection of two city-states in close proximity to Potidaea aroused Athenian resentment. A decree instigated by Cleon was passed by the *ecclesia* resolving the destruction of Scione and the execution of its male population. This harsh decision applied to Mende also when the news of its rebellion reached Athens. Nicias and Nicostratus were despatched at the head of an expedition made up of forty Athenian and ten Chian galleys, one thousand heavy infantry, six hundred archers, one thousand Thracian mercenaries, and some light infantry provided by the remaining allied communities in Thrace. They regained Mende almost at once, but the siege of Scione proved to be a lengthy operation.

Meanwhile Brasidas, since a portion of his soldiers' maintenance had been defrayed from the beginning by the Macedonian king, had been obliged to give some military aid to Perdiccas against the prince of Lyncestis and his Illyrian allies. The expedition was a failure and nearly brought Brasidas' troops to disaster. Then Perdiccas and he quarrelled. The king, convinced that nothing but disadvantages and expense had resulted from his entanglement with Sparta, returned to his former ally, Athens. The fragments of the peace treaty concluded between them are so imperfect that the terms cannot be stated with any certainty. The Athenians, however, certainly stipulated that the king should export timber to no one but them.[1] This preferential treatment was especially valuable at this juncture because the loss of Amphipolis had cut them off from the forest lands beyond Lake Cercinitis. Perdiccas, moreover, influenced the Thessalians to bar the progress through their country of Peloponnesian troops that were being sent to Brasidas. It was also no doubt a result of the improved relations between

---

[1] Cf. *I.G.*, I², 71. For a restoration of the central portion with a full commentary see J. J. Hondius, *Novae Inscriptiones Atticae*, III.

Perdiccas and Athens that a number of Bottiaean communities, which had seceded from their alliance with Athens at his instigation in 432, now concluded a new treaty of amity with the Athenians.[1]

When the year's truce came to an end in the spring of 422, the Athenians voted a second expeditionary force of thirty triremes, one thousand two hundred hoplites, and three hundred cavalry. Allied troops increased the military force to more than double this number. The command was entrusted to Cleon. He first sailed to Scione, which was still being blockaded. He withdrew some of the hoplites from the besieging army and hurried on to Torone. Assured by deserters that Brasidas was not in the immediate vicinity, he attacked the city by land and sea and captured it. A Spartan officer and small garrison in the town were also taken. Cleon deserves all credit for quick decision and rapid action; without them he would not have started his campaign with a very notable feat. For at the time when Torone was taken, Brasidas, who was hastening to its relief, had advanced to within five miles of the town. The Spartan then retired to Amphipolis, not doubting that this would be the next objective of the Athenians. Cleon, however, having made Eion his base of operations, attempted unsuccessfully to recover Stagirus; but he took Galepsus by assault. From Perdiccas he requested military support and also engaged some Thracian mercenaries.

In the interval Brasidas with a part of his army had taken up a position on a hill situated on the right bank of the Strymon between Amphipolis and Argilus. The rest of the available troops remained in Amphipolis; they were commanded by Brasidas' lieutenant, Clearidas. The Athenian commander was prepared to wait until the reinforcements from Macedonia and Thrace had arrived. But he reckoned without his men, whose discipline was of the worst. Fear of Brasidas' military reputation and distrust of their own general's capacity made them mutinous and Cleon's hands were forced. He ordered a cautious advance towards Amphipolis, whereupon Brasidas observing his advance withdrew with his detachment into the city. He determined to attack at once with his whole available force. Cleon,

[1] Tod 68.

however, was misled by his opponent's manœuvre. He should have followed one of two courses : to retire at once to Eion or to draw up his men in battle order. Instead he delayed on the rising ground above Amphipolis and did not give the sign to retreat until it was too late. Hardly had his troops begun to move when two separate bodies of the enemy, one led by Brasidas the other by Clearidas, advanced rapidly from different gates of the city and simultaneously attacked the Athenian centre and right wing. The Athenians were taken unprepared ; their left wing, which was furthest away from the city, took to flight when the centre was attacked. The centre and right wing stood their ground for a short while before they too were routed. Cleon, flying with his men, was killed. It was a complete victory for Brasidas, but he himself received a mortal wound and expired shortly after he had been carried back to Amphipolis. Scione did not capitulate until the following year after peace between Athens and Sparta had already been concluded. The original decision of the Athenian *demos* was ruthlessly carried out, for the men were executed, the women and children sold into slavery. The city's territory was then assigned by the Athenians to the surviving population of Plataea and their descendants.

§ 10. THE PEACE OF NICIAS

The desire for peace which had been general enough in Sparta and Athens to bring about a truce in 423, only to be stifled again temporarily by the course of events in Thrace, made itself felt with greater intensity in the winter of 422–421. The Spartan government, in addition to the anxieties and disappointments of the war, was becoming acutely conscious of problems nearer home. The Helots were restive and not infrequently deserted. If this movement should gain strength and they could enlist outside support, Sparta would be faced with a situation of grave peril. Moreover, the thirty years' peace concluded with Argos in 451 was almost at an end. The Argives coveted territory, now Spartan, which they had formerly possessed ; if they abandoned their neutrality and joined the enemies of Sparta, especially if, as was not unlikely, they were able at the same time to detach neighbours like Corinth and Sicyon from the Peloponnesian

League, the military hegemony of Sparta was doomed. The refusal of Brasidas to be bound by the truce may have been an embarrassment to the home government, which, save in the case of one or two kings, had never encountered such independence, indeed we may call it insubordination, in a citizen. Still, though his critics might describe Brasidas as an obstacle to peace, it cannot be gainsaid that his Thracian campaign was the severest blow inflicted on Athens in ten years of war.

Cleon's death was probably a misfortune for Athens; for, whatever his faults, he had shown singleness of purpose in his conduct of affairs. In spite of his traducers, we may believe that he was animated by genuine patriotism, not by mere personal ambition. Had he lived longer, the Athenians might never have become the dupes of an unscrupulous adventurer like Alcibiades. Cleon's death, however, left Nicias the most influential man in Athens, and he was ready enough to take up the negotiations with Sparta begun two years before. At Sparta the king Pleistoanax, who in 446 had fallen into disgrace for what were regarded as culpable conversations with Pericles, and had lived two decades in exile before he was recalled and reinstated as king, was not less eager to bring about a satisfactory settlement in order to rehabilitate himself in the eyes of his countrymen. The negotiations therefore proceeded apace, and in the spring of 421 a peace of fifty years was concluded. By its terms Sparta and her allies were to surrender Amphipolis and Panactum, a fortress on the Boeotian-Attic border seized by a Boeotian contingent in 422. The cities in Chalcidice that had fallen away from Athens were all to be independent—political autonomy was guaranteed to a few that had been Athenian dependencies—but they were at liberty to rejoin Athens as free allies if they wished. The Athenians for their part agreed to evacuate the three bases in the Peloponnese —Pylos, Cythera, Methone—and several minor posts elsewhere. They demanded, however, to retain Nisaea, as well as Sollium and Anactorium in north-western Greece. There was to be an exchange of prisoners. Further clauses in the treaty dealt with the independence of Delphi and the inviolability of its sanctuary, besides other religious matters; permitted the free departure of any citizens who wished to do so from cities handed over to Athens; and provided for subsequent alterations and additions in the treaty by mutual consent, the annual renewal of the oaths taken by the contracting parties, and the publication of the treaty in five sanctuaries.

From the Athenian standpoint the so-called Peace of Nicias, even had it not proved abortive, would have been as unsatisfactory as the settlement of 445. For the retention of Nisaea and two naval bases on the Ionian sea was a poor return for the losses in men and wealth caused by a decade of fighting, to say nothing of the permanent damage suffered by Athenian interests in the " Thraceward regions." On the other hand, Sparta had far less cause for satisfaction in 421 than twenty-five years before. At that time the terms that she imposed on her opponents were approved by her allies and her military hegemony in Greece was unimpaired. But in 421 Pleistoanax and the board of ephors proved curiously optimistic or obtuse. They misjudged the temper of their allies; for, while they expected Corinth and other states to accept certain sacrifices, they did not propose that Sparta should forego anything. Thus their conduct of the peace negotiations produced the very political upheaval in the Peloponnese that they had hoped to avert by ending the war.

## CHAPTER V

## THE PELOPONNESIAN WAR: SECOND AND THIRD STAGES, 420 TO 405 B.C.

### § 1. THE DISCONTENT OF SPARTA'S ALLIES AND RENEWED WARFARE

FOR four years after the Peace of Nicias the politicians in the more influential states of Greece experimented with diplomatic moves and countermoves. In the end the political and military power of Sparta was stronger than it had been for two generations, while the position of Athens in European Greece was once again isolated. When these two states signed the peace in 421, no less than five of Sparta's allies had grievances sufficiently serious to prevent them from accepting the settlement. Corinth, the prime mover on the Peloponnesian side in precipitating the war ten years before, resented the retention by Athens of two Corinthian colonies in Ambracia. The Megarians clamoured for the return of Nisaea, while the cities of Boeotia, headed by Thebes, were in no mood to hand over the fortress on the Attic frontier that they had but recently acquired. In the north-western Peloponnese, Elis, whose growth since the political unification half a century before seems to have been remarkable, was vexed with Sparta over a matter unconnected with the war, the Spartan support given to Lepreum when this city quarrelled with Elis. Finally, Mantinea, hitherto the most constantly loyal to the Spartans amongst the Arcadian cities, feared their resentment because she had during the war enlarged her frontiers at the expense of weaker neighbours. There remained the unknown quantity, Argos, whose peace treaty with Sparta was about to end.

In face of such widespread discontent the Spartan government was incapable of carrying the provisions of the peace agreement into effect. The Boeotarchs declined to hand over

Panactum to Athens; the Amphipolitans, even after the
Spartan garrison had withdrawn, determined not to revert
under Athenian control. The Athenians for their part
declined to proceed with the evacuation of the bases that they
held in the Peloponnese. To secure at least the return of the
Sphacterian prisoners the Spartan government thereupon
proposed a defensive alliance to the Athenians, who accepted
the proposal and gave up the captives whilst retaining the
Peloponnesian bases. Reaction in the Peloponnese to what
seemed a cynical disavowal by Sparta of her allies was not
slow in following. The lead in the opposition was taken by
the Corinthians, who began diplomatic conversations with
the Argives. By tradition Argos had been for centuries
unfriendly or hostile to Sparta, but her weakness during the
fifth century had compelled her to combine peaceful relations
with her neighbour with neutrality in the face of inter-state
rivalries. By their long abstention from warfare the Argives
by 421–420 had regained much of their old vigour; yet their
democratic constitution lacked the stability of the Athenian,
and the spectre of *stasis*, laid to rest while they had only
their domestic problems to handle, began to walk abroad as
soon as they again participated in the wider political life of
Hellas.

Corinth was only partially successful in trying to bring
about concerted action against Sparta. Her decision to ally
herself to Argos was followed by similar agreements between
Argos and Elis, Mantinea, and the Chalcidians. The Megarians
and Boeotians, however, were too cautious to join the
coalition at once, the latter especially being unwilling to
reach a decision until they felt more certain about the outcome of the Spartan-Athenian *entente*. Their hesitation was
justified. When a new board of ephors entered on office in
the autumn of 421 it soon became apparent that Sparta's
foreign policy would undergo an early change.

Meantime, though the conclusion of peace filled the Attic
population with a sense of deep relief, to which Aristophanes
gave expression in his play, the *Peace*, political circles were
acutely divided on the question of Athens' future foreign
relations, for the pacific and pro-Spartan policy of Nicias
soon found a challenger in the person of Alcibiades. First
cousin once removed and ward of Pericles—his father, Clinias,

had fallen in 447 on the field of Coronea—he entered public life at about the same age as Cimon. Like that statesman, he was a member of an old Athenian family and had seen considerable military service before he began his political career, for Alcibiades had fought first at Potidaea and more recently at Delium. Both men enjoyed great personal popularity; but, whereas in Cimon an iron sense of duty and profound love of his country were the guiding influences of his public life, in Alcibiades self-interest was throughout his career the overmastering passion. His youthful extravagances and an arrogant disregard of every convention were condoned as high spirits by a public fascinated with his personal beauty and, when he chose to exert it, his great charm of manner. Extremely gifted by nature, he must in adolescence have acquired not a little insight into public affairs through his close connection with Athens' master statesman, Pericles. His intellectual intercourse and friendship in early manhood with the middle-aged Socrates sharpened his wits; it could not mend his morals. When the first phase of the Peloponnesian War drew to a close, Alcibiades was just beginning to make his mark in the political arena.[1] He had desired that the Spartan government should appoint him their *proxenos* in Athens, as his grandfather had been before him; but his efforts to gain the distinction had failed. It was characteristic of the man that personal pique should at once become the motive force of his political conduct. By 420 the would-be representative of Spartan interests in Athens was amongst the most prominent opponents of Nicias and Nicias' pro-Spartan programme. The young aristocrat gave his adherence to the war party whose spokesman at the moment was Hyperbolus. Like Cleon, this man was of obscure, even humble origin; unlike Cleon, he appears to have been of mean ability and few convictions.

The general discontent at Athens after a few months with the policy of the peace party was mirrored in the elections for the *strategia* for 420–419, held in the spring of 420, for while Nicias failed to be re-elected, Alcibiades was amongst those chosen for office. In the interval the policy of the

---

[1] If one could be sure that the allusion to young politicians who bait their elders in Aristophanes (*Acharnians*, 680 ff.) is a reference to Alcibiades, it would show that he was already active politically in 426 or 425.

Spartan government had undergone a steady change, and early in 420 it adjusted its differences with the Boeotians. Contrary to their undertaking of the previous year, the Spartans entered into an alliance with the northern neighbours of Athens. The indignation of the Athenians was increased when the Boeotians, though indeed they now evacuated Panactum, razed the fortress to the ground instead of handing it over intact. The immediate reply of Athens was a refusal to cede Pylos. The Spartans, anxious to recover their base and alarmed lest the Athenians repudiate their alliance with them entirely, sent representatives to reassure the Athenians and arrive at a satisfactory understanding. It was chiefly owing to Alcibiades that this manœuvre failed. Very soon afterwards occurred the very development that the Spartan government had hoped to prevent. The Athenians concluded what was technically a hundred years' defensive alliance with Argos; in fact this step could only be regarded as a break with Sparta. The adherence of Athens to a coalition, some members of which, like Elis and Mantinea, were already at war with Sparta, was bound sooner or later to commit her to offensive operations. It has also been remarked that the anti-Spartan movement in Greece would have gained greatly in effectiveness if Corinth had followed up her original negotiations with Argos by joining the new coalition; but she now held aloof.[1]

In truth the quadruple alliance belongs to those diplomatic achievements, not rare in ancient or modern history, that in theory and on paper are in the highest degree impressive, but because they take insufficient account of actually existent conditions, mean little or nothing in practice. An effective coalition between the naval power of Athens and a considerable part of the military strength of the Peloponnese would have rendered Sparta harmless and would have been a match for even a Lacedaemonian-Boeotian combination. But Greek governments were notoriously unstable, and an alliance of this sort could only have proved workable, if the respective governments had followed a consistent policy over a period of years and could at the same time have collaborated to a degree unknown in Greek history down to that time. Various

[1] The text of the quadruple alliance given by Thucydides (V, 47) is confirmed by the actual treaty-stone found at Athens (Tod 72). There are only slight verbal differences between the two versions.

weaknesses in the agreement very soon became apparent. At Athens, although there was no immediate desire to break openly with Sparta, the political parties were divided on the question how to interpret their new obligations. While Nicias and his supporters believed in construing the treaty strictly as a defensive measure, the war party, with Alcibiades as their most effective spokesman, favoured the enlargement of the anti-Spartan *bloc* in the Peloponnese. Their programme carried the day. The Athenians prepared to support the Argives in the war that they now began against Epidaurus. The mobilization of a Lacedaemonian army to help this loyal member of the Peloponnesian League proved an effective check, so that the war between Argos and Epidaurus remained a quarrel between neighbours. Then during the winter of 419–418 the Spartan government sent a garrison to the help of its ally.

In Athens the imminence of war produced a reaction. In the spring Alcibiades, who had been re-elected *strategus* in the previous year, was not chosen for a third term of office. But the change in public opinion at Athens came too late to avert war. Nevertheless, the Spartan government, counting on the influence of Nicias to maintain strictly the terms of the Argive-Athenian alliance, delayed military action until the summer, when the new board of *strategi* had entered on office. Then King Agis invaded the Argolid with an army that can hardly have been less than twenty thousand strong. Boeotia, Corinth, Sicyon, Phlius, and Pellene had all sent contingents to co-operate with the Lacedaemonian brigades. The Argive army was augmented by detachments from Mantinea and Elis. They took up their position close to the frontier and astride the road from Argos to Phlius. The Spartan king divided his men into three sections, each entering the enemy's territory by a different route. The advance was carried out under cover of night, so that on the morrow the Argives and their allies found themselves in danger of being completely surrounded and cut off from their base, with Agis and the pick of the Lacedaemonian troops between them and Argos, and the other two corps approaching from the north and north-east. At this point one of the Argive commanders and another Argive who was Lacedaemonian *proxenus* sought an interview with Agis. The Spartan king,

influenced partly by the fact that one of his corps was late,
so that an immediate battle might prove dangerous, especially
if reinforcements from Argos attacked from the rear, partly
by the knowledge that the two Argives were prominent in
the oligarchic faction of their state, which desired to restore
peaceful relations between Sparta and Argos, agreed to a
four months' armistice preparatory to a permanent settlement. Agis withdrew and disbanded his army, his conduct
exposing him to severe criticism from the Spartan government. The rank and file of the Argives on their side were
full of indignation, as rightly or wrongly they believed that
their chances of settling with Agis by force of arms had been
good and they had been betrayed by two of their own leaders.
Thus, when an Athenian force at length arrived, accompanied
by Alcibiades not as commander but as a plenipotentiary,
the astute Athenian was able to overcome the annoyance of
the Argives at the tardy appearance of their allies and prevail
on them to break the truce.

Hostilities began afresh with the capture of Orchomenus,
a loyal member of the Peloponnesian League. It was a grave
error of judgment to offer such direct provocation to Sparta.
Besides this, however, the weakness of a coalition in which
each member tended to put his own before the common
interest was made clear by the defection of the Eleian regiments, when they were unable to persuade their allies to
join with them in an attack on Lepreum. The capture of
Orchomenus roused the ephors to order an immediate
mobilization. Agis was retained in the chief command, but
was saddled with an advisory council of ten elected by the
Spartan citizen body. At Tegea the Lacedaemonian brigades
were joined by regiments from that city and from several
others. An engagement took place before troops from the
more distant allies, like Corinth and Boeotia, could arrive.
The Argives and their allies, using Mantinea as their base,
had taken up their position on a hill (Alesion) immediately
to the east of the city. Their numerical strength may have
been approximately 11,000 men; the Lacedaemonians and
their allies probably numbered nearly 12,000.[1] Agis
advanced from Tegea and began by an attack on the heights

---

[1] See the calculations of W. J. Woodhouse, *King Agis of Sparta and his
Campaign in Arkadia in* 418 B.C. (Oxford, 1933), excursus B.

where the enemy was stationed. This move was, however, a feint and was followed by the retirement of his whole army, when the Argives made no move to descend to level ground against him. The king calculated that his sudden withdrawal would puzzle his opponents and lead them to believe that the Lacedaemonians were afraid to risk an engagement. His surmise proved correct, for the Argives and their allies after Agis' departure descended into the plain south of Mantinea. Next day Agis, whose army had bivouacked in Tegean territory, returned to the attack. In the ensuing battle the Mantinean regiments were opposed to the Lacedaemonian left wing, the Athenians to the enemy's right wing. The centre was formed of a picked corps of 1000 Argives and the less highly trained citizen militia of Argos. Opposed to them was the Lacedaemonian centre, made up of the best regiments and the king's body-guard of 300. By leaving a gap in his line Agis tempted the 1000 Argives to advance too far and join with the Mantinean troops in encircling the left wing of their opponents which was composed mainly of Helots serving as hoplites. Thereby the attack of the most formidable Argive troops was diverted to a subsidiary operation. The Lacedaemonians and allies forming the centre and right wing routed their opponents. Then Agis, instead of following them up, wheeled about and came to the rescue of his hard-pressed left wing, whose losses had been very heavy. In face of this onslaught the Mantineans and the Argives with them were hopelessly outnumbered and their short-lived success was followed by precipitate flight. Agis' victory would have been even more complete had not two of his regimental commanders disregarded orders and failed to carry out a flank attack on the Argives and Mantineans before Agis came to the rescue with his centre and right wing. Even so the battle completely rehabilitated the military reputation of Sparta as well as the personal prestige of Agis.[1] Moreover the political consequences of the Spartan victory were far-reaching, for before the end of the year Elis and Mantinea hastened to make their peace with Sparta and rejoined the Peloponnesian League. Argos came to terms with Sparta also and repudiated her alliance with Athens.

[1] The account of the battle of Mantinea in the text follows the reconstruction given with great wealth of detail by W. J. Woodhouse, *op. cit.*, 66 ff.

A few months later a revolution, backed by Spartan military force, established an oligarchy in power at Argos. But in the summer of 417 a counter-revolution, attended by much bloodshed, restored the democratic government. The Athenian-Argive alliance was renewed for fifty years, while the efforts of Sparta to restore the oligarchs to power in Argos, though unsuccessful, resulted in fitful hostilities between the two states for several more years.

### § 2. ATHENIAN AFFAIRS AT HOME AND IN THE EMPIRE

The defeat of Mantinea and the political consequences that flowed from it led to bitter recriminations at Athens. Alcibiades and his supporters complained that Nicias and the peace party were responsible for the half-hearted assistance given to Argos at a critical time. To this their opponents retorted with a general condemnation of the war party's aims. At the same time Hyperbolus, whose mediocre abilities had been thrown into the shade by the more brilliant talents of Alcibiades, urged the assembly to have recourse to ostracism in order to test popular sentiment. His motion was carried; but, when at the appointed time a vote was taken, it was found that not Alcibiades but Hyperbolus himself had been condemned to ten years' exile. Although the ancient accounts of this episode do not entirely agree, it is clear that Alcibiades had been clever enough to come to a private understanding with Nicias; both then prevailed upon their supporters to vote for the banishment of Hyperbolus. Ostracism as a method of easing a tense political situation was thus reduced to an absurdity, and the Athenians, realizing this themselves, after this occasion allowed the institution to fall into disuse.

For some years affairs in the Peloponnese had absorbed most of the attention of Athenian politicians, so that the restoration of Athenian authority in Thrace was neglected. If the Athenians at first hoped that Amphipolis would be restored to them without trouble the inhabitants thought differently. Four years after the peace Nicias at last led an expedition to Chalcidice; but his plans were upset by the defection of Perdiccas on whose co-operation the Athenians had relied. Using Methone as a base they so effectually blockaded the Macedonian coast that in the following year the king came to terms. He then gave some help when the Athenians attacked Amphipolis. But it proved impossible to take the place by assault, whereupon a blockade was instituted. The Amphipolitans must have made timely preparations to meet such a contingency, for they held out for two years and were still undefeated when the Athenian government, influenced by bad news from the Sicilian expedition, recalled the forces operating in Thrace.

If the Athenians failed to recover what was a key position, strategically and economically, in the empire, they added to their maritime possessions by the conquest of Melos. The Melians had consistently declined to ally themselves to Athens. Yet the geographical position of the island and its admirable harbour—one of the best in the eastern Mediterranean—had long since aroused the cupidity of the Athenians. We have seen how an expeditionary force raided Melos in 426,[1] but the inhabitants refused to be intimidated. In 425–424 the Athenians actually included the Melians in the tribute list, but the latter sturdily refused to pay.[2] At length in 416 another expedition was sent off to coerce them. Thirty-eight triremes and more than three thousand troops were brought into play. The Melians despatched representatives to Athens to protest against this unjustifiable threat to their liberty, but accomplished nothing. Refusing to submit voluntarily they were closely blockaded. When starvation compelled them to surrender, the Athenian assembly, on the motion of Alcibiades, voted the execution of all the adult males and the enslavement of the women and children. The fate of the Melians resembled that of Scione or Mende. Yet in the case of the Chalcidic towns Athenian brutality was to some extent condoned by contemporary opinion because a faithless ally merited condign punishment. For Athens' treatment of the Melians there was no such excuse. It was a cynical avowal that no weaker power had the right to live, if its existence stood in the way of Athenian ambition. Five hundred colonists were subsequently despatched to the island from Athens. The conviction that this episode was the most illuminating, as it was the worst, example of the excesses to

---

[1] See above, p. 99.
[2] They were assessed for fifteen talents (Tod 66, p. 152).

which unrestrained imperialism could give rise, led Thucydides to present in the form of dramatic dialogue the arguments for and against the doctrine that right is might. Nor is it accidental that the artist has juxtaposed the fate of Melos with the unprecedented disaster that within three years befell the Athenians.

The public expenditure of Athens continued to be heavy and so far more than 4000 talents had been borrowed from the sacred funds. Nevertheless, it is probable that in 421–420 the assessment of tribute was substantially lowered, so that the total was perhaps two-thirds of the total in 425–424.[1] Whether the rate was raised again in 416–415 is uncertain. In spite of these ample revenues from the empire, the Athenian government continued to borrow considerable sums from the Treasury of Athena every year from 418 to 414.[2]

A notable feature of the period is the increased attention paid to religion. Yet the forms in which it was manifested suggest, on the one hand, a carefully calculated effort to impress the world with the glory of Athens, and, on the other, a desire to divert the people's minds from criticism of their leaders by providing scapegoats to popular discontent or war hysteria. Temple-building which had been suspended in 431 was revived on the Acropolis soon after the Peace of Nicias, if, as seems probable, some progress was made with the building of the Erechtheum at this time, as well as with the small temple of Athena Nike. In 416 elaborate regulations were issued to ensure ample means for the sanctuary at Eleusis. While it was made obligatory on all Attic farmers and also on the cities of the empire annually to render as first-fruits to the Eleusinian deities one six-hundredth of their barley and half that amount of their wheat, other Greek states were also invited to contribute.[3] It was probably in the same year that the sophist Protagoras published his treatise, *On the Gods*. His philosophical position was that of an agnostic, for he argued that it was impossible by any

---

[1] The totals for the years 421–420 and 416–415 are lost. Cf. *A.T.L.* II, 34 and 39 and references there given; also Tod 71 and pp. 264–266.

[2] Tod 75. The largest amount borrowed was over 353 talents in 415–414; a part of this was used in connection with the Sicilian expedition.

[3] Tod 74. For the date of this inscription see W. B. Dinsmoor, *The Archons of Athens* (Harvard University Press, 1931), p. 338 ff.

process of reasoning to demonstrate the existence or non-existence of supernatural beings. He was, however, prosecuted and condemned for atheism and official steps were taken to destroy his book. Protagoras left Athens for Sicily, but was shipwrecked and drowned on the way to the island. In the next year the poet and philosopher Diagoras was the victim of a similar attack. He was charged with various offences against religion and forced to fly the country. It may well have been that, as he was a native of Melos, he became, no doubt undeservedly, an object of popular suspicion when the Athenians reduced that island.[1] The excitement caused by these trials was, however, as nothing compared to that which, as will be seen in the next section, swept over Athens in the summer of 415.

### § 3. THE ATHENIAN EXPEDITIONS TO SICILY

We have seen how before the war the Athenians under Pericles' guidance had entered into treaty relations with more than one city-state amongst the western Greeks. In those years, too, the Syracusans, after a period of civil unrest, at last composed their differences. With greater stability at home, moreover, there soon awoke a desire to re-establish the political supremacy of their city in the island. The old rivalry between communities of Dorian and of Ionian origin again became acute. The Dorian cities, solidly aligned behind Syracuse, certainly formed the stronger group and had, besides, the support of Locri across the straits. Rhegium, an Ionian foundation and the consistent rival of Locri, was in the opposite camp. By 427 the situation had become so grave for Leontini and her allies that an embassy, headed by the Sophist, Gorgias, was despatched to Athens to ask for help. The Athenians sent twenty triremes under the joint command of Laches and Charoiades. Their only substantial success was the capture of Messana, though the presence of the Athenian vessels also served to hold the Syracusans in check, as Syracuse's naval strength had been allowed to decline. An attack on Inessa failed disastrously. Raids on the territory of Locri could not be said to redress the balance in favour of Athens' western allies. When Charoiades had been killed in action, Laches remained for a

[1] So E. Derenne, *Les procès d'impiété*, p. 63.

while in sole charge. But in the winter of 426-425 he was
superseded by Pythodorus and on his return to Athens
was prosecuted for misappropriation of public funds. He was
apparently acquitted. Meanwhile the Syracusans had been
repairing their navy. In reply to an urgent request from
their allies for additional help to meet this new danger, the
Athenians despatched a second naval squadron under
Sophocles and Eurymedon. But owing to delay at Pylos
and Corcyra these reinforcements did not reach Sicily until
the end of the summer (425). In the interval Messana had
gone over to the enemies of Athens. Fighting in the island
went on spasmodically for another year, but it is not known
what Sophocles and Eurymedon accomplished during the
first few months after their arrival. When in 424 they
attempted to unite the Ionian cities into an effective anti-
Syracusan coalition, it was already too late ; for a pan-Sicilian
congress met at Gela at which representatives of the city-
states in Sicily sought at length to adjust their quarrels by
peaceful discussion. The most influential speaker at the
meeting was the Syracusan representative, Hermocrates.
The keynote of his policy was to debar all outside states from
intervening in Sicilian affairs. His arguments were sufficiently
convincing to lead to a settlement, for the time being, of
outstanding differences between the Sicilian cities. Thereupon the late allies of Athens intimated to Sophocles and
Eurymedon that their aid was no longer needed. So the
Athenian forces returned home ; but the Athenian assembly
was so incensed with the generals' conduct that it exiled
Sophocles and Pythodorus and punished Eurymedon by a fine.

Within two years peace in Sicily was again broken. Civil
war in Leontini was followed by the expulsion of the democrats. The oligarchs, who owed their success to Syracusan
intervention, for a time joined the Syracusan polity ; then
they occupied a part of the territory of Leontini, holding it
as a Syracusan dependency. In the light of these events the
Athenians thought it worth while to send Phaeax and two
colleagues to Sicily, to examine on the spot the chances of
promoting an anti-Syracusan coalition. Phaeax's reception
in Camarina and Acragas was favourable ; in southern Italy
he established more friendly relations with Locri. While the
attitude of these cities—two of them were Dorian—suggests

that they were becoming suspicious of the Syracusans, whose intervention in Leontini did not harmonize well with their pacific professions at the congress of Gela, the mission of Phaeax and his colleagues effected nothing further.

Six years elapsed before the Athenians again turned their attention westwards; when they did so it was in a different mood to formerly. No longer did they propose to send a small expeditionary force, when envoys from their old ally, Segesta, then involved in a war with Dorian Selinus, and from the exiled democrats of Leontini appealed for help in the winter, 416–415. Earlier expeditions to Sicily had after all been no more than subsidiary operations during the war. But in 416–415 dreams of a prostrate Syracuse and an Athenian empire in the west excited the popular imagination. The cautious counsels voiced by Nicias in the assembly for the most part fell on deaf ears. The Segestans undertook to pay for the cost of an Athenian expedition and the *ecclesia* in the first instance sent representatives to Sicily to investigate the situation. When they returned to Athens in the spring they reported with enthusiasm on the wealth of their Sicilian ally. No stronger incentive was needed to decide a people already favourably disposed to embark on the western venture. Foremost in urging the despatch of a large armament was Alcibiades. Ironically enough, when Nicias, in the desperate hope of deterring his countrymen altogether from the undertaking, argued that only an exceptionally large fleet and army could possibly succeed, he produced exactly the opposite effect to that which he had intended. The assembly demanded to hear what forces he considered necessary and hearing his reply promptly voted them. The preparations for the expedition were then set in train and carried through with such speed and enthusiasm that all was in readiness by the last days of June. The command was entrusted to Alcibiades, Lamachus, and Nicias.[1]

Shortly before the fleet was due to sail a serious act of sacrilegious vandalism caused general excitement and depression in Athens. One morning it was discovered that during the previous night impious hands had hacked and mutilated nearly all the busts of Hermes which stood in many of the shrines and in the vestibules of private houses through the

---

[1] This is the order of the names in *I.G.*, I², 302 (Tod, p. 187, line 51).

city. The wildest rumours gained immediate currency. Some believed that the oligarchic faction in Athens was responsible for the act, preliminary to attempting a revolution, others that traitors in the city were in league with the enemies of Athens, notably Corinth, in the hope that the Athenians under the influence of a most ill-omened occurrence would abandon their projected attack on Syracuse. For weeks there was ample scope for informers to ply their dirty trade and numerous prosecutions took place. But the most serious element in the situation was the attempt made by the enemies of Alcibiades to exploit popular excitement for their own ends. Information was laid concerning other acts of sacrilege reported to have occurred in the past, notably a mock celebration of the Eleusinian Mysteries staged in a private house with Alcibiades in a leading role. Alcibiades, who could rely on the loyalty of the soldiers and sailors, demanded an immediate investigation ; but his enemies were successful in postponing the inquiry, with the result that, since the departure of the Sicilian expedition could not be delayed, one of its commanders was compelled to set out for the west with a serious prosecution hanging over him. In the end the responsibility for the mutilation of the Hermae was supposedly brought home to the members of an oligarchic club (ἑταιρεία) presided over by a certain Euphiletus. One of its members was Andocides who, on promise of immunity, came forward with the necessary information. Nevertheless his action caused him to be boycotted to such an extent that he soon afterwards went into voluntary exile.

Some time before this sensation, however, the Athenian armament had left for Corcyra (end of June, 415). There a review was held and then the fleet sailed for southern Italy in three detachments. The total force of the Athenians, augmented by some of their allies, amounted to 134 triremes with 130 smaller vessels for supplies, 5100 hoplites, 1300 light-armed troops, and 30 cavalry, so that the total personnel cannot have been far short of 30,000 men. The inclusion of 250 Arcadian mercenaries amongst the fighting men was an innovation for Athens. The reception encountered by the Athenians amongst the south Italian city-states was almost uniformly unfriendly. Even at Rhegium the gates of the city were shut against them, although they were permitted to encamp outside.[1] Three vessels, which had been sent in advance of the main fleet to Segesta, at this point returned and reported unfavourably on their experiences. Only thirty talents were available, for the rest they made it clear that there was little hope of further pecuniary assistance and that the Athenian envoys in the previous winter had been grossly and wilfully misled. The three generals thereupon held a council of war which revealed at once that a more ill-assorted trio could hardly have been chosen by the Athenian assembly to conduct so great an undertaking. Alcibiades, grandiose as ever in his plans, was in favour of winning as many allies in Sicily as possible, before beginning active operations against Syracuse. The essential weakness of this plan, apart from the uncertainty of gaining many allies, was that it entailed considerable delay which would be of immense value to the Sicilian enemies of Athens. The cautious Nicias urged that they ought to confine themselves to their treaty obligations and proceed at once to help Segesta against Selinus. Lamachus, a good soldier but no politician, advocated an immediate attack on Syracuse, the real enemy and in all likelihood still unprepared. There is little doubt that his plan was the best of the three, but that of Alcibiades was forthwith adopted. The results achieved by Alcibiades' course of action were quite incommensurate with the time and effort expended. An attempt to gain possession of Messana failed; Naxos, however, joined the Athenians, and then, under duress, Catana, which was thereupon used by the expedition as its base. Next, an effort to gain control of Camarina met with no success. When Alcibiades returned to Catana he found an Athenian state-trireme (the *Salaminia*) waiting to take him back to Athens to stand his trial for sacrilege. He departed in his own ship in company with the *Salaminia*, but on the way to Greece gave his escort the slip and made his way to the Peloponnese.

With his departure the conduct of affairs passed into Nicias' hands. He tried to carry on Alcibiades' scheme after his own fashion by winning allies in the north of the island. He visited Segesta and tried, but without success, to bring

[1] Possibly their ally's lack of cordiality was inspired by jealousy of Locri, whose relations with Athens had been improved by Phaeax eight years before. See E. Ciaceri, *Storia della Magna Grecia*, II, 385.

Himera into the alliance. His only achievement was the capture of Hykkara, whose population was sold into slavery. The proceeds—about 120 talents—were some compensation for the poverty of Segesta.

During these months the Syracusans had not listened to the advice of their most experienced leader, Hermocrates, and, underrating the reality of the danger that threatened them, did little to prepare to meet it. The prolonged inactivity of Nicias at Catana finally encouraged them to march out against that city. But the Athenian commander, who had wished for precisely such a move, and had kept himself informed of the Syracusans' movements, set sail for Syracuse. The armada sailed into the Great Harbour and the troops were landed and then encamped on slightly rising ground to the south of the city, whence they had an uninterrupted view of Syracuse and the plateau of Epipolae behind. They also seized and destroyed the bridge across the Anapus. On the next day a general engagement was brought on by the Athenians in which the Syracusans were worsted. The action, however, taught Nicias one weakness in his force, the lack of an adequate body of cavalry of which the enemy had no lack. This was one of the reasons that he gave in a despatch to Athens announcing his withdrawal from Syracuse back to Catana for the winter months. He also cited the season of the year and the hope of enlarging the number of allies to the Athenian cause as grounds for postponing further operations against Syracuse until the spring. Nevertheless, Nicias' conduct is hard to explain, for, though unusual, winter campaigning was not unknown, and in Sicily was perfectly feasible. Moreover, although delay might conceivably strengthen the Athenians by the accession of cities in the island or in southern Italy, it also gave the enemy, who had now been aroused from their earlier lethargy, an opportunity of improving their situation. If he hoped that his countrymen would be satisfied with a demonstration, such as had just occurred, against Syracuse, he was soon to be disillusioned, for the *ecclesia* voted large additional funds and sent off 280 mounted troops, thirty of whom were mounted archers. During the winter 400 additional horsemen from several Sicilian towns joined Nicias, so that his weakness relative to the Syracusans in this arm of the service became less marked. For the rest, the months of waiting produced little result; a second attempt to win over Camarina was no more successful than the first had been.

The Syracusans after Nicias' withdrawal became more active. They constructed a wall to enclose the district called Temenites and at the same time connected it with the already fortified outer city (Achradina and Tyche) and inner city (Ortygia). In their engagement with the Athenians, moreover, the Syracusan troops had been far from steady. At the instance of Hermocrates steps were taken to improve the discipline of the soldiery. To secure more unity of action in the Higher Command the board of fifteen *strategi* was superseded by three generals, of whom Hermocrates was one. Above all, a ship bearing Syracusan envoys made its way safely to Corinth. The Corinthians sent legates of their own to accompany them to Sparta and urge the head of the Peloponnesian League to frustrate the Athenian plans. Their arrival in Laconia synchronized with that of Alcibiades, who, on reaching Greece, had probably visited Argos before making his way to Sparta. Besides apologizing for his own traitorous conduct, he gave the Spartan government some shrewd advice—to help Syracuse directly and to embarrass Athens at home, notably by fortifying Decelea. The ephors, being unready openly to transgress the treaty that was still in force between Sparta and Athens, for the moment did no more than nominate one of their ablest officers, Gylippus, to take command of the troops that Corinth was preparing to collect and send to the west, and, when he reached Syracuse, to assume supreme direction of the operations against the Athenian invaders.

Before the new campaigning season opened, the Syracusans had taken some further measures for defence. They protected the shore of the great harbour with a palisade and stationed a detachment of troops in the Olympieum which lay on rising ground at a little distance to the south-west of the city. But while they thus guarded against another attack from the sea they neglected the approach to Syracuse on the land side from the north until it was too late. At the west end of the triangular terrace Epipolae, which overlooked the city in the plain, was the high point of Euryalus. It was only by a track which came up from the coast over this summit that

MAP III

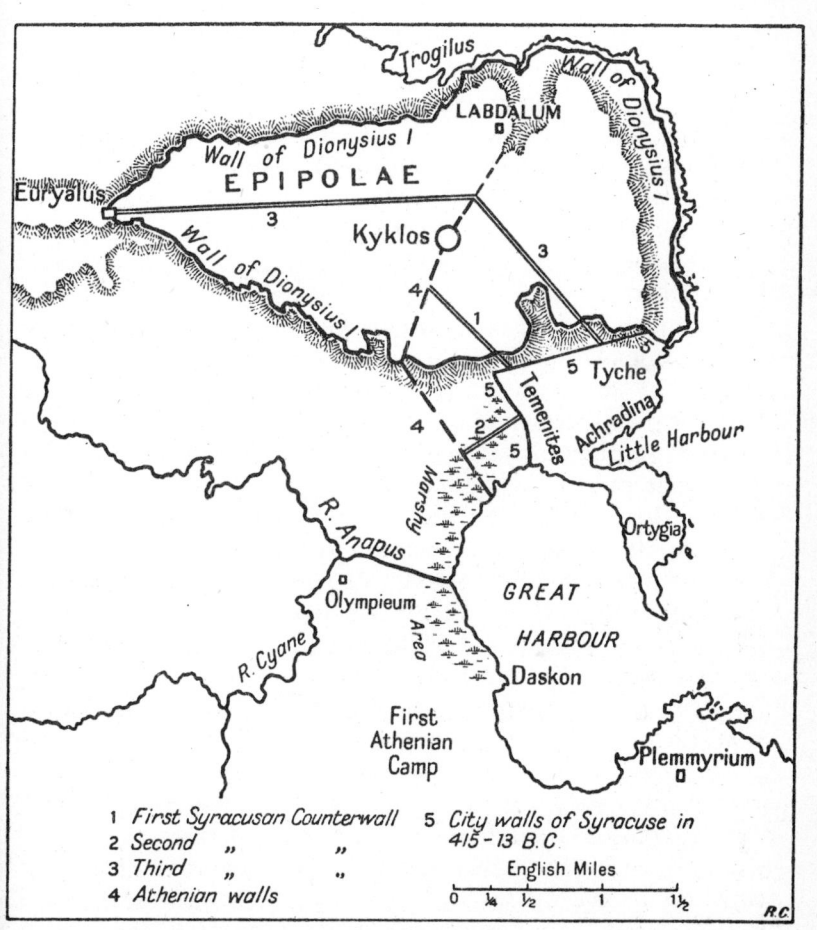

ANCIENT SYRACUSE
(The size of Syracuse in 415-413 B.C.)

Epipolae was accessible to an army approaching from the north. Nicias, we may suppose, had employed scouts to keep him informed of Syracusan activity. One night in May the fleet started out from Catana for Leon on the coast northwest of the Syracusan peninsula. Next morning the army was landed there and gained the top of Epipolae before the Syracusans were fully aware of their danger or could take steps to avert it. They were unable to dislodge the Athenians, but were driven back with loss into their city. Without delay the Athenian commanders proceeded, according to the usual method at this time, to construct a line of fortification which would completely shut off Syracuse on the land side; with the Athenian fleet in command of the sea a complete blockade would then be established. They began by building a fort, Labdalon, to be used also for storage purposes, on the north side of Epipolae. Then they pushed on to Syke, a point situated in the south-central portion of the plateau. From there they set themselves to run a double wall, with a passage between, southwards to the harbour and northwards to the sea a little east of Labdalon. The Syracusans, after failing to stop their opponents' progress by cavalry raids, settled down to the recognized defensive measure against such a blockade. Twice they essayed to prevent the Athenians from completing their wall by erecting counter-walls across the projected line of that fortification. The first extended westwards from the north-west corner of Temenites, but it was destroyed by a picked body of Athenian troops after they had driven back the builders. On the second attempt the Syracusans ran a palisade and fosse from the west side of Temenites to intersect the course of the Athenian works not far from their southern end. But this defence work too was stormed by the Athenians after considerable fighting in which Lamachus lost his life. At the same time the Athenian fleet had sailed round and entered the Great Harbour.

The loss of Lamachus was a serious blow for the Athenians. On the other hand, continued failure had caused grave depression amongst the people of Syracuse, so that the question of making peace was actively canvassed. It is possible, too, that they were having some trouble at this time with their slave population.[1] Some reports of the situation within

[1] Polyaenus, I, 43. Modern writers have generally rejected this story, yet Polyaenus' source may eventually go back to a Syracusan source like Philistus.

the city seem to have reached the ears of Nicias, who was the more confident that the war would be speedily terminated. But his optimism was premature. At this most critical juncture a single Corinthian ship slipped into Syracuse unobserved. Its commander announced that Gylippus had reached the west and would soon arrive with reinforcements. The Spartan officer, who had been distracted by conflicting rumours about the fate of Syracuse that had reached him in southern Italy, landed at Himera. He was well received by the inhabitants and recruited additional men until his total force numbered nearly 3000. He now hurried to the relief of Syracuse and, inexplicably enough, found the land approach by way of Euryalus unguarded. Moreover, the Athenians, though they had finished the southern end of their circumvallation some time before, had not completed the northern end. Thus the relief force from Himera was able to enter the city. A little later twelve Corinthian ships, after sailing through the straits of Messana, also reached Syracuse unmolested, a welcome accession of strength to the Syracusan navy. It is hard to account for what has the appearance of gross neglect on the part of Nicias. Even if there had not been time to complete the northern end of the Athenian walls, elementary considerations of prudence demanded a strong guard at Euryalus. Less serious perhaps, but hardly less strange, was the ease with which enemy triremes were able to reach their destination, for the Athenian fleet was large enough to have enabled the commander-in-chief to detail a squadron to bar the sea approach to Syracuse.

Gylippus began his command auspiciously by storming the fort at Labdalon. He then spurred on the Syracusans to construct with all speed a counter-wall, running from the northern end of the outer city (Tyche) in a north-westerly direction, so as to cut across to the north of Syke where the enemy's walls were still unbuilt. The Athenians indeed were making all haste to remedy their previous error, but they were too late. Gylippus, though repulsed at first, was more successful at a second venture, and the Syracusan counter-wall was carried past the danger spot and subsequently extended to Euryalus. Shortly before, Nicias had made Plemmyrium at the south-eastern end of the Great Harbour his naval base and had constructed several forts there. But it soon proved a far from satisfactory position; for the enemy, emboldened by their recent successes, sent out cavalry detachments which constantly threatened the parties of Athenians detailed to bring fuel and water to the base from a distance. In short, the Athenians, owing to the energetic direction of the enemy's tactics, were now on the defensive. As the winter progressed their difficulties increased. Many of their ships were badly in need of caulking and other repairs, while the non-Athenian portion of the personnel and of the army now began to show dangerous signs of discontent.

Already in October Nicias had sent off a report to the home government in which he gave an unvarnished account of his plight. Of the two alternatives which he submitted—immediate abandonment of the Sicilian venture or the despatch of a second expeditionary force—the latter was adopted by the Athenians. They may have felt that with heavy reinforcements the situation in Sicily could be retrieved, while, on the other hand, a withdrawal, tantamount to a defeat, would have a disastrous effect on Athens' prestige within the empire. If their action in voting a new armament was defensible and perhaps the best strategy, the retention in his command of Nicias—he had asked to be superseded on the ground of illness—was pure folly. A new expedition would take some time to equip. Eurymedon was therefore sent off to Sicily about December 24 with ten galleys to hearten the Athenians at Syracuse with the news of the assembly's decision and to share the responsibility of command with Nicias.[1] The enemies of Athens in Greece also became more active. Further reinforcements were sent to Gylippus, and before the end of March, 413, a Spartan army under King Agis reopened hostilities by invading Attica and seizing Decelea.

Soon after, warfare began afresh in Syracuse. The townsfolk had spent the winter months in overhauling their ships and practising their crews. In the spring Gylippus planned a double attack on the enemy, a land assault on the forts at Plemmyrium while the navy engaged the enemy's fleet. The storming of the largest fort was followed by the surrender of the others; at the same time Gylippus captured a quantity of ships' tackle and stores. Thus the Athenians,

[1] Eurymedon left Athens about the time of the winter solstice. This is one of the few precise dates given by Thucydides (VII, 16).

who had managed to hold their own on the water, were
compelled to retire to that part of the coast lying immediately
under the southern end of their own double walls. The subsequent efforts of Eurymedon and Nicias to destroy the
Syracusan ships met with little success because Hermocrates
had seen to it that the Syracusan docks were strengthened
by a kind of palisade, part of which was submerged and
therefore very perilous for any hostile vessel attempting to
enter. News of the imminent arrival of the second Athenian
expedition reached not only Nicias but Gylippus, so that the
latter planned a determined effort to crush the Athenians on
their own element before help actually arrived. The first of
two fights in the harbour was indecisive, but two days later
the Syracusans at last proved the superiority of their more
heavily built triremes in a confined space where the swifter
but more vulnerable Athenian galleys were unable to carry out
their normal tactics. The Athenians lost seven ships outright,
but many more were disabled. Worse than that, the enemy
now controlled the sea (July, 413). The situation of Nicias,
Eurymedon, and their men would have been quite desperate
had not the second expedition arrived the day after the
naval fight. Demosthenes brought with him 73 triremes,
5000 hoplites, and 3000 miscellaneous light-armed troops,
so that, as far as naval and military strength is concerned,
the odds were probably again slightly in the Athenians'
favour.

Demosthenes prevailed on his colleagues to act with
energy and speed. The first necessity was to destroy and
capture the Syracusan counter-wall. Then the circumvallation of Syracuse could be completed and the blockade of
Syracuse made absolute. But the attempts to carry the
enemy's wall by direct assault failed; the only chance of
success, therefore, lay in an encircling movement. That,
however, entailed a march of some distance. Moreover, the
Syracusans had established guard posts at several points
near Euryalus. Hence, as the element of surprise was essential to its success, the attack could only be carried out at
night. On the appointed date the Athenians reached
Euryalus without accident, probably ascending to the plateau
at a point somewhat south-east of Euryalus, where the ground
sloped gradually upwards in contrast to the inaccessible

cliffs on either side.[1] One fort was taken but some of its inmates escaped and raised the alarm. Then a general fight ensued on the plateau. At first the Athenians secured an advantage; but those in the van pressed on too far and were driven back on their comrades by Syracusan reinforcements hurrying up to the rescue of their hard-pressed fellows. The whole Athenian army was thrown into disarray and in the end was put to flight with heavy casualties, perhaps as many as two thousand men.

Demosthenes rightly foresaw that Gylippus would follow up his victory by a new offensive and therefore pressed for the immediate departure of the whole Athenian armament. But Nicias demurred, influenced, it would seem, by rumours of a philo-Athenian cabal in Syracuse which might betray the city even yet, as well as by fear of the Athenian *ecclesia*, if he and his colleagues retreated ignominiously. The insistence of Nicias won the day and the Athenians remained inactive for three weeks. In the interval their situation steadily worsened, while Gylippus' army was strengthened by additional troops from other parts of Sicily and some from Greece. At last even Nicias was convinced that the only alternatives were instant departure or annihilation. But on the night appointed for the withdrawal (August 27) the moon was eclipsed. The soothsayers in Nicias' train asserted that nothing must be done until twenty-seven days had passed. We do not know whether the advice was mere superstitious folly or whether some of them were traitors to the Athenian cause. But Nicias obeyed their instructions and his colleagues were powerless to move him from this resolve. Gylippus, on his part, had quickly learnt of the intended withdrawal of the Athenians and of their decision to remain after the eclipse. He thereupon laid his plans for blocking every land route from Syracuse and at the same time prepared to make a grand assault on the Athenian navy. In their first attack the Syracusans drove the Athenian galleys ashore, so that although their own losses had been heavy they were once again masters of their own harbour. They then closed its entrance with galleys and other craft securely moored

---

[1] So K. Fabricius, *Das antike Syrakus*, 16, who questions with some justification the accuracy of Thucydides (VII, 43), when he says that Demosthenes went all the way round Euryalus and ascended by the path used by Nicias in 414 and afterwards by Gylippus.

together, since they expected that their opponents, as soon as they had repaired their fleet, would attempt to break the blockade and escape by sea. And so it proved. In the last engagement in the harbour the Athenian fleet, so far from breaking through, was completely defeated with heavy loss. Demosthenes urged that a second attempt be made with the sixty triremes that remained ; but the crews were thoroughly demoralized and refused to embark. A retreat by land was the only alternative, but Gylippus had laid his plans well. For six days the Athenians struggled on in two divisions, closely followed and continuously harassed by the enemy. Finally the two divisions became separated. That commanded by Demosthenes was first completely surrounded and compelled to surrender on the seventh day. On the day following Nicias' army was all but annihilated as it was desperately fighting its way across the Assinarus river. The Syracusans, embittered by two years of war, were merciless to their captives. Nicias and Demosthenes were executed, Eurymedon had fallen fighting in the retreat ; the rest were imprisoned in stone quarries near Syracuse, where most of them perished after weeks of untold suffering. A handful of cavalrymen had eluded the enemy in the final stage of the retreat and eventually reached Catana. They, and a few fugitives who were fortunate enough to escape from their captors and make their way to the same friendly city were all that may after many months have returned home. For the rest, the two Athenian expeditions with their personnel of 50,000 persons had ceased to be—a disaster such as no Greek city-state had suffered down to that time.

### § 4. ATHENS IN STRAITS

When certain news of the unexampled disaster in Sicily filtered through to Athens her citizens came face to face with such a crisis as they had not experienced since the epidemic in 430. There can have been few Attic families that were not directly affected by the casualties in the west. In the midst of the general mourning popular discontent was directed partly against the war politicians, partly against the soothsayers and quack prophets who had foretold a successful ending to the expedition. A direct outcome of this dissatisfaction with their leaders was the appointment by the

Athenians of ten commissioners (πρόβουλοι), one chosen from each tribe. They appear to have taken over many of the more important duties of the Council of Five Hundred, which included the direction of finance, negotiations with foreign states,[1] and the superintendence of naval construction. As a matter of practical convenience, too, a small board of ten was clearly better adapted to direct public business in an emergency than the Council or one of its relatively large committees. Again, the election in 412 of no less than four persons with pronounced oligarchic sympathies to the board of *strategi* shows that the popular revulsion from the extreme democratic programme was not purely ephemeral. Two of the ten commissioners are known by name, the poet Sophocles and Hagnon, father of Theramenes. Both were men of advanced years.

The course of the war on the home front during the next two years also gave some strength to the anti-democratic movement. The Spartans, angered by an Athenian raid on Laconia in 414, in the following spring occupied Decelea, so that Athens came to resemble an armed camp in a state of siege. From Decelea—a dozen miles from Athens and about the same distance from the Boeotian frontier—the enemy raided all northern Attica and cut the direct route from Athens to Oropus and to Euboea. They also made incursions into the southern portion of the peninsula, so that it became difficult and finally impossible to carry on the mining of silver at Laurium. Cattle and flocks were destroyed or carried off by the enemy, and Attic slaves to the number of 20,000 and more seized the occasion to desert. There was of course no hope of starving the Athenians into surrender as long as they controlled the sea; and, as an added measure of precaution to ensure the safe arrival of the grain ships, they fortified Cape Sunium in the winter, 413–412. But their losses, as the war continued, were severe and fell most heavily on the wealthier portion of the citizen body, the very persons who had already borne the heaviest burden, next to the allies and subjects, in financing the war. And this was the class which,

[1] In Aristophanes' *Lysistrata* (980 ff.), produced in 411, the Spartan herald has an interview with one of the *probuli*. Under normal conditions the emissaries of foreign states appeared before one of the committees of the Council. Aristotle (*Politics*, 1299B) informs us that the authority of the ten commissioners was superior to that of the Council.

even in normal times, was most likely to be critical of the extreme democratic programme.

Finance was indeed one of the most pressing problems for Athens at this time. On top of the losses in Sicily came the failure of the revenue from Laurium, and at the end of 413 only the reserve fund of 1000 talents set aside at the beginning of the war remained in hand. Already in the previous year the need of drastic action had become apparent. But it was too dangerous to increase the *phoros* at a time when the subjects of Athens were displaying signs of unrest. The Athenians therefore replaced the tribute by a five per cent tax on all sea-borne commerce, and collection of the *phoros* was not resumed until 410 when Athens had partially recovered. Yet, if this way of raising revenue was less objectionable than the tribute, the concession, such as it was, did not suffice to arrest the revolt of many states from Athens. In the winter the cities of Euboea and Lesbos got into touch with King Agis, while Chios and Erythrae sent representatives direct to Sparta. It had become known that the Spartans had embarked on a programme of naval building, and, in addition, their maritime allies in the Peloponnese and central Greece were preparing to send quotas of ships. Once the Peloponnesian armada appeared to dispute Athenian supremacy in the Aegean, not only the four states already named but many others were ready to join in the attack on Athens. Hermocrates, too, persuaded his countrymen to participate actively in the war, and a Syracusan squadron of twenty galleys—two of them were furnished by Selinus—arrived in the middle of 412 to co-operate with the Peloponnesians. During the previous winter the Athenians strained every nerve to put what triremes they had ready built into commission; then in the spring, when through the defection of so many cities and especially of Chios they appeared in danger of losing their naval hegemony, they resolved to use the reserve fund to construct and equip new triremes.

### § 5. THE INTERVENTION OF PERSIA

There was, however, one further development in the political situation after the Sicilian catastrophe which was calculated to cause the Athenians greater anxiety than any of the preparations being made by their Greek enemies—

the intervention of Persia. The peaceful relations that had existed between the Great King and the mistress of the Aegean had recently suffered a rough jar. Pissuthnes, the satrap of Lydia, had been in revolt against his master and was only brought to book by the combined efforts of Tissaphernes, who succeeded him in the satrapy, and two other grandees.[1] Pissuthnes' son Amorges had also started trouble in Caria where he had received some support from Athens. Doubtless Darius II, who had come to the throne in 424, had kept himself informed of the progress of the Greek war. Hence, when the power of Athens in the Aegean seemed to be tottering to its fall, he judged the proper time had come to re-establish Persian authority throughout the Asia Minor littoral. Tissaphernes and the satrap of Dascylium, Pharnabazus, received instructions from Susa to collect tribute from the Greek cities in that area. It was an inherent weakness in the Persian imperial organization that the satraps, while virtually minor potentates in their provinces, depended too much for their position on the caprice of the monarch and hence were prone to allow their own advancement or security to outweigh other considerations. Thus, in the winter, 413–412, Pharnabazus and Tissaphernes, so far from acting in concert, made approaches independently to Sparta. Whereas the former aimed to deprive Athens of her subjects in the Hellespont and Propontis, since these lay nearest to his satrapy, it was in Tissaphernes' interest to promote the defection of Ionia. Hence he seconded the request of Chios for Peloponnesian aid. Alcibiades also gave his support to the Chian petition, as he rightly calculated that the secession of the sole remaining independent ally of Athens, and one, moreover, with a considerable navy, would be an even more severe blow to the Athenians than the loss of their dependencies on the Asiatic side of the Hellespont and Propontis. The ephors decided to assist Chios before attempting to deprive Athens of other parts of her empire. But Spartan preparations for naval warfare were necessarily slow. Besides, shortage of funds was, we may surmise, responsible for much delay; for the subsidies from Athens' revolted subjects or from the Persian satrap would not become effective

[1] Ctesias (ed. Gilmore), § 83, gives their names as Spithradates and Parmises.

until the Peloponnesian fleet appeared in Asiatic waters.
About July, 412, five Spartan ships commanded by Chalcideus, who was accompanied by Alcibiades, reached Chios.
The Corinthian fleet of thirty-nine triremes which should
have participated was intercepted by the Athenians and
blockaded on the coast of Argolis. The Chians were misled
into believing that the main Peloponnesian fleet would
shortly arrive and openly revolted. Their example was
followed by Erythrae. Within a few weeks Clazomenae,
Miletus, Ephesus, Lebedus, and Teos followed suit, and then
the secession movement spread northwards; for Cyme,
Phocaea, and Lesbos also joined the enemies of Athens. At
Miletus Tissaphernes and the Spartan admiral drew up a
treaty of alliance.

Meanwhile the Athenians by using the reserve fund of
1000 talents had greatly speeded up their ship-building
programme. Their decision to make Samos the base for the
naval war initiated in Ionia by their opponents, if dictated
by necessity, was also strategically sound. But to ensure
the absolute loyalty of the island to their interests they gave
back their autonomy to the Samian *demos* and supported
them in an anti-oligarchic revolution. Some two hundred
oligarchs were killed and double that number were driven
into exile, their property being confiscated. Any of the old
landholders that remained found themselves excluded from
ordinary civic rights. An Athenian fleet of fifty galleys was
by that time in Asia Minor; thither, before the end of the
summer, a second squadron of equal strength, with 3500
Athenian and allied hoplites, was despatched. Chios and the
other insurgents, however, had also been reinforced by more
than fifty Peloponnesian galleys, the Spartan admiral-in-
chief for 412-411 being Astyochus. The operations carried
out during the ensuing months by both sides were indecisive.
The Athenians recovered Lesbos and Clazomenae. The
Clazomenians who had been instrumental in bringing about
the secession from Athens withdrew to Daphnus. A treaty
between them and the Athenian commanders was finally
ratified some years later by the *ecclesia*.[1] But though the
Athenians also destroyed or captured a portion of the Chian
fleet and raided the island, they failed to recover it. Nor

[1] Tod 89, part of a decree moved by Alcibiades in 408.

were they more successful at Miletus, for an initial success against the inhabitants could not be followed up as the approach of a Peloponnesian fleet made a withdrawal to Samos advisable. A second attempt to reduce Chios also failed, but the Athenians seized and occupied the fort of Delphinium some miles to the north of the main city on the island.

In the interval the Spartans, although they had no reason to be dissatisfied with the conduct and growing number of their new allies, were not in harmony with Tissaphernes. In the late autumn a fresh agreement was drawn up with the satrap; by its terms he took over more directly the financial responsibility of maintaining the Peloponnesian fleet whilst in the service of his master. Shortly before, moreover, Alcibiades had been received by Tissaphernes in friendly fashion. The Athenian, who had a bitter enemy in King Agis and had recently become an object of suspicion to the Spartan government, had got wind of a plot to have him removed quietly. He therefore sought the protection of the satrap. Tissaphernes, thinking of Persian interests, had no intention of allowing a Peloponnesian naval supremacy to replace the Athenian in the Aegean. A prolonged war between the two groups of Greek combatants which would exhaust both would leave the Persian king as *tertius gaudens*; whereupon he would re-establish his suzerainty in Asia Minor with the minimum of effort. But if Tissaphernes was not unwilling to make use of Alcibiades for his own purposes, the Athenian, under pretence of supporting the satrap in opposing the unreasonable demands of the Spartan commanders, was in reality working to secure his recall to Athens.

Before the winter was out Athens suffered further losses. Cnidus joined Tissaphernes and Sparta; not long afterwards Rhodes also revolted. The course of events at home and abroad during eighteen months had given strength to the movement at Athens for constitutional reform. And while the number of responsible citizens favouring a modification of the democratic *régime* increased, the oligarchs of old standing, whose subterranean activities had been carried on for years in their secret clubs without any appreciable influence on public affairs, were straining every nerve to make capital out of the "present discontents" and overthrow the constitution. The real director of this movement was Antiphon, a man who combined great legal knowledge with an unusual gift of organization. But he remained in the background. Others, like Pisander and Phrynichus, who were less suspect because they had in the past been democratic politicians, or else were, like Theramenes, known to favour a compromise between the extremes of oligarchy and democracy, worked more openly to bring about a change. With some of them Alcibiades entered into communication during the winter, promising that he could detach Tissaphernes from Sparta and even win his active help for Athens, if the Athenians would abandon or seriously modify their democratic institutions which were both distasteful and suspect to a satrap of the Great King. By the close of the winter the Athenians were sufficiently convinced that this was the only course to avoid certain disaster that they empowered a commission of eleven, headed by Pisander, to negotiate a formal agreement with Tissaphernes and Alcibiades. But the craftiness of the Oriental was more than a match for the Greek proposals; for Tissaphernes, while continuing to treat Alcibiades with the utmost courtesy, set his demands so high that the negotiations came to an abrupt halt. Even had an oligarchy already been in power at Athens, it would scarcely have agreed to the cession of Ionia and the neighbouring islands to Darius or acquiesced in the unhindered navigation of the Aegean by Persian vessels. For the moment the person most adversely affected was Alcibiades. He had to realize that Tissaphernes was more than his match in diplomacy and that the Athenian representatives as a whole, and not merely Phrynichus, were now hostile to him because they blamed him for the disappointment of their hopes. The last-named, indeed, had been distrustful of Alcibiades from the first and had, though ineffectually, warned the Athenians of treating with a renegade who cared neither for one type of constitution nor the other, but had only his own interests in view. Soon after these fruitless conversations Tissaphernes and the Spartans once more composed their differences and concluded a third agreement. It was an innovation that Pharnabazus also signed this treaty as a representative of Persia.

## § 6. THE OLIGARCHIC REVOLUTION AT ATHENS

No obvious reason for a change in the character of the Athenian government now existed as the hope of an advantageous foreign alliance had been destroyed. Nevertheless Antiphon, Pisander, and their associates had no intention of abandoning their plans, the more so as, in addition to having prepared the ground at Athens, they had found the trierarchs and officers of the Athenian forces at Samos in the main sympathetic to their aims. In Athens itself recourse was had to methods of intimidation. Outspoken opponents of oligarchy—the most prominent was Androcles, who had taken a leading part in the prosecution of Alcibiades four years before—were assassinated. Yet the mass of the people, seeing that there were many moderates amongst the advocates of reform, seems to have regarded these violent measures rather as instances of summary justice against persons dangerous to Athenian welfare.

Meanwhile the revolutionaries at Samos were not idle. After explaining to the Athenian forces their programme of reform, some of Pisander's associates went off to promote the change from democratic to oligarchic government amongst the subjects of Athens. Pisander himself with some others left for Athens. On their way they, too, set up oligarchies in several places and at the same time raised some military levies to assist them in their *coup d'état*. At Athens they found that the way had been well prepared by their confederates. A proposal to increase the existing board of ten commissioners by twenty others above forty years of age was carried in the assembly. These thirty *probuli* were then empowered to draw up a constitutional scheme for the security of the state and bring it before the people on the fourteenth of the month Thargelion (April–May). On this day the assembly was convened at Colonus. With Pisander's armed supporters in evidence and the rest of the voters only partly present the proposals of the commission were carried without difficulty. The franchise was for the duration of the war to be limited to those citizens who were able to bear arms and financially independent, to the number of not less than 5000.[1] One hundred persons were to be chosen—ten

[1] Aristotle (*Const. of Ath.*, 29) is supported by Lysias (XX, 13) against Thucydides (VIII, 65), who says not more than five thousand.

from each tribe—to compile a list of those entitled to citizenship on those terms. A new council of Four Hundred was to be appointed. Finally pay for office was to be abolished save in the case of the archons and the chairmen ($\pi\rho\upsilon\tau\alpha\nu\epsilon\hat{\iota}\varsigma$) of the council. The Four Hundred were constituted at once; for the rest, it was agreed that they should summon the Five Thousand when it should seem good to them to do so. A new board of *strategi* was also elected. Two factors above all made the failure of this new *régime* inevitable from the first. There was a fundamental difference in aims amongst the revolutionaries themselves. The out-and-out oligarchs regarded the election of a civic body of Five Thousand as a mere blind; from the outset they intended that the government should pass absolutely into their own hands. A minority whose spokesman was Theramenes, on the other hand, seem to have been striving genuinely for a mixed constitution, that is, they desired the Five Thousand to become a reality as soon as the list of eligibles had been drawn up. In the second place, it was assumed that the constitutional upheaval at Athens would be approved without question by the Athenians at Samos. But precisely the opposite happened. An oligarchic plot, ushered in by the murder of Hyperbolus who was spending his exile in the island, was defeated by the Athenian troops and crews. They entrusted the direction of affairs to one of the trierarchs, Thrasybulus, and to a certain Thrasyllus, who was serving as a hoplite. When, a little later, news came that the Four Hundred were fully in the saddle at Athens, Thrasybulus and Thrasyllus bound all at Samos, the Athenians, irrespective of their political affiliations, and the islanders also, to remain faithful to the democracy, to refuse recognition to the usurpers at home, and to prosecute the war against the Peloponnesian states with all vigour. They deposed their commanders and elected others in their place, chief amongst them being Alcibiades, whom Thrasybulus and his associates recalled to Samos after formally voting his pardon. With his help they still hoped to bring about a rupture between Tissaphernes and Sparta. The satrap was, indeed, not to be won over; but he abstained from active hostilities, although a large Phoenician fleet had come to Pamphylia to be under his orders. Nor did he at this time lend any support to his Greek allies.

In contrast to the resolution and good sense displayed by the Athenians in Samos, the revolutionaries in Athens were distinguished by ineptitude and violence. Eight days after the meeting at Colonus the Four Hundred forcibly expelled the old council and took complete charge of the government, although the machinery for setting up a citizen body of Five Thousand was not openly set aside. But the Four Hundred had to think of external as well as internal enemies of the state, and the solution they sought was not heroic. Representatives were sent off to secure peace with Sparta. But neither King Agis nor the ephors were disposed to treat even an oligarchy at Athens with clemency. Doubtless they hoped that internal dissension would soon make the Athenians an easy prey for Sparta and her allies. In consequence, the Spartan reply was a demand for the dissolution of the Athenian empire, a stipulation that they well knew would be refused. The next move of the oligarchs was to bring about a reconciliation with the Athenians in Samos, but the latter were for sailing home at once to overthrow the usurpers. Had they left Samos, the rest of their dependencies in Ionia and the Hellespont would have been lost, indeed the position of Athens would have been almost as desperate as if the peace terms suggested by Sparta had been accepted. Whatever his motives, Alcibiades did his countrymen a service when he dissuaded them from acting so precipitately and insisted that a conciliatory answer be sent to Athens, approving the constitution of the Five Thousand but demanding the suspension of the Four Hundred and the restoration of a normal council of Five Hundred. Alcibiades could not but be aware that this would strengthen the hands of Theramenes and his fellow-moderates. The extremists thereupon sent twelve of their best men to Sparta, ostensibly to treat once more for peace, in reality to express their secret willingness to betray Athens to the enemy. They also proceeded to fortify the mole called Eetioneia on the northern side of Piraeus, so as more easily to admit a Peloponnesian fleet when it arrived.

But they had overreached themselves. The return from Sparta of the delegates who reported the failure of their mission, and the suspicious fortification of Eetioneia, enabled Theramenes to work upon the smouldering resentment of a

cowed citizenry.  Phrynichus was assassinated in the
Athenian agora.  The troops engaged on Eetioneia turned
against the extremists and set themselves to pull down the
very fortifications which they had lately erected.  A few days
later, when a meeting was held in the theatre of Dionysus to
reconstitute the government in such a way as to entrust
sovereign authority to the Five Thousand, a Peloponnesian
fleet was sighted in the neighbourhood of Salamis.  The
meeting broke up, as all hastened to the defence of Piraeus.
But the Spartan admiral, Agesandridas, passed on to bring
about the revolt of Euboea.  Thirty-six Athenian galleys
were manned at once and sent off in pursuit, but they were
defeated heavily off Eretria.  That city and the rest of
Euboea, with the exception of the Athenian cleruchy at
Hestiaea, thereupon went over to the enemies of Athens.[1]
The situation of the Athenians was now desperate, and they
were only saved from ruin by the inept conduct of their
enemies.  Had Agis and Agesandridas made a concerted
attack by land and sea on Athens and its harbour, the war
would have ended then and there.  But while the Spartans
did not use their chances to the full the disastrous loss of
Euboea had one good result at Athens.  For the citizens
vented their anger and alarm on the Four Hundred who were
forthwith deposed.  Antiphon and another were tried, found
guilty of treason and put to death ; but most of the leading
extremists escaped to Decelea.  One of their number,
Aristarchus, with a small body of archers tricked the garrison
of Oenoe into coming out for a parley and then betrayed
this border fortress to the Boeotians.

The government instituted by Theramenes and his supporters was an interesting constitutional experiment which
won the approval of Thucydides and Aristotle.[2]  The citizens
who actively participated in public affairs were about nine
thousand—roughly those belonging to the first, second, and
third Solonian classes—and formed both assembly and
council.  But to facilitate the transaction of business the

---

[1] The grateful Eretrians bestowed special favours on Hegelochus of
Tarentum, who took a prominent part in liberating Eretria (Tod 82).

[2] The identity of this constitution with that given in Aristotle's *Const.
of Ath.* (30) has been questioned.  But it is probable that at least it formed the
basis of Theramenes' constitution.  Cf. M. Cary in *J.H.S.* 72 (1952), pp. 56–61,
and G. Vlastos in *Amer. Journ. Phil.* 73 (1952), pp. 189–198.

total number of those with full civic rights was divided into four councils, each of which served in that capacity for one year. Each council, which had a full session once in five days, was subdivided into ten committees, each functioning for a tenth part of the year and carrying on the business in the intervals between the full meetings of the council. Other reforms included the appointment of the archons, like the generals, by election instead of by lot, and the institution of two committees, composed of ten and twenty members respectively, to take charge, in one case, of the religious, in the other of the secular funds of the state. The juries in the courts of justice, moreover, were recruited from the members of the three councils that were not serving as councillors in any given year. Payment for office was abolished; instead, regular attendance at council meetings was enforced by fining absentees. This constitution remained in force for about eight months (September, 411–April, 410).

One of the early acts of the new government was to confirm the appointment of Alcibiades as *strategus*, made by the troops at Samos. Nor had it been long in power before a naval victory in the Aegean brought fresh courage and hope to the Athenians in their difficulties. Owing largely to the aloof and unhelpful attitude of Tissaphernes, the Spartan admiral, Astyochus, had effected little during the spring and summer of 411 except to bring about the revolt of Byzantium. The secession of Thasos from Athens was unconnected with any Peloponnesian intervention. Astyochus' successor, Mindarus, altered the Spartan tactics, inasmuch as he aimed to deprive Athens of her control of the Hellespont—a plan which, if successful, would have meant starvation for the population of Attica. In furtherance of this objective he fostered good relations with the satrap Pharnabazus. Cyzicus and perhaps some other cities seceded from Athens on his approach, but the Athenian naval commanders at Samos, fully aware how critical a situation had arisen, followed the Spartan fleet and forced it to fight in the narrow waters of the Hellespont. Although the site of the engagement, off the promontory of Cynossema, placed the Athenians at some disadvantage, as their naval tactics to be most effective needed ample room, they defeated the enemy. The Peloponnesians only escaped with relatively small loss because they were able to withdraw

to Abydos which had joined Sparta some months before.
The Athenians followed up their victory by recovering
Cyzicus. Late in the autumn they again showed their naval
superiority in an action off Abydos.

The turn which events had taken and the transference of
Peloponnesian naval activity to the Hellespontine region led
Tissaphernes during the winter to reopen negotiations with
the Spartans. Alcibiades, on seeking an interview with him,
found himself put under arrest and was detained at Sardes
for a month before he made good his escape. As usual,
hostilities were suspended until the spring. Then Mindarus
began again by capturing Cyzicus a second time. The
Athenian fleet, which was operating in three detachments in
different areas, was quickly united at Sestos under the supreme
direction of Alcibiades. Taking advantage of poor visibility
caused by heavy rain his eighty-three galleys took the enemy,
sixty triremes strong, by surprise. Mindarus ran his ships
ashore and his men at first fought stoutly. But they were
outnumbered and outmanœuvred, and at last broke into
headlong flight. Mindarus himself died fighting. The
Peloponnesian galleys fell into the hands of the Athenians;
only the Syracusan detachment had succeeded in firing their
vessels before retreating (April, 410).

### § 7. THE RESTORED DEMOCRACY AT ATHENS

The victory of Cyzicus and more especially the return of
the fleet, many of whose rowers belonged to the disenfranchised class, produced a strong reaction at Athens. The
constitution of the Five Thousand was set aside, the poorest
class of citizens recovered their full civic status, and the
Council of Five Hundred, recruited and organized as of old,
was restored. But while the Athenians thus reverted to the
type of government under which they had become masters
of half the Hellenic world, they retained the recently established boards of financial officials and other minor innovations
made at the same date. Yet it would have been better for
Athens if the government of Theramenes had endured a
little while longer. The Spartan government, when the total
loss of the Peloponnesian fleet became known, made peace
overtures to Athens. An exchange of Decelea for Pylos
was proposed; for the rest, each side was to retain what

possessions remained to it. For Athens this would have meant, it is true, the loss of virtually all Ionia, Caria, and the Propontis, as well as of five of the larger Aegean islands. The new leader of the *ecclesia*, Cleophon the lyre-maker, backed by the citizens who had just restored to Athens her naval supremacy, brought about the rejection of the Spartan terms. This action was to prove a disastrous mistake. It is likely, though it cannot be demonstrated, that the government of the Five Thousand would have proceeded more cautiously and so would have saved Athens from her final humiliation. Cleophon's hand can also be detected soon after in the provision of work for impoverished labourers by resuming building operations on the Acropolis and by the institution of a small dole of two obols a day (διωβελία) to needy citizens, of whom at this time there must have been many. No details of the extent and organization of this state aid are known; but the relatively small sums borrowed for the purpose from the treasury of Athena suggest that the number of recipients was strictly limited.[1] Payment for office was, of course, revived, for this had been an essential feature of Athenian democracy for nearly half a century. Furthermore, a commission was appointed to revise and publish afresh the laws, a task that was carried on fitfully and was still unfinished at the end of the war.[2] It was to be expected that the restoration of democratic government should bring in its train hardship and injustice to individual citizens. But the experiences of the past few years and the continued strain of the war produced a bitterness and suspicion that were more than temporary, so that all the worst features of ancient democracy were accentuated and in some respects perpetuated. The citizens who had been disenfranchised by the Four Hundred and then by the Five Thousand were not disposed, when they had recovered their full rights, to let bygones be bygones. Indeed, something like a reign of terror was called into being. Not only were prominent members of the two short-lived governments, like Critias, exiled, but their supporters amongst the rank and file became objects of suspicion and then, with increasing frequency, of persecution. Professional informers, long since an unpleasing feature of Athenian society, thrived exceedingly,

[1] See the two financial inscriptions of 410–409 and 407–406 (Tod 83 and 92). [2] Cf. Tod 87, part of Draco's law on homicide.

the more so as the responsibility of instituting a prosecution against wrongdoers and suspected persons rested with the individual citizen. A long series of judicial murders, exiles, confiscations, and lesser penalties, such as heavy fines, partial disenfranchisement, and the imposition of other civil disabilities, must be laid to the charge of the leaders of the people and to the popular jury-courts. And, as the impartial jurisdiction of the *dicasteria* declined, so they became more corrupt. When Anytus was arraigned for negligence because he had not prevented the Spartans from regaining Pylos, he secured an acquittal by extensive bribery of the jurors who had to try his case. One specially repugnant feature of the new *régime* was, as we shall see, the lack of confidence and even gross injustice shown by the Athenians to their military leaders during the closing years of the war.

The chief theatre of operations continued to be in the Propontis. There Sparta had received most support from the neighbouring satrap; there also Athens' most vital interests lay. Using Cyzicus as his base, Alcibiades during the campaigning season of 410 levied a contribution to the war on Selymbria and perhaps recovered Perinthus. As he did not feel strong enough to besiege either Byzantium or Chalcedon, he erected a fort at Chrysopolis, close by Chalcedon. A naval detachment under Thrasybulus remained there to levy a ten per cent toll on cargoes coming from the Euxine. A smaller squadron was on guard in the Hellespont. In that way naval superiority could again ensure a safe passage for the Pontic grain ships as well as some revenues for the depleted Athenian treasury. In the winter the Spartans, at the instance of King Agis and in the expectation of ensuring the permanent loss to Athens of Byzantium, sent a harmost, Clearchus, with some troops to that city. When the campaigning season of 409 opened, the Athenians began to operate over a wider area. In the Propontis Alcibiades led an attack on Selymbria, which had refused to admit him the previous year when it paid its contribution to the war, and with the help of a disaffected group in the city captured it. On this occasion only his personal courage and great presence of mind turned an imminent disaster into a notable success.[1] A treaty between the citizens and the Athenians was then

---

[1] Plutarch (*Alcib.*, 30) relates the story at some length.

arranged, although it was not ratified till 407 when Alcibiades had returned to Athens.[1] The siege of Thasos may have been begun in 409, although the island did not capitulate to Thrasybulus until 408. The Athenians were helped in their operations in that region by the loyalty of Neapolis (now Cavalla). Its citizens had remained loyal to Athens throughout, and shortly before Thrasybulus' arrival had successfully repelled a combined Thasian and Peloponnesian attack. The Athenian *ecclesia* formally voted its gratitude and bestowed certain privileges on its ally.[2] An expedition of fifty triremes, 1000 heavy- and 5000 light-armed troops commanded by Thrasyllus in 409 attempted to recover some of the cities of Ionia. But, although he won Colophon, his assault on Ephesus was repulsed by the citizens supported by a considerable body of Persian cavalry and foot sent by Tissaphernes. In view of this unexpected show of force by the satrap, Thrasyllus deemed it wiser to withdraw from that area and joined Alcibiades in the Hellespont. Their attempt to recover Abydos failed.

In 408 Athens' good fortune was again in the ascendant. Alcibiades concentrated all his efforts on regaining complete control of the Bosphorus. Chalcedon was invested first and forced to capitulate in spite of Pharnabazus' efforts to relieve it. Byzantium, however, would probably have withstood every assault had not some of the population betrayed it into Alcibiades' hands during the temporary absence of Clearchus. Thrasybulus, in addition to his success at Thasos, also won back Abdera. Compared to these gains Athens' loss of Pylos and Nisaea at this time was trifling. Finally there seemed some hope of bringing the hostility of Persia to an end; for Pharnabazus, after the Athenian capture of Chalcedon, agreed to procure a safe passage to the Great King at Susa for an Athenian and Argive delegation.

### § 8. THE CLOSING YEARS OF THE WAR: CYRUS AND LYSANDER

The confidence of the Athenians was premature; for if the Spartans after the defeat of Cyzicus and the rejection of their efforts for peace seemed to have become inert in the main theatre of war, they had not abandoned hope of a more effective alliance with Persia. In the winter of 408–407

---

[1] Tod 88.   [2] See the two decrees in Tod 84.

Spartan delegates were sent to Susa. Seeing that part of their diplomatic mission was to protest formally against Tissaphernes' conduct, their arrival in the Persian capital was singularly opportune. The noble family of which Tissaphernes was a member had incurred the implacable hatred of the queen and had recently been all but extinguished. Darius was consequently ready enough to accept the Spartan version of Sparta's unsatisfactory relations with the satrap. Over and above this the king, under the influence of his consort Parysatis, desired to invest his son Cyrus with greater responsibilities than were usually accorded to the younger son of a reigning monarch. Moreover, by appointing Cyrus to be governor-general of all the satrapies in Asia Minor, with his headquarters in Tissaphernes' old province of Lydia, Darius expected to attain a single-minded direction of the war against Athens, such as had hitherto been conspicuously lacking owing to the rivalry between Tissaphernes and Pharnabazus. Over and above the regular revenues from the satrapies that he was to control, Cyrus received five hundred talents for the specific purpose of financing the rebuilding of the Spartan fleet. Cyrus had already reached Gordium in Phrygia when the Athenian and Argive delegates appeared on their way to Susa. They not only learnt that their mission was too late but were detained so that the new policy of the Great King might not become known in Athens prematurely. If the pro-Persian policy of Sparta was more indefensible than ever before, it must at least be admitted that the ablest man available was chosen to co-operate with Cyrus in the Near East.

Lysander, the son of a Spartiate father and Helot mother, was among the Spartan officers serving during the war second in ability only to Brasidas and Gylippus. Quite unscrupulous as well as ruthless in the means that he used to attain his ends, he had acquired a rare insight into men's characters and motives. Sparta rarely bred astute politicians, but in Lysander she produced a diplomat of the first rank, the very person to reach a cordial understanding with an Oriental prince. Lysander spent the autumn and winter, 407–406, in winning the confidence of the Greek communities in Ionia as well as of Cyrus himself. The headquarters of the fleet, which by the spring of 406 numbered ninety triremes, was Ephesus,

Moreover, the Persian was generous in his subsidies, so that Lysander could pay the rowers whom he recruited in Ionia better wages than they could hope to receive in the service of Athens.

The seriousness of these developments was not lost on Alcibiades. After eight years' exile he had returned to Athens in the early summer of 407, to be rapturously received by his compatriots. In applauding his recent naval and military successes, they forgot for the moment the injuries that they had suffered at his hands. Yet even in his hour of triumph he must have been aware that he had implacable enemies waiting for the first opportunity to remove him. The penalties against him were revoked and he was appointed commander-in-chief of all the Athenian forces for the ensuing Attic year. When he set out once more for Asia Minor, after some four months' stay at home, he was in command of 100 galleys, some 1500 hoplites and 150 cavalry. Owing to the presence of Lysander at Ephesus, Samos once more became the Athenian headquarters; but Alcibiades did not feel strong enough to risk an offensive before the spring.[1] In March at length he moved the greater part of his fleet to Notium, whence he could control the approach to the harbour of Ephesus. At the same time Thrasybulus with a small squadron began the blockade of Phocaea. During the temporary absence of Alcibiades from the grand fleet—he was bringing up some hoplites to co-operate with Thrasybulus—his second-in-command, Antiochus, disobeyed his orders, at all costs to avoid an open engagement, and took the offensive against the Spartan fleet. He was defeated off Notium and lost fifteen ships. If the Athenian reverse was slight, the consequences to Alcibiades, who was held responsible, were not. The Athenians quickly forgot their recent enthusiasm and Alcibiades' personal enemies doubtless became very active, for at the elections held soon after at Athens for the next year's *strategia* Alcibiades was not chosen. Instead, a full board of ten was appointed. He knew the temper of the Athenian democracy too well to risk a return to his native city, but withdrew to the Thracian Chersonese where he had long since acquired two castles in case of future need.

[1] I have followed Ferguson (*C.A.H.* V, 483–484) and others in dating Notium in the early part of 406. Bengtson, *op. cit.*, 232, adheres to 407.

Meantime Lysander had been superseded by Callicratidas, as his reappointment was not allowed by the Spartan system. The new admiral's relations with Cyrus were far from cordial. Nevertheless he carried out his duties with great determination. Transferring his base to Miletus, he collected ships from Rhodes, Chios, and some other cities, so that by the summer his total naval force reached the unparalleled number of 170 galleys. He ousted the Athenian garrison from Delphinium on Chios; then he attacked and captured Methymna on Lesbos. Conon, who had superseded Alcibiades in command at Samos, tried to retrieve the situation at Lesbos but lost thirty of his triremes in a fight against the Peloponnesian navy. With the remainder he was blockaded in the inner harbour of Mytilene. Nevertheless, he succeeded in sending an urgent despatch home, detailing his plight and the resources of the enemy. The Athenians had plenty of warships in reserve but not enough citizens to man them. So resident aliens and slaves were pressed into service with promises of high rewards. The treasury was empty. In order to finance a fresh naval expedition to Ionia the gold and silver plate in the temples on the Acropolis was melted down and minted into gold and silver currency. Even copper coins were issued as token money on the future credit of the state. Within little more than a month a fleet of 150 Athenian and allied vessels was on its way to relieve Mytilene. It encountered the Peloponnesian fleet of 120 galleys—fifty had remained behind to continue the blockade of Conon—near the Arginusae Islands situated between the southern end of Lesbos and the mainland. The number of warships engaged in this encounter was greater than in any sea-fight known down to that time between Greeks. The Spartan ships, though fewer than the enemy's, seem to have been better disciplined and more speedy. They attacked strongly in a single line with the object of breaking the Athenian centre and then enveloping their two wings. But the Athenians countered these tactics by forming a double line, in such a way that the ships in the rear were behind the gaps left between those in the front line. As the original Spartan plan thereby became impracticable, they next assaulted their opponents strongly on both wings. But the Athenians completely defeated the enemy's right wing, while their own right wing resisted tenaciously until the sinking of Callicratidas' own galley—the admiral perished like his men— threw the Peloponnesian left into confusion. Thus the Athenians won a striking victory. No less than sixty-nine of the enemy triremes had been sunk with all hands on board; they themselves had lost only twenty-five galleys. Of these, twelve were still afloat after the battle, but by that time a strong north wind had made the sea very choppy, so that the Athenian admirals failed to save the crews on board. Thus the Athenian casualties were increased by more than two thousand men. Though their rescue may in the circumstances have been impossible, public feeling at Athens imputed gross negligence to the admirals. The adverse weather also made it impossible for the Athenian navy to follow up the victory by annihilating the squadron that had been left behind to blockade Conon. Instead, this detachment withdrew to Chios and united with what remained of the Spartan grand fleet. Consequently the Athenians still had to reckon with a hostile fleet in the Aegean almost as numerous as their own.

The Athenian assembly deposed the eight *strategi* who had commanded jointly at Arginusae and transferred the Aegean command to Conon and two colleagues. All eight commanders were then impeached, but only six stood their trial, the other two deeming voluntary exile a safer choice. The admirals' defence that the trierarchs—amongst these were Thrasybulus and Theramenes—had been at fault, though it may have been true, availed them nothing. Not an ordinary court of law but the assembly itself tried the accused men, and after two sittings pronounced sentence of death and confiscation of property on all of them together. The six who stood their trial were then executed, amongst them being Thrasyllus and Pericles, the son of Pericles and Aspasia (October, 406). Not only was the penalty excessive, but the procedure followed was quite contrary to established usage at Athens by which each defendant should have been given a separate trial. The slaves who had served loyally as rowers in the recent fight were liberated and enrolled as citizens of the same category as the survivors of Plataea in 427.

The Athenian people now had one more opportunity of concluding peace. The Spartan government was not merely

## THE PELOPONNESIAN WAR

overwhelmed by the recent naval defeat, but, as Cyrus was withholding further subsidies, had not the money wherewith to keep their Aegean fleet in commission. So the Spartans proposed a cessation of war, each side retaining what it held at the time, save that they agreed to give back Decelea to Athens. Once more Cleophon proved the evil genius of his country. He argued strongly for the rejection of the Spartan proposals and a majority of his countrymen, intoxicated by their victory at Arginusae, followed his ruinous advice. The alternative demand of the Athenians that their opponents should relinquish all the places that they had won in the war was naturally refused.

A revival of better relations between the Spartan government and Cyrus followed at once, for while the Persian prince had no desire to withdraw from the contest, he demanded a congenial Spartan commander-in-chief with whom to cooperate. The Spartans, although there were not a few influential persons opposed to that course, agreed to send Lysander back to Asia Minor, nominally in a subordinate position, actually as the real director of operations. When Lysander arrived at Ephesus he found Cyrus prepared to be generous with funds. In consequence, by the summer of 405 the Spartan fleet had been reconstructed and enlarged to some two hundred vessels. After some subsidiary actions Lysander sailed for the Hellespont with the object of striking at Athens in her most vulnerable point. He passed the straits which were unguarded, and sailed for Lampsacus, which he captured. The Athenians meanwhile had renewed their offensive against Chios; but on learning of the Spartan move they hastened with all speed to the Hellespont. They took up their position in the straits at Aegospotami on the European side opposite to Lampsacus, their object being to force the enemy to engage. But the position was not free from danger if Lysander should attempt a surprise attack. Alcibiades in exile had watched developments with solicitous interest. Having a thorough knowledge of Lysander's abilities, he visited the Athenian commanders and urged them to withdraw to Sestos, where they would have a safe and convenient base for all emergencies. But the six *strategi* in charge of the Athenian fleet refused to listen to his advice, intimating also that his presence was not welcome. For several days the Athenians tried to draw their opponents out to give battle, but in vain. Then they became less watchful, and on the fifth day of these manœuvres the admirals allowed most of the crews to land after their ineffectual cruise outside Lampsacus. Lysander, who had closely observed the habits of his enemy, at once sailed out with his full fleet and took the Athenians completely by surprise. He captured 160 of their galleys; the twenty which alone were in readiness to give battle managed to escape. The crews of the captured vessels were gradually rounded up in the following days and the Athenians amongst them—more than three thousand in all—were ruthlessly executed. Conon, who was in command of the twenty triremes that escaped, sent twelve to Athens; with the rest he sailed to Salamis in Cyprus, to become for some years the guest-friend and retainer of the ruling prince, Evagoras.

It was the end of Athens' naval supremacy. To construct and equip a new fleet was impossible; besides, all the communities that had up to that time remained faithful to her now fell away, save one. The Samians killed off their oligarchs and communicated with the Athenians, promising to stand by them to the end. The Athenians responded by bestowing their citizenship on the Samians and undertaking to respect the independence of the islanders. The two states further agreed on a common course of action in war and peace, though actually it was too late for any co-operation to be feasible.[1] Of the former subjects and allies of Athens the more important were occupied by officers of Lysander. The Spartan commander-in-chief, moreover, compelled the Athenian cleruchs settled in Chalcidice and elsewhere to return to Athens on pain of suffering the same fate as the Athenian captives after Aegospotami. Their arrival at home swelled the population of Athens, which, after the first shock of consternation at the catastrophe in the Hellespont, set to with the energy of despair to prepare Athens and Piraeus to withstand a siege. But Lysander intended not to attempt a costly assault but to starve the Athenians into surrender. He spent some months in establishing complete control in Thrace and the Hellespont, so that it was not till the very end of the year that the Spartan fleet appeared in the Saronic Gulf to blockade

[1] Cf. the important decree, Tod 96.

Piraeus from the sea. The Spartan government had shortly before mobilized its land forces, and the garrison of Decelea under Agis and a Peloponnesian army under Pausanias united for an invasion of Attica. Shortage of food was already beginning to have an effect on the besieged, and an effort was made to win terms short of unconditional surrender from Sparta. But when the reply was that the Athenians must level a part of their Long Walls, the Athenians under the guidance of Cleophon refused. Nevertheless the more reasonably minded citizens so far prevailed as to procure the despatch of Theramenes to Sparta. The blockade continued until April, 404. Only then did Theramenes return, ostensibly because he had been detained forcibly, in reality because he hoped to attain some measure of goodwill as well as support from Lysander, if he and his supporters effected a change of government at Athens. During his absence the sufferings that they were enduring brought about a sharp cleavage of opinion amongst the Athenians. The extreme supporters of democracy lost ground, especially after Cleophon had been indicted by his political opponents, condemned and executed. Thus when Theramenes at length returned to Athens the situation in the starving city was more favourable for his plans. He and nine others were sent off to Sparta to secure what terms they could.

At a congress of Peloponnesian states and their allies which was convened in the spring there were some who demanded the complete destruction of Athens. But Sparta would not consent to forget Athens' services in the past to the cause of Hellenism and opposed the exasperated ferocity of the Boeotians and Corinthians. The terms actually imposed left Athens an autonomous state and that was all. Starved into surrender, the Athenians were obliged to destroy the fortifications of Piraeus and the Long Walls; they were deprived of all territory save Attica and Salamis and lost their navy save only twelve galleys; and they were obliged to recall all their political exiles, a measure fraught with serious consequences in the immediate future. When Lysander had received the formal surrender of the Athenians he sailed to Samos and forced the islanders to submit after a siege of several months.

## § 9. THE THIRTY AT ATHENS AND THE RESTORATION OF THE DEMOCRACY

With the departure of Lysander Athens became the scene of bitter party struggles. The upholders of democracy, though deprived by the death of Cleophon of their most prominent leader, fought hard to prevent constitutional changes. But the return of political exiles had greatly added to the number of men with pronounced oligarchic views. The most conspicuous was Critias, who had taken part in the government of the Four Hundred and the Five Thousand, but had been forced to go into exile when the democracy was restored. Against a coalition of extreme oligarchs and men like Theramenes, who was working for the restoration of his favourite polity, the democrats were bound to succumb, especially as their opponents in the last resort could appeal for Spartan intervention. And this was precisely what occurred. Lysander, when he had completed the reduction of Samos, returned to Athens and threatened severe penalties, if the government at Athens were not reconstituted on the lines proposed by Theramenes. An appearance of legality was given to his threats because the raising of the walls had not been finished and the Athenians had therefore not fully carried out the terms of the peace. A body of thirty persons was then set up (summer, 404) to draw up afresh the old constitution and to act as an interim government until that constitution could be put into effect. Of these persons ten were nominated apparently by Lysander, ten by Theramenes, and ten by the Athenians. Although Theramenes himself was amongst them, a majority, like Critias who was also chosen, had no more intention than had the Four Hundred seven years earlier of carrying out the first part of their duties. Once in the saddle, they intended to rule for an indefinite period as autocrats. The council of Five Hundred was reconstituted so that it was composed solely of men who would not oppose the Thirty. Similarly the magistracies were filled with their nominees. A special board of Ten was appointed to govern Piraeus under the presidency of Charmides, and the eleven police commissioners headed by Satyrus were also uncompromising supporters of the extremists.

The Thirty began by attainting and executing the chief democrats; they also removed some prominent informers and other persons of bad character. But Critias and his supporters did not feel strong enough to carry out their further plans without adequate armed support. So they applied to Sparta for a garrison 700 strong under a Spartan harmost, Callibius, who occupied the Acropolis.[1] Feeling that their position was now secure, Critias and his fellows began a systematic attack on the wealthy, whether citizens or resident aliens. Judicial murder was followed by confiscation of property, which was a primary reason for their reign of terror. The citizen body was next restricted not to all able to serve as hoplites but to 3000 only of whose support the extremists felt sure. The remainder were completely disfranchized and by a tyrannous enactment could be put to death without trial. Not a few of those who saw themselves without any civic rights were men who saw eye to eye with Theramenes, who himself had consistently opposed the ruthless programme of Critias. Deprived of the bulk of his supporters, Theramenes became an easy prey. Critias struck his name from the list of citizens and Theramenes was promptly handed over to the Eleven and forced to drink the hemlock. The most vivid picture of the excesses that followed is preserved not in the *Hellenic History* of Xenophon but in two extant speeches composed by the orator Lysias, when the democratic government had been restored, against one of the Thirty, Eratosthenes, and against an unscrupulous informer, Agoratus, who had been in the pay of the oligarchs.[2] The orator himself had suffered bitterly; his brother had been a victim of the Thirty and the family property was confiscated, while Lysias only barely escaped execution. Besides the continued persecution of potentially dangerous citizens, the murder of persons solely for their wealth was intensified, so that later writers estimated the number of persons done to death at no less than fifteen hundred.[3] Among the exiles were Alcibiades and Thrasybulus. The former, since Lysander was rounding up Athenian exiles

---

[1] Xenophon, *Hell.*, II, 3, 14. Aristotle (*Const. of Ath.*, 37) wrongly narrates the introduction of the garrison after the death of Theramenes.
[2] Lysias, XII and XIII.
[3] Aristotle, *op. cit.*, 35; Isocrates, VII, 67; XX, 11.

everywhere, took refuge with Pharnabazus; but the satrap when asked to do so handed him over to Spartan agents and he was executed by Lysander's orders. Thrasybulus was more fortunate, for he found a friendly welcome with other exiles in Thebes, until recently the most savage of Athens' enemies. The changed attitude of the Thebans and the Boeotians generally must be attributed to serious dissatisfaction with the terms of the peace, which reacted on the political parties in Boeotia and quickly produced an anti-Spartan majority. Thus the Thebans, by harbouring Athenian exiles and defying Sparta's demand for their surrender, became indirectly responsible for the overthrow of the Thirty; for during the winter Thrasybulus and about seventy other democrats occupied Phyle, a fortress on Mount Parnes, which like other Attic fortresses had but recently been dismantled. The Thirty sent their whole available force against them, and since the fortress was too inaccessible to be taken by assault, prepared to isolate the occupants by constructing a blockading work and starving them into submission. But severe wintry weather compelled them to desist before their task was finished and they made no further effort to oust Thrasybulus and his companions until the spring of 403. But by that time the army of exiled democrats had increased to ten times its original number. They carried out a surprise attack on an army composed of part of the Lacedaemonian garrison and two squadrons of cavalry who were on guard in the neighbourhood of Phyle to prevent the raids of the democrats. The oligarchs lost 123 men and were driven into flight. Not long afterwards Thrasybulus, whose men now numbered a round thousand, descended on Piraeus. But this was now an open town and his force was not large enough to defend all approaches to it. The democrats therefore encamped on Munychia. A fight between the oligarchs and Thrasybulus' men soon followed, in which the latter routed their opponents, who also by the death of Critias lost their foremost leader. In Athens counsels were divided, but in the end it was decided to replace the Thirty by a smaller body of ten to carry on the direction of the government. Of these only two had been members of the board of Thirty. The remainder of the Thirty withdrew to Eleusis, which they had seized a little while before after massacring the inhabitants. But the Ten and the democrats in Piraeus were unable to come to any understanding. Thrasybulus' army had been swelled not only by many adherents from Piraeus but by disenfranchized residents of Athens who had been driven out of the city by the Thirty. Thus for some months civil war went on fitfully between the two cities. But the democrats were slowly but steadily gaining the upper hand, so that at last the Ten and the Thirty at Eleusis appealed to Sparta to intervene. Naval and military forces were despatched under Lysander to crush the Athenian democrats, but once more a fortunate chance saved Thrasybulus. The blockade of Piraeus by Lysander's forces had hardly been begun when he was superseded by the Spartan king, Pausanias. For some time the opposition to Lysander and his ambitious schemes had been growing at Sparta, and at this juncture, which was so critical for Athens, it became strong enough to effect his recall. Pausanias was pacifically inclined, and after an initial demonstration of force agreed to a truce during which emissaries were sent to Sparta. The Spartan government, after hearing the contending parties, entrusted the settlement to Pausanias and fifteen Spartan commissioners. Thus peace was at last restored in Attica. A general amnesty was proclaimed, from which only the surviving members of the Thirty and Ten, the police commission of the Eleven, and the Ten who had ruled at Piraeus were excluded. Eleusis was to continue a separate state to which those oligarchs who wished could withdraw. With the constitution thereafter to be set up in Athens Pausanias did not interfere, so that a fully democratic *régime* in which all the citizens had political rights again came into being. The party differences which soon made their appearance were of the healthy constitutional type and threatened no renewal of *stasis*. Among the moderate leaders were Thrasybulus, Anytus, and Archinus, while the spokesmen of the extreme democrats were Epicrates and Cephalus. In 401–400, after the Thirty who for two years had been at war with Athens had been cornered and executed, Eleusis was reincorporated in the Athenian state. The Spartan government, which in truth had more pressing internal and foreign problems to solve at that time, made no move to interfere.

## CHAPTER VI

## SPARTA AS AN IMPERIAL STATE

### § 1. SPARTA AND HER EMPIRE

NO one would deny the far-reaching effects of the Peloponnesian War, yet to estimate them justly is far from easy. The accusation of decadence sometimes levelled against the Greeks of the fourth century has as much justification as the same indictment when directed against a whole people at any other period of the world's history, that is, none at all. Intellectual activity during the fourth century found expression in new forms, but it was not for that reason inferior to that manifested in the Age of Pericles, nor was the earlier epoch superior in its material culture, rather to the contrary. And the examples of monarchic rule on the one hand, and, on the other, the increasing number of leagues and federations during the fourth century, are proof that the political life of Hellas, though a record of failures, was at least not stagnant.

We cannot with the inadequate data at our disposal appraise with any accuracy the material consequences of the Peloponnesian War to the various combatants. That Athens among the major states had been the most severe sufferer—quite apart from her ultimate defeat—is not open to doubt. Three episodes—the epidemic during the early years of the war, the disaster in Sicily, and the execution of several thousand of her citizens after Aegospotami—together caused casualties which alone were far in excess of those suffered by any other single combatant during the entire length of the war. Similarly, the expenditure and material losses borne by Athens, partly because she was a naval power, partly because of the greater diversity and more ambitious nature of her undertakings, were incomparably heavier than Sparta's. On the Spartan side no single engagement probably took a heavier toll of lives than Arginusae, when upwards of 12,000 men were drowned. Yet the bulk of the crews in the sixty-nine vessels that were sunk were recruited from the Asiatic cities or islands which only shortly before had joined the enemies of Athens. For the rest, although their losses had at times been appreciable—for instance, on Sphacteria and at Mantinea—neither the Spartans nor the other members of the Peloponnesian League nor yet the Boeotians had kept up a sustained effort all but continuously over twenty-seven years. One can conclude, then, that while the end of the war left all concerned in a condition of partial exhaustion, a few years would have sufficed, given a general absence of hostilities, to restore even the most exhausted states to their former strength and prosperity.

The really irreparable harm done by the Peloponnesian War was neither the wastage of lives nor the impoverishment of the combatants but the destruction of the balance of power in the Hellenic world. The fact that before the war the majority of Greek states were either directly members, or else drawn into the sphere of influence, of one of two groups, headed respectively by Sparta and by Athens, had made for political stability and had promoted the security and prosperity of the smaller states, irrespective of whatever faults and weaknesses may have existed in the Peloponnesian League and the Athenian empire. The defeat of Athens left Sparta with the choice of making good her promise to liberate Hellas or of uniting the majority of Greek states under her own leadership. The former alternative, in view of the pact that had existed with Persia since 412, would have meant going back on the undertaking given to the Great King and to Cyrus. When they bargained away the Asiatic Greeks, so that these became once more the subjects of an Oriental ruler, the claim of the Spartans to be the liberators of the Hellenes was at once seen to be a mockery. And men were not slow to contrast their conduct with that of Athens after the Persian wars. The second alternative was manifestly impossible unless Sparta was prepared drastically to alter her institutions. But her first architect of empire was Lysander, whose method was to perpetuate in peace-time a system of military control and compulsion only tolerable and justifiable under war conditions. Though Lysander was in many ways unlike the average Spartan, he was thoroughly typical of the breed in applying the methods of the Laconian barrack to the problems of imperial government. The late members of the Athenian empire were not treated like the allies in the Peloponnesian League. Many of them had already received garrisons under a Lacedaemonian officer (harmost) during the concluding years of the war; in many others this military occupation followed hard on Sparta's triumph in 405.[1] The really objectionable feature of the Lysandrean *régime* was the general overthrow of democratic constitutions, often, as in Miletus, after a ruthless massacre of democrats, and their replacement by oligarchies. Many of these, moreover, were oligarchies only in name; for, since the government was placed into the hands of boards of ten, whose members, though natives of their cities, were commonly the blind creatures of Lysander, it was in reality a terroristic autocracy, similar in character to the rule of the Thirty at Athens or of the Ten in Piraeus. Such a system of imperial administration could not have lasted, but would have provoked sooner or later a general secession movement amongst the cities. And when, by the end of 403, Lysander's influence at home had declined and he relapsed into a subordinate position, the Spartan government, warned by the numerous complaints that they had received, acquiesced in the substitution of oligarchies of normal type for the detested decarchies. The garrisons with their harmosts drawn at least in part from the enfranchised Helot class ($\nu\epsilon o\delta\alpha\mu\omega\delta\epsilon\hat{\iota}\varsigma$) continued to be maintained.[2] To keep their authority in the maritime dependencies the upkeep of an adequate naval force was essential. Since Persian subsidies were no longer forthcoming, the expense had to be defrayed by levying tribute from the cities themselves. Even if the statement that the amount assessed yearly by Sparta against them exceeded 1000 talents deserves to be regarded with the utmost suspicion,[3] the late subjects of Athens must before long have asked themselves whether they were not worse off under

---

[1] It is probable that the harmosts in the Ionian cities were withdrawn at the end of the war, as by the agreement with Cyrus they passed under Persian control. On the harmosts in general cf. the careful essay by H. W. Parke in *J.H.S.*, L (1930), 37–79.

[2] On Helot harmosts cf. Parke, *op. cit.*, 54 ff.

[3] Only Diodorus (XIV, 10, 2) gives this information.

Spartan than under Athenian control; and further, whether, sentimental considerations apart, their kinsmen living as subjects of the Great King were not in better case.

## § 2. THE EXPEDITION OF CYRUS THE YOUNGER

Meantime the course of events within the Persian empire was destined to add to the difficulties of Sparta in the Aegean area. On the death of Darius II in 404 his elder son, Arsaces, ascended the throne as Artaxerxes II, in spite of the efforts of the queen-mother to secure the succession for Cyrus. Soon after, this prince was accused by Tissaphernes of treasonable designs; through his mother's influence his life was spared and he was sent back to his old command in Asia Minor. Tissaphernes remained on the watch in Lydia. Whatever the extent of his guilt before, Cyrus on returning to the West began secretly to plan the overthrow of his brother. While he hoped to win considerable Oriental support in the western satrapies, he determined that the backbone of his army should be composed of Greeks. He had made not a few friends amongst them during his previous stay in Asia Minor, and with their help he began to raise bodies of mercenaries, though without stating his real objective. Of the 13,000 Greeks enlisted in his service 10,700 were hoplites, the remainder were light infantry. They were drawn from all parts of the Greek world, though more than half seem to have been recruited from Arcadia and Achaea. Sparta, too, sent a contingent at Cyrus' request, although this was never officially admitted by the government. Amongst the Greek commanders the chief was the Spartan Clearchus, who had been military governor of Byzantium but had since been exiled for misconduct. Others were Menon, who commanded the Thessalian detachment, and the Boeotian Proxenus, at whose invitation the young Athenian Xenophon became for a time a soldier of fortune and later the historian of the expedition. The number of Cyrus' Oriental troops is hard to determine; probably they were about as numerous as the Greeks, so that Cyrus' total array at Cunaxa may have amounted to between 25,000 and 30,000 men.[1]

[1] The estimates of Xenophon (100,000: *Anab.*, I, 7, 10) and Diodorus (70,000: XIV, 19, 7) are equally impossible. Cyrus could never have fed so vast a host on his march from Sardes to Mesopotamia.

The expedition started from Sardes in the spring of 401, but the greater portion of the Greek regiments only joined at various points on the march through Phrygia. At this stage Clearchus alone had been apprised of Cyrus' real purpose; the rest were informed that their services had been hired to reduce the hill tribes of Pisidia. The satrap Tissaphernes, however, who had kept himself closely informed of the prince's preparations, suspected the truth. At the head of a troop of 500 cavalry he hastened to Persia to confide his suspicions to the king. One effect of Cyrus' reticence towards his army was that the Greeks, once they began to doubt his veracity, became restive on more than one occasion. By dint of persuasion and several increases in pay Cyrus kept the mercenaries together, but further trouble was caused by the mutual jealousy of the several commanders and their men which once nearly led to a fight between the regiments of Clearchus and of Menon. Cyrus' route lay through Phrygia and Lycaonia into Cilicia and thence by the Cilician gates to Tarsus. The governor of the district offered only formal opposition, sufficient to safeguard himself if Cyrus should fail, while his wife had secretly provided the prince with funds. From Tarsus the army kept close to the coast to Issus and Myriandrus and then struck south-eastwards until it reached and crossed the Euphrates at Thapsacus. The long march on towards Babylon through the desert was attended by many hardships. Baggage animals were lost through famine and the supply of grain for the troops ran so low that they were obliged to abandon their normal vegetarian diet and subsist on meat. When they were not far off the point where they might expect to fall in with the royal army, Cyrus discovered that one of his Oriental generals was plotting to desert to Artaxerxes with a body of cavalry. The officer was tried, found guilty, and executed. When at last they came to the village of Cunaxa, some eighty miles north of Babylon, Cyrus learnt with certainty that his brother was approaching.

His tactical dispositions in preparation for the coming battle were faulty.[1] He assigned the right wing to his Greek regiments under the supreme command of Clearchus, its right flank resting on the river, while the Oriental infantry was

[1] I have followed the interpretation of W. W. Tarn in *C.A.H.*, VI, 7–8.

stationed on the left wing. The centre was taken by Cyrus himself with his body-guard. This arrangement, however, took insufficient account of the invariable disposition of Persian armies, in which the finest troops, composed of the cavalry and mounted guardsmen, commanded by the king in person, occupied the centre. Cyrus was also handicapped by his weakness in cavalry, for he had less than three thousand mounted men. Realizing his tactical mistake when the engagement was about to begin, the prince tried to remedy it by passing the word to Clearchus to incline his battalions to the left, so that they might after all direct their attack against the centre of the enemy. But the Spartan refused to comply, not so much because it was an unusual tactical manœuvre for Greek hoplites, as because by so doing their right flank would cease to rest on the river and would be liable to be rolled up by Artaxerxes' cavalry. Thus, although the Persian left wing was overwhelmed by the Greeks, their advance in pursuit of the enemy created a gap in Cyrus' line, since the troops on Clearchus' left were held by their opponents. At this critical juncture Tissaphernes directed the cavalry squadrons under his command into the gap and retrieved the day. Cyrus, on his part, had with his body-guard charged at that part of the Persian centre where the king himself was; but though Artaxerxes was slightly wounded, Cyrus was killed. As his death became known his Oriental regiments took to flight; and when the Greeks returned from their victorious pursuit they found that the cause was lost and they themselves, though undefeated, were without a leader or a purpose in the heart of a foreign and hostile country (September, 401).

But the presence of the Greeks was an embarrassment also to Artaxerxes. After a parley, in which he failed to induce them to surrender, he entrusted the further conduct of affairs to Tissaphernes. The satrap undertook to escort them on their way homeward by another route which would avoid the desert march, and on which they would have no difficulties with the commissariat. He guided them to Sittace and thence over the Tigris and northwards along that river as far as its tributary, the Greater Zab. But the Greeks were suspicious of the satrap's intentions and at that point Clearchus sought an interview with him. Tissaphernes invited Clearchus and his fellow-generals to a conference on the following day. Unwisely enough they trusted him; for, once they were in his power, he arrested them and sent them off to Susa under escort. There they were executed. The satrap probably calculated that the Greeks, deprived of their senior officers, would at last lay down their arms. But he was mistaken. They elected the Spartan Cheirisophus, Xenophon, and several others to lead them and see them through to the end of the adventure. Then they made their way onwards without serious or organized interference from Tissaphernes until they reached the mountainous country of the Carduchi (Kurdistan). At that point the satrap abandoned the desultory pursuit of the Greeks entirely, no doubt anticipating that climate and the wild hillsmen in the country that they were about to enter would combine to cause their destruction. The march in mid-winter through the highlands of Kurdistan and Armenia deserves to rank amongst the great feats of human endurance in history. At length, in the early spring of 400, 8600 survivors arrived at Trapezus on the Black Sea. Their troubles were not yet over. To the Greek city-states on the Euxine the presence of so large a body of mercenaries could not but seem a menace. Moreover, the solution proposed by Xenophon, that they should settle down and found a new city in those regions, met with little support. After months and various adventures which still further reduced their numbers, they reached Europe partly overland, partly by ship; and, since the Greek cities and the Persian satrap, Pharnabazus, alike would give them no welcome, the majority finally entered the service of the Thracian king Seuthes. Somewhat later these men fought once more against Persia under the command of a Spartan general.

The effect of Cyrus' failure has often been exaggerated, for it seems very doubtful whether, had he taken his brother's place on the throne of Persia, the course of Greek history would have been appreciably altered. At most, it may be surmised, Persia's hold over the Greeks of Asia Minor would have become as complete as before and after the Ionian revolt. But the exploit of the Greek mercenaries in defying Persia and making their way back to the Greek world by hard and devious ways was an episode of great historical significance. It demonstrated the efficiency and endurance

not merely of the Greek hoplite, but of a professional army
as compared with the ordinary citizen militia of the average
city-state, and thereby contributed not a little to the development of mercenary service during the fourth century. It
also showed that the Persian empire was no longer the
formidable power that it had once been, but was vulnerable
to hostile invasion. Regarded in this light, the achievement
of Xenophon and his comrades can claim to have been the
prelude to Alexander's conquest of western Asia.

### § 3. SPARTA AND PERSIA AT WAR

The death of Cyrus and the return of Tissaphernes to his
satrapy reacted swiftly on the political situation in Asia
Minor. Sparta, though unofficially, had lent some aid to
Cyrus; a Spartan had been his most trusted general; above
all, the Asiatic Greeks, with the exception of the Milesians,
had sided with the insurgent prince, so that they might
expect reprisals from Tissaphernes who had been promoted
by Artaxerxes to supersede Cyrus as governor-general in
Asia Minor. In the circumstances their one hope seemed to
be Sparta; but their petition for help placed the Spartan
government in a difficult position. It had undertaken to
acknowledge the suzerainty of Persia over the Asiatic Greeks
and had left Cyrus a free hand to do as he wished. The
demand of Tissaphernes, who inaugurated his new governor-
ship by an unsuccessful attack on Cyme, that Sparta should
support him in carrying the terms of the Spartan-Persian pact
into effect, was reasonable. But whereas Cyrus had been
frankly philo-Laconian, the Spartans' past memories of
Tissaphernes were far from cordial. So they repudiated the
agreement, and in so doing were perhaps not uninfluenced by
the thought that they would be wiping out the stigma which,
in the eyes of a large part of the Hellenic world, attached to
them for having entered into alliance with the traditional
enemy of Greece.

In the winter, 400–399, a Spartan officer, Thibron, was
despatched to Asia with a little over 5000 men. Arrived at
his destination, he raised additional troops from the Greek
cities and in the spring took into his service the 6000 mercenaries of Cyrus who had found the Thracian Seuthes a

poor paymaster. With this army Thibron had some success in Aeolia; but, for a Spartan, he was a poor disciplinarian. The home government, being apprised of his incompetence through the complaints that reached it of excesses committed in the Greek cities by his men, sent out Dercyllidas in his stead. This officer derived advantage from the lack of co-operation amongst the servants of the Great King which had long been a flaw in the Persian imperial administration and which under the irresolute rulers of the fourth century became a chronic weakness. Thus, after patching up a truce with Tissaphernes, Dercyllidas descended with all his available men on the Troad and wrested substantial territory from Pharnabazus, including the fortified city of Scepsis. Best of all for his immediate needs was the capture there of accumulated treasure which sufficed to pay his troops for many months. After wintering in Pharnabazus' satrapy, Dercyllidas in 398 crossed the Hellespont and rebuilt the fortifications on the narrowest portion of the Thracian Chersonese. Later he besieged Atarneus on the mainland opposite to Lesbos. The city had been seized by exiles from Chios who were terrorizing the countryside. After an eight months' siege he reduced the place and, after leaving an officer in charge, moved on into Ionia. At Ephesus orders reached him from home to open hostilities against the main enemy, Tissaphernes; for, after the successes in the Troad, the Spartan government by agreement with the satraps had sent delegates to Susa, hoping that some compromise could be reached which would rid it of further responsibility, while ensuring the independence of the Asiatic Greeks. These conversations came to nothing. Furthermore, in 397 Pharnabazus undertook to co-operate with Tissaphernes. But the campaigning season passed without any military event of importance, and Tissaphernes, says Xenophon, rather than risk an engagement with a Greek army largely made up of those who had served under Cyrus, again proposed a truce.[1]

In truth, there were profounder reasons for the Persian tactics of temporizing. Pharnabazus on a recent visit to Susa had prevailed on Artaxerxes to sanction the equipment of a great naval armament to deprive Sparta of her supremacy

[1] Xenophon, *Hell.*, III, 2, 18.

in the Aegean. The satrap was granted five hundred talents to carry out his plans and proceeded to Cyprus, which was to serve as chief naval base. There he enlisted the assistance of the prince of Salamis, Evagoras, at this time still a loyal feudatory of the Great King; and, with the royal consent, he offered the command of the Persian fleet to the Athenian exile who for eight years had resided at Evagoras' court. Conon gladly accepted the appointment which provided him with an opportunity of trying to avenge the defeat of Aegospotami and which would further, as he hoped, the renascence of the Athenian state and make possible his own return to his native city. The preparations of Pharnabazus were well under way, before the Spartan government learnt of them.[1] A meeting of the Peloponnesian League was summoned, and it was decided to despatch a fresh expeditionary force to Asia. Through the influence of Lysander the command was entrusted to the king who had but recently succeeded to one of the vacant kingships. On the death of Agis in 398 his son, Leotychidas, was set aside, because his legitimacy was questioned. Agesilaus, brother of the late king, was appointed in his place. In that intrigue Lysander had played a leading part, hoping that the new ruler would be content to be a figurehead, while he himself recovered the dominant position in Spartan affairs that he had held during the closing years of the previous century. But it soon became apparent that Agesilaus had no intention of subordinating himself to any man, least of all to Lysander.

In 396 Agesilaus departed for Ephesus with some 8000 men, more than two-thirds of them being taken from the Peloponnesian allies of Sparta. It was significant of the political situation in Greece that both Corinth and Thebes declined to send contingents. When Lysander attempted to make himself the real director of operations, the king made a point of humiliating him before his staff of Spartiate officers, so that Lysander, seeing himself foiled in his aims, was glad to proceed on a mission to the Hellespont. There he did useful work for the Spartan cause. Meantime the king at first renewed the truce made by his predecessor with

---

[1] According to Xenophon (*Hell.*, III, 4, 1) the first information that reached Sparta came from a Syracusan merchant who reported unwonted naval activity in Phoenicia.

Tissaphernes and Pharnabazus. But before the date of its expiry Tissaphernes transgressed the agreement. Thereupon Agesilaus opened hostilities. But instead of attacking Caria, as the enemy expected, he marched into Phrygia and invaded the satrapy of Pharnabazus. Much spoil but no military consequences of importance resulted from this campaign. Agesilaus' cavalry, however, had suffered severely in a brush with the mounted troops of Pharnabazus near Dascylium. While wintering in Ionia, therefore, the king took special pains to strengthen this branch of his army. His foresight was justified in the sequel. When he advanced on Sardes in the spring of 395 and engaged the enemy by the Pactolus River near the capital, the decisive defeat that he inflicted on Tissaphernes' army was primarily due to a force of 1400 cavalry which he had placed in an ambush, with orders to attack the Persians in the rear at a given time. The Persian camp and much spoil were taken, but Agesilaus, though he raided the open country right up to the outskirts of the town, did not venture to assault Sardes itself. Perhaps the most important sequel to the Persian reverse was the recall of Tissaphernes. His failure to achieve results gave a welcome handle to his bitter enemy, the queen-mother Parysatis, who had never forgiven him his enmity to Cyrus. Through her influence Tithraustes was sent in the summer to western Asia. Acting on the royal instructions he arrested his predecessor at Colossae and executed him. Then he opened negotiations with Agesilaus, but the king was disinclined to enter into a permanent agreement on his own responsibility. He therefore would not do more than conclude a six months' truce while the home government was being consulted. Strangely enough the territory administered by Pharnabazus was not held to be exempt from attack under the terms of the truce. The king spent the remainder of the campaigning season in an elaborate raid through Phrygia and Pharnabazus' satrapy of Dascylium. He passed the winter months in that region, intending in the following spring to advance yet further into the interior of Asia Minor; for an interview with the satrap, though marked by courtesies on both sides, was barren of results.[1]

[1] This interview is described in considerable detail by Xenophon (*Hell.,* IV, 1, 29–38) for the purpose of illustrating the chivalrous side of his hero, Agesilaus.

During the years of Agesilaus' stay in Asia the naval preparations of Persia had progressed but slowly. Conon, like other Greek commanders before him, discovered that to be in the service of the Persian government had its drawbacks. Its methods were leisurely, and the absence of harmony between provincial governors made a concerted effort on a large scale difficult of accomplishment. During the first year of his appointment the Athenian admiral's movements were necessarily restricted. With forty vessels he had sailed as far as Caunus in Caria, only to find himself blockaded there for a time by a far stronger Peloponnesian squadron whose headquarters were at Rhodes. The arrival of reinforcements from Cyprus doubled Conon's fleet and raised the blockade. In the summer of 395 a substantial success was achieved. The city-state of Rhodes, which took its name from the island, was a recent foundation. It had come into being about 408 by the synoecism of the three older settlements of Lindus, Camirus, and Ialysus. Governed by an oligarchy, at whose head was the family of the Diagorids, it had rendered valuable help to Sparta in the last years of the Peloponnesian War and had remained an ally thereafter. But the oligarchic *régime* met with increasing opposition from the democratic faction, until finally a conspiracy was formed to overthrow the government. Conon, if not actually the instigator of this plot, was at least privy to it. It succeeded perfectly, although Conon withdrew part of his fleet to Caunus so as not to witness the inevitable bloodshed. The Diagorids and some other prominent oligarchs were massacred—the Spartan fleet had been previously scared away, as it would seem through Conon's naval activity—and a democratic government was set up. Its first act was to repudiate the alliance with Sparta.

With good reason the Spartan government took a serious view of this secession movement, which, in the absence of energetic reprisals by Sparta, was likely to spread to other important cities in the Aegean. Agesilaus was therefore nominated to take over general direction of the naval as well as the military operations. With characteristic energy the king pushed on the construction of new triremes in the dependent cities of Asia Minor, so that by the spring of 394 a fleet of 120 galleys was able to take to the high seas.

Pisander, the king's brother-in-law, was appointed admiral-in-chief, a choice that proved disastrous since, though personally courageous, he was utterly lacking in the experience necessary for so responsible a post.

That same winter (395–394) Conon's difficulties became so acute that he paid a personal visit to Susa. Some months before lack of funds and the clamour of his men whose pay was heavily in arrears had compelled him to seek an interview with Tithraustes and Pharnabazus. The former furnished some financial relief.[1] But before long the Athenian was again in difficulties; and besides, his relations appear to have become strained with some of his Persian officers who resented their subordination to a Greek admiral. His visit to Susa, thanks to the good offices of the Greek physician, Ctesias, who had the ear of the queen-mother, was eminently successful. His plan of campaign was approved and a large sum of money was put at his disposal. At Conon's request Pharnabazus was instructed to share the naval command. Naval building and equipment were now pushed on to such good purpose that by the summer of 394 a large fleet, numbering probably not less than 200 galleys and possibly more, set out to dispute Sparta's naval supremacy in the Aegean. Off the peninsula of Cnidus, Pisander was provoked to risk an engagement. His fleet was utterly defeated, more than sixty of his ships being either captured or sunk. The admiral himself died fighting. The political consequences of Conon's great victory were far-reaching. Cos, Nisyros, Teos, Samos, Chios, Ephesus, Erythrae, Mytilene, and other lesser cities took the opportunity of proclaiming their independence of Sparta. Samos, Cnidus, Iasos, Ephesus, Rhodes, Byzantium, Cyzicus, and Lampsacus concluded a maritime alliance *c.* 393 and issued coins bearing on the obverse a common type, while the reverse was reserved for the type of the issuing city.[2] Sparta's naval hegemony was at an end; more than that, the political situation in the Greek homeland had during the previous months become so threatening that

---

[1] The author of the *Hellenica Oxyrhynchia* (14, ed. Grenfell and Hunt) in chronicling this interview introduces some general comments on the shortcomings of the Great King as a paymaster.

[2] For these coins cf. G. F. Hill, *H.G.C.*, nos. 32 and 33; *C.A.H.*, Plates II, 4 k-p.

the ephors had been forced to recall Agesilaus and his army from Asia.[1]

## § 4. ANTI-SPARTAN COALITIONS IN GREECE

It was inevitable that the adverse effects of the Peloponnesian War on economic life should be widely felt throughout European Greece. In general, however, the social and political structure of the city-states was sufficiently elastic for their economic recovery to be rapid. But Sparta was different. Her institutions had remained virtually unchanged for a century and a half, and nothing was more abhorrent to the ruling class than " to move with the times." Partly from jealousy and distrust, partly as the result of the rigid social-economic system, the number of citizens with full rights had steadily declined. At the beginning of the fourth century there were no more than two thousand of them. On the other hand, the class of Inferiors ($\dot{v}\pi o\mu\epsilon iove\varsigma$), composed of those who through inability to contribute their share to the common messes had forfeited a part of their civic rights, had grown apace. The disparity between rich and poor was further accentuated by the inflow of wealth in the form of spoils won in the war. The treasure brought back to Sparta by Lysander became the property of the state, but some individuals had acquired not a little material wealth for themselves. This was, however, subversive of the communism under which the Spartiates lived, and the government introduced legislation to prohibit the possession of precious metals by citizens. In 397 the growing discontent of the Inferiors nearly brought about a social revolution in Laconia, which would have involved the dependent and serf population as well. But Cinadon, the ringleader, who was one of the Inferiors, was unguarded in his conversation. The ephors got wind of the conspiracy, Cinadon was arrested, and then under torture gave away the names of his chief accomplices. They were promptly rounded up and, like Cinadon himself, were forthwith executed. Thus this particular danger passed. Yet it is surprising that no further attempts were made to overthrow the ruling class. Apart from the effect of Spartan

---

[1] Interesting epigraphical records from this time are an Erythraean degree in honour of Conon (Tod 106) and an Athenian psephism which bears witness to friendly relations between Athens and Carpathus (Tod 110).

discipline enforced from earliest youth, the all but constant warfare, especially in the fourth century, by causing the withdrawal from Laconia and Messenia of a considerable number of Helots, Perioeci, and Inferiors, diverted their minds from their grievances and thereby reduced the risk of revolution.

In addition to domestic problems, the Spartans were faced with a growing opposition to their hegemony in the Peloponnese and beyond. The strained relations with their northwestern neighbours, the Eleans, had resulted in a desultory war between the two states through several seasons (401-399), consisting mainly in predatory raids led by King Agis in person into Elean territory. When the Eleans finally sued for peace they were deprived of considerable tracts of land, including the port of Cyllene, and were required to raze the fortifications of their chief city.

More serious for Sparta was the growth of hostile sentiments among some of her chief allies. As after the peace of Nicias, so at the conclusion of the war, states like Corinth and Thebes felt a justifiable grievance because they had received no return commensurate with their loyal co-operation with Sparta. And, although no immediate movement for secession developed, the latent discontent needed only some external stimulus to break out into active opposition. This was finally provided by Persia; for, as part of a more determined attack on Sparta, the satrap Pharnabazus in 396 sent a Rhodian agent to Greece to distribute largesse and stir up an anti-Spartan movement in Argos, Corinth, Thebes, and Athens.[1] In all these states the anti-Spartan party appears to have been in the ascendant. Corinth and Thebes had declined to support the expedition of Agesilaus to Asia, and the Thebans must have felt both resentment and fear at the activity recently displayed by Lysander at Heraclea in Trachis and in southern Thessaly, where he introduced a Spartan garrison. Athens in her defenceless position had to walk warily. Yet when Conon began his operations under the aegis of Persia, a ship containing arms and equipment

[1] The account in the text follows *Hellenica Oxyrhynchia*, 2, 5. Xenophon (*Hell.*, III, 5, 1) makes Tithraustes responsible; but in that case the mission could not have taken place till late in 395, when general hostilities had already begun in Greece. The version in *Hell. Oxyrh.*, besides presenting no chronological difficulties, receives support from a later source (Polyaenus, I, 48).

was sent off to him secretly. The council was in the plot but subsequently denied complicity; for the most influential politicians, like Thrasybulus and Anytus, in view of the near presence of a Spartan harmost on Aegina, advocated greater caution. A border dispute between the Locrians on the Corinthian Gulf and the Phocians, which was probably instigated by the Boeotians, precipitated more general hostilities; for, when Thebes supported Locris, the Phocians turned to Sparta.

The Spartans were very willing to chastise their recalcitrant ally and determined on a twofold attack, in which one body of troops under Lysander was to operate from Heraclea, while King Pausanias with another army invaded Boeotia from the south. The intervention of Sparta impelled the Thebans to seek their former enemy, Athens, as an ally. The Athenians, who may have been influenced by the news of Conon's early successes as well as by a feeling of gratitude for the protection that the Thebans had afforded Thrasybulus and his fellow exiles nine years before, decided to risk the anger of Sparta. An alliance in perpetuity was therefore concluded between the Boeotians and the Athenians.[1] The Spartan plan of campaign miscarried, even as the venture of Hippocrates and Demosthenes had gone awry in 424, because of a hitch in the prearranged time-table. When Lysander invaded Boeotia from the north his army was augmented by a detachment from the people of Orchomenus, who supported him because they resented the Theban leadership of the Boeotian League. But on his reaching Haliartus, where the army corps from the Peloponnese was to unite with his, Pausanias had not yet arrived. With less than his usual caution, Lysander attacked the town without waiting for his colleague. The Haliartians, with the assistance of a Theban relief expedition, repulsed the enemy and Lysander's troops were forced to retreat to rising ground at some distance from the town. Moreover, they were left without a leader, as Lysander had been one of the casualties of the fight. A day or two later Pausanias appeared on the scene; but by that time Thebes and her ally had been reinforced by an Athenian regiment commanded by Thrasybulus. Consequently the Thebans declined to hand over the corpse of

[1] Cf. Tod 101 for fragments of the agreement.

Lysander until the Spartan king had evacuated Boeotia. To this demand Pausanias felt obliged to agree, and the Spartan venture in central Greece for that year ended ingloriously. Pausanias, sensing the temper of the home government, did not himself return to Laconia, but retired to Tegea, where he ended his days as an exile.

The union between Thebes and Athens was now enlarged to a quadruple alliance by the adherence of Argos and Corinth. The Thebans captured Heraclea in Trachis and the anti-Spartan coalition in Greece was further strengthened when several new allies from amongst the lesser states joined.[1] When the campaigning season of 394 opened the allies mustered at the Isthmus of Corinth with a view to barring the advance of a Lacedaemonian army. Close to Corinth an engagement was fought which in a strictly military sense was indecisive; for, though the losses of Sparta and her allies were far lighter than those of their opponents, they failed to force the passage across the Isthmus.[2] Late that summer Agesilaus entered Boeotia, after having skirmished his way through Thessaly where anti-Spartan feeling ran high. Under the walls of Coronea his army, swelled by some troops from Laconia transported by sea across the Gulf, by Phocians and by Orchomenians, engaged an army made up of Boeotians, Argives, Corinthians, Athenians, Locrians, and some small units from the Sperchius valley and Euboea. Although Agesilaus, who was himself wounded in the battle, remained the victor at the end of the day, the honours of battle rested with the Theban regiments. In spite of heavy losses, they withdrew in good order.[3] The Lacedaemonian army retired into Phocis and subsequently crossed to the Peloponnese by water, since the land route to the Isthmus was blocked.

The Spartans were now in a tight place. Fortunately for them no other members of the Peloponnesian League followed

---

[1] Cf., for example, the treaties made by Athens with the Opuntian Locrians and with Eretria (Tod 102 and 103).

[2] For Athenian funeral inscriptions relating to this war, cf. Tod 104 and 105.

[3] Diodorus (XIV, 84, 2) puts the Spartan losses at 350, those of their opponents at 600. Xenophon (*Hell.*, IV, 3, 15-20) gives no figures, and his account of the battle, in which he may have fought himself on the Spartan side, is singularly unsatisfactory.

the example of Corinth. That circumstance and their iron discipline which was never more striking than in adversity saved them from disaster. Yet their difficulties were formidable; for, apart from the fact that the campaigns in Greece during 395 and 394 had brought them only Pyrrhic victories, the naval defeat off Cnidus, of which Agesilaus had received intelligence on the eve of Coronea, in addition to its effects in the Aegean, had repercussions in Greece itself. Thus in 393 the Persian fleet cruised in Hellenic waters and raided the Peloponnesian coast. Then, while the satrap returned to Asia, he entrusted the bulk of his fleet to his Greek colleague with the understanding that he should use it and a considerable sum of money provided by Pharnabazus to promote the restoration of Athens. Even before 393 the Athenians had begun the reconstruction of their fortifications.[1] But fear of Sparta and an exhausted exchequer had been obstacles to rapid progress with the work. Conon was received with enthusiasm by his countrymen, and the rebuilding of the Piraeus defences and of the Long Walls was pushed on with such energy that they were completed before the year drew to its close. The recovery of a fortified naval base was followed by a swift increase in the political influence of Athens. She recovered Scyros, Lemnos, and Imbros, islands that had been amongst her earliest extra-Attic possessions. Within a very short time the Athenians were strong enough to take an active part both by land and sea in the war against Sparta.

## § 5. THE KING'S PEACE

An early and unequivocal settlement with Persia seemed to the Spartan government the most pressing need, and, since Tiribazus was disposed to be friendly, the chances of success appeared to be good. When an Athenian delegation headed by Conon arrived in Asia Minor to undermine the influence of Sparta, the satrap promptly arrested the Athenian commander. However, the tentative agreement arranged by Tiribazus and the Spartan plenipotentiary, Antalcidas, during the winter of 393-392 was not sanctioned by the Great King.

---

[1] Cf. the inscriptions given in Tod 107, the former belonging to 395-394, the latter to 394-393. Clearly the defence works at Piraeus were first taken in hand.

Tiribazus was superseded by Struthas and the war in Asia dragged on for five more seasons. The Spartan officers who were sent out to operate in that theatre of war had some successes and some reverses, while the conduct of the war on the Persian side was half-hearted. The most spectacular gains, though they were not to be enduring, were won by Athens. Conon, it is true, passed from the scene. He had escaped from captivity and once more sought the hospitality of his old friend Evagoras. Shortly afterwards he died (c. 388). In 389 Thrasybulus with a fleet of forty triremes cruised in the northern Aegean and revived the maritime league of Athens by winning as allies, Byzantium, Chalcedon, the Thracian Chersonese, Thasos, and Samothrace. By the establishment of friendly relations also in Chios, Lesbos, Clazomenae Athenian influence once more began to be felt in Ionia, and Thrasybulus was strong enough to reintroduce the five per cent toll on merchandise which had become familiar during the last stage of the Peloponnesian War.[1] A surprise attack of an Athenian force operating from the Chersonese and directed by Iphicrates ended in the defeat and death of a Spartan harmost and gave the Athenians control of the entry into the Hellespont. In some degree the Athenian successes were furthered, as in Lesbos, by Pharnabazus. It was therefore unfortunate that Evagoras of Cyprus, who had openly rebelled against his overlord, Artaxerxes, now asked for Athenian support. In view of his past favours the Athenians, who some years before had formally voted their thanks to him and bestowed their citizenship upon him,[2] could hardly do other than send him some support; but indirectly they were playing into the hands of Sparta by antagonizing the Persian king. It was, further, a grave misfortune that in 388 Athens lost her ablest man, Thrasybulus—a combination of statesman and soldier more characteristic of the fifth century than of the fourth. The more lawless elements of his troops abused the inhabitants of Aspendus, which he visited in process of seeking to enlarge the maritime alliance, and in revenge certain of the townspeople murdered him one night.

Meanwhile the war in the Greek homeland had continued

---

[1] Cf. Tod 114 with the reference to τὴν ἐπὶ Θρασυβούλου εἰκοστήν.
[2] Cf. the fragmentary decree, Tod 109.

fitfully and indecisively. Most of the fighting took place in
the neighbourhood of Corinth which had entered into a close
federal union with Argos. In the end the Spartans, by capturing Lechaeum, the Corinthian port, were able to keep open
the passage from the Peloponnese to Boeotia. But they also
suffered reverses, the effect of which was still more to diminish
their already waning military reputation. Of these defeats
the one that perhaps impressed contemporary Greek opinion
most was inflicted almost under the walls of Corinth by the
Athenian Iphicrates with a body of light infantry (peltasts),
supported by some hoplites. By repeated skirmishing he
inflicted heavy losses on a Spartan regiment of hoplites, six
hundred strong, and eventually routed the survivors (summer,
390). It has already been seen how the same officer in the
following year effectively used 1200 peltasts in the Hellespont.
It was some solace to Spartan pride that in 388 Agesilaus led
a successful expedition into Acarnania and compelled its
people to become the allies of Sparta. In 387 the Athenian
Chabrias, by a well executed raid on the island, at last put a
stop to the interference with Athenian merchantmen which
the Spartan harmost on Aegina had maintained very effectively for several seasons. Yet a graver danger threatened
the food supply of Attica, when the blockade of Abydos that
Iphicrates was maintaining was turned by a Spartan fleet
into a blockade of the Athenian commander. On that occasion
the Spartans were reinforced by twenty Syracusan galleys
sent by Dionysius I, with whom Sparta had concluded an
alliance some years before.[1] The Athenians, faced by the
danger of partial starvation, were thereupon very ready to
come to terms with their old enemy.

Sparta was at last nearing the attainment of the objective
for which she had striven for six years. In 387 Antalcidas
was once more despatched to treat with Persia, and his
reception by Tiribazus was cordial. The Great King was
finally prevailed upon to sanction a settlement, while
Pharnabazus, whose hostility to Sparta had hitherto been
the chief obstacle to peace, was recalled to Susa. With

[1] The date of the alliance is uncertain but it was earlier than 394–393,
for in that year the Athenians, at the instance of Conon, pronounced a
laudatory decree on Dionysius and sent a delegation to Syracuse hoping to
win him as an ally. In this they failed, although Dionysius at that time
promised not to help Sparta actively. Cf. Lysias, XIX, 20; Tod 108.

Athens anxious to end the war, the rest of the anti-Spartan coalition in Greece was not in a position to carry on the struggle. Thus in the late autumn delegates from the various city-states obeyed the summons of Tiribazus to a congress at Sardes. There the satrap read the manifesto which the Greek historian has briefly summarized in these terms:

> Artaxerxes the king deems it just that the city-states in Asia and the islands of Clazomenae and Cyprus be his; and that the rest of the Greek city-states, small and great, be left independent by him, save Lemnos, Imbros, and Scyros. These shall belong to Athens as of yore. Whosoever shall reject this peace, against them I, together with those who are of my mind, will make war by land and sea, with my fleet and my wealth.[1]

At the beginning of 386 the several Greek states ratified the treaty by oath, the reluctance of Corinth and of Thebes being overcome by Agesilaus' threat of immediate mobilization against them.

It is usual to describe the King's Peace as a deep humiliation for the Greeks, since, instead of a settlement by negotiation, they were forced to submit to the ukase of an Oriental despot. That was certainly the view of publicists, like Isocrates, but it may be questioned whether such bitter feelings were general. The Asiatic Greeks, after their experience first of Athenian and then of Spartan rule, both of which had involved them in frequent and costly wars, may well have looked forward under Persian suzerainty to peace and prosperity such as they had not known for half a century or more. In Greece the odium that the Spartans might have incurred for making Artaxerxes the arbiter of Greek affairs was more than offset by two very positive gains. They were freed from a ruinous war of attrition on two fronts and they knew that they had complete liberty to enforce the terms dictated by the Great King according to their liking. The history of the decade and a half that followed the King's Peace is the story of the misuse that they made of their prerogative. As for the leading members of the anti-Spartan coalition, Argos and Corinth, apart from a certain injury to their pride, were not substantially harmed, although the close

[1] Xenophon, *Hell.*, V, 1, 31.

political union of the two states had to be abandoned. Corinth not long after seems to have been constrained to rejoin the Peloponnesian League.[1] The states that had lost most by the peace were Athens and Thebes. The former had, indeed, won the concession of retaining the three islands in the northern Aegean, but the maritime league brought into being by the energy of Thrasybulus came to an abrupt end. This loss, apart from its political aspects, plunged the Athenian government once more into the financial difficulties that were to become chronic in the fourth century. Worst of all was the experience of the Thebans, who saw themselves deprived at one blow of their hegemony in Boeotia, and had to acquiesce in the disruption of the political structure that they had built up during the past half century. Sparta's short-sighted policy towards her former ally in central Greece —Agesilaus seems to have been primarily responsible for it— was to prove her own undoing.

### § 6. SPARTAN POLICY IN GREECE

It was not long before the Spartan government showed the world in what manner it proposed to interpret the provisions of the King's Peace. While paying lip-service to the principle that every *polis* should be autonomous, it did not hesitate to bring states into alliance with Sparta, if necessary by force, to secure a pro-Spartan policy in cities by setting up oligarchies, and in one case to break up a flourishing league, ostensibly because it violated the terms of the peace, actually because its continuance was regarded as a potential danger to Spartan interests.

The first example of Sparta's high-handed policy occurred in 386. On quite inadequate grounds an ultimatum was presented to the Mantineans requiring them to raze their fortifications. When they refused, Agesilaus' colleague, King Agesipolis, laid siege to the Arcadian city. By damming at its lower end a stream which ran through Mantinea, he caused a flood which helped to undermine the walls of sun-dried brick and hastened its capitulation. Mantinea was broken up into five villages, that is, it reverted to the loose political organization existing prior to the synoecism of *c.* 460. That,

---

[1] This may be inferred from an allusion to the Corinthians in Xenophon (*Hell.*, V, 3, 27).

however, was not all, for each village was required to furnish a contingent of troops to Sparta and these were under the supervision of Spartan officers (ξεναγοί). Soon after, the people of Phlius were peremptorily bidden to recall their oligarchic exiles. The order was obeyed; but, as the Spartans had doubtless foreseen, the return of the exiles in a little while led to *stasis*. In 381 Agesilaus intervened and blockaded the city which held out for twenty months. When it finally surrendered, a Spartan garrison was placed in the town, while a commission decided on the fate of the leading democrats and framed a new constitution favourable to the oligarchs.

Of deeper significance for an understanding of Sparta's narrowly selfish policy were contemporary events in Chalcidice and Macedonia. The Macedonian kingdom had increased greatly in political stability and in material prosperity under its able ruler Archelaus (c. 413–399).[1] On his death, however, dynastic quarrels and attacks by the half-civilized Illyrian neighbours of Macedonia reduced that kingdom to anarchy. Hence when Amyntas III ascended the throne in 393–392, he was confronted with a task of exceptional difficulty and peril.[2] Needing a substantial ally against the Illyrians he opened negotiations with the Olynthian League.[3] This federation, centred originally in Olynthus, had steadily grown since its inception, and at the time when Amyntas became king it embraced many of the cities of the Chalcidic peninsula. A treaty for fifty years was concluded between the king and the League, either party undertaking to assist the other in case of an attack on its territory. Alliances with states outside, whether in Chalcidice or elsewhere, were only to be formed by either side after a mutual agreement with the other. The treaty further lays down regulations regarding the export of timber. Almost immediately after these negotiations Amyntas appears to have been forced by an Illyrian invasion to flee from his kingdom. But the danger passed as rapidly as it had come, and the king regained his throne. He received more help from Thessaly at that time than from the Chalcidic League, although he had temporarily ceded some Macedonian territory to the latter as a guarantee of

[1] For the reign of Archelaus see below, p. 220.
[2] Cf. F. Geyer, *Makedonien bis zur Thronbesteigung Philipps II*, pp. 108–115; for the Chalcidic League, cf. Larsen, *Representative Government*, pp. 42–45.
[3] A portion of the treaty has survived. See Tod 111.

good faith to his allies. Thus a number of coastal towns on
the Gulf of Therma and even Pella in the interior joined the
federation of which Olynthus was the head. Contemporaneously efforts were made to enlarge the League by winning
over coastal towns eastwards of the Chalcidic peninsula.
While some joined, two at least, Acanthus and Apollonia,
declined; and when they feared coercion, they laid a complaint before the Spartan government. Intervention from
that quarter might have been delayed or even denied, had
not Amyntas soon after demanded back the communities in
Lower Macedonia recently enrolled in the League. But
Olynthus and her allies were now disinclined to weaken the
organization by abandoning the cities on the Thermaic Gulf.
They refused Amyntas' legitimate demands and entered into
communication with Thebes and Athens. Their action drove
the Macedonian king into the arms of Sparta. The appeal
of Amyntas, following hard on the protests of Apollonia and
Acanthus, induced the Spartan government to declare war
on a federation which seemed to be becoming dangerously
strong and which could be interpreted as a contravention of
the King's Peace. An advance force of 2000 enfranchized
Helots under Eudamidas was despatched to the north in
382. The war against the Chalcidic League lasted until 379,
when Olynthus was at last forced to capitulate. But the
venture had cost Sparta dearly, for two additional expeditionary forces had been needed to win the war, casualties had
been heavy, one Spartan commander had fallen in battle,
and the king, Agesipolis, died of fever in 380. The federation
was broken up and each of its constituent members was
enrolled as an ally of Sparta, with the obligation of furnishing
troops when required. Lower Macedonia, however, passed
back under the control of Amyntas. Sparta's action in
destroying this federal union in the north was not only indefensible in itself but exceedingly bad statecraft; for the only
power capable of profiting by the destruction of the Chalcidic
League was Macedonia, once the internal government of that
kingdom had been stabilized.

But the most shocking abuse of power of which Sparta
was guilty in the opinion of ancients and moderns alike was
her unprovoked attack on Thebes. A Spartan officer,
Phoebidas, while passing through Boeotia in 382 with

reinforcements destined for the Lacedaemonian army in Chalcidice, entered into conversations with the leader of an oligarchic minority in Thebes named Leontiadas. A plot was hatched to admit the troops of Phoebidas into the Cadmea, the citadel of Thebes, on the festival of the Thesmophoria. As this was a women's festival, the men of Thebes on that day were rigidly excluded from the Cadmea. The treachery of Phoebidas and Leontiadas succeeded perfectly. The women were rounded up without opposition and then held as hostages for the good conduct of their male relatives. The next step was to arrest the leader of the democratic party, Ismenias, who was subsequently arraigned on a charge of medism and put to death. The conduct of the Spartan government leaves no room for doubt that Agesilaus, and perhaps the ephors also, were privy to the plot. For, though Phoebidas was deposed from his command and fined, the Spartans decided to hold the Cadmea with a Lacedaemonian garrison, while the oligarchs ruled the city in the interests of Sparta. The mass of the Thebans were too cowed to offer any opposition, the more so as they could expect no aid from other Boeotian towns. But some three hundred of the democratic faction had escaped at the outset and taken refuge in Athens. With pro-Spartan oligarchies already existing in Thespiae, Orchomenus, and Plataea, which had been restored soon after 387 by bringing back against their will survivors of the old city and their descendants, Sparta's control of this region in central Greece was irresistible.

The Athenians, unable to risk a single-handed struggle against their old enemy, were very circumspect in their foreign policy. They entered into alliance with Chios, but it is noticeable that its terms were so framed that they could in no way be interpreted as contravening the King's Peace.[1] Friendly relations with a Thracian prince of the Odrysae are attested by a decree passed in his honour.[2] It was a tentative effort of the Athenians to recover influence in an area where their control had once been unquestioned. An alliance with Olynthus just before the first Spartan expedition remained without result.[3] But after 387 they were unable to help their old friend Evagoras of Cyprus. He received valuable

---

[1] Tod 118.      [2] Tod 117.
[3] Only a small and mutilated fragment of this treaty survives (Tod 119).

support from Egypt which revolted from Persia in 386. For
a short time he gained control of almost the whole of Cyprus,
only to lose it again when Persia made a more determined
effort to regain the island. Finally in 380 he came to terms
and became once more the vassal of the Great King. This
war is mainly of interest because it demonstrates the military
weakness of Persia at this date, for it is surely remarkable
that Artaxerxes only recovered Cyprus after a decade of
fighting and at an enormous cost. Evagoras lived on until
374. He was succeeded by his son, Nicocles, the friend and
in some sense the pupil of the Athenian educator and political
thinker, Isocrates. Though thoroughly Greek in sentiment
and culture like his father, Nicocles seems to have been
greatly Evagoras' inferior in both military and political
ability.

### § 7. THE RISE OF THEBES AND THE SECOND ATHENIAN CONFEDERACY

By the summer of 379 the power of Sparta in Greece may
be said to have reached its zenith. The outward form of the
Peloponnesian Confederacy was maintained, but her control
extended across central Greece from eastern Locris and
Boeotia to Acarnania in the west. Some of the Thessalian
cities or their oligarchic factions sought to maintain a pro-
Spartan policy as a safeguard against tyranny; and in the
far north the cities of the Chalcidic League had become
dependencies. It was a significant innovation that the
Spartan government now permitted her so-called allies in
many cases to substitute cash payments for military service.
The monies thereby raised could under the rapidly changing
conditions of warfare in the fourth century be effectively
used to hire mercenaries in time of war. To administer the
new system, as well as to facilitate the general supervision
of the empire, the Spartans arranged their " allies " in ten
groups.[1]

[1] They are given as follows by Diodorus (XV, 31, 2): 1, Lacedaemon;
2 and 3, Arcadia; 4, Elis; 5, Achaea; 6, Corinth and Megara; 7, Sicyon,
Phlius, and some communities in the Argolid independent of Argos; 8,
Acarnania; 9, Phocis and Locris; 10, Olynthus and other communities in
Thrace. Diodorus, who relates the organization under the year 378, omits
Boeotia, where the fight for freedom from Sparta had begun in the previous
winter.

But Sparta's imperial structure was built on sand and at the first serious shock began to crumble. In the winter of 379–378 the plans of the Theban exiles at Athens were ready for a determined effort to liberate their native city. In view of the presence of Spartan garrisons in Plataea and Thespiae the utmost secrecy was necessary. The Athenians, though not officially involved, were sympathetic, and two of the generals assembled a body of troops and led them to the Attic frontier. Seven Thebans, led by Melon and Pelopidas, entered Boeotia and managed to enter Thebes in disguise. They lodged with a fellow citizen who was a strong patriot. Yet even so the conspiracy could hardly have succeeded, had not the secretary to two of the polemarchs, Phyllidas, lent his aid. He gave a banquet to the leading magistrates and then introduced the conspirators in female disguise, but armed with daggers. Then the three oligarchs were struck down, and subsequently Leontiadas and another leading oligarch suffered a similar fate. The next step was to proceed to the prison and free and arm the prisoners. In the morning a mass meeting of the citizens was called and Melon, Pelopidas, and their late host, Charon, were elected Boeotarchs. Messengers were despatched to Attica, and the rest of the Theban exiles together with a number of Athenian volunteers hastened to Thebes. Meanwhile the Spartan commanders of the garrison had communicated with their colleagues in Thespiae and Plataea. But the troops sent out from these two towns were waylaid and driven back by the Thebans, who next prepared to besiege the garrison on the Cadmea. It is a matter of surprise that the officers in charge agreed to evacuate Thebes, provided they were allowed to withdraw unmolested. Thus the Thebans regained the full control of their city and put to death some of the principal supporters of the Spartan *régime*. Of the three officers lately in command of the garrison at Thebes two were put to death and the third was exiled by the Spartan government. Its action was justifiable, for a garrison fifteen hundred strong should have been able to hold the fortress at Thebes until a Spartan army could come to its assistance. The Spartan king, Cleombrotus, next invaded Boeotia with a Peloponnesian army. It was no more than a military demonstration without concrete results and lasted little more than a

fortnight. Then he withdrew, leaving a portion of his men
to strengthen the garrison at Thespiae. Sparta also lodged a
protest at Athens and demanded that the generals who had
actively helped the Thebans be severely punished. The
Athenian government was still sufficiently intimidated to
obey. One of the two *strategi* was tried and executed, the
other made good his escape across the frontier before it was
too late. The restored democracy at Thebes also did not feel
too sure of itself and attempted to negotiate with Sparta.
But the Spartans refused their offer to join the Peloponnesian
League and prepared for further hostilities. The only hope
of the Thebans now seemed to be an alliance with Athens,
but the Spartans had foreseen this possibility and had sent
delegates to Athens to secure her neutrality or, if possible,
her active co-operation. It is difficult to say what the outcome of these negotiations might have been under normal
circumstances. They were completely wrecked by the precipitate and apparently unauthorized action of the Spartan
general commanding the garrison in Thespiae, Sphodrias, who
invaded Attica under cover of night and attempted to seize
Piraeus. The scheme failed and Sphodrias was forced to
beat a hasty retreat back into Boeotia. The Athenians
promptly arrested the Spartan delegates and only released
them on the understanding that Sphodrias be severely
punished. But the Spartan government, swayed by the
unscrupulous insistence of Agesilaus, later acquitted him.
The political results of this episode were momentous. The
Athenians were now very ready to listen to their philo-Theban
politicians and concluded an alliance with Thebes. In the
remaining military operations in Boeotia during 378 an
Athenian force under Chabrias co-operated with the Theban
army and foiled the attempt of Agesilaus and a Peloponnesian
army to reduce Thebes. Even more noteworthy, however,
was the resumption by the Athenians of their plans to found
a new maritime league. Amongst the charter members of the
new confederacy were Rhodes, Chios, Byzantium, Thebes,
and a few others; for Mytilene and Methymna on Lesbos
and Chalcis in Euboea joined early in 377.[1] In that year,
moreover, a more general invitation was sent to the Aegean

---

[1] Cf. Tod 121 (Byzantium); 124 (Chalcis); 122 (Methymna).

islands and to northern Greek communities. Before the end of the official Attic year, 378–377, the Athenian people ratified the terms to which they had agreed when the confederacy was inaugurated a few months earlier. This decree, proposed by a certain Aristoteles, has happily survived, and on it our knowledge of the league primarily depends.[1] Some years later—the precise year is uncertain—a rider which is unfortunately lost was added, and on the reverse of the stone is a supplementary list of members. From the available evidence it would seem that within three or four years the membership roll of the confederacy contained the names of some sixty city-states.[2]

The formulated purpose of the Second Athenian Confederacy was " to compel the Spartans to allow the Greeks to live in freedom and in enjoyment of autonomy and in secure possession of their territory." Any state was at liberty to join, provided it was not subject to the Great King, so that the Asiatic Greeks were automatically excluded. To have done otherwise would inevitably have provoked a new alliance between Persia and Sparta and would have ruined at the outset the chances of the League to survive. The Athenians specially bound themselves to renounce all claim to any landed property in the territory of the allies and declared any future attempt to acquire such property illegal. In the main this was a guarantee that they would not try to revive the cleruchies which had been the most unpopular feature of their earlier empire. A fear that the history of the Delian Confederacy might be repeated doubtless accounts for the existence of two theoretically sovereign authorities in the League, for the allies had their own federal council from which the Athenians were excluded. In this council each ally had but one vote. The council met in Athens and it is not improbable that the official delegates resided there permanently. In the early years of the confederacy it is clear that any measure of importance required the ratification of

---

[1] The failure of Xenophon to relate the formation of the confederacy is one of the most glaring omissions in his *Hellenica*. The account of Diodorus (XV, 29–30) is inaccurate and vague and would be of little use without the epigraphic evidence. For the decree see Tod 123.

[2] Diodorus (loc. cit.) speaks of seventy cities besides Athens who were members in 377, that is, he wrongly ascribes to the first year of the League a list of allies which was not a reality before c. 373.

this council and of the Athenian assembly.[1] A federal treasury was instituted to which each ally contributed; but the amounts of these payments (συντάξεις) separately or in bulk are unknown.[2] The executive of the League was from the beginning in Athenian hands, so that it devolved on the *strategi* to undertake the supreme command of the naval and military forces of the federation and to carry out whatever policy had been decided by the Congress of the allies and the Athenian assembly. Any person who tried to stultify the provisions of the League was to be tried " by the Athenians and the allies." It is uncertain whether such cases came before a joint court or whether, as is perhaps more probable, the allies tried only offenders in their respective territories. Certain weaknesses in this confederacy, which unlike the Confederacy of Delos was purely defensive, are at once apparent. It was an error to label it as an anti-Spartan organization in view of the frequent and sometimes violent shifts in the balance of power among the states of European Greece. It was not conducive to efficiency that there were two sovereign bodies, the Congress of the allies, and the Athenian assembly, in control. The truly federal solution would have been a single Congress with proportionate representation according to the size and importance of the constituent members, of which Athens would have been one. Even as the League was constituted, it would have been more equitable if the voting power in the Congress of the allies had been proportionate. Lastly, it was regrettable, though probably inevitable, that the executive power was vested entirely in the Athenians; for it was this more than any other cause which enabled Athenian politicians in time to exceed their legal powers, and ultimately plunged Athens in a disastrous war which deprived her permanently of her most powerful maritime allies.

While the Athenians were thus fully occupied the balance of power on the mainland was undergoing a gradual change. A second invasion of Boeotia by Agesilaus was met by the

[1] Corcyra became a member in 375–374. See Tod 127, lines 11–15: πόλεμον δὲ καὶ εἰρήνην μὴ ἐξεῖναι Κορκυραίοις ποιήσασθαι ἄνευ Ἀθηναίων καὶ τοῦ πλήθους τῶν συμμάχων· ποιεῖν δὲ καὶ τἆλλα κατὰ τὰ δόγματα τῶν συμμάχων.

[2] Isolated statements regarding the total funds collected from the allies are to be found in the orators (cf. Demosth., 18, 234; Aeschines, 2, 71), but they refer to the declining years of the League.

Thebans with some Athenian support in the same defensive way as before, so that the Spartan king returned home without any positive achievement. Then, in 376, the Peloponnesian army was commanded by Cleombrotus; but on reaching Cithaeron he found that the enemy had occupied all the passes into Boeotia strongly and he did not venture to force a passage. It became increasingly clearer that the Spartan method of annual invasions during the campaigning season, while during the rest of the year only one or two relatively weak garrisons were stationed in the country, was wholly inadequate to ensure Spartan control over Boeotia. Nothing but a permanent army of occupation could have coerced all that area into obedience. It was under the influence of their fight for freedom and under the inspired leadership of two men, Epaminondas and Pelopidas, that the Thebans at this time introduced military reforms whose full effect was not appreciated by their enemies for some years to come. The creation of a special corps of 300 hoplites taken from the best families of Thebes was a noteworthy innovation, for it gave Thebes a guards regiment of professional soldiers in addition to her ordinary citizen-militia.[1]

Foiled in their attempts to crush Thebes, the Spartans in 376 tried to strike an effective blow at Athens and her new maritime allies. A fleet of sixty-five galleys was equipped and entrusted to the Spartan nauarch, Pollis. His immediate orders were apparently to blockade the Saronic Gulf and confront the Athenians with the spectre of famine. But Chabrias was sent off with eighty-three triremes to frustrate this plan and rescue the grain ships from Pontus which had reached the vicinity of Cape Sunium. A naval battle was fought in the straits between Naxos and Paros in which the Athenians displayed their old naval superiority (September, 376). The Spartans lost more than half their fleet, while only eighteen of the Athenian ships were sunk or disabled. Impressed by Chabrias' prowess, most, if not all, the Cyclades enrolled as members of the League, and the Athenian admiral returned in triumph to Athens with many prisoners and

---

[1] The formation of this Sacred Band, as it was called, was due to one of the Boeotarchs for the year 378. On him and on the significance of this reform from a military point of view cf. H. W. Parke, *Greek Mercenary Soldiers*, pp. 91–92.

prize vessels and with the substantial sum of 160 talents in cash. In the following year the Athenians put out a great effort to enlarge the confederacy further and at the same time to deprive Sparta of some of her dependencies. Their two ablest admirals were chosen for the purpose. Chabrias sailed for Thrace and won over Thasos, Samothrace, Abdera, and other cities to the League, including in all likelihood the cities that formerly had belonged to the Chalcidic League.[1] At the same time Timotheus operated in western Greece. In addition to defeating a Peloponnesian squadron, he persuaded Corcyra, Cephallenia, and the Acarnanian cities to join Athens. But if the Athenians were fortunate in possessing two commanders of more than average ability they were all the while hampered by lack of funds. This circumstance and a growing estrangement with Thebes disposed them to seek an understanding with Sparta in 374. By this time the energy and military successes of Epaminondas and Pelopidas had brought all but three of the Boeotian cities together once more to form a league under Theban guidance. Indeed the recreated Boeotian Confederacy appears to have partaken more of the character of a single state with Thebes as the seat of government.[2] The partial sacrifice of independence made by the other cities was more than compensated for by the greater military and political security which resulted for all. It was small wonder that to the Athenians their northern neighbours, who had recently refused to contribute money towards the cost of Timotheus' campaigns in the west and were also casting covetous eyes on the Athenian border town of Oropus, seemed a greater danger than Sparta. The negotiations between Sparta and Athens towards the end of 374 led to a treaty of peace, but it was broken almost immediately by Timotheus' action in supporting a body of democratic exiles in Zacynthus against the ruling oligarchy. As Sparta's protests in Athens were ignored, war was resumed. The Spartans, with some help from Syracuse, now made a determined effort to recover Corcyra. The Athenians, at the urgent request of the Corcyraeans, deputed Timotheus to sail

---

[1] The Chalcidians in Thrace appear in the list of members appended to the decree of Aristoteles (Tod 123).

[2] For the Boeotian coins of this period bearing a uniform type and the name of the responsible Boeotarch see G. F. Hill, *H.G.C.*, no. 36. Cf. also below, p. 369.

west. But it was left to him to raise the necessary men and money from amongst the allies, a difficult task, seeing that the states in the Aegean were not unnaturally unwilling to support a venture in the north-west in which their interests were not in the least involved. Great delay ensued for which Timotheus was held responsible. He was deprived of his command and impeached on his return to Athens. He owed his acquittal mainly to the intercession of the Thessalian prince, Jason of Pherae, and his vassal, Alcetas ruler of Epirus. Both were personal friends and both at this time members of Athens' maritime League. Iphicrates was appointed to succeed Timotheus in the west, and with such limited resources as he could raise had some successes; but the Corcyraeans were by this time out of danger, since the Spartans had abandoned their operations against the island. In Athens the general regret at the failure of the peace of 374 grew apace as Thebes gained possession of Thespiae and Plataea. When the Plataeans rather than join the Boeotian federation planned to ally themselves closely with Athens, as their forebears had done, they were forcibly expelled by a Theban force and compelled to seek the hospitality of Athens. To the Spartans the growth of the political and military power of Thebes also seemed a more formidable menace than the League of which Athens was the head. For the interests of Athens and her allies were maritime and did not threaten the position of Sparta as head of the Peloponnesian League. Moreover, recent developments in northern Greece made it not unlikely that Thebes would soon find a powerful ally in that quarter. To these we must now turn.

### § 8. JASON OF PHERAE

Thessaly was one of those areas in Greece whose continuous history is utterly obscure. Very occasionally an oblique light is shed for a few years on its fortunes, generally because they impinge on those of other and better known Greek states. From ancient times the country had been governed by aristocratic clans and families which formed a minority and held the rest of the population in political subjection. In earlier days this dependent majority was made up mainly of agricultural serfs ($\pi\epsilon\nu\acute{\epsilon}\sigma\tau\alpha\iota$), for at that time the organization of the four divisions of Thessaly proper and of outlying regions under Thessalian control (περιοικὶς) was tribal. The immediate government was normally in the hands of a single ruler belonging to a principal clan, like the Aleuadae at Larissa or the Echecratidae at Pharsalus. By the beginning of the fifth century that organization had given place to one that was essentially urban, but the steps in what must have been a gradual transformation can no longer be traced. Certain other changes are adequately attested. The civic, as distinct from the rural population, though still lacking political influence, enjoyed a somewhat freer status, comparable perhaps to that of the Perioeci in Laconia and Messenia. In place of a despot the government passed at times into the hands of an oligarchy composed of the aristocratic clans. Again, the political unity of the country under the presidency of a military head (τάγος), which had existed, if not continuously, at least for periods of considerable length in the seventh and sixth centuries, had come to an end, and was doubtless one of the reasons why the country submitted to Xerxes without a struggle. As the *tagus* in the old days had been regularly one of the Aleuadae at Larissa, some loss of political influence on the part of this city probably resulted. Nevertheless after the Persian wars Larissa appears to have been the chief promoter of an alliance coinage, struck on the Aeginetan standard.[1] All the cities except Pharsalus appear to have participated. This economic measure did not endure, for soon after the middle of the century Pherae, which owed much of its importance to control of the sea-port of Pagasae, and also Scotussa issued independent coinages. In the fifth and early fourth centuries the Thessalians, so far as they were drawn into inter-state politics, were rather at the mercy of other powers with a better political and military system. Their disunion amongst themselves was shown, for example, in the fifth century, when for a time Larissa was allied to Athens and Pharsalus to Sparta. At other times they were drawn into the Macedonian sphere of influence[2] or brought into semi-dependence on Sparta. As late as *c.* 375 we find

[1] On the Thessalian coinage in the fifth century cf. the recent articles of Heichelheim and of Herrmann in *Zeitschrift für Numismatik*, 40, 16 ff.; 33, 33 ff.; 35, 1 ff.

[2] For instance, under Perdiccas II and again under Archelaus. Cf. F. Geyer, *Makedonien bis zur Thronbesteigung Philipps II*, p. 94.

the Macedonian king, Amyntas III, acting as arbiter in a Thessalian frontier dispute.[1] Yet that was at a time when the genius of a single man was recreating in more modern fashion the united Thessalian state of archaic times.

Jason's earlier life is unknown save for a tradition that in youth he was a pupil of Gorgias. When he first appears in history soon after 380 he was already despot of Pherae, had won the allegiance of almost the whole of Thessaly, and was acknowledged as overlord by the Epirot princes, Alcetas and Neoptolemus. Pharsalus alone stood out for her independence and its ruler, Polydamas, when threatened with war by Jason, sought to procure Spartan intervention. When this was refused he too submitted and Jason was installed as *tagus* of all Thessaly. Amyntas III, who had concluded an alliance with Athens in 375 or 374,[2] not long afterwards entered into a friendly agreement with Jason, who had already been enrolled as a member of the Second Athenian Confederacy. From this, however, he withdrew two or three years later at the time when it suited his interests better to cement good relations with his neighbours on the south, the new Boeotian state created by Epaminondas and his colleagues. Jason appears to have revived the old military and financial organization of the sixth century and to have adapted it to his ends.[3] During his rise to power he had employed professional soldiery on an exceptionally lavish scale. Once he became *tagus*, he was to some extent a forerunner of Philip II of Macedon in that he instituted a national army of not less than 20,000 hoplites, 8000 cavalry, and a large auxiliary force of peltasts. Besides this formidable array, he appears to have retained his mercenaries, 6000 strong. With such resources he may well have cherished as his ultimate aim the invasion of Persia at the head of a Panhellenic army.[4]

### § 9. THE ABORTIVE PEACE OF 371 AND THE CAMPAIGN OF LEUCTRA

It was the Athenians who finally took the initiative in seeking to end the war in Greece. After informing Thebes

[1] Cf. Geyer, *op. cit.*, p. 125; Stählin, P-W., XII, col. 850.
[2] Tod 129.
[3] On this cf. the article of H. T. Wade-Gery in *J.H.S.*, 44 (1924), pp. 55–64.   [4] Cf. Xenophon, *Hell.*, VI, 1, 12, and Isocrates, V, 119–20.

of their intention they sent their most prominent statesman, Callistratus, with two colleagues to Sparta in the spring of 371. The Thebans followed suit, their chief spokesman being Epaminondas. Broadly speaking, one may describe the peace agreement that emerged from the negotiations as a restatement of the King's Peace. Coupled with the undertaking that the autonomy of each and every Greek city be respected, the idea of a joint hegemony in Greece by Sparta and Athens was vaguely revived. Yet the Peloponnesian League and the maritime confederacy headed by Athens were to remain intact. The continuance of these unions of states, contradictory as it might seem, was justified by the provision that military or naval co-operation by constituent members would be purely voluntary. Neither Sparta nor Athens could use coercion towards their allies, and the Spartans undertook immediately to withdraw any Lacedaemonian garrisons that still existed in any allied or hitherto dependent state. But apart from the fact that not only cynics might question the possibility whether such a settlement could have any elements of permanence, the agreement between Sparta and Athens shows a naïve ignorance of realities that, in retrospect at least, is positively astounding. Sparta took the oath on behalf of herself and the Peloponnesian League, while the Athenian delegates appear to have done the same in conjunction with representatives from the Congress of allies. Both states intended and believed that the Thebans would be intimidated, as they had been in 386, into allowing each city of Boeotia to swear separately to the peace. But Epaminondas made it clear that Thebes considered Boeotia to be a single political unit and demanded that he and his colleagues should ratify the peace on behalf of all the Boeotian communities. Through the influence of Agesilaus Epaminondas' demand was summarily dismissed, and, when Epaminondas refused to recede from his position the name of Thebes was deleted from the list of signatories. Thus, although the war between Athens and Sparta was ended, the action of Sparta meant a continuance of hostilities in central Greece; for the Spartan government treated the refusal of Thebes to conform to its demands as a *casus belli* and ordered King Cleombrotus who was already in Phocis to invade Boeotia. The truth was that the Spartans had not yet learnt that the Boeotian army at this date was a very different thing from what it had been in former days when Boeotia was an ally. The all but consistent successes of Thebes between 378 and 371, of which the most striking had been the decisive victory of the Sacred Band over a Lacedaemonian force twice its number at Tegyra in 373, seem to have made singularly little impression on the Spartan High Command. It may also have been felt that Boeotia was dangerously isolated, a calculation that left out of account that Thebes now had a powerful ally in the ruler of Thessaly. And indeed, when the Thebans were threatened with a Peloponnesian invasion, they appealed to Jason for assistance.

Cleombrotus' army was stationed not far from the borders of Phocis and Boeotia in the region of Chaeronea. Epaminondas and his fellow commanders, knowing that his objective would be Thebes, led their men to occupy the main road into Phocis which in the neighbourhood of Coronea ran through a narrow pass between Lake Copais and Mt. Helicon. But the Spartan king was too wary to make this obvious move. With superior strategy he led his men through southern Phocis across the southern slopes of Helicon to Thisbe. A weak Boeotian force was overpowered and the near-by port of Creusis was seized, so that the Spartans had direct access to the sea and were in no danger of being attacked from the rear. The Theban army meantime had changed its position to meet the new situation and the two combatants came to grips in the vicinity of Leuctra. The numbers engaged were not exceptionally large, even if the figures transmitted— 10,000 Peloponnesian against 6000 Boeotian troops—are more approximate than exact. In cavalry the Boeotians were greatly superior, as was proved at the very outset of the battle, when the defeat of the Lacedaemonian squadrons caused some confusion in the hoplite ranks. But the tactical dispositions of Epaminondas were novel. It had long been the Theban practice to mass the heavy infantry in a deep and close formation. But he concentrated his best troops led by the Sacred Band on his left wing so as to form a column forty shields deep. The centre and right wing were left correspondingly weak since their role was to be a strictly defensive one. The left wing carried all before it, and after a bitter hand-to-hand fight the Spartan right wing was completely shattered.

The rest of the Peloponnesian army thereupon retreated precipitately to their entrenched camp situated on an eminence a little to the south. The Lacedaemonian losses are said to have been a thousand men, including no less than four hundred of the Spartiate class. On receiving news of this disaster the Spartan government at once mobilized a relief expedition which hastened past the Isthmus and through the Megarid to join forces with the survivors of Leuctra, whose commander, Cleombrotus, had been one of the casualties. But meanwhile Jason of Pherae with a picked force of 1500 infantry and 500 cavalry passed Thermopylae and swept through Phocis. With this ally the Thebans were more than ready to try conclusions with Sparta a second time. But the Thessalian preferred the role of mediator, and on his advice the Thebans agreed to a truce with Sparta. Thereupon the entire Peloponnesian army withdrew homewards. Jason on his return to Thessaly destroyed the fortifications of Heraclea, thereby facilitating any future march into central Greece. But within a year his plans for extending his suzerainty over a wider area, as also his immediate preparations for presiding at the Pythian festival in 370, were cut short by death. At a military review he was assassinated. The political structure, that he had created within less than a decade, passed nominally to two brothers, but in fact crumbled to pieces almost at once. Its stability had, as so often, depended entirely on the personality of the creator.

Leuctra deserves to rank as one of the most decisive actions in Greek history. It ended the political supremacy of Sparta which had endured some thirty years; but it also reduced her from the first military state in Greece, a position that had been hers for nearly two centuries—to one of the second rank. The consequence was that before long the entire political situation in the Peloponnese and in central Greece was profoundly modified. While it might with justice be said that the Spartans deserved their fate, their political decline and the partial breaking up of the Peloponnesian League destroyed the most permanent federation in Greece and thereby caused irreparable harm at a time when political unity was of vital moment.

## CHAPTER VII

## THE HEGEMONY OF THEBES

### § 1. EPAMINONDAS IN THE PELOPONNESE

THE death of Jason of Pherae caused no regrets in Greece. He had been allied to Athens for a few years, but had then withdrawn from that commitment, though without any overt break in peaceful relations with the maritime league or its head. His more recent support of Thebes had been welcome at the time, but the rise of that state to first place among the military states of Greece would not have been possible as long as its northern neighbour was a strong and united Thessaly ruled by a prince ambitious for a wider supremacy. The political results of Jason's murder were soon apparent. By the end of 370 all central Greece from sea to sea, with the exception of Aetolia and, of course, Attica, had passed under Theban influence. Athens was more isolated in Greece than ever, and even Euboea had gone over to the victors of Leuctra. Out of this amalgam of states the Thebans created a confederacy, the allies being represented in a congress distinct from the government of the Boeotian state. As this league was for defensive purposes only it did not theoretically run counter to the Athenian Confederacy; and, though there was no rupture between Athens and Thebes, an effective alliance between the two had ceased to be possible. The Athenians from apprehension of Theban designs, and from a desire to emphasize their own claims to be regarded as the leaders of Hellas, a few months after Leuctra convened a congress of delegates from the Peloponnesian cities. The terms of the King's Peace were reaffirmed and a rather loosely defined defensive alliance between the Second Athenian Confederacy and the former members of the Peloponnesian League, with the exception of Elis, was brought about. But the project was still-born, if only because it presupposed a degree of political harmony in the Peloponnese which the recent defeat of Sparta very soon rendered impossible.

Sparta's downfall was the signal for a widespread agitation on the part of the democratic parties in many Peloponnesian cities and for the return of numerous democratic exiles. In Corinth, Phlius, and Sicyon the oligarchic *régime* was too firmly established to be uprooted, but elsewhere *stasis* and bloodshed were followed by a change of government. The worst excesses, however, occurred outside the Peloponnesian League. A revolution of exceptional violence broke out at Argos, in the course of which a thousand of the richest citizens were massacred. The greatest activity and also the most constructive statesmanship was displayed in Arcadia. The Mantineans began by reuniting their scattered villages and rebuilding their city. But their most prominent statesman, Lycomedes, had more ambitious plans than the renascence of his native town. He was the prime mover in the creation of a pan-Arcadian League, and his ideas found favour with many of the lesser communities of Arcadia. Orchomenus, Heraea, and Tegea held aloof. But the Mantineans were prepared to use force to attain their ends, and with their help the supporters of Sparta in Tegea were expelled and fled for refuge into Laconia. This occurrence provoked the Spartan government to intervene. A Lacedaemonian army, strengthened by some contingents from Lepreum and Heraea, took the field under Agesilaus' direction. It accomplished little of military importance, but the action led to important political results. At the first threat of danger the Arcadian federation, supported by Argos and Elis, asked for Athenian co-operation. But the Athenians chose to disregard their recent defensive alliance and elected to remain neutral. The only alternative open to the Arcadians was an appeal to Thebes. It is indicative of the lack of political vision among the Athenian politicians at that time that the possibility of an entente between Arcadia and Thebes was overlooked or set aside as unimportant. Yet Athenian intervention might well have decided the Spartans to play for safety and to abandon their aggressive tactics, whereas the presence of a Boeotian army in southern Greece might produce incalculable consequences, not merely in the Peloponnese but for Athens herself.

The Theban reply to the Arcadian appeal was not delayed. In December, 370, contrary to the normal usage of Greek warfare, Epaminondas led a large army, composed of Boeotian troops reinforced by regiments from Thebes' central Greek allies, to the Peloponnese. When he appeared in Arcadia, the Spartans had already retired; but he decided to take the offensive against Sparta.[1] An invasion of Laconia would be a fitting reply to the many inroads that the Spartans had made into Boeotia during the past two decades. At the first news of the peril that impended, the Spartans sent pressing messages to those communities that still held staunchly to them, Corinth, Sicyon, and Phlius on the Gulf, Orchomenus and Heraea in Arcadia, Troizen, Hermione, and Epidaurus in the Argolid. King Agesilaus organized the defence so well that, though all Laconia was overrun and ravaged by the enemy moving southwards in four columns, the town of Sparta, protected by a desperate population and by the River Eurotas fed by winter rains, remained inviolate until the arrival of the allies in all haste convinced the Theban general that its capture was not practicable. Nevertheless the coming of Epaminondas was the signal for widespread disaffection among the Helots and the Perioeci, especially in Messenia. A portion of northern Laconia was permanently annexed to Arcadia. Messenia after centuries of serfdom recovered its independence. Epaminondas remained long enough to see the construction of a new capital city at the foot of Mount Ithome begun. Extensive remains of the town walls and fortified towers stand to this day and are amongst the most impressive examples of Greek military architecture.

Athenian public opinion was profoundly affected by the swift march of events in southern Greece; and, when the Spartans in the winter 370-369 turned to them for assistance, they voted to despatch an expeditionary force under Iphicrates. His arrival, however, was too late to have any serious influence on the course of the war. Sparta was safe, and, though his

[1] Xenophon (VI, 5, 23) states that Epaminondas, finding that the Spartans had evacuated Arcadia, proposed to return home, but was persuaded by the Arcadians, Eleans, and Argives to attack Sparta. It is difficult to believe that the Thebans would have mustered so large an army if an offensive against Sparta had not been projected from the first. Diodorus (XV, 62, 5) in rather ambiguous language makes the invasion of Laconia the result of a joint conference between Epaminondas and the generals of the three Peloponnesian states involved. In that case the initiative may have come from Epaminondas.

skirmishers inflicted some minor losses on the Boeotian army as it passed the Isthmus, he did not attempt to dispute the enemy's withdrawal into Boeotia. Then, a month or two later, a formal alliance between Sparta and Athens was concluded. Thus once more the balance of power in Greece had shifted. By their action the Athenians were led into war with Thebes and joined the opponents of the Arcadian federation.

### § 2. THE ARCADIAN LEAGUE AND THE WAR IN THE PELOPONNESE TO 364 B.C.

After the crushing blow inflicted on Sparta by Epaminondas the organization of the new Arcadian League could be completed. There were in Arcadia, besides the greater city-states, many smaller communities whose separate existence in a federal organization was not feasible. The founding of a new city, Megalopolis, in the centre of southern Arcadia, brought these insignificant and scattered units together to form one polity. But, in addition, this city became the federal capital of the League, for the obvious danger of inter-city jealousy precluded the choice of one of the older *poleis*, like Mantinea or Tegea, for this purpose. The site chosen was, moreover, singularly well adapted to be a political and military centre, for the geographical position of Megalopolis made it a nodal point in the heart of the Peloponnese, through which the main routes through the peninsula passed. The fate of this once handsome city recalled to the mind of a Greek traveller in the age of the Antonines the transitory nature of man's handiwork. " Megalopolis, the foundation of which was carried out by the Arcadians with the utmost enthusiasm and viewed with all the highest hopes by the Greeks, now lies mostly in ruins."[1] Of its buildings the most striking were a large theatre and the Thersilium, a covered hall supported within by pillars. It served as a meeting-place for the federal assembly or Ten Thousand. Every adult male citizen of each constituent city in the League was a member of this body, which exercised the sovereign authority in all major questions affecting the federation. It also elected the military head of the confederate army ($\sigma\tau\rho\alpha\tau\eta\gamma\grave{o}s$) and fifty executive officials ($\delta\eta\mu\iota\text{ουργοί}$), whose duties and powers are unknown. Nor is there any clear information about a council,

[1] Pausanias, VIII, 33, 1.

beyond the fact that it existed.¹ Provision was made for a permanent body of heavy infantry (ἐπάριτοι or ἐπαρίται), controlled by the federal government and maintained out of the federal treasury. Their strength is uncertain, as they were distinct from the citizen militia of the constituent cities.² By 368 the Arcadians were in the position to coerce Heraea and Orchomenus, so that these two important cities joined the federation. Thus it became truly Pan-Arcadian and at the same time Sparta lost two more valuable allies.

Epaminondas in the meantime had invaded the Peloponnese a second time in the summer of 369. He had fought his way past the Isthmus, where a joint army from Laconia and Athens had massed to bar his passage, but had not yet completed its defence works. Then he had occupied Sicyon and Pellene, but had failed in his attack on Phlius. On his return to Thebes his political enemies were strong enough to have him impeached. When his trial came on, the influence of friends inside and outside Boeotia sufficed to bring about his acquittal; but he was not re-elected to the Boeotarchy for the next year. Partly for this reason, partly because Thebes became involved in the affairs of Thessaly, the year 368 saw no Boeotian intervention in Peloponnesian affairs. But the peninsula continued in a disturbed condition. In the late summer an Arcadian force suffered a reverse at the hands of Sparta.³ At Sicyon civil war broke out and lasted intermittently for several years, interrupted by two short periods of tyrant rule under Euphron.

It is of more interest to note the efforts made by the chief states at this time to win the support of foreign rulers. The Spartans had long been in alliance with Dionysius I of Syracuse, and in both 369 and 368 he had lent them mercenary troops. Their recent victory over the Arcadians was

[1] Some modern writers have equated the δημιουργοί with the council, but this interpretation finds no support in the ancient sources. A council of fifty would be an exceedingly small deliberative body unparalleled in any other Greek state.

[2] H. W. Parke, *Greek Mercenary Soldiers*, p. 93, note 1, is justified in doubting whether the figure 5000 given by Diodorus (XV, 62, 2) can apply to the ἐπάριτοι alone. It would be an exceptionally large number for a permanent military force.

[3] This was the so-called "Tearless Battle," because no soldier in the victorious army was killed. Yet, if Xenophon (*Hell.*, VII, 1, 32) is to be trusted, tears were shed, but they were tears of joy at Sparta when this slight success became known.

in part due to these timely allies. In 368 the Syracusan ruler concluded an alliance with the Athenians, since they were at that time on the same terms with his ally, Sparta.[1] Some months before, the Athenians had passed a decree in his honour and had conferred their citizenship on him and on his sons.[2] He was, moreover, represented at a congress held in the early part of the year at Delphi. Its actual convener was the satrap of Phrygia, Ariobarzanes, acting through a Greek agent; but it is possible that the proposal originated at Athens. While it was not unwelcome in theory to any of the major city-states, its deliberations produced no results. The Athenians were as eager as ever to regain Amphipolis; Sparta refused to accept the independence of Messenia; and Thebes, while agreeing to no modifications of her own power, resisted the claims of both her rivals. In the following winter not only these three states, but Argos, Elis, and the Arcadians engaged in an unseemly scramble for the favour and moral support of the Great King. Of the various Greek envoys who thronged the court at Susa Pelopidas was the most persuasive. He returned home with a Persian rescript which approved the reconstituted Boeotian League and the new Messenia, ignored Arcadia, and opposed the Athenian pretensions to Amphipolis. The efforts of Epaminondas to convene a Hellenic congress at Thebes to reaffirm the terms of the King's Peace as modified by the latest rescript, awakened no response amongst the other states. In truth, these abortive negotiations with Artaxerxes only led to more active warfare in Greece.

Epaminondas, who had been re-elected to office in 367, during the summer months invaded the Peloponnese for the third time. His main purpose was to counteract the growing power of the Arcadian League whose leaders were dissatisfied equally with Artaxerxes' rescript, in which no acknowledgment of their new federation had found a place, and with the Thebans as interpreters of the Great King's will. The Thebans passed the Isthmus with the co-operation of an Argive corps which had guarded the passes to the south of Corinth before either Sparta or Athens could step in. The attitude of the Argive government at this time may have been dictated partly by enmity to Sparta, but it was chiefly prompted by jealousy of Lycomedes and his colleagues. Epaminondas

---

[1] See Tod 136.　　　[2] *Ibid.*, 133.

marched into Achaea and won over its cities to the side of Thebes, making separate agreements with their oligarchic governments. But the opponents of Epaminondas at home were still strong and forced through a systematic policy of expelling the oligarchs in Achaea and entrusting the conduct of affairs to the democratic factions. This ill-considered interference had the double result of producing *stasis* in the cities and of causing the oligarchs when they had fought their way back to power to ally themselves to Sparta. About the same time Pellene also severed her friendly relations with the Boeotian League.

The conclusion of a defensive alliance between Athens and the Arcadian League was yet a further blow at the supremacy that Thebes was seeking to establish in Greece. This agreement, the last act of Lycomedes, who was murdered by some Arcadian exiles on his return from Athens to the Peloponnese, was in some sense an Athenian reply to Thebes' seizure of Oropus some months before (spring, 366). It created an anomalous situation, seeing that the Athenians were now allied to two states, Arcadia and Sparta, who were themselves at war. Although neither Lycomedes nor Callistratus, acting as Athens' chief representative in the negotiations, can be blamed for lack of foresight, the alliance, taken in conjunction with the death of the Arcadian statesman, prepared the way for the political disintegration of the Arcadian League. However, Thebes soon after achieved a diplomatic success by concluding peace with Corinth, Phlius, and the cities on the coast of the Argolid; for, although they did not ally themselves to the Boeotian League, they now followed a policy of strict neutrality, thereby depriving Sparta of valuable support.

For more than two years Epaminondas and his colleagues abstained from further meddling in southern Greece, and parts of the peninsula were more tranquil than they had long been. But the north-western portion of the Peloponnese now became the scene of a bitter war between the Arcadians and Elis. In spite of some help from Sparta in the second year of the war (364), the Eleans were no match for their adversaries. In the summer the festival at Olympia, normally the period of a sacred truce observed by all Greek states, was ruined by fighting and bloodshed on the Altis itself; for the Eleans tried unavailingly to recover by force of arms the control over the holy places which the Arcadians had entrusted to the people of the ancient but politically insignificant town of Pisa. Sympathy was still further alienated from the Arcadians because they followed up their military successes by laying hands on part of the sacred treasure in the sanctuaries and using it for their own military purposes. This, the most disgraceful, may also be said to have been the last, act of a united Arcadian federation.

### § 3. THE RELATIONS BETWEEN THEBES AND NORTHERN GREECE

Although the death of Jason and the immediate collapse of the political unification that he had created may have encouraged Thebes at no distant date to strive for an extension of her influence northwards, the first move towards exploiting disunion in Thessaly was made by Alexander II of Macedon. The government of Pherae had passed into the hands of Jason's two brothers, Polydorus and Polyphron. The last-named assassinated Polydorus within a few days and then ruled about a year before he fell a victim to Polydorus' son, Alexander. But though the murderer secured the throne of Pherae he was not acceptable to the other Thessalian cities as successor to Jason. A number of Larissaean exiles who had been expelled from their city by Polyphron invited Macedonian intervention. Alexander II promptly replied by occupying Larissa and Crannon not as an ally but as a conqueror. Thereupon the Thessalians turned to Thebes. By the time that Pelopidas appeared with a Boeotian army at Larissa, Alexander II had withdrawn to his kingdom where civil war had broken out during his absence. The Theban general who had entered Larissa without difficulty was now requested to act as arbiter in the dynastic disputes of Macedonia. He threw his influence on the side of the reigning prince against Alexander's brother-in-law, Ptolemaeus, who had the powerful backing of the queen-mother, Eurydice. An alliance between Thebes and Macedonia formed the epilogue to these negotiations. But a few months later Alexander II was murdered and the war between pretenders to the throne began afresh. Eurydice exerted herself to secure the succession for the surviving sons of

Amyntas III, Perdiccas and Philip. Since both were minors, she for the present desired the regency of Ptolemaeus, whom she had married, and strove to defeat the attempts at usurpation of Pausanias, a more distant kinsman of the former king. In her difficulties she turned not to Thebes but to the Athenians. With the help of Iphicrates, who had been sent at that time in charge of a naval squadron to promote Athenian interests in Chalcidice, the queen obtained her object; but the intervention of Athens called forth a second Boeotian expedition into Thessaly in 368. This time Pelopidas, while recognizing the regency of Ptolemaeus, prevailed on him to renew the alliance with Thebes made by Alexander II. To this venture there was an unexpected sequel. In 369 Pelopidas, besides mediating in Macedonia, had smoothed out the affairs of Larissa and other Thessalian cities. They organized themselves into a loose confederacy under the general protection of Thebes. On his return from Macedonia in 368 Pelopidas attempted to win over Pharsalus, but the appearance of Alexander of Pherae at the head of a formidable army compelled him to seek a settlement by negotiation. Alexander, however, who as a counter-stroke to the alliance between Macedonia and Thebes had just concluded a friendly agreement with Athens, detained Pelopidas and his fellow-general, Ismenias, in honourable captivity. The first attempt made by Thebes to rescue their commanders was in the autumn of that year but failed, and the troops barely escaped disaster at the hands of Alexander. The credit for extracting his fellows from a dangerous position seems to have belonged to Epaminondas. He was serving in the ranks, but his fellow-hoplites, seeing the incompetence of their senior officers, unanimously handed over the command to him. His formal re-election to the Boeotarchy for 367 was the natural sequel, and a fresh expedition under his direction ended in a pact with the despot of Pherae. The legitimacy of Alexander's rule not only over Pherae but over a great part of southern and eastern Thessaly was acknowledged by Thebes and in return Pelopidas and Ismenias were liberated.

So far the results of Boeotian intervention in Thessaly and Macedonia had been modest enough. Probably the most powerful obstacle to a more ambitious policy of conquest was lack of money, for the Thebans had neither wealthy allies nor large natural resources to draw upon. It was thus to their advantage that their northern neighbours should be disunited and that no single city or despot should weld Thessaly into a single state as Jason had done. For several years fruitless negotiations with Persia and affairs in southern Greece kept the leading statesmen of Thebes fully occupied, a circumstance of which Alexander of Pherae took the fullest advantage. That " unjust robber by land and sea " is depicted for us as a monster of cruelty who butchered the population of two Thessalian towns in cold blood and put his individual victims to death with torments. Politically his ambition was to make himself master of the cities in the north, and in the fighting he was so successful that in 364 the hard-pressed Thessalians appealed once more to Thebes. Pelopidas with 300 volunteer cavalry entered Thessaly in the summer and with the Thessalian allies marched against the tyrant of Pherae. A prolonged engagement was fought at Cynoscephalae, a range of hills commanding the road from Pherae to Larissa. Alexander after a stubborn contest was defeated, but Pelopidas by too rashly exposing his person in the last stage of the battle was killed. When the news reached Thebes grief at the loss of one of their two ablest men was mixed with indignation. In the following spring an expeditionary force nearly 8000 strong was mobilized and sent against Alexander, who after his recent defeat was not in the position to risk another engagement. Thus he was constrained to come to terms; and it is significant of Theban policy that, instead of being compelled to abdicate, he was merely required to give up all the territory that he had held, save only Pherae. Like the cities of the Thessalian League, he agreed to acknowledge the general suzerainty of Thebes.

## § 4. ATHENIAN NAVAL OPERATIONS

For several years after Leuctra information about the Second Athenian Confederacy is exceedingly scanty. If the alliance of the Acarnanians with Thebes in 371–370 can hardly be counted a great loss to the League, the adherence of the Euboean cities to the Boeotian federation was a serious blow to Athens. Here and there a new member may have joined Athens, as Leucas did in 368;[1] but it was not till 366 that

[1] Cf. Tod 134.

the Athenians, partly under the influence of the loss of Oropus, but in the main because an opportunity of co-operation with a Persian satrap seemed to promise substantial advantage, made a serious effort at maritime expansion. The capture by Thebes of Oropus, moreover, was made the ground for an attack by his political opponents on Callistratus. The Athenian statesman, who had been prominent in Athenian politics for the best part of two decades, was impeached but secured an acquittal. Nevertheless he never recovered his former influence, but four or five years later was again accused, this time on the general ground of having misled the Athenian people. He went into exile and was condemned to death in his absence, a sentence that was actually carried out a year or two later, when he unwisely came back to his native city in the guise of a suppliant.

It may be surmised that Athens' previous lack of enterprise was due to shortage of funds, just as financial weakness had hampered Sparta in her plans before 371, and Thebes after that date. With a weak ruler at Susa disaffection in the Persian empire became increasingly common during the fourth century.[1] In 367–366 a rebellion against Artaxerxes broke out in which the satraps of Armenia, Phrygia, Lydia, and Caria participated; they received some support from Egypt. To further their ends these viceroys relied mainly on professional soldiery recruited from Greek cities, and in particular sought to engage Greek military commanders of established reputation. At the outbreak of the Satrapal Revolt Ariobarzanes of Phrygia tried to recruit both Spartans and Athenians in his service. The Spartans, who could spare no fighting men for such an enterprise, authorized King Agesilaus to proceed to Asia Minor alone. His military experience would be of no little value to the satrap and success would bring material rewards to fill the empty Spartan treasury. The Athenians, seeing a chance of both spoil and imperial expansion, despatched thirty triremes and some 8000 men under Timotheus, whose political ascendancy dated from the time of Callistratus' first trial. His instructions, if vague, were also somewhat contradictory, to assist Ariobarzanes without violating the truce existing between Athens and Artaxerxes. His first operation was an attack on Samos,

[1] Cf. below, pp. 291–292.

which had been recently annexed by Persia although, being an island, it was not included among the states that had reverted under Persian control in 386. After a ten months' siege Samos capitulated in the summer of 365. The Athenians thereupon sent 2000 settlers to the island at once, while additional contingents went out in 361 and again nine years later. But by reviving the military colonization they antagonized the members of their maritime confederacy; for, although the terms of the pact were not violated, since Samos was not a member of the League, the conduct of the Athenians savoured too much of their old imperialism.

Timotheus was next heard of in the Hellespont, and in return for his services to Ariobarzanes, of which we have no clear record, received both money and the cession of Sestos and Crithote. In view of these achievements the Athenians next appointed him to succeed Iphicrates in Chalcidice. There, too, his successes were substantial, if short-lived. He effected an alliance with Perdiccas III, who had attained his majority and the throne in 365, and with the king's connivance won over a number of Greek towns of which Pydna, Methone, Torone, and Potidaea were the most important. The last-named city was colonized three years later by Athenian settlers (361–360). But Timotheus' efforts to occupy Amphipolis failed, although he appears to have received some military and financial assistance from a Macedonian princeling.[1] An attempt to secure complete control of the Thracian Chersonese at that time was equally unsuccessful, mainly because of the Thracian ruler, Cotys, whose aim was to keep foreign powers away from the Thracian seaboard. The increased naval activity of Athens, however, had one unexpected consequence. On the advice of Epaminondas, who rightly saw in the maritime power of Athens the most serious rival to Theban supremacy in Greece, the Thebans occupied Larymna on the coast of Ozolian Locris and feverishly took to naval construction. The new fleet under Epaminondas' personal direction sailed for the Hellespont in 364. Byzantium was persuaded to secede from Athens, but negotiations with Chios and Rhodes bore no fruit, nor did the Theban commander seek an engagement with the Athenian fleet. Two of the Cyclades, Ceos and Naxos,

[1] Cf. Tod 143 and 146.

became the scene of internal revolution and joined Thebes. But the attempt to meet Athens on her own element and to sow disaffection amongst her maritime allies ceased as suddenly as it began; for in 363 the political situation in the Peloponnese took a turn so prejudicial to Theban interests that Epaminondas and his colleagues had needs to concentrate all their efforts on a land war. Byzantium remained outside the Athenian League, but the revolt in Ceos was suppressed after two military interventions.[1] The islanders suffered some diminution of their right of jurisdiction, and a few years later the existing agreement between Athens and the Cean cities regarding the export of red ochre ($\mu\iota\lambda\tau os$) from the island was made more stringent, so that the Athenians obtained a monopoly of the mineral which was used both as colouring matter and for medicinal purposes.[2] Naxos also seems to have been regained without difficulty; but hardly had quiet been restored among the islands when Alexander of Pherae, influenced by the decline of Thebes after Epaminondas' last campaign, disowned his treaty with Athens and carried out a series of raids in the archipelago on allies of Athens (362–361). In the following year the Thessalian League concluded an alliance with the Athenians, the text of which still survives.[3]

### § 5. THE CAMPAIGN OF MANTINEA

The Arcadian League's " borrowing " from the treasure at Olympia in order to pay its federal army brought to a head disagreements within the federation that had probably been latent for some time. As far as the use of temple funds was concerned, it might indeed be said that to borrow from such a source was a recognized Greek practice where the temple was within the territory of the borrower. Of that procedure the most obvious instance were the Athenian loans from Athena Parthenos during the Peloponnesian War. But Olympia, whether administered by the people of Elis or of Pisa, had long been a Panhellenic centre, and the religious scruples against the use of its wealth by any state or group of states had been shown in 431.[4] It may be guessed that when the Mantineans protested against the annexation of

[1] Cf. Tod 142.  [2] *Ibid.*, 162.
[3] *Ibid.*, 147.  [4] See above, p. 80.

temple funds, even though the money was officially borrowed, they were influenced by a more deep-seated discontent with the federation to which they belonged. For the moment, after a hostile but ineffective demonstration against Mantinea, the Arcadian League compromised by disbanding its paid army and enlisting a body of volunteers from the wealthiest class in the constituent cities. Then, while peace was patched up with Elis, a minority of the executive officers in the League invited Theban intervention. But the Theban commander who marched with a small contingent to the Peloponnese mismanaged or exceeded his instructions. He was forced to retire ignominiously, feeling against the Boeotian League in parts of Arcadia was greatly accentuated, and a fresh rupture within the Arcadian Federation, coupled with the decline of Theban authority in southern Greece, was the inevitable outcome.

In view of this situation Epaminondas had no difficulty in persuading his countrymen to mobilize *en masse*, when the campaigning season began. By that time the rift in the Arcadian League had been irremediably widened. Mantinea and northern Arcadia allied themselves to Sparta. Elis stood in with them, and Athens, technically allied to both Sparta and the Arcadian League, followed suit. Tegea, with bitter memories of Spartan aggressions, Megalopolis, and other communities in southern Arcadia, remained loyal to Thebes. Argos and Messene of course also sided with the enemies of Sparta. Megara and Corinth remained neutral and offered no opposition to the Boeotian army when it passed through their territory on the way to Arcadia. After waiting in vain close by Nemea to intercept the Athenian regiments that were expected to join the Mantineans, Epaminondas marched to Tegea, where he joined his Peloponnesian allies. The enemy's meeting-place was Mantinea, and he at first planned to reduce the city before the Spartan army could arrive. When this proved impracticable, because the town was strongly defended, he determined to make a sudden descent into Laconia while denuded of its fighting men. But Agesilaus who commanded the Lacedaemonian forces received news from a deserter of what was in the wind and instantly led his men back home by a forced march. Thus Epaminondas' second invasion of Spartan territory failed completely in its object, and he returned with all speed to Mantinea to rejoin his allies and a portion of the Boeotian army that had not taken part in the raid on Laconia. An attempt to surprise the city Mantinea by a cavalry attack might have met with some success had not a cavalry detachment sent by Athens reached the city just before. Amongst the Athenians who staunchly repulsed the Boeotian attack was Gryllus, the son of Xenophon.

Epaminondas now remained quiescent long enough to allow the main Athenian army to join their allies at Mantinea. At last, as the problem of feeding his men became acute and they showed some impatience to end their foreign service, he prepared to attack. Drawing up his army in the formation already used with such devastating effect at Leuctra, so that the offensive would devolve mainly on his left wing, he adopted a very effective stratagem; for, by setting out in a northwesterly direction, he led the enemy to believe that he was retiring or at least shifting his ground, and so that he would not attack on that day. Thus, when he wheeled round and advanced to the attack, his opponents' battle-order was to some extent disarranged, giving him a valuable initial advantage. Although the armies involved were more than twice as great—it has been estimated that about 25,000 men fought on either side—the battle of Mantinea seems to have been a repetition of Leuctra, save that the Boeotian cavalry played a more decisive part in 362 than in 371. The Lacedaemonian and Mantinean infantry could not in the long run resist the massed attack of the Theban left wing, and when they gave way the battle was as good as over. But in following up the enemy Epaminondas himself was mortally wounded, and so completely did the Boeotian army depend on the guidance of their commander-in-chief, whose place no other senior officer seems to have been competent to take in an emergency, that the pursuit of the enemy was abandoned. Through the death of their leader the Thebans lost all the fruits of their overwhelming victory and were glad to follow Epaminondas' dying advice to come to terms with the enemy. At the congress summoned for this purpose the peace was again based on the old formula of autonomy for each city-state. The Arcadian League remained split up into two federated groups. The independence of Messenia was confirmed, but the Spartans, rather than agree to this condition, withheld their assent to the peace negotiations—an impotent gesture that had no influence on the general policy of the other states. The Boeotian and Athenian Confederacies continued as before, but the former soon showed that it lacked the cohesion and driving force which had distinguished it for a decade under the inspired leadership of Epaminondas and Pelopidas.

There is a striking unanimity in modern estimates of Epaminondas' character and achievements. That he belonged to the small company of outstanding military leaders in the Ancient World is clear. He, together with Jason and especially Dionysius I, prepared the way for the more revolutionary changes in the art of war effected by Philip and Alexander of Macedon. But as the political mentor of Thebes and in constructive statesmanship his performance was mediocre. If it be maintained in his defence that his failure to give permanence to Theban imperialism was due to the limited resources of the Boeotian League and to the absence of unanimous backing by his countrymen, these excuses are but an admission that he gravely miscalculated the financial strength of Thebes and her allies; and that, although his personal charm and personality were great, he lacked those dynamic qualities which in Pericles had borne down all opposition and made that statesman a benevolent autocrat for the last fifteen years of his career. In short, in 360, when exhaustion and war-weariness in Greece were greater, while peace and co-operation were more imperatively needed, than ever before, all the political combinations that had in the past guaranteed at least a partial stability were either destroyed or moribund. Sparta was impotent and the Peloponnesian League broken up; the group of states formed in central Greece in 370 came to an end with the death of Epaminondas; and even the Athenian Maritime Confederacy was in rapid decline and, five years later, collapsed entirely. Finally, of Epaminondas' two most constructive achievements —his action in standing godfather to the Arcadian League and his creation of an autonomous Messenia—the one proved a failure even in his lifetime, while the other, however admirable as an act of abstract justice, in fact introduced one more element of discord into an already gravely disunited Peloponnese.

# CHAPTER VIII

# THE RISE OF PHILIP OF MACEDON

§ 1. MACEDONIA BEFORE THE TIME OF PHILIP

THE history of Macedonia before the accession of Philip II is wrapped in a darkness that is only lighted up occasionally and for brief periods when its rulers are drawn into the orbit of Greek politics. Thus we have already had occasion to note the foreign policy pursued by several of them.[1] In general, Macedonia from the Persian wars to the death of Perdiccas III was too weak and too loosely organized to do more than watch its more powerful neighbours and seek to be on good terms with the strongest. This is the explanation of Perdiccas II's vacillating and apparently perfidious relations with Athens. One king, Archelaus I (413–400 or 399) made a serious, and for the time being successful, effort to create a united state out of a large geographical area in which tribal loyalty had hitherto predominated. As Thucydides (II, 100) observes, Archelaus did more for the security of his kingdom than all his eight predecessors on the Macedonian throne. He improved the organization of his army, perhaps partially anticipating Philip II in making more use of his infantry. He built or rebuilt fortified posts and constructed roads to connect strategic points. He was himself a lover of Hellenic culture who invited prominent artists to his court at Aegae, which, in spite of its somewhat remote location, remained the capital till the time of Philip II. Amongst Archelaus' visitors were the poets, Agathon and Euripides, the painter Zeuxis, and Timotheus, the musician and lyric poet. Indeed, two of Euripides' dramas were directly inspired by his sojourn in

[1] For the earlier relations of Macedonia with Greek states see above, pp. 50 ; 107 ; 211,

Macedonia, the *Bacchae* and the *Archelaus*.[1] It is unlikely
that the Hellenic culture promoted by the king touched more
than the royal circle and courtiers. As a whole the population, made up of a landed aristocracy and a free peasantry,
lived the simple, rough life of their forebears. To the Greek
observer the Macedonian government and institutions recalled
those which existed in Greece during the heroic age, a
monarchy limited only by customary law and by the necessity
of holding the loyalty of the clan chiefs. That Archelaus was
able to advance several steps towards making a first-class
power of his kingdom was no doubt in part the result of
unusual ability and force of character. But an additional
reason why he was able to succeed where his predecessors
had failed was that the keen struggle of the leading Greek
states in his day left them neither the time nor the resources
to concern themselves greatly, as they had often done in the
past, with the north Aegean area.

Towards the close of his reign Archelaus felt sufficiently
strong to attempt the enlargement of Macedonia at the
expense of his immediate neighbours. But, owing to his death
at the end of 400 or early in 399, his aggressions in Chalcidice
and northern Thessaly had no permanent consequences. For
the next forty years the condition of Macedonia was more
insecure than at any time in the fifth century. Of seven or
eight rulers only one, Amyntas III, occupied the throne for
any length of time. But during his reign of twenty-four years
(393–370) he was beset by constant dangers. The tribes of
Orestis to the west and of Lyncestis in the north-west denied
to him the allegiance that they had owed to Archelaus and
were ready, when opportunity offered, to make common
cause with the hill peoples of Illyria and Paeonia, to whom
they seem to have been racially akin. The king, harrassed
by dynastic conspiracies and the invasions of the Illyrians,
whose frequent depredations could only be checked by the
payment of an annual tribute, was glad, even at the sacrifice
of some coastal territory, to ally himself with the Chalcidic
Greeks. In the later part of his reign his foreign policy,

---

[1] The hypothesis of Ridgeway, *Class. Quart.*, XX (1926), 1–19, that the
*Rhesus* was composed by Euripides for Archelaus can no longer be maintained, since R. Goossens has shown (*L'antiquité classique*, I, 93–134) that that
play contains plain allusions to the relations between Athens and Sitalces
of Thrace.

dictated by necessity, was as varied as that of Perdiccas II; for he was at different times the ally of Athens, Jason of Pherae, and Thebes. After his death Macedonia was once again the scene of dynastic disputes in which Thebes intervened more than once.

The accession in 365 of Perdiccas III coincided with the renewal of naval activity by the Athenian Timotheus in the north Aegean. By giving substantial support to that commander, the Macedonian king once more altered Macedonian foreign policy and substituted a maritime for a military ally. As, however, the good relations with Athens ceased rather abruptly after Timotheus' recall homewards in 362, it may be surmised that the personality of the Athenian officer and his initial successes were mainly responsible for Perdiccas' temporary change of policy. Early in 359, when he had been on the throne for six years, he determined to end his ignominious clientage to the Illyrians. He concentrated all his forces against them; but the complete absence of precise information about the military operations and the strength of the combatants makes it impossible to say whether his campaign was really feasible or the foolhardy venture of a desperate man. Certainly the Macedonian army was disastrously beaten, and more than four thousand dead, including the king himself, were left on the field of battle. It may be that Perdiccas was an indifferent commander, for both Philip II and his son in due course inflicted chastisement on the Illyrians. But they did so with an army of superior organization and discipline.

### § 2. SUCCESSION AND EARLY CAMPAIGNS OF PHILIP II

Macedonia never had greater need of a strong hand than on the morrow of the Illyrian catastrophe. While the victors made preparations for a mass invasion into the territory of their defeated foe, their neighbours in Paeonia did not delay, but at once ravaged the Macedonian districts on their border. Serious as was the threat from external enemies, the Macedonians were at the same time distracted by dynastic struggles. The heir to the monarchy, Perdiccas' son, Amyntas, was an infant, and no less than six members of the royal house aimed to secure the regency or seize the throne outright. Philip, however, the youngest brother of Perdiccas, had sufficient backing to assume at once the regency for his nephew. Little is known of his earlier career. His fifteenth to his seventeenth year (367–365) he passed as a Macedonian hostage in Thebes. A Pythagorean in the household of Epaminondas acted as Philip's tutor and stimulated an appreciation of Hellenic culture in his apt pupil. Even more decisive, however, for the boy's future was the opportunity of sitting at the feet of Thebes' two outstanding citizens, Epaminondas and Pelopidas, and of observing closely what was at that time the best military organization in Greece. A year or two before his death Perdiccas III appears to have entrusted to Philip the administration of a district in Macedonia. Philip lost no time in improving the discipline and organization of such military forces as his new position put at his disposal. Thus he was able to try on a small scale the innovations that he was soon to extend to all Macedonia, and at the same time he strengthened his own position sufficiently to maintain his rights to the regency in 359 against the other claimants.

He was faced with the immediate task of checkmating five pretenders, his three half-brothers, Argaeus, and Pausanias, who six years before had nearly succeeded in dispossessing Perdiccas III and who in 359 relied on Thracian support to attain his end. Argaeus, on the other hand, had the backing of the Athenians, to whom he had promised, in the event of his accession, to hand over Amphipolis. Although the Athenians had during the past decade recovered some measure of their old hold on Chalcidice they had failed signally in their effort to recover the city on the Strymon. Also, the furtherance of their interests on the Thracian coast had been hampered by the hostility of the Thracian ruler, Cotys, against whom their military operations had been uniformly unsuccessful. On the death of Cotys in 360 the Odrysian kingdom passed to his son, Cersobleptes; but two pretenders, Berisades and Amadocus, with the help of Greek commanders enlisted in their service, compelled him to acquiesce in a partition of Cotys' realm. At the same time the Athenians tried to extort the cession of the Thracian Chersonese; but as they did not back their demands with an adequate display of force they were foiled in their endeavour. Their alliance with the Macedonian Argaeus was at best half-hearted; for, although an Athenian fleet accompanied him to Methone, he was aided in his attempt to occupy Aegae only by a body of mercenaries and a few Athenian volunteers. The truth was that Philip had already given an example of that diplomatic adroitness—his enemies called it perfidy—for which he was afterwards so famous. He had withdrawn the Macedonians placed in Amphipolis shortly before and had agreed to acknowledge Athens' claims to that city. When he had disposed of Argaeus, he sent the Athenians in the pretender's army home, protesting at the same time his friendly feelings for Athens. The Thracian Berisades, who had promised to assist Pausanias in his plot to secure the throne, appears to have been bought off by Philip. Of the other three claimants to power one was put to death, the other two sought safety in exile.

Philip was no less dexterous in dealing with his more formidable neighbours in the north-west. At first he dissuaded the Paeonians by fair words and largesse from further hostilities. Then, a year later (358), when their king died, he led an expedition into Paeonia, and, after inflicting a decisive defeat on them, compelled them to swear allegiance to the Macedonian crown. He had now made trial of his troops twice in actual warfare, first against Argaeus and then against the Paeonians, and he was satisfied that they were ready for a severer test. Instead of accepting the offer of the Illyrians to conclude peace on the basis of the *status quo* he led all his available men into their territory and after a long and desperate contest defeated them. Then he imposed his own terms on the beaten enemy, which included the evacuation by the Illyrians of all territory lying eastwards of Lake Ochrida.

§ 3. PHILIP'S REFORMS AND EARLIER RELATIONS WITH ATHENS

It has already been suggested that Philip made his first experiments in military reorganization during the closing years of Perdiccas' reign. He had also as a boy studied the tactical innovations in hoplite warfare which had for a while made Thebes the first military state in Greece. But, in the absence of any evidence to the contrary, we may attribute to his original genius fundamental changes which altered the character of Greek warfare for generations and whose political results were hardly less momentous. While the perfecting of the new Macedonian army must necessarily have taken a number of years—indeed, we may suppose that Philip, like his son, never ceased to experiment and strive after greater efficiency—the troops with which he won his early successes against Paeonians and Illyrians must already have been to a great extent organized and equipped according to his new principles. Earlier Macedonian rulers had relied mainly in their wars on the cavalry recruited from the nobility and land-owning class; the infantry, levied from the peasantry, always played a very subordinate part. While Philip continued to employ his cavalry as his first weapon of offence, he also created a highly trained infantry which could cooperate effectively with the mounted troops and, if occasion demanded, could be trusted to initiate and sustain the attack as capably as the best hoplite regiment. The chief infantry unit was the phalanx. Each of its battalions was, as far as possible, made up of men from the same tribe or local division, so that loyalty to the group formed the starting point for the growth of a wider national sentiment, a consciousness on the part of each soldier that he was also a Macedonian. These troops wore defensive armour, while their chief weapon of offence was a spear (σάρισσα), some twelve to thirteen feet in length. The tactical formation of the phalanx seems for some time to have been variable, until under Alexander the Great a depth of sixteen men became the normal. It differed from a Greek hoplite force in being more mobile and in its ability to keep a more open order when in action, improvements that were made possible by superior training and also because the defensive armour of the phalangite was somewhat lighter. A special force of heavy infantry, distinct from the phalanx, was that composed of the hypaspists (ὑπασπισταί), but it is uncertain how far their tactical organization and armature differed from those of the infantry of the line.[1] We are scarcely better informed

[1] I follow W. W. Tarn, *Hellenistic Naval and Military Developments*, 16–17, in rejecting the common interpretation that the hypaspists were lightly armed and resembled the Greek peltasts. Nevertheless some recent writers still uphold this theory, although it is unsupported by satisfactory evidence. Cf. J. Kromayer and G. Veith, *Heerwesen und Kriegsführung der Griechen und Römer*, 99; H. W. Parke, *Greek Mercenary Soldiers*, 156; U. Wilcken, *Alexander der Grosse*, 28.

about Philip's use of light-armed auxiliaries whose systematic employment in the Macedonian army does not antedate the time of Alexander. The cavalry comprised a *corps d'élite*, about one hundred strong, of royal horse-guards and the rest of the mounted troops, which as before were recruited from the propertied class, but were now, like the infantry, organized into smaller territorial squadrons.[1]

Philip kept his troops in constant training, and, when not engaged in actual warfare, personally directed their drill, practice in tactical evolutions, and manœuvres. Nor did he, like most Greek governments or commanders, restrict his campaigning to seven or eight months of the year. In thus creating a national army out of the Macedonian tribesmen he also perfected an instrument of war immeasurably superior to any that had preceded it. A system of rewards and promotions fostered a healthy spirit of emulation; and the confidence that the commander-in-chief himself would take cognisance of merit ensured for Philip, and later for his son, the personal devotion of his men, with whom he also shared every hardship. Philip did not neglect other measures to bring about the greater security and solidarity of his kingdom. Like Archelaus before him, he built roads and fortresses; but the surviving sources record only the occupation of strongholds that lay in newly acquired territory. At his accession the theoretical frontier of Macedonia on the east was still what it had been since the reign of Alexander I, namely the Strymon. But an inscription found at Epidaurus corroborates the scanty literary evidence to show that, on the death of Perdiccas III, Macedonian control along the coast did not extend beyond Therma, while Methone and Pydna were still independent.[2] Next to securing his northern and north-western boundaries Philip's main objective at the beginning of his reign was to make the theoretical frontier to the east a reality, and even to advance it further. This policy of necessity brought him into conflict with more than one Greek community. He had begun his reign with a conciliatory gesture towards the Athenians in spite of their relations

---

[1] The term Companions (ἑταῖροι), which was originally applied to the mounted escort of the king, was now used with a wider meaning for the whole cavalry. The *corps d'élite* of horse-guards, though also Companions, were more specifically described as τὸ ἄγημα.

[2] Cf. Geyer, *Makedonien bis zur Thronbesteigung Philipps II*, 138-139.

with Argaeus (p. 223). But in the summer of 357 on some
pretext he declared war on Amphipolis and laid siege to it.
Having breached its walls in one place, his troops forced their
way into the town, which capitulated after some skirmishes.
Philip's task appears to have been simplified by the circumstance that a good proportion of the townsfolk were pro-
Macedonian in their sympathies. Philip's leading opponents,
who were now exiled, had previously addressed an urgent
appeal to Athens. But it remained unanswered, because
Philip promised to hand the city over to the Athenians on
the secret understanding that they should surrender Pydna
to him. It has been usual to portray the Athenians as merely
the credulous dupes in this negotiation, since it is not open
to doubt that the Macedonian ruler never intended to carry
out his promises. But, though it is probable that the Athenian
government had not yet taken the full measure of Philip, it
is surely more reasonable to see the real reason for Athens'
policy of abstention from Chalcidic affairs in the imminent
collapse at this time of her maritime federation.

Philip's activity in Thrace caused great uneasiness among
other Greek cities in this area. Olynthus approached Athens
with a request for alliance, but was no more successful than
Amphipolis had been. In 356 Philip, after negotiating with
traitors in the town, made himself master of Pydna. Then,
after concluding a treaty with Olynthus, he attacked Potidaea
and, after a siege of many weeks, took it. As a token of his
good will he handed over this new conquest, after he had sent
the Athenian part of the population to their own country,
and also the district of Anthemus, to the Olynthians. By
this time the Athenians were sufficiently aroused by developments in the north to conclude a treaty with three chiefs who
were amongst the hostile neighbours of Macedonia, the
Thracian Cetriporis, Lyppeius of Paeonia, and the Illyrian
prince, Grabus.[1] But again Philip had acted more swiftly;
for, at the time when the agreement was signed, he had
already occupied Crenides. The settlers who had come from
Thasos a few years before seem to have asked Philip's protection against the natives. Crenides was superseded by a
new and larger town hard by, colonized by subjects of Macedonia. Before the end of the year Parmenio, Philip's ablest

[1] Tod 157, dated July, 356.

general, had decisively defeated the three princes who had
allied themselves to Athens. The Athenians were now
technically at war with Macedonia. In the summer of 355
they made an agreement with their old ally, Neapolis;[1]
for the rest, the war with their allies precluded the possibility
of more energetic action against Philip. The Macedonian
colony near Crenides, under its new name of Philippi, became
the centre of a flourishing gold-mining industry, from which
after a few years the king is said to have derived an annual
income of more than a thousand talents. Soon he began the
issue of a gold and silver currency bearing his name on the
obverse. His gold staters were the first regular gold currency
to be struck on the European side of the Aegean. They were
slightly heavier than the Persian darics, whose place they
very soon took on the mainland. The stater was equivalent
to six of his silver tetradrachms, which were struck on the
Phoenician standard.[2]

### § 4. ATHENS AND HER MARITIME ALLIES

Although Philip's operations in Chalcidice met with little
effective opposition from the Athenians, they had some minor
successes in the year 357. The city-states of Euboea which
had been dependent allies of Thebes for more than a decade
were at this time preparing to secede. When a Boeotian contingent landed in the island to re-establish Theban authority,
the islanders appealed to their old mistress, Athens. The
Athenians, to whom the loss of Euboea had been particularly
galling for both political and economic reasons, on this occasion acted promptly. An expeditionary force composed
partly of citizens, partly of mercenaries was rushed across
the straits. The Theban force was expelled and the Euboean
communities were in due course enrolled as members of the
Athenian confederacy.[3] The mercenaries of Athens, commanded by Chares, were then sent north to enforce the terms
of the partition to which Cersobleptes had been compelled to
assent, and the Thracian Chersonese, but without Cardia at
its northern extremity, was at length recovered. Athenian

[1] Tod 159, dated towards the end of the Athenian year, 356–355.
[2] Cf. *C.A.H.*, Plates II, 6 1–p.
[3] For two fragmentary inscriptions referring to the renewed alliance between Athens and the Euboean cities see Tod 153 and 154.

# THE RISE OF PHILIP OF MACEDON

satisfaction at these gains was soon displaced by profound and justified alarm; for in the summer or early autumn of this year (357) several of the strongest members of the maritime league seceded and formed an alliance against Athens. In part their action was a protest against Athenian domination of the League, for it was felt with some justice that Athens had for some time greatly exceeded her rights as laid down in 378–377.[1] But her power had been sufficient to deter her allies from secession or active protest until they could rely on outside support. At length in 357 an opportunity for this presented itself.

The rebellion of satraps in the western provinces of the Persian empire which had begun in 367–366 had lasted fitfully until 359 and finally broke down owing to lack of co-operation among the participants. Early in 358 Artaxerxes II died and was succeeded by his son, Artaxerxes III (Ochus), who, though ruthless, appears to have possessed more vigour and initiative than his father. Although his authority in western Asia was not at once fully re-established, only two of the governors continued to be actively disloyal. Egypt, however, remained independent for another fifteen years. Of the loyal satraps the most notable personality was Mausolus, who from his capital at Halicarnassus ruled as a native dynast over a wide area, comprising all Caria and some portion of Ionia to the north and Lycia to the south. His resources seem to have included a substantial fleet, by means of which he aimed to annex the islands off the coast of his principality. But, instead of opening direct hostilities which might have entailed a war not only with states like Cos and Rhodes but with the whole Athenian confederacy, he was skilful enough to exploit for his own ends the discontent of the islanders with Athens. At last, relying on his support, Rhodes and Chios withdrew from the League, being joined at once by Byzantium and soon after by Cos, whose several communities had a few years before united to form a single political entity. The Athenians replied to this challenge by putting a garrison on Andros to safeguard the Cyclades[2]—a step approved by the Congress

[1] Cf. pages 215–216 above.
[2] Cf. Tod 156. This decree relating to the payment of the garrison was passed about May–June, 356. The precise date when the garrison was placed in the island is not known, but is likely to have been a good many months earlier, that is to say, soon after the beginning of the war with the allies.

of the allies who remained faithful—and sent off an expedition to Chios which had been chosen as the headquarters of the insurgents. The chief command was vested in Chares, who landed his mercenary army to attack the chief city by land, while Chabrias in command of the fleet operated by sea. But the double assault failed and Chabrias himself fell fighting. Chares was, however, able to re-embark his men and withdraw from the island without heavy casualties. More serious than the material losses was the moral effect of this reverse. Other defections from the Athenian side took place, including that of the strategically important Sestos. The allies followed up their initial advantage by raids on the islands that still held to Athens. Meantime Chares seems to have withdrawn to the Hellespont and prevented the Byzantines from co-operating with their allies.[1] It might have been well if the Athenians had listened to the advice of the ageing publicist, Isocrates. In his treatise, *On Peace*, he urged his countrymen to seek a peaceful settlement with their late allies and to abandon once for all their dreams of naval hegemony.[2] But the *ecclesia* thought otherwise and Isocrates incurred much acrimonious criticism by his pamphlet. In the summer Timotheus, Iphicrates, and Menestheus, the son of Timotheus, who were probably all on the newly elected board of *strategi* for 356–355, were put in charge of a supplementary fleet and ordered to join forces with Chares.[3] To finance the war and at the same time to distribute the main burden of its cost more evenly amongst the well-to-do citizens, a system similar to that long in force for the collection of war-tax was introduced for the trierarchy. Twenty groups, called symmories, were established, each with sixty members. In each symmory the less wealthy members were formed into smaller groups, made up of a varying number of persons from three to seven, and each of these smaller aggregations was charged with the maintenance of a trireme. Although the financial liability

---

[1] Cf. *Syll.* 199, a decree in honour of a citizen of Sestos who gave valuable information about the movements of the Byzantine fleet to Athens.

[2] Cf. F. Kleine-Piening, *Quo tempore Isocratis orationes quae περὶ εἰρήνης et ἀρεοπαγιτικὸς inscribuntur compositae sint* (Paderborn, 1930). Though not all of his arguments are equally sound, he makes out a strong case for dating the publication of the treatise in question after the disaster at Chios but before the election of *strategi* at Athens, i.e. in the spring of 356.

[3] Diodorus (XVI, 21) assigns sixty vessels to Chares and sixty to the others.

## THE RISE OF PHILIP OF MACEDON

of the individual was thus on a proportionate basis, in actual practice the system seems to have pressed unfairly on the poorer members. Two years later Demosthenes advocated certain changes which would have ensured a more equitable distribution of the burden. But the advice of a new-comer to political life was disregarded and the needful reforms were not introduced until 340-338.

Meanwhile the enemies of Athens had concentrated on the reduction of Samos. When the second Athenian squadron was ready it joined that of Chares. Then the whole fleet turned its attention on the Hellespont, primarily to keep the straits open and force the capitulation of Byzantium, partly in the hope that the enemy would abandon the siege of Samos, as actually happened. But though the allies sailed for the Hellespont, they refused to risk an engagement, either because they had the worse position or, more probably, because they were numerically weaker. Instead, they retired once more to the vicinity of their headquarters at Chios. The Athenians, determined on attack, pursued them and prepared to take the offensive in the straits between Chios and Erythrae, a city which was clearly numbered amongst the enemies of Athens since its citizens at this time passed a decree in honour of Mausolus as their benefactor.[1] Lack of agreement between the Athenian admirals had unfortunate results; for when, owing to rough weather, Timotheus and his two associates postponed operations, Chares nevertheless attacked the enemy, and being unsupported, was repulsed with loss.[2] To save his own face, Chares charged his colleagues with deliberate treachery—they were supposed to have been bribed by the enemy to act as they did. Two of the three commanders managed to secure an acquittal; but Timotheus, who, in spite of many services to his country, was not a popular figure with the masses, was condemned to pay a heavy fine. He went into voluntary exile and died two years later at Chalcis.

The further conduct of the war now devolved on Chares, since the Athenian democracy's faith in him seems to have been in no way shaken by recent events. Lack of funds was,

[1] Tod 155.
[2] Diodorus (XVI, 21, 4) telescopes two distinct operations and puts the naval action in the Hellespontine region. There is, however, no doubt that the site of the battle was Embatum, between Chios and the mainland.

however, a pressing problem, as the treasury was almost empty. In this predicament Chares enlisted in the service of Artabazus of Phrygia, one of the two satraps who had not yet submitted to Artaxerxes III. For his signal services in inflicting a severe defeat on a royal army Chares was well rewarded by the satrap and thus was enabled to pay his troops. But Artaxerxes was not the man to submit tamely to such a challenge. He protested formally to the Athenian government. In addition he levied fresh troops for service in western Asia, so that the Athenians, fearing to be embroiled in war with Persia, recalled their commander and abandoned any hope that they may have held till then of coercing their late allies. Instead they opened negotiations and before the end of the Attic year, 355–354, agreed to a peace, by which their late opponents retained their independence and ceased to be members of the Second Athenian Confederacy. As other important cities were encouraged by the course of events to secede also, the League by the end of 354 numbered amongst its members only Athens, Euboea, a few of the Cyclades, the northern Sporades, and some towns on the Thracian coast.

We do not know how far the naval successes of the allies were won through the active co-operation of Mausolus. But, now that the Athenian League was broken beyond repair, the Carian dynast carried out his ulterior plan and annexed Rhodes and Cos. Following the example of other despotic governments, he expelled the democratic factions and set up oligarchies on whose loyalty he could rely. On his death (353) he was succeeded by his widow, Artemisia; but she survived him only two years and the sceptre then passed to his brother, Idrieus. An appeal addressed to Athens, perhaps in 352–351, by the Rhodian democrats to carry out their restoration and recover the island from Artemisia was refused. It was the wisest course that the Athenians could pursue, although Demosthenes, who had recently begun his public career in Athens, spoke on behalf of the Rhodian exiles in what is one of the earliest of his purely political speeches.[1]

[1] Dionysius of Halicarnassus dated Demosthenes' speech, *On the Liberty of the Rhodians*, in the year 351, but many modern critics on a variety of grounds maintain that it was delivered two years earlier. It is, however, clear that Artemisia had succeeded her husband at the time when Demosthenes addressed the assembly. Moreover, the way in which the orator refers

## § 5. THE RISE OF PHOCIS AND THE SACRED WAR

Even before the war between Athens and her allies had terminated a grave crisis had developed in central Greece. In a short time the peace that had reigned in most of the states of European Greece since Mantinea and the hopes entertained by the more optimistic statesmen, that arbitration would replace armed intervention as a means of settling inter-state disputes, were rudely destroyed. Above all, disunion in Hellas played directly into the hands of Philip II. Most societies of respectable antiquity are familiar with institutions that have become anachronistic survivals, but usually such are not politically dangerous. The Amphictionic League was, however, an exception. Its origin reached back to the beginning of Greek history, to an age when all over the Hellenic world religious leagues, mostly of no great size, sprang up to foster the cult of some divinity. Many of these unions survived into late historic times, but since their activities never extended beyond the purpose for which they were first formed, they are rarely heard of in the ancient sources and exercised no influence on the public life of the Greek city-states. Two circumstances marked out the Amphictionic League as different from the others. Its twelve members were tribes not cities, and, though the original place of its periodic meetings had been the temple of Demeter at Anthela near Thermopylae, it had in the archaic period gained control of Delphi. Thereafter one of the two annual meetings was held in Anthela and one at Delphi; above all, the League assumed a general guardianship of the most venerated shrine in the Hellenic world. Since Delphi, unlike most other Greek sanctuaries, was of national importance and its oracle was consulted not only by individuals but by governments, the League, and not alone the Delphic priests, might easily be drawn into the turmoil of Greek politics. At the deliberations of the League each tribe had two votes so that, in theory, states like Athens or Sparta counted only as parts of the Ionians or Dorians.

---

to Artaxerxes' plans to recover Egypt (§ 11) suggests that the expedition to Egypt had either started out or at least was well under way. But Tarn (*C.A.H.*, VI, 22) very tentatively dates the Persian invasion of Egypt in 351. Thus it seems likely that Demosthenes' speech belongs to the Attic year 352–351,

In practice the leading states determined the voting of the tribes to which they belonged and not uncommonly that of other tribes as well. Thus in the fourth century, ever since Thebes had advanced to the front rank of Greek states, she had been able to rely on the votes of tribes in central Greece and Thessaly and thereby to exercise a controlling influence in the councils of the League.

About 357 B.C. the Amphictions passed a resolution condemning a number of wealthy Phocians to a heavy fine, probably for sacrilege.[1] Such action was no novelty, for after Leuctra the Spartans had been condemned, for their violation of the Theban Cadmea, to pay a heavy indemnity. In that case it had been found impossible to enforce the Council's decision. The Phocians, however, were the close neighbours of the Boeotians whom they had been constrained to join as dependent allies after Leuctra. Since the decline of the Theban power they had indeed reasserted their freedom of action ; but it was not to be expected that they could offer any prolonged resistance, if the League or its chosen instruments had recourse to military measures. The secession of Phocis in 362–361 caused deep resentment among the Boeotians, so that, backed by the Thessalians, whose dislike of Phocis was equally marked, they seized on the first convenient pretext to deal a crushing blow through the Amphictionic League at their hated neighbours. But at this juncture Phocis produced a series of military leaders—their contemporaries referred to them as despots or tyrants—whose energy brought their country temporarily into the full glare of the political limelight and indirectly caused a disturbance of the peace over a far wider area than central Greece.

We know nothing of the earlier career of the Phocian Philomelus. In 356 he was sufficiently popular with his countrymen to arouse their patriotism, so that they refused to submit tamely to the ultimatum of the Amphictions. When he appealed to Sparta—a fellow-sufferer at the hands

---

[1] According to Diodorus (XVI, 23) the Phocians had encroached upon and cultivated lands sacred to Apollo. Justin (VIII, 1) alleges that they had devastated Boeotian territory, while in Athenaeus (560 B) the abduction of a Theban woman is given as the cause of the trouble. The vague and contradictory testimony of these writers merely shows that these so-called reasons were no more than pretexts, the real reasons for the action of the League lying much deeper.

of the Amphictionic Council—its government declined to side with Phocis openly; but the king, Archidamus, privately put some mercenaries and a sum of money at his disposal. With this help and from his own resources Philomelus brought together a small force of mercenaries to co-operate with a Phocian citizen body of one thousand peltasts. With this small army he seized Delphi and its sanctuary. An attempt made by the Locrians of Amphissa to recover the shrine led to a bloody engagement in the vicinity of the temple, but was completely repulsed. In spite of these initial successes Philomelus could not hope to maintain himself without additional troops. He therefore exacted heavy contributions from the wealthy citizens of Delphi and with these funds engaged more professional soldiery. By the following year he had addressed a general appeal to the more influential Greek states. His presentation of the Phocian case, which included an appeal to the Homeric Catalogue of Ships in which the Phocians were described as lords of Delphi, was impressive enough to secure both Sparta and Athens as nominal allies. But for the moment neither state was prepared to send active help. The Achaeans, however, not merely expressed their sympathy with Phocis, but by the following year (354) despatched troops across the Corinthian Gulf.

Meanwhile the Amphictions under Theban guidance had not been inactive, but formally declared a sacred war against the sacrilegious violators of Delphi. In the second campaigning season the Phocian army had been augmented to some 5000 men. To facilitate the defence of the Delphic sanctuary, Philomelus fortified it with a wall. Then he took the offensive and invaded Opuntian Locris with the double purpose of ravaging the country and preventing a junction between the Boeotians and their Thessalian allies. But the ancient accounts of this and of two subsequent expeditions, in one of which the Boeotians appear for the first time to have taken part in the fighting, while the other was directed against the Thessalians, are so vague that it is impossible to determine what Philomelus' plans of campaign really were (or to identify the sites of several engagements) in all of which Philomelus worsted his adversaries. At length the tide of success turned and at Neon among the northern foot-hills of Parnassus the

Phocian army, now augmented to 10,000 mercenaries and supported by 1500 Achaeans, suffered a heavy reverse at the hands of the Boeotians.[1] Philomelus himself was slain, but his adjutant, Onomarchus, rallied the remnants of the army and brought them safely back to Delphi.

The serious disaster to their arms produced some wavering among the Phocians. But many of the doubters were deterred by Onomarchus' ready eloquence from treating for peace, and he then procured his election as generalissimo in place of Philomelus. Secure in his authority, he caused the arrest of any that continued hostile to his policy and impounded their property. It is probable that Philomelus had already begun to " borrow " from the temple-funds at Delphi in order to carry on the war and especially to double his mercenary army.[2] His successors certainly availed themselves freely of the all but inexhaustible treasures of the temple, gold and silver objects being turned into currency, which bore the names of Onomarchus and later on of Phalaecus, while bronzes and iron dedications were melted down and converted into weapons and defensive armour.[3] Onomarchus next reconstructed his army by engaging fresh mercenaries. He invaded both eastern Locris and western Boeotia, his most noteworthy achievement being the capture of Orchomenus. He also used some of the abundant monies now at his disposal for other military purposes, when he secured the alliance of Lycophron, tyrant of Pherae, by a gift

---

[1] Diodorus (XVI, 25) places the invasion of Locris in 355 and the catastrophe at Neon in 354. On the chronology of 357–351, see now N. G. L. Hammond in *J.H.S.* 57 (1937), pp. 44–78.

[2] Most modern writers state that Philomelus at some time before his death began to use the Delphic treasure. H. W. Parke, *Greek Mercenary Soldiers*, 135, note 4, after pointing out that the two versions in Diodorus (XVI, 30, 1 and XVI, 56, 5) are contradictory, would follow the latter and exonerate Philomelus from that sacrilege. But it is difficult to believe that Philomelus could have paid all his expenses from the resources of Phocis and from the sums that he squeezed out of the wealthy Delphians, even if we allow also for his having captured a good deal of booty from the enemy. During the second campaign his army, according to Diodorus, was swelled to 10,000 mercenaries. Parke (p. 140) himself points out that the maintenance of some 8000 men would cost about 2 talents a day. Thus it is preferable to assume that Philomelus set the example of taking funds from the temple. And why should the man who was sacrilegious enough to use violence towards the Delphic priestess (Diod., XVI, 27) in order that she should vaticinate about his future, be too scrupulous to use the temple treasure ?

[3] Cf. Hill, *H.G.C.*, 50–51 ; *C.A.H.*, Plates II, 8 *b* and *c*.

of substantial subsidies. To exploit the disunion of the
Thessalians in that way was an astute move, but it overlooked one grave responsibility. The Thessalian League, in
view of the double threat from Pherae and from Phocis,
turned to Philip of Macedon. The king entered Thessaly and
marched against Lycophron, who appealed to his new ally.
A Phocian corps, seven thousand strong and commanded by
Onomarchus' younger brother, Phayllus, hurried to the rescue
but was routed by Philip. Thereupon Onomarchus with all
his available men invaded Thessaly and defeated Philip on
two occasions (353). But the tables were turned in the
following year. It opened auspiciously enough for Onomarchus as he began by capturing two additional towns in
Boeotia. But then the Thessalian situation again demanded
his attention, for Philip had returned with augmented forces
to co-operate with his Thessalian allies. A decisive engagement was fought near the shores of the Gulf of Pagasae. The
opposing infantry seem to have been about equal in strength,
but Onomarchus had only a few hundred cavalry to oppose
to three thousand mounted Thessalians and Macedonians.
Philip inflicted a crushing defeat, Onomarchus himself was
killed and nearly a third of the Phocian army was wiped out.
In addition some three thousand were taken prisoner and
subsequently executed by Philip as sacrilegious robbers.

Once again a brief period of success was followed by a
crisis in the affairs of Phocis. Phayllus took his brother's
place and continued to spend the Delphic treasure freely.
To obtain enough mercenaries to make good the heavy
casualties recently incurred, he offered double the normal
rate of pay. Then, too, he repeated the requests of his predecessors to other Greek states to intervene on behalf of
Phocis. The Athenians had already acted; for, after his
victory, Philip had first captured Pherae and expelled its
ruler and then moved through Thessaly, preparatory to an
invasion of Phocis. As soon as his intention became known,
the Athenians mustered a force of citizens, composed of 5000
heavy infantry and 400 cavalry, and despatched them with
all speed to defend the pass of Thermopylae. To have overcome this opposition would have been very costly, and Philip
could afford to wait; so he withdrew again into Macedonia.
Achaea and Sparta by this time had also sent some troops

to the assistance of Phayllus.[1] Meanwhile the affairs of central Greece had reacted on the Peloponnesian states. The Spartans had been laying plans to overpower Megalopolis and then to recover Messenia at a time when the natural champions of these states, the Thebans, were too occupied on their own frontiers to intervene. Megalopolis appealed to Athens, but in spite of Demosthenes' advocacy the Athenians declined to meddle with Peloponnesian quarrels. By 352 each side had, however, found allies. Sparta was aided by three thousand men from Phocis and by contingents from Elis, Achaea, Phlius, and Mantinea. A year later Thebes also sent some help. But the other Arcadian cities, Messenia, and Argos aligned themselves with Megalopolis. Intermittent but on the whole indecisive fighting disturbed the peace of the Peloponnese probably for two years. In the end the political situation remained unchanged and Sparta was no nearer attaining either of her objectives.

In the interval the war in central Greece had continued. Phayllus, after suffering three reverses in western Boeotia, was more successful against his northern neighbours in Locris, whose towns he conquered one by one, only to be worsted once more by the Boeotians. Soon afterwards he died and was succeeded by Phalaecus. That the Boeotians did not press home their advantage more effectively may have been due partly to inefficient leadership, and it is perhaps significant that the name of not one of their military leaders has survived. But they were also hampered by lack of funds. They had indeed collected some contributions from allies;[2] but it was not till 351 that their finances were somewhat improved by a substantial gift from Artaxerxes III. For, although a Theban mercenary force had crossed to Asia Minor some years earlier to support the rebel satrap, Artabazus, Thebes subsequently made her peace with the Great King, who then sent 300 talents. In return he requested a loan of hoplites to take part in his Egyptian expedition.

[1] Diodorus (XVI, 37, 2) enumerates together the Athenian force, 1000 Lacedaemonians and 2000 Achaeans. He relates the defence of Thermopylae in another place (XVI, 38, 2) without giving any numbers. As there is no hint in any other source of two Athenian interventions in Phocis at this time it may be assumed that the 5400 held Thermopylae and then returned home. What part the Spartan and Achaean regiments played in any operations is nowhere stated.    [2] Tod 160.

Phalaecus was the son of Onomarchus. As he was either still a minor or barely of age, his uncle before his death had nominated an older man, Mnaseas, to act as his guardian and military advisor. The Sacred War continued fitfully until 347, but degenerated more and more into a series of border raids by the Phocians into Boeotia and by the Boeotians into Phocian territory. If the honours in the field appear to have been fairly evenly divided, the Phocians kept their hold not only on Delphi but on several towns in western Boeotia. In view of the lavish use that they made of the Delphic treasure it is interesting to find that the rebuilding of the temple, which had been wrecked by an earthquake about 373, was, though occasionally interrupted, not suspended. This is proved by the extant records of the "temple-builders" (ναοποιοί), a board whose members were drawn from various parts of the Greek world, including Delphi itself.[1] Wellnigh half a century elapsed before the new structure was completed.

## § 6. PHILIP IN CHALCIDICE AND HIS WAR WITH ATHENS

Philip's anti-Phocian activities, although they did not meet with uniform success and involved him in some temporary loss, in the end brought him considerable advantage. Nor did these matters absorb all his time and thought. In 354 he strengthened his hold on Thrace by the capture of Maronea and Abdera. Then, in the following year, before he suffered defeat at the hands of Onomarchus, he had laid siege to Methone and captured it. Its inhabitants were permitted to leave, but the city itself was destroyed and its territory incorporated in Macedonia. Later, after he had crushed Onomarchus, he had seized Pagasae, thereby winning a valuable port and gaining control of the peninsula of Magnesia. Then for perhaps two years he was busy increasing his influence in the interior of Thrace by winning over one or other of its native rulers. His friendly relations with Cersobleptes did not, however, last long, for that prince very soon turned to Athens. Philip replied by seeking the friendship of Amadocus and allied himself with Byzantium and Perinthus. Next he laid siege to the strong fortress of Heraeon Teichos situated

---

[1] Tod 169 reproduces the records for 346–343. There are other lists of later date.

in Cersobleptes' domain. These operations in the vicinity of the Thracian Chersonese produced a warlike reaction in Athens. Under the guidance of Eubulus, who towards the end of the war with the allies had become a member of the board which controlled the Theoric Fund and, through his exceptional skill in finance, had rapidly gained an ascendancy in the *ecclesia*, the Athenians had for some years pursued a policy of peace and retrenchment. Philip's threat to Thermopylae had indeed been answered by a prompt mobilization, so that the king's plan to enter central Greece had for the time being been frustrated. But we have seen how Athens refused to be drawn into a Peloponnesian war and had declined to come to the aid of the Rhodian democrats. Nevertheless, when Philip attacked Heraeon Teichos, preparations were hurriedly made to send an Athenian armament of forty triremes to Thrace to protect Athenian interests and assist Cersobleptes. Before it could sail, news came that Philip was dead. Actually he had fallen sick and had abandoned the siege. Lulled into a false sense of security, the Athenians gave up the projected expedition. It was perhaps in the same year (352) that Sestos was recovered by Chares. Subsequently a body of Athenian settlers was sent to occupy the town.[1] Whatever the nature of his illness, Philip had recovered by 351. He secured the Illyrian frontier of Macedonia by the establishment of new military posts and compelled the prince of the Molossi in Epirus to acknowledge his overlordship. His admirals prosecuted the war actively against Athens by raiding her island dependencies and capturing a grain fleet as it rounded the southern end of Euboea.

Above all, Philip turned his attention once more to Chalcidice and the Olynthian League. The friendly relations between him and the Olynthians had undergone a change. The latter, acting from motives that are obscure, had given asylum to two of Philip's old rivals for the Macedonian throne. Besides this, they had approached Athens with a view to an alliance, although it might have been thought that Athenian policy during the past five years did not encourage hope of

[1] It was perhaps at this time that some Samian exiles found refuge in Rhodes. See the Samian decree in honour of a Rhodian published by A. Maiuri in *Nuova Silloge epigrafica di Rodi e Cos*, 3–4.

# THE RISE OF PHILIP OF MACEDON

military and naval support sufficient to act as an effective check on Macedonia. And, merely by treating with Athens, they were communicating with a state that was at war with Philip, thereby increasing his suspicions and even exasperating him. As usual, however, he avoided precipitate action. He had protested to Olynthus in 352 but without effect. Then in 349, after the conclusion of his operations in the west and north-west, he repeated his demands. When they were again refused he proceeded to break up the federation. Most of the constituent towns of the Olynthian League appear to have surrendered without fighting, although some, like Stagirus, offered resistance. The Olynthians, now filled with extreme alarm, once more turned to Athens, this time with an urgent appeal for immediate military aid. The Athenians were divided in their counsels. A majority were still disposed towards non-intervention, but a growing minority, whose chief spokesman was Demosthenes, favoured more vigorous measures. Reference has already been made to certain of Demosthenes' earliest political utterances. Born in 384, he had, when seven years of age, lost his father. Of the substantial patrimony of fourteen talents which should ultimately have been his, the bulk was lost owing to fraud or mismanagement on the part of his legal guardians. As a youth he became a pupil of Isaeus, then the leading authority on testamentary suits, and in 363 pleaded his own case against his guardians. Although the jury returned a verdict in his favour, it is doubtful whether he ever recovered more than a small fraction of his property. He took to professional speech-writing and thereby deepened his knowledge of Athenian law. Also by assiduous practice he succeeded in overcoming certain physical disabilities which would have militated against his success as a public speaker. In addition he was a keen observer of affairs, so that by 355 he was already taking a prominent part in a political trial. His first speech in the assembly was, as we have seen, delivered in the following year, when he advocated a reform of the symmories. His first oration on the relations between Athens and Philip of Macedon—the so-called *First Philippic*—was probably spoken in 351. It begins with a broad review of Philip's past activities, from which the orator draws the conclusion that nothing but instant action could forestall the imminent danger threatening Athens from the Macedonian king. He then brings forward his concrete proposals, namely, to have a fleet of fifty vessels constantly in commission to counter the naval activities of Philip's admirals,[1] and to have a small army of 2000 hoplites and 200 cavalry ready for every emergency : of this corps a quarter shall be composed of Athenian citizens.

Although Demosthenes developed the full powers of his political oratory in this speech, it failed to bring about any change of policy. Two years afterwards, when the Olynthians addressed their appeal to the Athenians, it was Demosthenes who championed their cause. In his three orations on the affairs of Olynthus he enlarged again on the danger to his countrymen from the Macedonian king, advocated the despatch of an immediate armament to the north, and considered what was probably the most urgent problem connected with such an expedition, finance. While in the first speech he is still sufficiently guarded to make alternate proposals—for he was treading on dangerous ground—in the third he bluntly demands the repeal of the existing laws governing the Theoric Fund and its employment for naval and military purposes. The appeal of Olynthus an_ the speeches that it called forth belong to the period immediately preceding the siege of Olynthus itself, when Philip was still engaged in annexing the other towns in the federation. Athenian public opinion was veering round towards intervention ; yet, instead of acting swiftly, as they had done when Philip threatened Thermopylae, the Athenians continued for months to deliberate. Before their minds were fully made up, Philip dealt a very shrewd blow at his opponents, by persuading the cities of Euboea, with the exception of Carystus, to secede from Athens. The king had calculated rightly that the Athenians would place the recovery of the neighbouring island before the claims of Olynthus, although Demosthenes' voice at least was raised against an Euboean expedition.[2]

---

[1] Somewhat later in the speech (§ 32) Demosthenes advises the Athenians to use Lemnos, Thasos, and other islands in that region as bases from which to harry the vessels and ports of Philip.

[2] It was at this time that a supporter of Eubulus, Meidias, who had differed acrimoniously from Demosthenes about the advisability of an Euboean expedition, publicly assaulted the orator when he was acting as choregus during the Dionysiac festival. At the instance of Demosthenes a vote of

Nevertheless it was sent under the leadership of Phocion, who won a Pyrrhic victory but failed to recover the cities. They remained independent and the Athenian maritime confederacy thereby lost several of its few remaining member.

At length in the summer of 348 Philip invested Olynthus. In answer to one more appeal from the city an Athenian force of 2300 was sent off under Chares, but by the time that it neared its destination Olynthus had fallen. It was destroyed and its inhabitants enslaved. Destruction was also visited on the other communities in Thrace—according to a statement made by Demosthenes seven years later there were thirty-two in addition to Apollonia and Olynthus itself.[1] The king's reasons for this barbarous severity are obscure, as it ran counter to his usual policy. He must have been convinced that that area would never be completely controlled by Macedonia as long as it contained communities which, if merely allied to him, would always strive to recover their freedom of action and would naturally gravitate towards other Greek states to attain that end.

### § 7. THE PEACE OF PHILOCRATES

The surviving records of the eighteen months after Philip's capture of Olynthus are a tangle of diplomatic moves and counter-moves. This confusion is due to the nature of the sources. There is no reliable historical account of these events, for Diodorus is at his worst in telling the story, and his moral reflections on the deserved fate of the sacrilegious Phocians are a poor substitute for what he does not give us— an intelligent and intelligible narrative. For fuller information it is necessary to turn to the Athenian orators, but their versions of the negotiations with Philip were not published till several years later, and are so obviously written from a party point of view and so filled with personal recriminations that the truth is not easy to determine.

---

censure was passed on Meidias by the *ecclesia*. In addition, Demosthenes prepared to prosecute Meidias for sacrilege. But the extant speech against Meidias was never delivered; for when the trial, after much delay, was at last due to take place in 347, Demosthenes was supporting the policy of Eubulus. Hence it was probably for political reasons that he did not press the charge further, but accepted damages of thirty minae from the defendant.

[1] *Philipp.*, III, 26.

The destruction of Olynthus and the Chalcidic League produced something like consternation at Athens. For the time being the spokesmen of opposite political parties were united in their action for the common weal. Representatives were sent to various states in the Peloponnese. Amongst them was Aeschines, whose earlier career, though hardly distinguished, had at least been varied. After some experience as a school teacher and an actor he had become clerk of the Athenian assembly. He now emerged as a supporter of Eubulus and a powerful speaker. But his efforts and those of his fellow envoys to persuade the Peloponnesian cities to unite against Philip met with no response. It has indeed been suggested that the action of Eubulus in approaching the other states of Greece was merely a device for satisfying public opinion in Athens. But the extant evidence does not seem to justify so cynical a view; and we may credit Eubulus and his supporters with a genuine desire to arouse Greek sentiment to what they were at last convinced was a national danger. With the failure of these negotiations the wisest, indeed the only, course was to seek an agreement with the enemy. This appeared the more feasible because Philip had himself sounded the Athenians on the subject of peace even before the fall of Olynthus. His motives in working for an accommodation with Athens are obscure. One can only surmise that he did not yet consider the time ripe to crush his most formidable opponent. His management of the negotiations and his later conduct make it clear that in 347–346 he was playing for time. Unhappily for Athens the situation in Phocis had undergone a sudden change. Phalaecus' conduct of the Sacred War dissatisfied his countrymen. He was replaced by a board of three commanders; but, being enabled to keep a great part of his mercenaries, he established himself near Thermopylae and acted independently of the Phocian government. His depredations in Boeotia were so severe that Thebes appealed to Philip to intervene. The Phocian government, on the other hand, approached both Sparta and Athens. Both states responded with military aid, but Phalaecus, ignoring the action of his countrymen, refused to co-operate with the Athenian and Lacedaemonian contingents, who thereupon returned to their respective homes. To the Athenian assembly the conduct of

Phalaecus, apart from its discourtesy, was suspect; and events soon showed that they were not entirely wrong.

However, the immediate result was that the *ecclesia* authorized direct negotiations with the Macedonian king. Among the envoys were Philocrates, who had proposed the motion to appoint a delegation, Aeschines, and Demosthenes, who was a member of the Council of Five Hundred in 347-346. Arrived at Pella, they were treated with great consideration by Philip, but the terms which they reported to the assembly amounted to no more than a recognition of the *status quo* by Macedonia and Athens and by their respective allies. There were, moreover, two reservations. Philip, while agreeing that each side should retain what it held, insisted on the exclusion of Phocis and of the sea-town of Halus in Thessaly which he was engaged in reducing at that time. At two meetings the assembly deliberated. Finally, on the motion of Philocrates, Philip's terms were accepted. Demosthenes, however, carried a proposal to delete the clause excluding Phocis and Halus from the pact, which would at least leave their future status undetermined. But the representatives of Philip, who had appeared in Athens to administer the oath to the Athenians and their allies, made it clear that their master would not consent to this change. In the end the assembly followed the counsels of Eubulus and accepted the original terms.

It then became necessary to send a delegation to receive the oath from Philip and his allies. The personnel was the same as before, but proved far from harmonious. Since it was believed that the peace would date from the time when the king swore to the agreement, Demosthenes exerted himself to expedite matters as much as possible; for any conquests that Philip might make in the interval he would certainly insist on retaining. But Demosthenes' colleagues set the pace. After an initial delay at Athens they made their way slowly to Pella, and, when they found the king still absent in Thrace, awaited his arrival instead of going on to meet him. But even when Philip had returned to his capital, the real business of the mission was postponed. Besides, other states had sent representatives to his court to secure advantages for themselves, and the king appears to have excelled himself in charming all that he met without giving anything away. What Demosthenes had feared had indeed happened. While the Athenian mission had delayed, Philip had subdued Cersobleptes and greatly strengthened his hold on Thrace. At Pella Philip was not slow to notice the lack of agreement amongst the Athenian legates; for, while Demosthenes cared little for the future of Phocis and was mainly desirous of safeguarding the political integrity of the Boeotian League, his colleagues, and especially Aeschines, continued to plead on behalf of the Phocians. The king's assurances that Phocis would not suffer at his hands finally convinced Aeschines, who, in common with his fellow ambassadors, except Demosthenes, was also ill-advised enough to accept the gifts which Philip pressed on them. The envoys then accompanied Philip and his army into Thessaly and at Pherae the oaths were at last taken by him and by his allies. Then the Athenian delegation returned home after an absence of two and a half months (April–June, 346).

Heated debates followed. Demosthenes immediately laid his version of the transactions before the assembly, at the same time charging his colleagues with corrupt and treasonable practices. But the deep impression made by him momentarily on his hearers was completely dispelled a few days later when Aeschines, quoting the promises of Philip and even presenting a despatch from him, triumphantly vindicated himself and his fellows. The *ecclesia* accepted his assurance that Philip's designs were directed against Thebes not against Phocis, and passed a resolution of thanks to the Macedonian king. At the same time the Athenians called upon the Phocians to surrender Delphi to the Amphictionic Council. Meanwhile the situation in central Greece had undergone a swift change. While still in Thessaly, Philip communicated with the Athenians and invited them to send a military force to Thermopylae and to co-operate with him in settling the affairs of Phocis and Boeotia. On this occasion the Athenians followed Demosthenes' advice and refused. Instead, they were content to notify the king of the resolution that had just been passed by the assembly. Yet it would have been wiser if they had listened to Eubulus, who wished Athens not to isolate herself politically, but to take the part to which her position among the Greek states entitled her in adjusting the differences among her northern neighbours, which had disturbed the peace of Hellas for more than a decade. Philip, however, had not waited for their reply. He had suddenly appeared at Thermopylae and received the capitulation of Phalaecus on terms. The Phocian leader and his mercenaries were allowed to depart whither they would.[1] Deserted by the essential part of their army, the Phocians could only submit to Philip, although a few communities put up some resistance. Then Philip brought the question of their fate before the Amphictionic Council. When sundry proposals of varying severity had been ventilated, it was resolved that their towns should be broken up and the inhabitants dispersed in open villages. They were disarmed, and a heavy tribute spread over a number of years was imposed to make good the sums that had been taken from the Delphic sanctuary.[2] The Phocian votes in the Amphictionic League were transferred to Philip, who, in addition, had himself chosen to preside at the Pythian festival that was about to be celebrated.

These events had once more thrown the Athenians into a turmoil. It was not allayed by a despatch from the king justifying his action against Phocis, seeing that that state had been expressly excluded from the treaty between himself and Athens. Then, when the Athenians intimated that they were not sending the usual official delegates to the Pythia, he replied by demanding Athens' recognition of himself as a member of the Amphictionic League. The assembly was disposed to answer with a curt refusal, but on this occasion Demosthenes convinced his countrymen of the folly of provoking the king and perhaps bringing on themselves the combined hostility of Philip and the Amphictions. The peace must be kept at all costs and it would be more

[1] The Phocian leader and his men after various experiences found their way to Crete, where they participated in the local warfare. Phalaecus was killed at the siege of Cydonia. A part of his troops later returned to the Peloponnese and entered the service of Elean exiles. But they suffered defeat, and those that were captured were enslaved.

[2] Diodorus (XVI, 56, 6) estimates the total sum taken from Delphi at 10,000 talents. The annual tribute imposed on the Phocians was originally 60 talents a year, but such was their poverty that they did not pay the first instalment till 343. In 338, when Philip helped to restore the Phocian cities, the Amphictions reduced the tribute to 10 talents. This sum continued to be paid annually to 322. Cf. the lists in Tod 172.

than impolitic for the Athenians, who had already been compelled to acquiesce in so many losses, to remain obdurate in face of Philip's determination. Later events were to show that Demosthenes did not intend permanent submission to the will of the Macedonian ruler, but hoped by present concessions to pave the way for an anti-Macedonian coalition at a more favourable time. From this date on his ascendancy in the *ecclesia* became more and more marked, whereas until 346 he had generally represented a minority opinion.

The views of Isocrates are in strong contrast to Demosthenes' estimate of the political situation in 346 and of the future. The aged publicist issued his *Philippus* soon after the Peace of Philocrates.[1] He had long been convinced that an amicable alliance of the leading Greek states—Athens, Sparta, Argos, and Thebes—which would guarantee the peace of Hellas could not be brought about by any of these states, and he called upon Philip to create such a $συμμαχία$ and, when he had reconciled the cities with each other and with himself, to lead a combined expedition against Persia. It is not too much to say that Isocrates had a clearer notion of Philip's greatness than any of his Greek contemporaries. At the same time it must be admitted that his point of view is narrowly Hellenic. Philip is merely to be president of the $συμμαχία$ and its military leader; he is not to exercise any sovereignty over his Greek allies. Such a programme could not satisfy Philip, to whom the political dependence on himself of Greece was both an end in itself—the last step in his conquest of the Balkan peninsula—and a necessary preliminary to wresting from Persia her provinces in western Asia. Nevertheless Philip must have valued the support of so widely read a political essayist as Isocrates. The *Philippus* must always rank as a discourse of outstanding interest since its author to a great extent foresaw what his contemporaries failed to discern, the political future of the Hellenic world.

[1] The date of publication, after the peace and before the destruction of Phocis, i.e. between April and July, 346, is fixed by internal evidence (*Philippus* §§ 9 and 50).

# CHAPTER IX

# THE TRIUMPH OF PHILIP

## § 1. THE RIVAL DIPLOMACIES OF DEMOSTHENES AND PHILIP

FOR five years after the Peace of Philocrates Athens was the scene of an embittered party warfare engendered by divergent views on foreign policy. Nor did Demosthenes and his chief supporters—prominent among them were two younger men of great talent, Hyperides and Lycurgus—fight their battles only in the assembly; they sought to cripple the opposition by instituting legal proceedings against its leading men. Soon after the peace had been signed by all Demosthenes gave notice of his intention to charge Aeschines with corrupt and treasonable conduct, but unwisely he associated with himself in the prosecution a certain Timarchus. Aeschines, on the principle that attack is the best means of defence, at once brought an action against Timarchus under a law which disqualified any citizen from speaking in the assembly who had been guilty of gross profligacy. Not only did he secure Timarchus' conviction by the jury, but indirectly he threw discredit on Demosthenes, who found it expedient to postpone his attack on Aeschines to a more favourable time.

The next eighteen months are a blank in our records; but by 344 the diplomatic activity of Philip in the Peloponnese led Demosthenes to urge counter-measures on his countrymen. The king, taking into account the irritation felt in certain states against Athens for continuing to foster good relations with Sparta, made friendly overtures to the Messenians, Arcadians, Eleans, and Argives and backed up his advances by sending them money and mercenaries. In this way he won over the governing factions in these states. The efforts of Messene and Megalopolis to be admitted to the Amphictionic League about this time did not succeed, even though

Philip may have supported the applications. As a consolation prize they were formally voted benefactors of Apollo and the Amphictions, since they had regularly contributed to the rebuilding of the temple.[1] Philip's negotiations in the Peloponnese soon became known at Athens. On the motion of Demosthenes the assembly voted that he and some others be sent to the pro-Macedonian cities to win them back to the Hellenic cause. Demosthenes himself visited both Argos and Messene. His public references to the king of Macedonia were so embittered that, when they came to the ears of Philip, he entered a diplomatic protest. The arrival of the Macedonian envoys at Athens coincided with that of representatives from Argos and Messene, who came to urge on the Athenians the abandonment of their friendship with Sparta. Demosthenes took the opportunity of making an uncompromising attack on Philip's policy in the presence of these various delegates.

The *Second Philippic*, delivered in the autumn of 344, begins with a severe condemnation of the Athenians for their love of words instead of deeds. The speaker then strives to show that Philip, in spite of protests of friendship, is in reality directing all his efforts against Athens, and the Peloponnesian states are warned of the danger of trusting Macedonia's ruler. " Every king, every despot is the enemy of freedom and the foe of law. Beware lest, while you seek to be rid of war, you find a master."[2] The end of the speech contains veiled allusions to his political opponents at Athens, whom Demosthenes holds chiefly responsible for Philip's steadily growing influence in Greek affairs. The official reply of Athens to the Macedonian and Peloponnesian governments has not been preserved.

In the following year a dispute over Halonnesus strained still further the relations between Philip and Athens. This small island between Peparethus and Scyrus had formerly belonged to Athens, but had lately been seized by a pirate gang. Philip expelled the interlopers, but then annexed the island. The Athenians demanded its restoration, but Philip countered by sending Python of Byzantium, a former pupil of Isocrates, to Athens offering to reconsider the terms of the Peace of 346. The anti-Macedonian party at Athens put their

[1] Cf. *Syll.*, 224.  [2] *II Philipp.* 25.

demands so high that all the negotiations came to nothing, but an open rupture between the two states was still avoided.

Demosthenes and his associates now took advantage of the growing hostility in Athens to Macedonia and its king to eliminate their most influential opponents. Hyperides began by indicting Philocrates for treason. The defendant, foreseeing that he had a hopeless case, departed into voluntary exile and was condemned to death *in absentia*. Demosthenes then brought a similar charge against Aeschines, who, relying on the still considerable influence of Eubulus, his political chief, elected to stand his trial. The extant speeches of the prosecutor and the defendant are our chief source for the diplomatic conversations that led up to the Peace of Philocrates, although that of Demosthenes differs somewhat from the form in which it was delivered in court. He had undertaken a difficult, indeed a dangerous task, seeing that he had himself taken a part in the peace settlement of 346 which his political views of 343 led him to disclaim. Moreover, though he laboured with success to establish a strong presumption of Aeschines' guilt, he was unable to bring forward definite proofs. But his oratory in the existing state of public opinion was so effective that Aeschines was acquitted by a very small number of votes only. That he was actually guilty of treason or gross corruption is neither proven nor probable. If he, in common with some of his associates, accepted gifts from Philip, his conduct was not condemned by ancient standards of political morality, unless he actively tried to bring about the overthrow of the state whose representative he was. That he ever meditated so doing there is not a shred of evidence. To veer round from an anti-Macedonian to a pro-Macedonian point of view may argue instability of political convictions, but was no crime. If it be true that the Athenian general, Phocion, lent the weight of his influence to secure Aeschines' acquittal, then it is even harder to believe that the orator had been guilty of criminal conduct. For Phocion's reputation for rigid integrity, which was as proverbial as that of Aristides had once been, would not have allowed him to condone a flagrant piece of corruption even in a political associate.

By this time Philip had seen the impossibility of winning the Athenians for his designs by the way of friendship. He therefore sought to isolate them yet further by bringing Megara and Euboea to his side. But, although he overthrew the existing democracies in Oreus and Eretria, replacing them by his own supporters, he failed against Chalcis. A similar conspiracy, aided by his mercenaries, to seize the government at Megara was scotched by prompt action on the part of the Athenians. They sent troops under Phocion to occupy Nisaea and prevented an oligarchic *coup d'état* in Megara itself. During the winter of 343–342 Philip's influence in the Peloponnese began to wane owing to the renewed efforts of Athens to create an anti-Macedonian alliance. Messenia, Argos, Megalopolis, and Achaea entered into close relations with her, though apparently without repudiating their earlier alliances with Macedonia. About the same time an Athenian expedition was sent in haste to support the Ambraciots in resisting Philip's advance to the northern shores of the Corinthian Gulf.

## § 2. PHILIP IN THESSALY AND THRACE

The Macedonian king's varying relations with Athens and other states in southern Greece between 346 and 342 were only a part, and from the Macedonian point of view not the most important part, of his ceaseless activity. His northwestern frontier still required a watchful eye and, on occasion, a strong hand. Early in 344 he invaded Illyria and returned with substantial spoils, but we can only guess that this was a punitive raid to punish earlier incursions into Macedonian territory by the enemy. Of greater significance is his ascendancy in Thessaly which by this year had become so unquestioned that the Thessalians voluntarily accepted him as their *archon*. Though these communities continued nominally to count as allies, Thessaly in reality became a Macedonian province. It was divided into four administrative units, each under a Macedonian governor, and the Thessalians undertook to make fixed contributions of troops and funds to the king. Shortly after the failure of his negotiations with Athens Philip once more crossed swords with Arybbas of Epirus, the uncle of his wife Olympias, and deposed him. Her brother, Alexander, replaced him as the president of an Epirot League, whose territory Philip enlarged at the expense of its neighbours. Thereby he secured Macedonian control of this area

almost as effectively as he had previously done in Thessaly.
Arybbas with two sons made his escape and found a home in
exile at Athens.[1] But Philip's attempt to dominate all of
north-western Greece to the Gulf and to secure Naupactus for
the Aetolians, after adding them to his steadily mounting list
of allies, was frustrated by an Athenian expedition to
Ambracia. Only a costly and lengthy series of operations
could have brought him a victorious issue in that difficult
country. Evidently he did not consider the advantages to be
derived from success in such an enterprise commensurate with
the sacrifices that it would entail.

Instead he turned his attention once again to the Thracian
hinterland. Only the vaguest statements regarding his
campaigns there have survived, notwithstanding that they
lasted the best part of a year (342–341). He deposed Cersobleptes, thereby openly violating for the first time the Peace
of 346 to which the Thracian had been a party. Then he
advanced far into the interior in the direction of the Euxine.
Another native prince was deprived of his throne and the
whole of this conquered country was incorporated in
Macedonia. To make his new possessions safe Philip founded
a new city on the upper Hebrus (Maritza), called after himself,
Philippopolis, and established other fortified posts. With
Perinthus and Byzantium he had been allied for some years;
now he made agreements with more remote outposts of
Hellenism, like Odessus, and with native tribes in the interior,
like the Getae. Aenus on the Thracian coast opposite
Samothrace, which had hitherto held to Athens, also joined
Philip at this time.

This rapid expansion of Macedonian supremacy eastwards,
which promised to give Philip before long control of the
western shores of the Black Sea, even without other complications was calculated to cause grave alarm at Athens and to
lead to war. Actually it was a renewal of the dispute about
the Thracian Chersonese which led to an open rupture with
Philip. Although by the Peace of Philocrates that territory
had been recognized as an Athenian dependency, the city of
Cardia, situated on the western shore of the neck of the
peninsula, had been expressly excluded and was an ally of

[1] See the remains of a decree passed by the Athenian assembly in his
behalf, Tod 173.

Macedonia. Twice within a decade—in 353 and 343—Athenian settlers had been sent to the Chersonese, where they seem to have lived harmoniously with the earlier population.[1] On the second occasion, however, some of the new immigrants quarrelled with the people of Cardia. The Athenian mercenary captain, Diopithes, was sent with a few ships to help the colonists and attacked the Cardians, who promptly applied to Philip and received a Macedonian garrison. Diopithes, in order to raise money to pay his troops, plundered merchantmen and levied contributions on the coast towns. Then he carried out a raid into Macedonian territory. At this juncture Philip notified Athens of his intention to stand by the Cardians and at the same time protested formally against the aggressions of Diopithes. It is obvious that Diopithes' conduct had been entirely unjustifiable, and voices were raised in the Athenian assembly demanding his dismissal and calling for a conciliatory answer to Philip's just demands. But Demosthenes, who had been instrumental in having Diopithes sent to the Chersonese, not merely defended that officer's actions and warned the Athenians against dismissing so efficient a soldier, but took the opportunity of urging a vigorous prosecution of the war against Philip. In truth, Diopithes and his affairs play only a subordinate part in Demosthenes' superb oration, *On the Chersonese*. In it and in the *Third Philippic*, delivered somewhat later in 341, the orator resumes with full vigour and unsurpassed mastery of phrase his open crusade against Philip and all his works. The second speech aroused his countrymen to such a pitch of energy as had not been seen in Athens for more than a decade. At last it was the turn of deeds, not words.

### § 3. Renewed War between Athens and Philip

In the last section of the *Third Philippic* Demosthenes had formulated the course of action which the Athenians should follow to meet the existing crisis. They must send immediate reinforcements to the Chersonese, while preparations on a greater scale were being pushed on at home, and they must make one more effort to unite as many Greeks as possible into

---

[1] Cf. the Athenian decree of 340 (Todd 174) appointing Chares to safeguard the interests of Elaeus in the Chersonese, " so that the Elaeans, in possession of their property, may live fairly and equitably with the Athenian settlers in the Chersonese."

an anti-Macedonian coalition. This last proposal the orator
had already enunciated in the speech *On the Chersonese*. He
himself now visited Byzantium and won its citizens over to
the Athenian side. Hyperides exerted himself in the same
sense in Rhodes and Chios, and though we hear of no formal
alliance with Athens, both islands sent aid to Byzantium
some months later when the city was besieged by Philip.
Meanwhile help was despatched to Diopithes, and a squadron
commanded by Chares sailed for the northern Aegean. A
military expedition under Phocion and Cephisophon recovered
Oreus and Eretria. A confederacy of all the Euboean cities
came into being. Its congress met at Chalcis and an alliance
was made between this League and Athens. In the winter
Demosthenes and others strove to arouse the mainland states
to their danger. The result of their efforts was disappointing;
for the Hellenic League which was convened at Athens in the
spring of 340 included, besides Athens and the Euboean
Confederacy, only Corinth, Megara, and Achaea of the
Peloponnesian states, and from north-western Greece,
Acarnania and Ambracia, Corcyra, and Leucas.

In the summer Philip brought matters to a head by calling
on his nominal allies, Perinthus and Byzantium, to assist him
in a campaign against the Chersonese. Both cities declined,
whereupon he began by besieging Perinthus. Its citizens
received substantial help from Byzantium and also from
Arsites who had succeeded Artabazus in the Phrygian satrapy.
The circumstances in which Persia was thus drawn into the
war on the side of the Greeks are extremely obscure, but it is
possible that the Athenians had been diplomatically active
in the previous year. Perinthus, which was situated on the
steep cliffs of a little peninsula and joined to the mainland
only by a narrow strip of land, for several months staunchly
resisted all the newest siege artillery, including movable
towers and catapults which discharged arrows, that Philip's
engineers had devised for him. Foiled in his efforts to take
the town, the king suddenly withdrew his army and attacked
Byzantium. But this city also was not unprepared. The
Athenians, supported by the remaining members of their
maritime league,[1] sent one naval squadron under Chares and

---

[1] Cf. the decree (Tod 175) rewarding the Tenedians for their services at
this time.

soon after another under Phocion, while Chios and Rhodes also came to the rescue of their ally. Although Philip's operations appear to have been protracted into the early part of 339, he was no more successful than he had been at Perinthus, mainly because, compared with his opponents' naval strength, his own was negligible and an effective attack from the sea side was impossible. He withdrew his army and, after a punitive expedition against a Scythian tribe and a brush with the Thracian Triballi, who inflicted severe losses on the Macedonian troops, he returned to his capital.

### § 4. A NEW SACRED WAR AND THE CAMPAIGN OF CHAERONEA

Philip's double failure in the Propontis was the most serious set-back that he had suffered since his accession. Nevertheless he was by this time too familiar with Greek politics and with the resources of his antagonists to doubt the ultimate success of his plans. He must soon have become aware of Demosthenes' inability to create a solid anti-Macedonian *bloc* on the Greek mainland, and he might well wonder whether Athens herself would or could sustain the effort that she had recently begun at the behest of her foremost patriot. It is reasonable to suppose therefore that in any event a decision would not long be delayed. At the same time the naval power of Athens and her new and old allies was such that he must concentrate all his strength on a military attack. It was Philip's good fortune—unless we are to assume that his intrigues brought about the crisis, which is possible but not demonstrable—that almost immediately he was able to utilize a wrangle in central Greece to attain his ends.

Even before the king's return to Macedonia from the Propontis a dispute had broken out in the Amphictionic League. The Council, at the instance of the Locrians of Amphissa, had begun by imposing a fine on Athens for making an unlawful dedication in the Delphic sanctuary, but had then been persuaded by Aeschines who was the Athenian representative on the Council to divert its attention to the people of Amphissa who had themselves been guilty of sacrilege in cultivating land sacred to the god. After some actual fighting between the people of Amphissa and Delphi, a special meeting

of the Council was convened at Thermopylae. Persuaded by
Demosthenes the Athenians abstained from sending representatives to it. The Thebans, although by prevailing on the
Locrians to propose their anti-Athenian resolution they had
been the real instigators of the trouble, also held back from
the meeting. The League, lacking the support of two of its
strongest members, turned to Philip and invited him to
punish Amphissa. But the plans of Philip, who lost no time
in marching through Thessaly into Doris, were far deeper than
a mere punitive expedition against an insignificant Locrian
community. From Doris, instead of marching on Amphissa,
he turned off into north-eastern Phocis to occupy and fortify
the dismantled fortress of Elatea which commanded the
main road into western Boeotia. Then he sent a delegation to
Thebes informing her people of his intention to invade Attica.
He asked either for the active co-operation of the Thebans or
at least for an unopposed passage for his troops through
Boeotia.

Bad news travels fast, and Philip's occupation of Elatea
had quickly become known at Athens. Nine years later
Demosthenes in his speech, *On the Crown*, vividly recalled to
his countrymen the evening and night of panic after the
receipt of those ill-tidings and reminded them how at the
meeting of the assembly on the following day no man was
willing to begin the debate until finally he himself came
forward.[1] His advice in the emergency was the immediate
despatch of a delegation to Thebes to offer a military alliance
and to counteract the demands of Philip. It seemed a
counsel of desperation, seeing that the relations between the
two states had rarely been other than bad. In adopting it the
Athenians must have pinned their hope on Demosthenes, who
was one of the ten delegates deputed to hasten to Thebes, and
to their expressed willingness to make important concessions
to her. The arrival of the Athenian and Macedonian envoys
at Thebes coincided and both parties stated their case
before the Theban assembly. After mature deliberation the
Thebans accepted the alliance offered by the Athenians, who
had undertaken to bear two-thirds of the cost of the war and
to leave the supreme direction of the military campaign to
the Theban High Command. In addition they withdrew all

[1] Demosthenes, *On the Crown*, 169 ff.

claims to the frontier town of Oropus which had long been a source of contention and recognized Thebes' hegemony over the Boeotian League.

The efforts of the new allies to obtain assistance from the rest of Greece met with only limited response. The Peloponnesian cities held aloof, and only those states which had already allied themselves with Athens in the preceding year promised their support. At Athens the proposal that Demosthenes had first mooted at the time of the Olynthian War was at last adopted, and the Theoric Fund was converted for the time being into a war-chest. Its direction and that of the city finances in general were in the hands of Lycurgus, a staunch supporter of Demosthenes. Once the military preparations were completed, the allies occupied the various passes from Boeotia into Phocis, while a corps of 10,000 mercenaries under Chares was detailed to bar the road leading from the Gulf of Corinth and Amphissa into Doris. But although some minor skirmishes occurred during the autumn and winter months, Philip made no serious military effort until the year 338 was well advanced. By that time he had received reinforcements from home and from his Thessalian allies which brought his army up to some 30,000 infantry and 2000 cavalry. When at last he struck, it was with characteristic swiftness and certainty of aim. He carried out a lightning campaign against Amphissa, which he took after crushing the battalions of Chares. By following up this stroke with the seizure of Naupactus and transferring it to the safe-keeping of his Aetolian allies, he gained direct access to the Gulf. At the same time he forced his enemies to reconsider the disposition of their troops, since there was now a possibility that he might execute a rear attack.

The Greek commanders decided to withdraw their men from the passes and massed all their troops in the vicinity of Chaeronea, with their right flank resting on the River Cephisus. Here Philip, who had returned to Elatea and then advanced through the pass of Parapotamii, whence his opponents had lately withdrawn, met them in the summer (August 2 ?) of 338. The Greek army, which was numerically about as strong as the Macedonian, was disposed in such a way that the Theban battalions, headed by the Sacred Band, were stationed on the right and the Athenians on the left wing. The centre was made up of mercenaries and contingents from a few of the allies who had lately joined Athens. The Macedonian left wing, composed of the pick of the phalanx and supported by cavalry on its flank, was commanded by Philip's son Alexander, while Philip was on tue right. Stubborn as was the resistance of the Theban troops and especially of the Sacred Band, whose soldiers stood their ground until they were cut down to a man, they were gradually overwhelmed by the Macedonian phalangites. At the same time Philip executed a feigned retirement before the Athenians. Then, when they already seemed to see victory in their grasp, he turned to attack and broke their line. Lastly the Greek centre was enveloped by the victorious left and right wings of the enemy.

The victory at Chaeronea put southern Greece at Philip's mercy. The Athenians, it is true, in the expectation that a Macedonian army would forthwith invade Attica, made feverish preparations to stand a siege. The rural population was transported inside the fortified area and every man under sixty was summoned to the defence of the city. But the king had no intention of forcibly subjugating Athens. Of his late enemies Thebes had incurred his deepest displeasure, seeing that she had been his ally for some time. He doubtless also regarded the continued existence of a united Boeotian Confederacy as a potential threat to his own hegemony in Greece. The main strength of Athens, however, was on the sea. To reduce the city, so long as her navy was intact, would have been both difficult and costly. Besides, to carry out his future plan of wresting western Asia from the Great King, he needed the naval co-operation of Athens. Thus it came about that Philip's treatment of his two chief opponents diverged widely. The Thebans were deprived of their hegemony in Boeotia. Their leading anti-Macedonian politicians were banished and the government was handed over to an oligarchy of three hundred, on whose loyalty to himself Philip could rely. In addition, a Macedonian garrison was placed in the Cadmea and another in Chalcis on Euboea. Hardly less humbling to Theban pride was the restoration of hated cities, like Orchomenus, Thespiae, and Plataea.

The Athenians received their first intimation that Philip's

attitude towards themselves was likely to be more clement from their politician Demades who had been amongst the 2000 Athenian prisoners taken by the king after Chaeronea. Demades had been sent as an emissary to Athens and was then deputed to return in company with Aeschines to obtain the best terms possible from the conqueror. Philip, who sold his Theban captives into slavery, sent back his Athenian prisoners without ransom. The Athenian maritime confederacy was disbanded and the king retained the Chersonese. But Lemnos, Scyros, and Imbros, together with Delos and Samos, he permitted the Athenians to retain. He also gave them back Oropus and then enrolled them in the list of his allies. With the exception of Sparta, the Peloponnesian states, most of whom had in any case stood aside from the late war, accepted Philip's supremacy. The Spartans were left to their policy of intransigent isolation, but had to look on helplessly at the loss of frontier territory to their neighbours in the Argolid, Arcadia, and Messenia. Corinth, in view of its strategic position at the Isthmus, received a Macedonian garrison.

### § 5. Congress of Corinth and Death of Philip

The victorious soldier of Chaeronea, having made the most necessary dispositions to ensure the compliance of the several Greek communities to his will, now gave place to the constructive statesman. Towards the end of the year Philip summoned a congress of Greek states to Corinth, which was attended by delegates from all over Greece to the Macedonian border and from the Aegean islands. Sparta alone remained aloof. The programme that Philip laid before the delegates provided for an offensive and defensive alliance between the several Greek states and Macedonia.[1] In case of war the supreme command was vested in Philip and each constituent member of the federation undertook to furnish a certain quota of soldiers or ships. It is probable that in addition the Greek allies were also bound to each other by mutual alliances.[2]

[1] The valuable document (*Syll.*, 260) which preserves part of the oath taken by the allies has been re-edited by U. Wilcken in *Sitzungsberichte*, Berlin : phil.-hist. Klasse, 1929, 317. Cf. Tod 177.

[2] Though nowhere stated, this has been assumed by analogy with the League formed by Demetrius in 302, which revived the League formed by Philip. On this later federation cf. M. Cary in vol. III of this *History*, p. 38, and the references there given.

Provision was made for a *synedrion* of the allies, the number of representatives from each *polis* being variable and, in all likelihood, proportionate to its military strength. Its meetings, whether held at Corinth or at one of the centres of the national athletic festivals, were under the direction of five chairmen (πρόεδροι). Philip himself was not a member of this Council, just as Athens had been excluded from the *synedrion* of allies in the Second Athenian Confederacy. Transgressors against the symmachy were to be punished by the military forces of the allies and Philip. The internal governments of the constituent members were to remain as they were at the date when the League was formed, and the independence of each *polis* was guaranteed. Nor were any cities to receive garrisons, although there can be no doubt that an exception was made in the case of those places in which Philip had already placed military establishments—Chalcis, the Cadmea, Corinth, and Ambracia in north-western Greece. Severe penalties were ordained against any citizen who attempted to subvert the constitution of his city or who entered the service of, or conspired with, any foreign power. These regulations were framed specifically to put an end to *stasis* and to stop the enlistment of Greeks as mercenaries in the service of Persia. Technically the Macedonian king was merely, as generalissimo, the chief executive officer of the federation, while all major decisions were the responsibility of the *synedrion*.[1] It need hardly be said, however, that in actual fact, Philip retained in his own hands the direction of the League's foreign policy. The Council of the allies also acted as the supreme judicial court; but it was, of course, within its competence to delegate the task of arbitrating in a dispute between two cities to one of the constituent members of the League. An actual instance of such procedure occurred about this time when the Argives, "in accordance with the resolution of the *synedrion* of the allies," arbitrated between the islands of Melos and Cimolos.[2]

It is clear that, while Philip was primarily concerned to unite the Greeks in a military alliance with himself, he had the secondary aim of promoting their internal harmony—of

---

[1] Thus, if Wilcken's readings be adopted, the League will proceed against any transgressor of the alliance καθότι ἂν δοκῇ τῷ κοινῷ συνεδρίῳ καὶ ὁ ἡγεμὼν παραγγέλλῃ.

[2] See Tod 179.

securing that good understanding (ὁμόνοια)—for which Isocrates had already pleaded eight years before. The orator, who had died at the age of ninety-eight some weeks after Chaeronea, did not live to see the unification achieved by the Macedonian ruler. But Philip had also been perfecting his plans for an attack on Persia, though it is probable that he kept them discreetly in the background until the Hellenic federation was in being. In the spring or early summer of 337 the new *synedrion* was summoned for the first time in order that he might lay before it his military plans. If Diodorus, or rather his source, be correct, then Philip tried to give a Hellenic complexion to his expedition against the Great King by representing it as a war of vengeance for the sacrilegious destruction of holy places in Greece by the armies of Xerxes.[1] The Council acquiesced in his proposals—it could hardly have done otherwise—and formally voted him commander-in-chief of the expedition, thereby authorizing him to requisition the needful troops from the Greek allies. The rest of the year was taken up with military and naval preparations. Then in the spring of 336 an advance army of 10,000 men, commanded by Parmenio and Attalus, crossed the Hellespont. Their task was the double one of preparing for the arrival of the main Macedonian and confederate Greek army and of promoting the secession of the Asiatic Greeks from Persia. Several cities—Chios, Ephesus, Cyzicus—appear to have joined without delay, and others would doubtless have followed suit, when the news of Philip's assassination reached the Macedonian generals. Parmenio thereupon returned home, while his colleague withdrew his battalions to the Hellespont, pending the accession of a new ruler.

The relations between Philip and his son by Olympias had recently become strained and the two men had quarrelled bitterly in 337 when the king, whose marriages to several wives had hitherto been tolerated by Olympias, who alone

[1] Diodorus, XVI, 89, 2. U. Wilcken's contention (*Alexander der Grosse*, 44, repeating what he had already stated at greater length in *Sitzungsberichte*, Berlin : Phil.-hist. Klasse, 1929), that it was an idea of genius (*idealer Gedanke*) on Philip's part to justify his Persian expedition by this appeal to Greek religious sentiment, seems to the present writer a gross exaggeration. Philip's Greek contemporaries were neither so simple-minded nor so religious as to be deceived by this flourish ; nor is there any reason to believe that the Greek confederates entered on the Persian war with any enthusiasm.

had presented him with an heir, married the niece of his
general, Attalus. Alexander and his mother had both
withdrawn for a space from the court; but some months
later a reconciliation between father and son was brought
about, and the possible anger of Olympias' kinsman,
Alexander of Epirus, was assuaged by offering him in marriage
Olympias' daughter, Cleopatra. It was at the celebration of
this wedding in July 336 that one of Philip's own officers
stabbed him to death. The ancient testimonies disagree
about the author and motives of the murder. That the
assassin was avenging a personal injury which Philip had not
troubled to have righted, though it lay in his power to do so,
need not be doubted. But we cannot accept as proven either
the story that Olympias was the real instigator or the version
which made the episode a Persian plot to prevent Philip's
forthcoming expedition to Asia. Both rumours, even if
wholly false, were bound to arise very soon in view of the
existing situation.[1]

Philip's life-work consists of two parts, though he himself
would have regarded the second simply as the logical sequel
of the first. His creation of a united Macedonia would alone
entitle him to a place in the front rank of ancient statesmen.
But he had all but succeeded, at the time of his premature
death, in bringing most of the Balkan peninsula under the
control of one directing mind. His detractors, ancient and
modern, have consequently traduced him as a foreign despot
who wrought the destruction of Greek liberty. We cannot
tell how the Hellenic federation would have prospered, had
Philip lived to old age. But there is no reason to believe that
he would have abandoned that partnership of Greece with
Macedonia for a more absolute form of rule over the Greeks.
Indeed, though larger questions of foreign policy in the
city-states would always have been decided at Pella, there
was little danger that the king would interfere with their
internal autonomy. And such interference was precisely
the rock on which every Greek state had hitherto foundered

[1] Modern critics have judged variously. The most judicial appraisal of
the evidence is that by Tarn (*C.A.H.* VI, 354). Pickard-Cambridge (*ibid.*,
269) is more non-committal. Wilcken (*Alexander der Grosse*, 53) and Schachermeyr (*Alexander der Grosse*, 87) are disposed to believe in Olympias' guilt,
while H. Berve (*Griechische Geschichte*, II, 158) uncritically accepts it as
proved.

when it embarked on the troubled sea of imperialism. The Greek genius of the fourth century, as expressed in literature, philosophy, and the arts, was not inferior to that of the fifth. But Greek political institutions had not proved adaptable to changed conditions. That many Greeks were aware of the inadequacy of the *polis* as a self-complete organism is shown, not merely by the writings of a few theorists, however eminent, but by the numerous experiments in some kind or other of federal union. But there was not one league or federation that did not succumb sooner or later to local jealousies or the too narrow patriotism of the *polis*. With singular insight Isocrates, even before he addressed his famous appeal to Philip, had discerned the truth, that unity could not be imposed on the Greeks from within. Where Athens, Sparta, and Thebes had failed Philip had succeeded. Judged by the highest ethical standards, his methods and political morality, like his private life, were not seldom open to criticism. He could be ruthless, as towards Olynthus or the Phocian prisoners taken from Onomarchus' army; yet he was guilty of less brutality than Athens during the Peloponnesian War. His diplomacy to attain a certain end could be tortuous and knew no scruples; but he was no worse than the greatest statesman ever produced by Athens, Themistocles. In short, if Philip has often had less than justice done to him, it is mainly for two reasons: his greatness has inevitably been overshadowed by the even greater genius of his son, while his bitterest opponent was the foremost orator of antiquity, whose highest flights of eloquence were attained in the very speeches of which Philip was the central theme.

# CHAPTER X

# THE GREEKS IN THE WEST DURING THE FOURTH CENTURY

## § 1. SICILY AFTER THE ATHENIAN EXPEDITION

WE have seen in the foregoing pages how political separatism, often combined with lack of internal stability, sapped the strength of the city-states in European Greece. Among the western Greeks these weaknesses were even more marked; for there we find as an added factor of disunion the survival of a sharp antipathy between Dorian and Ionian groups which in the rest of the Hellenic world was hardly of more than antiquarian significance. At the same time Hellenism itself was exposed to graver dangers in the west; for, while the Asiatic Greeks had reverted under Persian suzerainty, they had been left on the whole to their own devices. Nor was there ever any danger that the Persian rulers of the fourth century would renew the attempt to conquer European Greece. But the city-states of Sicily and southern Italy were surrounded by non-Hellenic peoples who were at all times ready to take advantage of disharmony among their Greek neighbours. Syracuse had more than once paid lip-service to the ideal of a Hellenic union of the Greek *poleis* in Sicily, but we are left with the impression that even the Congress of Gela in 425 was no more than an astute political move of Syracusan politicians to further the temporary interests of their own city.

After the triumphant defeat of Athens in 413, if ever, the Syracusans could have tried to give effect to their plans, had they been more than hollow pretence. Instead, they were sufficiently ill-advised to join in the war against Athens in the Aegean by sending a naval squadron under Hermocrates to co-operate with Sparta.[1] In the light of what then

---
[1] Cf. p. 141 above.

happened at Syracuse one is tempted to believe that the despatch of the expedition was due more to the machinations of Hermocrates' political enemies than to a desire to participate in the defeat of Athens. In his absence the democratic party at Syracuse secured a majority and reformed the constitution. More particularly they introduced election by lot for all the magistracies. They further passed a resolution banishing Hermocrates and his immediate associates in their absence. But it was a singularly inopportune time either for military commitments overseas or for party warfare. The Carthaginians, who since their defeat by Gelo had been content to retain a few naval bases in the north-west of Sicily, were not slow to take advantage of a good opportunity for intervention and possible aggrandisement. With the failure of the Athenian expedition the old antagonism between Selinus and Segesta, now deprived of her Athenian allies, broke out with renewed violence. The Segestans in their isolation turned to Carthage for aid, undertaking to remain her allies in the future. The Carthaginians, swayed by the counsel of one of their suffetes, Hannibal, the grandson of the Hamilcar who had fallen at Himera in 480, sent an advance force for the immediate relief of Segesta.

Some months later a large armament sailed for Sicily. Hannibal, who himself commanded the expedition, began by laying siege to Selinus.[1] The city being in a bad state of defence collapsed after a few days. A relief force from Syracuse arrived too late to save the city, whose inhabitants, irrespective of age or sex, were put to the sword. No less terrible was the vengeance wreaked by Hannibal on Himera, in memory of his grandfather. He laid siege to the city and captured it, but only after a part of the population had been rescued by a Syracusan naval squadron. Even so three thousand captives were sacrificed to Baal and the city itself was levelled to the ground (summer? 409).

After this Hannibal withdrew his army to Africa without attempting further conquests. His departure synchronized with the return of Hermocrates to the west. He had utilized

[1] Little reliance can be placed on the estimated size of the Carthaginian army given by Diodorus (XIII, 54, 5). He states that, according to Ephorus, there were 200,000 infantry and 4000 cavalry, according to Timaeus, a total of not much more than 100,000. Even this figure is likely to be considerably too large.

a substantial gift from Pharnabazus, the satrap of Dascylium, to acquire five galleys and a thousand mercenaries. Landing at Messana, he first attempted to re-enter Syracuse by force. When he had failed in this, he led his little army, soon to be reinforced by exiles from Himera and elsewhere, to the site of Selinus. From there he organized raids into Punic territory; yet, even after these services against the common enemy, the Syracusans declined to rescind their decree of banishment. A second attempt to occupy Syracuse and overthrow his political enemies failed like the first; in the fighting Hermocrates lost his life. But his activities in western Sicily had provoked the Carthaginian government; and when the Syracusans sent envoys to Carthage disclaiming responsibility for Hermocrates' actions, they received an equivocal reply, while preparations for an expedition to Sicily were put in train. A colony of Punic and Libyan settlers was also founded not far from Himera. It was named Thermae, in allusion to the hot springs hard by, and subsequently absorbed a considerable number of Greek settlers also.

Once again it was Hannibal who directed the Carthaginian armament that sailed for Sicily in the spring of 406, but a younger kinsman, Himilco, was associated with him in the command. This time their attack was directed against Acragas. This city was strongly fortified; in addition, its citizens engaged a thousand mercenaries under the Spartan, Dexippus, and also some Campanians who had once fought on the side of Carthage. Help was sent by Syracuse and other Greek cities. Months passed during which these combined forces gave a good account of themselves. An epidemic took a heavy toll of the besiegers and their supplies began to run out. Moreover, owing to the death of Hannibal, the supreme command devolved on Himilco. Having foiled his antagonists' attempt to storm his entrenched camp, he succeeded in intercepting some Syracusan ships that were bringing food supplies to the beleaguered city and in sinking the convoy. If these military actions redressed the balance between the two enemies and the danger of famine in the Carthaginian army was averted, the withdrawal of their Sicilian allies and of the Campanian mercenaries rendered the situation of the Acragantines hopeless. Some eight months after the beginning of the siege they evacuated the city one night, leaving the Carthaginians to loot its treasures and destroy its buildings. The fugitives found temporary homes at Gela and Leontini.

### § 2. THE RISE OF DIONYSIUS

The action of the Syracusan army in withdrawing from Acragas at a most critical juncture aroused widespread indignation among the Sicilian Greeks. In Syracuse itself it led to an embittered attack on the military commanders by a former adherent of Hermocrates' party. Dionysius, who was not without influential supporters—amongst them was the historian, Philistus—by his pertinacity caused the Syracusans to elect a new board of generals, of whom he was one. But this arrangement did not endure for long. His ascendancy in Syracuse was soon so marked that he procured the passing of a decree recalling political exiles to the city. His next step was to take advantage of a request for military aid from Gela. He made sure of the loyalty of his Syracusan troops by promising high pay and by similar means attached to himself a body of mercenaries in Gela who, under the command of Dexippus, had been sent to that city by Syracuse after the fall of Acragas. At the same time he brought about a democratic revolution in Gela. All the while he had been intriguing against his fellow-commanders. Then, on returning home from Gela, he secured enough popular support to bring about their deposition and his own appointment as sole general. Not long afterwards, by giving currency to a plausible tale that an attempt had been made on his life, he even induced the Syracusans to assign him a body-guard of six hundred men. It was later increased to a thousand.

In the interval Himilco, who had wintered in Acragas, had attacked Gela preparatory to an assault on Syracuse itself. Dionysius proceeded to the relief of the city, intending to carry out a simultaneous naval and military onslaught on the Punic army. But the execution of his strategic plan went all awry. The attack of his mercenaries and of his citizen forces did not synchronize, so that, after a part of his army had been severely mauled, he prevailed on the Geloans to abandon their city. The people of Camarina, who would be the next to be exposed to Carthaginian fury,

followed suit, with the result that Himilco became master
of the entire southern sea-board of the island. The conduct of
Dionysius nearly cost him his own position. The citizen
cavalry of Syracuse, composed of the younger members of
wealthy families, broke away and started a revolution in the
city to depose him. Nevertheless, as his mercenaries remained
loyal, he was able to overcome the insurrection. Syracuse
was not, however, in a state to resist a determined attack
by the Punic army. Hence Dionysius, taking advantage of
Himilco's anxiety about his troops, whose efficiency was again
being impaired by sickness, patched up a truce with the enemy.
Under its terms Carthage retained all the territory recently
won in the north and south of Sicily. Dionysius, moreover,
bound himself to respect the autonomy of the Sicel communities,
Messana, and Leontini, at this time largely settled by refugees
from Acragas. In return the Carthaginians recognized him
formally as the ruler of Syracuse.

It was natural that even his contemporaries should suspect
him of having played a double game, of having sacrificed
Gela and Camarina deliberately, to come to terms with the
enemy and secure his own absolute position; and though
the only ancient account that we possess is far from clear
and uniformly hostile to Dionysius, the charge was probably
just. Even now his position at home was unstable. He
dismissed the Lacedaemonian mercenary captain Dexippus,
whose behaviour at Acragas had been, to say the least,
equivocal. Then, continuing to rely for his personal safety
and political ascendancy on professional troops, he occupied
Ortygia and, by the construction of massive fortification
walls and towers, converted it together with the smaller
harbour of Syracuse into an impregnable fortress. But when
he next led a military expedition against the Sicel town,
Herbessus, his Syracusan troops mutinied and he was forced
to flee back to his stronghold. Some of his mercenaries now
deserted him in return for the promise of citizenship, and a
large reward was offered by the Syracusans for his capture.
But Dionysius had his wits about him. He succeeded in
sending a message to a troop of a thousand mercenaries whom
he knew to be in Sicily but in Punic service and promised
large rewards for their help. In the meantime he opened
negotiations with the citizens and asked for leave to sail

away with five vessels. They not only granted him these terms but were foolish enough to relax their vigilance. Consequently the Campanian mercenaries to whom he had sent a message were able to force an entry into the citadel and were reinforced by three hundred others who came by sea, presumably from some part of Italy. With such reinforcements and with the men who had remained loyal to him throughout Dionysius risked a sortie and completely defeated the citizens. Some fled to Aetna, the rest accepted the situation, and the victor wisely abstained from any punitive measures against them. The Campanians were then paid off and dismissed. They made their way to Entella in the west of the island, and, after being admitted as new citizens of that town, treacherously attacked and slew all the adult males and married the women.

During the next five years Dionysius consolidated his own power and made a beginning of that territorial expansion which for a few years made Syracuse the strongest military state of the Hellenic world. His first aggressions were directed against the Sicel communities in the interior of the island westwards from Mount Aetna, although these, like his subsequent conquest of Greek cities, contravened the recent truce with Carthage. But his efforts to master the Sicel strongholds by force failed and were not renewed for nearly a decade. He was more successful against Aetna, filled with refugees, and against the Greeks of Catana and Naxos. In both these towns there was a disaffected section whom he bribed to betray their respective states, and the alliance which the Catanians had lately made with Leontini did not save them. Dionysius sold the population of both towns into slavery. He peopled Catana with Campanian mercenaries and, after destroying the buildings of Naxos utterly, handed over the territory to a body of Sicel settlers. Terrified by these events, the citizens of Leontini, who had at first refused to admit Dionysius, reconsidered their decision and opened their gates. They were transplanted to Syracuse and enrolled as citizens.[1]

---

[1] Bury (*C.A.H.*, VI, 119), who all through his account of Dionysius is unduly biassed in his favour, minimizes his ruthless conduct when he writes that the inhabitants of Catana and Naxos were driven from their homes. Diodorus (XIV, 15, 3–4; cf. also 40, 1) expressly states that they were enslaved. In his earlier work (*History of Greece*, 647) Bury reproduced his source correctly.

Now that Syracuse no longer had any reason to fear opposition from her Greek neighbours, Dionysius carried out on a grandiose scale a programme for naval and military defence. The high ground above the city—the plateau of Epipolae culminating in the eminence of Euryalus at the western end—was enclosed with a massive stone wall, while a strong fortress was erected on Euryalus itself. Thus the possibility of a surprise attack from the interior was eliminated. The walled-in area did not, however, form a new residential quarter of Syracuse but, as a recent writer has well expressed it, served a somewhat similar purpose to the territory inside the Long Walls at Athens. In time of war and siege the fortified plateau could temporarily house troops provided by the allies or dependents of Dionysius.[1] Not less impressive were the measures that he took to build up his naval and military strength. His navy when completed is said to have exceeded two hundred men-of-war, including perhaps some of a larger and swifter type than the trireme.[2] His timber he procured partly from the forests around Aetna, partly from Italy. He also imported craftsmen from there, as well as from Greece and even from Carthage, paying liberally for their services. By such means he accumulated a great store of weapons and defensive armour. He also assembled various siege engines such as no Greek commander before his time is said to have used, namely, movable towers, catapults which discharged arrows, and large battering rams. It may be that for the construction of much of his siege apparatus Dionysius relied primarily on the Carthaginian workmen whom he had hired;[3] but it is also possible that at this time or later in his reign he was

---

[1] Cf. K. Fabricius, *Das antike Syrakus*, 26, whose reasoning seems quite conclusive. H. Berve, however, still adheres (*Griechische Geschichte*, II, 86) to the old notion that Epipolae was an inhabited area forming part of a great metropolis (Riesenstadt).

[2] Diodorus (XIV, 41, 3) credits Dionysius with the invention of quadriremes and quinqueremes. There is, however, much justice in Tarn's scepticism (*Hellenistic Military and Naval Developments*, 130-2), since quinqueremes are not heard of again until the time of Alexander the Great. I would suggest that Dionysius may have had one or two vessels of a larger pattern for ceremonial purposes, for Diodorus relates (XIV, 44, 7) that the tyrant had his bride fetched from Locri in the first quinquereme to be built. As it was ἀργυροῖς καὶ χρυσοῖς κατασκευάσμασι κεκοσμημένη, it was clearly a state barge rather than a fighting ship.

[3] So W. W. Tarn, *op. cit.*, 102-3.

indebted for some of his ideas and perhaps for some of his Italian artificers to the philosopher-statesman, Archytas of Taras.[1] The personnel of Dionysius' army was very varied, but the insufficiency of the ancient sources renders it impossible to trace the gradual process by which he built up his formidable host. Diodorus, it is true, credits him with 80,000 infantry and over 3000 cavalry in 397, but these figures are suspiciously large. At all events, his army then and later was a mixed force, composed partly of mercenaries, partly of citizen-militia, partly of contingents from allied or dependent states.[2] The enormous cost of these preparations and indeed of the military autocracy wielded for so many years by Dionysius was met in a variety of ways. Crushing taxation was imposed on the Syracusans and doubtless also on subject communities. Conquered states, like Rhegium in 389, were required to pay large indemnities. Occasional military successes brought the conqueror spoil and captives whose sale in the slave-market or ransom to their relatives was no inconsiderable source of income. Nor did Dionysius scruple to despoil temples of their treasures when opportunity offered. It is possible that he also had recourse to that favourite expedient of extravagant despots and spendthrift governments, depreciation of the currency, but the numismatic evidence does not unequivocally support ancient assertions to that effect.[3]

[1] Cf. E. Ciaceri, *Storia della Magna Grecia*, II, 439, who points out that Plutarch (*Life of Marcellus*, 14) calls Archytas and his pupil Eudoxus precursors of Archimedes in the science of mechanics. Unfortunately the date of Archytas' *floruit* at Tarentum is very uncertain, so that it is impossible to say when he could first have been in communication with Dionysius.

[2] Diodorus XIV, 47, 7. Cf. the analysis of H. W. Parke, *Greek Mercenary Soldiers*, 67 ff. But Parke's estimate that " perhaps from a quarter to a third " of the army in 397 was mercenary seems an understatement.

[3] Pseudo-Aristotle, *Oeconomica*, 2, 20, and Pollux, 9, 79, assert that Dionysius at one time issued tin tetradrachms. On the other hand, though there seems to be no doubt that the number of silver tetradrachms issued during Dionysius' reign was decidedly less than in the preceding period, some of the fine medallion coins which were first minted after the Athenian expedition continued to be struck in the early years of the fourth century. The only known example of a base metal issue is a decadrachm of doubtful authenticity. Thus, if the numismatic evidence is inconclusive, it at least does not bear out the categorical assertions of the pseudo-Aristotle and Pollux. Cf. G. F. Hill, *Coins of Ancient Sicily*, 115, and A. Evans in Freeman's *History of Sicily*, IV, 230–8. Evans' efforts to reconcile the numismatic with the literary evidence are not wholly convincing.

## § 3. THE FIRST PUNIC WAR

Dionysius' recent conquests in Sicily had been effected in total disregard of his agreement with Himilco. By 398 his elaborate preparations for war were completed. Moreover, he received information that a severe epidemic was causing heavy mortality in Libya, so that it seemed a peculiarly favourable moment at which to take the offensive against Carthage. His plans seem to have been received with a fair amount of enthusiasm by the Syracusans, whose hatred of Carthage for the time being overmastered their dislike of the autocrat under whom they lived. In an outburst of popular fury the property and trading-vessels of Punic residents were despoiled and they themselves ill-treated, and it was a mere formality when Dionysius sent envoys to Carthage offering the alternative of war or surrender of all Greek cities in Sicily. Obviously the Carthaginians would not submit tamely to the loss of their dependencies on the island. Having received a refusal to his demands, Dionysius opened hostilities at once by attacking the Punic fortress-town of Motya in the extreme west of Sicily. It was situated on an island connected with the mainland by an artificial causeway. This the inhabitants destroyed, in the hope that the enemy would be compelled to rely entirely on a naval attack. But Dionysius, calculating that some months must pass before a relief expedition from Africa could appear, gave orders for the construction of a mole, to enable him to bring his siege-train to bear on the city. While this work was under way he himself was busy in winning over by fair words or force the towns subject to Carthage. Gela, Camarina, and Acragas in the south and some smaller communities in the interior had joined him at the very outset of his campaign; others opened their gates when his troops appeared at their gates. Segesta and Entella, however, held out and were blockaded, while he returned to carry on the assault on Motya. By that time a Punic naval force under Himilco had appeared in the offing, but his attempts to destroy Dionysius' fleet and constrain him to abandon the siege failed. Since he had no land-army adequate to cope with his opponents he withdrew to Carthage.

The Syracusan despot was now free to concentrate on

battering down the defences of Motya with the use of rams and catapults fired from his movable towers. But the defenders fought desperately to the last and only succumbed finally to an unexpected night attack. When Dionysius' troops at last entered the city they massacred all that came in their way. Some Greek mercenaries taken prisoner by Dionysius were crucified by his orders. Remarkable as was Dionysius' capture of the fortress, his lack of forethought in leaving only a Sicel garrison there was more remarkable still. Active operations were suspended till the following year, when he again led his army to the west of the island. His first action was to convert the blockade of Segesta into an active siege. But the Carthaginians had bestirred themselves during the winter and a large expedition had sailed to Panormus in the spring of 397. Himilco who was again in command recovered Motya and other towns, and his opponent, apparently fearing to risk an engagement in the open, abandoned the siege of Segesta and retreated to Syracuse. Thus he left Himilco free to found a new Carthaginian stronghold at Lilybaeum at the southern end of the bay on which Motya stood ; for this city was left by him in ruins. He then advanced eastwards and attacked Messana, whose capture would for the time give his fleet command of the strait. Its inhabitants for the most part fled to the near-by hills, since their city was not in a condition to stand a vigorous siege. But Himilco, having occupied it without difficulty, did not prepare for a permanent occupation but razed it to the ground. A new stronghold, Tauromenium, was built by him in the hills to the north of Naxos, to whose Sicel inhabitants he entrusted it. Thus, by fostering good relations with the older population of the island, he hoped to increase the difficulties of his Greek opponents, between whom and the Sicels there had never been any cordiality.

In the meantime Dionysius prepared to bar the advance of Himilco at Catana, but his fleet, commanded by his brother, Leptines, was so severely beaten that, rather than risk a second engagement on land, he withdrew to Syracuse. An appeal for help sent by him to Sparta was answered by the despatch of thirty galleys from the Peloponnese, who eluded the vigilance of the Punic fleet and entered the small harbour ; for by that time Syracuse had for weeks been beleaguered by the enemy. The arrival of these allies was highly opportune also to Dionysius personally, since it prevented a popular revolution in Syracuse against his authority. Once again the most deadly enemy with which Himilco had to contend was disease. A severe epidemic attacked the Carthaginian army as it lay encamped in the marshy territory to the south of the city.[1] When the sickness was at its height, Dionysius planned a double attack on the enemy. While Leptines with eighty ships sailed against the Punic fleet at dawn, Dionysius, who had led his men out from the city while it was still dark, timed his onslaught on the Carthaginian lines and forts to synchronize with his brother's operations. The plan succeeded perfectly. The Punic army sustained a crushing defeat and the bulk of the fleet which had been caught unawares was destroyed. But in the hour of his triumph Dionysius was swayed solely by motives of self-interest. Calculating that his own security as ruler of Syracuse depended on the realization by the citizens that he was indispensable as their military chief as long as there was a powerful enemy in Sicily, he was unwilling to follow up his victory by annihilating Himilco and his men as he could have done, but connived at the secret departure of the Carthaginian commander with forty triremes and what remained of the Punic part of his army. Himilco's Greek mercenaries were basely left in the lurch. Those that were not killed were rounded up by the Syracusans and sold as slaves, save for a few Iberians whom Dionysius took into his own service.

On his return to Carthage Himilco was a ruined man. But the Carthaginians do not appear to have sought a formal pact with Dionysius. Their heavy defeat in Sicily, however, reacted on their native dependencies in Africa, and it was only after a hard struggle that they succeeded in restoring their authority over the Libyan tribes. That was doubtless one main reason why three or four years passed before they made any effort to recover what they had lost in Sicily. Dionysius used this interval to gain control over the greater part of the island. The Sicel communities, with the exception of Tauromenium,

---

[1] It was most probably malaria, or possibly enteric; but the highly coloured description of Diodorus (XIV, 71) reads like a rhetorical exercise based on Thucydides' famous description of the " plague " at Athens.

which he failed to take, ended by acknowledging his overlordship.[1] The Greek cities, till lately subject to Carthage, passed under his control, and even the Punic fortress of Solus came into his hands through treachery. On the site of Leontini he settled ten thousand of his mercenaries. Then he restored Messana, preparatory to carrying his arms across the strait. But at that point he was forced temporarily to abandon his plans of conquest by the appearance in the vicinity of Messana of an army under Mago, who commanded the Carthaginian troops stationed in western Sicily. Mago suffered defeat, but, probably in the following year (392?) received reinforcements from home. No particulars of the ensuing campaign have survived, but it seems clear that Dionysius, largely because of the efficient help that he received from the Sicels, had the best of it. At length the Punic general sued for peace. The resulting treaty may be said to have regularized the situation that existed in Sicily before Mago's intervention. Carthage, while retaining her fortresses in the west—it may be presumed that she recovered Solus—acknowledged Dionysius' suzerainty over the Greek and Sicel communities. She even recognized his right to Tauromenium, from which he promptly expelled the Sicel inhabitants. In their place he established a body of his own mercenaries.

### § 4. DIONYSIUS IN ITALY

Dionysius' interest in Italian affairs, and especially in the control of the strait, went back to the early years of his reign. Of the city-states in Italy lying nearest to Sicily Rhegium had been traditionally hostile to the Syracusans, whereas her neighbour and rival, Locri, had maintained good relations with them. The people of Rhegium, doubtless because they realized that Syracuse would be more dangerous to their interests if ruled by a despot, had sent a naval squadron to assist the Syracusans when they ineffectively staged a

---

[1] Bury (*C.A.H.*, VI, 118) conjectured that the title, ἄρχων τῆς Σικελίας, by which Dionysius is described in several Athenian decrees (Tod 108, 133, 136), was originally bestowed on him by Sicels and referred to his overlordship over them. When he described the title as highly unusual, Bury seems to have forgotten that at a somewhat later date Philip II of Macedon was accepted as ἄρχων by the Thessalian cities. Thus there is no reason why Dionysius' title should not have referred to his suzerainty over the Greeks also.

rebellion against Dionysius in 403. This circumstance did not deter him a year or two later from seeking to gain control of Rhegium by a peaceful alliance. He proposed to aid its citizens in enlarging their territory in return for a wife, the daughter of one of their leading men, but the offer was firmly declined. Thus there were personal as well as political reasons for the rancour subsequently shown by Dionysius towards that city.[1] For the moment he was content to cement good relations with Locri, and married Doris, daughter of the Locrian Xenetus.[2] His restoration of Messana (c. 395 ?) was the first step towards getting a foothold in Italy, but, as we have seen, further operations had to be postponed owing to the renewal of the war with Carthage. Thus it was not till *c.* 390 that he led an expedition against Rhegium, using the territory of Locri as a base. But Rhegium received help from other Greek cities in southern Italy, who were at this date united in a defensive league aimed primarily against the hill-tribes of Lucania.[3] Dionysius suffered a serious naval reverse and abandoned his campaign until the following year. Then he allied himself to the Lucanians whose threat to the independence of the coastal communities was becoming exceedingly formidable. They had already taken Posidonia and they followed up this stroke by capturing Laus and Pyxus (*c.* 390). Thus in 389 the Italiot Greeks were exposed to a double attack. The Lucanians inflicted a crushing defeat on Thuria, while Dionysius, who had attacked Caulonia, won a no less decisive victory near the stream Elleporus over a force 27,000 strong sent by Croton to relieve her ally. His capture of Caulonia and Hipponium followed, perhaps before the end of the year.[4] The inhabitants were transplanted to Syracuse to swell the citizen population, while the

---

[1] There is a quaint, though no doubt apocryphal, tale in Diodorus (XIV, 107) that the Rhegines in answer to Dionysius' request said that the only girl that they would offer him was the hangman's daughter!

[2] It is uncertain what Aristotle's statement, that this union destroyed the constitution of Locri, is meant to imply (*Pol.*, 5, 1307a38). But Ciaceri's conjecture (*Storia della Magna Grecia*, II, 411, note 2), that Timaeus was Aristotle's source, is chronologically impossible.

[3] Thus Croton was issuing coins whose reverse—the infant Heracles strangling serpents—was an alliance type found elsewhere in the Hellenic world at this time (Grose, I, plate 54, 19–20).

[4] Diodorus (XIV, 107, 2), however, relates the capture of Hipponium in the next year (388) before the final attack on Rhegium.

territory of the two towns was assigned by him to his Locrian allies. Seeing so many of their friends beaten or even destroyed, the people of Rhegium also submitted. They surrendered their navy of seventy vessels and agreed to pay a heavy indemnity. As surety they handed over to Dionysius one hundred hostages. But in the next year he reappeared in Italy and, treating the refusal of the Rhegines to provision his troops indefinitely as a *casus belli*, he laid siege to their city. He strove to batter down its walls with his engines, as he had done at Motya ten years before; but the citizens, knowing that they could expect no mercy, held out heroically for nearly a year and only capitulated when famine drove them to it. With characteristic brutality the conqueror enslaved the survivors, after he had tortured their commander-in-chief and finally killed him with all his kin (spring 387?). Although the city itself ceased to be, its fortifications must have remained, since Dionysius treated the territory as his own and erected pleasure grounds on the site.[1]

Directly or indirectly Dionysius now controlled a large part of southern Italy.[2] With Taras, the most powerful of the Greek city-states that were still independent, he seems to have concluded an alliance. The most influential member of its government—a blend, it would seem, of oligarchy and democracy—was a remarkable personality, Archytas. An adherent of the Pythagorean philosophy and a mathematician of distinction, he was no less versed in public affairs and enjoyed the deep respect and whole-hearted trust of his fellow-citizens. Contrary to an existing law, which prohibited a second tenure of the office, they elected him *strategus* no less then seven times. It may be guessed that the good relations between Dionysius and Archytas had been put on a firm footing before the former embarked on an ambitious scheme for extending his influence along both shores of the Adriatic. Before the beginning of a new war with Carthage (*c.* 383) he had established colonies or outpost-settlements at Ancona,

[1] Ciaceri, *op. cit.*, II, 429.
[2] It has frequently been assumed (e.g. by Bury, *C.A.H.*, VI, 130) that all southern Italy was dependent on Dionysius, but the numismatic evidence is against this, for Taras, Metapontum, and Thuria all continued to issue their own coinage at this period, a clear mark of sovereignty. At Taras it is the age of the famous "horsemen." Cf. Grose, I, 79 ff.

Hadria at the mouth of the Po, and some other sites on the east coast of Italy, and at Issa and Pharus in Illyria. An alliance with Alcetas, prince of the Molossians in Epirus, also dates from this period. Unfortunately we have no means of knowing whether his success in these distant regions was purely transitory or whether he retained control over the settlements till his death.

### § 5. THE LATER YEARS OF DIONYSIUS

If the record for the first half of Dionysius' reign is far from complete and reliable, the last fifteen years of his life are so obscure that no continuous narrative is possible. Even about the two remaining wars with Carthage little definite information has survived. Thus the reasons for an outbreak of hostilities *c.* 383 are unknown. Although modern writers have commonly followed Diodorus and represented Dionysius as the aggressor, the military policy of the Carthaginians at this date raises the legitimate question whether the first step was not taken by them.[1] They concluded an alliance with cities in Italy and, though Diodorus gives no names ,it is probable that Croton and Thuria were both involved.[2] Dionysius was thus threatened on two fronts. A Syracusan fleet was destroyed by a storm off Thuria, and, with Carthaginian aid, the exiles of Hipponium were enabled to rebuild their city.[3] They appear to have remained independent hereafter. But in the same year the Syracusan ruler captured Croton. Though not destroyed, the city lost its autonomy.[4] In Sicily the fortune of war went markedly in favour of Carthage ; for though Dionysius won an engagement in which Mago lost his life, he suffered a crushing defeat at Cronium in the north-west of the island. His losses were so heavy that he was compelled to conclude a highly disadvantageous peace with the enemy. In addition to paying a heavy indemnity, he had to cede considerable territory to the Carthaginians, so that Selinus in the south and Thermae in the north reverted under Punic control and the river

---

[1] Diodorus, XV, 14, 4 ; 15, 1.
[2] *Ibid.*, XV, 15, 2.
[3] For coins of Hipponium after its restoration cf. Grose, 209.
[4] Croton issued no coins between *c.* 380 and 366.

Halycus became the eastern boundary of the Carthaginian sphere in Sicily.[1]

Nothing further is recorded of Dionysius until the last year of his life when, thinking to profit by Carthage's renewed troubles with the Libyan dependencies and the outbreak of an epidemic in Africa, he once more organized an expedition to the western parts of Sicily. Selinus, Entella, and Drepanum with the neighbouring hill stronghold of Eryx passed into his hands, but Lilybaeum proved impregnable. At this point a Punic fleet appeared and captured a great number of Syracusan galleys anchored in the harbour of Drepanum. Very soon after, before peace between the two states had been signed, Dionysius died. The unsatisfactory nature of our sources makes a just appraisal of him far from easy; yet it may well be questioned whether the estimate of his character and achievements which many modern critics have formed is not unduly favourable. From first to last he appears as a ruthless egotist, as a man consumed with a passion for power, without the redeeming qualities of the autocrat who uses his absolute powers at least in part to advance the greatness and welfare of his people. Obscure as is his policy of alternating war and peace with Carthage, whose hold on western Sicily he could have ended once for all, it can only be explained on the assumption that he could not maintain his position save by diverting the minds of his oppressed subjects periodically from their just grievances with fighting against a hereditary foe. It is a wilful perversion of the known facts to regard him as a champion of Hellenism or of Europe against the Semitic power of Carthage, the more so as his ruthlessness was not confined to one enemy. His treatment of Rhegium or Naxos is indeed far harder to condone than the horrors of Motya. It is even harder to judge rightly his military capacity. Against Carthage he failed almost as often as he succeeded; and his most spectacular conquests

---

[1] The chronology is very uncertain. Diodorus puts all the fighting in Sicily in one year (383-382), but relates the restoration of Hipponium in 379, making it clear that Dionysius and Carthage were still at war at the time. On the other hand, if Dionysius of Halicarnassus (*Excerpt.* 20, 7) is correct, Dionysius held Croton for twelve years, in which case he must have taken it in 379. But he can hardly have done so immediately after his disastrous defeat at Cronium; so that it seems preferable to assume that Diodorus has put the restoration of Hipponium a year or two too late, and that this event and the peace with Carthage occurred in 382 or 381.

were against the city-states of Magna Graecia, whose resources were limited and who relied chiefly on their citizen armies for defence. Thus one is led to conclude that Dionysius won his victories rather because he had the means to keep up an unprecedentedly large body of professional soldiers than by any unusual qualities as a strategist or tactician. Indeed, the extensive use that he made of mercenaries is the most significant feature in the military history of his reign. That he advanced the science of siege warfare is likely, although his capture of Motya by the employment of novel artillery is offset by his failure to take Rhegium, which was starved out, not taken by assault. That he was able to maintain his position as head of the Syracusan state for nearly forty years was at least in part due to the fact that, though he placed heavy financial burdens on the citizens, he was free from those private vices which more often than not have been the cause of a tyrant's downfall. But, unlike Gelo or Hiero in the previous century, Dionysius appears to have done little to further the arts of peace at his court or in his realm, while his own efforts as a poet were mediocre. In short, we may believe that the ancients who appraised him as a tyrant with few redeeming qualities were in the main justified and far nearer the truth that those modern writers who have portrayed him as the forerunner, both in statecraft and military genius, of Philip and Alexander of Macedon.

## § 6. THE WESTERN GREEKS AFTER THE DEATH OF DIONYSIUS I

On the death of Dionysius, his son, who bore the same name, succeeded to his position without popular opposition. Although nearly thirty years of age, the new ruler of Syracuse had no experience of the art of government since his father, with the characteristic jealousy of a despot who suspects even his nearest kin, had excluded him rigorously from any participation in public affairs. It was therefore inevitable that Dionysius II should become the centre of court intrigues carried on by older relatives or friends anxious to exercise a directing influence on their young kinsman. Amongst the earliest acts of his reign were the conclusion of a peace treaty with Carthage, which reaffirmed the previously existing territorial division of Sicily, and the making of suitable promises to the professional soldiery on which his position as successor to Dionysius I depended. Of the older men at his court two stand out—Dion, brother-in-law of Dionysius I, and Philistus, who, after many years of faithful service given to that ruler, had fallen into disfavour and had for some years been living in exile. Unhappily for Syracuse the two men had quite different aims; for while Philistus after his recall sought to perpetuate the despotism of the Elder Dionysius, with the sole difference that he would be the indispensable minister of the young prince, Dion, a friend and pupil of Plato, had hopes of converting the young Dionysius into the semblance of a philosopher-king of a Platonic Utopia. At first Dion's influence was paramount, especially as Plato himself rather unwillingly accepted an invitation in 367 to come to Syracuse. More than twenty years earlier he had visited the court of Dionysius I, but the temperaments of the two men had been too divergent to allow of a real understanding. Though outwardly polite, Dionysius I had taken a suitable opportunity of ridding himself of his guest, who had been deported on a Lacedaemonian ship and put ashore at Aegina at a time when that island and Sparta were at war with Athens (388). Plato had been treated as an enemy captive and sold as a slave, but a friend, Anniceris of Cyrene, finding him in this unhappy situation, bought his liberty. His second sojourn in Sicily seemed to open auspiciously. Dionysius II was interested in the philosopher's teaching and flattered by the notion of having so famous a man at his court. But others were not so contented at the prospect of a government inspired by Dion and his friends. By 366 Philistus and his supporters were strong enough to procure Dion's banishment on a charge of having had disloyal communications with Carthage. Plato extended his stay after his friend's departure to Greece, in the hope of smoothing over the quarrel between Dionysius and Dion. When this proved impossible, he too left the island.

For several years after this our records of Sicilian history are almost blank. Dionysius retained some hold on southern Italy, where he restored Rhegium under the new name of Phoebia and founded two outposts on the Apulian coast. Nearer home he seems to have recalled some of the Syracusans who had been exiled by his father for their political opinions, and he is also credited with having remitted some part of the taxes which bore so heavily on the citizens. In 361 Plato once more visited the West, having yielded to the invitations pressed on him more than once by Dionysius. He found that conditions in Syracuse had changed much for the worse during five years. The ruler, after having vainly tried to reduce the cost of his military establishment, was terrorized by his mercenaries and encouraged in self-indulgence by the court faction opposed to Dion. Its influence finally poisoned Dionysius' mind against Plato himself, who found himself treated more as a prisoner than as an honoured visitor. In 360, thanks to the intervention of Archytas, he was permitted to return home.

Meantime Dion, who had been allowed to retain his property in Sicily, had been living in Athens in comfortable circumstances, but planning for his ultimate return to Sicily. He visited other parts of Greece also and made many influential friends. At last, swayed by what he had heard from Plato and from Plato's disciple and future successor in the Academy, Speusippus, about the Syracusan situation, he determined to attempt a military intervention. In making his preparations he was assisted by Heraclides, a former commandant of Dionysius' mercenaries who had fallen into disfavour and fled for his life first to Africa and then to Greece. At last, in 357, Dion set out with a part of the mercenaries that he had raised, it being agreed that Heraclides should follow as soon as possible with the rest. At Zacynthus, whence Dion started out with only a few ships and eight hundred fighting men, he had been so highly esteemed by the government that it permitted him to issue Zacynthian silver staters bearing his name, in order to pay his troops.[1] After a stormy journey the small company landed at Heraclea Minoa on the southern coast of Sicily. Their appearance in the island aroused considerable enthusiasm among the Greek cities, and many volunteers joined Dion on his march towards Syracuse. Dionysius was in southern Italy at the time, so that Dion, when most of the tyrant's mercenaries had deserted to Leontini and Aetna in the belief that their towns would be the first to be attacked, was able to enter Syracuse without fighting. A week later Dionysius appeared with his fleet,

[1] Cf. G. F. Hill, *H.G.C.*, No. 45.

but the Syracusans and Dion's men together defended the city so desperately that he finally abandoned the assault and withdrew into his fortress on Ortygia. The Syracusan populace now elected Dion and his brother, Megacles, together with a committee of twenty *strategi*, to carry on the defence and government of the city. But Dion's difficulties had only begun. The freedom of Syracuse would not be a reality until the tyrant had been driven from his stronghold and his navy off the seas. Moreover, among the more influential citizens there were not a few who distrusted Dion, believing, though probably quite unjustly, that he was merely seeking to supersede Dionysius as absolute ruler. The last-named, having got wind of this, tried to undermine Dion's popularity still more. He contrived that a letter should fall into the hands of the Syracusans in which he praised Dion's past services to his family and urged him to assume despotic powers.

The arrival of Heraclides with a few additional vessels and 1500 more mercenaries created a temporary diversion. But, though he was officially appointed admiral to co-operate with Dion, and in the course of 356 defeated Dionysius' navy decisively, Heraclides soon began to intrigue against his senior colleague. Dionysius, after the defeat of his fleet, tried unavailingly to come to terms with the Syracusans. In the end he made his escape to Locri, leaving his son, Apollocrates, in charge of the garrison on Ortygia. Before the year closed the democratic faction in Syracuse had become so strong that Dion, taking his professional soldiery with him, withdrew to Leontini, only to be recalled to Syracuse a little later when its citizens were hard pressed by Apollocrates. The intervention of two Spartan officers, whose diplomatic mission is quite obscure, led to the departure of Apollocrates and to the establishment of an oligarchic constitution at Syracuse in which Dion was the leading figure. Once again the settlement was of short duration and Syracuse became the scene of new plots and counter-plots. Dion himself was assassinated already in 354, soon after he had acquiesced in the murder of Heraclides, at that time the leader of popular opposition. The Syracusans were incapable of evolving a settled form of government, after sinking their differences, with the result that first the sons of Dionysius and finally Dionysius himself recovered Syracuse (347).

## § 7. THE EXPEDITION OF TIMOLEON

The *régime* of the tyrant after his return to Sicily was far more ineffective than before, when the political control of Syracuse over the Greek part of the island had at least been maintained unimpaired. But about 345 the Carthaginians were on the war-path in Sicily, when their ally, Entella, attempted to secede. Soon after, they were actively threatening Syracuse and the Greek parts of the island. The lack of political stability in Syracuse seems to have communicated itself to the cities that were still, nominally at least, within the Syracusan sphere; for when help from Greece at last arrived many were ruled by tyrants.[1]

In the extremity of their impotence, and especially in view of the threat from Carthage, the Syracusans at length appealed, as they had done in the past, to their mother-city, Corinth. At the same time they made what was to prove a costly error when they invited Hicetas, at that time despot of Leontini, to aid them in expelling Dionysius. For Hicetas, who had once been an associate of Dion, while accepting the invitation to head the Syracusan struggle for liberty, and also outwardly approving the petition to Corinth, was in secret aiming to become himself sole master of Syracuse, if need be, with Carthaginian assistance. The Corinthian government was moved by the distressful situation of an erstwhile colony and authorised the despatch of seven hundred mercenaries—most of them, it would seem, had lately served in the Phocian army—under command of Timoleon. Though a highly respected citizen, Timoleon, who for personal reasons had been living in retirement for many years, does not appear to have had any special qualifications, save a detestation of tyranny, for the difficult task that he now undertook. The success, political and military, of his mission was all the more remarkable. As he was able to obtain a little additional support from Leucas and Corcyra, his total force on reaching

---

[1] R. Hackforth (*C.A.H.*, VI, 285-286), following Meltzer, argues that Punic intervention in Sicily was at first purely defensive, i.e. caused by the action of Entella. But the ancient evidence is too slight to allow of any certain conclusions about Carthaginian policy at this date. On the other hand, one wonders what authority H. Berve (*Griechische Geschichte*, II, 121) could quote to support his assertion that Carthage had recovered Acragas, Gela, and Camarina before Syracuse appealed for help to Corinth.

Tauromenium, after successfully tricking a Carthaginian squadron that tried to bar his progress at the strait, amounted to ten vessels and 1000 men. But his appearance in Sicily at first aroused little enthusiasm and few volunteers joined him. Then, by a fortunate chance, he was invited by a faction in Adranum to intervene in the affairs of that town. The opposing faction had already turned to Hicetas who arrived first but was routed by the much smaller force of Timoleon. The news of this victory of the Corinthian spread swiftly, and many new volunteers flocked to his standard. Several cities opened their gates to him and one, Catana, now became his headquarters. It was a further piece of good fortune that Dionysius, realizing the hopelessness of his own position, since his guards had recently suffered a reverse at the hands of Hicetas and his men, preferred to surrender to Timoleon than to his rival for tyranny. It is evident that Hicetas' military dispositions were very imperfect, seeing that a body of 400 men sent by Timoleon were able to take over Ortygia. Dionysius, having surrendered to Timoleon in person, was transported to Corinth where he lived for some years longer in humble circumstances.

Timoleon's position had now become perceptibly easier. He was master of the Syracusan fortress, his army was increased by the two thousand mercenaries of Dionysius who now entered his service, and he acquired a valuable collection of arms and armour, a part of the stock originally laid up in Ortygia by Dionysius I. Moreover, on receiving information of his success, the Corinthian government at once despatched 2200 additional soldiers to Sicily to reinforce him. Nevertheless he had two enemies to contend with, Hicetas, still master of the city of Syracuse, and the Carthaginians, who since 344 had been acting in concert with Hicetas. During the winter months (344–343) Timoleon, still operating from Catana, and his colleague, Leon, who had charge of the garrison on Ortygia, more than held their own, although beleaguered by greatly superior forces. Leon even succeeded in capturing the district of Syracuse known as Achradina. In the spring, with the arrival of the reinforcements from Corinth, who, like Timoleon before them, tricked the Punic fleet stationed off Rhegium, Timoleon ventured to march on Syracuse and encamped close to the city. For reasons that are entirely obscure the Carthaginian commander-in-chief, Mago, abandoned the siege there and then, and the whole Punic armament sailed away. As Mago subsequently committed suicide, it is evident that he had not acted on instructions from Carthage, when he retired from Syracuse. The city passed into the hands of the deliverer, but Hicetas made good his escape to Leontini (autumn, 343).

The winter months were presumably passed by Timoleon in beginning his constitutional reforms and in repairing the worst of the material damage which successive conflicts had wrought in the city. During the next campaigning season he had both successes and failures. He was unable to dislodge Hicetas from Leontini, but he won over some Sicel towns in northern Sicily and even raided the Carthaginian parts of the island. This activity called forth a new expeditionary force from Carthage, composed partly of citizens, partly of dependents and mercenaries. It is said that 200 galleys and 80,000 men participated, but, as usual, little reliance can be placed in the figures given by the ancient writers. The troops were landed at Lilybaeum in the spring of 341, but the plan intended by their commanders, Hasdrubal and Hamilcar, is not known. At all events their progress into the eastern half of the island was barred by Timoleon who, with an army that was perhaps not more than one-sixth as strong, gave battle to the enemy on the eastern bank of the Crimisus river between Segesta and Entella. The disparity in numbers was to some degree neutralized by natural features of which the Greek commander was not slow to take advantage. Descending from hilly ground above the river, Timoleon was able to take his opponents unawares because of a heavy mist that enshrouded his advance. Then during the action itself a violent rain-storm swept the plain. The difficulties of the Punic soldiers, who faced the tempest and whose heavy equipment weighed them down, were still further increased by the state of the ground, which became water-logged from the torrential downpour and the flooding of the river. The Carthaginian lines broke, and in the ensuing rout as many were swept away by the flood as were cut down by the Greeks.

But Carthage did not at once abandon the war. Hostilities seem to have continued until 339, in which the Punic commanders received some support from the tyrants of

Adranum, Messana, and Leontini, though all had previously sided with Syracuse. Yet, in spite of some minor reverses, Timoleon, playing upon the lack of co-operation shown by his opponents, in two or three years expelled every tyrant in the island. Seeing the defeat of their Greek allies, the Carthaginians before the end of 339 came to terms which left the territorial division of the island much as it had been before. But they engaged to abstain for the future from alliances with the ruler of any Greek city in Sicily and agreed to allow any Greeks within the Punic section of the island to leave, if they so desired.

It remains to notice the work of Timoleon as a restorer of peace and order. Already after his capture of Syracuse he had, in order to remedy the depopulation there and in other towns, appealed to his home government to promote the emigration of settlers to Sicily. The response was notable, if it be true that the male immigrants alone numbered 60,000, drawn partly from Greece, partly from Italy. The settlement of citizens in Syracuse was accompanied by a redistribution of the land. The fortifications on Ortygia were razed and the site was reincorporated in the city. A new court of justice was set up where once had stood the palace of Dionysius. Little information has survived concerning the form of government instituted by Timoleon. It appears to have been a blend of oligarchy and democracy, seeing that the council of six hundred was recruited from the wealthiest citizens, whereas all alike were members of the assembly. The chief magistrate was the priest of Zeus Olympius, who was chosen in rotation by lot from one of three clans. Associated with him in the executive was a board of *strategi* ; but it was further provided that, if the Syracusans were involved in a serious foreign war, they should receive a commander-in-chief from their parent-city, Corinth. Clearly the object of this provision was to prevent for the future any attempt at tyranny. After the conclusion of the Carthaginian War the restoration and resettlement of other Greek cities proceeded apace, notably at Acragas, Gela, and Camarina. It is likely that these cities adopted constitutions similar to the Syracusan. Their renascence as independent city-states is clearly shown by the fact that they again began to strike their own coins. Those issued at Syracuse, moreover, reflect the

influence of Corinth both in weight and in the types used—
a helmeted Athena and the winged Pegasus. Especially
noticeable also is the multiplication of mints in Sicily at this
time ; for smaller communities, some of them Sicel, now began
to issue their own, or else alliance, coins of silver or bronze.[1]

Although Timoleon retired into private life *c.* 336, he continued to reside in Syracuse, enjoying the deep veneration of
its inhabitants until his death (*c.* 330 ?). Remarkable as was
his achievement, it failed to bring about a lasting settlement ;
for, as in the East, so in the West the independent city-state
had become an anachronism. Timoleon, although he had
restored to the Sicilian *poleis* a temporary prosperity, had not
devised adequate safeguards against a renewal of despotism
or attempted to form a federal union which would have given
them lasting security against a foreign invader. Within
a dozen years of his death Timoleon's work was undone by the
personal ambition of Agathocles.[2]

### § 8. THE ITALIAN GREEKS AFTER THE DEATH OF DIONYSIUS II

During the years that Sicily was distracted by civil strife
and foreign aggression the situation of the Greeks in southern
Italy became steadily more precarious in face of the pressure
exerted by the hill-peoples of the interior. As early as 356
the Bruttians, taking advantage of Dionysius II's difficulties
and the consequent weakening of Syracusan control, organized
themselves into a federation with its capital at Consentia.
They conquered most of the Greek communities lying between
the River Siris and the Isthmus of Scyletium. Even the
Thurians perhaps succumbed for the moment ; but if so, they
regained their freedom soon afterwards.[3] About twelve
years later the Lucanians and Messapians threatened the
independence of Taras and her neighbours. Deprived some

---

[1] It was probably Alaesa which for a time minted coins with the legend
KAINON ( = κοινὸν). Cf. Grose, 248. Centuripae, Herbessus, and Adranum
first struck their own *c.* 340. Abacaenum and Tauromenium had begun to
do so some years before the arrival of Timoleon in the West.

[2] Cf. M. Cary in Vol. III of this work, 166 ff.

[3] Diodorus (XVI, 15) includes Thuria among the places conquered by the
Bruttians, but other ancient writers and the numismatic evidence show that
Thuria was an independent state as late as 330. Cf. Beloch, *Griechische
Geschichte*, III, 1, 594, and Ciaceri, *Storia della Magna Grecia*, III, 2–3.

years before of the wise counsels of Archytas,[1] the Tarantines applied for aid to their parent-city, Sparta. In reply Archidamus came over with a body of mercenaries.[2] Nothing is known of his campaigns save that the last ended in complete disaster. The king with most of his army was destroyed by the Lucanians and Messapians near Mandonium (338). Though apparently safe for the moment, the people of Taras after four or five years were again in difficulties. This time they appealed to Alexander the Molossian, ruler of Epirus and uncle of Alexander the Great. Like Pyrrhus fifty years later, Alexander accepted the invitation with the object of uniting southern Italy and Sicily into a single kingdom under his rule. For two or three years he fought with marked success, defeating both Bruttians and Lucanians in several engagements and capturing Consentia, Terina, and other towns of the enemy. But these military achievements filled the people of Taras, Thuria, and Metapontum with apprehension that he would not scruple to deprive them of their independence. Thus involved in a war with his late allies, Alexander was more than a match for them and seized Heraclea, a Tarantine colony. But while he was engaged in this way, the Lucanians and Bruttians renewed their attacks and at the battle of Pandosia Alexander's army suffered a heavy reverse. The king himself was assassinated by a Lucanian renegade who had previously served under him.

Taras and her neighbours preserved their political independence for several more decades before they finally succumbed before the power of Rome in the early part of the third century.

[1] The date of his death is unknown. Ciaceri (*op. cit.*, III, 4) suggests that had he still been alive in 346 he would have prevented the massacre of the wife and daughters of Dionysius II by the Locrians when they inaugurated their new democratic constitution. But this is a mere guess.

[2] As Ciaceri observes (*op. cit.*, III, 4), it is not without significance that at the very time that Taras applied to Sparta the Greek towns of Campania were turning to Rome for help against the Samnites.

# CHAPTER XI

# THE CONQUESTS OF ALEXANDER

## § 1. THE PERSIAN EMPIRE IN THE FOURTH CENTURY

THE empire that Darius I had organized, and that he and his immediate successors had governed, suffered serious diminution in the fourth century. Although no ancient source describes the circumstances, it is beyond dispute that the far eastern provinces fell away, so that the Hindu Kush marked the limit of Persian authority. Similarly, northern Armenia and the regions bordering on the southern shores of the Euxine became independent. It was some compensation that since the Peace of 386 the Greek cities of Asia Minor had reverted to their old position of tributaries. Nevertheless, the material advantages that accrued to Persia from the King's Peace were in some degree lessened by the disaffection which, like a wasting disease, undermined the prosperity of the western satrapies. In the south Egypt had revolted in 404 and remained independent for seventy years under the rule of native dynasts, who, not content with holding Egypt, might on occasion lend support to insurrections elsewhere. Thus Evagoras, the Hellenized prince of Salamis in Cyprus and patron of the Athenian Conon, received some Egyptian help when he seceded from Persia in 389. For several years he controlled nearly the whole island, only to succumb in the end (380) to the vastly greater resources of Artaxerxes II. Again Egypt was implicated in the Revolt of the Satraps, an insurrection that was supported by the governors of Phrygia, Armenia, Lydia, and Caria. Had they known how to co-operate effectively, the result might well have been the permanent loss to Persia of her western provinces. As it was, the authority of the Great King was approximately restored after seven years (366–359). With the accession of Artaxerxes III in 358 the policy of Persia became more vigorous. But even he did not recover Egypt until 343–342. That the country did not relish its relapse into the status of a Persian province is suggested by the feeble opposition that it offered to Alexander ten years later. For the military history of the period it is important to note that all concerned—the Great King as well as his disloyal satraps —relied for their fighting material primarily on Greek mercenaries; and temporary service in Persian pay was sometimes a source of profit to the governments of Greek city-states, who permitted one or other of their leading generals to fight for the ancestral enemy of Greece.

### § 2. EARLY TRAINING AND CAREER OF ALEXANDER

On the death of Philip II, Alexander was twenty years of age. That he handled with consummate skill a situation which would have tested the powers of a far older man was due in part to the admirable training of his youth. That the son of Philip should excel in hunting and all physical and military exercises will occasion no surprise; but Philip had also taken care to develop the intellect of his heir. Aristotle, the son of a physician of Stagirus employed at the Macedonian court, was the tutor of the young prince for several years, and, though we do not know the curriculum that he laid out for his royal pupil, it is evident that it included some scientific as well as literary and philosophic studies and imbued Alexander with a lasting love and admiration of what was best in Hellenic culture. At sixteen Alexander filled his first responsible post, when his father entrusted to him the regency in Macedonia, while he himself was engaged on a campaign in the interior of Thrace. Two years later Alexander shared prominently in the victory of Chaeronea. But then, as we have seen, the relations between father and son were strained for some years.[1] An outward reconciliation had taken place before Philip's death.

It is clear that Alexander, who had already shown his mettle as a soldier, was popular with the fighting men of Macedonia. In addition, he could rely on the unswerving loyalty of Philip's two most experienced and trusted generals, Antipater and Parmenio. Thus he was proclaimed king by the troops

[1] Cf. above, p. 262.

before any revolution or dynastic struggles could develop. Those who had been guilty of conspiracy against his father were punished, and one or two persons of royal blood who might prove dangerous in Alexander's absence were removed. Amongst them was Amyntas, whom Philip had set aside after the first years of his regency. The news of Philip's death was the signal for general unrest in Greece and amongst the Thracian tribes subject to Macedonia. Alexander lost no time, but led an army into Greece, where his appearance sufficed to stop the anti-Macedonian movement at the outset. Attalus, the Macedonian general, was adjudged guilty of treasonable correspondence with the Athenians and executed. Alexander was elected in his father's place, first, as archon of Thessaly, and then towards the end of the year as commander-in-chief of the League of Corinth. But the situation in Thrace was not so easily smoothed out. In 335 Alexander conducted his first independent campaign with conspicuous success. Starting out in the spring from Amphipolis he advanced against the Triballi and defeated them in an engagement. A swift and brilliantly executed raid across the Danube against the Getae, who were preparing to help the Triballi, decided the latter to submit and become Alexander's vassals. In the meantime he had heard that the Illyrians under their prince Clitus had invaded Macedonian territory. By forced marches he took his men to Pelium and, after a narrow escape from being surrounded by a superior force, inflicted a decisive defeat on Clitus.

Vague rumours of these distant campaigns filtered through to Greece; one in particular, that Alexander had been killed, produced an immediate reaction. A body of democratic exiles from Thebes recovered control of their city and blockaded the Macedonian garrison in the Cadmea. Athens, the Aetolians, and several states in the Peloponnese prepared to join in the rising. But the Greek plans were completely upset by the sudden appearance of Alexander in Boeotia. He had not delayed an instant when he heard of the Greek insurrection and led his men in two weeks from northern Macedonia to the gates of Thebes. He began by calling on the citizens to submit and to honour their oath to the League. Only when his demand met with no response did he order an attack. The Thebans, after fighting gallantly under the walls of their city, were driven back pell-mell and pursued so closely that the victors were able to force their way into the city close on their heels. Attacked also by the Macedonian garrison, the Theban troops made a last stand, but were cut down with tremendous losses. Technically the fate of the city was left by the conqueror to the decision of the League members, but all that were on the spot, from the other cities of Boeotia and from Phocis, were bitter enemies of Thebes. It has never been doubted that the complete destruction that they decreed, from which only the temples and the house of the poet Pindar were exempted, was in accordance with Alexander's own decision. The territory of Thebes was divided amongst the other Boeotian towns, while the Cadmea continued to be occupied by a Macedonian garrison. A few Thebans had managed to escape across the frontier into Attica; the rest of the survivors were sold as slaves. Further than this Alexander's punitive measures did not go. The Athenians, with good reason expecting severe measures, hastened to congratulate the victor on his safe return from the north and the suppression of the Theban revolt. Contemptible as was their conduct, when one considers not only their previous anti-Macedonian agitation, but the fact that three years before, Thebans and Athenians had fought shoulder to shoulder on the field of Chaeronea, it saved them. And Alexander was even persuaded to desist from his first demand that Demosthenes and other leaders of the anti-Macedonian propaganda be surrendered to him. The motive for exercising such clemency was perhaps not so much a sentimental regard for Athens as the chief representative of Greek culture, as the need of her naval services in the war against Persia. With peace restored in Greece—for the fall of Thebes had been followed by an immediate cessation of anti-Macedonian acts throughout Greece—Alexander spent the winter months in perfecting the arrangements for an Asiatic expedition.

### § 3. THE CAMPAIGNS AGAINST DARIUS III

The army which crossed from Sestus to Abydus in the spring of 334 composed not less than 30,000 infantry and 5000 cavalry. Of the former 12,000 were Macedonians, while the hoplites furnished by the Greek allies and the mercenaries,

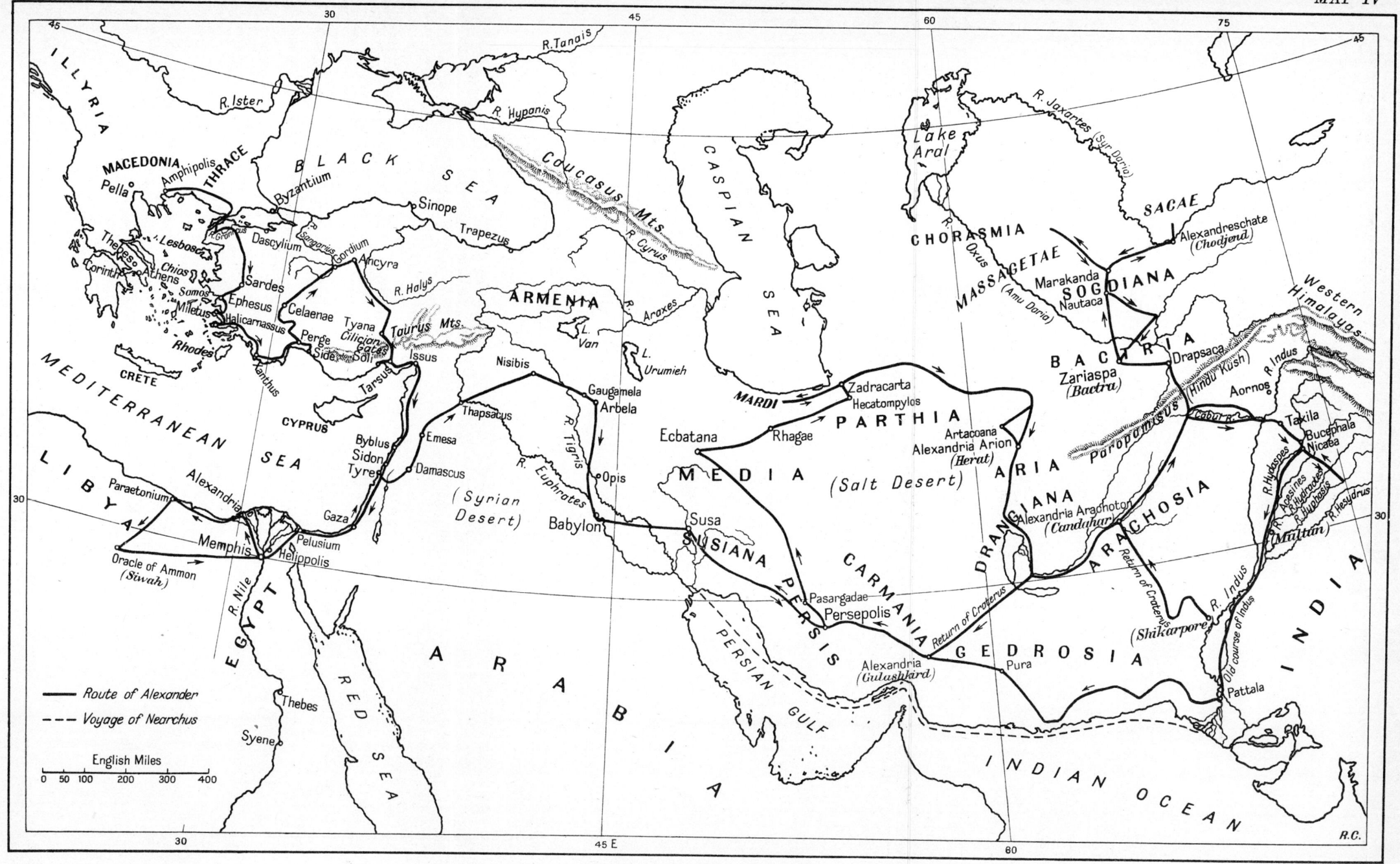

THE CONQUESTS OF ALEXANDER

# THE CONQUESTS OF ALEXANDER

partly armed as hoplites, partly as peltasts, amounted to about the same figure. The remaining 6000 men were a miscellaneous force of slingers, javelin-throwers, and light-armed skirmishers. The Macedonian cavalry was about 2000 strong, the Thessalian mounted contingent not much less, the rest being furnished by other Greek states. An artillery and engineer unit under the direction of Diades completed the land army. Besides his military staff Alexander took with him Eumenes and Aristotle's nephew, Callisthenes, the one to keep the official journal of the expedition (ἐφημερίδες), the other to write its history. Important in the later stages of his advance was a number of scientific observers who accompanied the expedition to record the *flora, fauna*, and natural resources of the countries traversed. Alexander's navy amounted to no more than 160 galleys supplied by the Greek League.

Although the threat of a Macedonian invasion had been in the offing for some years, no serious steps to repel it had been taken by Persia. It may be guessed that a recent double change of rulers was a prime cause of this lack of preparedness. Artaxerxes had been assassinated by Bagoas in 336, who, after elevating the late king's son to the throne, shortly afterwards murdered him like his father. Then the king-maker elevated to the throne Darius III, a member of a collateral branch of the Achaemenid House, only to fall himself a victim to a poison cup administered by the new ruler. When Alexander landed in the Troad, the governors of the four nearest satrapies, Dascylium, Lydia, Cappadocia, and Phrygia, collected such forces as they could muster. In addition, Memnon, the general who had successfully checked the Macedonian advance columns sent to Asia by Philip in 336, had some mercenaries for field service after placing strong garrisons in Miletus and Halicarnassus. Memnon, with more military sense than the satraps, urged that they should retreat into the interior, destroying all crops as they went, thereby rendering Alexander's advance into Asia very difficult at the outset. But the satraps overruled him and prepared to bar Alexander's progress on the lower reaches of the River Granicus. There the cavalry took up its position on the steep banks which overhung the southern bank, while the infantry, consisting of Greek mercenaries, was stationed a little to the rear. It has been suggested that their reason for this unusual and tactically indefensible disposition was that they staked all on surrounding Alexander himself and killing him.[1] Had their gamble succeeded, the Macedonian invasion would have been checked at the very beginning. Against the advice of Parmenio Alexander gave the order to attack as soon as he reached the river. He himself commanded the right wing composed of the Macedonian cavalry supported by light-armed troops, while Parmenio was in charge of the allied horse on the left wing. The heavy infantry was in the centre. It was pre-eminently a cavalry engagement in which the heaviest fighting was borne by the right wing. The Macedonian attack proved irresistible, although the plan of the Persian generals nearly succeeded; for Alexander was only saved from death at the hands of Spithridates by the swift action of Clitus, the colonel of the first, or Royal, squadron of the heavy cavalry. After the defeat of the mounted troops the Greek infantry in Persian service was no match for the Macedonian phalanx. They were surrounded and the greater part was cut down. Some 2000 were made prisoners and subsequently condemned by Alexander to forced labour in Macedonia as a punishment for entering Persian service in contravention of the provisions laid down by the League of Corinth. The immediate sequel to Alexander's victory was that Sardes was surrendered without fighting by its Persian commandant, and that the majority of the Greek cities in or near the coast declared for Macedonia, especially when it became known that Alexander favoured the restoration of democratic governments. The Greek communities were not slow to depose the tyrants or oligarchies who had ruled them under Persian suzerainty. But Miletus and Halicarnassus were only taken after a siege. At Miletus the timely presence of Alexander's fleet off Lade prevented the far more numerous Persian navy from effecting the relief of the city. The Milesians were enrolled amongst the Greek allies. The capture of Halicarnassus, where Memnon himself was in command, was a lengthier operation, until finally the Persians evacuated the city. While Alexander had so far entrusted the government of the satrapies that he had conquered to Macedonian officers, he reinstated Ada, the widow of Idrieus, as Carian dynast. But her authority was

[1] Cf. Tarn in *C.A.H.*, VI, 361.

limited to the civil government, the command of Alexander's garrison being assigned to one of his own officers. It was after the capture of Miletus that Alexander decided to dismiss the bulk of his naval force. By occupying and garrisoning the more important maritime cities he had rendered it difficult for the Persian fleet to operate effectively in western Asia Minor. Besides this he calculated rightly that Persian attempts to draw the Greek states of the islands and the European mainland on to a general anti-Macedonian rebellion would prove futile. If he took a risk, it was only after a mature consideration of all the circumstances. To create a fleet approximately equal to the enemy's was far beyond his financial resources at this time; and, besides, the real decision rested with the army. Only the defeat of Darius in the field could break the power of Persia.

During the winter months Alexander divided his forces. The newly married Macedonians were sent home on leave. Parmenio conducted the allies and heavy cavalry to Sardes, with orders to join up with Alexander in Phrygia at the beginning of spring. Alexander himself then led the rest of his army into Lycia and Pamphylia, where he received the submission of the various coastal cities. When he turned north from Side into the mountainous interior on his way to Phrygia he met much resistance from the hill tribes. After a brief stay at Celaenae, where he left a small garrison, he pushed on to Gordium. Here his whole army was reunited and augmented by three thousand additional men from Macedonia. But his most dangerous opponent, Memnon, who had withdrawn from Halicarnassus to the fleet at Cos, had not been idle during the winter. Chios was surrendered to him by the oligarchic faction. Then he laid siege to Mytilene, after the rest of Lesbos had surrendered without a struggle. Even if it be true that these operations were only a preliminary to inciting the European Greeks to secede from Macedonia, it may be doubted how far this greater plan would have succeeded. For the hands of the Athenians were tied because Alexander had retained twenty of their galleys with the crews, and these were hostages for the loyalty of Athens. Many of Memnon's own rowers, again, were drawn from the cities of Asia Minor which had recently set up democracies and so were disaffected. His most serious threat might have been to gain control of the Dardanelles, thereby endangering Alexander's lines of communication and compelling him to send back some part of his army to their defence; for the troops left at home under Antipater—some 12,000 infantry and 1500 cavalry—were needed to ensure the safety of Macedonia and Thrace and to overawe the Greeks. Thus it must have been with some sense of relief that Alexander received news at Gordium that Memnon had died of disease while still at Mitylene. Since Darius recalled the Greek mercenaries who had hitherto served under Memnon, leaving to his successor a mere 1500 fighting men and the fleet, Alexander thereafter had far less cause for anxiety about the situation in the Aegean area.

On leaving Gordium he marched first to Ancyra and then turned southwards through Cappadocia into Cilicia. The speed of his advance took his opponents so completely by surprise that he was able to secure the impregnable pass called the Cilician Gates and then to occupy Tarsus itself without striking a blow. After a short but sharp bout of fever and some subsidiary operations against the hill tribes, Alexander advanced first to Issus, where he left his sick and wounded, and thence to Myriandrus. But it soon proved that he had acted on faulty information concerning the movements of Darius III. The king had in person led an army into northern Syria, there to bar the progress of the invader in the wide plain on which his cavalry and archers could be used with most effect. Only when the enemy did not appear for some time did he give orders to march on into Cilicia. Thus it came about that his troops actually traversed the Amanus by one pass while Alexander crossed the range by another. As soon as Alexander received certain information that the enemy were between himself and his base, he hastened back to Issus. The Persian army was drawn up on the right bank of a stream, the Pinarus, with its right wing resting on the sea and the left on rising ground. Alexander's battle order was similar to that adopted at the Granicus. The size of the armies engaged in this memorable encounter was much exaggerated in antiquity and cannot be determined with certainty. As Alexander had been obliged to leave garrisons in various place in Asia Minor, it is to be presumed that, in spite of having received substantial reinforcements in 333, he actually had fewer troops than in his first engagement, perhaps 25,000 men all told. The Persian array, composed partly of Orientals, partly of Greek mercenaries, may have been 35,000 strong. The Persian archers on the left succumbed almost at once before the charge of the Macedonian cavalry, but the Persian guard and the Greek hoplites fought gamely and caused their opponents heavy loss before they too were forced to give way. On the left Parmenio fought a stubborn defensive action until his adversary, apprised of the precipitate flight of Darius himself and the retreat of the centre, also gave ground (end of October, 333).

Although the onset of darkness cut short the pursuit, so that a great portion of the Persian army escaped, it was a great victory for Alexander which had profound political consequences. The unrest still latent amongst the European Greeks might have developed into a general rising against Macedonia, had Alexander suffered a reverse. On the other hand, the news of his victory took the wind out of the sails of anti-Macedonian politicians. Even more momentous for Alexander's future plans was the reaction of Darius' defeat at Issus on Syria and Egypt, regions—if we except Phoenicia—whose loyalty to Persia had never been strong and had very rapidly declined as Alexander's triumphant progress through Asia Minor became known. Thus it was that Syria, save for two cities, passed into his hands without resistance. Byblus and Sidon submitted voluntarily, and their fleets, together with squadrons from Rhodes, south-western Asia Minor, and Cyprus deserted the Persian cause and joined the conqueror. But Tyre refused to surrender and its reduction proved one of the hardest tasks and greatest achievements of Alexander's career. After a siege of seven months, during which his new artillery was tested to the utmost and the Tyrians countered assault after assault, the Tyrian fleet was captured or destroyed and a part of the city wall was breached. Once inside the city the Macedonians, infuriated because some of their companions, who had been taken prisoner, had been killed by the Tyrians, indulged in an orgy of carnage. Those citizens who escaped death, and the women and children, were sold into slavery. By the autumn of 332 Gaza, the gateway to Egypt, also fell after a spirited resistance. But before this diplomatic exchanges had taken place between

Darius and Alexander. The Great King was prepared to cede all territory west of the Euphrates and to pay a large indemnity, asking in return that his wife and daughters who had been taken captive after Issus be returned to him. He even offered one daughter in marriage to the conqueror. But it is probable that after his victory in October Alexander had begun to envisage the conquest of the Persian empire, an ambition which had only been strengthened by the relative ease with which he became master of Syria. Hence he refused Darius' terms and made plans for the invasion of Mesopotamia in the following spring.

The end of the year saw Alexander in Egypt. The Persian governor, Mazaces, knowing that the Egyptians were thoroughly disaffected to Persia, surrendered Memphis with its garrison and its state treasury containing the ample sum of 800 talents. The people received the conqueror, whom they regarded as a liberator, with acclamation and accepted him as the legitimate successor of the Pharaohs. But the most momentous consequence of his visit to Egypt was the foundation of Alexandria on the territory between the Island of Pharos and Lake Mareotis, a little to the west of the most westerly mouth of the Nile. The site was peculiarly adapted for the growth of a great port and exchange-mart, because the sea harbour, unlike the Nile estuaries, was never in danger of being silted up, and because the lake could at the same time serve as the terminus of river traffic. Though Alexandria was only one of many cities founded by, and often named after Alexander, it surpassed them all and has retained its importance as a commercial port to this day. The visit paid by Alexander to the famous oracle of Ammon, situated at the oasis of Siwah in the Libyan desert, has been very variously interpreted in ancient as in modern times. While it is true that Ammon had been equated by the Greeks with Zeus and that his oracular seat at that time enjoyed a prestige among the Greeks hardly inferior to the renown of Delphi and Dodona, it is more reasonable to interpret Alexander's consultation of Zeus-Ammon as the outcome of a romantic or mystical impulse of his nature rather than an act dictated by policy, still less as an attempt to impose the belief in his divinity upon the Hellenic world. Before he set out from Egypt for his next campaign he arranged for the government of Egypt. He retained the native governors and officials but entrusted the general direction of finance to a Greek, Cleomenes of Naucratis. Some troops—we do not know their number—remained stationed in the country, even as Macedonian garrisons had been left in the previous year in Tyre and Gaza. It was also welcome news that the last remnants of the Persian fleet had been rounded up by Alexander's admirals, Hegelochus and Amphoterus, who had been active in the Aegean ever since Memnon's death.

Alexander left Egypt in the spring of 331 and went to Tyre where administrative duties detained him for some months. By the middle of summer he was at Thapsacus on the Euphrates. There he met Parmenio, who had preceded him with orders to construct a bridge across the river. A Persian advance force, stationed on the eastern bank under command of Mazaeus for purposes of reconnoitring rather than for defence, withdrew on the arrival of Alexander's main army and continued to retire before him as he advanced through northern Mesopotamia and past the Armenian foothills to the Tigris. This river also was crossed without hindrance, Mazaeus having hastened on to report Alexander's movements to the Great King. Darius had used the winter to reorganize his army. To make good the loss of all but 2000 of his Greek mercenaries—the rest had withdrawn from his service after Issus and ultimately found their way back to Greece—he had a number of scythed war-chariots constructed, machines that had long been obsolete but which he hoped would inflict severe damage when sent against the formidable Macedonian infantry. Cavalry contingents of high quality had been collected from the eastern and north-eastern provinces of the empire, and it was on his numerous mounted troops that Darius relied to give him victory. In order that they and especially the chariots might operate on the most favourable ground, he had marshalled his host near Gaugamela, on the flat plain lying a little to the north-east of the modern town of Mosul. There is again much uncertainty about the size of the armies engaged. Both were somewhat greater than those which fought at Issus. But the disparity was also more marked; so that Alexander, fearing that his decidedly smaller force might be outflanked—it probably did not much exceed 40,000 all told —took special precautions. While his general dispositions were similar to those that he had employed in his two previous battles, he placed behind each wing a deep reserve column made up partly of infantry, partly of cavalry and auxiliaries. These columns served a double purpose : they could be used to strengthen and extend his wings or, if there were danger of encirclement by the enemy, they with the front line troops would have formed three sides of a hollow square. Furthermore, he posted reserves composed of Greek mercenaries behind the phalanx, and these had orders in an emergency to form front to the rear and thus complete the square.

On the last day of September, 331, Alexander encamped some four and a half miles from the enemy and gave his men a good night's rest. Then on the morning of October 1st he moved forward to the attack. Observing as he advanced that his right wing would come opposite to the Persian centre, he inclined to the right so as to deliver his main thrust at the enemy's left, at the same time bringing his guards' regiment of infantry opposite to the scythed chariots arrayed before the Persian centre. The actual fighting opened with an attack of the Scythian and Bactrian cavalry on Alexander's right flank, and, while a sharp cavalry encounter developed at this point, Darius ordered the chariots to charge. But this manœuvre failed. Alexander's skirmishers shot down many of the drivers or pulled them from their seats and, as the chariots approached the Macedonian front, the hypaspists opened out their ranks to let them roll by harmlessly. Meanwhile in the contest on his right flank Alexander had more than held his own, so that Darius found it necessary to detach more and more mounted troops to help his hard-pressed Bactrians and Scythians. But through this transference a gap was made in his left wing, a weakness of which Alexander at once took advantage. He ordered his infantry to a frontal attack while he himself at the head of his Companions charged the gap. Before this double assault the Persian line broke and Darius himself, as at Issus, wheeled his chariot about and fled precipitately. But on the other wing Parmenio was fighting desperately. His line was broken by the enemy cavalry and the phalanx would have been surrounded, if the Persian and Indian horsemen who had broken through had not ridden straight on to attack the Macedonian camp instead of crushing the Macedonian left wing. Alexander's second line now showed its mettle. It re-formed and attacked them in the rear, compelling them to retire. At this juncture Alexander, who had received an urgent message from Parmenio, came on the scene with his Companions and barred the progress of the Persian horse. In this final cavalry action Persians and Indians fought desperately for their lives and inflicted heavy casualties on their opponents before they succeeded in breaking through and escaping. In the interval Parmenio, thanks to the gallantry of his Thessalian horse, had ended by driving back his opponents also. The whole Persian army was now in flight. The victor ordered a pursuit until darkness fell and resumed it after midnight. But although he pressed on at top speed until he reached Arbela, more than sixty miles away, he was too late to capture Darius.

Alexander now continued his march to Babylon. Mazaeus, who had retired there after Gaugamela, opened its gates and went out to meet the victor. The Babylonians received him, as the Egyptians had done, with enthusiasm, and, in return, Alexander gave them back their native customs, which Xerxes had suppressed, and gave orders for the rebuilding of the temple of Marduk (Esagila). About a month passed before he left the city for Susa, leaving Mazaeus in charge as civil governor, but associating with him two Macedonians, one to command the garrison, the other to take charge of the financial department.

### § 4. THE CONQUEST OF MEDIA AND PERSIS

Susa capitulated without a struggle as Babylon had done. There Alexander obtained possession of great quantities of gold darics and gold and silver bullion that the Persian rulers had accumulated. As in Babylon so at Susa he reinstated the Persian commandant, but appointed two Macedonian officers to co-operate with him. To celebrate his victorious entry into the Persian capital he offered a great sacrifice to the gods of Macedonia and held an athletic contest and torch race in the Greek manner. At Susa he also received substantial reinforcements from home. For the march on Persepolis he divided his army, sending the Greek allies under Parmenio by the main road, while he himself led the Macedonians by a shorter route through the mountains. He found the pass, called the Persian Gates, barricaded off by a wall and guarded by a strong force under the governor of Persis, Ariobarzanes. In spite of the winter season Alexander left his heavier troops under Craterus to engage the enemy, while he himself took a picked body of men by a mountain path to attack Ariobarzanes in the rear. The manœuvre succeeded, and the satrap, attacked from two sides, was compelled to give way. Alexander then hastened on to Persepolis which its commandant handed over without fighting. There, and at Pasargadae which also surrendered, Alexander found treasure and bullion exceeding by far what he had already annexed as the victor's spoil in Susa. At Persepolis he spent perhaps two months (February–March, 330).[1] As an act of deliberate policy symbolizing the end of Achaemenid rule he caused the royal palace at Persepolis to be burnt.[2]

During the winter months Darius had taken refuge in Ecbatana, where he had with him the Bactrian troops, led by Bessus, a number of other grandees from the eastern provinces, and the Greek mercenaries who had fought at Gaugamela. He seems to have expected substantial military aid from his more distant satrapies, a hope that was not, however, fulfilled. Media was thus Alexander's first objective when he left Persepolis about the end of March, 330. At his approach Darius took to flight once more in the direction of Bactria, and reports reached Alexander that reinforcements were on the way to aid the fugitive. In this way Ecbatana also passed into the conqueror's hands as the other royal cities had done, without bloodshed. From there he sent his Greek troops home. He also in effect removed Parmenio, with whom his relations had for some time been less cordial than formerly, from his position of second-in-command, although he retained him in a most responsible post. He was left in Media with a force of mercenaries and Thracian auxiliaries to guard the lines of communication, and to supervise the safe transport

[1] For the chronology of the years 330–327, I have accepted the conclusions of C. A. Robinson, Jr., *The Ephemerides of Alexander's Expedition* (Brown University Studies, 1932), Appendix, 74–81. He rejects the isolated statement, irreconcileable with the other sources, of Plutarch (*Alex.*, 37) that Alexander stayed four months in Persis.

[2] So our two best authorities, Tarn (*C.A.H.* VI, 383) and Wilcken (*Alexander der Grosse*, 134), rightly. Schachermeyr (*Alexander der Grosse*, 236–237) is non-committal. But Berve (*Griechische Geschichte*, II, 185) accepts the legend (of Clitarchus ?) that the fire was an accident which occurred during a drunken bout of Alexander and his Macedonians.

of the treasure from the palaces to Harpalus, whom Alexander had entrusted with the supreme direction of finance.

After settling the most necessary business in Ecbatana, Alexander pressed on at incredible speed into Hyrcania and to the Caspian Gates, where he received news that the satraps were holding Darius a prisoner after having deposed him from his kingship. Taking only a small portion of his army with him, Alexander continued the pursuit. At last near Hecatompylus he came upon the dying monarch, who had been stabbed and left to perish by his companions. The dead body was treated with all honour and sent to Persepolis for burial in the tombs of the Persian kings.

### § 5. THE CAMPAIGNS IN CENTRAL ASIA

The appearance of Alexander's army in Zadracarta, the Hyrcanian capital, following on the news of Darius' death, led to the voluntary submission of many satraps and high officials, including the governors of Hyrcania and Parthia. A military expedition to the mountainous region lying close to the southern shore of the Caspian Sea reduced the Mardi to obedience. Moreover, the Greek mercenaries who had remained faithful to Darius almost to the last, now surrendered. While those who had been in Persian pay before 338 were allowed to go free, the rest, as they had transgressed the provisions of the League of Corinth, were compelled to enter Alexander's service.

Alexander's intention now was to push on direct to Bactria in search of Bessus. But he had not advanced far from Parthia when he learnt that a national rising was afoot in the central provinces of the empire. This necessitated a complete change of plan and a march into Aria and Drangiana. The governors fled at his approach and the conquest of these regions was for the moment assured. A rising in Aria some months later, when Alexander was already in Bactria, was suppressed not without some difficulty by one of his lieutenants. At Phrada, the royal residence in Drangiana, Alexander was faced for the first time with the danger of disloyalty from his staff. His considered policy of conciliating the peoples that he had vanquished by appointing or reinstating Oriental governors in the satrapies, though it showed unusual breadth of mind and a true understanding of the only way to hold together a vast and heterogeneous empire, was alien to Greek and Macedonian habits of thought and displeased some of his Macedonian officers. Alexander's adoption after Darius' death of Oriental dress and court ceremonial on state occasions was even more distasteful to them. At Phrada a conspiracy against his life was discovered. A number of officers was implicated, of whom the most conspicuous was Parmenio's son, Philotas, a general of the Companions. Tried by the army, he was found guilty of treason and executed. Obscure as is the evidence, it looks as if Alexander's action in this case was justified. But it is impossible to condone the sequel. Alexander, fearing to leave Parmenio in his position of high responsibility in Media, sent orders to his other generals in Media and had him put to death.

If Alexander now introduced certain changes in the higher commands and in the tactical formation of his army, he acted from a variety of motives. The division of the Companions into two hipparchies, each under its own colonel-in-chief, may have been a safeguard against entrusting all the guards' cavalry to a single man who, like Philotas, might prove dangerous. But there was also a strictly military aspect of these changes. Scanty as our records are about Alexander's campaigns in Afghanistan and Turkestan, it is at least clear that he had to devise a completely new strategy to meet the special character of the country and the tactics of the enemy, which were to carry on a ceaseless guerilla war and give no opportunity for full-dress battles such as Alexander had fought in western Asia. In these conditions he must needs divide his army into a number of columns or units, whose commanders at times were thus entrusted temporarily with independent commands.

After the conspiracy of Philotas Alexander moved on into Arachosia. At its capital he founded a new city, Alexandria Arachoton, on the site of the modern Candahar. Then, leaving to Menon with a sufficient military force the task of subduing Arachosia, he advanced past Ghazni, where a second city was founded, and Cabul to the southern slopes of the Hindu Kush. In this vicinity he passed some months in winter-quarters and there, too, he laid the foundations of yet another city, Alexandria ad Caucasum. Early in the spring of 329 he crossed the Hindu Kush on his way to Bactria where Bessus, who had assumed the royal style and title, Spitamenes of Sogdiana, and Oxyartes of Bactria were waiting to dispute his passage. Although the march across the mountains imposed great hardships on the troops—besides the rigour of the climate so early in the season, supplies were short because the enemy had laid waste most of the territory through which they passed—casualties appear to have been few. Moreover, Alexander outmanœuvred Bessus, who was stationed at Aornos (Tashkurgan), whereupon the self-styled king of Persia retreated beyond the Oxus (Amu Daria). By the summer Bactria had submitted and Alexander advanced from the city of Bactra to the Oxus. The associates of Bessus now betrayed him and he fell into Alexander's hands. The regicide was subsequently tried, mutilated and put to death. Late in the summer Alexander had entered Marakanda (Samarcand) in Sogdiana. From there he turned eastwards towards the Jaxartes (Syr Daria) which marked the north-eastern frontier of the Persian empire. But during his absence a rising in Sogdiana showed that the apparent submission of this province had been but a lull before the storm. He had to detach a column for the relief of Maracanda which was being besieged by Spitamenes, while he himself set about building a fortified outpost on the Jaxartes to which was given the name of Alexandreschate. This, and hard desert fighting with the half nomadic horsemen on the farther bank of the Jaxartes, may have occupied him for a month or more, when he learnt that the force sent against Spitamenes had been destroyed by that national leader almost to a man. By forced marches Alexander reached Maracanda with a picked body of men in a few days, but on his approach Spitamenes had again withdrawn into the surrounding steppes. As the season was now far advanced hostilities were suspended and Alexander withdrew to Bactra as his headquarters for the winter (329–328). There heavy reinforcements from both Europe and Asia Minor joined him. The former partisans of Bessus were rounded up. An alliance offered by the paramount chief of Chorasmia, Pharasmanes, was accepted. For the rest, Alexander prepared for further intensive campaigns during the coming year. Spitamenes, who wintered at Bokhara, was still a danger; in addition, Alexander was evolving plans for recrossing the Hindu Kush and attempting the invasion of northern India.

For none of Alexander's campaigns are the records poorer than for those of 328. Nevertheless there is no doubt that the reduction of Spitamenes and the pacification of these distant regions were tasks of the greatest difficulty, and Alexander's plans for entering the Punjab had to be postponed for another season. All through 328 the army was subdivided into several columns and operated in the country to the north of the Oxus, where many fortified posts were established that steadily lessened Spitamenes' power of free movement. But supported by the Massagetae, who dwelt in the steppes to the north-west of Bokhara, he continued to cause Alexander both anxiety and material losses. The Macedonian king passed the winter of 328-327 with the bulk of his troops in Nautaca, although some detachments under command of Coenus were left behind in Sogdiana. Then near the end of 328 Alexander was rid of his most dangerous foe, a piece of good fortune that he could hardly have foreseen. Coenus had inflicted a decisive defeat on Spitamenes, whereupon this chief's own allies turned against him, murdered him, and sent his head to Alexander. Oxyartes also was forced to surrender during the winter months. He received honourable terms, while his daughter, Roxane, was taken to wife by the conqueror. But this year of achievement, filled, as it was, with strenuous warfare and with military and administrative problems of the first class, demanding Alexander's unceasing vigilance, was overshadowed by two tragic episodes. At a banquet during the summer he quarrelled violently with his friend Clitus when both were in their cups, and in the extremity of his passion killed him. For three days and nights the king, stricken with profound remorse, refused all food, and only then was with difficulty persuaded to resume his normal life. This tragedy was perhaps symptomatic of the deep dislike which some of his closest associates amongst the Macedonians continued to feel for the Oriental ceremonial of Alexander's court. A few weeks after the death of Clitus, the official historian of the expedition, Callisthenes, offended Alexander deeply by refusing to conform to his demand that the Greeks and Macedonians in his circle should, like the Orientals, perform the ceremonial of prostration ($\pi\rho o\sigma\kappa\dot{\nu}\nu\eta\sigma\iota\varsigma$) when they came into his presence. Although the king was prudent enough not to insist on this procedure in future, because he sensed that by persisting he would alienate many of his trustiest officers, he never forgave Callisthenes. Near the end of the year some of the royal pages, because one of their number had by Alexander's orders received a whipping for a breach of etiquette, formed a conspiracy against his life. The plot was detected and the guilty were put to death. But suspicion had also fallen on Callisthenes, who acted as tutor to some of the boys and was believed to have discoursed to them on the evils of despotism, that he had instigated or abetted the culprits. He was imprisoned and subsequently was put to death. If the guilt or innocence of Callisthenes is a question of secondary importance, the later hostility to the king manifested by the Peripatetics, of whom Callisthenes as the nephew of Aristotle was one, had grave consequences; for it was the Peripatetics who first circulated in their writings a thoroughly unfavourable portrayal of Alexander's career and character, and this exerted a lasting influence on the historical literature of the Hellenistic age.

If Alexander's relations to those nearest to him were not wholly harmonious during the most difficult years of his career, the loyalty and affection of the rank and file remained unshaken for a leader who expected no man to endure hardships which he would not undergo himself, and of whose personal interest in their lives and fortunes he at all times gave ample proof.

### § 6. ALEXANDER IN INDIA

When Alexander decided to attempt the conquest of India, he was to some extent influenced by the circumstance that in the time of Darius I an Indian satrapy had formed a part of the Persian empire. Although the precise boundaries of that province are unknown, it cannot have comprised more than a portion of the Punjab. Alexander, moreover, in common with all his contemporaries, had entirely erroneous notions about the geography of the Far East. He believed that when he reached the Syr Daria he was not far from the ocean that encircled the earth on the east, and that the valley of the Indus and its tributaries was likewise bounded by the same vast and uncharted sea. Thus to subdue India was to him merely to round off his eastern conquests. His anger and disappointment in 326, when his troops refused to advance beyond the Beas, becomes the more intelligible if we remember that he believed himself to be but a short distance from his goal when compelled to turn back.

In preparation for his expedition, as well as to provide for the security of the lands that he had already conquered, he had enlisted many native troops and had introduced further changes in his military organization. It was thus an army of varied race that he led about May, 327, from Bactra across the Hindu Kush, leaving some thirteen thousand men behind under command of the Macedonian general, Amyntas.[1] The territory that now corresponds to the North-west Province, western Cashmir, and the Punjab was in Alexander's day occupied by many small independent states or principalities, whose mutual relations were generally unfriendly and whose inhabitants differed to some degree in their customs and even in race. At least one of the native princes had been in friendly communication with Alexander before he left Bactra. At or near Cabul this ruler, whose capital was at Taxila between the upper reaches of the Indus and the Hydaspes (Jhelum), appeared in person and made his submission to Alexander, an example that was followed by other native chiefs from west of the Indus. The invading army left Cabul in the late autumn of 327 in two divisions. The smaller, commanded by Hephaestion and Perdiccas, proceeded with the baggage through the Khyber Pass to the Indus with instructions to construct a pontoon bridge across the river. Alexander himself with the larger division set out through the mountainous district in the North-west Province stretching northwards from the Cabul River; for the reduction of that area was essential to secure his communications and to protect the division under Hephaestion. Months of hard fighting in difficult country followed against tribes who relied on their

[1] Tarn (*C.A.H.*, VI, 401) estimates the army that invaded India at 35,000 men. In 326 Alexander received the submission of many Indian chiefs who then sent detachments of native troops to serve under him. The traditional number of those encamped on the Jhelum River—120,000—very probably, as Tarn suggests, included many non-combatants. Wilcken, however, speaks (*Alexander der Grosse*, 165) of an army of 120,000.

hill fortresses to repel any invader. After defeating the
Aspasii, Alexander entered Swat and there encountered the
most bitter resistance from the Assaceni. After a sharp
struggle he captured their stronghold of Massaga and lesser
settlements ; whereupon they retreated eastwards and withdrew to the mountain fastness of Aornos. This seemingly
impregnable site lay in the *massif* of Pir-Sar some five thousand feet above sea-level.[1] Only after Alexander's engineers
had constructed a dam across a ravine which lay between
him and the fortress, so that he could approach close enough
to bring his catapults to bear on the defenders of the high
plateau, did the Assaceni submit (Jan.–Feb., 326 ?). After
this, one of his most spectacular achievements, Alexander
joined his other division on the Indus, leaving Nicanor in
charge as governor of the newly conquered province. The
troops were now given a month's rest to recuperate from a
campaign which the nature of the country and the winter
season had combined to render one of unexampled severity.

After this Alexander crossed the Indus and advanced to
Taxila, the capital of his most valuable ally amongst the
Indian princes. His next objective was the kingdom of
Porus on the eastern side of the Hydaspes, a powerful rajah
with whom the ruler of Taxila had had a long-standing feud.
When he reached that river towards the end of June he found
the enemy drawn up on the opposite bank to prevent his
crossing. Since a direct attack, such as he had risked at the
Granicus, was impossible in face of Porus' brigade of two
hundred elephants, Alexander for several days sent detachments of troops hither and thither along the river bank, to
give the impression of an imminent attack. Several times,
too, he made as though he were about to send his troops across.
While Porus was in this way kept in suspense and mystified
by what proved again and again an idle threat, Alexander
had the boats in which he had crossed the Indus transported
in sections to a point some eighteen miles upstream, where
the Hydaspes made a wide bend and where, besides, there
was a wooded islet in the river. At length one night, when
Porus' vigilance after many false alarms was relaxed, the
Macedonian king set out with some five thousand cavalry and

[1] The site of Aornos was identified by Sir Aurel Stein. See his book,
*On Alexander's Track to the Indus* (London, 1929).

double the number of infantry to the spot where the pontoons had been assembled and succeeded in effecting a crossing. Craterus was left behind with the rest of the army and had been instructed to cross the Hydaspes only if Porus were defeated or moved his army, and especially his elephants, away from the river bank.

On the morning after the crossing Alexander, having routed an advance troop of Indians, proceeded to attack Porus. The rajah reformed his army in the plain behind the river so that the centre was occupied by the infantry drawn up on either side of the elephant brigade, while chariots and mounted troops were stationed on the two flanks. Alexander's force was a match for the enemy in cavalry alone; he had fewer foot soldiers and no elephants. He therefore laid his plans to win a decisive advantage at the outset by a cavalry engagement. As he massed all his cavalry on one wing, Porus followed suit and moved the mounted men on his right flank to his left. Meantime Alexander, having detailed his mounted archers to harass and hold the infantry on the enemy's left, faced the Indian mounted troops with two hipparchies. At the same time Coenus with the other two cavalry units rode off towards Porus' right. Misled by this manœuvre, as Alexander had intended, Porus' cavalry launched a vigorous attack against Alexander, which the two hipparchies withstood with great steadiness, while Coenus with his now executed a semi-circular movement and bore down on the Indian horsemen from the rear. Thus attacked on two sides, Porus' cavalry was forced to fall back. At that point the whole Macedonian line moved forward and a desperate struggle ensued. At first the elephant brigade inflicted severe casualties on the Macedonians, but still they hung on grimly until many of the beasts had lost their riders or being wounded ran amok, trampling all that came in their way underfoot. In this stampede the Indian troops suffered more heavily than the hypaspists, and Alexander, although his losses had been very heavy, broke their last resistance. They fled, only to be pursued for some distance by Craterus, who had brought his reserves across the river when he saw how the action developed. Porus, who fought to the last and then rode off the field on his elephant, was persuaded to surrender. He was treated by his conqueror with great consideration and reinstated in his principality. But Alexander, besides numbering the two most powerful rajahs, one on either side of the Hydaspes, amongst his vassals, provided further for the security of these regions by founding Bucephala on the western and Nicaea on the eastern side of the river.

He now left Craterus in charge of the two cities and a part of the army, while with the rest he pushed on during July and August into the eastern Punjab. Only one of the tribes that he encountered appears to have offered serious resistance. The Cathaei defended their chief town, Sangala, with determination and only capitulated after they had inflicted heavy loss on their opponents. Having entrusted the protection of this region to Porus, Alexander led his troops on to the River Hyphasis (Beas). Here the endurance of his men came to an end. Already wearied by the strain of continuous campaigns in difficult country and exhausted by the extremes of an unfamiliar climate, they had, since their battle with Porus, been marching for many days through the unceasing downpour of the monsoon rains. When their leader proposed to penetrate the unknown regions beyond the Beas they refused to follow. Alexander for three days remained in the retirement of his tent, hoping that this sign of deep displeasure would change their minds. But they were obdurate and he had to yield to their will. After causing twelve altars to the Olympian deities to be constructed on the river bank, he ordered the return march to the Hydaspes.

It seems to have been his intention from the first to come back to that point after completing his eastern conquests and from there to descend the Jhelum and then the Indus to its mouth. With that aim in view Craterus had been ordered to prepare a large flotilla of transports and small fighting ships during Alexander's absence. On his return from the Beas, Alexander found that these preparations were far advanced. The departure took place in the late autumn. While a part of the army was conveyed by water, the rest marched along the river banks in three divisions commanded by Hephaestion, Craterus, and Philippus, for Coenus had died shortly before. The naval command over some eight hundred miscellaneous craft was entrusted to the Cretan, Nearchus, of whose unusual abilities Alexander had long been convinced, though hitherto he had not employed him in any outstanding capacity. It soon became apparent that the progress of this host—for not a few Indian allies escorted Alexander—would meet with opposition. Alexander received advice that two powerful tribes, the Malli and Oxydracae, were preparing to give trouble. He therefore halted at some point south of the confluence of the Hydaspes with the Arcesines (Chenab) and with a part of his army marched against the Malli. After a series of desperate fights they and the Oxydracae tendered their submission. But Alexander had lost heavily in the assaults on their strongholds and had himself been so severely wounded in the last assault that he had to be carried back to the fleet on a litter. Once more his iron constitution pulled him through; but it is not unlikely that his health was permanently impaired, so that his powers of resistance were insufficient two years later to fight down an attack of fever.

When he was convalescent the army and fleet continued their advance, reaching the Indus itself about February, 325, and Patala near its mouth some five months later. The tribes near the river submitted, though not always without some show of resistance, and two new cities were established in this region by Alexander's command. From a point near Shikarpore Craterus was sent to the west with the artillery, the baggage, and the wounded. He proceeded by the Mulla Pass to Candahar and thence through southern Drangiana into Carmania, where he joined Alexander in the following year at Gulashkird.

### § 7. THE LAST PHASE: RETURN AND DEATH OF ALEXANDER

Patala was designed by Alexander to become a far-eastern counterpart of Alexandria in Egypt, and during the two months that he remained there he began to construct harbour works, quays, and docks. Furthermore, he assigned to Nearchus the honourable, if hazardous, task of taking the fleet back from the mouth of the Indus to the head of the Persian Gulf. The observations that the admiral took on the voyage were of great scientific value to the next generation and added very appreciably to the geographical knowledge of Hellenistic scholars. But Alexander's primary object seems to have been to develop for commercial purposes a direct sea-route from the estuary of the Indus to the Euphrates. The start of Nearchus' voyage and Alexander's departure for the west overland took place towards the end of September, although the former soon after leaving the Indus was delayed for several weeks by adverse winds. Alexander, with such of his army as was not left behind for garrison duty or given to Nearchus for the defence of the naval expedition, passed through the land of the Arabitae and Oritae into the Gedrosian desert (Mekran). It was his intention to keep close to the sea-shore, in order to maintain contact with Nearchus and aid him by sinking wells and establishing depots for provisions. But he did not know the country, and his guides proved unreliable and lost their way. Shortage of water and oppressive heat added to the trials of the army and the miscellaneous body of camp-followers, women, and children following in its train. It was thus only a fraction of those who had set out from Patala who, some two months later, reached Pura, the capital of Gedrosia, alive, although it is probable that the casualties amongst the troops were substantially fewer than amongst the non-combatants. After a rest at Pura Alexander passed on into Carmania where he was joined by Craterus. There, too, he was relieved to see Nearchus again. After various adventures the admiral had reached the estuary of the River Amanis. Leaving the fleet anchored there he had proceeded inland until he had found his master. After this the fleet continued on its way without accident to the mouth of the Shat-el-arab and then up-stream to Susa. Its arrival (Feb.–March, 324) synchronized with that of Alexander, who had taken his army by way of Persepolis to the Persian capital.

What proved to be the last year of his eventful life was passed by Alexander partly in Media and Elam, partly in Mesopotamia; for there were many problems of imperial administration to solve, the more so as many of the men whom he had left in positions of authority during his absence in the Far East had proved unworthy of his trust. The victorious return of the army and navy was celebrated at Susa with lavish festivities. There, too, he carried on with his plan of welding the eastern and the western portions of his empire more closely by intermarriage. He himself took to wife a daughter of Darius and a daughter of Ochus. Hephaestion at the same time married another daughter of Darius and many of the Macedonian officers contracted alliances with the daughters of Persian aristocrats. Then the Macedonian rank and file followed suit in wedding native women, it is said, to the number of ten thousand. But this policy of promoting racial intermixture was but one aspect of his grandiose scheme. He had some years earlier given orders that suitable youths of native families should be trained for military service in the Macedonian fashion. Now on his return from India thirty thousand of these Oriental troops were summoned to parade before him at Susa. Even the Macedonian cavalry regiments were diluted with men of Iranian stock. These innovations, however logical and necessary they might seem to Alexander, aroused the deep resentment of his veterans. In the summer, when he stopped at Opis on his way to Ecbatana, the discontentment came to a head; for when he proceeded to discharge ten thousand Macedonians who were no longer fit for active service and announced that they would be sent home with a pension, the Macedonians gave voice to their anger. This mutiny awoke his fullest anger and he formally discharged all his Macedonian troops; besides this he transferred the names of the old Macedonian regiments to his new Oriental army. After three days his old comrades in arms tendered their submission and a great feast of reconciliation was held, at which Alexander prayed for concord (ὁμόνοια), for a union of Hellene and non-Hellene, a practical exemplification of the brotherhood of man.[1] After that Craterus took the veterans back to Europe, while their king undertook to have the children by native women, who remained behind in Asia, trained after the Macedonian manner.

After spending the hot season in Ecbatana, where he was deeply afflicted by the death of his most intimate companion, Hephaestion, Alexander went to his headquarters at Babylon for the winter. Administrative questions continued to engage much of his attention. The plan of leaving Oriental governors in the provinces had failed disastrously in many instances. They had abused their power to oppress the population, and

[1] See W. W. Tarn in *Proceedings of the British Academy*, XIX (1933) and in his *Alexander the Great*, II, pp. 399 ff.

some had even attempted to make themselves independent rulers. Alexander punished these grave offences by the extreme penalty. But even some of the Macedonians in high positions had failed in their duty. Several generals had misconducted themselves, while the treasurer, Harpalus, had absconded with large sums, after a riotous career in Babylon. He made his way first to Tarsus and later on to Greece, where he was soon to stir up serious trouble. But during the winter Alexander also elaborated plans for a maritime expedition to explore the Arabian coast. By the spring the preparations were far advanced, but at the beginning of June he contracted a fever from which, worn out by the tremendous exertions of a decade, culminating in the dangerous wound that he had received in India, he never recovered. After nearly a fortnight's illness he died on the thirteenth of the month in the thirty-third year of his age.

## CHAPTER XII

## THE EMPIRE OF ALEXANDER

### § 1. ALEXANDER'S ACHIEVEMENT AND ITS EFFECTS

IT is singularly unfortunate that all the ancient writers on Alexander's career address themselves almost exclusively to its military aspects. As long as his campaigns took him further and further east his system of administration was provisional and experimental, and, when at last he returned to Susa, it was apparent that much would have to be changed before a stable government throughout the empire could be assured. But about his future plans, as about new schemes of conquest, we learn but little that can be called reliable. Even his conquest of the empire of Darius I was unfinished at the time of his death, since northern Asia Minor as far as the Caspian Sea and also Armenia had been left untouched by him. It is, indeed, idle to speculate on what Alexander's plans for the future may have been. There is no satisfactory reason for believing that even in 323 he had envisaged the possibility of conquering the western Mediterranean; for his supposed ambition to be a world conqueror rests on a late and unsound tradition, a part of that Alexander legend whose wide vogue is perhaps the most remarkable phenomenon in all literature. The Arabian expedition, had it taken place, would merely have rounded off his Asiatic conquests, even as it would have supplemented the scientific *data* already gathered by Nearchus and others; that more than this was ever intended we are not justified in assuming on the existing evidence.

It is, then, only of Alexander the general that posterity has been able to form a clear judgment. Granted that he started out with the initial advantage of inheriting from his father the most scientifically trained and equipped army that the world had yet seen, his own military genius is apparent in every undertaking from the Granicus to the Hydaspes. If the basic plan of attack in each of his pitched battles was that which he had learnt from Philip, he on each occasion modified or changed his dispositions to meet the special circumstances of the day, be it the danger of encirclement by a larger force, as at Gaugamela, or the unfamiliar peril of Porus' elephant brigade. The same unfailing ability to devise means to overcome every obstacle, however great or strange, is seen in his siege operations; for no two problems could have been more dissimilar than Tyre and Aornos. In central Asia his ultimate success, after perhaps the hardest sustained fighting of his life, was due to his power of improvising the right measures against the guerrilla tactics of his opponents, in short, of beating them at their own game. And, finally, if we except the error before Issus, which was quickly rectified, and the march through Gedrosia, there was never any hitch in military organization.

What Alexander would have proved to be as the ruler of an empire we cannot even guess. It is possible that, if he had lived another decade or two, he could have welded its disparate parts into a harmonious whole and secured unity in diversity. While he lived, his subjects regarded him in different ways. To the Macedonians, even after the adoption of Oriental ceremonial, he remained the king whom the army had acclaimed after Philip's death. To the Greeks, though in fact they were forced to recognize in him a master rather than an ally, he was until 324 legally the commander-in-chief of the Corinthian League. In Asia he was the successor of the Achaemenids, in Egypt of the Pharaohs and, like them, an incarnation of Ra. In one sense one might call his achievement the most impressive failure in history, for the basic weakness of the magnificent structure that he had raised was that its continuance depended absolutely on one man—himself. And yet the effect of his conquests was to change the world, since it was these that made possible the spread of Hellenism in all its aspects over Asia. Greek ideas and customs, and in many of the cities Greek law, were diffused far and wide during the following centuries, even when politically there was constant change and large sections of his empire had again become independent states under native dynasties. Again, much of the scientific achievement of the Hellenistic Age would have been impossible of attainment in the older, geographically restricted, Hellas. We have already noted the value to geographical studies of Nearchus' observations.

Similarly many data collected by the scientists who accompanied Alexander to India were subsequently utilized by Theophrastus in his botanical researches; and it may well be that the information gathered by Gorgos on the mineral resources of the far-eastern provinces were no less valuable, scientifically and economically, to later generations. Then, too, one must not forget the infiltration into the West of eastern ideas during the centuries after Alexander, and the profound influence that they exerted on philosophic, and especially on religious, thought.

Before many generations had passed Alexander began to become a figure of legend. The earlier part of the process by which this came about can be descried but dimly. But few men can have written so influential a book as the author of the historical romance, composed in the Roman imperial age and going under the name of the pseudo-Callisthenes. Two Latin versions, made respectively in the fourth and the tenth centuries, made this mixture of fact and fancy—for it had a historical kernel traceable ultimately to Clitarchus—the common property of the West, and in time inspired the poets and writers in the vernacular languages of medieval Europe. But there exist also versions in Syriac, Egyptian, Abyssinian, Arabic, and Persian, so that the heroic Iskendar is a familiar figure in the literature and myth of the Islamic world. Alexander, whom the genuine Zoroastrian literature designated as " the accursed Alexander the Roman," occupies in the great epic of Persia, Firdausi's *Shah-name*, a special place of honour as the last of the old Persian kings with whom the glorious period of the ancient monarchs drew to a close.[1]

### § 2. THE IMPERIAL ADMINISTRATION

It will be apparent from what has already been said that no comprehensive account can be given of Alexander's system of government in Asia. As far as possible he seems to have left intact the administrative units that had existed under Persian rule. More than that, although the satrapies of Asia Minor were entrusted to Macedonians, those further east were at first mostly put in charge of Orientals. At the same time it is important to note that the Persians always,

[1] Cf. E. G. Browne, *A Literary History of Persia*, I, 118 ff.; R. Merkelbach, *Die Quellen des griechischen Alexanderromans* (Munich, 1954).

and the Iranian satraps frequently, were civil governors only. The Persians proved less satisfactory than the aristocracy of the more distant provinces, and, with one exception, it would seem that no Persian was promoted to the highest office in a province after 328. Of those Orientals who were in high office when Alexander returned to Susa in 324 the majority were deposed and punished for maladministration or other abuses, so that at the time of his death only three of the provincial viceroys were Asiatics. The military authority in each satrapy was regularly vested in a Macedonian. In addition there were many fortresses, like Sardes, Pelusium, Babylon, Persepolis, whose Macedonian commandants were responsible to Alexander alone. But division of responsibility and authority was carried even further, for Alexander appointed a separate body of financial officials. These presided in the taxation districts which were separate from, and mostly larger than, the satrapies; so that Cilicia, for example, formed a single financial area with Phoenicia and Syria. The state treasury at Babylon, moreover, over which Harpalus presided for five years, was quite distinct from the military chest.

Important innovations in the currency were introduced, which in the long run must have greatly facilitated commercial transactions within the empire and which in the remoter provinces caused the older exchange of commodities to be largely superseded by a money economy. Unlike the Persian kings, who alone had issued gold while allowing their satraps to coin silver, Alexander introduced throughout the empire a uniform silver currency on the Attic standard. His tetradrachms were struck in many different mints, the two chief being in Amphipolis and in Babylon. In general no other issues were admitted, but in a few cases, as in Phoenicia and at Babylon, the older coinage of the country was allowed to circulate, so as to avoid an abrupt change which might have hampered, instead of promoting, trade in these highly commercial areas.

An essential part of Alexander's policy to fuse East and West was the foundation of cities, even where in the first instance military considerations may have determined the choice of a particular site. Thus, while they helped to insure the safety of the empire, they also did much to disseminate

Hellenic culture and institutions in the East. There are said to have been no less than seventy of these settlements, but little more than a third of that number are certainly known. Many were named after the conqueror himself, and, since they controlled main caravan routes or other arteries of communication, have retained much of their importance to this day; Chodjend (Alexandreschate), Herat (Alexandria Areion), and Candahar (Alexandria Arachoton) are instances in point. There was, however, one feature in particular which distinguished these towns from the *poleis* of Greece and Asia Minor: they did not enjoy complete local autonomy, but were under the direction of a governor appointed by Alexander. The laws of the city were framed on the Greek model and applied also to the non-Hellenic groups within it, which in some other respects had privileges of their own. But it must again be emphasized that these arrangements were probably regarded by Alexander as provisional. He may have aimed at giving these new foundations ultimately more liberty of action, thereby bringing them into line with the older city-states of Greece. Finally, it may be observed that there were not a few districts or communities which occupied a special position in the empire. Apart from Tyre, the Phoenician cities continued to be administered by their own princes who owed allegiance to Alexander. His relation to the Indian rajahs and to some of the powerful chiefs of central Asia was that of the overlord to the feudatory. We have seen how he permitted the Babylonians to resume their native laws and customs, and there are other instances which show that he was wisely ready, like the Romans at a later date, to continue existing institutions, even those which conferred some political power, if they could be made to fit into his larger scheme of imperial government.

### § 3. ALEXANDER AND THE GREEKS

Until near the end of his life Alexander's relation to the Greeks is adequately defined by saying that he succeeded his father as *generalissimo* of the League of Corinth. His conquest of Asia Minor for a while caused extensive political unrest amongst the Greek city-states there. In general their adherence to his side, whether voluntary or under duress, was accompanied by constitutional changes, since he promoted the establishment of democracies and the suppression of despots or oligarchic factions which were generally pro-Persian. But for a few years Persian influence in the Aegean had still to be reckoned with, and more than one city became the scene of *stasis*. Less than a year after Chios had become a democracy, its government, owing to the intervention of Memnon, was overthrown and the oligarchic *régime* was restored. But by 332 the democrats with Macedonian aid had expelled the Persian garrison and had driven the oligarchs into exile. An extant rescript shows that Alexander himself had taken a hand in the settlement of the island.[1] He ordained that any of the oligarchs who might be captured should be tried before the Council of the Corinthian League for medizing, and he placed a garrison in Chios for a year or two until the government was stable and worked smoothly. The liberation of the Lesbian cities in 334 from the rule of pro-Persian tyrants was short-lived, for in 333 despotism was restored and lasted for several years.[2] Erythrae suffered similar internal disturbance, and it is likely that, if more records had been preserved, they would show such unrest to have affected many other communities in the Aegean.[3] The attachment of the cities to Alexander was commonly attended by their enrolment as members of the Corinthian League.

In European Greece it was Sparta under her king, Agis III, who broke the peace. That state had chosen to remain aloof from the League in 338 and again in 336. A few months before Issus Agis was actually in communication with Persia, but Alexander's victory over Darius in the autumn prevented any effective anti-Macedonian coalition. Nevertheless the Spartan king had received considerable funds with which he was able to build up a mercenary force of appreciable size. Efforts to enlist Athens as an ally failed, but he obtained support from some of the Peloponnesian states. In the summer of 331 he attacked and defeated a Macedonian force in the Peloponnese and then marched against Megalopolis, which, like Messenia and Argos, had remained loyal to Alexander. But Antipater, although he had first to quell some disturbances in Thrace, collected League troops in Thessaly and central Greece to augment his Macedonian army and invaded Arcadia before the end of the year. Close to

[1] Tod 192.  [2] *Ibid.*, 191.  [3] *Ibid.*, 184.

Megalopolis he inflicted a crushing reverse on the Greeks. Agis died on the field of battle and the rising against Macedonia collapsed. Antipater left the punishment of Sparta to the League Council; but when the Spartans appealed from its decision to Alexander himself, the king was content to punish only the leaders of the insurrection and to impose a fine to be paid as compensation to the Megalopolitans.

Although the virtual hegemony of Macedonia over the Greeks was far from popular and Antipater especially was widely disliked, caution dictated quiescence at least during Alexander's lifetime. Even at Athens, where opinion on many questions of policy was sharply divided, a majority was in favour of avoiding any provocative action against Macedonia. Since Demosthenes for a few years after 336 kept himself in the background, Hyperides became the chief spokesman of the minority overtly hostile to Alexander. For a dozen years, however, the most influential man at Athens was the finance minister, Lycurgus, to whom the other financial officials were subordinate.[1] It was due to his initiative that the public income of Athens increased substantially and that much of the available money was wisely spent. The fortifications of Athens were thoroughly repaired, additions were made to her naval force, including some vessels of the newest type—quadriremes and quinqueremes—and the arsenal was replenished with arms and tackle. The training of the young men between eighteen and twenty ($\dot{\epsilon}\phi\eta\beta\epsilon\iota\alpha$) which appears to have been organized more systematically at this time, also had as its aim greater efficiency in time of war.[2] Much money was also expended on public works, not all of which served naval or military purposes; for, if

[1] There is no doubt about Lycurgus' direction of Athenian finances. I follow Kunst (P.-W. s.v. Lykurgos 10) in believing that he was ἐπὶ τῇ διοικήσει τῶν χρημάτων, but others (cf. Tarn, *C.A H.*, VI, 441; Cary in Vol. III of this *History*, 277) argue that that office was a later creation, so that they are forced to believe that Lycurgus held some extraordinary post whose title has not survived.

[2] To say, as some have done (e.g. Tarn, *C.A.H.*, VI, 442), that the reformed *ephebia* aimed at training the mind as well as the body, is to attribute to the institution as it was at the end of the fourth century a function that, to judge by the epigraphic evidence, it did not yet perform. It is only the inscriptions of the later Hellenistic age which record that a part of the duties of *ephebi* consisted in attendance at the schools of rhetoric and philosophy. This change came at a time when the *ephebia* had lost much of its military character and was no longer obligatory.

it was now that Philo's arsenal and docks were finished, it was also now that the theatre of Dionysus was reconstructed in stone throughout and the Panathenaic stadium was built.

Agis' venture in 331, although disastrous, served to stir up popular feeling afresh at Athens; and, though the Athenians as before avoided giving direct offence to Macedonia, the law-courts were kept busy with political trials. The most famous of these was the indictment of Ctesiphon by Aeschines. The former had after Chaeronea moved that Demosthenes' patriotic services be rewarded by the bestowal of a gold wreath. This proposal, which had been confirmed by a resolution of the *bule*, was declared illegal by Aeschines who gave notice that he would prosecute Ctesiphon. But, owing to Philip's death, the trial had not taken place; the decree of the council, on the other hand, was never carried into effect. But after six years Aeschines brought forward his indictment, and Demosthenes, against whom the attack was really levelled, undertook Ctesiphon's defence. The trial is of interest solely because the speeches of both men have survived and because that of Demosthenes is a long and eloquent vindication of his whole public career. Though not free from a certain unevenness of treatment and marred at times by gross personal abuse, the speech, especially in its later sections, is filled with the highest patriotism and convinces the modern reader, as it convinced Demosthenes' contemporaries, that failure may be more glorious than success. Aeschines lost his case and, retiring from Athens to Rhodes, died in exile soon after.

Considerable obscurity surrounds the affairs of Athens for several years after the *cause célèbre* of 330. The most serious problem confronting the government appears to have been a food-shortage, caused primarily by the extensive requisitions of grain made by Alexander. Although other parts of Greece may well have been affected also, the lack of wheat and barley was most serious for the Athenians who at this time depended almost wholly on imported grain. In 326 this situation was perhaps exploited by the political opponents of Lycurgus, although by then the danger of famine seems to have receded.[1]

---

[1] The Athenians honoured Heraclides of Salamis in Cyprus, giving him the rights of a metic of the privileged class, because he had helped them greatly during the famine period (*Syll.*, 304). They were still nervous about

It is possible that Alexander's absence in the Far East and the belief that he would never return to the West also strengthened the hands of the war party. At all events Lycurgus was not re-elected, and his successor at the head of the finance department was a political enemy. Two years later, at a time when Demosthenes was again the most influential man of his party, the relations between Athens and Alexander were strained almost to breaking-point. We have seen how Harpalus had absconded from Babylon after embezzling huge sums from the royal treasury. In the spring of 324 he appeared with a small fleet and a body of mercenaries off Piraeus, but it was decided not to admit him. He then sailed to Taenarum, where he left his troops, and returned to Athens in the character of a suppliant or refugee. This time the Athenians allowed him into their city. With him he brought a very substantial sum. But the Athenians soon found themselves in an awkward predicament, when Alexander's admiral in the Aegean demanded the extradition of the absconded treasurer. Instead of surrendering a suppliant, they put him in prison and placed his stolen money in the Parthenon in trust for Alexander. But the sum there deposited proved to be only half of the amount which Harpalus stated that he had on his arrival, and it was generally believed that he had bribed various public men in order to win them over to an anti-Macedonian war. Harpalus escaped from prison and returned to Laconia, where he was soon afterwards assassinated by one of his own officers. But in Athens public feeling continued to run high and an investigation into the whole transaction by the Areopagus was voted on the proposal of Demosthenes. Six months elapsed before the court yielded to popular clamour and indignation and presented a report. It consisted of a list naming nine persons, headed by Demosthenes, and specifying the sums received by each. A legal prosecution followed. Demosthenes, with two others, was found guilty and fined; but being unable to pay he withdrew to Aegina. The circumstances of this trial are far from clear, and the guilt or

the grain supply in 325–324, for they sent a body of colonists into the Adriatic under a strong naval escort. The site of the settlement is uncertain, but its purpose was to secure trade in general and grain in particular, and to obtain a base to protect their merchantmen against sea-raiders from Etruria (Tod 200).

innocence of Demosthenes cannot be established with any degree of certainty. And, if he did fall short of the standards of an Aristides or a Pericles, we can safely assume in the light of his career that he accepted Harpalus' money not for personal gain but for political ends.

Some time before the conclusion of this melancholy episode in Athenian public life great excitement had been caused, not only in Athens but generally in Greece, by a rescript from Alexander in which he assumed an authority greater than that conferred on him as general of the League. When he sent Nicanor to the Olympian festival to communicate to the assembled Greek delegates his decree that the Greek cities should recall their political exiles, he was interfering with the autonomy of his allies. At the same time he asked that divine honours be paid to himself. Most of the states acquiesced in his demands;[1] but the Aetolians and the Athenians offered serious opposition. The former had recently expelled the Acarnanian inhabitants from Oeniadae, and, if they had obeyed the rescript, they would have been obliged to evacuate the city in favour of the people that they had dispossessed. Similarly, the Athenians feared that compliance would mean to them the loss of Samos which, after the expulsion of the old inhabitants, had been settled by cleruchs some twenty-five years before. By voting without delay the deification of Alexander, they hoped to keep him in a good humour, while they procrastinated on the more important question. It was still unsettled in June, 323, and became one of the causes for the Greek insurrection against Macedonia known as the Lamian war.[2] By demanding the restoration of some twenty thousand exiles to their respective cities, Alexander had tried to put into effect his general policy of reconciling divergent groups within the empire. But to the Greeks it merely seemed that he was assuming autocratic powers over themselves to which he was not entitled. Even so most of them did as they were told. His request for deification was a political expedient to justify his interference with Greek autonomy by placing himself above the law and above his agreement with the League.

[1] The return of the exiles to Tegea and to Mytilene is illustrated by two inscriptions (Tod 201 and 202).
[2] Cf. Cary in Vol. III of this *History*, 4 ff.

# PART II

## CHAPTER XIII

## GREEK WARFARE

### § 1. RECRUITMENT OF ARMIES AND CONDITIONS OF SERVICE

APART from the increased use of mercenaries, which dates from the closing years of the fifth century, the armies of the Greek city-states down to the death of Alexander were constituted much as they had been before the invasions of Darius and Xerxes. The essential fighting force was the heavy infantry (hoplites) recruited from the adult male citizen population and, in the case of Sparta, from the free males dwelling in Laconia and Messenia. It is therefore impossible to form any certain estimate of the effective fighting strength at the disposal of a given *polis*; for any calculation necessarily involves the question of population for which, save perhaps in the case of Athens, no adequate *data* exist. Moreover, the figures occasionally given by historical writers of the armies engaged or the casualties in a particular battle are, with rare exceptions, approximate rather than accurate, when indeed they are not gross exaggerations. The size of the armies opposed in some of the more noteworthy engagements were modest enough. At Tanagra in 457 a Peloponnesian force of 11,500, of whom only 1500 were sent by Sparta, fought against an army of 14,000 made up mainly of Athenians with 1000 Argives and some other allied contingents. The Boeotian field-army at Delium was 18,500—7000 hoplites, 10,000 light-armed, 1000 cavalry, and 500 peltasts. The Athenians on this occasion were numerically about the same, but Thucydides observes that the light-armed troops were irregulars and, though more than those of the enemy, were not properly armed.[1] The most recent estimate of the armies which fought at Mantinea in 418 assigns to Sparta and her allies some 12,000 men and to her opponents about 11,000.[2] At Leuctra 6000 Boeotians are said to have defeated 10,000 Peloponnesians. At Mantinea in 362 the number of combatants was considerably greater, if it be true that either side mustered some 25,000 men. Lastly, at Chaeronea, if, as seems probable, the Greek confederates were numerically not inferior to Philip's host, the army formed by Thebes, Athens and a few allies somewhat exceeded 30,000. Valuable as these figures may be, they obviously never represent the complete fighting strength of any city; since, even when Thucydides states that the Athenians marched out in full force ($\pi\alpha\nu\delta\eta\mu\epsilon\grave{\iota}$ or $\pi\alpha\nu\sigma\tau\rho\alpha\tau\iota\hat{\alpha}$) this means no more than all those available at a given time in Attica for active service on a particular campaign.[3] There might be some fit for foreign service fighting on another front and, in addition, a certain percentage of the youngest and the oldest men were normally retained for home defence. The same historian estimates the military resources of Athens at the outbreak of the great Peloponnesian War as follows: 13,000 hoplites for active service, 16,000 for garrison and guard duties in Attica, including an unspecified number of resident aliens, and 1200 cavalry and mounted archers.[4] This estimate, attributed to Pericles, represents the military strength on paper, based on the demotic lists, and it is clearly necessary to assume that these figures in actual practice included some who were unfit for any service.[5]

Until 371 by far the most efficient of the Greek armies was by universal consent that of Sparta. The reason for this was obvious; for, although the Spartan army was not in the

[1] Thuc., IV, 93.   [2] Cf. above, p. 121.
[3] Cf. Thuc., I, 107; IV, 90.   [4] Ib., II, 13.
[5] This point is rightly emphasized by A. W. Gomme, *The Population of Athens in the Fifth and Fourth Centuries, B.C.*, p. 4. I cannot agree with W. W. Tarn, *Hellenistic Military and Naval Developments*, p. 3, who would almost eliminate the possibility of some men being unfit. Gomme, however, seems to err in reckoning the troops in frontier forts as separate from the 16,000 for home defence. This is an unnatural interpretation of Thucydides (II, 13, 6): ἄνευ τῶν ἐν τοῖς φρουρίοις καὶ τῶν παρ' ἔπαλξιν ἐξακισχιλίων καὶ μυρίων. The total 16,000 is surely meant to include both τῶν ἐν τοῖς φρουρίοις and τῶν παρ' ἔπαλξιν. Quite apart from the interpretation of the Greek words, it would be strange for Thucydides to be vague about the frontier guards, when he goes out of his way in this chapter to give precise figures for all the Athenian resources.

strict sense professional but composed of citizens and *perioeci*, the entire system of education was directed towards securing the maximum of military efficiency. The total field force of Sparta in the fifth century has been estimated at about 6000 men—this figure includes a small cavalry detachment of 300 or 400—divided into eight regiments (λόχοι). One of these is commonly named separately in our sources and was recruited entirely from the region called Sciritis and situated on the northern frontier of Laconia. By the beginning of the next century certain changes had been introduced. The seven regiments were reduced to six and were called μόραι; the mounted troops were increased to 600, 100 being attached to each μόρα. Sparta's regular army was composed of full citizens, Inferiors, and *perioeci*. What proportion of the dependent population was normally drafted for a campaign is quite uncertain and must have varied according to circumstances. But, since the *perioeci* were indispensable to the economic life of Laconia and Messenia, one must assume that only a relatively small number was called up for military service at one time. With the decline in the number of full citizens, which was especially marked in the fourth century, the Spartan government found itself obliged to modify its earlier practice. The use of a hoplite regiment composed of Helots is first mentioned in connection with Brasidas' expedition to Thrace.[1] In the fourth century liberated Helots (νεοδαμώδεις) were used in considerable numbers on foreign expeditions; for 3000 served under Agesilaus in Asia Minor in 396.[2] In the campaigns undertaken by Sparta outside her own territory only a part of her regular forces was employed; for the rest of the total army her allies of the Peloponnesian League were responsible. Thucydides frequently refers to a two-thirds levy of the Peloponnesian army in the early years of the Peloponnesian War.[3] At Leuctra only four *morai* were engaged. While the age of service was from 18 to 60, it was the oldest classes who would normally be retained for home defence.

The military resources of the various Peloponnesian allies are not recorded; nor is there much definite information

[1] Thuc., IV, 80.
[2] If Xenophon is correct (*Hell.*, VI, 5, 29), 6000 Helots were under arms in 370 when Epaminondas invaded Laconia.
[3] e.g. Thuc., II, 10; III, 15, *et al.*

about the man-power of Argos. The defeat and death of 6000 Argives at Sepeia in 494 crippled that state for more than a generation. In 457 one thousand Argives fought at Tanagra. On the other hand, during the Corinthian War at the beginning of the following century the Argives could put 7000 hoplites into the field. One feature at Argos is noteworthy. Towards the end of the fifth century there existed one corps, a thousand strong, of picked men who formed a standing army.[1] The remainder of the citizens, who were called upon as needed, seem to have been distributed into five regiments.

For the states of northern and central Greece the *data* are again very scanty. The military strength of Athens in 431 has already been stated. For each of the ten Athenian tribes a careful register was kept of all those who were of military age, namely, between eighteen and sixty; but the members of the fourth Solonian class—*thetes*—were exempt from hoplite service in the fifth century.[2] It was on them that Athens primarily relied for rowers in the navy. The home defence force was made up of citizens between eighteen and twenty and between fifty-five and sixty, together with a certain number of resident aliens whose financial rating was not less than that of a zeugite. The use of *metoeci* for foreign service was exceptional and only adopted in emergencies. The two youngest classes were technically known as the ἔφηβοι. From eighteen to nineteen they were practised in drill and in various military exercises; from nineteen to twenty they performed guard and patrol duties in the fortified areas and along the frontiers of Attica. Their training and supervision was the duty of a special official. During the administration of Lycurgus this system of compulsory military service was reorganized and the number of trainers and technical teachers was increased. At the end of their two years the ἔφηβοι were paraded in a solemn review and, if they had passed all their tests, were presented with a spear and shield in token of their efficiency. The Athenian cavalry in our period was normally 1000 strong. They were picked partly by compulsory enlistment, partly on a voluntary basis

---

[1] The evidence is for the Mantinea campaign in 418 (Thuc., V, 72).
[2] The Athenian casualty lists were also arranged by tribes; cf. Tod 26 and 48.

from the wealthiest families who were called upon to maintain horses as one of the state services, or liturgies, to which the richer citizens were liable. The subject states of the Athenian confederacy in the fifth century, in addition to paying tribute, were obliged to furnish contingents of troops. But how often the Athenians requisitioned men, and what percentage of the fighting force in a subject city was drafted, is quite obscure. The neighbours of a new colony, too, might be required, if need arose, to come to the assistance of the recent settlers.[1]

The military strength of the Boeotian League headed by Thebes was substantial. From the middle of the fifth century the Theban hoplites were probably superior to all save the Lacedaemonian. Their defeat of Sparta in 371 and 362 was principally due to the tactical innovations of Epaminondas; but the formation a few years before Leuctra of a standing battalion three hundred strong—the Sacred Band—was a contributory cause. The Boeotian cities, furthermore, made more use than most other Greek states of light-armed troops and of cavalry. Yet their horsemen, though numerous by Greek standards, mostly played only a subsidiary part in action. The victory of Pagondas at Delium, which was won by a timely use of mounted troops against enemy infantry, appears to have been exceptional.

Of the resources of Thessaly, whose cavalry was famous throughout the Hellenic world, little is heard save during the short rule of Jason. At that time (c. 375) Xenophon estimates their military strength at 10,000 hoplites and 8000 horsemen.

Two important innovations introduced during the second part of our period must here be recorded. The first was the use of peltasts. Originally the name was applied to light armed auxiliaries drawn from Thrace and used in small numbers as javelin-throwers by Athens, Boeotia, and other states already in the fifth century. Early in the next century a larger body of such troops was organized by Athens and, when supported by heavy infantry, was employed with great effect even against Lacedaemonian hoplites.[2] Soon after their equipment was improved and to some extent changed. Instead of javelins they used a thrusting spear, and they were provided with a certain amount of defensive

[1] Cf. Tod 44, 14–15.  [2] Cf. above, p. 185.

armour. The new peltast was, in short, a lighter and more
mobile edition of the hoplite. The second novelty in Greek
warfare had more far-reaching consequences, namely, the
use of mercenaries. From early times adventurous Greeks
had embraced arms as a profession and hired themselves
out to foreign princes.[1] In the fifth and fourth centuries
the kings of Persia attracted many such *condottieri* into their
service by the offer of high wages and on occasion even
engaged Greek military commanders of outstanding reputation. The expedition of the younger Cyrus and its aftermath
revealed to the Greek world at large both the advantages and defects of professional troops in large numbers.
They were drawn especially from the poorer and more outlying regions of the Hellenic world, like Arcadia, Achaea, Aetolia,
and Crete. Their greater efficiency in war led many Greek
states, when they could afford the cost, to strengthen their
citizen militia by supporting it with a corps of mercenaries.
In the west Dionysius I and, after him, Timoleon won their
successes largely with the aid of professional soldiery, while
in central Greece Phocis for a decade defied her neighbours
by paying for more and more such troops out of the Delphic
treasure. This last named state at one time probably paid
for as many as 10,000. Those in Dionysius' service must have
been far more numerous, even if, as is probable, the ancient
estimate of his military resources is much exaggerated.[2]
While some of the mercenaries were always equipped as
hoplites, an increasing number, as the century progressed,
fought as peltasts, when the greater mobility of this lighter
infantry had been thoroughly tested by experience. In the
end their use contributed greatly towards the development
of a more scientific type of warfare, so that they may be
said to mark an intermediate stage between the amateur
Greek armies of Miltiades and Pericles and the standing
national army created by Philip and perfected by Alexander.

## § 2. STRATEGY AND TACTICS : SIEGE OPERATIONS

To the time of Epaminondas the tactics adopted for a set
engagement in the field (ἐκ παρασκευῆς μάχη) were simple and

[1] Cf. the Greek mercenaries of Psammetichus : Tod 4.
[2] Diodorus (XIV, 47, 7) speaks of 80,000 infantry and 3000 cavalry
all told.

almost unvarying. Two opposing bodies of hoplites marched against one another and delivered a direct frontal attack. Normally either army was drawn up eight deep in three divisions—centre, right wing, and left wing. Occasional deviations from this practice are, however, recorded.[1] The decision rested with whichever side kept the best order and could put most weight into its assault. It was thus the aim of every Greek commander to bring about an engagement on level ground, and it is only in exceptional cases, and where other troops than hoplites could be used decisively, that advantage might be taken of rising ground or other natural features of the landscape. Thus at Delium Pagondas made effective use of a hill which concealed the movements of his cavalry until it delivered its flank attack on the Athenian right wing.[2] Most Greek generals ordered their infantry to accelerate their march as they drew close to the enemy. The Spartans avoided such shock tactics. They advanced at the ordinary marching step until they engaged. The advantage of this method over the other was that it avoided the danger of the line becoming disordered, as might happen to a force eight deep when it suddenly quickened its pace some fifty or sixty yards from the opponent. The Spartans calculated that the shock of the assault delivered by a faster moving enemy could be neutralized by the perfect discipline kept by their own line. The place of honour in the battle was ordinarily on the right wing.

The only serious modification of these tactics in a hoplite battle before the Macedonian period was introduced by Epaminondas. Theban commanders before his time had favoured a deeper formation than eight or even twelve ranks. But it was Epaminondas who, instead of a direct frontal attack all along the line, concentrated his main attack in one wing—the left—where he massed his best troops into a column or wedge fifty deep, at the same time protecting them with a body of cavalry on their flank. The centre and right wing remained strictly on the defensive, while the deep left wing crushed the force opposed to it and then executed a flank attack on the centre of the enemy. Both at Leuctra and at Mantinea in 362 these tactics were

[1] The Spartans at Leuctra were drawn up twelve deep (Xen., *Hell.*, VI, 4, 12); the Thebans at Delium were twenty-five deep (Thuc., IV, 93).
[2] Thuc., IV, 96.

entirely successful against what till then had been regarded justly as the finest infantry in Greece; and at Leuctra, although the exactness of the ancient figures may be open to doubt, there seems to be no doubt that the Thebans and their allies were numerically weaker.

In more irregular fighting effective use might be made of light-armed and mounted troops. The former consisted of javelin-throwers, bowmen, and slingers. Such troops when fighting in hilly country could be employed with deadly effect, as Demosthenes found to his cost when pitted against the Aetolians in 426. The final reduction of the Spartan hoplites on Sphacteria was carried out by light-armed soldiery who wore the enemy down by a long-range attack before closing in. In the first expeditionary force sent in 415 by Athens to Sicily 480 archers and 700 Rhodian slingers were included. On the other hand, although we hear of the presence of auxiliaries at Delium and again at Mantinea in 418, they do not seem to have played any decisive part in these battles. In the rather irregular campaigning carried on by Agesilaus in Asia Minor archers and peltasts had a place beside the heavy infantry. These peltasts were probably, like those employed by Iphicrates, of the older type—skirmishers armed with javelins and protected by a light round shield. The later type of peltasts who approximated more to the hoplite and, as they were generally mercenaries, were highly trained, were admirably adapted for all operations other than engagements of the formal Greek type. Their employment in a line of battle together with hoplites was tried more than once, but it did not prove satisfactory. With his usual insight Alexander did not use these troops for a purpose for which they were unfitted.

Cavalry, with which most of the Greek states were but poorly supplied, was useful chiefly for scouting, for harassing the enemy's forage parties,[1] and for preventing the occupation of level country by a hostile body of infantry. Occasionally horsemen took an active or even a decisive part in the larger battles, but always, like the infantry, in a frontal attack. The scientific use of mounted troops in war, especially for carrying out flanking movements, was not achieved until the Macedonian period.

[1] As, for instance, at Syracuse (Thuc., VI, 4, 6).

It has often been remarked with what wealth of detail Thucydides, who elsewhere shows the utmost economy of phrase, depicts the siege operations during the Peloponnesian War. As early as 462 the Athenians enjoyed an unusually high repute for their skill in this type of operation. Their failure against the Messenians on Ithome at that time may have been due mainly to disagreement between the Spartan and Athenian commanders. Yet the capture of any fortified place by assault was rare, even though most city-walls were built wholly or largely of crude brick and wood, not of stone. The engines to which Thucydides refers from time to time were rams, ladders, and fire-throwing devices; for the use of stone-throwers and arrow-shooting catapults is not attested before the fourth century. Since most fortified places contained a good deal of wood in their construction, a favourite device was to set fire to the enemy's works with lighted arrows or a flame-throwing apparatus.[1] Occasionally mining under walls was attempted. A particularly effective stratagem was adopted by Agesipolis against Mantinea, when he diverted a part of the local stream against the city-walls and so compelled the surrender of the inhabitants. Nevertheless, the great majority of cities captured in war were either starved into submission or betrayed to the attackers by a disloyal faction inside. Even where assault was tried, it was in conjunction with the other method, which consisted in cutting off the townsfolk from all communication with the outside world by the construction of walls, palisades, or other fortified lines which could be held by relatively small bodies of troops. Thus it is noticeable that the Spartan technique at Plataea was of this type, although for a time it was combined with various devices to facilitate a forcible entry into the city. Although the engineer employed by Pericles had constructed special rams to batter down the defences, the Samians in 439 yielded only

[1] At the siege of Plataea the inhabitants hung out skins as a protection against the burning arrows of the Lacedaemonians (Thuc., II, 75). An incendiary μηχανή. was employed by Brasidas in Thrace (*Ib.*, IV, 115). In the following century Aeneas Tacticus describes a similar method (*edd.* Hunter and Handford, xxxv): " You yourself may make a fierce fire, which it is impossible to put out, with the following materials : pitch, sulphur, tow, pounded gum of frankincense, and pine sawdust. Put these in a vessel, and apply them to any articles belonging to the enemy which you wish to catch fire."

to the threat of starvation. The most elaborate instance in our period of the use of fortifications and counter-fortifications was at Syracuse in 414. Twice its inhabitants failed to interrupt the progress of the Athenian walls intended to shut off the town from the interior of the island. But on the third occasion they succeeded, thanks to an error of Nicias in not first completing the northern end of his fortification. They ran their counter-wall diagonally across the end of the Athenian wall, thereby rendering the Athenian blockade by land incomplete. The operations of Dionysius against Motya mark a distinct advance in siege warfare. He employed ladders, movable towers from the stages of which catapults fired arrows against the defenders, and an improved type of battering ram. In view of his success against the Punic stronghold, it is surprising that he failed at Rhegium, which fell in the time-honoured way, before the imminent danger of starvation.

The betrayal of a town by a disaffected party within happened frequently. That the Greeks themselves regarded it as a grave danger was natural enough, seeing that the weaker side in party politics was often ready to have recourse to sedition, and *stasis* resulted. Moreover, this particular peril to the safety of a town is especially stressed in the fourth-century treatise on siege warfare by Aeneas Tacticus.[1] The same writer also warns against the danger of quartering allied troops all together when these are admitted inside a city and against hiring bodies of mercenary troops numerically stronger than the civic army.[2]

### § 3. THE INNOVATIONS OF PHILIP AND ALEXANDER OF MACEDON

With the rise of Macedonia to the position of a first-rate power a complete change came over the warfare of the ancient world. In earlier times the effective fighting force of the Macedonian kings had been the mounted troops, the natural result of the quasi-feudal relations existing between the monarch and the tribal and family heads. Although some attempts to improve the foot-soldiers may have been made by his predecessors, notably by Archelaus, the real

---

[1] Aeneas, chapters 11, 17, 29.  [2] *Ib.*, 12.

credit of creating regiments of highly trained heavy infantry belongs to Philip II. The general method followed by him to form a national army has already been described.[1] That achievement alone would entitle him to a prominent place amongst the great leaders of history. But he did more than this; for, once his new tool was ready, he proceeded to use it in an entirely novel way. Then the principles of strategy and tactics that he had adopted were widened and perfected by his son. The novelty in tactics lay in the balanced combination and use of cavalry, heavy infantry, and various types of auxiliaries.

The pick of the mounted troops who, in combination with the phalanx, had already been employed with overwhelming results against the Theban hoplites at Chaeronea, in the pitched battles of Alexander became the chief weapon of offence. In all three of the battles fought against the armies of Darius III the main plan of the Macedonian attack was the same. The attack was opened by the right wing composed of the Companions and led by Alexander in person, its right flank being protected by light-armed auxiliaries, mounted and on foot. In the second stage of the fighting the frontal attack of the phalangites prepared the way for the flanking movement of the cavalry and the rolling up of the Persian line. The vagueness of the surviving accounts makes it impossible to determine with any precision Alexander's strategy during most of his campaigns in central Asia and India. Were fuller information available, it would probably show that his military genius was even more conspicuously displayed against Spithridates and Oxyartes than against the generals of Darius. " He was the ablest judge of the course to be pursued in a sudden emergency." " Even where he had no experience he was quite competent to form a sufficient judgment." These words, in which, Thucydides evaluates the statecraft of Themistocles, can be applied to the generalship of Alexander. His success in the Far East was due more particularly to speed of movement, made possible by a superbly organized line of communications, to his Macedonian cavalry, and to his consummate skill in the use of light-armed troops of all kinds. Moreover he was the first great captain who surrounded himself with a staff technically

[1] See above, pp. 225 ff.

as expert as himself. When he fought in all actions himself instead of superintending operations from behind the lines, he followed the traditional practice of ancient warfare down to and even after his time. It was the only major instance of conservative thinking in his career. The concept of the commander-in-chief who was the directing brain of an action without personally participating in it was only evolved at a much later date.[1]

Of the novelties encountered by Alexander perhaps the greatest was the use of elephants in warfare, and he proved equal to the emergency created by their use on the Hydaspes. It would be interesting to know whether, if he had lived longer, he would have thought them of sufficient value in war to have acquired an elephant brigade himself. His successors, and the Carthaginians also, employed these beasts for attack, in siege warfare, and as a protection against the cavalry of their opponents.[2]

The changes introduced by the Macedonian kings in the conduct of sieges were scarcely less revolutionary than their innovations in field tactics. Unfortunately the two sieges in which Philip II used a greatly improved siege-train are imperfectly known. Clearly, however, his son in his operations against Tyre, Gaza, and other places, improved methods with which his father had already been to some extent familiar. That Philip failed against Perinthus and Byzantium was, we may suspect, due not so much to the insufficiency of his artillery as to the inadequacy of his fleet. The engines used by Alexander with such effect were movable towers, catapults, and battering rams. The towers constructed for the siege of Tyre are said to have been 150 feet in height, but they were quite unusually tall. Ordinarily they seem to have been only half as high or even smaller. They carried archers and catapults to hurl arrows or stones against the defenders, and also to prevent them from putting the battering rams out of action. This could be done by igniting them or by drawing them up with a hook in a perpendicular direction. We hear

---

[1] Cf. the excellent remarks of Tarn on the subject (*Hellenistic Military and Naval Developments*, 30 ff.).

[2] Cf. Tarn, *op. cit.*, 95 ff. The comparison of elephants to the modern tanks, instituted by Lieut.-Colonel H. G. Eady, R.E. (*United Services Journal*, 1926, 81 ff.), is superficially attractive, but, as Tarn has shown, is misleading, because the use of elephants was far more varied.

also of boarding bridges which were devised to be lowered from a stage on the tower to the top of the enemy's wall and to afford the attacking troops a direct passage on to the battlements. Used from ship-board these bridges could be very effective for scaling the sea-walls of a city.

The older type of catapult, with which both Dionysius I and Philip were familiar, fired arrows and was therefore only serviceable for sniping at the opponent, its range being considerably greater than that of an ordinary bow. It was some catapults of this kind that Alexander carried with him in the Punjab, in spite of difficulties of transport, and utilized with good results against the defenders of Aornos. More deadly in an assault on strong fortifications were catapults which hurled stones. Their certain use cannot be proved before the time of Alexander. The best torsion catapults, which were fired by releasing heavy cables, could hurl a stone weighing half a hundredweight for some two hundred yards. Used in conjunction with rams, they could effectively breach the massive stone walls which during the course of the fourth century had gradually replaced the older structures of brick in all the more important cities.

### § 4. NAVAL WARFARE AND TACTICS

It is surprising how sparse accurate and reasonably detailed information is concerning Greek naval warfare, when one considers how great a part it played in the history of the fifth and fourth centuries. If the tactics and progress of most land engagements in that period are incompletely known, the descriptions of sea-fights in our sources are almost without exception of the vaguest character. Nor is it possible to be certain about the size of the navies maintained by particular states. The truth probably is that the number of galleys in commission at different times fluctuated within wide limits. The root problem was not, in fact, the ships, but the crews. The all but universally used man-of-war was the trireme, a long narrow vessel of shallow draught, propelled by a single bank of oars arranged in threes and requiring a total personnel of some two hundred. The Athenian trireme, which was built primarily for speed, was approximately $120 \times 20$ feet, as is clear from the measurements of the shipyards at Munychia.

Triremes carried some auxiliary sailing tackle ; but this could only be used with a fair following wind, and not at all when the ship went into action. Clearly it was possible for a state, like Athens, to possess a very large number of such galleys in her shipyards, provided that she could procure the necessary timber. To ensure an adequate supply of it was one of her chief reasons for colonizing Amphipolis and for fostering good relations with Macedonia.[1] But to find 60,000 persons to man three hundred triremes at one time was virtually impossible, even if the expense of maintaining such a fleet could be met by the trierarchy. The Athenian navy was manned by the members of the fourth Solonian class and by citizens of allied and subject states recruited for the purpose. Resident aliens and slaves were only employed in times of crisis, as, for instance, at Arginusae. In practice, 200 triremes on active service at one time was a very large number, while 250 is mentioned by our most reliable authority as quite exceptional.[2] About two hundred participated in Cimon's expedition to the Eurymedon, and later on the same number were sent to Cyprus. In short, the strength of the opposing fleets in most of the naval encounters was appreciably less. At Sybota, in 433, 110 Corcyrean opposed 150 Corinthian galleys. At the battle of Cyzicus less than one hundred fought on either side, while at Arginusae 120 Peloponnesian ships were attacked by 150 Athenian ; for the Spartan admiral had detached 50 from his total force to continue the blockade of Lesbos. At the battle of Cnidus the Spartans had perhaps 120 ; the fleet of Pharnabazus and Conon was larger, but by how much we do not know. Eighteen years later 80 Athenian triremes fought 60 from the Peloponnese at Naxos. When the Thebans in 364 followed the advice of Epaminondas and attempted to strike at Athens in the most vulnerable spot by getting control of the Dardanelles, they built one hundred galleys. At the height of his power Dionysius I is reputed to have sent two hundred ships to sea at one time.

Though a very effective fighting machine in a naval battle, if properly handled, the trireme had certain very substantial defects which limited its usefulness on other occasions. It could not cruise at night. The amount of food and water

[1] Cf. Thuc., IV, 108 ; Tod 91 and 129.
[2] Cf. above, p. 80.

needed for so large a crew compelled the commander to be always within easy reach of a friendly base.[1] Indeed, the very restricted accommodation on board, where most of the available space was needed for the rowers, was a further reason for going ashore every night. It followed also that it was difficult to intercept single ships or small detachments belonging to any enemy, when they attempted to run a blockade. The naval history of the period offers many instances like the arrival of a few Corinthian vessels at Syracuse after eluding the vigilance of Athenian patrols. Even moderately rough weather prevented triremes from continuing their voyage or endangered them if they were unable to put into port without delay. The enforced wait of the Athenian squadron at Pylos in 425 and the heavy losses of the Athenian fleet after its victory at Arginusae are familiar cases in point.

The older naval tactics, by which the ship's captain brought his boat alongside one of the enemy and tried to board her, had become almost obsolete in the fifth century. Thucydides points out that at Sybota this old method was followed, and adds that the encounter resembled a land-fight rather than a naval battle, being conducted with great vigour but little science.[2] The normal tactics, however, consisted in trying to disable the enemy's fleet by ramming. The favourite method adopted and perfected by the Athenians was the manœuvre known as the διέκπλους. When carried out successfully, the attacking fleet at maximum speed broke through the opponent's line, each galley seeking to pass an enemy ship so close as to put its oars on one side out of action. This movement had to be timed with great precision so that the oars of the attacking ship could be drawn in at the right moment and then released again as soon as she was clear. Having crippled and passed its opponent, the victorious trireme swept round in a semicircular course and rammed the disabled galley amidships. To counter the first of these manœuvres you drew in your oars just before the hostile ship passed you. To meet the second, it was necessary to steer quickly out of the way or else to swing round so that your vessel received the

---

[1] Thucydides (I, 48) goes out of his way to mention that the Corinthians before Sybota provided themselves with rations for three days.
[2] Thuc., I, 49.

# GREEK WARFARE

impact on its prow. With this aim in view the Corinthians and Syracusans built their prows of exceptional strength, although by so doing they somewhat reduced the speed of their men-of-war. But there were, besides, two tactical formations against the threat of the διέκπλους. In one a second line of ships was drawn up behind the first so that each rear galley was immediately behind one in the front line. It was then the business of the triremes in the second line to ram the opponents before they could complete their circular attack on the galleys in the front. Even more effective, since it made the διέκπλους impossible of execution, was the method adopted by the Athenians at Arginusae. They staggered their rear line in such a way that each of its triremes was opposite the gap between two front-line ships. Thus any attempt by their opponents to charge through the gaps of the front line would have been met by a head-on charge from the triremes behind.

An unusual, and, as it proved, a disastrous expedient was adopted in 429 by the Corinthian squadron of forty-seven against the twenty triremes of the Athenian Phormio. At the threat of attack they adopted a circular formation with the prows of their boats turned outwards, keeping five of their best vessels within the circle to act as reserves and assist any ship of the line, if it should be in difficulties. Phormio replied by sailing round and round the enemy in single file, making feints at them and crowding them as much as possible. He had calculated rightly that soon after sunrise a strong breeze would spring up, which would increase the difficulties of the Corinthian squadron. And so it turned out. The Corinthian galleys, already hampered for room, were driven against one another and in the choppy sea became quite unmanageable so that they were completely at Phormio's mercy. This circular formation (κύκλος) seems by that time to have been generally discredited as too dangerous even against a weaker force. Half a century before, it had been used with partial success by the Greeks at Artemisium; but on that occasion it had not been adopted from choice but had been forced on the Greeks by the superior numbers of the Persian fleet which threatened their two wings.[1] Although vessels larger than the

---
[1] For a full account see the interesting essay of A. Köster, *Studien zur Geschichte des antiken Seewesens* (*Klio*, Beiheft 32 [1934]), 87-96.

trireme began to be built in the fourth century, their history and their influence on naval warfare belong essentially to the Hellenistic Age.[1]

### § 5. THE RULES OF WAR

The account of military and naval operations in the earlier part of this volume will have shown that the wars of the Greeks were at times accompanied by a good deal of brutality. After a battle, it is true, the victors generally granted a truce to the vanquished to collect and bury their dead. When this was refused, the reason was that the defeated side had been previously guilty of sacrilege or impiety, as was the case with the Phocians in the fourth century. Ordinarily fatal casualties on land do not seem to have been unduly heavy. At sea loss of life was greater, since often it was the object of the stronger side not merely to disable the ships of the other, but to sink them and drown the crews. But the worst sufferers in war were the inhabitants of captured cities, especially of those which had been the allies or subjects of the conqueror. Death or enslavement were the alternatives that they had to expect, and more clement treatment was the exception rather than the rule. The fate of Scione or Melos at Athenian hands, Sparta's punishment of Plataea, and Philip's vengeance on Olynthus are familiar examples. The people of Mitylene narrowly escaped a similar fate in 427, while the Athenians themselves would have suffered what they had done to others, if the Thebans had had their way in 404. Some of the most gruesome excesses were committed in the civil wars which occurred so frequently in the city-states of the classical period. It would be difficult to point to a more ghastly narrative than Thucydides' account of the Corcyraean revolutions between 427 and 425.[2] In the fourth century communities often endured spoliation and worse excesses at the hands of mercenaries. It seems to have been difficult for the general in command to maintain strict discipline among the professional soldiery, and in this respect the generals of the Hellenistic period were, with occasional exceptions, much abler. To make matters worse, in the fourth century the city governments

---

[1] Cf. W. W. Tarn, *Hellenistic Military and Naval Developments*, 124 ff.; M. Cary in Volume III of this *History*, 240–241.

[2] Thuc., III, 72–84; IV, 46–48.

which employed mercenaries too often kept the commander insufficiently supplied with funds. He had to shift for himself, and to satisfy his men had to permit them or even encourage them to loot not merely hostile but sometimes neutral towns. The excesses committed by Alexander's troops at the capture of Tyre were an act of revenge for the savagery of the townsfolk towards Macedonian prisoners and were condoned by Alexander. Aside from the episodes on the Beas and at Opis his control over his heterogeneous army was never in doubt. Always solicitous for his men's welfare, he could on occasion punish serious transgressors with exemplary severity. If he was ruthless and brutal to the people of Thebes and Tyre and to certain communities in India, in general his treatment of captured towns was marked by greater humanity than was shown by the Greeks to one another.

## CHAPTER XIV

## THE GOVERNMENT OF THE CITY-STATES

### § 1. TYRANNY AND OLIGARCHY

NOT the least of the consequences flowing from the Greek victory over the hosts of Xerxes was a widespread movement amongst the city-states towards constitutional reform. Tyranny, which lingered on into the fifth century in Asia Minor and in the western Mediterranean, within twenty years of Salamis had become virtually obsolete, though it might be regarded as a possible danger in a constitutionally governed state.[1] In the fourth century despotism was revived under a somewhat different form, made possible more especially by the growth of mercenary armies. Those absolute rulers of whom Dionysius I was the outstanding example were military autocrats whose position from the first depended not on the good will, or at least tolerance, of a part of their subjects but on the professional army that they were able to bring and hold together. To some extent this type of military tyranny can be deemed characteristic of the western Greeks; for the mercenaries in Gelon's service at the time of the Carthaginian invasion are said to have made up more than a third of his military strength.[2] But there is no reason to suppose that after Himera he or his successor continued to maintain a large body of professional soldiers. In the fourth century despots reappeared in various parts of the Greek world. Several of the Thessalian cities passed into their hands. The leaders of the Phocians during the Sacred War were hardly distinguishable from military autocrats and were actually described as τύραννοι by hostile contemporaries. Even in the Peloponnese *stasis* occasionally threw up a tyrant, although his career, like that of Euphron at Sicyon or Timophanes at Corinth, was usually very short. Such absolute

[1] Cf. the decree regulating the constitution of Erythrae (Tod 29, 33-34).
[2] Herodotus, VII, 158.

rulers became more numerous in Greece during the later years of Philip II, who promoted their establishment as a support to his own Hellenic policy. Alexander pursued a different course, and the ephemeral tyrannies that sprang up in Asia Minor in his day or in the preceding decade were usually the result of Persian intervention or support. At the same time the weakness of Persian control in western Asia sometimes made possible the rise of local dynasties. Nominally a vassal of the Great King, Mausolus was really an independent ruler. The cities of Assos and Atarneus in the Troad passed into the hands of a certain Eubulus in 360, but the circumstances in which this tyranny was established are unknown. After ten years Eubulus was succeeded by his former slave, Hermias, who, as a freedman, had spent some years in Athens and had there been a member of Plato's Academy. In 348 he invited Aristotle and Xenocrates to his court, and some years later the former married the adopted daughter of the tyrant. In 345 Hermias was betrayed into the hands of Memnon. He was sent to Susa and executed. Of greater permanence was the monarchy established in Heraclea on the Black Sea by Clearchus, who in his youth had been a pupil of Isocrates at Athens. He appears to have come to power as a popular champion against the ruling oligarchy. But he could not have attained his object without a strong body of mercenaries paid with Persian gold. He ruled for a dozen years and founded a dynasty which lasted into the third century. That it endured for so long was due to the fact that, although Clearchus and his immediate successor, Satyrus, governed with great severity, the later princes of the line abstained from persecution of political opponents, and, as Aristotle remarked of Peisistratus, ruled constitutionally rather than tyrannically.

The time was long past when full civic status and political privilege were restricted to those of noble birth and ancient lineage. In oligarchies the possession of some wealth, usually in the form of landed property, was necessary to entitle a man to the full exercise of civic rights. In the fifth and fourth centuries the number of those participating in the citizenship of oligarchic states was in most cases moderately large. The wielding of power by a very small and despotic group, like the Thirty at Athens or the decarchies set up by Lysander, was exceptional and ephemeral. The extreme paucity of existing sources renders it impossible to determine what proportion of city-states were ruled by oligarchies. Aristotle, indeed, approaching the subject from the point of view of the political theorist, gives an elaborate classification of different types of government by the Few; but his illustratory examples are usually too brief and often too allusive to justify broad deductions. One generalization is, however, borne out by the known facts. It has been previously pointed out that by the middle of the fifth century the majority of city-states in Asia Minor, the Aegean, and Greece—apart from certain remote and backward areas—were drawn into the orbit of either Sparta or Athens. While we are not justified in assuming that the Athenians regularly, or even frequently, used open compulsion to make their allies or subjects conform to their own type of government, it is clear, nevertheless, that democracies were the rule in the city-states within the Athenian empire. It is significant, moreover, that in the years immediately following the disaster in Sicily, when many of her subjects revolted from Athens, they also changed from a democratic to an oligarchic constitution.[1] Similarly, association with Sparta commonly, but not invariably, implied that the city was governed by some form of oligarchy. It was under the influence of Sparta and at the time of the Athenian expedition led by Hippocrates that an oligarchy was established at Megara, while for three years after the battle of Mantinea (418) the Spartans supported a movement in favour of that type of rule in Argos. But there the democratic party in the end prevailed. Similar variations can be traced during the fourth century whenever one of the leading Greek states suffered a substantial reverse or, conversely, won a notable success. The Spartan defeats at Cnidus and at Leuctra and the formation of Athens' Second Confederacy were each followed by constitutional changes in some of the smaller city-states. Of the inner working of a typical oligarchy we are singularly ignorant. Contemporary opinion appears to have regarded the government of Corinth as equitable and an excellent example of its kind, since power, though in the hands of a minority, was exercised in the interests of the whole community. Yet its distinctive features are unknown. Legally the sovereign power in an oligarchy must always have

[1] Thuc., VIII, 64.

rested with the entire body of those who were full citizens, but in practice the authority of the council, whose size varied considerably in different states, was often all but absolute. Unfortunately it is not possible always to distinguish clearly between the full civic body and the council. Thus when we hear that in certain cities the constitution was in the hands of one thousand—to judge by the numerous cases in which this figure is recorded, this seems to have been the regular number in oligarchic states of moderate size—the reference is no doubt to an assembly of all privileged citizens. The council in such cases was a much smaller body elected from the older citizens. Election not sortition was the rule in oligarchies. Membership in the council was for long periods or for life and was restricted to men of middle life or over.[1] In Massilia the Six Hundred did not make up the whole of the privileged class; nevertheless they, in conjunction with an executive body of fifteen, carried on the government. The number 180 recorded for Epidaurus must mean the governing body or council, not all those with full civic rights.[2] The councils in most cases had a membership of less than a hundred and worked in close association with a yet smaller executive committee. At Corinth the responsibility was shared between the council of eighty and eight πρόβουλοι. In the mixed constitution that had long been characteristic of Sparta the γερουσία, including the two kings, numbered thirty persons. During the fifth and fourth centuries these elders and the five ephors divided virtually all power between them; for, after the time of Cleomenes I, the kings could rarely act independently of the ephors, while the *apella*, or assembly of Spartiates, was only a confirmatory, not a deliberative or legislative body. Indeed it appears to have been the general practice in oligarchies to limit the powers of the citizen assembly to the ratification or rejection of decisions formulated by the council or the executive committee.

In Boeotia during the fifth and fourth centuries oligarchic rule existed in conjunction with confederation. In each constituent city of the Boeotian League there were four

[1] Not only at Sparta, but in Corinth and elsewhere the council was significantly called γερουσία.
[2] Plutarch, *Greek Questions* 1, has confused the council of 180 with the civic body, and the *artynoi* with the council. The *artynoi* would correspond to the *probuloi* elsewhere.

councils (βουλαί). The administration was carried on by each of these in regular rotation and for a fixed period. The members of all four councils together formed an assembly in which sovereign power was vested. What the minimum census qualifying for election was is uncertain. A reasonable assumption would be that it was property sufficient to enable a man to provide his own equipment and serve in the heavy infantry. Moreover, in Thebes and in some other cities there seems to have existed a law which excluded from office any person who had within ten years practised as a craftsman or shopkeeper.[1] The magistrates in oligarchic states, like the members of the council, were elected. In some cities all full citizens were eligible; in others eligibility was confined to certain families or to those who were of the third generation of citizens. Jurisdiction was exercised by the council and the magistrates or by specially chosen judges, who, however, tried civil suits only. The elaborate system of trial by large juries of citizens that was characteristic of Athens was peculiar to democracies, and the suspension of the δικαστήρια at Athens was amongst the earliest acts of the oligarchies when they attained to power in 411 and 404.

### § 2. ATHENIAN DEMOCRACY IN THE FIFTH CENTURY

The two essential features of a fully developed Greek democracy were that the sovereign power should rest with an assembly of all the adult male citizens, and the existence of popular courts of law. For half a century after the time of Clisthenes the legitimate son of an Athenian father attained the status of a citizen on completing his eighteenth year. It was then that the young Athenian was enrolled in his father's deme, after the father had deposed on oath that his son had reached the necessary age and had been born in wedlock. But in 451 Pericles gratified the jealous spirit of the urban voters by proposing an act limiting Athenian citizenship to those of Athenian descent on both sides. How many of the so-called μητρόξενοι were disfranchised by this ordinance there is no means of guessing, but it may be noted that some of the most prominent men in the Athenian state during the

---

[1] Aristotle, *Pol.* 1278A25; Xenophon, *Oeconomicus*, 4, 3. Both writers are somewhat vague in their phraseology, but both artisans and tradesmen seem to be meant.

preceding period—for example, Themistocles and Cimon—had belonged to that class. In any case it must be emphasized that democracy in the Greek sense differed essentially from the modern; for even in an advanced democratic state, like Athens, the adult male citizens who were collectively synonymous with the government formed only a minority of the population. Scarcity of precise information makes all estimates of ancient populations notoriously uncertain. The most recent estimate of the Athenian population at the outbreak of the Peloponnesian War tentatively suggests about 43,000 adult male citizens and a total citizen body—allowing two children to each married couple—of 172,000. There was also a considerable colony of resident aliens (28,500 ?) and a large slave population (115,000 ?). Athens was never so populous a state again. The " plague " in 430-427, the losses in the war, and the resultant decline in the birth-rate may have reduced the total population of Attica by 400 B.C. by more than a hundred thousand persons. In the fourth century the numbers rose again gradually and the resident alien population especially became greater; even so the highest figure that can be postulated for the age of Demosthenes was appreciably less than the maximum in the fifth century.[1] At all events, whatever the exact size of the population may have been at any given date, the citizen body in the political sense never formed more than a fraction of the total inhabitants.

In an earlier chapter we have seen how the Clisthenic constitution, in which the nominal sovereignty of the assembly was in practice limited by the Council of the Areopagus and the restriction of the archonship to a wealthy minority, was converted into the Periclean democracy in which the authority of the people was absolute and in which, with insignificant exceptions, every citizen enjoyed equal opportunities for advancement.[2] The assembly (ἐκκλησία) was composed of all male citizens over eighteen years of age, but in practice youths of nineteen and twenty did not attend since they would be engaged in military training. For all major business the

---

[1] Cf. A. W. Gomme, *The Population of Athens in the Fifth and Fourth Centuries* and his note on Athenian slaves in *J.H.S.* 66 (1946), 127–129.

[2] See above, pp. 31 ff. Legally the archonship seems never to have been open to the fourth Solonian class or *thetes*; but *politically* the archonship from the time of Pericles was of little importance.

necessary *quorum* seems to have been 6000. Even the highest magistrates were responsible to the *ecclesia* ; for, just as after their appointment they had to undergo an inquiry (δοκιμασία) into their legal right to hold office, so at the end of the year they were subjected to an official scrutiny (εὔθυνα) into their administrative acts. Even in the fifth century several meetings of the assembly seem to have taken place in each month ; by the middle of the next century forty each year was the regular number. In addition, the president of the Council could summon an extraordinary meeting, if the *ecclesia* had so resolved at an earlier meeting, or if the Council and the board of *strategi* so voted.

Primarily the *ecclesia* was a deliberative body in which every member, provided that he had suffered no diminution of his civic status (ἀτιμία) as the result of conviction for a criminal offence, was entitled to speak and to propose resolutions. As an electoral body it was responsible for the choice of all those functionaries who were not appointed by lot. Actually this meant the election of the *strategi*—normally one from each of the ten Clisthenic tribes—of the financial officials, and of the holders of posts requiring technical knowledge, particularly in connection with military and naval affairs. The *ecclesia* exercised control over the executive magistrates and the members of the Council of Five Hundred by virtue of the annual scrutiny of their administrative acts. It was, moreover, the only legislative body ; for, although the initiative in law-making was taken by the Council, the ratification or rejection of proposed enactments rested with the assembly. Save in one instance, it did not function as a judicial body, since it was equivalent to the citizens acting collectively in a political capacity, whereas the *heliaea* was the people sitting as the judiciary. The one exception occurred when a citizen was charged with treason or conspiracy against the state. His indictment took place before the assembly, unless that body chose to refer the trial to the law-courts. From the time of Pericles the most important safeguard of the constitution was the practice of holding the proposer of a law or decree (ψήφισμα) responsible, if it proved to conflict with existing statutes. In that event he could be arraigned on a charge of unconstitutional action. His personal liability was held to cease one year after the passing of the questionable decree,

# THE GOVERNMENT OF THE CITY-STATES

but even after that date legal action could be taken to procure the annulment of the measure.[1]

It would have been impossible for so large a body as the assembly, meeting relatively rarely, to transact its multifarious business, if there had not been a Council. The βουλή consisted of five hundred citizens over thirty years of age who were appointed by lot and who could serve on it not more than twice and then not in successive years. Even this number was in practice too large for the transaction of routine business. Consequently it was divided into ten committees (πρυτανεῖαι) each of which was in continual session for one-tenth of the year. The chairmanship rotated from day to day amongst the members of the prytany, and during his brief tenure the chairman also acted as president of the Council and the *ecclesia*. As an executive body the Council acted in close concert with the magistrates, at the same time that it exercised a constant supervision over many of them. Since its duties were so multifarious it elected by lot from its own number various boards—they were usually composed of ten members, one from each tribe—to deal with specially important or technical business. Such were the ten accountants (λογισταί) who in each prytany checked the expenditure of the magistrates and the thirty ushers (συλλογεῖς) who kept a record of attendances in the assembly and saw to it that no unauthorized persons were present. All proposed legislation and all business intended for submission to the assembly were first considered by the Council, which then submitted appropriate resolutions to the citizen-body in the form of preliminary decrees (προβουλεύματα). But this function of acting virtually as a standing committee of the *ecclesia*, responsible and time-consuming as it was, was only a part of the work devolving on the councillors. As an executive body they co-operated closely with the senior magistrates—the board of generals—especially in that most vital matter for Athens, the upkeep and general direction of her naval resources. Equally important was the Council's control over expenditure. It kept a watchful eye on all

---
[1] There is a corresponding difference in technical terminology. Thus Demosthenes' speech against Leptines was delivered in a prosecution of this sort. Since more than a year had elapsed since the decree of questionable legality had been passed, his oration is entitled πρὸς Λεπτίνην not κατὰ Λεπτίνου.

officials who spent public money and each year it presented a report to the assembly on the financial condition of the state. It also exercised a general supervision over public buildings, sacred and secular, and over religious festivals. Certain of these duties might be delegated to a committee of ten chosen by lot from the councillors (ἱεροποιοί). The Council also sat as a judicial body. Indeed, during the fifth century it could not only impose fines for lesser offences, but could imprison and even execute traitors. More usually trials for treason came before the people; in that case, even if information had been laid in the first instance by a private citizen, the actual prosecution was conducted by the Council.

With few exceptions the magistrates and administrative officials held office for one year. Re-election was prohibited except in those offices which, like the *strategia*, were military in character. In the majority of cases the executive direction of a certain department was not entrusted to a single head but to a board, usually composed of ten persons. All its members were on an equal footing and the duty of presiding rotated. Occasionally one man was chosen to act as chairman for the whole tenure of his office, as was the case with the president of the ten Hellenotamiae or the chairman of the Treasurers of Athena (ταμίαι ἱερῶν χρημάτων τῆς Ἀθηναίας).[1] In the case of the *strategia* the presiding *strategus* came to be chosen from the whole body of Athenian citizens, the other nine being elected from the tribes. In practice, if not in theory, his authority seems to have been greater than that of his colleagues. For particular military or naval expeditions the *ecclesia* might designate one member of the board to take sole responsibility, but more usually several were appointed to act jointly, as were Alcibiades, Nicias, and Lamachus for the expedition to Sicily in 415. These boards of officials were exceedingly numerous. Their duties, from those of the archonship of venerable antiquity to those performed by committees of market or grain inspectors (ἀγορανόμοι, σιτοφύλακες) were purely administrative and their positions carried no political influence. The ten *strategi* from the first were in a different position. From the time of Pericles they

[1] Theoretically there were ten Treasurers, but in the fourth century the board was sometimes smaller. On inscriptions the reference is commonly to the chairman by name καὶ συνάρχοντες. Cf. Tod 75, 83, 92.

were the real executive of the state. They alone were entitled to take part in the meetings of the Council by virtue of their office. They were, however, responsible to the *ecclesia* for all their acts, and in most matters the Council acted as intermediary between them and the sovereign people. It was characteristic of Athenian democracy in the fifth century that the leading politicians, like Pericles, combined the informal leadership of the assembly with the tenure of the highest military office, from which indeed their real authority was derived. If not actually *strategus* in a given year, the unofficial spokesman of the people ($\pi\rho o\sigma\tau\acute{a}\tau\eta\varsigma\ \tau o\hat{v}\ \delta\acute{\eta}\mu ov$) would be likely to fill some other magistracy. Thus Cleon, though he became the most powerful politician in Athens soon after Pericles' death, is not known to have held the *strategia* before 425. But he was a member of the Council in 428–427 and in the following year acted as one of the ten Hellenotamiae.

A typical feature of Athenian democracy in its fully developed form was the *heliaea*. Its institution, indeed, went back to Solonian times, but its real development dated from the time of Pericles. According to the theory of an ancient democracy each male citizen of adult age was expected to take his share in the government of the state. Similarly the administration of justice was a responsibility which he must not shirk; and it was a part of his civic duties to have a general understanding of the laws under which he lived. Thus, too, if involved in litigation himself, he was required to conduct his own prosecution or defence. Judicial business increased enormously in Athens during the fifth century. Comic poets, like Aristophanes in his *Wasps*, made fun of the democratic Athenian's fondness for law-suits and jury-service. Moreover, the work of the courts included many disputes and litigations in which the members of allied or subject states within the Athenian empire were involved. The *heliaea*, or citizens in their judicial capacity, consisted in practice of six thousand of those in the civic body who were over thirty years of age, chosen by lot each year to act as jurors from those who gave notice of their desire or willingness to serve. An equal number was taken from each tribe. This large total was divided into ten sections, but the number of jurors engaged in a particular trial, though always large according to modern notions, varied. Panels of 201, 501, 701, 1001, and even some that were greater, are heard of, at least in the fourth century. Probably 501 was an average number, and larger panels were used only in trials of unusual importance, that is to say, in political *causes célèbres*. From the verdict of the dicasteries there was no appeal; for even the *ecclesia* could not reverse the finding of a popular jury, though it could extend a pardon to an offender who had been condemned to punishment. In certain cases, for instance, in testamentary suits and those concerned with illegal claims to citizenship, it was possible to obtain a re-trial, if the defendant could show grounds for believing that some part of the evidence brought by the prosecutor was insufficient or that some of his witnesses were untrustworthy. It is difficult to form a fair judgment of these courts. It was a not unreasonable belief that a citizen when tried by a large number of his peers would receive substantially equitable treatment. On the other hand, a clever speaker with a more intimate knowledge of law than the average juror could sway his hearers by appeals to popular prejudice or political passion, with disastrous consequences to the cause of true justice; for, though there was a presiding officer in the court, there was no judge in the modern sense to direct the jury. Obviously the danger of injustice was greatest in trials of a political or semi-political nature, and there were not a few instances where Athenian juries treated Athenian generals or public men with harshness. But there is no reason to suppose that litigations between ordinary citizens, which made up a majority of the cases to be tried, were not as a rule conducted fairly and decided equitably. In civil suits a simpler procedure was often followed. The litigants were able to submit their case to a public arbitrator ($\delta\iota\alpha\iota\tau\eta\tau\dot{\eta}s$), and it did not come into court unless either party refused to accept his judgement. The number of disputes settled in this way was probably considerable and to some extent relieved the pressure of business in the dicasteries.

§ 3. CHANGES IN THE ATHENIAN GOVERNMENT DURING THE FOURTH CENTURY

After the short-lived rule of the oligarchs came to an inglorious end in 403, it soon became clear that, barring outside interference, the old democratic *régime* would be reintroduced at Athens. But the Spartans took the liberal view that the Athenians must settle for themselves under what kind of government they wished to live. There was a group in Athens who desired to see restored the type of constitution which had been sponsored eight years before by Theramenes and had then worked well for a brief spell. But the proposal of Phormisius in 403-402, to make possession of some wealth a qualification for active citizenship and to limit to 5000 those in full enjoyment of civic status, was defeated. About the same time the law of Pericles, under which only those of Athenian parentage on both sides were reckoned as citizens, was again put into force. The people next decreed that a careful revision and codification of Athens' old laws be carried out by 500 *nomothetae*, assisted by the Council of Five Hundred. When the revised code was published, the only substantial innovations that had been adopted were in the sphere of judicial administration. Nevertheless during half a century or more the democratic constitution of Athens in practice altered perceptibly, and popular government in the time of Demosthenes differed very appreciably from Periclean democracy. The weakness of the former was in part the result of economic factors. The Peloponnesian War had impoverished many of the wealthier families in Attica, yet the burdens imposed upon them and their descendants by the state were proportionately heavier than before. Also the *demos*, though its income was less, did not correspondingly reduce expenditure, but rather added new items to it. No wonder that not a few of the better-class citizens showed a growing disinclination to shoulder civic responsibilities as understood in an ancient *polis*. A majority of the voters on whose support the politicians depended were urban and belonged to the poorest classes, yet they were the least fitted by training and temperament to have a deciding voice in the conduct of affairs. What in theory was government by the sovereign people, in reality was rule by a class for a class.

Many of the changes in Athenian government during the fourth century were minor modifications of procedure or dealt with administrative details. But there were, besides, certain broader aspects of democracy in that age which justify us in calling it more radical than the system that had preceded it.

### 358 THE GREEK WORLD FROM 479 TO 323 B.C.

If it were decided to sum up the difference in a sentence, it would be true to say that the well-balanced division of responsibility between *demos, boule,* and executive magistrates characteristic of Athenian democracy at its best, was gradually destroyed and replaced by a *régime* in which a more jealous and more irresponsible *ecclesia* regarded itself as self-sufficient and restricted the competence of both magistrates and Council. It is significant that the leading members of the assembly in the fourth century—men like Anytus, Callistratus, Aristophon, Eubulus—were politicians first and last.[1] Iphicrates, Timotheus, Chabrias, on the other hand, were amongst the most successful *strategi* produced by Athens at that time, but their political influence was either wholly negligible or else transitory. If the leader of the *ecclesia* held a high official position, it was most likely to be a financial office, as was the case with Eubulus for eight years and later with Lycurgus for an even longer term. The duties of the *strategi* tended to become again what they had originally been, mainly military or naval. In the trial of military offences they presided, as before, in the dicasteries where the cases were heard. Another symptom that even the senior magistrates were becoming simply heads of administration and nothing more is to be found in the gradual breakdown or abandonment of the principle of collegiality. From the middle of the fourth century special departments began to be assigned for their whole year of office to individual members of the Board of Generals.[2] It was a gradual innovation and not completed until the Hellenistic Age. The later fourth century also saw the creation of new officials with important duties. The prominence of the superintendent of the Theoric Fund dates from the time of Eubulus. Towards the close of his administration the war treasury was put in charge of a separate comptroller. When after Chaeronea the *ephebia* was reorganized, an annual supervisor (κοσμήτης) of magisterial status

---

[1] It is not implied that such men were never *strategi*. Callistratus was a general in 378–77 and again later, but his political career extended over thirty years.

[2] The earliest recorded instance seems to be the general acting as minister of defence in 352–351 (*Syll.*, 204, 20 : τὸν στρατηγὸν τὸν ἐπὶ τὴν φυλακὴν τῆς χώρας κεχειροτονημένον). The chief literary authority for these changes is Aristotle (*Const. of Ath.*, 61), but the dates when other special provinces were assigned to individual *strategi*—e.g. the general supervision of Piraeus—are uncertain.

was placed at the head. Perhaps the earliest instance, however, of such departmental specialization is to be seen in the secretaryship of the Council. This responsible post had been held by ten different persons in each year; for each prytany received a secretary chosen not from the members of that prytany but from the rest of the Council members. By 362-61 this method had been changed. An annual secretary was appointed by lot from those who submitted their names as candidates and he was not himself a member of the Council.[1] Very soon afterwards a second secretary was appointed in a similar manner. His functions appear to have consisted mainly in the copying and publication of the laws and of the decrees passed by the assembly.

The powers and duties of the Council continued to be wide and an essential part of the democratic machine in the fourth century. Nevertheless they were more circumscribed than they had been previously. At some date between 402 and 378 the presidency of the Council was taken away from the members of the prytany in office and assigned to nine *proedri* from the other councillors, one of the nine acting as chairman. The judicial competence of the Council was restricted and the punishment that it could inflict was limited to a maximum fine of five hundred drachmae. Even then the culprit had the right of appeal to the popular courts. Again, the institution of special financial departments to some extent reduced the responsibility of the *boule* in an administrative sphere in which it had once been all-powerful.

The Athenian democracy in the fourth century was often capricious and unwilling to trust the senior members of the executive after it had appointed them to office. There are many recorded instances—the cases of Callistratus and Timotheus are far from being isolated—of generals whose lack of success was at once made the ground for a criminal charge before the people; and, unless they chose exile before the trial, almost certain condemnation awaited them. Yet generally the real fault lay with the Athenians themselves. Unwilling to face the rigours of military or naval service themselves, they expected their commanders to do the impossible with insufficient men and inadequate funds. The suspicious attitude of the assembly also reacted on the

[1] Aristotle (*op. cit.*, 54) calls him an assessor—παρακάθηται τῇ βουλῇ.

individual, so that public men or generals put their own interests or safety first and did not hesitate to take a lead in prosecuting an unsuccessful or unpopular colleague.

In short, while much of the routine of administration was perhaps more efficiently conducted in the fourth century than in the fifth, the democratic government itself was not. The *demos* lived from day to day; for long periods it lacked a coherent or consistent policy, especially in foreign affairs. Demosthenes, even if we regard his policy as mistaken, commands our admiration because for a dozen years he fearlessly advocated what he believed to be right without stooping to court the favour of the assembly. Had we more data about other democratic governments in the Hellenic world, we might indeed find that they were inferior to that of Athens both in efficiency and stability; for, save during two short interludes, the Athenians were able to keep *stasis* out of their commonwealth for nearly two hundred years. But the predominance of the urban voters in the *ecclesia*, which meant that the will not of the whole *demos* but of a fraction prevailed, the use of the lot which put a premium on mediocrity, and the absence of anything like a second chamber which could at least retard hasty and ill-considered legislation and thus compel more careful discussion, were grave and ineradicable faults. They brought to decay a system of government that had once seemed the most admirably adapted to promote the happiness and welfare of a Greek city-state.

### § 4. FINANCIAL ADMINISTRATION IN ATHENS

Imperfect as are the existing records of public finance at Athens, they show that the methods adopted were singularly haphazard and that no complete co-ordination of the financial administration under the control of one department was ever achieved or even projected. There was no single state treasury under a minister of finance, nor was there any annual budget to include all income and expenditure for a given year. To the time of the Persian Wars both the annual revenues and expenses of the state were small; and when the silver mines at Laurium yielded a surplus, it was for some years distributed to the citizens. The political and economic development of Athens after 480, her leadership of the

## THE GOVERNMENT OF THE CITY-STATES

maritime confederacy, and the far-reaching reforms of Ephialtes and Pericles produced such startling changes in so short a time that much of the administrative machinery had perforce to be improvised to meet an immediate need. This was especially true of finance, and in such conditions no well thought out and carefully co-ordinated system could well have been devised. The Council of Five Hundred, as was noted above, supervised the expenditure of the magistrates. A very ancient board of officials whose name, " meat-carvers " (κωλακρέται), suggests that they had once helped at state sacrifices, in the fifth century received certain revenues—for example, court fines and fees—from which they were required to pay the fees of the jurors in the *heliaea*, as well as for certain religious rites and other charges. For reasons that are obscure they disappeared in 411 and their duties were taken over by the Hellenotamiae. These officials presided over what in effect became during the second half of the fifth century the Athenian war-chest, whose income was the tribute paid by the allies and subjects of Athens. At the conclusion of the Peloponnesian War this board was abolished, since the monies that it had controlled ceased to exist.

In addition to these two funds of the state great importance attached to the Sacred Treasury of Athena. Its revenues became exceedingly great, so that soon after 450 no less than 9700 talents had accumulated in it, while in 431, after several years of lavish spending, there still remained a reserve of 6000. Moreover, for nearly forty years—from 441–40 to the collapse of Athens—the government borrowed regularly from this source to meet a part of the costs imposed by the Peloponnesian War. It was controlled by a board of treasurers of the goddess.[1] In 434, as is known from a surviving decree proposed by a certain Callias, the treasure of the other gods, save only of the two goddesses of Eleusis, was given into the care of a second board of treasurers.[2] From this surplus the state also borrowed occasionally. The two boards were amalgamated in 406, only to be separated again in 385.[3] Several new funds and treasuries came into being during the fourth

---

[1] For extant records of these borrowings cf. Tod 50, 55, 64, 75, 81, 83, 92 ; also B. D. Meritt, *Athenian Financial Documents*, Chapters V–VII.

[2] Tod 51, with references there given.

[3] For the date, 406, see especially W. S. Ferguson, *The Treasurers of Athena*, 104–106.

century. Both the council and the assembly received their own *tamias*, the latter being created as early as 394. Separate funds for building triremes and for war purposes, each with its own official, were established somewhat later. The Theoric or Festival Fund came into special prominence under the administration of Eubulus. At that time all surplus revenues of the state were paid into it, so that its supervisor in effect acquired a general control over state finance. It was greatly to Eubulus' credit that by careful management he was able to restore to Athens some measure of financial stability at a most critical time when she was nearly bankrupt.

The expenses of the Athenian government comprised pay to members of the council, to the magistrates other than those few who, like the *strategi* and Hellenotamiae, were elected not chosen by lot, and to the jurors in the *heliaea*. At the beginning of the fourth century, in order to stimulate the declining attendance of citizens in the *ecclesia*, a small payment of one obol for each meeting was introduced on the motion of Agyrrhius. By the year 392 the amount had, at the instance of the same politician, been raised to three obols. It remained at this figure until *c.* 327, when it was doubled and for certain sessions even trebled. The resulting expense each year for this purpose alone was substantial, perhaps as much as thirty talents. It is possible that Pericles first instituted the payment of one drachma to the poorest citizens to enable them to attend the Greater Dionysia. In the fourth century the sum was increased, the number of recipients became greater, and similar disbursements were granted also for the Panathenaea and other festivals. It was this lavish spending on the pleasures of the people which aroused the strong disapproval of Demosthenes; but ten years or more passed before his suggestion to use the Theoric Fund for military and naval purposes was at last adopted by the assembly. During the closing years of the fifth century the government found it necessary to introduce a system of two-obol doles to the poorest citizens; but, although records of money paid out in this way exist, the total annual cost of this poor-relief cannot be estimated.[1] Sacrifices and religious celebrations were recurrent and heavy items of expense; so also was the erection of temples and other public buildings and their upkeep and

[1] For such payments cf. Tod 83, and especially 92.

# THE GOVERNMENT OF THE CITY-STATES

repair. During the days of their greatest prosperity the Athenians, as we have seen, did not hesitate to use for this purpose large sums from the tribute of their subjects. On the other hand, as will appear hereafter, much of the cost connected with religious festivals, as also a great part of the expenditure caused by the upkeep of the navy, was shouldered by the individual citizen of means.

The chief source of revenue during the fifth century was, of course, the tribute paid by allies and subjects. The financial organization of the Second Athenian Confederacy is obscure, but even at its zenith the income from contributions probably fell short of 200 talents.[1] After the war with the allies it probably did not exceed a quarter of that sum.[2] A regular income was obtained by the state from the proceeds of mines at Laurium and in Thrace, from rents for state-owned property, although this was probably never extensive, from confiscations, the sale of the sequestered property of debtors, court-fees, and fines. Resident aliens were required to pay a poll-tax of twelve drachmae *per annum*; resident alien women living on their own paid half that amount. Indirect taxes included market-dues, a small levy on country produce brought for sale to Athens and resembling the *octroi* still exacted in some European countries, a two per cent *ad valorem* tax on all imports and exports at Piraeus, and some others.

The citizens paid no regular direct tax, but the state was relieved of a part of the burden that it would otherwise have had to shoulder by the public services known as liturgies. The ordinary liturgies were undertaken by the wealthier citizens and by metics, provided their property qualification exceeded a certain minimum. The trierarchy devolved only on the citizens. The ordinary or recurrent liturgies were many and were chiefly connected with religious festivals. The *choregia* entailed the equipping and training of a chorus for the dramatic performances held each year at the Greater Dionysia and the Lenaea. The *gymnasiarchia* took care of athletes who were in training for athletic festivals. The cost of sending sacred embassies to Delos was only partly borne by the government; a liturgy (ἀρχιθεωρία) took care of the

---

[1] The estimate of J. Beloch (*Griechische Geschichte*, III, 2, 167–8), 200 talents, is an outside figure.

[2] Demosthenes (18, 234) speaks of 45 talents, Aeschines (2, 71) of 60.

balance. The performance of these services, at least in the more prosperous days of the fifth century, was a patriotic duty willingly shouldered by the wealthier citizens who made it a point of honour to be more lavish in their outlay than was actually required of them. An instance is on record of a citizen who in ten years spent six talents, 36 minae in this way.[1] The trierarchy involved the cost of equipping and keeping a trireme in good condition for one year. The state provided the hull and some tackle and paid a small sum to the crew; for all other expenses the trierarch was responsible, and he frequently augmented the sailors' pay as well. Towards the end of the Peloponnesian War it became impossible to find sufficient trierarchs to undertake this costly burden individually and it became necessary to divide the responsibility between two persons acting jointly. This method appears to have continued until 357 when, on the proposal of a certain Periander, an important change was introduced, modelled on a procedure that had already been in force for some time for collecting the extraordinary tax on property (εἰσφορά). By this enactment the 1200 wealthiest persons were divided into twenty companies of sixty. These companies were further split up into smaller groups, so that a varying number of persons—from two to ten or a dozen—contributed towards the upkeep of one trireme. The financial liability of the individual trierarch was probably assessed on a sliding scale. Even so abuses crept in, because the richer members of groups who acted as chairmen sometimes escaped with a smaller payment than was warranted by their property qualification. An enactment, brought forward by Demosthenes in 340–339, aimed at remedying such irregularities, but its provisions are not known.

But there was one other way in which the state exacted money from the wealthier citizens and resident aliens. The *eisphora* was a direct tax on property and was an extraordinary levy for war purposes. The earliest recorded instance of its use was in 428–427, and it was collected from time to time in the later stages of the Peloponnesian War. In the fourth century, when the income of Athens had shrunk, these levies became more frequent. In 378–377, when the total property, movable and immovable, of all the citizens and metics of

[1] Lysias, XXI, 1–6.

Athens was estimated at only 5750 talents,[1] a system of collecting the tax by companies (συμμορίαι) was introduced. Corporate property was liable to be taxed, as well as that of individual citizens, while metics paid at a higher rate; but it is uncertain what the lowest census was which brought a man into the taxable class. The rate seems to have varied according to circumstances, being usually not more than one or two per cent, but occasionally higher. When the symmories were instituted, each had a chairman, a treasurer, and a secretary or registrar, who listed the amount due from each member of the group. After 362–361, presumably because the payments by the symmories had not always been as prompt as the government wished, the council compiled a register of the wealthiest men in each deme and exacted from them the whole sum due. This so-called προεισφορά was regarded as a liturgy, and those who performed it were left to recover to the best of their ability the legal contributions from the other members of their respective symmories. The system inaugurated in 378–377 was intended to provide the Athenian share of the costs connected with the new maritime league. But the yield from the *eisphora*, together with the irregular and often reluctant contributions from the allies, did not suffice as a war-fund, and one of the strongest reasons for the rapid decline of the confederacy was the poverty of the Athenian state. It led to semi-piratical conduct on the part of Athenian commanders which alienated friends and neutrals, just as it prevented them on sundry occasions from following up a military or naval advantage legitimately gained against the enemies of Athens. The greatest weakness of Athens as a would-be imperial state in the fourth century was the absence of reserve funds, whether owned by the state or by Athena, such as she had possessed in the age of Pericles and his successors.

## § 5. LEAGUES AND FEDERATIONS

The voluntary coming together of a number of autonomous states for a common purpose had long been a familiar phenomenon in the Hellenic world; but, if we except the Delphic

[1] I follow W. S. Ferguson, *The Treasurers of Athena*, 166, note 1. Others have maintained that the figure applies only to the citizens and aliens liable to direct taxation. See Busolt-Swoboda, *Griechische Staatskunde*, II, 1213.

Amphictiony, the leagues which flourished in the archaic period of Greek history and continued to exist for centuries after were entirely religious. Their members met periodically to celebrate a festival or sacrifice to a deity who was the common patron of all, but the union had no political significance. On the other hand, there is no exact equivalent in English for what the Greeks described as a symmachy (συμμαχία), and the terms commonly used, league or confederacy, are only approximately correct descriptions. Essentially a symmachy was a defensive and offensive alliance between two states or a number of states for joint action in war and, by a natural extension, for a collective conduct of foreign affairs. This was the basic character of the Peloponnesian League, of the Confederacy of Delos, and of the Second Athenian Confederacy.[1] Theoretically all questions of war and peace, the general policy of the League, the admission of new members, and kindred topics were decided by an assembly in which each member had equal representation and equal voting power; or, in the case of the Second Athenian Confederacy, by the joint action of the Athenian *ecclesia* and the congress of the allies. It was, however, impossible that in any of these leagues the exact equality of all the members should be maintained indefinitely. There was, for one thing, too wide a difference in the strength and resources of the constituent states; and, again, and largely for that very reason, the executive was always in the hands of the same state. The consequence was that Athens in both the fifth and the fourth century, and Sparta notably between 404 and 371, ignored the terms of their respective leagues and took decisions without consulting the other members, or else overrode the resolutions of their allies. Furthermore, the smaller states might find their real status changed from that of free allies to that of dependents. The history of the Delian Confederacy offers the most complete example of this, but the career of Sparta as an imperial state in the fourth century is hardly less instructive.[2]

In spite of the passionate love of political independence

---

[1] J. Larsen in his careful study of the Peloponnesian League (*Classical Philology*, 28, 257–276; 29, 1–19) points out (28, 267) that whereas the two Athenian leagues were founded for a specific purpose, that of the Peloponnesian League was quite general, that is, not directed against any particular foreign power or powers.    [2] Cf. above, Chapter VI, §§ 1 and 6.

characteristic of the city-states in ancient Greece, it is possible to point to a substantial number of unions approximating to the federal type. In these the supreme direction of affairs was vested in a federal assembly whose control extended over the constituent communities and their citizens. If each of the members managed its own local affairs, it did so either because this was stipulated when the union was formed or because this power was delegated to it by the federal authority. Expressed in another way, we may say that the individual in such a federation exercised dual rights of citizenship—he was a citizen of one constituent state and also a citizen of the federation. Of this general type were the Boeotian League, the Arcadian League formed in 370, and federations in Phocis, Thessaly, Epirus, Acarnania, and Chalcidice. About most of these surviving information is too scanty to give a clear picture of their organization and practical working. It must suffice to consider more nearly the federations in Arcadia and Boeotia.

In the Arcadian League (τὸ κοινὸν τῶν Ἀρκάδων) the government of each constituent member exercised sovereign rights within its own boundaries. While a federal coinage was struck, the several cities of the League could also issue their own currency. At the same time the federal government had some judicial authority over the citizens of constituent states. It was composed, as we have seen,[1] of an assembly—the Ten Thousand—and of a council. The former was probably composed of all the full citizens of hoplite census in all the cities within the federation. Its decisions relative to war and peace and to all foreign affairs were binding on each member. Its judicial authority was operative in offences against the League whether committed by federal officials, or by magistrates or private individuals of a constituent city. It also adjudicated in disputes between its members unless it chose to refer the question at issue to a neutral arbitrator. The council, like the *boule* of a democratic city-state, prepared the business for the assembly and collaborated with the magistrates, chief of whom was the *strategus*, in the administrative and financial business of the League. The federal funds seem to have been made up only of contributions levied as need arose and not the product

[1] Cf. above, pp. 207–208.

of regular taxation.[1] This experiment in federalism was not a success. It lasted only a few years partly because of the jealousies and long-standing disagreements between two of its chief members, partly because Lycomedes, the one man who might have succeeded in evolving harmony out of discord, died within a few years of its inauguration.

The beginnings of a league of cities in Boeotia go back at least to the sixth century, when a uniform currency was already in use. This league was broken up by Sparta after the Persian wars, when Thebes and other cities had medized, and its reconstitution after Tanagra was almost at once made ineffective by the Athenian conquest of Boeotia. It was only after 447 that a new union came into being. It comprised nine independent cities: Thebes, Orchomenus, Thespiae, Haliartus, Lebadea, Tanagra, Coronea, Acraephia, and Copae. Smaller communities, of which there was a good number, were dependent on one or other of the nine, especially on Thebes. Soon after 424 Chaeronea, hitherto controlled by Orchomenus, became an independent member. The administrative organization of the League was unusually elaborate. Its entire territory was divided into eleven regions, of which four were assigned to Thebes, two each to Thespiae and Orchomenus, and one to Tanagra. Haliartus, Coronea, and Lebadea shared the tenth, and Acraephia, Copae, and Chaeronea the eleventh. The chief federal authority was a body of 660 persons, 60 from each region. The result was that Thebes alone sent more than a third of the delegates to this assembly or council. The delegates, it may be supposed, were elected or taken by lot in equal numbers from the four *boulae*, which were composed of all full citizens and which formed the government in each city.[2] The federal body of 660 was also divided into four *boulae*. Each carried on the administration of the League in turn and acted as a deliberative committee for the whole number with whom the final decision on policy rested. The chief executive officers were eleven Boeotarchs, one for each district, so that again Thebes exercised greater influence than the other cities. They were elected for one year by the councils of each constituent state.

[1] It has been pointed out above (p. 207) that the functions of the fifty δαμιοργοί are quite obscure.
[2] For these four councils in the cities cf. above, p. 350.

In the fourth century at least, if not before, re-election was permissible, and, in special cases, frequent; for Pelopidas held the office on thirteen occasions. Though they were primarily military officers, they also played an influential part in the conduct of foreign affairs, especially in the preliminary negotiations with other states. The funds of the Boeotian League were obtained in the form of a levy on property as occasion demanded, and not on the basis of a regularly recurrent tax. During the later fifth and early fourth century coinage was minted only in Thebes. This fact, and the position of Thebes as the federal capital, together with the large representation of that city on both the council of 660 and the board of Boeotarchs, in practice deprived the League of some of its federal character; for there is enough evidence to show that the policy of the League was determined by the Thebans and that they did not hesitate on occasion to coerce other constituent members of the federation, even as Sparta and Athens went beyond their rights in their dealings with their allies.

The reconstituted Boeotian state that came into being shortly before Leuctra no longer deserves the name of a federation. Not only had Thebes reduced Thespiae, Plataea, and Orchomenus and incorporated these territories in her own, but she controlled Boeotia as a whole to a degree unknown before. Of the seven Boeotarchs who now formed the executive, no less than four were Thebans. And the use of the name, Boeotians, as the official designation of the state cannot be taken as proof that it was still truly federal, the more so when the *damos* that exercised sovereign power is frequently called in the sources a Theban assembly.[1] A Boeotian League, presumably of the older type, existed after Chaeronea, when Thebes had succumbed to Philip and even after her destruction by Alexander. Its capital was probably Orchomenus.

---

[1] The character of the Boeotian state after *c.* 374 has been the subject of much controversy. For the literature cf. Busolt-Swoboda, *Griechische Staatskunde*, II, 1426–1428. I cannot agree with the authors that Boeotia was a true "Bundesstaat" at that time; for, to explain away the many references to the Theban assembly, they merely state that the assembly was so described because it met at Thebes. Larsen (*Representative Government*, 72) believes that a representative council had been superseded by a primary assembly meeting at Thebes.

The so-called federations in our period were confined to comparatively narrow areas whose inhabitants had long lived under similar conditions and with similar customs. Also, like the more loosely organized confederacies, they were imperfect and lacked permanence, either because one constituent member was stronger than the rest and tended unduly to dominate the others, or because the latent rivalries of several cities made a lasting fusion of interests for the common weal impossible of attainment. Only in the Hellenistic Age, with the formation of the Aetolian, and especially the Achaean Leagues, were true federal unions of enduring character achieved by the Greeks. Moreover, their membership roll extended far beyond the narrow geographical region within which they had first taken rise.

## CHAPTER XV

## GREEK ECONOMIC LIFE

### § 1. GEOGRAPHICAL FEATURES AND NATURAL RESOURCES

THE geographical features of Greece that had to a great extent determined the political and economic development of the city-states in the archaic period of Greek history continued to influence their life in the fifth and fourth centuries. A country with a total area of approximately 45,000 square miles, with no navigable rivers but an unusually long seaboard, with more hilly or mountainous than low-lying regions, of necessity made considerable demands on the energy and practical ability of its population. It was no accident that districts like Arcadia, Aetolia, and north-western Greece generally, being almost wholly mountainous or cut off from easy approach to the sea, as well as not too accessible by land, remained backward politically and culturally. With the growth of mercenary service many of their inhabitants, being poor if hardy, found it profitable to seek their fortunes in the pay of foreign governments. Though it is clear from the military operations in our period that the different parts of Greece were for the most part linked by adequate roads, trade was predominantly sea-borne, and some states owed much of their wealth to their geographical position; either because, like Corinth and Byzantium, they controlled important straits, or because, like Miletus or Ephesus, they were not only seaports but lay at the end of a main highway from the Middle East. In Asia Minor the great majority of purely Greek settlements were on, or in close proximity to, the sea and situated in level and fertile country. The economic prosperity that resulted from natural advantages greater than those enjoyed by many states of European Greece had contributed towards the more rapid political and cultural evolution of the city-states on the Anatolian sea-board, so that they became pioneers in the realm of thought and of art. But the nearness of powerful non-Hellenic kingdoms in the interior made their political independence at all times more precarious than that of their European kinsmen.

The natural resources of the Greek world were adequate but not lavish. Stone of all kinds suitable for building was plentiful; for, besides the all but ubiquitous limestone, green porphyry was quarried in the hills lying to the east and west of Laconia, while there were ample supplies of marble in Attica, in the islands of Paros and Naxos, and elsewhere. Metals, other than iron which existed in many places in modest quantities and in larger deposits in Laconia, Euboea, Seriphus, and in the hinterland of Sinope and Trapezus in Asia Minor, were relatively scarce. Gold was mined in Thasos and Thrace (Pangaeus). The ore of Siphnos seems to have been nearly exhausted by the fifth century, but gold was found in Xenophon's day in the neighbourhood of Abydos. There were also gold deposits and rivers containing gold dust in the interior of Asia Minor. The chief source of the silver supply was at Laurium in southern Attica. Other silver-bearing regions were Pangaeus, Damastium in Epirus, Dysoron in Macedonia, and, during the fifth century, Siphnos. There was abundant silver in Asia Minor and in Spain, but since these areas were controlled respectively by Persia and by Carthage, the ore can only have reached the Greeks of the Anatolian coast and those of Sicily and Italy by way of trade.[1] Copper was mined in parts of Asia Minor, but for European Greece the richest source was Cyprus. As that island was generally under Persian control, the metal formed an important article of commerce in times of peace. The regions from which the Greeks obtained tin are obscure. The largest deposits were in Spain and the ore must have reached the Greeks through Carthage. It is likely that some tin and silver also was mined in N. Albania and Bohemia and shipped to Greek ports down the Adriatic.[2] The best timber was procured in Macedonia and Thrace; smaller forested areas existed in Crete, Arcadia, and Thessaly. But the science of forestry seems to have received no attention, with the result that

---

[1] See M. Cary in *Mélanges Glotz*, I, 133–142.
[2] See R. L. Beaumont in *J.H.S.* 56 (1936), 181–194.

deforestation proceeded rapidly in many parts of the country. Attica, which had once contained good timber for building, in the fourth century had little or none.[1] Excellent lumber abounded on the slopes of Ida in the Troad, while in the West the hill regions of southern Italy supplied the Greek cities of the coast and probably those of Sicily as well where the forested areas were few and smaller.

### § 2. RESIDENT ALIENS AND SLAVES

No survey of Greek economic life would be complete without some reference to the non-citizen population in the city-states, upon whose labour much of the material prosperity depended. Resident aliens or denizens (μέτοικοι) probably were to be found in many of the Greek states, especially in those where industry and commerce offered most opportunity for gaining a decent livelihood.[2] It is, however, only in the case of the denizens at Athens that some particulars of their status and activities are known. The Athenian metics were free to pursue their calling provided that they conformed with certain regulations that were strictly enforced by the state. They had to register formally as aliens, a record being kept in each deme of the aliens residing there. They had to find an Athenian citizen who was willing to act as their sponsor (προστάτης) and through whom they were obliged to act in most cases of litigation. They also paid a small annual head-tax. Furthermore, they were liable to military service in Attica, and, if sufficiently wealthy, they were called upon to undertake the ordinary liturgies. At Athens, at least, grant of citizenship to metics was unusual and only made in very exceptional services. Thus some resident aliens who had fought on the side of Thrasybulus in 403 were rewarded two years later by the gift of civic rights.[3] More usual was the bestowal on prominent aliens of what was known as *isoteleia*. The recipient of this status was exempt from the head-tax, did not require the help of a patron

---

[1] Cf. Plato, *Critias*, 111C.

[2] M. Clerc long since traced the existence of metics in seventy city-states of the Greek world. This number can now be slightly increased. Cf. P.-W., XV, 1454–55.

[3] Cf. Tod 100. The inscription is badly damaged but the restorations are reasonably certain.

in the law-courts, and, in the matter of military and financial liabilities, was on a footing of equality with the citizens. From extant decrees conferring *isoteleia* it is clear that the grant was usually accompanied by a further privilege, that of owning landed property, which the ordinary metic was not allowed to do. The *isoteleis* thus formed a privileged minority of the resident alien population, being intermediate between the citizens and the ordinary denizens. The majority of the metics were, however, of humbler status, corresponding to the classes of *thetes* and *zeugitae* among the citizens. They were employed in trade and commerce and in a great variety of crafts. Thirty-five out of a total of seventy-one persons employed on the building of the Erechtheum in 408–407 were denizens.[1] The commercial litigants whose activities are recorded in the speeches of the Demosthenic corpus seem to be without exception members of the metic class. It is also noteworthy that five out of seventeen metics enfranchised in 401, whose calling is known, were described as farmers.[2] Unless they were already *isoteleis*, they can only have been hired farm-workers prior to the grant of citizenship. After that they would have the opportunity of becoming peasant proprietors. To judge by existing records, the metics during the greater part of our period were Greeks; only towards the end of the fourth century do non-Greek denizens make their appearance.

The vast majority of Greeks did not question either the propriety or the need of slavery as an institution, and it is well known that Aristotle essayed a philosophical justification of it. One must, however, distinguish between two types of servile population. In Laconia and Messenia, in Crete, and in Thessaly, as well as in a few city-states, like Heraclea on the Black Sea, there existed a serf population whose main function was to till the soil for their masters. Obscure as is the origin of the Helots or of the Thessalian Penestae, it is a reasonable assumption that essentially they represent the descendants of early inhabitants of Greece reduced to bondage by victorious invaders. The lot of the Helots appears to have been the hardest, and the Spartans never devised any better

[1] *I.G.*, I², 372–374.
[2] Tod 100. There are more than seventeen names on the inscription, but in some cases the professional description has been entirely destroyed.

method of controlling their agricultural workers and servants than by intimidation. In other parts of the Greek world the slaves were either captives taken in war or non-Hellenic persons purchased in the slave-market. It was only very slowly that sentiment grew against the enslavement of Greeks by Greeks. And while there was often the opportunity for a Greek captive to buy his ransom, this concession depended entirely on the whim of the victor, and, as we have seen,[1] did not apply at all to the members of allied or subject states which had revolted. The distribution of slaves in Greece varied greatly. Since the majority were employed either in domestic service or in industry, their numbers were greatest in the city-states where trade and commerce formed an important part of economic life. In the regions where the communities were predominantly agricultural, as in Arcadia and many parts of Boeotia, the growth of a servile population appears to have been much slower. In Athens in the years immediately preceding the Peloponnesian War the total number of slaves of both sexes was probably about one hundred thousand. As the mercantile and industrial activity there was at that time more highly developed than in many states, we may assume that the proportion of servile to free population in Athens was unusually high. The Attic slaves were employed in the silver mines of Laurium, in domestic service, and in the arts and crafts. Those used in the mines worked under appalling conditions and the wastage must have been high. The other classes of slave, on the other hand, seem to have been reasonably well treated, and manumission, though never as common as in Rome, was a not infrequent reward of faithful service. The status of the liberated slave was not unlike that of a resident alien. His former master became the freedman's patron, unless the liberation was testamentary. In that case the former slave became the client of the heir. The majority of slaves in Attica during the fifth and fourth centuries were non-Hellenic. They came by way of the slave-market from Scythia and from the interior of Thrace and of Asia Minor. Natives of other regions, like Africa or Syria, are rarely met with in the period. The employment of slaves in industry took various forms. A craftsman of civic or metic status might own one or more servile workers, who shared

[1] Cf. above, p. 344.

the work with him and his sons. On the other hand, men of wealth not infrequently invested capital in slaves. When properly trained, these could be hired out to the state or to private employers; or the owner might himself set up and equip a factory, leaving the actual management to an overseer, who more often than not was himself a slave. Finally, the owner of slaves skilled in particular crafts might prefer to set them up in business on their own, on condition that a certain part of their earnings was given up to him. Slaves treated in this way would need to be exceptionally trustworthy and after a lapse of years could look forward to their freedom, either by purchase out of their savings or by the gift of their master as a reward for faithful service. The best-known example of this was the money-lender and banker, Pasion. He began his career as a slave and ended it as a citizen of Athens. His successor and heir to the business, Phormio, likewise began as a slave. While it is beyond doubt that industry was very largely in the hands of slaves and ex-slaves, we lack data from which to determine the kind of influence that slavery had on the economic life of Athens, or, for that matter, of other Greek states; and it would be unwise to argue from analogies drawn from the experience of slave-holding societies at other times.

### § 3. AGRICULTURE

In many areas of the Greek world agriculture, though it brought only small profit, continued to be, as it had always been, the chief occupation of the people. Even if Pericles, as reported by Thucydides (I, 141), was thinking primarily of the contrast between Sparta and Athens, his generalization, that the Peloponnesian Greeks tilled their own land and did not accumulate riches either individually or as communities, was doubtless true of a majority of city-states in the Morea.[1] In Boeotia, too, and Thessaly land was the chief source of wealth, the former region producing field crops and garden produce in large quantities, the latter being especially noted

[1] The Spartans themselves were of course not αὐτουργοί, but their society was predominantly agricultural. It has also been inferred that the use of the word αὐτουργοί implies that in other farming areas of the Peloponnese there was little slavery. But, though the master was himself a farmer, it does not follow that he may not have had slave hands to work with him.

for its stock-raising. In many of the islands the chief article of export was wine, while in Asia Minor and in the western Mediterranean, cities like Miletus or Taras owed much of their commercial prosperity to sheep-raising. This provided the raw material for the woollen manufactures for which they were famous. Nevertheless, in many *poleis* it must have become increasingly difficult to make farming of any sort pay; for the disturbed political conditions and frequent wars affected the peasants more adversely than other members of the community. Lack of chemical knowledge, moreover, and the existence of serfdom or slavery hindered the development of scientific farming and the invention of tools and machinery which would have made agricultural processes less wasteful and rendered possible a more intensive cultivation of the soil. There was relatively little good pasturage for cattle in Greece, much territory being suitable only for sheep or goats. Hence animal manure was not too abundant. Other substances for enriching the ground were indeed known, such as decayed vegetation and the waste products from tanneries; or lupines and other green crops might be grown and then dug under and left to rot. But these were only subsidiary aids and not equivalent either to animal manure or to the chemical fertilizers of modern times. In consequence the normal procedure was to raise crops on a particular piece of land only in alternate years and to leave it fallow in the intervening periods. The cultivation of alternating crops was, even in the fourth century, the exception rather than the rule. Existing agreements between the lessor and lessee of a farmstead stipulate that the tenant in the last year of his lease shall not cultivate more than half of his acreage.[1] In that way a new lessee could work the other half as soon as he entered on his occupancy. The tools used were of the simplest pattern, To judge by representations on vases of the fifth century, the plough then used was as simple as in the ages of Homer or Hesiod. When the grain was ripe, it was cut by hand with the sickle and was separated from the chaff by the age-old process of turning oxen or mules loose to trample on it. The straw that remained standing was either burnt or used for

---

[1] Cf. R. Dareste and others, *Recueil des inscriptions juridiques grecques*, Ie série, p. 236, lines 18–20; also 238, 14 ff. On field crops generally cf. A. Jardé, *Les céréales dans l'antiquité grecque* (Paris, 1925).

manure. The two chief cereals grown throughout the Greek world were barley and wheat, but in European Greece land suitable for their cultivation was very limited. The rainfall for months in the year was uncertain and a torrential downpour in the summer season was likely to do more harm than good. In many districts the cultivation of the olive and the vine was found to suit existing conditions better. Vines could be grown on sloping ground, and both plants were hardy, so that the irregularity of the water-supply was of less consequence. Thus, if Laconia and Messenia, Boeotia and Thessaly were self-supporting in the matter of field crops, many other regions were not and depended on imports either from Sicily or Southern Italy or else from South Russia, Egypt, and in 330-326 from Cyrene. The greatest quantities of wheat in our period were obtained from South Russia, and it was not only Athens which sought to remain on friendly terms with the rulers of Bosporus and secure preferential treatment for trade in this commodity.[1]

Olives and vines, then as now, were to be found all over the Mediterranean area, even though their cultivation needed more capital at first; for vines did not begin to bear fruit till the third year and olives were not productive until the tenth. In many regions the wine and oil manufactured on the spot were ample for local needs; in many others considerable quantities were available for export. The Athenians were already exporting olive oil in the sixth century. Thasos Samos, Chios, Lesbos, Rhodes, Naxos, and Cos were all noted for their wines and sold them over a wide area.[2] These were by far the two most valuable products of the soil in Greek lands and as such were among the chief commodities of trade within the Mediterranean and with non-Hellenic peoples dwelling beyond. For the rest, horticulture and the raising of other fruit trees sufficed only for local requirements and for trade with neighbouring communities. Farms and estates were usually small, so that a property which produced in one year 1000 medimni of grain, over 800 measures of wine, and timber to the value of 3600 drachmae was accounted unusually

---

[1] Cf. Tod 167. Mytilene c. 350 received remission of part of the export tax levied by Leucon and his sons (Tod 163). For Cyrene, cf. Tod 196.

[2] For the Thasian trade see E. Ziebarth, *Beiträge zur Geschichte des Seeraubs und Seehandels im alten Griechenland*, pp. 75 ff.

rich.[1] The estates of the ruling aristocracy in Thessaly which were worked by the serf population were doubtless of greater extent, but in the absence of all information no estimate of their size can be attempted. The small territory of most city-states in any case precluded the formation of large estates even where the government was oligarchic, so that the political organization of the Greeks in the classical period, whatever its other drawbacks, at least saved them from the economic problems faced by Rome three centuries later.

## § 4. INDUSTRY AND COMMERCE

It is easy to exaggerate the character and extent of industrial development in the Hellenic world of the classical age; for, while the volume of production at Athens and doubtless in many other cities increased rapidly in the fifth century, to reach its maximum in the fourth, its methods did not alter appreciably. Athens and southern Italy might be famous for their pottery, Corinth and Chalcis for their metal work, Miletus or Taras for their woollen cloth and tapestries, Megara for its cloaks, but in each case the articles were mainly produced by master craftsmen in workshops that offered employment for only a few hands. In a city like Athens each group of craftsmen had its own quarters in the vicinity of the market-place. There the articles were made, there, too, they were sold. From the end of the fifth century one can trace the growth of production on a somewhat greater scale. Men who were not themselves artisans invested capital in small factories employing thirty or forty hands. The father of Isocrates owned an establishment of this sort for the manufacture of musical instruments. Demosthenes' father employed about fifty slaves all told in two workshops where arms and beds were turned out. The wealthy metic, Cephalus, father of Lysias, owned altogether 120 slaves; but, although it has often been assumed that all these were artisans in his shield factory, it is more probable that some were domestic slaves belonging to his home in Piraeus. Essentially, then, this innovation, which may have been paralleled in Corinth and elsewhere, was merely an extension of the older system, coupled with a somewhat more extensive

[1] Demosthenes, XLII, 20

use of slave labour. It may have driven some master craftsmen out of business, but the effect on the citizen population was probably slight. By that time industry, like commerce, seems to have been predominantly in the hands of noncitizens, free and servile. The citizen found employment in the assembly, as an official or a councillor, or in the dicasteries, and in each case received compensation from the state. Nor must it be forgotten that many homes, especially outside the towns, were still largely self-sufficient. The women of the household spun cloth and made the clothes for the family, and in the country most, if not all, the food was raised on the spot. The lamentable absence of precise information makes it impossible to state the proportion of citizens to resident aliens and slaves employed in industry either at Athens or elsewhere. In oligarchies, moreover, the artisan class would ordinarily not be in possession of full civic rights. It would be unsafe to draw deductions from an isolated record like the building inscription of the Erechtheum, which shows that out of a total of seventy-one workmen, each receiving a drachma a day, twenty were citizens, thirty-five were resident aliens, and sixteen were slaves. It is, nevertheless, probable that fifty years later a similar undertaking would have been carried out with the labour of fewer citizens and of more metics and slaves.[1]

The variety of arts and crafts was great and the technique highly developed. The surviving examples of ceramic fabrics, of bronze ware, and of the builders' and stonemason's work are sufficient proof of this. They also justify the belief that more perishable articles, such as textiles, were no less skilfully made. The potter, the bronze worker, the silversmith took a pride in his work and was an artist as well as a craftsman. And it was not famous sculptors but humble stonemasons who made many of the admirably sculptured tombstones in the Cerameicus at Athens. In the winning of raw materials lack of scientific knowledge and of machinery was a handicap. The process of mining and the smelting of the ore had to be effected with the simplest of equipment. Yet considerable skill was shown at Laurium in conserving the available water-supply and devising a system by which the

[1] Cf. *I.G.*², II–III, 1672. Of ninety-four employed at Eleusis, twenty were citizens, twenty were slaves, and no less than fifty-four were metics.

same water could be used over and over again for washing the ore.[1] And, if smelting was performed in a wasteful way, so that not so much ore was extracted as would be possible under modern conditions, the purity, for example, of the silver used in Greek coins of the best period is truly astonishing.

Merchandise not sold in the place of manufacture was traded chiefly by sea; for although there was no lack of roads, they were narrow and often in indifferent repair. The cost or transport by land was far higher, and beasts of burden or for draught were expensive and not too abundant. Maritime trade also suffered from certain handicaps. Ships were small, a merchantman of medium size displacing less than 100 tons. The average speed of these sailing vessels was four knots an hour or a little more. If a favouring wind enabled them at times to scud along at six or seven knots, the advantage so gained might speedily be neutralized by a sudden calm or by a shift of the wind that necessitated tacking and added to the length of the voyage. The risk to ships and cargoes from storms and, in view of frequent warfare, from danger of capture by an enemy were considerable. Piracy was an added hazard; for, though the maritime supremacy of Athens after the Persian wars virtually eliminated corsairs in the eastern Mediterranean, the policing of the seas during the fourth century was less complete and there was a recrudescence of robbery by sea. Moreover, some of the mercenary leaders, like Charidemus, though officially accredited to a state, sometimes combined their legitimate business with piratical enterprises. Little was done by traders during the winter months. The sailing season for commercial craft was from March to October. Whereas local trade, either in the manufacturing city or in the neighbourhood was mainly direct sale by the craftsman or the manufacturer to his customers, commerce by sea was, at least in the fourth century, predominantly in the hands of middlemen. Such a one might transport goods on his own ship ($ναύκληρος$) or he might accompany his merchandise on another's vessel ($ἔμπορος$). But both the shipmaster-merchant and the merchant travelling on another man's boat operated on borrowed capital. It was, in fact,

---

[1] Cf. generally the interesting paper of G. M. Calhoun, "Ancient Athenian Mining" in *Journal of Economic and Business History* 3 (1931), 333–361.

characteristic of business life in the Greek world that the owner of capital was distinct from the merchant and trader. The latter borrowed money in order to buy the commodities in which he traded. So, too, loans on bottomry were a popular form of investment with the owner of some capital. The risks were heavy, but the profits were correspondingly great. Partnerships between two or more persons, who sometimes lived in different ports, were not rare. The trader proceeded from port to port disposing of his wares wherever it seemed most advantageous to sell. In the course of a prolonged voyage—for instance, from Piraeus to the Crimea—he might change his cargo several times. He would try to bring back to his home-port such commodities as he could there dispose of to the greatest advantage.

There were certain well-defined trade-routes followed by Greek merchants. The northern and north-eastern route from Piraeus lay through the Euripus, and along the coast of Thessaly to Chalcidice, or by way of the Sporades to the Dardanelles, Byzantium, and the ports of the Black Sea. Ships proceeding from Athens to the cities of the Asia Minor littoral would call at some of the Cyclades on the way. Those whose destination was Syria or Egypt would thread their way through the Cyclades to Rhodes and pass thence to more distant ports. The voyager from the Peloponnese to the African coast would most likely touch at one or more points in Crete; while the ordinary route to the western Mediterranean followed the coast as far as Corcyra and thence passed across the Adriatic to the nearest point of Italy. As far as possible the captain of the vessel avoided crossing the open sea and kept in touch of land, a course dictated partly by the smallness of the ships and their limited power to face rough weather, partly because the size of the vessel imposed strict limitations on the supply of water that could be carried.

From the time when Themistocles persuaded his countrymen to fortify Piraeus to the foundation of Alexandria, Piraeus easily surpassed all other harbours for the volume of business there transacted. Athens' chief exports were oil, wine, honey, silver, and marble. In return she imported, besides great quantities of wheat, fish and skins from the Black Sea area, linen and papyrus from Egypt, iron and copper ore from Euboea and elsewhere, and a variety of manufactured articles, many for the luxury trade depending on the custom of a few wealthy citizens or metics, from different regions. There is no reason to doubt the substantial truth of the boast put in the mouth of Pericles by Thucydides and uttered a century later by Xenophon, that the produce of all the world found its way to Athens.[1] The trade of Corinth was carried on especially with her colonies and other states in the West. As an exchange mart this city was second in importance only to Athens amongst the states of European Greece; but we know too little about her trade and commerce and those of other city-states to particularize.

Nothing more clearly defines the gulf that separates ancient Greek from modern business than the attitude of Greek governments to industry and commerce. There was no legislation to protect the workmen or to formulate the relations between employer and employed, save that in the case of slaves at Athens gross mishandling of a slave by his owner might result in state interference. There is no clear evidence to suggest that any Greek government ever passed laws for the exclusive advantage of its mercantile class or subsidized any commercial or industrial undertaking from state funds. The Thasians in the fourth century, it is true, passed certain regulations to govern the wine-trade on which much of their prosperity depended. To prevent speculation it was forbidden to buy up in advance the harvest of a whole vineyard. State inspectors examined the full jars of wine to ensure that they contained the correct amount. Thasian ships were not permitted to load up with foreign wines between two stated points on the mainland coast off the island.[2] Probably the purpose of these ordinances was not so much to help the local wine growers as to enrich the state treasury by the imposition of duties which could only be levied effectively if the trade was rigorously supervized. Commercial treaties, so called, were made to ensure the importation of essential commodities, not to further the growth of commerce as such. Thus the Athenians were vitally interested in grain and timber. They entered into

---

[1] Thucyd., II, 38; Xen., *Ways and Means*, 1, 2 ff.
[2] Cf. the inscription which has been most recently studied by E. Ziebarth, *Beitrage zur Geschichte des Seeraubs und Seehandels im alten Griechenland*, 75; Anhang II, 10.

agreements with foreign states so that they might have no lack of either. Besides this they appointed a board of grain inspectors at Athens and Piraeus and legislated to prevent corners in wheat and excessive prices.[1] The people of Teos formulated a curse, to be solemnly pronounced by their magistrates each year, against anyone who prevented the importation of wheat.[2] Miletus bargained for privileges with the ruler of Bosporus in the matter of her wheat supply from South Russia.[3] The purpose and limitations of such pacts are obvious enough and they were framed for the welfare of the state as a whole and not for its commercial class. On the other hand, we do not hear of any Greek government attempting to regulate prices, while state monopolies of raw materials or of manufactures were a development of the Hellenistic Age.[4] We are thus justified in the belief that, compared with other branches of human endeavour, the economic life of the Greeks remained essentially simple in character and the methods of production and exchange had not passed, as it were, out of the adolescent stage. This backwardness will become even more apparent in the following section.

### § 5. MONEY-DEALING

We have already seen the somewhat crude methods of state finance employed by the Greeks of the classical period. A similarly undeveloped system of private finance existed in the fifth and fourth centuries; for what is commonly called banking in the Greek city-states scarcely deserves so imposing a title. The word τραπεζίτης, originally meant a money-changer and, in view of the multiplicity of Greek currencies, was a natural and early development from the invention of coinage. For a time the currencies in widest circulation were those of Corinth, Athens and Aegina, but with the loss of her independence in 457 the last-named city ceased to strike her own coins. During the earlier years of the Peloponnesian War Athens sought to compel the use of

[1] For Athens' control of the grain trade in the fifth century cf. above, p. 82.
[2] Tod 23A.     [3] Tod 163.
[4] Cf. M. Cary in Volume III of this *History*, 294 ff. Examples of monopolies in Greek cities are given in the pseudo-Aristotelian *Oeconomica*, but they are not dated. Probably all date from the end of the fourth century or later.

her "owls" throughout the empire.[1] Unfortunately it is not known for how long, and indeed with what degree of success, this ordinance could be enforced. In the fourth century the diversity of currencies was even greater than before, and neither Athens nor any other state could compel the use of its money in other communities. The government of Olbia on the Black Sea allowed the free entry of all gold and silver coins, but passed an enactment that all such foreign currency must be changed into local money. Clearly the state derived some profit from this regulation by claiming the agio wholly or partly for itself.[2] Although the Olbian inscription is unique, it is by no means improbable that other governments added to their revenues by similar regulations.

There was thus plenty of business at all times for the money-changer, especially in centres like Athens or Corinth, where trade was specially active and merchants from all parts of the Mediterranean congregated. The first private individuals on record as engaging in various forms of money-dealing are Antisthenes and Archestratus during the closing years of the fifth century. Under their successor, Pasion, the business grew to unusual dimensions. This is also the only "banking-house" before the Alexandrian period of which any details survive. In addition to the ordinary business of currency exchange, the firm engaged in pawnbroking, that is to say, it advanced cash on valuables deposited as security. It received money on deposit and operated with the capital of its clients as well as with its own. If Pasion and his successor, Phormion, and other money-dealers like them in Athens or elsewhere must have developed a careful system of book-keeping, it is surprising to find no mention of written receipts. The usual procedure was the more cumbersome one of carrying out transactions, such as the deposit or payment of sums of money, in the presence of witnesses. When a speaker in the courts could exclaim, "who would be so unwise as willingly to pay money to a person making a written application?", it is surely obvious that banking at that time was still in its infancy. There were no clearing-houses. There was no proper credit system and consequently no letters of credit, as the term is now understood, still less any system of payment by

[1] Tod 67.     [2] E. Ziebarth, *op. cit.*, App. II, 75.

cheque. The nearest approach to letters of credit was where a client deposited a sum of money with Pasion who then gave him a letter to an agent in Miletus authorizing the last-named to pay Pasion's client the like sum. Otherwise the transference of money or bullion was carried out literally by shipping it from one place to another. Another transaction to help the traveller is recorded by Isocrates. The plaintiff in the suit, who lived in Athens, had money in Bosporus on the Euxine which he wished to transfer to Athens. He found that a certain Stratocles was travelling to the Euxine and would need money while there. He therefore struck a bargain with Stratocles. The latter was to pay him money in Athens, while he gave Stratocles a letter to his father in Bosporus instructing the old gentleman to pay Stratocles an agreed sum when he arrived. In this case Pasion did not act as a banker at all, but merely witnessed the transaction. He was in fact a " surety for the foreign connections of a man in whom Pasion had financial confidence."[1] State and private economy, like most other human activities in the Greek city-states, were profoundly influenced by the conquests of Alexander. Vast quantities of bullion and coined money that had been hoarded in the royal treasuries of Persia passed into the victor's hands. Some 180,000 talents were put into circulation by him in the course of a decade, and this circumstance, coupled with the issue of a currency accepted throughout the empire, must have very radically effected business and money-dealing in the Hellenic world and beyond. It is not surprising therefore that the Hellenistic Age witnessed the growth of more ambitious methods in banking.[2]

---

[1] W. L. Westermann, *Journal of Economic and Business History*, 3 (1930), 42.

[2] Cf. M. Cary in Volume III of this *History*, 299–301; also W. L. Westermann, *op. cit.*, 44–54.

# CHAPTER XVI

# GREEK ART

## § 1. ARCHITECTURE

IT is not wholly accidental that surviving town sites in the Greek world are of Hellenistic or Graeco-Roman date. The cities of the classical period offered to any visitor the extremes of architectural magnificence and unrelieved squalor. Whereas temples were erected with infinite labour and distinguished by every artistic refinement, the towns themselves were aggregates of narrow and crooked streets. The houses were mostly small with at most one story above the ground-floor. How flimsy was their material, chiefly sun-dried brick, is illustrated by the tale of the Plataeans who, when they planned a rally against the enemy within the gates, in a few hours dug through the partition walls of their houses, like veritable burglars.[1] The irregularity of most cities was due to their age and to the fact that they had been enlarged very gradually. In the fifth century some new ideas became current. New cities were planned more regularly and laid out according to a geometric pattern, so that the side streets ran at right angles into the main thoroughfares. When Miletus was rebuilt after the Persian wars this innovation was followed. In 443 Thuria was constructed according to similar designs by Hippodamus of Miletus, who at Pericles' request had previously carried out some improvements in the Piraeus. The city of Rhodes, when completed soon after 408, was probably an even finer example of a town according to the new model, approximating more to those of the Hellenistic Age as known from excavations at Priene or Magnesia. But the great majority of cities were probably as dingy in the fourth century as they had been in the fifth. There was no proper drainage and sewage system, though in Athens, at least, a board of city inspectors

---

[1] Thucyd., II, 3. The Greek equivalent of a burglar is τοιχωρύχος.

(ἀστυνόμοι) supervised the disposal of rubbish. Water was sometimes brought from springs in the neighbouring country; yet the inhabitants of Piraeus as late as 430 depended on wells. That serious epidemics were rare under ordinary conditions may be attributed to a dry and sunny climate. The prevalence of marshy districts, however, at all times made malaria a serious menace. Even the houses of the wealthy seem to have been of modest size and unpretentious appearance, although the interior might be adorned by tapestries or by the murals of some fashionable painter. Houses of three or four stories are occasionally heard of; it was one of this type that Midias owned in Eleusis, and he incurred his neighbours' displeasure because it shut out the light from their own dwellings![1] The civic and business centre was the *agora* or market-place. On the eastern and western side of the Athenian *agora* stood the Painted Colonnade (στοὰ ποικίλη), decorated with frescoes by Polygnotus and Micon, and the Royal Colonnade (στοὰ βασίλειος). In the immediate vicinity were several municipal buildings, such as the Council House and the Metroon in which the public archives were kept. At a little distance, not far from the northern slopes of the Acropolis, stood the Town-hall. There is nothing to suggest that these structures, however adequate for utilitarian purposes, were in any way remarkable as buildings or comparable to the numerous examples of imposing secular architecture characteristic of the centuries after Alexander.

With few exceptions the monumental architecture of the fifth and fourth centuries as revealed by the extant remains was religious. During the first half of the period the Doric order was still in all but universal use in European Greece and among the Greeks of the West. The temple of Aphaia in Aegina was completed probably soon after the Persian invasions; the sculptured decoration more than the architectural features stamp it as the work of an age of transition. By *c.* 450 a new and imposing temple of Zeus was finished at Olympia. Even though it was the chief shrine in a national Greek sanctuary, it may perhaps also be regarded as an outstanding monument to the enterprise shown by the Eleans since they had reformed their state and changed their constitution. Many temples were raised in the first half of the

[1] Demosth., XXI, 158.

fifth century in the West, and the extant remains at Segesta, Selinus, and Acragas in Sicily and at Posidonia in Italy prove that the Greeks settled in these regions had little to learn from their kinsmen in the eastern Mediterranean. Though varying somewhat in size, these structures resemble one another closely in general plan. But the temple of Zeus Olympius at Acragas, which was still unfinished when the city was destroyed by the Carthaginians, was the work of architects seeking at all costs to avoid the conventional. In addition to being exceptionally large, the building had no peristyle. Instead, engaged columns were placed all round in the cella wall, seven on the short sides, fourteen on the long. The interior was divided lengthwise into three sections separated by rows of square pillars. Against the walls on the inside were pilasters, corresponding in position to the engaged columns on the outside. Yet a further novelty was the use of large sculptured figures, both male and female, to support parts of the architrave. But the example set at Acragas does not seem to have been followed elsewhere, so that the building remained an eccentricity.

But the finest examples of fifth-century architecture must be sought in Athens. Attica had suffered more severely than any other area in Greece at the hands of Xerxes and his men. During the last twenty years of his life Pericles set himself not merely to make good the destruction caused by the Persian wars but to beautify Athens' citadel in a manner worthy of an imperial state. The new temple in honour of Athena, the Parthenon, was begun in 447 and completed some nine years later. It was appreciably larger than the temple of Zeus at Olympia, the peristyle having eight columns on the short, and seventeen on the long sides compared with the six by thirteen columns of the earlier structure. Built entirely of white marble and decorated with three distinct sets of sculpture, it was the joint achievement of the architect, Ictinus, and the sculptor, Phidias, and represents Doric architecture in its most perfect form. Of the three sets of sculpture the metopes in high relief and the pedimental groups were normal features in Doric temples. But the continuous frieze which ran along the top of the walls of the cella on the outside was borrowed from Ionic structures. That there was in the latter part of the fifth century a growing taste for the Ionic order and that this style exerted some influence on contemporary Doric is abundantly clear. The great entrance gateway on the north-western side of the Athenian Acropolis, called the Propylaea, was the work of Mnesicles. Begun in 437, the main structure was finished by 432, but the complete design of the architect was never carried out owing to the outbreak of the Peloponnesian War. In this building Mnesicles combined the use of Ionic with Doric columns. The temple of Hephaestus, lying between the Dipylon Gate and the agora at Athens, was a Doric temple (6 × 13 columns) but contained some Ionic features. Finally the temple of Athena and Erechtheus (Erechtheum) and the small but graceful shrine of Athena Nike, both on the Acropolis, were built in the Ionic order throughout. An unusual feature of the Erechtheum was the use of six draped female figures (caryatids) in place of columns to support the architrave. This experiment, which recalls a similar use of human figures for strictly architectural purposes in the Olympieum at Acragas, does not appear to have been repeated.

But the influence of Ionic was not confined to Athenian buildings. Near Phigalea in Arcadia a fine Doric temple was constructed from the designs of Ictinus. In the interior of the cella he introduced engaged Ionic pillars, five a side. Between the last two stood a column with an acanthus capital, a very early example of Corinthian. In the fourth century the direct influence of Ionic on Doric proportions is very palpable, for the Doric columns used in the temple of Zeus at Nemea and in the temple of Athena Alea at Tegea are noticeably more slender than those found in the structures of Mnesicles and Ictinus. The temple at Tegea was the work of the sculptor-architect, Scopas, who, in addition to combining Doric with Ionic features introduced fourteen Corinthian half-columns in the interior of the cella.

In Asia Minor the fifth century seems to have been a period of artistic depression, since there are few traces of temple building at that time. But probably in 395 the old sixth-century temple of Artemis was burnt to the ground and was replaced by a handsome structure of approximately the same dimensions. No less than 127 Ionic columns were used in this dipteral temple. What almost appears to be a local taste was again satisfied by the architect when he decorated thirty-six of the columns with sculptured reliefs on the lowest drum; for similar ornamentation was used in the sixth-century building, but the fashion was not copied elsewhere. Somewhat later the people of Priene set up a small but beautiful temple to Athena, which was dedicated by Alexander the Great in 334.[1] The architect of this peripteral temple (6 × 11) in the Ionic order was Pythius, who also designed the grandiose tomb of Mausolus at Halicarnassus. This lofty building was composed of a substructure 42 feet in height, a cella surrounded by a colonnade of Ionic pillars resting on the substructure, and a stepped pyramid forming the roof and crowning the whole. On the summit stood a chariot, which may have contained statues of Mausolus and his consort, Artemisia. This was the second example in Asia Minor of an elaborate funerary structure in temple form—a conception more consonant with Egyptian than Greek ideas. Towards the end of the fifth century a small but graceful tomb in temple form had been erected at Assos in the Troad. It stood on a high podium and had an Ionic peristyle (4 × 6). The great decastyle dipteral temple of Apollo at Branchidae near Miletus was indeed begun in the fourth century, but was not finished till many years later, so that it belongs rather to the Hellenistic than to the classical age.

Secular structures in monumental architecture seem to have been rare in the fifth century and far from common even in the fourth. There was a certain general similarity in design in several covered halls intended for large concourses of people. The Odeum built by Pericles' orders in Athens was a rectangular auditorium whose roof was supported by some eighty interior columns. Much of its construction seems to have been of wood. More famous and roughly contemporary was the new and enlarged hall of initiation at Eleusis, the work of Ictinus. This *telesterion* measured 170 feet square and the roof was supported by six rows of seven columns. When, more than fifty years later, Megalopolis was built to be the federal capital of the new Arcadian federation, an assembly hall, called the Thersilion, was built. Its plan was rectangular and the roof was borne by interior pillars. Their disposition seems to have been

[1] Cf. Tod 184.

more skilfully contrived than had been the case in earlier buildings of the type, since they were arranged in radiating lines. In this way the view of fewer auditors was hampered and very possibly the acoustics also were improved. The interior pillars and the entrance porch of the building were in the Doric style.

In the age of Pericles, the golden age of the Attic drama, the theatres in Attica and elsewhere appear still to have been temporary structures of wood. Extant examples of stone theatres do not antedate the fourth century. One of the earliest, and in point of preservation the finest of all, was built at Epidaurus to the plans of the younger Polyclitus. The stone theatre at Athens, estimated to hold some 18,000 persons, was not completed until the time of Lycurgus. It is not known when it was begun. At Thoricus, not far from Laurium, a small theatre of somewhat eccentric plan can still be seen. That built at Megalopolis, though now but poorly preserved, seems to have accommodated even more spectators than the theatres at Athens or at Epidaurus. Not the least remarkable feature of these structures is their astonishing acoustic properties.

Military architecture in the fourth century is represented by the fine town walls of Messene built in the best ashlar masonry and strengthened at intervals by towers; by the remnants of town walls in Acarnania and of the walls across the Piraeus peninsula as restored after 394; by the defence works erected on Epipolae and Euryalus by Dionysius I; and by ruins of forts, such as can still be seen at Phyle in the foothills of Mt. Parnes. To this category also belongs the arsenal in Piraeus which was erected soon after 350 B.C. Though completely destroyed, it is known to have measured $55 \times 400$ Attic feet. The interior was divided into three longitudinal sections by seventy stone pillars, and light was admitted by a series of windows, measuring 2 feet by 3. There were three at each short end and one opposite to each intercolumniation in the side walls. There was also a wooden gallery running lengthwise on either side. The roof was timbered and covered with terra-cotta tiles. Externally the arsenal was unadorned save for two plain pediments and a triglyph frieze which was carried right round the building.

It cannot be said that the architecture of the fifth and fourth

centuries was characterized by any striking novelties. The
Doric order was perfected in the period and then slowly
declined in popularity as well as in technical excellence; the
Ionic order, which had almost always been used in Asia Minor
in preference to the other, made rapid headway in European
Greece, as we have seen, from *c.* 420 onwards. It remains
to mention one innovation, the Corinthian capital. Although
the full development of this architectural form was not
reached until the Hellenistic period, this type of capital was
used not infrequently in the fourth century for interior
decoration. The circular buildings, known as *tholoi*, at
Delphi and Epidaurus were externally Doric buildings; but
the former had in the interior ten slightly engaged Corinthian
columns, the latter, being considerably larger, had twenty-six
standing free. Yet another circular structure was the Philip-
peum in Olympia. It is supposed to have been built at the
order of Alexander the Great and had an outer colonnade
of eighteen Ionic pillars and twelve engaged Corinthian
columns in the interior. The use of Corinthian capitals in
the temples at Phigalea and Tegea has already been noted.
Lastly in the elegant Choragic monument of Lysicrates,
erected in Athens in 334, six engaged Corinthian columns
were used in conjunction with an Ionic entablature.

## § 2. SCULPTURE

No phenomenon in ancient history is more striking than
the manner in which the rapid political growth of Athens
after the Persian wars coincided with her emergence as the
artistic and intellectual leader of Hellas. The Asiatic Greeks,
pioneers of philosophical and scientific speculation, had been
foremost also in developing the arts. But before the middle
of the fifth century the chief artistic influences emanated no
longer from Miletus and Ephesus, Samos and Chios, but from
cities in European Greece, above all, from Athens. The list
of Greek sculptors who flourished in the one hundred and fifty
years after Xerxes' invasion is a long one. Yet, for the most
part, the modern student depends on literary notices of their
works and on copies of later date. Original examples of
sculpture in the round are relatively very scarce. Nearly all
that have survived are by unknown artists or else can be

assigned only tentatively to the "school" of this or that eminent sculptor. In consequence, the remains of architectural sculpture from temples of different date are peculiarly valuable, not merely because of their own worth, but because, being unquestionably genuine works, they illustrate beyond possibility of doubt at least some part of the artistic evolution of the period. The pediments of the temple of Aphaia in Aegina were finished before the first quarter of the fifth century had drawn to its close. The sculptured groups represented battle scenes of the Trojan War. The individual figures still betray a lingering archaism in the treatment of the face, but in the matter of pose they show an astonishing advance on the work of the previous generation. The artist, to prove that he is no longer bound by the trammels of a stiff frontality, has gone to the opposite extreme in seeking to portray every variety of motion; for, while some of the figures are at rest, others represent kneeling archers, or dying warriors, or even wounded men on the point of falling backwards. By an artistic convention, and in accordance with the Greek artist's love of the nude male form, the figures are naked save for their armour. Regarded as a whole these pedimental groups also mark the beginning of a new age. Earlier sculptors, as we know from the remains of archaic pediments from the Athenian Acropolis, had experimented long with only partial success to adapt a group of figures to a triangular space. The Aeginetan sculptor, by using kneeling and recumbent figures as a natural and integral part of his plastic subject, had at last solved the problem.

About thirty years separate the Aeginetan pediments from the sculptures of the temple of Zeus at Olympia. Twelve metopes in high relief portray the labours of Heracles. Although the general presentation is lively, there is a surprising amount of stiffness in the treatment of details. This is the more remarkable when they are contrasted with the pedimental groups. Indeed, the latter are so superior both in conception and technique that they must be from the hand of another artist. In the central figure of Apollo in the west pediment we see an ideal presentation of the young male athlete, a subject which in the next generation Polyclitus the Elder was to make peculiarly his own. The best preserved figure from the east pediment is an aged seer reclining on the ground and showing in his face an awful foreboding of misfortune to come. If there is still a slight archaism in the treatment of the hair, the expression demonstrates the complete mastery of the artist in the naturalistic presentment of the human countenance.

With the Parthenon sculptures we reach the finest achievement of the Greeks in architectural sculpture. Although the general design may be attributed with confidence to Phidias, its execution was entrusted to various hands under his general supervision. Forty-six metopes were adorned with scenes from several mythological episodes. The pedimental sculptures portrayed the birth of Athena from the head of Zeus and the contest of Athena and Poseidon for lordship over Attica. Finally, the Ionic frieze running round the cella wall brings vividly before us the central episode in the Greater Panathenaic Festival—the solemn procession of the Athenians from the city to the temple of the goddess on the Acropolis. Varied as is the treatment of the groups on the metopes and vigorous as is their conception, their technical execution both in the treatment of the nude and of the draperies is not flawless. But such imperfections are absent in the pedimental groups and the frieze. Shockingly damaged as the former are, so that the disposition of the whole and of the individual figures is far from certain, one can still marvel at the exquisite modelling of the reclining " Theseus " or the torso of Poseidon and the no less masterly handling of masses of drapery in the female figures. The frieze, carved in rather low relief, astonishes by its variety of subject no less than by its technical perfection. Old men and young, maidens and matrons, horsemen mounted and leading their steeds, beasts destined for sacrifice, form a symphony of rhythmic motion and a superb contrast with the stately repose of the seated deities who fill the frieze at the eastern end of the temple. No Greek artist ever executed a finer architectural relief. The frieze, which by a unique arrangement ran round the inside of the cella in the temple at Phigalea, so that the entire scheme could be viewed by the spectator from one spot, portrayed most vigorously the battle of Greeks with Amazons and the battle between Centaurs and Lapiths. But there is in the work an excess of violent motion and some lack of variety in the treatment of the groups. Individual figures, like that of a dying Amazon, are so contorted as to be both ugly and anatomically incorrect. The same subjects are treated on two friezes that decorated the Mausoleum at Halicarnassus. While there is more variety in the scenes than on the Phigalean frieze, the individual figures are more widely spaced. The effect is to increase the impression of restlessness and at the same time to interfere with the most essential quality of a frieze, continuity of action. The changed taste of the fourth century is also very apparent in the more slender proportions of both the male and female figures and in the modelling of the draperies which are of the lightest texture, fluttering in the breeze behind the female figures or blowing meretriciously aside to reveal the nude form below. Perhaps the most impressive example of sculpture in relief that has survived from the fourth century is the marble sarcophagus by an unknown artist found at Tyre in 1887. It dates from the second half of the century and is adorned on the two long sides with a battle between Alexander and the Persians, while the short sides are ornamented with another skirmish between Persians and Greeks and with a panther hunt. The figures are carved in rather high relief and are closely massed, the total effect being one of vigorous life without extravagance or striving after sensational effects. Other notable features of this work are the extensive remains of colour employed to enhance the effect and the life-like portrait heads of Alexander and Parmenio.

One of the most permanent influences on the statuary of the period was that of the athletic festivals, which caused not merely a fondness for depicting the nude male form, but, as we see especially in the work of the Elder Polyclitus in the fifth and of Lysippus in the fourth century, a desire to establish an artistic canon of male beauty. The tendency is already very marked amongst the predecessors of Phidias. Pythagoras indeed might take the titles of his subjects from Greek mythology, but the ancient descriptions of his lame Philoctetes, of his Apollo fighting the Pytho, or of his duel between Eteocles and Polynices, leave no doubt that these works were essentially variations of athletic types. His contemporary, Myron (*floruit c.* 460), was the author of the well-known discus-thrower—a work known to us only from later copies—and of a statue of the most famous runner of the day,

Ladas, which showed the athlete not in repose but on tip-toe and with every muscle set for the race. His figure of the satyr, Marsyas, shown as he is starting back in alarm before Athena, was yet another work in which he reproduced the male form in a state of extreme muscular tension. The greatest of the Peloponnesian sculptors during the fifth century, the Argive Polyclitus, was famed for the perfect symmetry of his athletes. His youth with a spear (Doryphorus) and his youth tying a fillet about his head (Diadumenus) were, like the works of Myron and Pythagoras, cast in bronze. Extant copies in marble show that both were studies, based on a profound knowledge of anatomy, of arrested motion. The weight of the body rested on one leg, while the other was lightly poised and drawn back a little way, the head being inclined towards the leg on which the weight rested. It was a characteristic of Polyclitus, and indeed of Peloponnesian artists in general, that they created a type of youth or young man of heavier build than that favoured by Attic artists. Polyclitus also made use of his favourite pose in an Amazon that was later to be seen in the Artemisium at Ephesus. To judge from extant copies, this work was as finely proportioned as the Doryphorus, but, as in that statue, the total effect was one of massive strength rather than grace.

In the fifth century many of the older cult-images, whose venerable age could not compensate for their artistic crudity, were replaced by statues from the hand of the greatest Hellenic sculptors. Most famous of all were the two masterpieces of Phidias, one in the temple of Zeus at Olympia, the other in the Parthenon at Athens. Both were of colossal size and fashioned in a rare and costly technique, gold and ivory applied to a wooden framework. It is impossible to form any conception of these works from late and small copies or from representations on coins, but the testimony of the ancients themselves was unanimous in praising their beauty and stressing the feeling of awe that they inspired in the beholder. Almost as admired as the Zeus and Athena of Phidias was the gold and ivory image of Hera at Argos, the work of Polyclitus. But the portrayal of members of the Greek Pantheon was not confined to cult statues; indeed it would be difficult to name any artist of note who did not portray one or more divinities. Calamis of Athens, the contemporary of Myron, was the author of one of the most highly prized statues of antiquity, Aphrodite, Saviour of men (Sosandra). An ancient critic singles out for special praise her "noble and unconscious smile" and "the comely arrangement and order of her drapery." Calamis seems to have cultivated a severe simplicity, and some modern critics have sought to assign to his school or influence the relief now known as the Ludovisi Throne and the magnificent life-sized statue in bronze of a charioteer, the most precious discovery of the French excavators at Delphi. Phidias' other portrayals of divinities included a colossal Athena in bronze which stood upon the Athenian Acropolis, his Lemnian Athena, regarded by Lucian as one of the sculptor's finest works, a gold and ivory statue of Aphrodite at Elis, and an Apollo Parnopius. The catalogue of deities represented plastically by Myron is even longer. The medium predominantly used by these sculptors for statues or groups in the round was bronze, and this fact is only one reason among many why later copies, which are generally in marble, can only give an approximate notion of those fifth-century masterpieces. The scarcity of life-size statues in bronze makes a recent discovery unusually precious. A statue slightly over life-size was fished out of the sea off Cape Artemisium in the autumn of 1928. On stylistic grounds it can be dated to c. 460 and represents a bearded male divinity striding impetuously forward. The raised right hand may once have held a trident or a thunderbolt, for critics are divided in their interpretation of the work, which may portray either Poseidon or Zeus. The modelling of the torso and of the hands and arms, which though broken off were also recovered, is extremely delicate; but the most striking feature is the head with its flowing locks and deep-set eye-sockets in which the eyes were once inlaid, as was the case with the charioteer from Delphi.

Towards the end of the fifth century marble, which hitherto had been used chiefly for architectural sculpture, began to be increasingly favoured for statues and groups in the round. Thus Agoracritus and Alcamenes, both pupils of Phidias, although they still worked largely in bronze, occasionally used the other medium to express their art. Fifty years later the opposite tendency is seen in an artist like Praxiteles, who worked both in marble and bronze but showed a decided preference for the former. His example does not seem to have been extensively followed; for of the two artists whom antiquity ranked with Praxiteles, Lysippus worked exclusively in bronze, and Scopas, though expert in the use of marble for architectural sculpture, as in the temple of Athena at Tegea, preferred bronze for his single statues. Of Praxiteles' art it is possible to form a clear conception from his extant statue of Hermes holding the infant Dionysus, which was found by the excavators at Olympia.[1] Contrasted with the athletes of Polyclitus, this study of the nude male is remarkable for its more slender proportions and for a greater delicacy in modelling the muscles and flesh. The head, too, as usual in the work of Attic artists, is less square and the features more finely chiselled. More famous in antiquity were Praxiteles' several statues of Eros, whom he portrayed as a youth on the threshold of manhood, and his Apollo Sauroctonus. All these works were essentially variations of a single theme—the young male figure, nude and in a placid, reposeful attitude. Of his female figures the most renowned was a statue of Aphrodite made for the Cnidians. He was an innovator in that he represented the goddess without draperies, a conception impossible in the previous century. The Cnidian Aphrodite is only known from indifferent copies, yet even these suffice to show that the work combined the outstanding characteristics of Praxiteles' art, calm beauty in pose and expression and an exquisite sensibility for form.

The art of Scopas appears to have been in many ways the very antithesis to that of his contemporary. The ancients themselves regarded his works as the very embodiment of passion and emotional depth, qualities that especially distinguished two of his most famous creations—a Bacchant shown in a state of inspired frenzy and a group of Eros, Himeros, and Pothos (Love, Desire, and Yearning) in which he personified three emotional states associated with the passion of love. It is difficult to judge Scopas' achievement adequately, for the heads from the pedimental sculptures at Tegea are badly preserved and afford only a very imperfect glimpse into the artist's manner. This lack of knowledge is

---

[1] The genuineness of this statue has been questioned by some archaeologists. Cf. *American Journ. Arch.*, XXXV (1931), *passim*.

the more to be regretted since it is very evident that his example inspired much of the greater realism and even extravagance in subject and treatment characteristic of some phases of Hellenistic art. Could one but be certain that the magnificent statue of a seated Demeter now in the British Museum was a product of the Scopaic school in the fourth century, one would have proof that Scopas could portray a calm deep pathos as finely as the more turbulent emotions.

The leading artist of the later fourth century was Lysippus. He was, moreover, a representative of Peloponnesian art, whereas Praxiteles was an Athenian and Scopas a native of Paros. True to the earlier traditions of Peloponnesian sculptors, Lysippus had a marked predilection for athletic figures. Their proportions, which were noticeably slimmer than those of the Polyclitan athletes, determined the artistic canon of the later fourth century, even as the Doryphorus was regarded as the norm in the fifth. But Lysippus' output of artistic creations was both large and varied. He made many statues of divinities, some of which, like the famous Heracles made for the people of Taras, were variations on the athletic theme, while his statue of Poseidon standing with one foot resting on a rock and holding a trident in his hand became the accepted type of the god of the sea. But the most important achievement of Lysippus in the history of art is his portraiture of Alexander the Great. He represented the conqueror many times and combined a realistic likeness with a certain idealization of treatment. These portraits permanently influenced the sculptural type of Hellenistic art and were an inspiration also to the engravers of coins. Moreover, merely as a portrait sculptor, Lysippus may be said to have initiated a new form of art; for, though Cresilas had made a likeness of Pericles, and the head of the Mausolus statue in the British Museum is clearly a realistic portrait, not an idealized type, portraiture was rare and found little favour in the classical period of Greek art.

Brief mention must suffice for a long series of Attic tombstones which prove that the love of plastic art was not confined to a group but had permeated the people as a whole. Most of them were made in the fourth century, but the artisans who carved them were for the most part conservative

# GREEK ART

and influenced by the architectural reliefs of the fifth century. Thus the tombstone of the young mounted soldier, Dexileos, on which he is depicted in the act of slaying his adversary, is clearly indebted for its general conception to the Parthenon metopes. It is on these tombstones that scenes from the everyday life of the deceased are portrayed. Such subjects, though common enough on vase-paintings, were too trifling for the sculptors of the fifth and fourth centuries. It was only in the Hellenistic Age that *genre* scenes plastically expressed attained a wide popularity.

### § 3. PAINTING AND THE MINOR ARTS

Painting is the one art practised by the Greeks of which a fair estimate is impossible. No number of references or descriptions in literature can compensate for the complete loss of the works themselves. Extant frescoes of Graeco-Roman date, like those found at Herculaneum and Pompeii, may sometimes be copies of paintings from the classical age. But their value for appraising these earlier compositions is slight, partly because the technique had changed not a little in the interval, but chiefly because artistically they are themselves of very inferior merit. Indeed it is probable that the designs on some Attic red-figure vases are a safer guide towards gaining some notion of the manner in which a painter, like Polygnotus (*c.* 470), treated mythological subjects.

A native of Thasos, Polygnotus was brought to Athens by Cimon. There he spent his artistic life and in due course was rewarded with the gift of citizenship. In collaboration with Micon and Panaenus, brother of Phidias, he was responsible for decorating several public edifices, of which the best known was the Painted Colonnade in the *agora*, with life-size frescoes. He executed similar commissions in several other cities, and at Delphi he adorned the walls of the Hall (Lesche) of the Cnidians. He took his subjects from the epic cycle, such as the Sack of Ilium which he depicted twice—at Athens and at Delphi—and the descent of Odysseus into Hades. His associate Micon's best-known work was a fresco of the battle of Marathon. These artists used only very few colours: black, white, red, and yellow, and they applied them flat so that there was no modelling of the figures. There was an absence of light and shade and little perspective. Since these compositions of Polygnotus, in spite of their obvious limitations, were greatly admired by contemporaries, and later critics praised especially his outstanding skill in expressing character in the face of his subjects, we must suppose that he was a superb draughtsman. Towards the end of the fifth century a noticeable advance in technique occurred. There is great significance in the nickname, Shadow-painter (σκιαγράφος), given to the painter Apollodorus. His experiments in chiaroscuro influenced both Zeuxis and Parrhasius. They paid great attention to shading and perspective and were no longer satisfied with the flat colours and two-dimensional art of an earlier generation. The subjects that they portrayed continued to be taken mainly from mythology. In addition, they were pioneers in a new fashion which preferred easel pictures to large murals. A slightly younger contemporary, Timanthes, was the author of a much-admired Sacrifice of Iphigeneia. A well-known fresco in Pompeii is probably a copy of Timanthes' picture.

According to the judgment of the ancients themselves painting reached its zenith in the later fourth century with Apelles. Like his predecessors, he occasionally essayed figure subjects on a large scale, and a Pompeian mosaic representing a battle between Alexander and Darius III is copied in all likelihood from one of his more notable paintings. But his fame rested even more on his portraiture, especially as he made several likenesses of Alexander the Great. In this branch of his art he was as much a pioneer as Lysippus was in portrait sculpture. Moreover, in showing a decided fondness for allegory and personification of abstract ideas Apelles was the forerunner of a widespread tendency in Hellenistic art.

Besides *tempera*, which was the usual method adopted by these various artists, the encaustic process had been fully developed by the beginning of the fourth century. In this technique the colours were mixed with wax and the mixture after being heated was applied with brush and spatula to either wood or ivory. The process, which was both slow and difficult, was only suitable for small pictures; but, though the size of an encaustic painting might be small, its colour effects were far more brilliant than anything that could be achieved in *tempera*. The first great artist in encaustic was Pausias, who painted children and still-life. Later in the fourth century Antiphilus showed his versatility by using both encaustic and *tempera* with success. His liking for *genre* was symptomatic of a new taste which, as has already been noted, was characteristic of the centuries that followed.

If our knowledge of classical Greek painting is limited to the names of artists and to certain general notions about their artistic aims and methods, the art of vase-painting can still be studied in the greatest detail from a mass of material. By the fifth century the manufacture of highly decorated vases appears to have become almost a monopoly of Attic potters and vase-painters. Other centres indeed continued to manufacture their own wares for ordinary household use and generally for local consumption. But the Athenian red-figured (R.F.) pottery which by the beginning of the century had quite superseded the older black-figure ware, was being exported to all parts of the Hellenic world. The shapes of R.F. pottery are very varied, from delicate low-stemmed cups and small oil bottles to large amphoras and mixing-bowls. Except for the absence of historical subjects there is hardly any limit to the diversity of the designs.[1] There are mythological scenes in endless profusion. Athletic scenes were always popular, while episodes from daily life, especially banqueting scenes, had almost as much appeal for the buying public. Of great interest also are scenes illustrating religious cults, especially the worship of Dionysus. As might have been expected, certain artists tended to specialize in certain types of subject. The cups of Euphronius, for example, are decorated with elaborate scenes from mythology and the epic cycle. It became increasingly common for two men to collaborate in the making of a vase, one being the potter the other the painter. In the vases of the severe style (*c.* 500–460), the signatures of potter or painter, and sometimes of both, occur frequently. For reasons that are obscure the fashion changed in time, so that in the vases of the free style (*c.* 460–420) this information is usually absent. In the more

[1] A vase now in the Louvre at Paris, which is decorated with a picture of Croesus on the funeral pyre, is the nearest approach to a vase ornamented with a historical design. But the voluntary immolation of the last Lydian king, a theme treated also by the poet Bacchylides in the fifth century, belonged to legend rather than to history.

ornate style which came into fashion during the last decades of the fifth century, one artist, Midias, signed his works. In his vases and those of his contemporaries certain innovations are to be observed : there is more subsidiary ornamentation, additional colours are used, though sparingly, and there is an over-elaboration in the main design which smacks of preciosity and contrasts with the freshness and naturalism of vases from the preceding periods. This tendency became more marked in the fourth century. The industry gradually declined and, though there was a slight revival after *c.* 350, within fifty years vase-painting at Athens was dead. During most of the fourth century, moreover, the Athenians had serious rivals in the potters and vase-painters of Apulia. The style of these south Italian wares was over ornate and there was a tendency to overcrowd the surface of the vase with subsidiary decoration. A special series of vases painted with scenes from the comic drama have an interest of their own. But in Apulia the vase-painter's art also disappeared soon after the opening of the Hellenistic Age.

Besides the R.F. ware, vases of a different technique enjoyed a considerable vogue in Athens during the second half of the fifth century. Oil bottles (λήκυθοι), intended for funerary use, and small cups were the two shapes regarded as suitable for polychrome decoration. That part of the vase which was to receive the design was covered with white or pale cream paint. On this light background the picture was applied in several colours. The general effect was very pleasing, but the painted decoration was far less durable than that of the R.F. ware.

Bronze statuettes and utensils were manufactured in various regions of the Greek world—at Corinth, Argos, and Athens, in Arcadia and in south Italy. The statuettes which are often of the most delicate workmanship reflect the prevailing fashions in sculpture. Thus there was found on the Athenian Acropolis a miniature reproduction of Phidias' Athena Promachus, while a whole series of small athletic figures from the later fifth century are of Argive make and clearly inspired by the works of Polyclitus. Similarly, in the next century the statues of Praxiteles and Lysippus were copied by the bronze-worker. Very admirable, too, was the *repoussé* work in bronze in which the Greeks of southern

Italy excelled. It reached its finest development in the fourth century with such works as the Siris bronzes now in the British Museum.

The engraving of gems and coins, like all the other arts, made rapid strides from the beginning of the fifth century. The influence of sculpture and painting is again very evident on the designs of gems, so that heroic and athletic themes predominate. Portrait heads are found occasionally, but do not become common till the Hellenistic period. Some of the engravers signed their works, and several of the finest extant gems from the fifth century bear the name of Dexamenus. The variety of coin types is as astonishing as their unsurpassed technical execution. The Athenians, indeed, seem to have cared little about the artistic merits of their tetradrachms, being concerned only with their commercial soundness, that is to say, the purity of the metal which remained unimpaired as long as Athenian independence endured. But in the majority of cities the coin engravers sought to give the fullest scope to their art. While it is possible to point to many fine designs on coins from the Greek homeland, a handsome head of Zeus on the coins of Elis, Hera on those of Argos, or Apollo on those of Amphipolis, the summit of achievement was attained by the Greeks of the West. No more beautiful coins have ever been produced than the medallions and tetradrachms of Syracuse during the last quarter of the fifth century; and the issues of other Sicilian and Italiot Greek towns were little inferior. Only in portraiture of the realistic kind did the Hellenistic Age have a new and striking contribution to make to the art of coin engraving.

### § 4. GREEK MUSIC

That music, as practised amongst them, was highly esteemed by the Greeks is beyond dispute. Singing was an essential part of education in Dorian as in Ionian states. Writers on educational theory, like Plato and Aristotle, were at pains to define what the character and limits of musical training for the young should be. Musical competitions were held regularly at the Thargelia, Panathenaea, Pythia, and other religious festivals. Music was an essential part of the choral interludes in tragedy and comedy, as it was of the

Epinician Odes and other poems of Pindar; and the chief reason for the uncertainty which scholars still feel about the metrical structure of Pindar's odes is our complete ignorance of the music to which they were sung. Choruses sang in unison or in octaves. The accompaniment on the harp (*cithara*), lyre, or *auloi*—pipes with the musical pitch of the middle and low registers of a clarinet—appears to have been of a simple contrapuntal type, and, where several instruments were employed, might be in two or more parts. Virtuosos on the *cithara*, like Phrynis, who won the first prize at the Panathenaic festival in 446, or Timotheus (*fl. c.* 390), had a large following of admirers. In their rhapsodic solos the words were subordinate to the instrumental part and, as can still be judged from the remains of Timotheus' *Persians*, were often vapid or bombastic, but so strung together as to afford the maximum opportunity for the arpeggios and roulades of the instrument. The variety of modes and scales was considerable. The theory of their interrelation and of acoustics attracted not a few inquirers from Pythagoras' time on. We learn that different modes expressed different emotional states, and Plato's strictures on certain modes as unsuitable for educational purposes are well known. Nevertheless the modern student, even if he is familiar with the difference between the major and minor keys of the modern diatonic scale and realizes that on a stringed instrument played with the bow a composition written in a key with four or five flats will tend to sound sombre, owing to the absence of open strings, will find it difficult, in the absence of actual choral or instrumental works from the classical period of Greece, to appraise the artistic merits and *nuances* of Greek music.

## CHAPTER XVII

## GREEK LANGUAGE AND LITERATURE

### § 1. SPOKEN AND WRITTEN DIALECTS

A BROAD classification adopted by specialists in philology divides the dialects of the Greek world into two broad groups, an eastern and a western. The one includes the several varieties of Ionic, Attic, the so-called Aeolic dialects of Thessaly, Boeotia, and Aeolis in Asia Minor, and the speech of Arcadia and Cyprus; the western group embraces many variants of Doric together with the kindred tongues of Phocis, Locris, Elis, and north-western Greece. In all there were some two dozen dialects which were still being spoken in the Hellenic world of the classical period. Had their use been merely oral we should know little of their characteristics, but they were also written. City-states customarily employed their local vernacular in official documents and there was no standard form of Greek speech universally used for diplomatic purposes. When a state acted as arbiter of a dispute between two others, the record of the arbitration was set down in the dialect of the arbitrator. Thus, when Argos gave a ruling on the differences between the people of Cnossus and Tylissus in Crete or adjudicated between the people of Melos and Cimolos, the settlement was recorded in the Argive dialect.[1] These numerous varieties of Greek had, however, little influence on the literary productions of the period, for the outstanding development of the fifth and fourth centuries is the triumph of Attic as the medium for dramatic poetry and for every type of prose. The literary dialect traditionally associated with choral lyrics had long been Doric with an admixture of Lesbian-Aeolic and epic forms. It was used by Pindar and by his younger contemporary, Bacchylides, but it was not a dialect that was spoken anywhere.

[1] See Tod 33 and 179.

Herodotus and the writings going under the name of Hippocrates are composed in a literary variety of Ionic; literary also was the Doric dialect favoured by writers belonging to the Pythagorean brotherhood in southern Italy. The native Sicilian comedy of Epicharmus, however, was written in the genuine vernacular of Dorian Syracuse. To a sophisticated audience of Athenians towards the end of the fifth century the appearance of a Boeotian or a Megarian or a Laconian speaking his particular *patois* in the plays of Aristophanes was a figure of broad comedy. The rapid advance of Athens to a position of political and intellectual leadership in Greece exercised a profound influence. The tragic and comic drama was the creation of Athenian playwrights who used their native tongue with amazing skill. Attic Greek next became the language of artistic prose, even though it owed so much of its earliest development to non-Athenians, like Gorgias. But the political domination of Athens in the Aegean also reacted in the matter of speech on her allies and subjects, with the result that Ionic was the first of the spoken dialects to become modified by Attic usage. This process of assimilation was, it is true, arrested for half a century because of the downfall of the Athenian empire. But with the rise of Macedonia, and especially as the result of Alexander's conquests, a more rapid change took place. In the interval, moreover, Attic speech had itself been affected in some respects by Ionic, and it was this language—the Attic κοινή —that was spread by Alexander's troops and under the successors of Alexander throughout the Near and Middle East. By the end of the fourth century Ionic had become virtually extinct and the κοινή had begun to modify other Greek dialects. Nevertheless their use by city-states in their documents and decrees continued for several centuries after Alexander's time.[1]

## § 2. ELEMENTARY EDUCATION

In Sparta and the city-states of Crete the educational system that had been in force for several centuries continued unchanged in our period.[2] Its sole purpose was to make

[1] For the κοινή in the Hellenistic Age cf. M. Cary in Volume III of this *History*.
[2] For the Spartan " agoge " see H. Michell, *Sparta*, ch. vi.

hardy, " eugenic " men and women out of the children of the community—to fit the boys for soldiering when they had grown up and the girls to become the healthy mothers of lusty sons. Little attention seems to have been paid to intellectual training, although tuition in choral singing is mentioned as a regular feature of Spartan education. Nevertheless it is obvious that at least some of the Spartiates must have learnt to read and write ; but universal instruction in the three Rs is nowhere attested. In the rest of Greece the state assumed no responsibility for the education of its future citizens. At Athens, indeed, the sons of citizens who had been killed in battle were educated at the public expense ; but even for Athens there is no unequivocal proof that the state compelled its citizens to educate their boys.[1]

Schools for elementary education were uniformly private undertakings, and there were no ordinances to ensure that the teachers were properly qualified. In consequence we must suppose that the standard of instruction varied greatly, although competition probably soon drove an utterly incompetent schoolmaster out of business. Boys attended such schools from the age of seven to thirteen or fourteen years. They learnt to read and write and then went on to study a fair selection of the poetic literature of Greece. Homer had the place of honour in the school curriculum ; and, when it is remembered how important a role memorization played in the teaching of literature, at a time when none but the master had a copy of the poem to be studied, it is safe to say that Niceratus, who could repeat the whole of the *Iliad* and *Odyssey*, was not by any means unique amongst his contemporaries.[2] Portions of Hesiod, selections from the Lyric and Gnomic poets and, in the fourth century, also from the great tragic dramatists of Athens, together with Aesop's *Fables* and the *Maxims of Cheiron*, which must have been a very typical school *Reader* of the improving sort, were the other works ordinarily studied by schoolboys. Some attention was also given to music, at least in the better schools. This took the form of instruction in choral singing and in playing on the seven-stringed lyre, and occasionally in playing the *aulos* or

[1] The passage in Plato, *Crito*, 50D, hardly proves more than that universal education was customary for Athenian boys. The Solonian laws cited in Aeschines, *In Timarchum*, § 9 ff., are almost certainly spurious.
[2] Xenophon, *Symposium*, 3, 5.

pipe. But though boys learning to play this wind-instrument were often represented on the R.F. vases during the first half of the fifth century, this type of music later fell into disfavour in Athens. It came to be regarded as unsuitable for youth because of its associations with religious cults of an orgiastic kind and with the frivolous entertainments of the banquet. In Boeotia, however, the *aulos* was found unobjectionable. It may be questioned whether arithmetic was part of the regular school curriculum before the second half of the fourth century. But the average boy, whether he learnt it in the class-room or outside, became acquainted with the weights and measures in daily use and was taught to do simple sums with the use of his fingers. More elaborate sums were worked out with the aid of a reckoning-board or *abacus*, in which the different pebbles had varying values according to their position. During the fourth century drawing was also included occasionally among school subjects.

No less important in the eyes of the Greeks than the education of the mind (μουσική) was the training of the body (γυμναστική). Although theorists, like Plato and Aristotle, advocated that μουσική and γυμναστική should be taught at different stages in a boy's life, in ordinary practice these two branches of education were carried on concurrently. The gymnastic training was graduated according to the age and strength of the boys, beginning with lessons in deportment and simple physical exercises and then passing on to recognized sports, like wrestling, sprinting,[2] jumping, and boxing. At the age of thirteen or fourteen the sons of the poorer citizens and resident aliens ended their formal education. They then went on to their father's farm or were apprenticed to a trade. The Higher Education provided from the last quarter of the fifth century onwards by the Sophists entailed considerable expense, so that only the wealthier members of the community could afford to let their boys take advantage of the opportunities for intellectual development that it offered.

There is no clear evidence that girls before the Hellenistic

---

[1] Plato, *Republic*, 537B ; Aristotle, *Politics*, 1339A7.

[2] Whether schoolboys practised long-distance running may be doubted. At any rate at the Olympic Festival boys could only participate in a short race of about 200 yards.

Age ordinarily shared in such educational benefits as were enjoyed by their brothers. Rather they were instructed in domestic duties by their mothers in the home. For a girl to have learnt to read and write or to have any intellectual accomplishments was rare. Women with literary or artistic tastes in the classical period formed a very small company indeed. The mother of the Cyrenaic Aristippus was herself interested in philosophic questions, Lesbos had produced Sappho, and Thebes was the home of Corinna in the late sixth and of Erinna in the early third century. Aspasia, the Milesian, mistress of Pericles, was treated by him and the members of his circle as an intellectual equal. The Greek dramatists portrayed not only masterful women, like Clytemnestra or Medea, but gave the world a gallery of heroines of more virtuous mould in Deianira, Antigone, Iphigeneia, Electra, and Andromache. It may be argued that the appreciation of Athenian audiences for these female characters affords some index to their own attitude to womanhood; and it is no doubt true that the average Greek was a reasonably good husband, brother, or son. Nevertheless, under Athenian law—and there is no reason to suppose that the laws of other city-states were substantially different[1]—women were under various disabilities. They took no part in public, and very little in social life. The prevailing attitude towards women did not pass wholly unchallenged. That greater freedom for the sex was beginning to be debated in some quarters is suggested by the publication of Aristophanes' *Women in Parliament* (393 B.C.). It is a satire on women's rights—dramatically it is the weakest of Aristophanes' extant plays—which would have been pointless if feminist ideas had not been in the air at that time. A little later Plato in his ideal commonwealth gave the women of the Guardian class virtual equality with the male Guardians in the matter of physical and intellectual education; but at the same time he advocated community in women and children as well as in property. But in the main the position of women in the fourth century did not differ from their position in the fifth, and Ischomachus'

---

[1] The testamentary laws of Gortyn were, however, somewhat more liberal towards women. A woman's property did not pass wholly into her husband's hands when she married, although he had the use of it. On a man's decease the daughters received some share of his personal estate.

well-trained young housewife corresponded pretty closely to the popular notion of what a woman should be and of what was her proper sphere.[1]

### § 3. LYRIC POETRY

At the beginning of our period lyric poetry was obsolescent. Sappho, Alcaeus, and Anacreon had no successors, and it was only the choral lyric, developed in the earlier age especially by Alcman and Stesichorus, that found its greatest exponent in the fifth century. Simonides of Ceos, though he did not die until *c.* 467, belongs essentially to the older generation. But his example of commemorating in choral odes victories won at the athletic festivals, instead of confining himself, like earlier poets, to the praise of gods and heroes, found an imitator in the Theban Pindar (*c.* 518–446). Although Pindar experimented with almost every type of lyric composition suited for choral presentation, his fame now rests on forty-four *Epinician Odes*. Nearly all were written for victors at one or other of the four major festivals—the Olympian, Pythian, Nemean, and Isthmian Games. It may be added that his great reputation in antiquity was won primarily with these poems. He had many aristocratic patrons—the Alcmaeonidae at Athens and Aleuadae in Thessaly, Arcesilas of Cyrene, above all, the Sicilian rulers Hieron of Syracuse and Theron of Acragas, at whose courts he resided for two years. Himself filled with aristocratic pride, he was a thorough conservative in both his political and religious outlook. While he occasionally strove to rationalize a myth or to gloss over a legend of the gods, if it portrayed them in a base light, he was apparently unaffected by the philosophic and scientific ideas of the sixth and fifth centuries. On one of the rare occasions that he strays away from orthodox religious ideas it is not philosophy but the mystic doctrines of the Orphic sect, with their promise of reward and punishment after death, on which he expatiates at length. In politics he was an admirer of autocracy and aristocracy, forms of government that became rapidly extinct in the fifth century. The spread of democratic ideas after the Persian wars filled him with distaste, since the society in which they flourished had nothing in common with the nobility that he

[1] See Xenophon, *Oeconomicus*.

idealized. His *Odes*, then, are, save rarely, not remarkable for profound ideas on religion or on political and social questions. But no Greek poet had a more astounding wealth of poetic diction or enriched his theme with a more varied and lofty imagery. And the finest of the myths that he introduced into his *Odes* as a link between the present and the heroic past are unforgettable for the swiftness of their imagination and their epic splendour.

The discovery in 1897 of a papyrus in Egypt made known to the world some poems by Bacchylides, a younger contemporary of Pindar who had hitherto been little more than a name. Thirteen epinician odes and six hymns in honour of gods or heroes were recovered in various states of preservation and prove him to have been a tuneful minor poet. The narrative portions of his poems, as when he describes the self-immolation of Croesus or the adventures of Theseus, are agreeable and melodious. But his poetry, taken as a whole, lacks both the dignity and the grandeur of Pindar's work.

### § 4. THE DRAMA

The origins and earliest development of the Athenian drama lie outside the scope of this volume. Dramatic performances had been a central feature of the Greater Dionysia for some decades before the close of the Persian Wars. The festival was organized by the state and strict regulations, for whose observance the archons were responsible, governed the whole procedure. Three poets were chosen to compete for the tragic prize and three for the prize for comedy, since it was probably not until the early years of the fourth century that the number of authors competing for the latter was increased to five. The choice of the trainers of the choruses and of the chief actor, when the poet himself did not fulfil this function, as had been customary in early days, rested, like the choice of the poets, with the archons. The formal routine of dramatic representations at the Greater Dionysia had, then, become fixed by 501-500. Similar ordinances were introduced at the old rustic festival of the Lenaea when performances began to be given there, first of comedy (*c.* 446) and a few years later (*c.* 433 ?) of tragedy. But the drama itself at the close of the Persian Wars was still in a formative stage. Only two actors were used in tragedy and the chorus played a leading part in the dramatic action. This simple form of play can still be studied in the earliest of the extant plays of Aeschylus, the *Suppliants*. The introduction of a second actor was traditionally ascribed to him, but it was not until a third actor was added *c.* 468 that a more elaborate dramatic technique became possible. The tragic poet who was chosen to compete at the festival was required to offer a trilogy of three tragedies followed by a satyric drama. For some time the three plays of the trilogy dealt with successive or related episodes of the same story, but Sophocles abandoned this convention and presented three tragedies, each of which treated a separate subject. Not only his younger contemporaries and successors but also Aeschylus followed his example, although the last-named reverted to the older practice in his last work, the great trilogy, *Agamemnon, Libation Bearers, Eumenides*, which is both the supreme achievement of the poet and the only extant example of a trilogy. Sophocles is credited with two other innovations—the introduction of a third actor and the enlargement of the tragic chorus from twelve to fifteen members. The subject matter of tragedies was almost exclusively taken from mythology and the stories of the epic cycle, a fact trenchantly expressed in the *mot* attributed to Aeschylus, that his plays were slices from the banquets of Homer. Historical subjects were rarely used. Phrynichus, an older contemporary of Aeschylus and famed especially for his lyrics, in his *Capture of Miletus* had portrayed the last tragic episode of the Ionian revolt and had been prosecuted and fined by the Athenians. In 476 his *Phoenician Women*, which dramatized the campaign of Salamis, won a prize. Four years later Aeschylus successfully treated the same theme in his extant play, the *Persians*. In the main, however, the tragic fortunes of the Atreidae and of the House of Labdacus and similar legends provided the plot and afforded the poet the opportunity for the development of character and the conflict of will or personality which formed the essence of the tragedy. To judge by the numerous titles that survive of lost Greek tragedies, the number of heroic stories treated was relatively small and the same subject was chosen by different poets, who showed their originality in their portrayal of the characters and in the interpretation that they placed on the actions and motives of the chief persons. How great the difference between two poets dramatizing the same legend might be can still be seen, if one compares the *Electra* of Sophocles with the play of the same name by Euripides.

In Aeschylus (524–456) the recurrent theme is the conflict between human endeavour and Pride and Fate or the Will of God, which can nullify the one and abase the other. The gods are jealous of human insolence ($ὕβρις$) and visit it with condign punishment. Sin can be atoned for only by suffering and it is by suffering that men can attain to wisdom. Zeus in the poet's conception is not just the father of a divine family, as he is seen in Homer, but an all-guiding power acting in accordance with reason and striving for righteousness. Yet at times Aeschylus seems to think of even Zeus as ruled by Fate or Necessity. A champion of freedom, the poet is at the same time a staunch upholder of law and order and justice against tyranny and injustice. This part of his message is seen most clearly in *Prometheus Bound* and in the *Eumenides*, in which the avenging Furies at the behest of Apollo, who stands for justice tempered with compassion, abandon their pursuit of Orestes, the innocent victim of Fate, and are transformed into the Eumenides or Kindly Goddesses. As a poet Aeschylus rivals Pindar in grandeur of language and in boldness of imagination, as revealed especially in his choral odes. But he is not satisfied with the Boeotian poet's rather conventional outlook on life. He seeks for a deeper explanation, half philosophical, half mystical, as befits an initiate of the Eleusinian Mysteries, of the basic problems that confront humanity. His greatest characters are cast in the heroic mould, and, to judge by his extant plays, he was most successful in his portrayal of women. Clytemnestra and Cassandra in the *Agamemnon*, Atossa in the *Persae*, belong to that small gallery of tragic heroines whose immortality is secure.

Sophocles (496–406) won his first victory in 468. Of his vast literary output, which is said to have well exceeded one hundred plays, only seven tragedies and substantial portions of one satyric drama survive. But the fact that he won the prize on twenty-four occasions against the thirteen victories of Aeschylus and the five of Euripides is a gauge of the appeal that his art and conception of dramatic poetry had for his contemporaries. A friend of Pericles and his circle, he embodied in himself the best qualities of the remarkable society to which he belonged; and it has often been observed that his dramas are distinguished by the same perfect restraint and flawless symmetry that is found in the sculptures of the Parthenon. The plot of his plays was taken from heroic legends in their traditional form. His characters, while they lack the almost superhuman proportions of Aeschylus' figures, are men and women with human virtues and human failings, who speak and act at all times in strict consistence with their situation. Sophocles was not enslaved to any single formula in fashioning his plays. *Oedipus the King*, in point of dramatic structure the finest of all extant Greek tragedies, has a plot that can fairly be called intricate, yet there is nothing superfluous. In that play, as in the earlier *Antigone*, each episode and each speech marks a step towards the tragic climax of the play. In *Oedipus at Colonus* and *Philoctetes* the plot is very slight. There the interest of the drama centres in the psychological analysis of the leading characters—the old blind Oedipus and his impetuous son; Philoctetes, the young and chivalrous Neoptolemus, and Odysseus, the experienced and not too scrupulous man of affairs—and in the conflict of will with will and passion with passion. Sophocles' choral odes are marked by great lyric beauty and an exquisite felicity of phrase; but the participation of the chorus in the dramatic action, though never in doubt, is noticeably less active that in the Aeschylean tragedies. Sophocles made of Attic Greek a perfect medium for expressing every mood and thought, revealing in this as in his dramatic technique a superb artistry devoid of mannerisms or exaggeration and always harmonious. In his philosophy of life he, like Aeschylus, believes in a moral order which directs the world and in a divine justice that punishes the guilty and rewards the righteous. But unlike the older poet, he does not stress the operation of Fate or Necessity in human affairs. Man is free and responsible and his misfortunes follow as the natural consequence of his own acts. By repentance the human will is brought into harmony with the Divine Law.

In the year in which Aeschylus died Euripides (480–406)

competed for the first time at the Dionysia and won third
prize. It is not a mere coincidence that nineteen of his
plays have survived;[1] for, although he was less highly
esteemed and much less successful in his lifetime than either
Aeschylus or Sophocles, his popularity steadily grew during
the century after his death. His influence on the drama of
the Hellenistic and subsequent ages was incomparably greater
than theirs. The tragic poet who enjoyed the special approba-
tion of Alexandrian playwrights and critics in time was
adapted and imitated by the Roman dramatists who cared
little for Sophocles and nothing for Aeschylus; and it was
the Euripidean play as transformed by Seneca which ultimately served as a model for the French classical tragedy.
Euripides was responsible for several novelties in the structure
or technique of his tragedies. The chorus frequently, though
not always, became a mere adjunct to the play, and the choral
odes, though often exquisite as poetry, have little or no
connection with the plot. He experimented with metres and
in his later plays introduced monodies, that is, solo lyrical
passages, for his actors. Furthermore he increased the
length and importance of the prologue, making the speaker
of it explain in detail the precise situation at the opening
of the dramatic action. The beginnings of his plays in consequence tend to be tedious and lacking in dramatic interest;
but by following this convention the poet secured for himself
greater freedom in his treatment of the story to be dramatized.
Up to a point Euripides was bound by religious conserva-
tism and traditions in the material that was regarded as
suitable for tragedy. So his plots, like those of Aeschylus and
Sophocles, were taken from the tales of the heroic age.
But, unlike the older poets, he did not idealize his characters
in any way. He did not hesitate to put into their mouths
his own views on contemporary problems, political, social,
or ethical. He was strongly influenced by the philosophic
thought and the Sophistic teaching of his day, with the
result that he often offended public opinion by attacking
current views on religion or morality. The sceptic and
rationalist was also believed by his contemporaries to be a
hater of women and was so burlesqued by Aristophanes.

[1] The *Rhesus* has been counted as a genuine play by Euripides.
Cf. R. Goossens in *L'antiquité classique*, I, 93 ff.

Yet the truth is that his greatest characters are all female; and he achieved a greater sympathy for them and a deeper insight into their character than either Sophocles or Aeschylus. New also was the romantic and even melodramatic handling of some of the old stories. Such innovations, which to a majority of his contemporaries were discordant and distasteful, were precisely the features of his work that endeared him to later generations and made his influence on dramatic writing after his time so profound.

In the fourth century tragedies were composed by Theodectes and many others, but they were all inferior to the three great masters. Plays abounding in rhetorical refinements of speech and argument were more suited for reading than for presentation, and, as Aristotle remarks,[1] with the audiences in the theatre the performers counted for more than the authors. It is a proof of the established position of Aeschylus, Sophocles, and Euripides as "classics" that in 386 the Athenians decreed that one of the old masterpieces should be revived each year at the Dionysiac festival.[2]

The complete evolution of Athenian comedy was not achieved until the second half of the fifth century. Performances by a κῶμος or troop of mummers who celebrated the god in a song had long been a feature of the Greater Dionysia; and the leader of the band commonly followed this up by a jocular address on topics and personalities of the day. In time this performance, which began by being a private venture, was regulated by the state and the training of the κῶμος became a *choregia*. It was, however, not until c. 450 that these shows were transformed into regular comedies; for, although earlier comic poets are known by name, the real founder of this form of dramatic writing was Cratinus. His productivity extended over many years, seeing that as a very old man he defeated Aristophanes in 423. The performances of comedies, like those of tragedy, were controlled by the state and were organized on a competitive basis, each playwright nominated by the archons presenting one comedy. The number of actors was normally three, though a fourth actor was occasionally necessary for small parts in the plays of Aristophanes. The chorus was composed of twenty-four members and was often divided

---

[1] Aristotle, *Rhetoric*, III, 1403b.  [2] *Syll.*, 1078, lxxxvii.

into two half choruses. Of the three most distinguished authors of comedies, Cratinus, Eupolis (*floruit c.* 429–411) and Aristophanes (*c.* 448–388) only the last named can be properly estimated. Eleven of his comedies survive and in the judgment of the ancients he was the greatest exponent of his art. His earliest plays, written and produced when he was still a very young man, were brought out under another name. Both the *Banqueters* and *Babylonians* are lost, but their general tone and character seem to have been similar to what can still be studied in the earlier of his extant works. The *Banqueters* was a satire on education as practised by the Sophists, the *Babylonians* contained a bitter attack on Cleon and Cleon's imperialism, and was presented at the Greater Dionysia when the revolt of Lesbos was a recent memory and Athens was full of visitors. More than one attempt had been made, notably in 440–439, to curb the licence of comic poets by legislation, but without success. Aristophanes, however, was prosecuted, but seems to have got off on promising in future to produce his plays at the Lenaea, a purely local festival unattended by visitors from foreign parts.

The earliest of his comedies that we possess is the *Acharnians* (425). Like two of his later works, the *Peace* (421) and the *Lysistrata* (411), it was a plea for peace. The *Knights* (424) was a fresh attack on Cleon, a politician of whom Eupolis also made fun in one of his comedies. The *Clouds* (423) attacked the intellectual movements of the age as represented, on the one hand, by men like Anaxagoras or Leucippus, and, on the other, by the Sophists. Somewhat unjustly the poet burlesqued Socrates as a typical specimen of the new thought and portrayed him as a danger to religion and morals. Soon afterwards the Athenians' love for litigation and their passion for jury-service was pilloried in the *Wasps*. Later plays, like the *Birds* (414), *Women at the Thesmophorian Festival* (411), and *Frogs* (405), with its brilliant criticism of the tragic poets, reflect the condition of the times, inasmuch as the poet avoids political topics and abstains from attacking leading men of affairs. The *Birds* is generally and rightly regarded as his masterpiece. Its subject, the founding of a bird-commonwealth by two Athenians who are thoroughly tired of the life and bustle of their own city, enabled the poet to give free rein to his poetic fancy, as well as to his love of broad fun. Taken together, these plays are a brilliant commentary on the manners and foibles of Aristophanes' countrymen. His own views on contemporary affairs he commonly placed in the mouth of the chorus leader when he came forward to deliver the choral interlude ($\pi\alpha\rho\acute{\alpha}\beta\alpha\sigma\iota\varsigma$) near the middle of the play, which was one of the most characteristic features of the Old Comedy. Unlike his fellow-writers of comedy, he was not content with invective against prominent men who displeased him, but at times gave way to a more reflective mood or struck a note of high patriotism.

After the production of the *Frogs* nothing is known of Aristophanes' activities for twelve years. During the fourth century political comedies were out of favour nor was the same licence of speech permitted as in the preceding age. This change in the character of the comic plays is already apparent in the *Women in Parliament* (393), while *Plutus* (388) stands completely apart from Aristophanes' other works. The characters are wholly imaginary, the choral odes have disappeared, and the chorus only participates in the dialogue. Of other writers of comedy in this century, like Antiphanes and Alexis, nothing remains except the titles of some of their plays and a few fragments. Personal satire was on the whole discarded, even if a philosopher was occasionally singled out to be the butt of the poet. Instead these authors dealt with types of character and professions. They parodied literature and philosophical tenets and even mythology. The occasional introduction of a love interest in the plot pointed the way towards the Hellenistic comedy of intrigue.

§ 5. HISTORY AND GEOGRAPHY

The beginnings of historical writing in the Greek world reach back to the sixth century when, under the influence of the Ionian enlightenment, men began to question the traditional beliefs about cosmology, to draw up genealogies with some attempt at critical method, and to compose local chronicles. They were compilers of material, partly historical, partly legendary, and inevitably they were not infrequently at fault. Such studies attracted some minds in the fifth and even in the fourth century. Thus Hellanicus (c. 480–397) gave his attention to local myths and lists of athletic victors; he also put together an Attic chronicle whose inaccuracies drew a rebuke from Thucydides.[1] Other works on the legends, archæology, and history continued to be written after Hellanicus' time. But their authors cannot be ranked as historians, since they merely collected and sifted the raw material of history. Moreover, their merits are hard to determine, seeing that only fragments, and those for the most part very brief, of their compilations survive.

Historical composition begins with Herodotus of Halicarnassus in south-western Asia Minor. Most of his life (484–424?) was spent away from his native city; for, in addition to living some years at Samos and later at Athens, he travelled extensively in Greece, visited Phoenicia and Babylon, sailed the length of the Black Sea, and explored Egypt as far south as Elephantine. In 443 he joined the colony that set out for Thuria. Ten years later he was back in Athens where, so far as is known, he spent the remainder of his days. His death probably occurred in 424 or thereabouts.[2] His *History*, as it has come down to us, falls into two unequal parts, the present division into nine books being later than the author's time. The second part (Books VI–IX) narrates the relations between Persia and the Greeks from c. 500 to 479; that is to say, a relatively brief account of the Ionian Revolt and the expedition of Datis and Artaphernes is followed by a more detailed presentation of Xerxes' invasion of Greece. Books I to V contain a record of the manners, institutions, monuments, and history of various Oriental peoples within the Persian Empire. There is much variation in the treatment of the subjects in these early books. Thus, while Egypt is described at great length, Lydia and the Scythians receive only a comparatively small amount of space. The reason for these disparities is not far to seek. Herodotus had himself visited Egypt, had studied its ancient monuments, had talked with its inhabitants, especially the priests, and had perhaps acquired some knowledge of its written records.

[1] Thucyd., I, 97.
[2] The attempt of J. Wells (*Studies in Herodotus*, 169 ff.) to prolong Herodotus' life to c. 414 has not met with general acceptance. Though ingenious, the theory rests on a very flimsy foundation.

In his account of Lydia he concentrates on the political history; the absence of any discussion of Lydian customs or archaeology may be due to lack of first-hand information or else to the belief that the culture of the Lydians, owing to their nearness to the Asiatic Greeks, would be sufficiently familiar to his readers. For Scythia—a vague term covering modern Rumania and the southern part of European Russia—there were, it may be presumed, no written documents. Herodotus had sailed as far as Phasis, but it is improbable that he visited any part of the interior. Thus he depended on such oral statements as he could collect on his voyage.

Modern scholars have been divided greatly in their views, first, of the order in which the extant *History* was composed, and, secondly, of its merits as a historical composition. Regarding the first of these questions, the widely held opinion that Herodotus wrote the later books first, which incidentally implies that Herodotus' primary interest was in history, seems to the present writer arbitrary and, indeed, untenable. The hypothesis that Herodotus' " first love " was geography, archæology, and ethnography has far more to recommend it, and it is not improbable that the early books of the *History*, as we have it, grew out of lectures about his travels that he gave at Athens and possibly elsewhere.[1] If these assumptions be correct, then it was only in his maturer age that Herodotus set himself to the composition of history and utilised the material that he had gathered about different regions in the Persian Empire, to put together what is in effect an elaborate introduction to the purely historical part of the existing work. There is more unanimity about his merits as a historian; for few scholars would now defend the severe judgment passed on him by Plutarch and by many critics of the nineteenth century. Herodotus has undeniable weaknesses. He has little understanding for military tactics and strategy. Like many another ancient historian he gravely exaggerates the size of armies. Himself a rather pious soul, he shows an amount of respect for oracles and alleged supernatural phenomena that is surprising at the date when he wrote. When he deals with Greek affairs, especially those of Athens, he at times allows his personal prejudices to bias

[1] The writer finds himself in substantial agreement with the masterly monograph by Jacoby in P.-W., Supplementband II, 205-520.

his judgment. His unfair estimate of Themistocles and his defence of the Alcmaeonidae are well-known examples of this weakness in the historian. These defects are, however, quite outweighed by his numerous excellencies. He is an inimitable teller of tales, writing in an easy graphic style that never lapses into triviality and that recalls not a little the manner of the epic poets. Those of his statements which were made from personal knowledge, especially where he treats of the material remains of an ancient culture like the Egyptian, have been proved over and over again by archæological discoveries to be substantially accurate. While it is certain that he used the geographical work of Hecataeus, his other sources of information were probably mainly oral; for the attempts made by some modern writers to prove his use of various chronicles, if ingenious, are entirely unsupported by any ancient evidence. The result, then, is that where Herodotus depends on what he was told by others—and it is clear that he was indefatigable in entering into conversation with every passing stranger—he was at the mercy of his informants. He is critical within certain limits. If a tradition or assertion seems to him suspect, he may reject it. If he is in doubt and there are several traditions about the same event, he may reproduce them all, leaving the decision to his readers while sometimes, though not always, indicating his own. One of his most admirable traits, and one that was rare amongst the Greeks, at least before Hellenistic times, is the fair-mindedness that can appreciate many aspects of an Oriental civilization like the Egyptian or Persian and can do justice to the customs of a semi-barbarous people like the Scythians. In short, Herodotus wrote what he deemed to be the truth, and, if he failed to envisage the larger problems of history, he was the first to set down in a connected form the traditions and accounts of historical events and to weld his material into an artistic whole.

If Herodotus' outlook on men and affairs still belongs in the main to the age of the Persian Wars, Thucydides is pre-eminently a product of the intellectual movements which centred in Athens during the second half of the fifth century. Little is known of his life beyond what he has himself chosen to relate. Born *c.* 471, he must have taken a fair part in the public life of Athens before his election to the *strategia* for

**425-424.** He was in Athens at the beginning of the Peloponnesian War; for he fell a victim to the epidemic which wrought such havoc in Attica between 430 and 426, but, unlike many others, he was fortunate enough to recover. As *strategus* he was stationed in 424 at Eion, in charge of a naval detachment. His failure to relieve Amphipolis, though probably not his fault, brought on him a decree of exile. During the next twenty years he lived partly on his estate in Thrace, partly he travelled in Greece and possibly in the western Mediterranean to collect materials for a history of the war. With the restoration of the democracy in 403 he was able to return to his native city. He died not many years later, leaving his book unfinished.

His *History* covers the period from 431 to 411. Of the eight books into which it was subsequently divided the first is introductory to the main narrative. In it he sketches the earlier development of Hellas, and especially the growth of the Athenian maritime empire from 478 to 445. He also presents a circumstantial account of the diplomatic exchanges and military episodes that immediately preceded the outbreak of the Peloponnesian War. Two strong influences combined to shape the mental outlook of this remarkable man. He was deeply affected by the scientific trends of his age as represented by the atomic theory of Leucippus and Democritus and the rational and empirical methods in medical practice advocated by Hippocrates and his school. In consequence Thucydides approached his historical investigation as a philosophic rationalist. He discarded legendary and mythical accounts of early Greek history, in so far as they were not susceptible of a rational explanation, and his sketch of pre-Hellenic and early Hellenic conditions has been shown by archæological discovery to be substantially correct. His remarks on the evolution of the city-state after the migrations form, together with the philosophical analysis of primitive society in Aristotle's *Politics*, the most valuable observations on sociology and political science penned by any ancient writer. The second influence which played strongly on Thucydides was the Sophistic movement, but in this case it was not so much the historical investigator as the literary artist who was indebted to the new teaching. The debt which his prose owes to the stylistic and linguistic theories of the Sophists is most apparent in the speeches that the historian has introduced into all parts of his work except the eighth book. Yet his style, so far as we can judge, is all his own. The careful distinction of synonyms and the antithetical structure of his sentences derive from his acquaintance with the Sophists, but not the compressed treatment in which the maximum of ideas finds expression in the minimum of words, so that the reader cannot allow his attention to stray for one moment for fear that he will lose the thread of the argument. He justified the introduction of speeches into his narrative by pointing out that he only inserted them on those occasions when he had good reason to know that they had actually been delivered; and, further, by explaining that he had attempted, not to give the actual words of a speaker, but to reproduce the substance of his argument on the basis of the most accurate information that he had been able to obtain.

With regard to the general conception of a historian's duty he stresses the difficulty of securing reliable information, especially about the earlier period of Greek history. The truth about contemporary events, moreover, was sometimes not easy to disentangle, because two or more eye-witnesses of the same occurrence might vary greatly in their version of what they believed to be facts and in their interpretation of them. The historian assures us that he has avoided all meretricious adornment of his narrative and that he has taken the utmost pains to obtain accurate data. It can confidently be said that he has lived up to his high standards. The number of cases where it can be shown that he has erred in matters of detail or has gone astray on some larger question are very few. Because he tried to probe deeply and to ascertain the causes underlying the actions of governments and their leaders' mental attitude which conditioned those actions, he is the first and ranks amongst the greatest of philosophic historians. And there are few writers of history who have been able to maintain so objective an attitude towards their subject. There are but three or four places where Thucydides expresses a personal judgment directly, as in the case of Cleon and Theramenes, or by implication, as with Themistocles and Pericles. For the rest, the facts that he has assembled, whether in the narrative portion of the *History* or in the speeches, provide sufficient evidence to enable the reader clearly to understand the motives and characters of the actors on the stage of history.

After the death of Thucydides Greece produced no critical historian of the first rank until the exiled Polybius took to writing in the later part of the Hellenistic Age. Ancient critics were, it is true, accustomed to group Xenophon with Herodotus and Thucydides, a distinction which the amiable soldier of fortune cannot be said to have deserved. His association with the two leading historians of the fifth century may be explained in part by the circumstance that he consciously set himself to continue the unfinished work of Thucydides. Born *c.* 431, Xenophon in his thirtieth year entered the service of the younger Cyrus and took part in the ill-starred expedition of that prince against his brother. After the execution of Clearchus and other senior officers, Xenophon was chosen with several other men to lead the Greek mercenaries back to safety. They owed their safe arrival at Trapezus after months of hard fighting and many hardships in the Armenian highlands to the Athenian who at a crisis revealed great qualities of leadership. Later he entered the service of Agesilaus, for whom he conceived an extravagant admiration, and fought in the Lacedaemonian army at Coronea. In the circumstances his formal banishment from Athens causes no surprise. For more than twenty years Xenophon divided his time between the pleasures of country-life and literary pursuits on an estate near Elis granted him by the Spartan government. After Leuctra he withdrew to Corinth, and there he probably continued to reside until his death *c.* 355. But when Sparta and Athens became allies some two years after Leuctra, the decree of exile against Xenophon was lifted, so that his sons were able to return to Athens. One of them lost his life fighting on the Athenian side in the battle of Mantinea.

Xenophon's most ambitious work was his *Hellenic History*, in which he took up the history of Greece at the point where Thucydides broke off, and carried it down to 362. The expedition of Cyrus and its sequel he described in a separate work, the *Anabasis*. These two books together form our chief source for the history of Greece during the hegemonies of Sparta and Thebes. The *Anabasis*, especially in its later portions, is a terse and vivid narrative, such as one would expect in modern times from an efficient war-correspondent. Because Xenophon was an eye-witness of the episodes that he relates and because he had a fluent pen, the book has the straightforward appeal of a good adventure story. As a historian, however, Xenophon must be judged primarily by his *Hellenic History*. Its merits consist in the clear concise presentation of the material, combined with a marked skill in bringing to life the actors in the historic drama. This is particularly true of his portrait of Agesilaus, of whom he also wrote a short biography. But he over-stressed the biographical element in history, and, further, through excessive admiration of Sparta and her king, composed a very one-sided account of much of Greek history between 404 and 386. His chronology is often confused. His omissions of notable events are serious. Thus the early history of the Second Athenian Confederacy is ignored, the description of the Leuctra campaign is unsatisfactory, and Epaminondas is mentioned no more than three times and then only in the last book of the *History*. In spite of his own military experience, he is greatly inferior to Thucydides or Polybius in describing campaigns; while the rather tangled inter-state politics during the period that he is portraying are very imperfectly comprehended by him. The result is that, although he strove to be honest and accurate, he failed to bring before his readers a well-balanced and coherent picture of the earlier fourth century. Nor was he capable, like his great predecessor, of appraising and interpreting the motives and policies of states and statesmen during his time.

Of his other works the *Education of Cyrus*, though in form it resembles a historical novel, is partly an educational treatise inspired by admiration of Spartan methods, in part it is a manual on generalship and the art of war. The *Reminiscences of Socrates*, which purport to give in dialogue form that philosopher's views on many topics, is valuable chiefly in revealing Xenophon's own character and varied interests; for, while he did come under Socrates' influence in his youth, his acquaintance with that great man and his understanding of him were strictly limited. Some shorter treatises by Xenophon are the fruits of his experience as a country gentleman during several decades.

Ephorus and Theopompus, both pupils of Isocrates, in antiquity enjoyed a high reputation as historical writers. As only fragments of their works survive, a just estimate of them is difficult. Like Xenophon, Theopompus essayed to continue Thucydides' uncompleted *History* and wrote a *Greek History* from 410 to 394. But his *magnum opus* was the *Philippica*, a history of Macedonia and Greece from 362 to 336. It was executed on a large scale, being in fifty-eight books, and, as shown by the title, had Philip II as its central figure. Ephorus undertook the difficult task of compiling a general history of the Greeks from the earliest times to 340. The archaic period was treated rather briefly. Then, the nearer the historian came to his own times, the greater the detail of his narrative. Both Ephorus and Theopompus had been deeply affected by the political theories and Panhellenic outlook of their teacher, Isocrates. It was this influence that impelled the one to attempt a general history of the Greeks and the other to divine the greatness of Philip and his achievement, even though he bitterly criticized his private life and some of his public acts. In addition, Theopompus seems to have absorbed some of the Cynic's puritanism; for it is remarkable how many of the surviving fragments of his works contain strictures on the manners and morals of individuals and of whole peoples. It is some recommendation of Ephorus that Polybius, no easy-going critic, seems to have regarded him more highly than other historians of the fourth century. Nevertheless, both Ephorus and Theopompus began the fashion, which became so disastrous later on, of subordinating historical accuracy and source criticism to literary form, and, further, of embellishing their histories, in order to give them popular appeal, with anecdotes and declamations that catered to the popular admiration of rhetorical display but had little relation to historic fact or even historic probability.[1]

The geographical knowledge of the Greeks during most of the classical period was almost confined to the Mediterranean, which only ceased to be a *mare clausum* during the age of Alexander. Moreover the lack of scientific instruments and ignorance of the difference between the magnetic and astronomical pole were responsible for many errors in

[1] For some other historians in the period see the Appendix on Sources.

geographical descriptions even of familiar areas. Herodotus' geographical lore was based in part on the work of Hecataeus of Miletus, whose περιήγησις was an explanatory commentary on the world map of Anaximander, enlarged by some data on flora, fauna, and ethnology, in part on his own observations. His travels up the Nile had taken him to the neighbourhood of Assouan and his voyage on the Black Sea to Phasis at its eastern end. While he was acquainted with the explorations conducted by Scylax along the Arabian coast and in the Persian Gulf and Red Sea, he is silent regarding the voyages of Carthaginian explorers, like Hanno and Himilco. Information about the hinterland of the Greek or Graeco-Iranian cities situated on the north shore of the Euxine, as about the regions bordering the middle and upper reaches of the Danube was vague and inaccurate. And, though the discovery in France of Macedonian coins or of Gaulish pieces struck in imitation of the Philippeia makes it probable that there was some commercial activity of Greeks up the valley of the Rhone and beyond, the data that might have been gathered by this means concerning the physical aspect and resources of the country remained lost to science. The central and eastern parts of the Persian Empire, similarly, were quite unknown to the majority of Greeks, who were thus prepared to swallow the fables retailed by Ctesias regarding India, a country that he had certainly never visited. However, Ctesias' long residence at the Persian court enabled him to learn and pass on to his countrymen some particulars of trade routes between Asia Minor and India and Asia Minor and Bactria. The expedition of the Ten Thousand, it is true, seeing how many participated in it, must have helped to enlarge the general stock of knowledge about the Armenian Highlands; but it was only Alexander's conquests and the voyage of Nearchus that demonstrated to the Greeks how small was the portion of the inhabited world with which they had hitherto been familiar. In view of these facts it is not surprising that there was no literature of importance on geographical topics before the Hellenistic Age.

## § 6. ORATORY

The decline of dramatic and other poetry coincides chronologically with the evolution of artistic prose and oratory. Again it was the Athenians whose contributions in the new art-forms stand forth in solitary eminence. The development of oratory was intimately connected with the rise of constitutional government, and especially of democracy, after the Persian Wars. The Athenian citizen of adult years participated directly in ruling his country, if only as a member of the assembly, while, as a juror, he took his part in the administration of justice. If he were himself involved in litigation, it behoved him to conduct his own case. Although tradition associated this requirement at Athens with the venerated name of Solon, it was in reality a regular feature of ancient Greek democracies. Actually it was in Sicily that two men, Tisias and Corax, first thought of formulating rules for the guidance of those who would speak in the law-courts, and in consequence they were regarded as the founders of rhetoric. Once a beginning had been made by them, it was not long before others entered the field both as teachers and writers. Not only the technical structure of written and spoken prose, but grammar and syntax thus became subjects of scientific study. In that way the creation of the new prose was in a great measure the work of the Sophists.[1]

Leading Athenian statesmen, like Cimon and Pericles, could carry their hearers with them by their eloquence, which, to judge by the few recorded phrases that they used, was strongly tinged with poetic diction and imagery. Cleon, too, was a powerful and compelling speaker; but his style was less restrained and was accompanied by violent gestures and the tricks of the demagogue which, though effective with large crowds, lacked dignity. Nevertheless the statements of a biographer like Plutarch, or the satiric comments of Aristophanes, do not suffice to give us a very clear impression of Athenian oratory before the closing years of the fifth century. The canon of Ten Attic Orators, established by the scholars and critics of Alexandria in the Hellenistic

---

[1] The contributions of the leading Sophists to knowledge are further considered in the next chapter.

Age, begins with Antiphon of Rhamnus (*c.* 480–411), the prominent oligarch who suffered death for his part in the Revolution of the Four Hundred.[1] Three of his extant speeches were written for actual trials. His three tetralogies, on the other hand, were exercises, the fruit of his work as a teacher of forensic oratory. Each tetralogy consists of four speeches in brief outline, two stating the case for the prosecution, two for the defence. His orations with their stately periods and rugged diction suggest that the formal law-court speech was still in process of development. Antiphon seems also to have been the first to make a profession of composing for others. While each citizen was required to conduct his own case in the dicasteries, there was nothing to prevent him from employing the services of another, whose knowledge of law and of public speaking was greater than his own, to write a speech for him. In this way the writers of law court-speeches for clients in practice fulfilled some of the functions of the modern advocate. The successful λογογράφος must not only be well acquainted with legal procedure and the rules of forensic oratory, but must be able to adapt his speeches to suit the character of his clients. This combination of qualities was especially conspicuous in the case of Lysias (*c.* 457–380).

The son of the wealthy metic Cephalus, Lysias was deprived of his patrimony and nearly lost his life at the hands of the Thirty. Under the restored democracy, he took to speech-writing to earn his living and in the course of about two decades seems to have composed well over two hundred orations. Of the thirty-four that are extant under his name twenty-eight are probably genuine. They well illustrate both his attractive prose-style, subtle and vivid, yet little removed from the colloquial Attic of his day, and his unusual gift of reproducing the manner and characteristics of his clients, whatever their age and station in life. Of his contemporary, Andocides, who was implicated in the scandal over the mutilation of the Hermae in 415, and who spent a good many years of his life in exile, three genuine speeches remain. Their author, though not an orator of any marked distinction, at least could tell a story in a lively and convincing manner, as shown particularly in his defence against

[1] Cf. above, p. 149.

a charge of having participated in the Eleusinian Mysteries when disqualified by partial loss of civic rights.

Isaeus (c. 410–340 ?) illustrates a new tendency amongst λογογράφοι. Although he sometimes wrote speeches in other types of suit, in the main he specialized in inheritance cases. He was noted for his unrivalled knowledge of the laws of testamentary succession and could present even the most intricate case with masterly clearness. Eleven complete speeches survive, all of them concerned with litigation arising out of inheritances. The fragment of a twelfth oration was written as a defence for a man threatened with loss of citizenship. Furthermore, it was not the least of Isaeus' claims to be remembered that he was the teacher of the greatest orator of antiquity.

In Demosthenes political oratory, as represented by his three *Philippics*, the speech, *On the Affairs of the Chersonese*, and the speech, *On the Crown*, which contains a vindication of his public life down to 330, reached its zenith. But during the earlier years of his manhood he practised as a professional speech-writer. If this calling was forced upon him by the loss of most of his patrimony at the hands of dishonest guardians, it was also a valuable preparation for taking a part in public affairs. The best of his forensic speeches are masterly in their kind. In some of the shorter examples, such as the orations *against Conon* and *against Callicles*, he rivalled Lysias in the art with which he developed the argument in a manner suited to the peculiarities of his client. But it would seem that, as the fourth century progressed, less attention was paid to the fiction that every litigant was responsible for his own speech. In many of the law-court speeches Demosthenes speaks in his own person. A few of these are of great length, like the speech *against Aristocrates*, and, unless spoken by the orator himself, must have been shorter when delivered than in the published form. It is significant of Demosthenes' character also, especially when he is compared with the Roman Cicero, whose forensic speeches, with the exception of the *Verrines*, were all written for the defence, that with few exceptions his forensic orations were composed for the prosecution. While he had a complete mastery of the technical side of his art, it is never obtruded for its own sake. The structure of his longer orations, however elaborate, is never either obscure or diffuse. He commands every mood at will, from subtle irony to biting sarcasm, from complete objectivity, that lets the facts speak for themselves, to impassioned invective and partisanship. Whatever may be thought of his public policy, it is the high and moral earnestness of his various orations against Philip, when coupled with a consummate artistry in language and construction, that gives a unique quality to his oratory.

The teaching of Gorgias, whose pupil he was for some years, may be said to have reached its fullest expression in Isocrates (436–338). Forced by adverse circumstances to become a λογογράφος, he soon abandoned this profession and became a teacher of the Higher Education first at Chios and then in Athens.[1] Although his discourses—apart from a few early forensic speeches of which in later life he affected to be ashamed—are cast in the form of deliberative orations, they were meant to be read rather than spoken and partake rather of the character of political essays. His prose style exerted a profound influence not only on later Greek writers but on Cicero, through whom it was still later to affect the artistic prose of modern times. In spite of Isocrates' use of elaborate periods and florid diction, he is rarely obscure. No unbiased reader of the *Panegyricus* (380) or the best of his later discourses can fail to be impressed by the calm eloquence with which he unfolds and argues his case. Perhaps his most serious defect—and it is this that has reduced the number of his modern admirers—is that the man is always subordinated to the artist. Although his sincere conviction that he is advocating the right policy for Athens and for Greece is never in doubt, the clarity of his utterance and the cumulative force of his reasoned arguments cannot wholly compensate for his undoubted lack of passion.

The canon of the Ten Orators is completed by Aeschines, the bitter opponent of Demosthenes, by the two political associates of Demosthenes, Lycurgus and Hyperides, and by the Corinthian Dinarchus, who lived as a resident alien at Athens and followed the profession of λογογράφος. Aeschines, whom nature had endowed with a fine presence and an excellent voice, at his best was an impressive orator. As a defence of his actions the speech, *on the Embassy*, is little inferior

[1] For Isocrates' role as an educator see the next chapter.

to the oration of Demosthenes delivered on the same topic. But Aeschines relied too much on his natural gifts as a speaker and paid too little attention to artistic form. The result is that all three of his extant works contain periods of striking eloquence cheek by jowl with commonplace and uninspired passages. His greatest lack, however, as the ancients themselves were well aware, was the absence of moral fervour and innermost conviction that pre-eminently distinguished Demosthenes.

The single extant speech of Lycurgus *against Leocrates* (331 ?) is a dignified utterance which stylistically betrays the influence of Isocrates' canon. The fragments of six orations by Hyperides, of which two, *for Euxenippus* and *against Athenagoras*, are nearly complete, prove him to have been a brilliant and witty, if somewhat shallow speaker. Noticeable, too, is his frequent descent to colloquial speech and his use of bold metaphors that must have been more startling to his ancient hearers than to modern readers. For, whereas modern languages are so overloaded with metaphorical expressions that one is often unconscious of their use, the ancient prose-writers employed such figures sparingly and often with a parenthetic apology.[1] Three of Dinarchus' speeches survive. They show that he took Demosthenes as his model, but they are immeasurably inferior even to Demosthenes' less perfect works.

[1] Readers of Cicero, too, are familiar with his frequent qualification, *ut ita dicam*.

# CHAPTER XVIII

# GREEK SCIENCE AND PHILOSOPHY

## § 1. THE ELEATICS AND THE ATOMISTS

SCIENTIFIC and philosophical speculation had taken its rise in Ionia during the sixth century. Through the agency of immigrants to southern Italy from Asia Minor it had spread also to the Greeks of the West. The so-called Ionian physicists, from Thales to Heraclitus, had concerned themselves chiefly with the origin of matter and sought for the material cause of the Universe in one or other of what they regarded as primary substances or elements. Pythagoras of Samos, after he had settled in Croton, was led from his study of mathematics and acoustics to propound a semi-mystical theory of the Universe. He became the founder of a semi-mystical, semi-philosophical brotherhood which, as we have seen,[1] for many years played an important part in the political life of Croton and other Greek communities in Italy.

The founder of the Eleatic school of philosophy was Parmenides (*fl. c.* 480–450). The tradition that he was the pupil of Xenophanes, the poet and mystic who had bitterly attacked the religious beliefs of his day, is probably without foundation. It seems more probable that he began by being a Pythagorean, who later emancipated himself from the thought of his old teacher to set forth with rigid logic and great dialectic skill a new philosophic theory. Its basic concept was in direct opposition to the tenets propounded by the youngest of the Ionian physicists, Heraclitus, who had maintained that the ultimate Reality of the Universe was not Being but Becoming and that, owing to perpetual change, the world is constantly dying and constantly being reborn. Parmenides on the contrary distinguished between *what is*

---

[1] See above, Chapter III.

(τὸ ὄν), which is one and changeless, uncreated and indestructible, and an infinite number of modifications, the Many which become but are not. *What is* is likened to a sphere, and, since there is no empty space either within or without, all motion is illusory not real. The sense qualities which cause belief in change are only apparent and do not belong to ultimate reality. Thus, only *what is* can be the object of knowledge through the operation of pure reason, whereas change and becoming in their unending variety can only be the object of opinion. When Parmenides (in the second part of the hexameter poem in which he enunciated his philosophy) deals with phenomenal things about which knowledge is impossible, because together they make up *what is not*, he appears to be submitting to a rigorous scrutiny the dualistic concepts of the Pythagorean school, who divided the elements that make up the world of seeming into opposites, light and dark, fire and earth, and so forth.

The effect of Parmenides' philosophical thesis and of his method of proof was far-reaching. Two of his followers, Zeno of Elea and Melissus of Samos, set themselves to defend his teaching about the One which is the only Reality by logical proofs in which paradoxes played an important part. Melissus, moreover, turned the master's philosophical poem into prose. Other thinkers were stimulated by Parmenides' thought to oppose his doctrines. They questioned his doctrine of the Many and sought a solution more in conformity with the visible evidence of the senses. Thus Empedocles of Acragas (*c.* 495–440 ?) attempted to reconcile the views of Parmenides with those of Heraclitus, by assuming the existence of four roots, or elements, which are eternal and permanent—fire, earth, air, and water—and two moving causes, love and strife, which he seems to have thought of at the same time as elements. When love predominated entirely, the result was a perfect combination of the four elements, while a complete separation of them was achieved when strife prevailed. In the intervals between these two extremes love and strife combined to produce material worlds and all their component parts. Although much of his doctrine seems crude, Empedocles was the first to propound a theory of evolution based on the premiss of the survival of the fittest. His description of the gradual creation in several stages of living creatures with the

## GREEK SCIENCE AND PHILOSOPHY

power of reproducing their kind was four centuries later to inspire one of the most remarkable passages in Lucretius' poem, *On the nature of the Universe*. A scientific discovery of some importance made by Empedocles was that atmospheric air was distinct from the element so-called by the Ionian physicists and that their theory that water was liquid air was scientifically incorrect.

Almost contemporaneously with Empedocles, Anaxagoras of Clazomenae (*c.* 500–428) expounded the first of several atomic theories of the Universe. Rejecting the four elements as primordial substances, he postulated the existence of minute seeds (σπέρματα) of which all things in the ordered Universe are compounded. The Moving Cause he called Mind (νοῦς), thinking of it as an Intelligence, but confining its operation to giving the initial impulse in the form of rotatory motion to the totality of seeds (πανσπερμία) and thereby starting off the process of world-creation. His assumption of Mind as the moving cause, even though he limited its functions, was a bold innovation that profoundly influenced later thinkers, notably Plato. In contrast to Anaxagoras, his contemporary, Leucippus, and Leucippus' disciple, Democritus, whose long life extended through the first half of the fourth century, rejected the postulate of an intelligent moving cause and put forward a purely mechanical explanation of the Universe. According to their argument there exist two first elements, the void or space, and the full. The full is made up of tiny atoms, infinite in number and immutable, but varying in shape, order, and inclination. As these atoms fall through space, and as their velocity varies because it depends on their size, they collide with one another and set up a vortex in which similar atoms are brought together to form material objects and material worlds. There is no directing mind, the order in the Universe being the result of the necessary and undesigned collision and coalescing of the atoms in the void. The soul is made up of atoms which are extremely fine and light. When the living creature dies, the soul disintegrates into its component atoms even as the heavier atoms of the body separate. The views of Leucippus and Democritus do not seem to have exercised any profound influence on the thought of their contemporaries. Nevertheless they mark a very real advance in human ideas because of their attempt to explain the Universe according to strictly scientific principles.

### § 2. MATHEMATICS AND ASTRONOMY

While Pythagoras had been responsible for mathematical discoveries of basic significance, his innate mysticism also led him to combine science with purely fanciful theories concerning supposed qualities inherent in numbers. His pupils, however, made considerable advances and their example was followed by students in other parts of the Greek world. In this way the general properties of numbers were investigated and a theory was evolved by which numbers were represented geometrically. A triangular number was equivalent to the sum of the arithmetical series of the natural numbers starting from unity. Of solid numbers, that is, those that are the products of three numbers, the commonest was the cube. The products of two numbers were plane and could be either oblongs or squares. Plane and solid geometry were indeed the branch of mathematics in which the greatest advance was made by the Greeks of the classical period; and it is probable that most of the knowledge that was collected and systematized for a wider public by Euclid (*c*. 300) was already familiar to Plato and to the mathematicians of his time. In the matter of calculation and the representation of fractions the Greeks were handicapped by the lack of a simple but adequate system of notation. In any case what we now understand as arithmetic, called by them calculation ($\lambda o \gamma \iota \sigma \tau \iota \kappa \eta$), was generally regarded as a purely utilitarian accomplishment for shopkeepers and such, but unworthy of the mathematician's attention. In later times particular mathematical investigations were attributed to particular individuals, but the existing evidence is too scanty to permit verification of these statements. Thus Hippias of Elis is said to have tackled the problem of trisecting an angle. Menaechmus, a contemporary of Plato, is reported on somewhat doubtful authority to have studied conic sections and to have discovered the parabola and hyperbola from the sections of the right-angled and obtuse-angled cone respectively. Eudoxus, better known for his astronomical theories, sought to work out a system of proportion applicable to irrational numbers and devised a method of doubling the cube. Plato's contribution lay primarily in systematizing existing knowledge and in using the analytical in addition to the synthetic method of proving theorems and problems.

In astronomy, although certain notable deductions were made, progress was necessarily limited by the relatively undeveloped character of contemporary mathematics, and especially by the absence of mechanical aids, that is, instruments with which a philosophical or mathematical theory could be substantiated by observation. Also it not infrequently happened that a truth or partial truth discovered by one investigator failed to win general acceptance by his contemporaries or after. Pythagoras had already believed in a spherical earth and in a sphere of the fixed stars which rotated daily about its axis. Yet Anaxagoras, who rightly deduced that the moon shines by the borrowed light of the sun and thereby was able to give the correct explanation of eclipses, seems at the same time to have adhered to the old hypothesis of a flat earth. To one of the successors of Pythagoras in the fifth century—his identity is disputed— belongs the credit of first propounding a theory that was nearer to the truth than the old geocentric theory of the universe. According to this hypothesis the universe is both spherical and finite. At its centre is a fire around which ten celestial bodies revolve, namely, an imaginary companion of the earth, called the counter-earth, the earth, moon, sun, five planets and, tenthly, the sphere of the fixed stars. It is to be noticed, on the other hand, that Anaxagoras and the Atomists continued to accept the geocentric theory, although they differed in their views of the relative position of the sun, moon, and planets to the earth. Plato also appears during the greater part of his life to have favoured the incorrect hypothesis of a central earth; but it is possible that in old age he inclined to approve the Pythagorean theory. His contemporary and pupil, Eudoxus, however, devised a purely mathematical, that is to say, geometrical hypothesis of considerable complexity. In his desire to account for the stationary point and retrograde motion of planets he postulated a system of concentric spheres—three for the sun and moon, four for each of the planets—lying one inside the other and rotating uniformly about different axes. Another disciple of Plato, Heraclides of Pontus, discovered the important truth that Mercury and Venus revolve like satellites around the sun, and that the apparent rotation of the heavenly bodies is due to the earth's rotation about its own axis.

It remains to refer to a purely practical application of mathematical and astronomical *data* for the purpose of reckoning time and more especially to correlate the solar and lunar years. Meton, who flourished in the last quarter of the fifth century at Athens, devised a nineteen-year cycle with seven intercalary months. This was a great improvement on an older eight-year cycle, but still fell short of complete accuracy. About a century after Meton Callippus improved on the Metonic cycle by substituting for it a cycle of seventy-six years. He reckoned the solar year at $365\frac{1}{4}$ days, his cycle being four times the Metonic cycle less one day.

### § 3. HIPPOCRATES AND SCIENTIFIC MEDICINE

The rise of scientific medicine in the fifth century was to a great extent conditioned by current philosophical theories, more particularly by Pythagoreanism. The chief medical centres were at Cnidus and Cos in the eastern Mediterranean and at Croton in the West. While Hippocrates of Cos was regarded as the true founder of the science there are few eminent men about whom so little is known as about him. Born *c.* 460, he was a member of the Asclepiadae, a guild or family of priest-physicians. He seems to have travelled extensively in Greek lands but to have practised chiefly in Cos. He was the trainer of many other physicians and died at a ripe old age (*c.* 377 ?). The extensive body of writings known as the *Hippocratic Corpus* is a collection of treatises varying greatly in character and scientific outlook and composed at different times. It is, however, generally admitted that certain of these works reproduce a reasonably consistent doctrine of medical theory and practice and that they represent Hippocrates' teaching. As for the collection as a whole, it has been suggested not without probability that it forms the remains of a medical library at Cos.

Hippocrates' scientific view of life was that it consisted of the unceasing interaction of φύσις—nature in the sense of living organism—and environment. Even as the physical philosophers had determined that there were four elements which in various combinations made up all material substances,

so Hippocrates and his school took over and developed a
doctrine older than their time, that the body contained four
humours or body fluids : blood, phlegm, yellow and black
bile. In a perfectly healthy body, they said, these four were
in a state of perfect balance or mixture (εὐκρασία); excess
or lack of one (δυσκρασία) produced ill health. However
unscientific this particular theory, whose essential features
were accepted for many centuries, may seem, it was a great
advance in human thought when Hippocrates regarded
diseases as perversions of nature, or, in other words, as due
to a disorganization of the normal functions of the body ;
for medicine now became a part of natural knowledge and
was divorced from the supernatural and magical beliefs that
had stifled the progress of medical science amongst other
ancient peoples, like the Babylonians or Egyptians. Believing
that nature was the best healer, Hippocrates gave careful
attention to clinical observation and to prognosis, whereby it
was possible, by studying certain signs in the early stages of
a sickness, to determine with fair accuracy its further course
and probable outcome. No less remarkable than his work on
*Prognostics* was his treatise on *Air, Waters, and Places*, in
which the writer turned his attention to environment and its
influence on the natural organism. Thus, he found that
under certain climatic conditions certain diseases tend to
be endemic ; or again, that certain kinds of water are more
harmful to both a healthy and a sick person than other kinds.
Records of medical cases abound in the *Hippocratic Corpus*
and throw valuable light both on the treatment of disease
and on the character of the commonest ailments in the
Mediterranean World at that date. In the main the treatment
consisted in letting nature take its course and at the same
time in helping the process of healing by diet, fresh air, and
regulated bodily exercises. More drastic remedies, such as
drugs, cupping, and bleeding, were as far as possible avoided,
since recourse to them was only justified in extreme cases.
The most prevalent illnesses were fevers of various types—
mostly, it may be presumed, of malarial character—diseases
of the respiratory system, and intestinal ailments of varying
gravity. Of dangerous epidemics the most famous was that
which caused such heavy loss of life in Attica between 430
and 426. While it does not in Thucydides' clinical description

correspond exactly to any disease now known, it did resemble in some particulars typhus, whose spread would be particularly rapid under the crowded conditions existing at Athens at the beginning of the Peloponnesian War. From the Hippocratic *Epidemics*, moreover, it is clear that a number of sicknesses at times took on an epidemic character in a given area, for example, mumps, erysipelas, malaria, and perhaps bubonic plague.[1] There seems to be no certain proof of the occurrence of enteric, cholera, or Malta (Mediterranean) fever.

The structure of the human bones and joints was well understood, by the trainers of athletes as well as by physicians. While internal surgery can have been but rarely attempted and all but slight amputations are likely more often than not to have been fatal to the patient, a high degree of skill was shown in manipulative surgery and the setting of simple fractures. In conclusion we may note the lofty code of medical ethics observed by practitioners of the Hippocratic school. It finds expression not only in the so-called Hippocratic Oath which, with slight modifications, has remained in use down to our own time, but in many incidental passages in the *Hippocratic Corpus*. Little further progress in medical science was made until the Hellenistic Age, when a better understanding of human anatomy, which followed on the studies made in animal biology and embryology by Aristotle and his school, made possible improvements in both medical and surgical practice.

### § 4. THE SOPHISTS

From the middle of the fifth century a strong reaction began to make itself felt against the philosophic inquiries that have engaged our attention in the earlier part of this chapter. The rise of the teachers of Higher Education, whom the Greeks called Sophists (σοφισταί)—a word that at first had no derogatory meaning—offers a good example of the law of supply and demand. In the recently created democracies, where the task of government had passed into the hands of all the male citizens of adult years, the need was soon felt for some training for citizenship more advanced than the elementary schooling which ceased about the fourteenth year. Moreover, the prevailing trend in political development had

---

[1] For a malaria epidemic at Selinus cf. above, p. 63.

the effect of arousing the individual man to a consciousness of his rights and duties which were of far more immediate concern and interest to him than the origin of matter or the mechanism of the Universe. The Sophists, many of whom, ironically enough, seem to have received their education after the elementary stage from the very men whose speculations they later condemned as arid, left the macrocosm to take care of itself, denying the possibility of knowledge in the abstract, and concentrated their attention on man, the microcosm, and his relation to his social environment. Complete sceptics about the possibility of attaining to ultimate truth, they set before themselves a strictly practical aim, to educate young men for civic life. When they professed to train their pupils to excellence ($ἀρετή$) they meant not virtue or morality in the abstract, but practical efficiency. The young citizen must be shown how to manage his own family and the larger organism, the state, in the best manner. An inevitable result of the Sophists' practical aims was that they considered the evolution of ordered society and the relation of the individual to the state. Protagoras (481–411) especially deserves to rank as a pioneer in political science. He regarded the city-state as the result of conscious intelligence, having been created by law, not existing by nature. The careful attention that he gave to the meaning of law further entitles him to be regarded as one of the founders of jurisprudence. Justice, he held, was not an absolute quality but the outcome of social instincts which were ordered in accordance with its norm by each political organism. The purpose of punishment was not revenge but to deter others from criminal acts.

Another aspect of this occupation with the *polis* and its citizens was the Sophists' interest in different types of polity amongst the Greeks and, furthermore, in the institutions of non-Hellenic peoples. Thus they led the way towards that more cosmopolitan outlook—the Sophist Hippias is reputed to have called himself a citizen of the world—which in the next century profoundly influenced Isocrates and his disciples. Stimulating as was this new approach to political and social questions, it might generate an extreme scepticism towards established beliefs and institutions which to the more conservative Greeks seemed both dangerous and blasphemous. Protagoras, indeed, stressed as the two chief civic virtues a sense of law and a moral sense; for, although he denied the possibility of an objective criterion of knowledge, in practice he upheld the need of the individual to abide by the opinion of the majority. Yet he, who as a teacher upheld traditional morality and organized society, was prosecuted for impiety at Athens. Certainly when asked about the gods he replied that he did not know whether they existed or not; probably, however, he owed his indictment mainly to the doctrines put forward by other Sophists less scrupulous than himself. For example, the Sophist Antiphon expressed the antithesis between nature and law in its extremest form when he argued that "justice consists in not transgressing any of the ordinances of the state of which one is a citizen. A man would therefore make use of justice with most advantage to himself if in the presence of witnesses he upheld the greatness of the laws, but when there were no witnesses he upheld the laws of nature." Later in the same passage he remarks, "most of what is justice according to law is strongly opposed to nature." According to Gorgias every man is entitled to fix his own standard of truth. Or again, unless Plato is wholly unfair, being admittedly an unfriendly witness, then certain of the Sophists were prepared to justify philosophically the doctrine that might is right.

The Sophists from the educational aspect were the founders of what we should now call Humanism. They did not in the fifth century establish schools, but travelled from city to city, staying only a short time in each. Their instruction took the form of lectures to general audiences on literary, political, or historical topics, and of less formal tuition to regular pupils who were placed under their guidance for varying periods. Many of them were specialists in a particular subject. Gorgias of Leontini, who visited Athens in 427–426 as ambassador from his native town, gave all his attention to rhetoric and, as we have seen, became one of the founders of Attic prose. Prodicus of Ceos spent much of his time on the scientific study of grammar, investigating the meaning and proper use of synonyms and classifying all sentences under one of four heads—request or wish, question, answer or direct statement, and command. Hippias of Elis was a type of the successful polymath who can find a plausible reply to any question. He is credited with inventing a system of mnemonics and he compiled a list of Olympic victors from their statues, thereby laying the foundation for a method of recording events according to Olympiads which was ultimately adopted by some Hellenistic historians. Thrasymachus, like Gorgias, concentrated on rhetorical studies and embodied his views in a treatise. He seems especially to have stressed the psychological aspects of the art, a topic later treated with consummate mastery by Aristotle in his *Rhetoric*. The linguistic and stylistic investigations of the Sophists were both timely and valuable. Nevertheless in the hands of an unscrupulous teacher scientific rhetoric might easily be perverted to unworthy ends. Aristophanes in his *Clouds* indicted the Sophists as a class because through their teaching bright young men learnt to make the worse argument appear to be the better. Plato's distrust of them and of their methods continued until the end of his life;[1] while Isocrates, though himself a Sophist in the best sense, disliked to be so regarded because in his day moral education had no place in the teaching of the average Sophist, who in return for a fee taught his pupils the use of specious argument or vapid declamation and little else. The fact that all the Sophists received remuneration for the instruction that they imparted, however reasonable this may seem to the modern mind, created a prejudice against them among their contemporaries. Since only the sons of the well-to-do could enjoy the advantages of this Higher Education, the result after a time was to accentuate the difference between two classes in society, the poor and those in comfortable circumstances. This antagonism to the Sophists became more marked when, as sometimes happened, their pupils tended to develop oligarchic views or in other ways failed to conform to the political or moral sentiments of the majority.

### § 5. ISOCRATES

Very little is known about the Sophists of the fourth century, and the few references that survive are chiefly to be found in the writings of hostile critics, like Plato and Isocrates. Nevertheless Isocrates was himself the intellectual heir and successor of the fifth-century Sophists. A pupil of Gorgias, he started a school of Higher Education in Athens *c.* 387 and

[1] Cf., for example, Plato, *Laws*, X, 889E.

directed it with outstanding success for almost fifty years. In spite of the considerable extent of his surviving work we have little precise information about his methods of teaching and curriculum. His pupils after a while became very numerous and generally stayed with him from three to four years. Although he had many traducers, some being professional rivals, others opponents of his political views, he kept the loyalty of his pupils and the confidence of their parents. His educational philosophy—for he gave the name $\phi\iota\lambda o\sigma o\phi\iota a$ to his training—can be gleaned particularly from his three *Cypriote orations*, from the *Antidosis*, a literary autobiography in the form of a forensic speech, and from the *Areopagiticus*, which is a panegyric on Athenian government and society in Clisthenic days and a treatise on citizenship from the standpoint of an educator. Like Protagoras and his contemporaries, he regarded what men called knowledge as relative. His system of education had a threefold aim, the training of the intellect, the will, and the feelings. From Protagoras he took over and developed the antithesis between natural ability ($\phi\acute{v}\sigma\iota s$), training ($\pi\alpha\iota\delta\epsilon\acute{\iota}a$, $\epsilon\pi\iota\sigma\tau\acute{\eta}\mu\eta$), and practice ($\mu\epsilon\lambda\acute{\epsilon}\tau\eta$). On the intellectual side Isocrates strove to instil in his pupils a power of sure and correct judgment. As an educator of future citizens he inculcated in them that the sum of the virtues was to be found in justice ($\delta\iota\kappa\alpha\iota o\sigma\acute{v}\nu\eta$) and in a balanced self-control ($\sigma\omega\phi\rho o\sigma\acute{v}\nu\eta$); for whereas $\sigma\omega\phi\rho o\sigma\acute{v}\nu\eta$ lies at the root of, and is the sum of the virtues of man considered as an individual, justice is the sum of a man's virtues in relation to his fellows. Of the individual virtues he stressed particularly honour, self-control, obedience, modesty, and unflinching truthfulness. "At all times let men so see you honouring truth before all, that your mere word will be more trusted than other men's oaths."[1] "Teach your children to submit to control and accustom them as much as possible to practise this duty of obedience; for, if they have learnt implicit obedience, then they will be able to rule over many."[2] And in another passage he observes that man should not strive to govern other men until he has won the mastery over himself.[3] Although his system of intellectual training was based on the study of rhetoric, it had a far wider scope than what would now be understood

[1] *Ad Nicoclem*, 22.  [2] *Nicocles*, 57.  [3] *Antidosis*, 290.

by that term. Linguistic and literary studies, including grammar, syntax, composition, and style, are the way to a proper understanding and use of method. To develop your powers of speech is tantamount to developing your powers of reasoning. Here it must be remembered that the same Greek word, λόγος, signified both speech and reason; and it is λόγος which distinguishes man from the beasts.[1] But in addition the pupil must, if he is to become an intelligent and useful citizen, acquire some knowledge of history, contemporary political problems, jurisprudence, and religious beliefs and institutions. Unlike many instructors in rhetoric, Isocrates was exceedingly particular about the themes for composition that he set his pupils. If they were put to write on some historical topic of importance, or maybe a panegyric on some outstanding personality of the past, their character was being fortified by moral precepts and examples at the same time that their intellects were being trained. Isocrates' eminent success as a teacher, which even the bitterest of his modern detractors are unable to deny, was due to his personality and personal example to his students, and to the rare gift, even in old age, of understanding sympathetically the problems and aspirations of the young. The same man who told his fellow-citizens that the right education of young men is only possible in a community where the ideals and principles of the older generation are of the best,[2] at the age of seventy still retained his psychological insight into the mind of youth. His political discourse, *Archidamus*, is supposed to be an address delivered by the youthful Spartan king, and the illusion is perfectly maintained to the end. As the second founder of rhetoric and the true father of Humanism, Isocrates exercised an influence that it would be hard to overstress on the subsequent development of Higher Education.

### § 6. SOCRATES AND THE MINOR SOCRATIC SCHOOLS

There can have been few more familiar figures in the streets and public places of Athens during the last quarter of the fifth century than Socrates, the son of Sophroniscus. The son of a stonemason, he was born in 470–469. The certain facts about his life are few. He served as a hoplite through

---

[1] *Nicocles*, 5.      [2] *Areopagiticus, passim.*

the siege of Potidaea and in the campaigns at Delium and Amphipolis. In 406–405 he was a member of the Council of Five Hundred, and this, so far as is known, was the only occasion on which he held public office. When the trial of the generals who had fought at Arginusae came on in that year he was practically the only councillor who stood out against the illegal procedure that was adopted. In 399 he was charged by three accusers of impiety and of having corrupted the youth of Athens, and since he refused to placate the jury by being even momentarily false to his inmost convictions, he was condemned to death and executed. It is now a matter beyond dispute that Socrates was the innocent victim of the democratic reaction at Athens after the Peloponnesian War. Amongst his followers had been men like Alcibiades and Critias, and this association seemed to some of the narrower democratic minds sufficient proof that Socrates himself was politically dangerous. In his earlier years he seems to have followed his father's calling for a time; it is also likely that he was for a while deeply interested in contemporary theories about the physical world and a pupil of one of the less known physicist philosophers, Archelaus. It was, however, the last twenty-five years which were the significant part of his life. In 424 the Delphic oracle had expressed the view that no man was wiser than Socrates. From that time on he devoted himself to what was in his own eyes no less than a religious mission. He professed no formal system of education or ethics. He had no school, but engaged all classes of men in conversation wherever he found them. He started from the conviction that current beliefs about right and wrong were not equivalent to knowledge and that most men's actions are founded on opinions that are false and derived from others instead of proceeding from their own conviction. When he engaged a friend or stranger in talk he had two ends in view; or, to express his purpose in terms of method, there were two stages in his dialectic. In the first, by a skilful use of question and answer, he proceeded step by step to convince his companion that his opinions on the topic under discussion were erroneous, so that the companion was finally reduced to a state of complete perplexity ($ἀπορία$). If the discussion ended at this point, then at least he had been made conscious of his ignorance. If, however, he was not too discouraged or annoyed to continue the conversation the second stage in Socrates' dialectic method began. Again, by use of question and answer, and by starting from a number of particular instances, Socrates guided the other towards the formulation of a general proposition and in this way sought to induce ethically right concepts in his companion's mind. It is clear that Socrates deeply impressed his followers not only by his dialectic skill and the loftiness of his moral precepts, but by his own personality, which exemplified in practice his ethical principles.

Socrates himself left no writings, and it is, in consequence, difficult to determine with any certainty the scope and character of his thought; for though most scholars would now agree that Plato is our most reliable witness for the historic Socrates, it is exceedingly difficult to state how much that Plato puts in the mouth of Socrates actually represents Socrates' views. Thus while some would accept the Platonic *Apology* as an authentic estimate of Socrates' life and work, but would hesitate to accept any of Socrates' utterances in the Platonic *Dialogues* as purely Socratic teaching untinged by Platonism, others have gone so far as to attribute to Socrates the germ of the doctrine of Forms or Ideas, which has more commonly been regarded as wholly Plato's own. The *Apology*, however, lends no support to the view that Socrates ever gave serious attention to metaphysical problems. While we know that he conformed where necessary to the rites of the state religion, his allusions to God or to the gods in the *Apology* are in accordance with conventional phraseology and give no clue to his real beliefs; still less do they justify us in assuming that he believed in a Platonic Demiurge. His interest, in short, was in man and in human conduct. He equated happiness with virtue and virtue with knowledge. A man cannot regard the opinions of others as knowledge, for men are not agreed in their views of right and wrong. Hence knowledge can only come from a man's own soul, and it is implicit in Socrates' teaching that the human soul can intuitively perceive what is good. If a man chooses what is not good he does so because what he deems to be knowledge is not true knowledge at all but false opinion. Wrong action then is purely the result of an inability to distinguish truth from falsehood. Socrates bore witness himself by his life and by his death that this simple but lofty moral code was possible for man to follow. But it is obvious that there was not a little danger in the doctrine that each man is the only right judge of his conduct. It was one that could lead to definitely anti-social conduct, and, short of that, it could be, and actually was by some of Socrates' disciples, seriously misinterpreted.

Although Socrates formulated no system of ethics, still less of metaphysics, the influence of his personality and of his dialectic was so profound that a number of distinct philosophical schools were founded by his immediate followers. For Aristippus of Cyrene the one avenue to truth was through sensation. He defined pleasure as the supreme good or end of existence. Happiness consisted for him in a rightly balanced indulgence in the pleasures of sense and mind. Each man must judge for himself what is pleasurable for him and what not, and he must be the master, not the slave, of his pleasures. The Cyrenaic school founded by Aristippus won a certain number of adherents. In the history of thought its only importance is that it prepared the way for the more enduring theories of Epicurus.

Another disciple of Socrates, who started a new philosophic movement, was the Athenian Antisthenes. The founder of the Cynic school in his doctrines was the extreme opposite to Aristippus. Pleasure as the end of life he rejected as madness. He was the first advocate in the Greek world of an ascetic morality. The virtue which he defined as the *summum bonum* consisted in extreme simplicity of life, in contempt of the world and its affairs, and in a hardy, even brusque, independence of mind. Austere teaching of this kind will always attract certain temperaments and will flourish particularly in societies marked by the extremes of ostentatious wealth and economic misery. The strong revival of Cynicism in the Roman imperial age was no mere accident. Also, tenets like those of Antisthenes somewhat easily lend themselves to travesty. While he himself lived a life of rational self-abnegation, his follower, Diogenes of Sinope, who died in 323, carried his practice of the simple life to ridiculous extremes and prided himself in flouting the common decencies observed by men living in a civilized community.

Two further philosophical schools inaugurated by followers

of Socrates were founded respectively by Euclides of Megara and by Phaedo of Elis and Menedemus of Eretria. Both the Megarians and the Eleo-Eretrians devoted their attention to ethical questions without, however, formulating, as both Antisthenes and Aristippus had tried to do, any clear-cut guide to conduct. Both schools also were interested in the more precise definition of terms, and the Megarians especially followed methods of logical argument similar to those which had been used first by Zeno of Elea.

§ 7. PLATO

Aristocles, universally known by his sobriquet, Plato, was both the most eminent of Socrates' disciples and the only one to whom the full inwardness of the master's teaching was apparent. As a youth he studied with the Heraclitean philosopher, Cratylus, and on a visit to Cyrene some fifteen or more years later he deepened his knowledge of geometry under the guidance of the mathematician Theodorus. But the determining influence of his life was Socrates, with whom he first began to associate c. 407 when he was twenty years of age. After Socrates' condemnation and death he abandoned his intention, natural in one who through his father claimed descent from King Codrus and through his mother from Solon, of devoting himself to public affairs. He withdrew for a time from Athens. Journeys to Egypt, Cyrene, and to the Western Greeks followed, his first visit to Dionysius I ending disastrously.[1] He was back in his native city c. 387 and, save for his two later journeys to Syracuse, resided there until his death in 347 as head of a school of Higher Education of which he was himself the founder. It derived its name, Academy, from the gymnasium of Academus in which Plato first began to discourse to pupils. Next to nothing is known of the inner organization and educational aims and methods of the Academy. Nevertheless it can be assumed that the training of the Guardians in the *Republic* was to some extent an idealization of his own methods as a teacher. His approach, as distinct from that of his contemporary, Isocrates, was scientific, not humanistic, and the basic study of the Academy was mathematics, which was

[1] Cf. above, p. 282.

not only the necessary preparation for other sciences, but in Plato's opinion the best means of preparing the mind for abstract thinking.

In addition to teaching, Plato composed many writings, most of which were intended rather for the educated public than for his own advanced students in philosophy. All, except the *Apology of Socrates*, are composed as dialogues, and in most Socrates appears as the principal speaker. Thus Plato, adopting the Socratic methods of destroying false arguments and of building up a constructive theory by question and answer, created a new literary form. Although only his last work, the *Laws*, which was left unfinished at his death in 347, can be precisely dated, and the chronological order in which most of the dialogues were written is quite uncertain, a careful analysis of his style and language has made possible a broad division of all his works into three groups. To the earliest belong several short dialogues, sometimes called Socratic from the belief that their conclusions represent not so much the views of Plato as those of his master. In each some virtue or moral quality—piety, courage, self-control, friendship—is analysed and an accurate definition of it is sought. To the earliest group must also be assigned several longer works, like *Gorgias* and *Protagoras*, whose primary purpose is to controvert certain theories of the Sophists. The second period in Plato's literary career produced, besides several minor pieces, the *Phaedrus, Banquet, Meno, Phaedo*, and, above all, his universally acknowledged masterpiece, the *Republic*. In all of them, but especially in the *Phaedo* and *Republic*, we are confronted with the doctrine that forms the foundation of his philosophical thought, his theory of Forms or Ideas. According to this all objects of sense are unreal and transitory. The general Forms or Ideas, from which they derive their name, are alone real and existent, but can be apprehended only by the mind. The objects of sense are no more than copies of the archetypal Forms. The Highest Form or Idea is the Idea of the Good which Plato equates with God or the Demiurge. True knowledge, that is knowledge of the eternal Forms, is acquired by recollection, since the soul, before it begins its career in the human body, has known the archetype and can recollect it when it perceives its imperfect copies in the phaenomenal world.

# GREEK SCIENCE AND PHILOSOPHY    453

The application of his basic theory to various activities of man's life and thought led Plato, often almost incidentally, to discuss and illuminate problems of psychology, aesthetics, and education. Above all, in the *Republic* his life-long interest in human society and the art of government found its most idealistic expression. The first book of this work discusses the nature of justice. Many current theories are propounded but all are rejected by Socrates, until his interlocutors turn upon him and demand that he should abandon the role of destructive critic and provide an answer to the question under discussion. In the succeeding books Socrates, in order to investigate justice actually at work, and so to prepare the way for a better definition than had so far been offered, analyses early human society and then proceeds to construct an ideal city-state, characterized by complete communism in property, women, and children in the case of the ruling class and by a long and arduous system of Higher Education for the select minority on whom the real task of governing the state will devolve. In the later books of the *Republic*, after the ideal *polis* has been fully described, various types of constitution and the human characters that correspond to them are exhaustively analysed, according to a scale of progressive degeneration.

The dialogues of the latest group of Plato's writings, which are the maturest fruit of his metaphysical thought, contain much self-criticism; for it is true to say that he is his own severest critic. In the *Theaetetus, Sophist*, and especially the *Parmenides* he submits his theory of Ideas to a searching inquiry. The *Statesman* contains his later reflections on the art of government and modifies some of the views that he had previously expressed in the *Republic*. The *Philebus* takes up once more the question of what is human happiness, while the *Timaeus* is a cosmological and ontological treatise in which its author seeks to describe the process of world creation by the Demiurge when he imprinted the Forms on the formless matter of chaos. Finally, in the *Laws* Plato as an old man came back once more to political theory. At great length, and with a wealth of knowledge about contemporary and earlier Greek governments, he constructed a model city-state. It fell short admittedly of the ideal *polis* portrayed in the *Republic*, but in his opinion would be the best to which men could attain in practice. His sympathies throughout his life were for aristocracy, but it is noticeable that in his latest work he has so far modified his earlier attitude as to advocate a mixed constitution. Nevertheless, even in the state of the *Laws* most of the real power is to be exercised by a select minority. Plato's works taken as a whole owe their unique position in the world's literature to the perfection of their literary form, to the inexhaustible wealth of their ideas, and to the noble idealism of their author with its identification of the Good, the Beautiful, and the True.

On Plato's death the headship of the Academy passed to his nephew, Speusippus. Eight years later, in 339, he was succeeded by Xenocrates. Both were men of high character and ability; yet neither was equal to pursuing further the master's system in all its aspects. Speusippus, indeed, is reported ultimately to have rejected the Platonic theory of Ideas, to devote himself mainly to the less abstract pursuit of scientific classification. Xenocrates attempted to explain the Platonic metaphysics by the use of a mystic theory of numbers in which the number, three, was predicated of the Deity. His strange speculations met with little recognition, chiefly perhaps because they were subjected to a searching and highly destructive criticism by Aristotle.

§ 8. ARISTOTLE

Aristotle, the most eminent of Plato's pupils, was born at Stagirus in Chalcidice. His father, Nicomachus, for a time held the appointment of physician to the Macedonian court. His keen interest in biology later in life may thus owe its origin at least in part to his early environment, just as Nicomachus' connection with the rulers of Macedonia may have contributed to Aristotle's appointment to become the tutor of Alexander. Moreover, Aristotle's early life, spent in a Greek *polis* surrounded by non-Hellenic tribes, was perhaps responsible for the keen understanding that he subsequently showed for comparative anthropology. In his eighteenth year (367) Aristotle came to Athens. There he spent the next two decades first as a pupil, later as a teacher, in the Platonic Academy. The twelve years after Plato's death were spent

partly in travel, partly in Macedonia as Alexander's mentor.
When Aristotle at last came back to Athens in 335 or 334
he founded a philosophic school of his own. There he was
extremely active in teaching and writing until the news of
Alexander's death arrived in the summer of 323. It was the
signal for a strong outburst of anti-Macedonian feeling, so
that the former tutor of the dead king deemed it more prudent
to retire to Euboea. There he died less than a year later.

Of Aristotle's enormous literary output only a fraction
survives. All the works that were intended for a larger public
have perished save the short treatise on the Athenian constitution. The very substantial Aristotelian *corpus* that has
come down to us is made up of his lecture notes, either in the
form in which he himself left them at his death or else in a
revised form published subsequently by one or other of his
disciples. It was natural and inevitable that the man who
spent twenty years of his life in the Academy should be at
first a Platonist. The growth of Aristotle's mind, the process
by which he gradually drew away, and finally all but completely emancipated himself, from the fundamental doctrines
of his master, is a problem that is still only partially solved.
Specialists in Aristotelian thought would distinguish three
stages in the evolution of his philosophy. His earliest views,
so far as they can now be recovered, were still deeply influenced by Plato. In the middle stage the bond with his teacher
has become extremely loose, while in the maturest phase of
his thinking the rupture with Platonism seemed to him at
least to be complete and irrevocable. There was, moreover,
a fundamental difference in temperament and intellectual
approach between the two men. Where Plato was endowed
with a poetic imagination and insight and was in essence the
creative artist, Aristotle had the severely analytic mind of
the scientist, who is happiest when he is amassing data, that
is to say, empirical facts. Aristotle's unique importance is
due partly to his own fundamental contributions to several
branches of human knowledge, partly to the fact that he was
the first to devise a wellnigh complete philosophical system
which included all that could then be known of the physical
world as well as the realm of the mind. His works, in short,
for the first time provided men with an encyclopaedia that
was the product of one mind and in which each branch of

knowledge fitted into its place as part of a single philosophic whole. His scientific method consisted of three stages : to collect and test all current opinions or, in the case of the physical sciences, all available *data;* by induction to formulate a hypothesis or general law from the collection of particulars; and, thirdly, by deduction to apply the general law to particular instances. If at times he was unable to apply his method more than partially, this was not the fault of his system but of the relatively backward character of scientific observation and experiment.

He was the creator of formal logic, developed out of the dialectic method of Plato. The *Organon* is a collection of treatises setting forth the various parts of the science of reasoning, from an enumeration of the heads of predication (κατηγορίαι) to an analysis of the syllogism, from an investigation of propositions to a classification of fallacies. In all essentials the system elaborated by Aristotle has not been superseded to this day. Once the student has grasped the processes of rational thinking, but then only, Aristotle would lead him on to the study of his philosophic system. He would divide it into three branches, each aiming at a specific purpose. Speculative philosophy (θεωρητική) has as its aim truth, the end of Practical philosophy (πρακτική) is happiness, while Poetic, that is, Creative philosophy (ποιητική) aims at an artistic product. The first of these groups includes metaphysics, mathematics, and the physical and biological sciences ; the second is made up of ethics, politics, and economics ; the third is concerned with poetry, painting, and the other arts. The extant writings of Aristotle can be classified along similar lines, although some subjects, for example mathematics, are not there represented. The surviving treatises dealing with Speculative philosophy are the *Metaphysics*, the *History of Animals*, *On the Soul*, and several shorter works on biology and four books devoted to physics. The three treatises on ethics, *Nicomachean Ethics*, *Eudemian Ethics*, and *Magna Moralia*, of which the first is the most important because it preserves Aristotle's views in their purest form, and the *Politics* are concerned with πρακτική. Finally, in the partially preserved *Poetics* and in the *Rhetoric* we have the philosopher's theories on certain parts of ποιητική.

Although Aristotle abandoned Plato's theory of Ideas, the

Platonic Idea may be said to survive in the Aristotelian Form. But while the Platonic Idea was a primary and transcendental form which alone was real and existent, the Aristotelian Form is immanent in the matter that encloses it but does not exist apart from it. While Aristotle thus opposed Form to Matter he also distinguished between three aspects of Form, and thus reached his famous classification of the four Causes, the strictly Formal Cause ($\tau\grave{o}$ $\tau\acute{\iota}$ $\mathring{\eta}\nu$ $\epsilon\mathring{\iota}\nu\alpha\iota$), the Material Cause ($\mathring{v}\lambda\eta$, $\tau\grave{o}$ $\mathring{v}\pi o\kappa\epsilon\acute{\iota}\mu\epsilon\nu o\nu$), the Efficient Cause ($\tau\grave{o}$ $\mathring{v}\phi'$ $o\mathring{v}$, $\tau\grave{o}$ $\kappa\iota\nu o\mathring{v}\nu$), and the Final Cause ($\tau\acute{\epsilon}\lambda o\varsigma$, $\tau\grave{o}$ $o\mathring{v}$ $\acute{\epsilon}\nu\epsilon\kappa\alpha$). The four Causes may be defined as four kinds of antecedent condition necessary for the existence of each thing. One of the most profound and consequential aspects of Aristotle's philosophy is his enunciation, and at least partial demonstration, of an evolutionary doctrine according to which all forms of life progress from a lower to a higher state. The influence of Plato on his pupil is apparent in the fact that this process is not conceived by Aristotle as fortuitous or mechanical, but due to the deliberate design and act of the First Cause. Regarded from this aspect the First Cause or Formal Cause is equivalent to Plato's Idea of the Good. This Prime Mover is responsible for the development of each thing from a potential to an actual existence and is the object and end of all desire and all effort.

The two works of Aristotle which are still of the most universal interest are the *Ethics* and the *Politics*. To him, as to all Greek thinkers, there is a close connection between the two subjects; for while the one seeks to determine the Highest Good of the individual man and the means to attain, or at least to strive after, it, the other is concerned with the Highest Good of the community, and this end is more important in proportion as the state is more important in Aristotle's thought than the individual member of it. Aristotle maintains that conduct should be regulated by Law and, like Plato, had a good deal of sympathy for the system of state supervision actually existing in Sparta. " The Law," he remarks, " has compulsive power, while it is at the same time a rule proceeding from a sort of practical wisdom and reason. And while people hate men who oppose their impulses, even if they oppose them rightly, the Law in its ordaining of what is good is not burdensome." And again with special reference to the problem of education he observes : " But it is difficult to get from youth up a right training for virtue if one has not been brought up under right laws ; for to live temperately and hardily is not pleasant to most people, especially when they are young. For this reason their nurture and occupations should be fixed by Law, for they will not be painful when they have become customary."[1] Virtue aims at a mean between two extremes and is thus defined by Aristotle : " Virtue is a state of character concerned with choice, lying in a mean, *i.e.* the mean relative to us ; this being determined by a rational principle, and by that principle by which the man of practical wisdom would determine it."[2] Virtues and vices are evaluated more as they affect society than as they influence the individual, so that to Aristotle the civic virtues come first in any comparative estimate. The modern student of ethics is conscious of a certain limitation in Aristotle's treatment of the subject, since the inquiry is almost wholly confined to morality in its external aspects. Virtue and vice are distinguished according to their outward effect on the individual and his associates. There is no discussion of duty as such nor of the inward faculty by which man is guided in discerning good from evil. Though the opening chapters in the third book of the *Nicomachean Ethics* contain an investigation of the voluntary and involuntary moral virtues we miss a treatment of the will itself. Aristotle's avowed purpose was to determine what, in the light of man's nature and environment, was the most desirable plan of life. The fair critic will bear in mind this self-imposed limitation of the philosopher on the scope of his subject and will not expect an investigation of those aspects of moral science that have developed out of Christian theology and ethics. Aristotle placed first the intellectual virtues, at the head of which he put speculative wisdom, and the moral virtues second. These last include, for instance, courage, liberality, magnanimity, and justice, and their importance in Aristotle's eyes proceeds from the circumstance that we have already noted, that he tends to think of man not so much as an individual as a social being.

The *Politics* in its surviving form is a composite work

[1] Arist., *Eth. Nic.*, 1180a21.  [2] *Ib.*, 1106b36.

containing Aristotle's thoughts on political science at two
and possibly three different periods of his life. The result
is that there are some unreconciled contradictions; certain
topics, for example, the different types of constitution, are
treated twice over and from a different point of view; and
occasionally a promise to discuss a particular question is
never carried into effect. Thus, early in the first book he
defines three human relationships, that of husband and wife,
master and slave, father and child; but the first and third
of these are never brought up in the extant work for detailed
consideration. Yet, though the *Politics* is somewhat amor-
phous, and there is still no complete agreement among modern
critics about what portions represent the earlier and what
the later phases of Aristotle's thought, it is nevertheless the
profoundest contribution made by any ancient writer to
political science.

In the first book the author, after tracing the development
of the *polis* from the household and the aggregation of house-
holds that form a village ruled by the eldest progenitor,
considers in detail the relation of master and slave, this being
one of the three relations between ruler and ruled which he
enunciated at the beginning. After discussing slavery, however, he passes on to investigate the origin, meaning, and
use of wealth and property. This part of his work, together
with some brief passages in the *Ethics*, is all that survives of
Aristotle's views on political economy, for the *Oeconomica*
included among his writings are known to be a compilation
of Hellenistic date. In the second book of the *Politics* he
criticises earlier political thinkers—Phaleas, Hippodamus,
and Plato's theories in the *Republic* and the *Laws*—and also
existing constitutions or social organizations, notably those
of Sparta, Crete, and Carthage. Later in the *Politics* he
follows the lead of his master and portrays for us what
he would regard as an ideal city and an ideal city-state.
Although his Utopia differs in various ways from Plato's,
there are sufficient resemblances to justify the belief that this
part of the *Politics* represents a relatively early phase of his
thought. His views on education, which it is the business
of the state to organize and control, are unfortunately very
fragmentary; like Plato, however, he had considerable
admiration for the methods existing in Dorian states like

Sparta, save that the Spartan system, as it worked in practice, seemed to him too narrow in its aims. Of supreme interest are too long sections in which he classifies and analyses constitutions. There particularly it is clear that we are confronted with an earlier (semi-Platonic) and a later body of opinions. In the earlier scheme, besides three perfect forms of government, by the one (monarchy), by the few (aristocracy), and by the many (commonwealth), we are introduced to three perversions, tyranny, oligarchy, and democracy. Each of these is better or worse in proportion as it is better or worse suited to the nature and position of the people. But in his later classification Aristotle avoids any such hard-and-fast systematization. Instead, he passes in review a great many varieties of constitution and illustrates his theories by constant reference to historical examples. Since he supervised the publication of monographs on no less than one hundred and fifty-eight ancient constitutions, his generalizations, based on this vast accumulation of data, are exceptionally valuable. This is true also of the passages in which he inquires into the causes of political faction and *stasis*.

No inquiry into the art of the drama is more penetrating than the *Poetics* and none has had a more lasting influence on this branch of literature. Similarly his manual on rhetoric is the most scientific treatment of the subject that antiquity has bequeathed to us. Even his scientific works, more especially those on biology, though they have long since been superseded, were epoch-making in their day and are still mentioned with respect by those modern scientists who have taken the trouble to peruse them. " Nullum fere scribendi genus non tetigit, nullum quod tetigit non ornavit."[1]

---

[1] These words, which are frequently misquoted, occur on the epitaph of Oliver Goldsmith, composed by Dr. Johnson.

# CHAPTER XIX

# GREEK RELIGION

## § 1. THE STATE RELIGION

THE official religion in the classical Greek world was essentially a contract between men and the gods. The religion of the family, the clan, and the state was a matter of rites and ceremonies performed at fixed times and according to an accepted form. If men gave to the gods their due in prayer and sacrificial offerings, then the supernatural powers might be reasonably expected to do their part in helping and protecting their human petitioners. Conformity to the state religion was expected of those persons who held official positions; and it was the rule amongst the rank and file of citizens, but there is nothing to show that it was exacted or that failure to participate in the more important cults was punished. The few recorded cases of prosecutions for impiety occurred at a time of popular excitement or war hysteria, when a scapegoat was needed to allay the fears of the masses, or else were the result of political intrigue. To the former category may be assigned the trials of Protagoras and Diagoras and of the Hermocopids, to the latter the indictments of Anaxagoras, Alcibiades, and Socrates. But it should be noted that in the former also questions of politics were involved.

The intellectual movements of the fifth century undoubtedly did much to undermine old beliefs. The difference in attitude between the older and the younger generation is brought vividly before us if we contrast conservative minds, like Herodotus and Aeschylus, with thorough-going rationalists like Thucydides and Euripides. Nevertheless it would be difficult to maintain the thesis that the changing attitude towards the gods or, as in the case of the physicist and atomist philosophers, towards natural phenomena, appreciably

affected the mass of the population in Attica or elsewhere.
The ordinary people continued as before to observe the
prescribed forms of family worship, to take their part in
the state festivals, and even to accept and perpetuate the
superstitions which their fathers and grandfathers had
believed. Aristophanes might raise a laugh by making fun
of soothsayers in the *Birds* or treating Dionysus with thorough
disrespect in the *Frogs*; Euripides might represent Heracles
in the *Alcestis* with no semblance of heroic, let alone divine,
stature. The very audience which had applauded the wit
of the poets on one day would on the next sacrifice to
Heracles in due form or seek to ascertain the future with the
help of Bacis' oracles. Still more could an old-established cult
weather even a heavy storm. Apollo of Delphi may have
been temporarily under a cloud for " medizing " in 480, but
the credit of the Delphic sanctuary and oracle was not long
impaired. Greek religion, if we except a few mystery cults,
offered little or nothing to satisfy either the spiritual or the
emotional craving which other religions have at least partially
assuaged. But the inner life of the average Greek is to us
a sealed book. If he was not an initiate of the Mysteries,
as many were, we may suppose that he gained some satisfaction that was more than merely artistic from the various
forms of art—sculpture, architecture, and the drama—that
were pressed into the service of religion. In the sense that
some formal act was done or prayer was uttered, religion can
be said to have permeated the public and even the private
life of the Greeks. But there never existed a priestly caste,
still less was there any powerful hierarchy, such as was
familiar in the Oriental kingdoms of the Near and Middle
East. The *sacra* of the family, be it a sacrifice and prayer
at the family hearth or the pouring of a libation before
sitting down to meat, were performed by the head of the
family. The formal rites that preceded most public acts
were carried out by the presiding magistrate or by persons
whom he had designated for the duty. At meetings of the
Athenian assembly not only were the proceedings opened
by prayer and sacrifice, but the heralds pronounced formal
curses on any speaker who should intentionally deceive the
people. In Teos the magistrates each year uttered prescribed
imprecations against any one who should plot against the

state or against its individual members.[1] Priests or priestesses were in charge of the temples. Occasionally tenure of a particular priesthood was hereditary in one family. At Athens, for instance, the priest of Poseidon-Erechtheus and the priestess of Athena Polias were always taken from the family of the Eteobutadae. Such survivals of the days when the control of the state religion, like that of the government, was the exclusive privilege of an aristocratic minority, were probably few in classical times. At Athens, and probably elsewhere, especially in the democratic cities, most priesthoods were filled in a manner similar to that used for appointing the lesser magistrates. Most of the Athenian priests were appointed by sortition out of a number of previously selected candidates. During their tenure of a priesthood the incumbents received certain perquisites from the sacrifices and sometimes a small salary as well.[2] The religious head of the Athenian state was the King archon, that is to say a senior magistrate, not a priest. The appointment of committees or functionaries to deal with particular festivals was in the hands of the assembly or, in some cases, of the Council of Five Hundred. No new cult, whether Greek or foreign, could be officially started on Athenian soil without the approval of the people, whose authority held good wherever Athens was in control politically. Thus from the middle of the fifth century to 404 the sanctuaries on Delos were administered by an Athenian committee of ἀμφικτύονες. It was by orders of the *ecclesia*, acting on oracular advice, that a formal purification of the island was carried out in 426–425.[3] After the formation of the Second Athenian Confederacy Athenian influence again predominated in the Cyclades and the temples of Delos again passed under Athenian control.[4] Another instructive instance, somewhat later in date, of official direction is furnished by the case of the Amphiaraus cult in Oropus. When this border-town, after having changed hands several times during the course

[1] Tod 23.
[2] The priestess of Athena Nike was paid fifty drachmae a month. Cf. Tod 40 and 73.
[3] Cf. Tod 54 and 85; Thucydides, III, 104.
[4] Delos was freed by Sparta *c.* 403 (cf. Tod 99), but by 389 some Athenian officials were again in control of the temple of Apollo. For temple accounts after the formation of the Second Athenian Confederacy, cf. Tod 125.

of two centuries, finally reverted to Athens about 338, the management of the shrine and oracle of the hero and of the four-yearly festival in his honour was taken over by the *ecclesia* and *boule*.[1]

The state took cognizance of all offences against religion and exacted retribution from the culprit, from the condign punishment of homicide, which brought pollution on the country, or sacrilege, to the levying of fines on persons who pastured animals or committed a nuisance on temple-lands.[2] The administration of the four Panhellenic games was vested in the political power that controlled the territory where the celebration took place. On the other hand, there is at least one well-attested instance of inter-state action in a matter of religion. When the house of Apollo at Delphi was destroyed by an earthquake or by fire c. 372, the building of a new temple was defrayed in part from the treasure of the god, partly by contributions from all over the Greek world. The control of this international fund was entrusted to a board of "temple-builders" (ναοποιοί) whose duty it was to supervise the spending of the money by the Delphic council. As the extant inscriptions show, the board was made up of appointees from various Greek cities, although Delphi itself always had some representatives of its own.[3]

There appears to have been no diminution during the fifth and fourth centuries in the popularity of oracles. There were many lesser oracular seats in addition to those few—Delphi, Dodona, Branchidae near Miletus—whose importance was Panhellenic. The consultants, as in earlier times, include state governments as well as individuals. The development of scientific medicine did not seriously impair the cult of Asclepius. At Epidaurus, the chief centre of his worship on the Greek mainland, incubation was extensively practised, and, to judge from official records, many miraculous cures were effected.[4] The worship of Asclepius had been officially introduced into Attica c. 420, but no accounts of the medical side of the Athenian cult have survived. At Piraeus certain

---

[1] *Syll.*, 287.  [2] *Ibid.*, 986.
[3] *Ibid.*, 236 ff. For a list of gifts to Apollo, cf. Tod 140.
[4] Cf. *Syll.*, 1168–1169. These inscriptions were carved in the last quarter of the fourth century, but they list cures occurring over a number of years. See generally R. Herzog, *Die Wunderheilungen von Epidauros* (Leipzig, 1931).

other divinities were associated with Asclepius in the rites, and even the temple dogs were regarded as sacrosanct.[1]

## § 2. RELIGIOUS FESTIVALS

The better known festivals of Greece were all deeply rooted in the past and in the main their development had been completed before the end of the sixth century.[2] Some had begun as purely local celebrations, but already at an early date, by the admission of visitors or participants from other Greek areas, had taken on a national or Panhellenic character. Such were the Olympian, Isthmian, and Nemean Games. Other festivals were from the first attended by groups of tribes or city-states who had formed a religious league for the common worship of some divinity. The institution of the Pythian Games was the act of the Amphictionic League, the only one of these religious federations that is much heard of during the classical period. Many of the others seem, nevertheless, to have continued an obscure existence into the Hellenistic Age. The most striking, as well as the best attested, feature in the history of the Greek festivals during the fifth and fourth centuries is the manner in which the leading Athenian celebrations changed their character. Before the Persian Wars the Panathenaea, the Greater Dionysia, and even the Eleusinia had little interest for any Greek who lived outside Attica. Before the death of Pericles all three were attended by visitors from all parts of the Greek world. Incidentally this circumstance is but another aspect of the close connexion between the state religion and politics. Similarly, one result of the political rehabilitation of the Argives towards the middle of the fifth century was that they arrogated to themselves the presidency of the Nemean Games that had hitherto been exercised by the people of Cleonae. Had Athens after the repulse of Xerxes remained a *polis* of the second or third rank, it is probable that her festivals would have appealed to few save her own citizens. In the case of her dependencies Athens, having become an imperial state, actually stipulated that they participate in the Athenian celebrations by sending contributions. The colonists at Brea

[1] *Syll.*, 1040.
[2] For the earlier history of some of these festivals see Volume I of this *History*.

undertook to despatch offerings both to the Panathenaea and to the Greater Dionysia.[1] Some ten years before the people of Erythrae had undertaken similar obligations. Finally, in 425–424 contributions for the Panathenaea were requisitioned from all the tributaries of Athens, who in this respect were put on the same footing as Athenian colonists.[2]

The rest of the Greek world was under no obligation to attend or patronize Athenian festivals. That it did so voluntarily was the reward reaped by Pericles, his associates, and successors who beautified Athens with new temples, enlarged the *telesterion* at Eleusis, and added new features to the festivals themselves. The full magnificence of the Greater Panathenaea, as held every four years, had been immortalized in the frieze of the Parthenon. It was at Pericles' instigation that the Odeum was built at Athens, and in it were held the musical contests that from his day formed an important feature of that festival. About the same time were introduced the Lesser Mysteries held at Agrae, a suburb of Athens on the Ilissus. Thereafter they formed a preliminary exercise to the Greater Mysteries at Eleusis. An inscription from the year 416–415 shows how at that time the Athenians were striving to win the same international support for Eleusis that they had already in a large measure achieved for the Panathenaea. For Athenian citizens and for the subjects of Athens the payment of first-fruits for the Eleusinian sanctuary was compulsory. But other Greek cities were invited at the same time to show their generosity and veneration for a cult that was all but unique by making similar gifts.[3] The Greater Dionysia owed their wide appeal to the phenomenal development of the Attic drama in the fifth century.

The love of the Greeks for religious celebrations, which brought together large concourses of people, was deeply rooted. At Athens seventy days in the year were given over to public festivals. From time to time additions were made

---

[1] Tod 44, lines 11–12.   [2] *Ibid.* 29, lines 1–4.
[3] *Ibid.* 74. For the date see W. B. Dinsmoor, *The Archons of Athens*, 338. The older view that the inscription antedates the Peloponnesian War and illustrates the imperialism of Pericles may now be discarded, although R. J. Bonner (*Aspects of Athenian Democracy*, 159) still adheres to it. But the only reference that he gives is to an article published by Foucart in 1880. For the older theories in general see Tod's commentary.

GREEK RELIGION 467

to a list that was already long. We have already referred
to the quadrennial Amphiarea at Oropus, held in the fourth
year of each Olympiad, and distinguished by games and a
procession in the hero's honour. Although our information
concerning festivals in other parts of the Hellenic world is
exceedingly scanty, it is probable that they were as numerous
in other cities as they were in Athens. Nor is there anything
to show that important celebrations peculiar to Dorian states
in general, or to Sparta in particular, like the Hyacinthia,
Carneia, and Gymnopaidia, were different in the classical
period from what they had been in the seventh or the sixth
centuries. In any event such accounts of these ceremonies
as survive are, without exception, preserved in post-classical
writers.

### § 3. MYSTERIES AND FOREIGN CULTS

Just as many festivals and games varied in character from
the small and simple *festa* of no more than local appeal to
national meetings to which all Greek cities sent delegates, so
too the number of mystery cults was exceedingly great, but
only a very few attracted devotees from a wide area. Before
the end of the fifth century the Eleusinia occupied the first
place in popular estimation. The general arrangements for
the various ceremonies which lasted eight or nine days were
the responsibility of the King archon, supported by a board
of assessors ($\epsilon\pi\iota\mu\epsilon\lambda\eta\tau\alpha\iota$). The chief religious offices connected with the cult were hereditary in two families, the
Eumolpidae and Kerykes. The preliminary rites, lustrations,
and processions, and the final initiation seem to have been
the same in the days of Pericles or Demosthenes as they had
been under Peisistratus. The only real innovation was the
institution of the Lesser Mysteries at Agrae. They were held
early in the year, about six months before the Eleusinia,
which took place in the autumn. Moreover, it became a rule
that no one could be initiated at Eleusis who had not first
been initiated in Agrae. As in the case of the national games,
so for the Eleusinia a sacred truce was proclaimed throughout
the Greek world to enable Greeks from all parts to take part
in the holy rites of Demeter and Core. Next in importance
to the Eleusinia came the Mysteries in honour of the Cabiri.
The headquarters of this cult was on Samothrace, but the

worship of these nature divinities is attested for various other areas, notably for Thebes, where the earliest remains of a Cabirion go back to the sixth century. During the classical period the Samothracian Mysteries seem to have been overshadowed by those of Eleusis, for it can hardly be a pure accident that nearly all the evidence about them belongs to the Hellenistic or Graeco-Roman eras. Like the Eleusinia, the Mysteries at Samothrace appear to have satisfied the emotional and spiritual yearning of the initiate and to have held out to him, as reward for a pure life on earth, happiness in the hereafter.

Orphism, which before the close of the sixth century had provided some of the esoteric doctrines for the Pythagorean brotherhoods in the West, had its adherents in the rest of the Hellenic world. Its devotees formed private associations of their own, for Orphism did not attain recognition as a state religion. Many of its adherents belonged to the lower strata of society, it was especially popular with women, and its practices often became overlaid with elements borrowed from eastern cults. Hence it is not surprising that both Plato and Demosthenes expressed a disapproval that was probably felt by a majority of their countrymen. In short it may be suspected that, side by side with the genuine and high-minded adherents of true Orphic teaching, there were many others who, under the name of Orphic initiates, indulged their fancy for orgiastic rites and magical hocus-pocus.

In the Greek homeland, in view of the multiplicity of genuine Hellenic cults, the acceptance by individuals or by states of non-Hellenic, that is barbarian or Oriental rites, was inevitably slow before the age of Alexander when all was swiftly changed by the opening-up of the Near and Middle East. In Asia Minor, however, the age-old proximity of non-Hellenic peoples had sometimes affected the religious beliefs and ritual practised in the Greek cities. The Ephesian Artemis had more of the characteristics of an Asiatic mother-goddess than of Apollo's virgin sister. What few Oriental cults can be traced, for example, in Athens, before the close of the fourth century owed their establishment at, least in the first instance, either to slaves or to resident aliens. The worship of Bendis, a Thracian goddess, though introduced by foreigners, in time received official recognition. The deity was identified with Artemis or Hecate and her festival, the Bendideia, held in the Piraeus, seems at least in the fourth century to have been attended by the whole population. More often these extraneous cults thrived more or less underground, tolerated but not sanctioned by the government. Such were the rites paid to the Thracian Cotytto, to the Phrygian mother-goddess, who in time became identified with Rhea, a divinity recognized by the state, to the Anatolian Adonis, and to the Phrygian Sabazios.

It is interesting to note from unequivocal examples how the *ecclesia* might be swayed on occasion by purely material interests to authorize the introduction of a foreign cult. It was a principle of Athenian policy that no metic or foreigner might own landed property in Attica, unless granted this privilege by the people. In 332-331 an application by merchants from Citium in Cyprus was favourably considered, and the *ecclesia* voted a grant of land on which these Citians were at liberty to erect a shrine to the Cyprian Aphrodite. The same inscription that records this decree also informs us that a similar grant had been made on some earlier occasion to Egyptian worshippers of Isis.[1] The motion before the assembly was proposed by Lycurgus himself. Clearly the action of the Athenians was determined, not by any religious motive, but by the wish to be gracious to a part of the foreign population in Attica that was valuable for promoting Athenian trade. One other example may be given. The oracle of Ammon at Siwah had long been familiar to the Greeks and had occasionally been consulted by travellers from Greek lands as early as the fifth century, if not before. At some date prior to 333 the worship of Ammon had been officially sanctioned in Athens.[2] We may guess that Alexander's well-advertised visit to the oracle in the Libyan desert did much to make the cult more widely known among the Greeks.

[1] Tod 189.      [2] *Syll.*, 281 and 1029.

# APPENDIX

## SOURCES AND AUTHORITIES FOR THE PERIOD, 478 TO 323 B.C.

(a) *Literary texts.*—For three-quarters of the period from 478 to 323 B.C. there survive virtually contemporary accounts in the *History* of Thucydides and in the *Hellenica*, *Anabasis*, and some minor writings by Xenophon. But the treatment or the space accorded to different parts of the whole epoch is far from uniform. Thucydides' work was planned as a detailed narrative of the Second Peloponnesian War (431–404); but it was never completed and breaks off in the year 411. In the opening book the historian provides the reader with a brief review of Greek history from 479 to 432, and also analyses in detail the ultimate causes of the Peloponnesian War as well as the political and military events and diplomatic conversations that immediately preceded the outbreak of hostilities. Xenophon's works cover the years from 411 to 362, but in a very uneven fashion, the treatment of the last decade especially being much briefer than of the earlier period. A discovery of some importance was made known in 1907, when portions of a historical work describing the early years of the fourth century were deciphered on a papyrus from Oxyrhynchus. They deal in considerable detail with Greek affairs in 396–395 and are valuable for two reasons. They provide completely new information about some matters previously very obscure—for instance, the democratic revolution in Rhodes at this time and the organization of the Boeotian Confederacy at the beginning of the fourth century—and their version of the relations between Persia and the Greeks differs from, and in some respects corrects, the narrative of Xenophon. The history, of which these fragments form only a small part, was evidently on a large scale, but it is uncertain what was the length of the period covered by the complete work. Nor is the author known; for none of the attributions hitherto made—Theopompus, Ephorus, Cratippus, and Daimachus of Plataea have all been suggested—is free from serious objections. All that can be said with certainty is that Ephorus not long afterwards used this work when composing his own history of Greece, Of historical works composed at a later

# APPENDIX

date the fullest is the world history of Diodorus (*circa* 80 B.C.). Books 11 to 17, covering the whole of our period, are preserved in their entirety. Their value, when all allowance has been made for the uncritical method of Diodorus and his carelessness in arrangement and chronology, depends upon the character of his sources, although these cannot always be determined with certainty. But much of his information is drawn from fourth-century writers now lost, especially from Ephorus.[1]

Fifteen of the *Lives* composed by Plutarch (*circa* A.D. 100) are devoted to statesmen and soldiers of the fifth and fourth centuries (Themistocles, Aristides, Cimon, Pericles, Nicias, Alcibiades, Lysander, Agesilaus, Pelopidas, Artaxerxes, Dion, Timoleon, Demosthenes, Alexander the Great, Phocion). They are brief biographies, and their author was writing with a moral purpose. As he himself observes:

> And the most glorious exploits do not always furnish us with the clearest discoveries of virtue or vice in men; sometimes a matter of less moment, an expression or a jest, informs us better of their characters and inclinations, than the most famous sieges, the greatest armaments, and the bloodiest battles whatsoever. (*Life of Alexander*, ch. 1.)

In consequence, anecdotes abound in the *Lives*, many being probably or certainly apocryphal. The chronology is often confused, and there is a lack of critical treatment of the sources. Nevertheless, just as each generation of readers, from Plutarch's own time down to the present, has been charmed by these inimitable pen-portraits, so the historical student will meet with substantial material not found elsewhere to supplement his picture of the classical Greek world. Some of Plutarch's sources, now no longer extant, were reliable accounts contemporary with the events related. Such, for instance, was the history of the Syracusan Philistus. It may be added that many of the *Lives* supplement one another, when indeed they do not reproduce some of the same material. This is the case, for example, with portions of the *Lives* of Pericles and Cimon, or those of Nicias and Alcibiades.

Little of value can be gleaned from the brief biographies of Themistocles, Alcibiades, and some other prominent figures in Greek history by the Roman writer Cornelius Nepos (*circa* 40 B.C.), nor yet from the anecdotes of famous personages in the *Varia Historia* of Aelian (*circa* A.D. 220). For the history of the western Greeks, apart from the Athenian invasion of Sicily in 415–413

---

[1] A new edition with commentary by F. Jacoby of the fragments of the Greek historians is in process of publication with the title, *Die Fragmente der griechischen Historiker*,

narrated in masterly fashion in the sixth and seventh books of Thucydides' *History*, we depend on Diodorus and on Plutarch's *Lives* of Dion and Timoleon. Diodorus, supplemented by Plutarch's biography of Artaxerxes, is also our informant about the relations between Persia and the Greeks from the Peace of Antalcidas (386) to the advent of Alexander the Great. For the rise of Macedon and the career of Philip II the surviving material is sadly insufficient; the loss of Theopompus' *Philippica* is especially to be deplored. As it is, we are obliged to depend mainly on the inexact narrative of Diodorus and on the hostile utterances of Philip's great opponent, Demosthenes. The commentary on certain public speeches of that orator by Didymus (circa 30 B.C.) is occasionally helpful. By far the most reliable account of Alexander's military achievements is contained in the seven books of the *Anabasis of Alexander* by Arrian (circa A.D. 160); for the writer, himself a man of some military experience, made full use of the diaries of Alexander's general Ptolemy and of other contemporary material. The *History of Alexander* by the Roman Quintus Curtius (circa A.D. 75) and to a great extent Plutarch's biography of the conqueror reproduce the novelistic, quasi-legendary accounts of Alexander which began to gain currency even before his death, and which Clitarchus, writing some decades later, particularly helped to perpetuate and to augment.

Judiciously used, the speeches of the Attic Orators are a most precious quarry for the student of fourth-century history. It will be obvious, however, that the political harangues of Lysias, Aeschines, and Demosthenes, and, in a somewhat less degree, the deliberative discourses of Isocrates, are all *ex parte* statements. Hence the authors' accounts and interpretations of historical occurrences, and especially of the actions and motives of their political opponents, must be received with due reservations. Even in the solitary instance where the utterances of opposing speakers in the same *cause célèbre* have survived, to wit, the speeches of Aeschines and of Demosthenes on the embassy sent to Philip in 346, the historic truth is often difficult to disentangle. The forensic speeches, too, are in the highest degree important for the economic and social history of their time. But again the modern reader must never forget that he is viewing only one side of a disputed case.

For constitutional and institutional questions, especially at Athens, the treatise written by an unknown writer of oligarchic sympathies about the year 430 B.C., which is preserved amongst the works of Xenophon, is of some interest; but the outstanding work in this field is Aristotle's *Constitution of Athens*. In those chapters, however, where Aristotle touches on political events, he is far from impeccable. Very valuable, on the other hand, are his observations, scattered through the pages of the *Politics*, on the actual working of Greek constitutions. Some light on economic questions is thrown by the oligarchic writer mentioned above and by the treatise entitled *Ways and Means* (of improving the revenues of Athens). It was published about 358 B.C., and its attribution to Xenophon, although it has been questioned, is probably correct.

A treatise by Aeneas Tacticus (*circa* 340) contains much interesting information about military tactics, strategy, and ruses of war, particularly during the fourth century when the author is dealing with events of his own time. Some help in the study of military history can also be derived occasionally from the *Stratagems* of the Macedonian Polyaenus who flourished in the age of the Antonines.

(b) *Inscriptions*.—There is a considerable number of these for our period, although the total is small compared with the epigraphic material for the Hellenistic and Graeco-Roman epochs. Even so they not only serve to check the accuracy of the literary sources, but considerably augment our knowledge. Often the additional information is on relatively small points of detail that are of more interest to the specialist than to the general student. But at times the epigraphic evidence is all or nearly all that we possess on leading topics. If it were not for the Athenian tribute lists from 454 to 419, or for the decree of Aristoteles passed in 378, we should know but little of the inner history and organization of the Athenian Empire or of the Second Athenian Confederacy.

(c) *Coins*.—Inasmuch as the issue of currency was the mark of an independent city-state and the sum total of autonomous communities in our period was very great, it is not surprising that there is an abundance and an astonishing diversity of coins. Besides their more obvious worth as artistic objects, and in special cases as records commemorative of notable events or of new colonial or civic foundations, they may be of the utmost service for reconstructing the commercial enterprises and policies of city-states, as well as for the history of alliances and inter-state relations.

(d) *Papyri*.—Apart from certain literary papyri that have already been named amongst the literary sources—for instance, the anonymous history of the years 396–395 and Aristotle's *Constitution of Athens*—this class of historical material, which is of such basic importance for the Hellenistic period, is virtually non-existent for the fifth and fourth centuries.

# SELECT BIBLIOGRAPHY

(Only a brief selection of works is given. For full bibliographies down to 1927, see *Cambridge Ancient History*, vols. V–VI. For works which appeared between 1926 and 1931, see T. Lenschau in Bursian's *Jahresberichte für das klassische Altertum*. For books and articles published after 1931, consult the pertinent sections in Marouzeau's *L'année philologique*. There are good bibliographies in the works of Bengtson and de Sanctis listed below, section A.)

## A. GENERAL

K. J. BELOCH, *Griechische Geschichte*, 2nd ed., vols. II and III, each in two parts. (Berlin–Leipzig, 1914–1923.)

H. BENGTSON, *Griechische Geschichte*. (Munich, 1950.)

H. BERVE, *Grieschische Geschichte*, 2 vols. (Freiburg i.B., 1931–1933.)

J. B. BURY, *History of Greece to the death of Alexander*. 3rd ed. revised by R. Meiggs. (London, 1951.)

J. B. BURY, S. A. COOK, and F. E. ADCOCK, *The Cambridge Ancient History*, vols. V and VI. (Cambridge, 1926–1927.)

G. GLOTZ and R. COHEN, *Histoire grecque*, vols. II and III. (Paris, 1931–1936.)

P. ROUSSEL, *La Grèce et l'orient des guerres médiques à la conquête romaine*. (Paris, 1928.)

G. DE SANCTIS, *Storia dei Greci*, vol. II. (Florence, 1939.)

U. VON WILAMOWITZ-MOELLENDORF and B. NIESE, *Staat und Gesellschaft der Griechen und Römer*, 2nd ed. (Berlin, 1923.)

## B. PARTICULAR STATES OR AREAS

(1) *Athens*

R. J. BONNER, *Aspects of Athenian Democracy*. (Berkeley, 1933.)

P. CLOCHE, *Démosthène et la fin de la démocratie athénienne*. (Paris, 1937.)

P. CLOCHE, *La politique étrangère d'Athènes de 404 à 338 avant Jésus-Christ*. (Paris, 1934.)

A. FERRABINO, *L'impero ateniese*. (Turin, 1927.)

B. W. HENDERSON, *The Great War between Athens and Sparta*. (London, 1927.)

# SELECT BIBLIOGRAPHY

A. E. ZIMMERN, *The Greek Commonwealth : Politics and Economics in Fifth-Century Athens*, 5th ed. (Oxford, 1931.)

(2) *Sparta*

V. EHRENBERG, *Sparta*, in Pauly-Wissowa-Kroll-Mittelhaus, *Realencyclopädie*, Zweite Reihe VI (1929), 1373–1453.
B. W. HENDERSON, as above.
H. MICHELL, *Sparta*. (Cambridge, 1952.)

(3) *Northern Greece, Macedonia, Philip II, and Alexander*

H. BERVE, *Das Alexanderreich auf prosopographischer Grundlage*, 2 vols. (Munich, 1926.)
F. GEYER, *Makedonien bis zur Thronbesteigung Philipps II*. (*Historische Zeitschrift;* Beiheft 19 [1930].)
A. MOMIGLIANO, *Filippo il Macedone*. (Florence, 1934.)
G. RADET, *Alexandre le grand*. (Paris, 1931.)
C. A. ROBINSON, Jr., *Alexander the Great*. (New York, 1947.)
F. SCHACHERMEYR, *Alexander der Grosse*. (Graz, 1949.)
W. W. TARN, *Alexander the Great*, 2 vols. (Cambridge, 1948.)
H. D. WESTLAKE, *Thessaly in the Fourth Century*. (London, 1935.)
U. WILCKEN, *Alexander der Grosse*. (Leipzig, 1931.) An English translation by G. C. Richards appeared in 1932.

(4) *The Greeks of the West*

E. CIACERI, *Storia della Magna Grecia*, vols. II and III. (Milan–Rome–Naples, 1927–1932.)
K. FABRICIUS, *Das antike Syrakus*. (*Klio*, Suppl., vol. 28, 1932.)
E. A. FREEMAN, *History of Sicily*, vols. II–IV. (London, 1891–1894.)

## C. SPECIAL SUBJECTS

(1) *Constitutions and Leagues*

G. BUSOLT and H. SWOBODA, *Griechische Staatskunde*, vol. II. (Munich, 1926.)
G. GLOTZ, *La cité grecque*. (Paris, 1928.)
C. HIGNETT, *A History of the Athenian Constitution to the end of the Fifth Century*. (Oxford, 1952.)
J. A. O. LARSEN, *Representative Government in Greek and Roman History*. (Berkeley, 1955.)
J. A. O. LARSEN, *The Constitution of the Peloponnesian League*. (*Classical Philology* 28 [1933], 257–276 ; 29 [1934], 1–19.)
F. H. MARSHALL, *The Second Athenian Confederacy*. (Cambridge, 1905.)

476   THE GREEK WORLD FROM 479 TO 323 B.C.

H. NESSELHAUF, *Untersuchungen zur Geschichte der delisch-attischen Symmachie.* (*Klio*, Suppl., vol. 30, 1933.)

L. WHIBLEY, *Greek Oligarchies.* (Cambridge, 1896.)

(2) *Military and Naval Affairs*

A. KOESTER, *Studien zur Geschichte des antiken Seewesens*, chs. II and V. (*Klio*, Suppl., vol. 32, 1934.)

J. KROMAYER and G. VEITH, *Antike Schlachtfelder*, vols. I and IV. (Berlin, 1903–1931.)

J. KROMAYER, G. VEITH, and others, *Heerwesen und Kriegführung der Griechen und Römer.* (Munich, 1928.)

E. and F. LAMMERT, *Kriegskunst*, in Pauly-Wissowa-Kroll-Mittelhaus, *Real-encyclopädie*, XI (1922), 1827–1858.

F. MILTNER, *Seekrieg* and *Seewesen*, in Pauly-Wissowa-Kroll-Mittelhaus, *Real-encyclopädie*, Supplementband V (1931), 864–962.

H. W. PARKE, *Greek Mercenary Soldiers.* (Oxford, 1933.)

W. W. TARN, *Hellenistic Military and Naval Developments.* (Cambridge, 1930.)

W. J. WOODHOUSE, *King Agis of Sparta and his Campaign in Arcadia in 418 B.C.* (Oxford, 1933.)

(3) *Economic History and Finance*

G. BUSOLT and H. SWOBODA, as under C (1).

G. M. CALHOUN, *The Business Life of Ancient Athens.* (Chicago, 1926.)

W. S. FERGUSON, *The Treasurers of Athena.* (Cambridge, Mass., 1932.)

G. GLOTZ, *Le travail dans la Grèce ancienne.* (Paris, 1920.) There is an English translation with the title, *Ancient Greece at Work.* (London and New York, 1926.)

A. W. GOMME, *The Population of Athens in the Fifth and Fourth Centuries.* (Oxford, 1933.)

J. HASEBROEK, *Staat und Handel im alten Griechenland.* (Tübingen, 1928.) There is an English translation with the title, *Trade and Politics in Ancient Greece.* (London, 1933.)

F. HEICHELHEIM, *Wirtschaftsgeschichte des Altertums*, 2 vols. (Leyden, 1938.)

B. D. MERITT, *Athenian Financial Documents of the Fifth Century.* (Ann Arbor, 1932.)

B. D. MERITT and A. B. WEST, *The Athenian Assessment of 425.* (Ann Arbor, 1934.)

B. D. MERITT, H. T. WADE-GERY, and M. F. MCGREGOR, *The Athenian Tribute Lists*, 4 vols. (Princeton, 1939–1953.)

# SELECT BIBLIOGRAPHY

W. L. WESTERMANN, *The Slave Systems of Greek and Roman Antiquity*. (Philadelphia, 1955.)

E. ZIEBARTH, *Beiträge zur Geschichte des Seeraubs und Seehandels im alten Griechenland*. (Hamburg, 1929.)

### (4) Law and Legal Procedure

S. ACCAME, *La lega ateniese del secolo IV a. C.* (Rome, 1941.)

R. J. BONNER, *Lawyers and Litigants in Ancient Athens*. (Chicago, 1927.)

R. J. BONNER and GERTRUDE SMITH, *The Administration of Justice from Homer to Aristotle*, 2 vols. (Chicago, 1930–1938.)

G. BUSOLT and H. SWOBODA, as under C (1).

G. M. CALHOUN, *The Growth of Criminal Law in Ancient Greece*. (Berkeley, 1927.)

J. H. LIPSIUS, *Das attische Recht und Rechtsverfahren*, 2 vols. (Leipzig, 1905–1915.)

P. VINOGRADOFF, *Outlines of Historical Jurisprudence*, vol. II. (Oxford, 1922.)

### (5) Art and Architecture

W. J. ANDERSON and R. P. SPIERS, *The Architecture of Ancient Greece*. (London, 1927.)

J. D. BEAZLEY, *Attic Red-Figure Vase-Painters*. (Oxford, 1942.)

J. D. BEAZLEY, *Potter and Painter in Ancient Athens*. (London, 1952.)

E. A. GARDNER, *Handbook of Greek Sculpture*, 2nd ed. (London, 1915.)

D. LAMB, *Greek and Roman Bronzes*. (London, 1929.)

A. W. LAWRENCE, *Classical Sculpture*, 2nd ed. (London, 1944.)

G. MACDONALD, *Coin Types*. (Glasgow, 1905.)

E. PFUHL, *Meisterwerke griechischer Zeichnung und Malerei*. (Munich, 1924.) English translation by J. D. Beazley (new ed., 1955).

C. PICARD, *La sculpture antique*, 2 vols. (Paris, 1923–1926.)

G. M. RICHTER, *Sculpture and Sculptors of the Greeks*, 3rd ed. (New Haven, 1951.)

D. S. ROBERTSON, *Handbook of Greek and Roman Architecture*, 2nd ed. (Cambridge, 1943.)

C. T. SELTMAN, *Attic Vase-Painting*. (Cambridge, Mass., 1933.)

C. T. SELTMAN, *Greek Coins*, 2nd ed. (London, 1955.)

M. H. SWINDLER, *Ancient Painting*. (New Haven, 1929.)

### (6a) Literature—General

W. VON CHRIST, W. SCHMID, and O. STÄHLIN, *Geschichte der griechischen Literatur*, 6th ed., 2 vols. (Munich, 1912–1924.)

# 478 THE GREEK WORLD FROM 479 TO 323 B.C.

A. and M. CROISET, *Histoire de la littérature grecque*, 3rd ed., vols. II–IV. (Paris, 1913–1947.)

A. W. GOMME, *Essays in Greek History and Literature*. (Oxford, 1937.)

H. J. ROSE, *Handbook of Greek Literature*, 4th ed. (London, 1950.)

T. B. L. WEBSTER, *Greek Art and Literature, 530–400 B.C.* (Oxford, 1939.)

(6b) *Drama*

M. BIEBER, *The History of the Greek and Roman Theatre*. (Princeton, 1939.)

V. EHRENBERG, *The People of Aristophanes: a Sociology of Old Attic Comedy*, 2nd ed. (Oxford, 1951.)

R. FLICKINGER, *The Greek Theatre*, 4th ed. (Chicago, 1936.)

P. W. HARSH, *A Handbook of Classical Drama*. (Stanford, 1944.)

H. D. F. KITTO, *Greek Tragedy*, 2nd ed. (London, 1950.)

A. W. PICKARD-CAMBRIDGE, *Dithyramb, Tragedy, and Comedy*. (Oxford, 1927.)

A. W. PICKARD-CAMBRIDGE, *The Dramatic Festivals of Athens*. (Oxford, 1953.)

(6c) *Oratory*

F. BLASS, *Die attische Beredsamkeit*, 3 vols. (Leipzig, 1890–1898.)

S. H. BUTCHER, *Demosthenes*. (London, 1891.)

E. DRERUP, *Demosthenes im Urteile des Altertums*. (Würzburg, 1923.)

R. C. JEBB, *The Attic Orators*, 2 vols. (London, 1893.)

(6d) *History and Geography*

J. B. BURY, *The Ancient Greek Historians*. (London and New York, 1909.)

M. CARY, *The Geographic Background of Greek and Roman History*. (Oxford, 1949.)

M. CARY and E. H. WARMINGTON, *The Ancient Explorers*. (London, 1929.)

C. N. COCHRANE, *Thucydides and the Science of History*. (Oxford, 1929.)

J. H. FINLEY, *Thucydides*. (Cambridge, Mass., 1942.)

T. R. GLOVER, *Herodotus*. (Berkeley, 1924.)

G. B. GRUNDY, *Thucydides and the History of his Age*, 2nd ed., 2 vols. (London, 1948.)

F. JACOBY, *Herodotus* in Pauly-Wissowa-Kroll-Mittelhaus, *Realencyclopädie*, Supplementband II, 205–520.

W. R. M. LAMB, *Clio Enthroned*. (Cambridge, 1911.)

J. DE ROMILLY, *Thucydide et l'impérialisme athénien*, 2nd ed. (Paris, 1951.)
J. O. THOMAS, *History of Ancient Geography*. (Cambridge, 1948.)

(7) *Science*

T. L. HEATH, *Manual of Greek Mathematics*. (Oxford, 1931.)
J. L. HEIBERG, *Geschichte der Mathematik und Naturwissenschaft im Altertum*. (Munich, 1925.)
W. KUBITSCHEK, *Grundriss der antiken Zeitrechnung*. (Munich, 1927.)
B. D. MERITT, *The Athenian Calendar in the Fifth Century*. (Cambridge, Mass., 1928.)
G. SARTON, *History of Science : Ancient Science through the Golden Age of Greece*. (Cambridge, Mass., 1952.)
C. SINGER, *Greek Biology and Greek Medicine*. (Oxford, 1922.)

(8) *Philosophy and Education*

E. BARKER, *Greek Political Theory : Plato and his Predecessors*, 4th ed. (London, 1951.)
A. BURK, *Die Pädagogik des Isocrates*. (Würzburg, 1923.)
J. BURNET, *Early Greek Philosophy*, 4th ed. (London, 1948.)
J. BURNET, *Greek Philosophy*, Part I, 5th ed. (London, 1932.)
G. C. FIELD, *Plato and his Contemporaries*. (London, 1930.)
G. M. A. GRUBE, *Plato's Thought*. (London, 1935.)
W. JAEGER, *Aristoteles*. (Berlin, 1923.) English translation by R. Robinson (2nd ed., 1948).
W. JAEGER, *Paideia*. Translated by G. Highet, 3 vols. (New York, 1939–1944.)
H. I. MARROU, *Histoire de l'éducation dans l'antiquité*. (Paris, 1948.)
G. MATHIEU, *Les idées politiques d'Isocrate*. (Paris, 1925.)
L. ROBIN, *Greek Thought and the Origin of the Scientific Spirit*. (London and New York, 1928.)
W. D. ROSS, *Aristotle*, 3rd ed. (London, 1937.)
P. SHOREY, *What Plato said*. (Chicago, 1933.)
F. SOLMSEN, *Plato's Theology*. (Ithaca, N.Y., 1942.)
A. E. TAYLOR, *Plato : the Man and his Work*, 6th ed. (London, 1950.)

(9) *Religion*

L. A. DEUBNER, *Attische Feste*. (Berlin, 1932.)
N. GARDINER, *Olympia*. (Oxford, 1925.)
W. K. C. GUTHRIE, *The Greeks and their Gods*. (London, 1950.)
W. A. LAIDLAW, *A History of Delos*. (Oxford, 1933.)
F. MAGNIEN, *Les mystères d'Eleusis*. (Paris, 1929.)

M. P. Nilsson, *Geschichte der griechischen Religion*, Vol. I, 2nd ed. (Munich, 1955.)
M. P. Nilsson, *Greek Popular Religion*. (New York, 1940.)
A. D. Nock, *Conversion*, chs. I and II. (Oxford, 1933.)
H. W. Parke and D. E. W. Wormell, *The Delphic Oracle*, 2 vols. (Oxford, 1956.)
F. Poulsen, *Delphi*. (London, 1920.)

# INDEX

Abacaenum, 289 n.
Abdera, 154, 197, 239
Abydos, 151, 154, 185, 294
Acanthus, 189
Acarnania, 39, 80, 91–3, 96–7, 98, 185, 191, 255
Achaea, 44, 46, 80, 101, 235, 237, 238, 252, 255
Achaemenes, 17
Acraephia, 368
Acragas, 54, 59–60, 62–3, 64, 65, 267–8, 269, 273, 288, 379
Ada, 297
Adranum, 286, 288, 289 n.
Aegina, 35, 44, 78, 82, 185, 384, 394
Aegospotami, 159, 160
Aeneas Tacticus, 336, 337
Aenus, 253
Aeschines, 244, 245, 246, 249, 251, 256, 325, 433–4
Aeschylus, 32–3, 414–15
Aesop, 409
Aethalia, 65
Aetna (Catana), 59, 61
Aetna (Inessa), 63, 64, 270, 283
Aetolia, 39, 91, 96–8, 327, 371
Agariste, 33
Agathon, 220
Agesilaus, succeeds to throne, 175; campaigns in Asia Minor, 175–6, 177; returns to Greece, 182; conquers at Coronea, 182; campaign in Acarnania, 185; blockades Phlius, 188; his anti-Theban policy, 190, 193, 201; fails to recover Thebes, 193; invades Boeotia again, 195–6; organises defence of Laconia, 206; enters service of Ariobarzanes, 214; defends Laconia, 217; admired by Xenophon, 426–7
Agesipolis, 187, 189, 336
Agis II, 120–3, 141, 149, 153, 161, 175
Agis III, 323–4
Agoracritus, 398
Agoratus, 163
Agrae, 466, 467
Agyrrhius, 362
Alaesa, 289 n.
Alcamenes, 398
Alcetas, 198, 279

Alcibiades, early training of, 118, 448; elected *strategus*, 118; anti-Spartan policy, 119, 120; leads expedition to Argos, 121; votes for death of Melians, 124; urges expedition to Sicily, 128; prosecuted for impiety, 129, 130, 461; proceeds to Sicily, 128, 354; his strategy, 130; escapes to Sparta, 130; advises Spartans, 132; sails for Chios, 142–3; flies to Tissaphernes, 144; communicates with Athenians and is recalled, 145, 147, 148; confirmed as *strategus*, 151; in Propontis, 153; recovers Chalcedon and Byzantium, 154; returns to Athens, 156; made commander-in-chief, 156; disobeyed by subordinate, 156; goes into exile, 156; warns Athenians at Aegospotami, 159; flies to Pharnabazus and is extradited and killed by Lysander, 164; estimate of, 118
Alcidas, 88, 94
Alcmaeonidae, 33, 423
Alexander I, 30, 50
Alexander II, 211, 212
Alexander III (the Great), early training of, 292; at Chaeronea, 259; quarrels with father, 262–3; accession and first campaigns, 293; suppresses Greek rising, 293–4; victory at Granicus, 296; conquers western Asia, 296–8; victor at Issus, 298–9; annexes Syria and Egypt, 299–301; marches to Tigris, 301–2; victory at Gaugamela, 302–3; conquers Media and Persis, 303–5; campaigns in central Asia, 305–9; invades Punjab and Swat, 309–11; defeats Porus, 311–12; marches to Beas, 313; returns to Patala, 313–14; sends Craterus to west, 314; marches through Gedrosia, 315; returns to Babylon, 315; suppresses mutiny, 316; decrees recall of exiles, 327; death of, 317; as an administrator, 320–2; his relation to Greek states, 293–4,

296, 322-7 ; aims and personality of, 318-20 ; legends about, 320 ; portrayed in art, 400, 402
Alexander of Epirus, 252, 263, 290
Alexander of Pherae, 211, 212, 213, 216
Alexandreschate, 307, 322
Alexandria, 300
Alexandria ad Caucasum, 307
Alexandria Arachoton, 306, 322
Alexandria Areion, 322
Alexis, 420
Amadocus, 223, 239
Amanus, 298
Ambracia, 80, 91, 92, 97, 98, 255
Amisus, 51
Ammon, 300, 469
Amorges, 142
Amphictionic League, 22, 233-4, 247, 249, 256-7, 366, 465
Amphilochians, 92
Amphipolis, 109-10, 112, 114, 117, 124, 226, 227, 321, 341
Amphissa, 235, 257, 258
Amphoterus, 301
Amyntas III, 188-9, 200, 212, 221-2
Amyntas IV, 222, 293
Amyntas (general of Alexander III), 310
Amyrtaeus, 18
Anactorium, 80, 98, 114, 116
Anaxagoras, 72, 419, 437, 439, 461
Anaxilaus, 57
Ancona, 279
Ancyra, 298
Andocides, 129, 431-2
Androcles, 146
Andros, 44, 229
Antalcidas, 183, 185-6
Anthemus, 227
Antiochus, 156
Antipater, 292, 298, 323-4
Antiphanes, 420
Antiphon, 145, 146, 149, 431
Antisthenes, 450
Anytus, 165, 181, 358
Aornos (Pir-sar), 311, 340
Aornos (Tashkurgan), 307
Apelles (painter), 402
Apelles (Syracusan commander), 65
Aphytis, 108
Apollocrates, 284
Apollodorus, 402
Apollonia (Chalcidice), 189, 243
Apollonia (Epirus), 73
Apulia, 404
Arabitae, 315
Arachosia, 306
Arbela, 303
Arcadians, 24-5, 46, 205, 207-8, 209-11, 216-17, 218, 249, 260, 367-8, 371

Arcesines, 314
Archelaus, 188, 220-1, 338
Archidamus I, 26, 77
Archidamus II, 290, 447
Archinus, 165
Archytas, 272, 278, 283
Areopagus, 31-2, 326
Argaeus, 223, 224
Argilus, 109, 112
Arginusae, 158-9, 341, 343
Argos, at war with Sparta, 24 ; destroys Mycenae and Tiryns, 25 ; makes alliance with Athens and Thessalians, 34 ; makes treaty with Sparta, 40 ; neutral in Peloponnesian war, 80 ; covets Spartan territory, 113 ; joins anti-Spartan alliance, 117 ; at war with Sparta, 119-22 ; revolutions at, 123, 205, 348 ; anti-Spartan policy of, 180 ; alliance with Megalopolis, 217, 238 ; relations with Philip II, 249 ; friendly relations with Athens, 249, 250, 252 ; army of, 331
Aria, 305
Ariobarzanes, 209, 214, 215, 304
Aristeus, 76
Aristides, 5, 27-8
Aristippus, 411, 450
Aristodicus, 33
Aristophanes, 89, 117, 355, 408, 411, 418, 419-20, 430, 462
Aristophon, 358
Aristoteles, 194
Aristotle, 149, 292, 348, 410, 424, 454-60
Armenia, 172, 291
Arrhabaeus, 109
Arsites, 255
Artabanus, 15-16
Artabazus (*circa* 478), 3
Artabazus (*circa* 350), 238, 255
Artaxerxes I, 15-16, 17, 20, 29
Artaxerxes II, 169, 170, 171, 173, 174, 184, 185-6, 209, 214, 229, 291
Artaxerxes III, 229, 232, 238, 291-2, 295
Artemisia, 232
Arybbas, 253
Asopius, 93
Aspasia, 72, 411
Assaceni, 311
Assinarus, r., 139
Assos, 347, 391
Astacus (Acarnania), 83, 93
Astacus (Propontis), 51
Astyochus, 143, 150
Atarneus, 174, 347
Athens, head of the Delian Confederacy, 5-7 ; prosecutes war

# INDEX

against Persia, 7, 8–9, 15–18, 19–20; converts Delian Confederacy into an empire, 10–15, 44–53; assists Sparta, 26–7; at war with Peloponnesian states, 34–40; makes truce with Sparta, 40; renews war and loses Boeotia, 42–3; concludes peace, 44; sends colonists to Thuria, 46, 70; makes alliance with Corcyra, 74–5; coerces Potidaea, 75–7; renews war with Peloponnesian League, 77–8; resources of, 79–81; operations in Peloponnese, 82–3, 99–103; coerces Mytilene, 86–91; operates in north-western Greece, 91–9; operates in Chalcidice, 107–13, 123; defeated in Boeotia, 103–6; in financial difficulties, 91, 106–7, 125, 141; makes peace with Sparta, 113–15; allied with Argos and others, 117–23; reduces Melos, 124–5; sends expeditions to Sicily, 126–39; at war with Sparta and Persia, 141–2, 153–60; capitulates, 161; joins anti-Spartan coalition, 180–3; naval activity of, 184–5, 190; forms alliance with Thebes, 193; organizes maritime league, 193–5; victorious at Naxos, 197; enlarges maritime league, 197–8, 200, 213–16; makes peace with Sparta, 201; makes alliance with Sparta against Thebes, 206–7; sends help to Sparta, 217; backs pretender to Macedonian throne, 223–4; refuses alliance with Olynthus, 227; at war with Macedonia, 228, 229; at war with maritime allies, 228–32; helps Phocians at Thermopylae, 237; further wars with Philip II, 239–43; sends expedition to Olynthus, 243; initiates peace with Philip, 243–8; strained relations with Philip, 250–2, 253–4; renews war with him, 254–5; supports Thebes at Chaeronea, 257, 260; joins League of Corinth, 260; submits to Alexander, 294; receives Harpalus, 326; votes divine honours to Alexander, 327; military and naval organization of, 328–9, 331–2, 341–4; administration and government, 31–4, 140, 146–52, 162–5, 351–60; financial organization, 360–5; alien and slave population of, 373–4, 375–6; trade and commerce, 378, 379–82, 383, 385–6; art, 389–90, 391–2, 395–9, 400–1, 401–2, 403–4; drama, 413–20; prose-writers, 422–7, 430–4; philosophy, 447–60
Attalus, 262, 293

Babylon, 170, 303, 316, 317, 321
Bacchylides, 407, 413
Bactra, 307, 310
Bactria, 304, 305, 307
Bagoas, 295
Bendis, 469
Berisades, 223, 224
Bessus, 304, 307
Boeotian League, renewal of, 37; disbanded by Athens, 38; reconstituted, 42; joins Sparta against Athens, 80; victory at Delium, 104–6; seizes Panactum, 114, 116, 119; demands destruction of Athens, 161; disbanded by Sparta, 190, 191; reconstituted by Thebes, 197, 201; victory at Leuctra, 202–3; military strength of, 332; constitutional organization of, 368–9.
*See also* Thebes
Boges, 7
Bosporus, 386
Bottiaeans, 112
Branchidae, 391, 464
Brasidas, 103, 107–13, 114, 331
Brea, 45, 465
Bruttians, 290
Byblus, 299
Byzantium, 3, 4, 48, 49, 150, 153, 184, 193, 215, 216, 229, 230, 231, 232, 239, 253, 255–6, 339, 371

Cabiri, 467–8
Cadmea, 190, 294
Calamis, 397–8
Cale Acte, 65
Callias (Athenian officer), 76
Callias (Athenian politician), 20
Callias (mover of decree of 433), 361
Callibius, 163
Callippus, 440
Callisthenes, 295, 308–9; pseudo-Callisthenes, 321
Callistratus, 210, 214, 358, 359
Camarina, 63, 130, 132, 268, 273, 288
Camirus, 177
Campania, 58
Campanians, 267, 270
Cappadocia, 295, 298
Cardia, 228, 253–4
Carduchi, 172
Caria, 9, 15, 48, 291, 296
Carmania, 314, 315
Carpathus, 179 n.
Carthage, 54, 266–9, 273–6, 280, 285, 286–8
Carystus, 10

Caspian Gates, 305
Catana, 59, 63, 130, 131, 134, 138, 270, 274, 286
Cathaei, 313
Caulonia, 67, 69, 277
Caunus, 177
Cecryphaleia, 35
Celaenae, 297
Centuripae, 289 n.
Ceos, 215–16
Cephallenia, 39, 83, 91, 95, 197
Cephalus (Athenian politician), 165
Cephalus (father of Lysias), 379
Cephisophon, 255
Cersobleptes, 223, 228, 239, 240, 246, 253
Cetriporis, 227
Chabrias, 185, 193, 196, 230, 358
Chaeronea, 42, 104–5, 258–9, 329, 338, 368
Chalcedon, 153, 154, 184
Chalcideus, 143
Chalcidic League, 109, 188–9, 191, 197, 212, 215, 221, 223, 227, 240–3. *See also* Olynthus
Chalcis, 10, 43, 193, 252, 255, 259, 261, 379
Chares, 228, 230, 231, 240, 243, 255, 258
Charmides, 162
Charoiades, 126
Charon, 192
Cheirisophus, 172
Cheiron, Maxims of, 409
Chimerium, 75
Chios, 6, 8, 48, 81, 83, 141, 142, 143, 144, 157, 158, 159, 178, 184, 193, 215, 229, 230, 231, 255, 256, 262, 297, 323, 378
Chorasmia, 307
Chromius, 57, 59
Chrysopolis, 153
Cilicia, 298
Cimolos, 261, 407
Cimon, early life, 7 ; takes part in forming Confederacy of Delos, 5, 7 ; becomes generalissimo of Confederacy and takes Eion, 7 ; captures Scyros, 7–8 ; leads expedition to Asia, 8–9 ; reduces Thasos, 11 ; is impeached but acquitted, 30 ; takes expeditionary force to Sparta, 26–7 ; is ostracized, 31 ; leads expedition to Cyprus, 19 ; besieges Citium, 19 ; death, 19 ; personality, 29–30 ; political ideas of, 30 ; oratory of, 430
Cinadon, 179
Citium, 19, 469
Clazomenae, 143, 186
Clearchus (Spartan officer), 169, 170, 171, 426

Clearchus (Tyrant of Heraclea), 347
Clearidas, 112–13
Cleippides, 47, 87, 88
Cleombrotus, 192, 196, 201–3
Cleomenes I, 349
Cleomenes of Naucratis, 301
Cleon, early career of, 89 ; his policy against Mytilene, 89–90 ; goes to Pylos, 102 ; supports venture of Demosthenes and Hippocrates, 104 ; leads expedition to Chalcidice, 112 ; defeated by Brasidas, 112–13 ; death, 113 ; estimate of, 114, 419, 425 ; his oratory, 430
Cleonae, 25, 465
Cleophon, 152, 159, 161
Cleruchs, 8, 14, 44–5, 53
Clinias, 117
Clisthenes, 33
Clitus (Illyrian chief), 293
Clitus (Macedonian officer), 296, 308
Cnemus, 92–3
Cnidus, 144, 178, 183, 341, 348, 399
Cnossus, 407
Coenus, 312, 313
Colonae, 4
Colophon, 13, 154
Conon, blockaded in Lesbos, 157, 158 ; escapes after Aegospotami to Cyprus, 160 ; commands Persian fleet, 175 ; helps revolution in Rhodes, 177 ; his victory at Cnidus, 178 ; returns to Athens, 183 ; death, 184
Consentia, 289, 290
Copae, 368
Corax, 430
Corcyra, quarrels with Epidamnus, 71 ; at war with Corinth, 73–5 ; makes alliance with Athens, 74, 80 ; revolution in, 93–5, 344 ; visited by Athenian expedition, 129 ; joins Athenian maritime league, 197, 198 ; gives help to Timoleon, 285
Corinth, quarrels with Megara, 34 ; at war with Athens, 35, 38–9 ; at war with Corcyra, 71–5 ; quarrels with Athens over Potidaea, 75–7 ; urges Sparta to mobilize Peloponnesian League, 77 ; suggests use of sacred treasure for war purposes, 81 ; loses Sollium, 83 ; naval operations in Corinthian Gulf, 92–3, 343 ; discontented with Peace of Nicias, 115 ; relations with Argos and Sparta, 117, 119–20, 121 ; urges Sparta to help Syracuse, 132 ; sends help to Syracuse, 132, 135 ; her fleet blockaded by Athenians, 143 ;

demands destruction of Athens, 161; joins anti-Spartan coalition, 180–2; returns to Peloponnesian League, 187, 206; makes peace with Thebes, 210; remains neutral, 217; receives Macedonian garrison, 260, 261; sends Timoleon to Sicily, 285, 288; oligarchic government of, 349; economic life of, 371, 379
Corinth, League of, 260–2, 264, 294, 322
Coronea, 42, 182
Cos, 178, 229, 232, 297, 378
Cotys, 215, 223
Crannon, 211
Craterus, 304, 312, 313
Cratinus, 418, 419
Cratylus, 451
Crenides, 227, 228
Crimisus, r., 287
Critias, 152, 162, 163, 164, 448
Cronium, 279, 280 n.
Croton, 46, 66–7, 69–70, 277, 279, 280 n.
Ctesias, 16, 18, 429
Ctesiphon, 325
Cumae, 58
Cunaxa, 169, 171
Cylon, 67
Cyme, 173
Cynics, 450
Cyprus, 2–3, 9, 15, 17, 19–20, 299, 372, 469
Cyrenaics, 450
Cyrene, 18
Cyrus the Elder, 427
Cyrus the Younger, 155, 157, 159, 167, 169–71, 172, 173, 333, 426
Cythera, 103, 114
Cyzicus, 150, 151, 153, 262, 341

Damastum, 372
Daphnus, 143
Darius II, 142, 145, 155, 169
Darius III, 295, 298–9, 302–3, 304–5, 338, 402
Dascylium, 176
Decelea, 132, 136, 140, 151
Delian Confederacy, 5–7, 10–11, 194, 195. *See also* Athens
Delium, 104, 105–6, 328, 332, 334, 335
Delos, 5, 463
Delphi, 9, 42, 78, 80, 114, 233, 235, 236, 237, 239, 256, 393, 448, 462, 464
Delphinium, 144, 157
Demades, 260
Democritus, 424, 437–8
Demosthenes (Athenian general), his campaigns in Aetolia, 95–9; at Pylos, 100–102; in Corinthian Gulf, 103–4; sent to Syracuse, 137–9; death, 139
Demosthenes (Athenian orator), early career, 241; first political speeches, 232, 241, 242; his efforts on behalf of Olynthus, 242; sent as envoy to Philip, 245–6; his anti-Macedonian diplomacy, 249, 250–1, 254, 255, 326; wins over Byzantium, 255; secures alliance with Thebes, 257; supports Ctesiphon, 325; implicated in Harpalus affair, 326–7; his oratory, 325, 432–3
Dercyllidas, 174
Derdas, 76
Dexamenus, 405
Dexippus, 267, 268, 269
Diagoras, 126, 461
Diagoridae, 177
Dinarchus, 433, 434
Diodotus, 90
Diogenes, 450
Dion, 282, 283–4, 285
Dionysia, 363, 413, 418, 465, 466
Dionysius I, becomes tyrant of Syracuse, 268; wars with Carthage, 268–76, 279, 280–1; wars and conquests in Italy, 276–9; alliance with Sparta, 185, 208–9; with Athens, 209; military and naval resources of, 271–2, 333; his siege-craft, 273, 281, 337; estimate of, 280–1
Dionysius II, 281–4, 285, 286
Diopithes, 254, 255
Dipaea, 24
Dium, 110
Dodona, 464
Doris, 37, 257
Doriscus, 7
Drangiana, 305, 314
Drepanum, 280
Ducetius, 63–4, 65
Dysoron, 372

Ecbatana, 304, 316
Echecratidae, 199
Egypt, 16–18, 291–2, 299-301, 421
Eion, 7, 110, 112, 113
Elaeus, 254 n.
Elatea, 257
Eleusinia, 129, 465, 466, 467
Eleusis, 125, 164, 165, 361, 388, 391
Elis, 23–4, 46, 116, 117, 119, 180, 205, 206, 209, 210, 238, 249
Elleporus, r., 277
Empedocles, 62–3, 436–7
Entella, 270, 273, 280, 285, 287
Epaminondas, at peace congress of 371, 201; strategy at Leuctra,

# 486 THE GREEK WORLD FROM 479 TO 323 B.C.

202-3, 334; supports Arcadian League, 206; invades Peloponnese, 206, 208, 217-18; restores Messenia, 206; fails to be re-elected Boeotarch, 208; extricates Boeotian army in Thessaly, 212; re-elected Boeotarch, 209; tries to summon Hellenic congress, 209; his foreign policy opposed, 210; builds fleet, 215; victory and death at Mantinea, 218; estimate of, 219
Ephebeia, 358
Ephesus, 143, 154, 155, 156, 159, 174, 178, 262, 371
Ephialtes, 32-3
Ephorus, 428
Ephyra, 75
Epicharmus, 61, 408
Epicrates, 165
Epidamnus, 73
Epidaurus, 83, 120, 349, 392, 393, 464
Epirus, 240, 252
Eratosthenes, 163
Erechtheum, 125, 390
Eretria, 10, 252, 255
Erythrae, 13, 141, 143, 178, 179 n., 323
Eryx, 280
Eteobutadae, 463
Etruscans, 58, 65
Euboea, 43, 140, 228, 242, 252, 255, 372, 382
Eubulus (Athenian politician), 242, 244, 251, 358, 362
Eubulus (ruler of Atarneus), 347
Euclides, 451
Eudamidas, 189
Eudoxus, 438, 439
Eumenes, 295
Eumolpidae, 467
Euphiletus, 129
Euphron, 346
Euphronius, 403
Eupolis, 419
Euripides, 220-1, 417-18
Eurydice, 211
Eurylochus, 97, 98
Eurymedon, 94, 95, 100, 127, 136, 137, 139
Eurymedon, r., 9, 341
Evagoras, 160, 175, 184, 190-1, 291

Galepsus, 112
Gaugamela, 301-3
Gaza, 299, 339
Gedrosia, 315
Gela, 61, 63, 128, 268, 269, 273, 288
Gelon, 54, 56, 346
Getae, 253, 293
Gordium, 297, 298
Gorgias, 126, 408, 444-5

Grabus, 227
Granicus, r., 296-7
Gryllus, 218
Gylippus, 132, 135-7, 138-9
Gythium, 38

Hadria, 279
Hagnon, 84, 140
Haliartus, 181, 368
Halicarnassus, 295, 296, 391, 396
Halieis, 25, 35
Halonnesus, 250
Halus, 245
Halycus, r., 280
Hamilcar, 287
Hannibal, 266, 267
Hanno, 429
Harpalus, 305, 317, 321, 326-7
Hasdrubal, 287
Hecataeus, 429
Hecatompylus, 305
Hegelochus, 301
Heliaea, 355-6
Hellanicus, 421
Hellenotamiae, 6, 354, 361, 362
Hellespont, 1, 15, 150, 153, 159, 160, 215, 297-8
Helots, 25-7, 113, 168, 331, 374
Hephaestion, 310, 313, 316
Heraclea (Italy), 70, 290
Heraclea (Trachis), 96, 109, 180, 182
Heraclea Minoa, 283
Heraclides (of Pontus), 439
Heraclides (Syracusan), 283, 284
Heraclitus, 435
Heraea, 205, 206, 208
Heraeon Teichos, 239, 240
Herbessus, 269, 289 n.
Hermae, mutilation of, 128-9, 461
Hermias, 347
Hermione, 206
Hermocrates, 127, 132, 137, 141, 265, 266-7
Herodotus, 408, 421-3, 429
Hesiod, 409
Hestiaea, 43
Hicetas, 285, 286, 287
Hieron, 56-61
Himera, 57, 59, 61, 65, 135
Himilco, 267, 268-9, 274-5
Hindu Kush, 291, 307, 308, 310
Hippias, 438, 444-5
Hippocrates (Athenian general), 104-5, 348
Hippocrates (physician), 408, 424, 440-2
Hippodamus, 70, 387, 459
Hipponium, 277, 279, 280 n.
Homer, 409, 414
Hybla, 64
Hydaspes, r., 311-12, 313

## INDEX

Hydros, 9
Hykkara, 131
Hyperbolus, 118, 123, 147
Hyperides, 249, 251, 255, 324, 433, 434
Hyphasis, r., 313
Hyrcania, 305

Ialysus, 177
Iapygians, 67, 68
Iasus, 178
Ictinus, 389, 391
Idrieus, 232, 296
Illyria, 221, 222, 224, 225, 240, 293
Imbros, 186, 260
Inaros, 16–18
India, 309–14
Indus, r., 310, 311, 313–14
Inessa, 63, 126. *See also* Aetna
Inferiors (Hypomeiones), 179
Ionia, 1, 6, 15, 142–3, 145, 156–7
Iphicrates, 184, 185, 198, 206, 212, 215, 335
Isaeus, 432
Isis, 469
Ismenias, 190
Isocrates, 186, 191, 230, 248, 264, 379, 428, 433, 445–7
Issa, 279
Issus, 170, 298–9
Isthmia, 465
Istone, 94–5
Ithome, 26–7, 206

Jason, 198–200, 202, 203, 204, 332
Jaxartes, r., 307

Kerykes, 467

Laches, 126
Lade, 296
Lamachus, 128, 130, 134, 354
Lampsacus, 29, 159, 160
Larissa, 199, 211, 212
Larymna, 215
Laurium, 141, 360, 363
Laus, 70, 277
Lebadea, 368
Lebedus, 143
Lechaeum, 185
Lemnos, 48, 186, 260
Lenaea, 363, 413
Leocrates, 35
Leon (Syracusan general), 286
Leon (anchorage near Syracuse), 134
Leontiades, 190, 192
Leontini, 46, 59, 66, 126, 127, 128, 269, 276, 283, 287, 288
Leophron, 57
Leotychidas (Spartan king), 1, 21–2
Leotychidas (son of Agis II), 175

Leptines (Athenian), 353 n.
Leptines (brother of Dionysius I), 274
Lesbos, 6, 48, 83, 86–91, 143, 184, 297, 323, 378
Leucas, 80, 91, 92, 95, 213, 255, 285
Leucippus, 419, 420, 437–8
Leuctra, 202–3, 329, 331, 334, 348
Lilybaeum, 274, 280, 287
Lindus, 177
Locri, 57, 67, 126, 127, 277, 284
Locris, 80, 97, 235
Lucanians, 277, 289, 290
Lycia, 9, 297
Lycomedes, 205, 209, 210
Lycophron, 236, 237
Lycurgus, 249, 324, 325, 331, 358, 392, 433, 434
Lydia, 176, 291, 295, 421–2
Lyncestis, 108, 111, 221
Lyppeius, 227
Lysander, co-operates with Cyrus, 155–6; recalled to Sparta, 157; returns to Asia Minor, 159; victorious at Aegospotami, 160; organizes siege of Athens, 161; nominates ten oligarchs at Athens, 162; rounds up Athenian exiles, 163; prepares to crush democrats at Athens, 165; his method of governing dependencies, 168; procures Spartan throne for Agesilaus, 175; is sent to Hellespont, 175; brings back treasure to Sparta, 179; operates in Thessaly and Trachis, 180; invades Boeotia, 181; killed at Haliartus, 181
Lysias, 163, 379, 431
Lysicrates, 393
Lysippus, 396, 400

Macedonia, organization and culture before Philip II, 221–3; in fifth century, 50; varying foreign policy of, 108; under Archelaus, 188; alliance with Sparta, 188–9; alliance with Jason of Pherae, 200; relations with Thebes and Thessaly, 211–12. *See also* Philip II *and* Alexander III
Maeandrius, 9
Magnesia-ad-Maeandrum, 29
Mago, 276, 279
Malaria, 62–3, 441–2
Malli, 314
Mandonium, 290
Mantinea, 24–5, 26, 117 119, 121–2, 187, 205, 206, 217, 218, 238, 329, 334, 335, 336, 348
Maracanda, 307
Mardi, 305
Marduk, 303

Mareotis, Lake, 300
Maronea, 239
Massaga, 311
Massagetae, 308
Massilia, 349
Mausolus, 229, 232, 347, 391
Mazaces, 300
Mazaeus, 301, 303
Megabates, 3
Megabyzus, 16, 18
Megacles, 284
Megalopolis, 207–8, 217, 238, 249, 252, 323–4, 391, 392
Megara, at war with Corinth, 34–5; renews alliance with Peloponnesian League 43, 80; Athenian decree against, 77, 78; invaded by Athenians, 82; revolution in, 103–4; refuses to join anti-Spartan coalition, 117; abortive effort of Philip II to control, 252; joins anti-Macedonian League, 255; famous for cloaks, 379; dialect parodied by Aristophanes, 408
Megara Hyblaea, 63
Meidias, 243
Melon, 192
Melos, 81, 124–5, 261, 344, 407
Memnon, 295, 296, 297, 298, 347
Memphis, 17–8, 300
Menaechmus 438
Menaenum, 64
Mende, 110, 111
Menedemus, 451
Menestheus, 230
Menon, 169, 170
Messana, 57, 65, 69, 126, 127, 130, 135, 269, 276, 277, 288
Messapians, 67, 68, 289, 290
Messene, 26–7, 206, 218, 219, 249, 250, 252, 260, 323
Metapontum, 278 n., 290
Methone (Argolid), 103
Methone (Macedonia), 108, 123, 215, 224, 226
Methone (Messene), 38, 83, 114
Methymna, 87, 91, 193
Meton, 440
Micythus, 57, 60, 67, 68
Midias, 388, 404
Miletus, 12, 47, 143, 144, 157, 295, 296, 371, 377, 379, 384, 387
Mindarus, 150, 151
Mnaseas, 239
Mnesicles, 390
Morgantina, 64
Motya, 273–4, 280, 337
Motyum, 64
Munychia, 23, 36, 164
Mycenae, 25

Myriandrus, 170, 298
Myron, 398
Myronides, 35, 38
Mytilene, 86–91, 157, 178, 193, 297, 298, 327 n., 344
Myus, 29

Naupactus, 27, 39, 44, 80, 92, 93, 94, 97, 98, 104, 253
Nautaca, 308
Naxos, 6, 10, 45, 196, 215, 216, 341, 378
Naxos (Sicily), 59, 63, 130, 270, 274, 280
Neapolis (Italy), 58
Neapolis (Thrace), 154
Nearchus, 313, 315, 429
Nemea, 390, 465
Neon, 235
New Sybaris, 70
Nicias, heads Moderates at Athens, 99; military successes of, 99; disagrees with Cleon, 102; captures Cythera, 103; sent to Thrace, 111; negotiates peace with Sparta, 114–5; his foreign policy, 118; joins forces with Alcibiades against Hyperbolus, 123; leads expedition to Chalcidice, 123–4; opposes Athenian expedition to Sicily, 128; is appointed one of its commanders, 128, 354; his proposed strategy, 130; directs operations after departure of Alcibiades, 130–6; sends despatch home, 136; opposes plans of Demosthenes, 138; is captured and executed, 139
Nicocles, 191
Nicostratus, 111
Nine Ways (Ennea Hodoi), 11, 49
Nisaea, 36, 44, 101, 103, 114, 116, 154, 252
Nisyros, 178
Notium, 156

Odessus, 253
Odeum, 52, 391
Odrysae, 49–50, 190
Oeniadae, 39, 91, 92, 98, 327
Oenoe, 82
Oenophyta, 39
Olbia, 385
Olpae, 98
Olympia, 80, 388, 389, 393, 465
Olympias, 252, 262–3
Olynthus, 76, 107, 109, 188–9, 190, 240–3, 344
Onomarchus, 236–7
Opis, 316
Orchomenus (Arcadia), 121, 205, 206, 208

Orchomenus (Boeotia), 42, 181, 190, 236, 259, 268, 369
Orestes, 39
Orestis, 221
Oreus, 252, 255
Oritae, 315
Oropus, 140, 197, 214, 258, 260, 463, 467
Orphism, 468
Oxus, r., 307
Oxyartes, 307, 308, 338
Oxydracae, 314

Paches, 88–9, 90
Paeonia, 221, 222, 224, 225
Pagae, 39, 44, 101, 103
Pagasae, 239
Pages, Conspiracy of the, 309
Pagondas, 105–6, 334
Palice, 64
Pamphylia, 297
Panactum, 114, 116, 119
Panaenus, 401
Panathenaea, 395, 405, 465, 466
Pandosia, 67, 69, 290
Pangaeus, 373
Parmenides, 436
Parmenio, 227, 262, 292, 301, 303, 304, 306
Parrhasius, 402
Parthenon, 52, 389–90
Parthia, 305
Parysatis, 169, 176, 178
Pasargadae 304
Pasion 376, 385
Patala, 314
Pausanias (circa 479), 2–4, 25–6
Pausanias (circa 400), 161, 165, 181
Pausanias (Macedonian pretender), 224
Pella, 245
Pellene, 120
Pelopidas, conspires to expel Spartans from Cadmea, 192; elected Boeotarch, 192; goes to Susa as envoy, 209; invades Thessaly, 211, 212; is captured by Alexander of Pherae, 212; is liberated, 212; invades Thessaly again, 213; is elected Boeotarch thirteen times, 369; death of, 213
Pelusium, 321
Penestae, 374
Peparethus, 250
Perdiccas II, 50, 76, 108–9, 111, 123
Perdiccas III, 212, 215, 221, 222, 223
Periander, 364
Pericles, early training of, 33; prosecutes Cimon, 30; joins with Ephialtes to prosecute Council of the Areopagus, 32; his democratic reforms, 33–4, 350; his official position, 355; leads expedition against Oeniadae, 39; decline of his influence, 40; promotes building of Long Walls, 36; tries to promote Panhellenic Congress, 41; foreign and colonial policy of, 41, 44–6; leads expedition to Euboea, 43; reaches accommodation with Pleistoanax, 43; is opposed by Thucydides, 44, 46, 47; virtual autocracy of his later years, 47; leads expedition to Samos, 47–8; visits Euxine, 49–51; his imperialism and its critics, 51–3; prepares for war with Sparta, 72, 74, 75; his decree against Megara, 77; his ultimatum to Sparta, 78; sets aside money and ships for emergency, 80; his strategy, 81–2; leads expedition to Argolis, 83; is prosecuted and deposed from office, 84–5; re-elected to office, 85; death and estimate of his achievement, 85; his oratory, 430
Pericles the Younger, 158
Perinthus, 239, 253, 255, 339
Perioeci, 26–7, 331; in Argos, 24 n.
Peripatetics, 309
Persepolis, 303, 304, 305, 315, 321
Persian Gates, 303–4
Petalism, 65
Phaeax, 127
Phaedo, 451
Phalaecus, 239, 244–5, 247
Phaleas, 459
Pharasmanes, 307
Pharnabazus, 142, 145, 150, 154–5, 172, 174, 178, 180, 183, 184–5, 267, 341
Pharsalus, 39, 212
Pharus, 279
Phaselis, 8, 12
Phasis, 422
Phayllus, 237, 238
Pherae, 199, 200, 211, 212, 213, 237, 238
Phidias, 72, 395, 397, 398
Phigalea, 390, 393, 395
Philistus, 268, 282, 477
Philip II, early training of, 223; becomes regent and king, 222, 223; Illyrian wars of, 224, 225, 240; his military reforms, 224–6, 338, 339, 340; seizes Amphipolis and Pydna, 227; at war with Athens, 227; opposes Phocis, 237, 244, 247; in Chalcidice and Thrace, 227–8, 239–42, 252–4; makes peace with Athens, 243–8; seeks support in Peloponnese, 249; becomes archon

490   THE GREEK WORLD FROM 479 TO 323 B.C.

of Thessaly, 252; quarrels with Athens, 254; attacks Perinthus and Byzantium, 255–6; supports Amphictionic League, 257; seizes Elatea, 257; defeats Greeks at Chaeronea, 258–60; summons congress at Corinth, 260–1; projects war against Persia, 262; assassinated, 263; estimate of, 263–4, 338
Philip (brother of Perdiccas II), 76
Philippi, 228
Philippopolis, 253
Philippus, 313
Philocrates, 245, 251
Philomelus, 234–6
Philotas, 306
Phlius, 120, 188, 205, 206, 210, 238
Phocians, quarrel with their neighbours in Doris, 37; attacked by Sparta, 42; allied to Sparta in Peloponnesian War, 80; send help to Agesilaus, 182; allied to Thebes, 204; fined by Amphictionic League, 234; seize Delphi, 234; at war with the League and Philip II, 234–9, 244–5; defeated and punished, 246–7; restored by Philip, 247 n.; their use of mercenaries, 236 n., 333
Phocion, 251, 255
Phoebidas, 189–90
Phoenicia, 299, 321
Phormio (Athenian admiral), 77, 92–3, 343
Phormio (Athenian banker), 376, 385
Phormis, 61
Phrada, 305, 306
Phrygia, 176, 291, 295, 297
Phrynichus (oligarch), 145, 149
Phrynichus (playwright), 414
Phrynis, 406
Phyle, 164, 392
Pindar, 59, 61, 294, 406, 412–13
Piraeus, 23, 36, 82, 387, 388, 392
Pisa, 216
Pisander (Athenian oligarch), 145, 146–7
Pisander (Spartan commander), 178
Pissuthnes, 48, 142
Pithecusa, 58
Pithias, 94
Plataea, 78–9, 85–6, 190, 192, 198, 259, 336, 369, 387
Plato, 406, 410, 411, 438, 439, 445, 449, 451–4, 455, 457, 459
Pleistoanax, 43, 114, 115
Pollis, 196
Polyaenus, 134 n., 479
Polyclitus the Elder, 396, 397
Polyclitus the Younger, 392

Polydorus, 211
Polygnotus, 388, 401–2
Polyphron, 211
Polyzalus, 56–7
Porus, 311, 312–13
Posidonia, 66, 70, 389
Potidaea, 75–7, 83, 84, 108, 111, 215, 227
Pontus, 50–1
Praxiteles, 399
Priene, 47
Prodicus, 444
Propylaea, 52, 390
Prosopitis, 18
Protagoras, 70, 125–6 443, 444, 446, 461
Proxenus, 169
Ptolemaeus, 211, 212
Pydna, 76, 215, 226, 227
Pylos, 100–3, 114, 119, 150, 153, 154
Pythagoras (philosopher), 406, 438, 439
Pythagoras (sculptor), 396
Pythagoreans, 67, 69, 408, 435, 436, 468
Pythia, 465
Pythius, 391
Pythodorus, 127
Python, 250
Pyxus, 67, 277

Rhegium, 46, 57, 60, 66, 67, 68, 69, 126, 129, 272, 276, 277, 278, 280, 282, 286
Rhodes, 177, 178, 193, 215, 229, 232, 255, 256, 299, 378, 382, 387
Roxane, 308

Sabazios, 469
Salaethus, 88, 89
Salamis (Cyprus), 19, 160, 175
Samos, 6, 13, 47–9, 71, 143, 146, 147, 150, 156, 160, 161, 162, 178, 215, 231, 327
Samothrace, 184, 197, 468
Sane, 110
Sangala, 313
Sardes, 176, 296, 297
Satyrus (Athenian oligarch), 162
Satyrus (despot of Bosporus), 51
Satyrus (despot of Heraclea), 347
Scepsis, 174
Scidrus, 70
Scione, 110, 111, 113, 344
Sciritis, 331
Scopas, 390, 399–400
Scylax, 297
Scyros, 7–8, 186, 250, 260
Scythia, 375, 421
Segesta, 46, 66, 128, 130, 266, 273, 287, 389

# INDEX

Selinus, 61, 62–3, 128, 130, 141, 266, 279, 280, 389
Selymbria, 153
Seriphus, 372
Sestos, 1, 4 n., 5, 159, 230, 240, 294
Seuthes, 172, 173
Sicels, 63–4, 65, 66, 269, 274, 275, 276, 289
Sicyon, 38, 39, 105, 113, 120, 208, 347
Side, 297
Sidon, 299
Sinope, 51, 372
Siphae, 104–5
Siris, 70
Sitalces, 49–50
Sittace, 171
Socrates, 118, 427, 447–51, 461
Sogdiana, 307, 308
Sollium, 83, 114, 116
Solus, 276
Sophists, 425, 442–5
Sophocles (Athenian commander), 95, 100, 127
Sophocles (playwright), 140, 414, 415–6
Sparta, condition and policy after Persian Wars, 1–2, 21–3, 23–5; sends Pausanias to Cyprus and Byzantium, 3–4; prosecutes Pausanias, 3–4, 25–6; faced with Helot rising, 25–7; declines to aid Thasos, 11; joins in war against Athens, 37–8; makes truce with Athens, 40; declines to attend Panhellenic Congress, 41–2; renews war with Athens, 43–4; diplomatic interchanges with Athens, 77–8, resources in Peloponnesian War, 80–1; invasions of Attica, 82; attacks Plataea, 85–6; admits Lesbos to Peloponnesian League, 87; sends officer to Mytilene, 88; operates in Acarnania, 92–3, 96, 97–8; founds Heraclea, 96; defeated at Pylos, 100–3; despatches Brasidas to Thrace, 107–11; concludes peace with Athens, 113–15; disagrees with her allies, 116–18; restores authority in Peloponnesian League, 120–3; sends Gylippus to Syracuse, 132; seizes Decelea, 140; treats with revolted allies of Athens, 141; makes agreement with Persia, 141–5; causes revolt of Euboea, 149; operates in Aegean, 150–1; sues for peace, 151–2; continues war, 153–4; sends Lysander to Asia, 154; suffers naval reverse, 157–8; treats anew for peace, 159; reappoints Lysander, 159; defeats and besieges Athens, 161; replaces Lysander by Pausanias, 165; imperial policy of, 167–8, 187–8; aids Cyrus, 169; at war with Persia, 173–9; is opposed by a coalition in Greece, 179–83, 185; makes peace, 183, 185–7; seizes Cadmea, 189–90; reorganizes Peloponnesian League, 191; policy in central Greece, 192–3; at war with Boeotia and Athens, 195–8; renews peace, 200–1; excludes Thebes from settlement, 201; defeated at Leuctra, 202–3; political weakness of, 205–6, 208, 218–19; relations with Dionysius I, 208–9, 274; allied with Athens, 207, 209; supports Elis against Arcadians, 210; refuses to recognize Philip II, 260; stands aloof from League of Corinth, 260; defeated by Antipater, 323–4; sends Archidamus to help Taras, 290; military organization of, 329–30; oligarchic government, 349; education, 409
Spartocus, 51
Speusippus, 283, 454
Sphacteria, 100–3, 335
Sphodrias, 193
Spitamenes, 307, 308
Spithridates, 338
Stagirus, 109, 112, 292
Strategi, 33–4, 354–5
Struthas, 194
Strymon, r., 7, 50, 109, 112
Susa, 303, 315, 321
Sybaris, 46, 66, 70
Sybota, 75, 341, 342
Syracuse, ruled by tyrants, 54–61; constitutional changes at, 62, 64, 265–6, 288; at war with Acragas, 64, 65; revolutions at, 62, 64; conquers Sicel communities, 66; heads Dorian states in Sicily, 126; earlier relations with Athens, 126–8; besieged by Athenians, 128–39; sends ships to join Sparta, 141, 151; wars with Carthage, 266–75, 279–80, 285, 287–8; civil war in, 282–4; liberated by Timoleon, 285–9; city of, 54, 271, 288

Taenarum, 326
Tanagra, 38, 105, 328, 331, 368
Taras, 66, 67, 68, 69, 70, 278, 289–90, 377, 379
Tarsus, 170, 298
Tauromenium, 274, 275, 276, 289 n.
Taxila, 310, 311

Tegea, 24, 121, 205, 206, 327 n., 390, 393
Temesa, 67
Ten Thousand, March of the, 169–73, 429
Teos, 143, 178, 462
Teres, 49
Terillus, 57
Thapsacus, 170, 301
Thasos, 6, 10–1, 30, 150, 154, 184, 197, 227, 378, 383
Thebes, becomes head of Boeotian League, 42 ; attacks Plataea, 79 ; its citadel seized by Sparta, 190 ; expels Spartan garrison, 192 ; reconstructs Boeotian League, 196, 197 ; leading military state in Greece, 204 ; at war with Phocians, 235–6, 238–9 ; forms alliance with Athens, 257–8 ; treatment by Philip, 259 ; siege and destruction of, 293–4. *See also* Boeotian League
Themistocles, responsible for naval expansion of Athens, 5 ; his anti-Spartan policy, 22–3 ; responsible for fortification of Peiraeus, 23 ; declining influence in politics and ostracism, 28 ; flies to Artaxerxes I, 28–9 ; death, 29 ; Herodotus' unfair estimate of, 423
Theodectes, 418
Theopompus, 428
Theorica, 362
Theramenes, 147, 148–9, 151, 158, 161, 162–3, 425
Therma, 76
Thermae, 279
Thermopylae, 237, 242, 247, 257
Theron, 54, 57, 58, 59
Thespiae, 190, 193, 198, 259, 368
Thessaly, 39, 80, 198–200, 211–13, 234, 236, 237, 252
Thibron, 173–4
Thoricus, 392
Thrace, 15, 45, 49–50, 223, 227–8, 239–40, 243, 293

Thracian Chersonese, 7, 45, 174, 184, 215, 240, 253–4, 255
Thrasybulus (Athenian), 147, 154, 156, 158, 163, 164–5, 181, 184
Thrasybulus (despot of Syracuse), 61
Thrasydaeus, 57, 60
Thrasyllus, 147, 154, 158
Thrasymachus, 445
Thucydides (historian), 81, 83, 84, 89, 106, 110, 149, 329, 330, 331, 337, 338, 376, 423–6, 427, 441
Thucydides (politician), 40, 46–7, 72
Thuria, 46, 70, 277, 279, 289, 290, 387
Thyrea, 82
Timanthes, 402
Timarchus, 249
Timoleon, 285–9, 333
Timophanes, 347
Timotheus (general), 197, 214, 215, 222, 230, 231, 358, 359
Timotheus (musician), 221, 406
Tiribazus, 183, 185–6
Tiryns, 25
Tisias, 430
Tissaphernes, 142, 144–5, 151, 154, 155, 169, 170, 171, 173, 174, 176
Tithraustes, 176, 180
Tolmides, 38, 42
Torone, 110, 112, 215
Trapezus, 172, 372
Triballi, 256
Troizen, 44, 101, 206
Tylissus, 407
Tyndarion, 64
Tyre, 299, 301, 322, 339, 345

Xanthippus, 1, 27
Xenocrates, 454
Xenophanes, 435
Xenophon, 163, 169, 172–3, 174, 175, 218, 233, 426–7
Xerxes, 15

Zab, r., 171
Zacynthus, 80, 95, 100, 197, 283
Zadracarta, 305
Zeuxis, 221, 402